Working at Archaeology

This is a volume in

Studies in Archaeology

A complete list of titles in this series appears at the end of this volume.

Working at Archaeology

Lewis R. Binford
Department of Anthropology
University of New Mexico
Albuquerque, New Mexico

1983

ACADEMIC PRESS

A Subsidiary of Harcourt Brace Jovanovich, Publishers
New York   London   Paris   San Diego   San Francisco   São Paulo   Sydney   Tokyo   Toronto

ACADEMIC PRESS, INC.
111 Fifth Avenue, New York, New York 10003

United Kingdom Edition published by
ACADEMIC PRESS, INC. (LONDON) LTD.
24/28 Oval Road, London NW1 7DX

Library of Congress Cataloging in Publication Data

Main entry under title:

Working at archaeology.

    (Studies in archaeology)
    Bibliography: p.
    Includes index.
    1. Archaeology--Philosophy--Addresses, essays, lec-
tures. 2. Archaeology--Methodology--Addresses, essays,
lectures. I. Binford, Lewis Roberts, Date.
II. Series.
CC72.W67 1982   930.1'01   82-18466
ISBN 0-12-100060-5

PRINTED IN THE UNITED STATES OF AMERICA

83 84 85 86   9 8 7 6 5 4 3 2 1

This book is dedicated to the memory of my father, Joseph Lewis Binford, and my son, Lewis Clinton Binford, who both died during the 1970s

Contents

Figures   *xiii*
Tables   *xvii*
Acknowledgments   *xix*

I. Paradigm Growth and Theory Building

1982
1. Working at Archaeology: The Late 1960s and Early 1970s   3

1968
2. Archaeological Theory and Method   21

1975
3. Sampling, Judgment, and the Archaeological Record   23
      Introduction   23
      Specific Comments   25

1977
4. General Introduction to *For Theory Building in Archaeology*   31

1978
5. On Covering Law and Theories in Archaeology   41

1982
6. Objectivity—Explanation—Archaeology—1981   45
      Paradigms Are Not Explanations   45
      Objective Evaluation   47
      Middle Range Research   48
      The Archaeological Record   49
      Some Misunderstandings   51
      The Linking Process   53

1982
7. Meaning, Inference and the Material Record   57

II. Interassemblage Variability: The Mousterian Problem

1982

8. Working at Archaeology: The Mousterian Problem—
Learning How to Learn   65

1966

9. A Preliminary Analysis of Functional Variability in the
Mousterian of Levallois Facies (with Sally R. Binford)   71

    The Method   73
    The Sample   76
    The Variables   76
    Results of Analysis   76
    Factor I   80
    Factor II   83
    Factor III   83
    Factor IV   87
    Factor V   87
    Redesign of the Cumulative Graph
      in Light of the Factor Analysis   91
    Flint-Working   96
    Analysis of Sites and Site Samples   99
    Summary and Conclusions   120

1969

10. Comment on "Culture Traditions and Environment
of Early Man," by Desmond Collins   125

1973

11. Interassemblage Variability—
The Mousterian and the 'Functional Argument'   131

    Arguments of Desmond Collins   132
    Arguments of Paul Mellars   134
    Arguments of François Bordes   140
    Conclusions and a Summary of the 'Functional Argument'   145

III. The Mousterian Problem: How to Research the Issue

1982

12. Working at Archaeology: The Debate, Arguments of Relevance,
and the Generation Gap   157

The Debate and Arguments of Relevance   157
The Generation Gap   161

1975
13. Historical Archaeology: Is It Historical or Archaeological?   169

1978
14. Introduction to *Nunamiut Ethnoarchaeology*   179

1977
15. *Olorgesailie* Deserves More Than the Usual Book Review   195

1982
16. On Arguments for the "Butchering" of Giant Geladas
    (with Lawrence C. Todd)   205

IV. Researching Formation Processes: My Style

1982
17. Working at Archaeology: The Generation Gap—
    Reactionary Arguments and Theory Building   213

1981
18. Behavioral Archaeology and the "Pompeii Premise"   229
        Was Distortion Going on at Pompeii?   233
        Paradigm Conflict: Describing Past Cultural Systems
            versus Reconstructing the Past   235
        Behavioral Archaeology at the Joint Site   237
        Do We Need a "Revisionist" Behavioral Archaeology?   239

1977

19. Forty-seven Trips: A Case Study in the Character
    of Archaeological Formation Processes   243
        Types of Trips and the Gear Carried   252
        Relationship between Distance Anticipated
            and the Quantity of Gear Carried   254
        The Hunters' Conception of the Gear   255
        Optional Gear   260
        The Archaeological Record of the Trips   262
        Summary Conclusions   268

1979

20. Organization and Formation Processes: Looking
    at Curated Technologies   269

    Active versus Passive Gear   270
    Embedded versus Direct Procurement Strategies   273
    Organization of Gear   275
    Looking at Procurement Strategies in Terms
      of the Organization of Gear   280
    Tool Design, Form Function Relations and Tool Use
      in Terms of Organizational Characteristics   281
    Looking at Disposal and Abandonment in Terms
      of Organizational Characteristics for Gear   283
    Implications for Intersite Variability   284

1978

21. Dimensional Analysis of Behavior and Site Structure:
    Learning from an Eskimo Hunting Stand   287

    Activities Conducted   289
    Technological Organization   293
    Disposal Modes   298
    Organization of Space   303
    The Archaeological Consequences of All This Behavior   315
    Conclusions   319

1978

22. Evidence for Differences between Residential
    and Special-Purpose Sites   325

    Evidence for Differences in Content Redundancy
      for Residential versus Special-Purpose Sites   325
    Evidence for Differential Temporal Patterning
      from Residential and Special-Purpose Locations   334

1980

23. Willow Smoke and Dogs' Tails: Hunter–Gatherer
    Settlement Systems and Archaeological Site Formation   337

    Collectors and Foragers   339
    Discussion   348
    Conclusions: Settlement Systems
      and Interassemblage Variability   353

1982

24. The Archaeology of Place   357

Economic Zonation   358
Mobility Patterning   360
Within- and Between-Site Variability   362
Consequences of Variable Site Utilization   366
Occupation and Deposition   366
Summary of Ethnoarchaeological Observations   369
Between-System Variability   370
Implications of This Study   371
Conclusions   377

1981

25. Long-term Land-Use Patterning:
Some Implications for Archaeology   379

V. Some Current Views   **387**

1982

26. Working at Archaeology:
Some Thoughts about the 1970s and Beyond   389

1982

27. Paradigms, Systematics, and Archaeology
(with Jeremy A. Sabloff)   395

Two Views of "Culture"   397
Projecting Views of Culture into the Past:
Our Observational Languages   403
Conclusion   407

1981

28. Middle-range Research and the Role of Actualistic Studies   411

The Paradigm—One's Guide to Describing the World   414
Theory—One's Guide to Explaining the World   416

1982

29. Some Thoughts on the Middle to Upper Paleolithic Transition   423

Bone-Working Technology   423
Subsistence Activities   424
Dimensions of Settlements   427

Population Densities   428
Differences in Interassemblage Variation   428
General Comments   432

References   *435*
Index   *451*

Figures

Figure 9.1   Model plots of factor loadings showing expected patterns for different relationships between factors.   79

Figure 9.2   Cumulative graphs of expected frequencies—Factors I–V.   82

Figure 9.3   Plot of factor loadings for "essential" variables— Factors I and III.   86

Figure 9.4   Plot of factor loadings for "essential" variables— Factors II and V.   90

Figure 9.5   Cumulative graphs of expected frequencies—Factors I–V.   93

Figure 9.6   Percentage of factor's diagnostics occurring in each factor.   95

Figure 9.7   Cumulative graphs of observer frequencies— Levels 2–8. Shelter #1 Jabrud, Syria.   104

Figure 9.8   Observed and expected frequencies for Levels 7, 8, and 3. Shelter #1 Jabrud, Syria.   105

Figure 9.9   Observed and expected frequencies for Jabrud Shelter #1. Levels 5 and 6.   108

Figure 9.10   Observed and expected frequencies for Jabrud Shelter #1, Levels 2 and 4 and for Shubbabiq, Unit 100.   111

Figure 9.11   Percentage graphs of factor determinacy for studied samples of "Levallois Mousterian."   115

Figure 9.12   Observed and expected frequencies for Houppeville (série claire) near Rouen, France.   121

Figure 14.1   Map of North Alaska showing location of research area.   193

Figure 15.1   Relationship between flake and angular fragment counts—Olorgesailie.   198

Figure 15.2   Relationship between "biface ratio" and the percentage of flakes represented by very small pieces—Olorgesailie.   199

Figure 17.1   The rock with eyes.   225

Figure 19.1   Frequency of trips of varying distance—Anaktuvuk Pass.   253

Figure 19.2   Number of items carried compared with the distance covered for all trips—Anaktuvuk Pass.   254

Figure 19.3   Percentage of classes of gear carried on trips of different distances (in miles).   258

Figure 19.4   Covariation among items carried on trips of different purposes.   259

Figure 20.1   Kaotah from Nunamiut sites.   279

Figure 21.1   Relationship between mean group size and time spent eating, playing cards, and talking—Mask site.   291

Figure 21.2   Relationship between mean group size and time spent in crafts and target shooting—Mask site.   292

Figure 21.3   Location of hearths and glacial boulders—Mask site.   304

Figure 21.4   Model seating plan.   305

Figure 21.5   Observed localization of eating and talking activities under variable wind directions—Mask site.   306

Figure 21.6   Observed localizations of card playing—Mask site.   308

Figure 21.7   Observed localization of craft activities—Mask site.   309

Figure 21.8   Observed localization of activities on the afternoon of June 5th—Mask site.   310

Figure 21.9   Observed localization of activities on June 6th— Mask site.   311

Figure 21.10   Observed localization of activities at noon on June 5th—Mask site.   311

Figure 21.11   Definition of activity areas W, X, Y, Z—Mask site.   312

Figure 21.12   Relationship between mean group size and the percent of total craft time spent within an "eating circle."   314

Figure 21.13   Distribution of bone—Mask site.   315

Figure 21.14   Distribution of spent cartridges and wood shavings— Mask site.   316

Figure 21.15   Artifact distribution—Mask site.   316

Figure 21.16   Bone distribution superimposed on model seating plan.   317

Figure 21.17   Artifact distribution superimposed on activity areas— Mask site.   318

Figure 23.1   Characterization of a foraging subsistence-settlement system.   340

Figure 23.2   Actual map of foraging trips made by !Kung San around base camps.   342

Figure 23.3   Characterization of a collector subsistence-settlement system.   345

Figure 23.4   Graph of the relationship between storage dependence and effective temperature.   353

Figure 24.1   Schematic representation of zones of economic activity around a residential camp.   360

Figure 24.2   Different idealized patterns of residential camp movement, with resultant spacing or overlap of foraging or logistical zones around camps.   362

Figure 24.3   Idealized pattern of site use and movement among sites at time t_1 (late summer).   363

Figure 24.4   Idealized pattern of site use and movement among sites at time t_2 (approximately 1.5 months later than t_1).   364

Figure 24.5   Idealized pattern of site use and movement among sites at time t_3 (early fall).   365

Figure 25.1   Traditional cycle of Nunamiut Eskimo land use.   381

Figure 25.2   Curve of use intensity for Sudden Shelter.   385

Figure 29.1   Channeled bone gnawed by wolves.   424

Tables

Table 9.1 Functional Suggestions for Tool Types Listed on
Bordes's Type List 77

Table 9.2 List of Variables Arranged According to a Descending
Order of Factor Loading—Factor I 81

Table 9.3 List of Variables Arranged According to a Descending
Order of Factor Loading—Factor II 84

Table 9.4 List of Variables Arranged According to a Descending
Order of Factor Loading—Factor III 85

Table 9.5 List of Variables Arranged According to a Descending
Order of Factor Loading—Factor IV 88

Table 9.6 List of Variables Arranged According to a Descending
Order of Factor Loading—Factor V 89

Table 9.7 Summary of Factors 92

Table 9.8 Expected Percentages for Variables Included in This Study
Arranged According to the Revised Ordering of Types
Suggested by the Factor Analysis 94

Table 9.9 Expected Values for Technical Ratios 97

Table 9.10 Observed and Expected Ratios for Samples in the
Study—Technical Characteristics 106

Table 15.1 Summary Data on Faunal Information from Olorgesailie 201

Table 19.1 Gear Carried by Hunters on 47 Trips 246

Table 19.2 Frequency of Dry Meat and Marrow Bones Packed by
Hunters on 111 Trips 250

Table 19.3 Frequency Distributions of Dry Meat Parts and
Marrow Bones Carried by Season 251

Table 19.4 Number of Trips on Which Dry Meat, Marrow Bones,
or Both Were Carried by Season 252

Table 19.5 Hunters' Categorisation of the 'Basic Trip' Gear 255

Table 19.6 Frequency of Items in Three Nunamiut Categories
Arranged According to Recognised Trips 257

Table 19.7   Two Categories of Optional Gear Divided According to
              Age of Hunters   261

Table 20.1   Disposition of Selected Gear, June 2–30, 1971   273

Table 21.1   Flow of Men through the Site   290

Table 21.2   Frequency of Activities Conducted on the Mask Site
              during Controlled Periods of Observation   290

Table 21.3   Data from the 23 Hours of Behavioral Observation as
              Regards the Items Observed and the
              "Activity" in Which They Were Used   294

Table 21.4   Comparison between Numbers of Items Observed
              Behaviorally and Archaeologically   297

Table 21.5   Comparative Inventories for Items Observed
              Ethnographically and Archaeologically—Mask Site   301

Table 21.6   Proportion of Man-Hours of Activities Performed by
              Men Seated in Circular Fashion around the Hearth   307

Table 21.7   Man-Hours of Activity Localized in Different Areas   313

Table 22.1   Frequency of Differentiated Use of Locations by
              Two Families during the Years 1947–1948   329

Table 23.1   Summary of Group Sizes and Annual Mobility for a
              Number of Equatorial and Subequatorial
              Groups of Hunter–Gatherers   341

Table 23.2   Cross Tabulation of Settlement Pattern as Evaluated by
              Murdock (1967) and Effective Temperature Values as
              Calculated from World Weather Records   350

Table 24.1   Comparative Usage of Place   367

Table 27.1   Old World and New World Paradigms   405

Table 29.1   Assemblage Variability by Type of Site in the
              Wabash River Drainage   429

Acknowledgments

I must acknowledge several sources of invaluable aid and inspiration for the work assembled here. The laboratory staff and students in F. Bordes's laboratory at Telance helped make the Mousterian problem "come alive," and F. Bordes himself provided immeasurable aid and support. The people of Anaktuvuk village, Alaska, patiently taught me much about the process of living by hunting and gathering tactics in an arctic setting. In addition, my students and colleagues at the University of New Mexico have been a continuous source of stimulation and inspiration to continue working at archaeology.

Several other people were extremely helpful in actually putting the book together. Martha Graham made copies of all the articles and inventoried the chapters, and did most of the work of combining the many bibliographies into a single reference section. Martha also reassembled all of the illustrations and prepared the reprinted articles for the publisher.

All of the new material was typed by Del Draper. Advice and comments on this material were offered by Jeremy Sabloff, Neale Draper, and Erik Ingbar, whose assistance I gratefully acknowledge.

PART I

Paradigm Growth and Theory Building

1

1983

Working at Archaeology:
The Late 1960s and Early 1970s

All except two of the articles in this collection were written between 1973 and 1983. I also published four books during this time: *For Theory Building in Archaeology* in 1977, *Nunamiut Ethnoarchaeology* in 1978, *Bones: Ancient Men and Modern Myths* in 1981, and *In Pursuit of the Past* in 1983. The problems addressed in these books are discussed in the articles as well, and the combined works provide a comprehensive picture of my research involvement since the early days of the new archaeology. I dealt with my role in that episode in the anthology of my papers published in 1972 (L.R. Binford 1972a). Everything in this volume represents avenues of research prompted by the issues raised under the rubric of the new archaeology.

So much confusion has been generated in the field of archaeology, particularly between 1968 and 1975, that many readers may not understand how my work and ideas related to the more populist view of the new archaeology, a view created by others during the early 1970s. The new archaeology as I originally conceived it was a reaction against what I then viewed as limitations crippling traditional archaeology.

In the framework in which I learned archaeology, the relationship of the things remaining in the archaeological record to past conditions was by convention a simple reflection of the social identity of the creators of those things.

> All archaeological data are expressions of human thoughts and purposes and are valued only as revelations thereof [Childe 1962:10–11].
>> Similar assemblages of archaeological types are found repeatedly associated together because they were made, used or performed by the same people at the same time. . . . Different assemblages of associated types occur at the same time because they were made by different peoples [Childe 1956:111].
> Cultural relationships which do exist have been brought about through the minds of living beings. . . . Inanimate products themselves do not reproduce, modify, copy, or influence one another culturally. It is the mediate agency of a mind that brings about the culture relationships between cultural products. Therefore any classification which attempts to portray the relationships of human cultural materials must do so in terms of the people who made, used, or possessed those materials. . . . since it will be a rare case in archaeological research when a single individual

WORKING AT ARCHAEOLOGY

can be identified as the agent, it follows that in our discipline a more general designation will usually have to be made, i.e., by groups of individuals [From Taylor 1948:143. Reproduced by permission of the American Anthropological Association, from *American Anthropologist* 50(3, Pt. 2—Memoir 69); 143, 1948.].

The metaphysics expressed here presupposed that the basic units of meaningful synthesis were recognizable by virtue of patterns of association among classes of things within sites. The cause of both formal variation in artifacts and variability among the contents of different sites was considered to be the different social identity of the producers of the artifacts. The metaphysics were simple:

1. The cause of formal variability in artifacts and in turn particular configurations of content among assemblages was seen as referable to variability in the social identity of their producers.
2. The cause of variability in the social identity of peoples—that is, the combined factors that impinged on the "mind of man" to condition the differential production of different things in different combinations in different places and at different times—was history!

The accidents of history conditioned the degree to which social units shared or did not share "culture." History was thought to consist of two major processes: (a) innovative events, in which new culture was generated and/or old culture reinterpreted, and (b) dispersive events, in which old culture was translated spatially and differentially incorporated into the cultural repertoire of spatially separated groups. The latter process was considered to occur by virtue of two possible conditions: (a) the migration of peoples, or (b) the diffusion of culture itself among otherwise stationary populations—that is, the exchange of ideas. Thus the culture of any given group at a given time was the vectoral sum of two forces, the innovative and the dispersive, with the relative strength of each being an accumulative function of the past combinations of sums that happened to have converged at that particular place and time. Explaining culture therefore entailed tracing the varying paths or trajectories of the culture's traits in both their innovative and dispersive modes, thereby exposing the pattern of their convergence at a given place at a given time. History was seen as the cause of the culture that was characteristic of any given time and place, and each place and point in time, each "configuration" of culture, was distinctive by virtue of its historical uniqueness. This might be viewed as the external source of uniqueness. Another justification for uniqueness, the internal source, was developed primarily under the guiding hand of Franz Boas. His argument was that man's active mind was continuously "reinterpreting" culture.

[We cannot] disregard the action of inner forces, that may lead two people of like cultural possessions, after their separation, to entirely distinct conditions [Boas 1911, in Boas 1966:300].

Anthropological research which compares similar cultural phenomena from various parts of the world, in order to discover the uniform history of their development, makes the assumption that the same ethnological phenomenon has everywhere developed in the same manner. Here lies the flaw. . . . for no such proof can be given. Even the most cursory review shows that the same phenomenon may develop in a multitude of ways [Boas 1896, in Boas 1966:272].

Boas was saying that similar things have different meanings to different people. I recall a Boasian instructor illustrating this point. When alarm clocks first reached a remote tribe in South America through an exchange network, he said, the natives interpreted the clock as a status item and each headman wore one around his neck as a mark of his social position. Clearly any projection of our notions of "clock" would not reflect the unique and interesting mental reality of this remote tribe! Similar things were not similar if different ideas were ascribed to them. The ideas that stood behind things were largely the playing out of the inner workings of minds, human psychology. No explanations were possible; all we could justifiably do was to appreciate each culture in its unique grandeur.

Given these views, construction of past conditions was not possible because it required an inferential argument. Similarity among things from different eras or places was considered illusory. One could never have confidence that things that looked alike had similar meanings. In like fashion, any inferential argument about the past that required a uniformitarian assumption was unjustified, because the present had different causes than the past—that is, it had a different history. This meant that no uniformitarian link could bridge the present and the past. Essentially all one could do was describe and inventory the contents of the archaeological record and then project it back in time to its correct place in history. We could ask questions about the reasons for the invention of things when they initially appeared in the archaeological record, or the reasons for the differential spread and association of things occurring in the archaeological record. Statements about aspects of the past *not* directly available in the record were not considered possible. This view was commonly shared by archaeologists working between 1930 and the mid-1960s.

> Prehistory reveals only material phenomena, and only part of them. . . . it determines accurately certain phases of technology and nothing else [Lowie 1937:22].
>
> Nothing pertaining to the intangible aspects of life can be rescued with the help of the spade. Thus we may learn about skeletal types, about implements and utensils used, about the steps in their manufacture; but no information is forthcoming to tell us about languages, customs, beliefs [Boas 1938:2].
>
> An archaeologist may recover material but not the substance of aboriginal artifacts. The exact meaning of any particular object for the living group or individual is forever lost, and the real significance or lack of importance of any object in an ethnological sense has disappeared by the time it becomes a part of an archaeologist's catalogue of finds [Griffin 1943:340].

Given such views, archaeologists continued to attempt to unravel "culture history" by classifying artifacts associated at places into assemblages, these into components, foci, phases, folk traditions, or whatever taxonomic unit of affinity is in current use (see Chapter 9).

Objections to this situation began to be voiced, particularly in the later 1930s (see Willey and Sabloff 1980:131–136), and was systematically presented to Americanists by Walter Taylor (1948). As I read the response to Taylor's appeals for the description of new types of archaeological data (affinities) and the interpretation of archaeological remains in behavioral terms, there was some sympathy with the desire to gain a richer picture of the past, but no one saw how this could be accomplished. The message that most archaeologists received from Taylor's appeal was that they ought to look harder and for more detail, because only new facts could expand their knowledge. The alternative was simply to speculate, and that in their view was unjustifiable.

During the early 1960s I came to reject the view that history causes history, accepting in its place the view that the events of history are the phenomena in need of explanation (see Spaulding 1968). I also rejected the strict inductivist's view of science, and came to believe that explanations are invented to aid us in understanding "facts," rather than generalized from facts. I accepted the view that there is no such thing as an external observer objectively looking down on nature and able to see nature "truly," unaffected by ideas the observer might have (see Chapter 7). In line with these beliefs, I rejected the view that the archaeological record is only amenable to discussion in terms of its manifest or strictly empirical properties. In short, I dismissed the view that the archaeological record in its obvious material poverty limits our discussions of the past to the same impoverished remnants. I suggested that the materials remaining to us were molded in their properties and patterned associations by the operation of past dynamics, none of which are preserved for us directly. Past dynamics, the molder of the archaeological record, I said, could only be known inferentially.

This point was made in two ways. First, my associates and I attempted to demonstrate that the facts of the archaeological record as traditionally described and interpreted could plausibly refer to a very different set of past conditions than was commonly considered by traditional archaeologists.[1] Second, we began to investigate methods for inference and their use.

The first approach was heralded in my 1962 paper "Archaeology as Anthropology." It was also the message, as I saw it, of the works of my students William Longacre (1963) and James Hill (1965). This point has been missed by many critics. For instance, it has been implied that these works were set forth as models for transforming archaeological research into a kind of ethnography of the past.[2] Although it is true that we frequently acknowledged that we would like to know what life was like in the past, it should have been clear that we sought to understand *processes,* particularly the processes that brought into being the facts of the archaeological record. In our view these processes were much more complicated than previously thought (or imagined).

The original critical work of Longacre was directed at the seriation of ceramic types, a very popular activity for archaeologists in the late 1950s. We reasoned that if variability in the frequency of pottery types could be shown to be responsive to the differential sizes of kin groups within a community, then the assumption that variability was a measure of stylistic change, or simple popularity, was clearly challenged. An additional point that the work of Longacre and Hill sought to make was that properties of the archaeological record were referable to properties of past systems not generally considered accessible by strict inductivists or empiricists. (See my discussion of the limitations of the archaeological record [L.R. Binford 1968a].)

Many critics have missed these essential points, and have attempted to discredit the models of the past projected by Longacre, Hill, and myself (Dumond 1977; Eggert 1976b; McHugh 1973), thinking that by so doing they were discrediting the validity of the new archaeology. This is rather silly, for it was not essential that our particular alternative views of the past be correct—only that they be reasonable given the information available. That was all that was required to illustrate that traditional interpretative conventions could be both impoverished and incorrect. By casting doubt we established the need for a way of testing the accuracy of alternative ideas. By showing that the traditional conventions could produce inaccurate results, we made it clear that we needed means for evaluating any interpretative conventions used for converting archaeological observations into statements about the past. *Only by the use of such means would it be possible to evaluate either the alternative views advanced or the traditional views being questioned.* In our view the testing of ideas was central to progress.

This position led directly to the second, the investigation of the methods of inference and how to use them—in my opinion the most constructive component of the new archaeology. Given that traditional approaches denied our ability to make meaningful inferences about the past, it is not surprising that the methodological problems associated with making inferences had been neither explored nor developed for archaeologists.[3]

I had accepted Raymond Thompson's analysis for epistemology as practiced among traditional archaeologists. As the reader probably knows the conclusion that Thompson set forth regarding the evaluation of inferences about the past was that "any archaeologist's cultural reconstruction must . . . be based on an appraisal of his professional competence [R.H. Thompson 1956:331]." Having reached that conclusion, Thompson proceeded to discuss the characteristics a person should possess to ensure high regard and a high "truth" rating by virtue of having been judged competent (see L.R. Binford 1981b: 82–84, 237–242). In Thompson's analysis, the most important criterion for judging someone's competence was the manner in which that person handled arguments from analogy.

> What actually happens is that he compares an artifact type which is derived from archaeological data with a similar type in a known life situation. If the resemblance in the form of the two artifact types is reasonably close, he infers that the archaeological type shares the technique, behavior, or other cultural activity which is usually associated with the ethnographic types [R.H. Thompson 1956:329].

In essence, inductive arguments from analogy and common sense (see Gardin 1980) were the methods used by traditional archaeologists for interpreting the past. This position was well stated somewhat later by K. C. Chang (1967), and was one of the points that I came to criticize (see L. R. Binford 1967, 1968a). Under a strict culture historical view, an argument from analogy could only be justified when the cultures were the same; that is, where there was historical continuity with little culture change between the ethnographic case cited and the past being interpreted. Robert Ascher (1961) was one of the first to champion the idea that there may be situations other than simple historical continuity for which inferences to the past based on arguments from analogy were warranted, and he cited the conditions under which such "new analogies" might be justified. The different approaches represented by the "direct historical method" and the "new analogy" of Ascher were later termed *continuous* and *discontinuous* analogies by Richard Gould (1974:38–39, 1978:254–256).

Although I was sympathetic to Ascher's approach, I could see no way to evaluate whether a "continuous" or a "discontinuous" argument from analogy was in fact accurate. As part of a demonstration of the problem, I accepted Thompson's criteria as to what rendered the use of analogy powerful and hence a measure of competence, and attempted to mount the strongest possible argument from analogy. In the "Smudge pits" article (L.R. Binford 1967) I argued in terms of all the traditional criteria, as I understood them, regarding the proper and prudent use of analogy. In my opinion it remains one of the strongest arguments from analogy I have ever seen in archaeology. *Yet my own conclusion was that it was inadequate* (L.R. Binford 1967:10). If argument from analogy was the method used by archaeologists to warrant their interpretations of the past, the implication was clear: *Archaeologists lacked appropriate methods for making accurate statements about the past based on archaeological observations.*

Leslie Freeman (1968) presented an extreme conclusion based on this type of argument—namely, that arguments from analogy were misleading because they were inadequate epistomological devices. He drew the conclusion that they had no place, at least in Paleolithic archaeology. In partial disagreement with Freeman, I said that arguments from analogy could be inspirational, and might well serve an important educational function for the archaeologist. Analogies could inform him or her of possible meanings to be given to observations. What was lacking was the means to evaluate alternative ideas beyond the warranting arguments that might be offered from the ethnographic analogies themselves. I suggested that an analogy should serve "to provoke certain types of questions which can on investigation, lead to the recognition of more comprehensive order in the archaeological data [L.R. Binford 1967:9]." At the time I had only one suggestion for evaluating existing propositions about the significance of archaeologically observed forms of patterning: that we "develop testable hypothese in a deductive framework [p. 9]." This appeared to be a tactical way out of the apparent dilemma that if argument from analogy was the only way we could give meaning to observations on the archaeological record, and if there was no way to evaluate the accuracy of such arguments, then the past became a construction dictated by our current ignorance, bias, or other subjective conditioners.[4] How could archaeology be more than opinion, and the accuracy of the constructed past rest on more than the prudence or competence of the archaeologist, as Thompson had suggested?

Central to my thoughts on this issue was the idea of explanation. *Explanation* was one of the words that I began using repeatedly in 1962. Although primarily tied to the debates of the 1950s concerning generalizing versus particularizing activities, it seemed to me that one principal weakness of traditional archaeology had been that the past was created to explain the facts of the present, the archaeological record. Our constructions of a past represented our particular little inventions, which, if true, would accommodate the observations we made on the archaeological record. History was considered to be composed of multiple unique events, hence our reconstructions were generally unique events said to explain the archaeological record. These unique "pictures" of the past constituted our constructed histories. The only test for accuracy was the degree of fit between the imagined events and the observations made on the archaeological record. (See my comments in Chapter 12, as well as the discussions of post hoc accommodative arguments in the *Bones* book [L.R. Binford 1981b].)

In the early 1960s I thought of explanation as something quite different. I had learned that an event or condition was said to be explained if it could be referred unambiguously to an established body of generally valid understanding. Such an event or condition was seen as a particular example of a generally understood phenomenon.

In the context of trying to generate an accurate past, I had a rather vague idea of explaining the archaeological record. If we could explain the archaeological record in the aforementioned terms, then we should be able to generate an accurate past with respect to at least some of its properties. I looked through the literature and could find no body of general understanding regarding the information of the archaeological record to which particular observations were referable in an explanatory sense. On the other hand, the particularly secure inferences that had been made to the past, particularly those concerning architectural reconstructions and the dating of remains, did seem to have the form I advocated. They were backed up by a secure body of theory that permitted the inference of causes from effects with some degree of accuracy.

This view was most explicitly stated in the context of the Sabloff and Willey (1967) discussion of the Maya collapse. These two authors basically accepted as an appropriate goal the achievement of a processual understanding of the past, but they insisted that we had to establish the nature of the past by methods different from those of processual studies.

> Only after a thorough understanding of the historical events which occurred in the late ninth and early tenth centuries A.D. in the Southern Maya Lowlands has been reached can the larger question of process be successfully broached. For if in our eagerness to change our goals from historical to processual ones, we relegate the reconstructions of historical events to a low priority role and ignore the importances of these events, then our efforts will be futile [Sabloff and Willey 1967:314].

In response to their position I tried to make several points. I stressed the view that historical reconstruction does not proceed from epistomological criteria different from those involved in the explanation of culture process.

> Explanation begins for the archaeologist when observations made on the archaeological record are linked through laws of cultural or behavioral functioning to past conditions on events [Binford 1968c:270].
> If we . . . appeal to unstated processual propositions in explaining observations we can have little confidence in the historical reconstructions offered. . . . If the propositions appealed to in explaining our observations of the archaeological record are correct, then we will have gained knowledge of the past [L.R. Binford 1968b:1].

Sabloff and Willey's suggestions seemed to me to be raising an archaeological double standard to new heights. I had always thought that traditional archaeology had operated with a kind of double standard regarding its procedures for giving meaning to archaeological observations. For instance, when the archaeologist observed patterned similarities, these were conventionally said to be particular manifestations of a general phenomenon called culture. Culture was considered to have certain essential characteristics that served to justify a number of conventions used in taxonomy and systematics for creating units of culture thought to have historical reality. When discontinuous differences were observed among such units in a sequence, the differences were said to derive from the unique events of history. Unique events were then created by the archaeologist to account for the observed differences or unexpected discontinuities observed among "cultural things" in the archaeological record. The double standard operated in that there was an ironclad set of conventions in use for interpreting *similarities,* and a wide-eyed, open-ended, undisciplined speculative approach operative when it came to interpreting *differences* among culturally defined units.

A similar double standard seemed to be inherent in the arguments made by Sabloff and Willey. They interpreted the facts of the archaeological record by intuition, analogy, convention, speculation, whatever came to mind, all with wide-eyed naiveté. Historical interpretations generated by these means provided us with our view of the past. Sabloff and Willey seemed to be saying that given such a history we would be in a position to investigate the processes that operated to produce that same past. Processual archaeology was only relevant after we had constructed a past by nonprocessual means! Just as I had taken exception to the double standard of traditional archaeological conventions, I objected to the double standard whereby the past was to be described by intuitive, traditional, and humanistic means, and then explained in processual terms. The very act of inferring the past from archaeological observations was a central problem in processual archaeology. Put another way, seeking understanding of the past processes that brought into being the phenomena remaining for us to observe archaeologically was central to the act of inferring a past. When I later referred to this problem in the development of inferential methods as the need for archaeological theory (see Chapter 1), I found that readers misunderstood. Many thought that I was referring to theories of culture change that might be employed to explain why the past had been the way it appeared to have been. For this reason I began developing the idea of *middle-range research*[5] or middle-range theory as opposed to general theory (see Chapter 3).

What came out of my exchange with Sabloff and Willey was a recognition of the importance of differentiating the problem of inference into at least two levels of discourse and concern; giving meaning to the archaeological record, and explaining the past as known. At this point the issues seemed clarified. Discussions about analogy had led to an exploration of the various ways one might provide an explanation, and a general search had begun for ways to evaluate ideas. In both of these undertakings the role of deductive reasoning began to appear more and more important. The Sabloff and Willey exchange had pointed to the necessity of separating the problem of explanation into at least two problems with differing tactics. The question at this point was what these tactics might be.

Into the middle of this state of reasoning, works by James Hill (1968) and Pat Munson (1969) forced me to evaluate still further analogy and the role of deductive reasoning. Hill's paper seemed to deal directly with the problem of analogy as I had outlined in the "Smudge pits" (L.R. Binford 1967a) paper. Hill was concerned with how we might increase the accuracy of the inferences we had originally justified through ethnographic analogy. He cited a number of properties that had been ethnographically documented as differentiating several classes of rooms within southwestern pueblos. These properties were observable in the archaeological record and could serve as the positive analogy between the archaeological and ethnographic records, permitting the interpretation of the archaeological rooms by analogical argument. Having accepted my arguments regarding the inadequacy of arguments from analogy, Hill introduced a number of additional arguments designed to test the accuracy of his initial argument from analogy. It is the nature of these "tests" that implicates a number of the arguments then current in the literature and others that would appear later.

> The procedure used here involved . . . an examination of the ethnographic literature to find out what kinds of activities are carried out in the different . . . present-day pueblo rooms, and what kinds of artifacts and other materials might be expected to occur in the respective room-types as a result of these activities; and secondly, an examination of the archaeological evidence to find out whether or not similar artifact clusters occurred in the supposedly analogous room at Broken K. If the proposition of functional equivalence is correct, the large, small, and special rooms at the site should contain similar cultural materials to the small, large, and special rooms in the modern pueblos. . . . Such a finding would, in fact confirm the proposition [J. Hill 1968:116].

Hill was searching for ways to evaluate his interpretative concepts. He developed both a procedure for expanding our archaeological definition of a concept (like "storage room") and, in another sense, means for increasing the "positive analogy" between an archaeological and ethnographic case, thereby increasing the strength of an argument from analogy! (See Chapter 3 for a discussion of this point.)

I had worked with Hill throughout his development of the storage room argument, and it was not until after it was published and it was cited as an example of "explicitly scientific archaeology" (P.J. Watson et al. 1971:37–45) an alleged example of a "nomological–deductive explanation" complete with "hypothetical general laws" and "deduced implications" that I began a serious reevaluation of the work that my students, colleagues, and I had been producing.[6] I can remember pointing out to a friend the lack of parallelism between what I had suggested in the "Smudge pits" (L.R. Binford 1967) paper and what Hill had done. I likened Hill's study to one that would seek to increase the number of attributes of smudge pits through a more exhaustive study of the ethnographic literature describing skin smoking. His argument was a new suggestion, and one that I had not considered at the time I wrote the "Smudge pits" article. In that paper, I had suggested the following:

1. An examination of the ethnographic context, seeking to recognize other characteristics that would correlate with, for instance, skin smoking and might also be recognized archaeologically.

2. Given an argument (that the features were skin-smoking pits) "and the knowledge of the formal, spatial, and temporal correlates of the activity designated in the postulate, the specification of a number of hypotheses as to the predicted mode of variation expected between the archaeologically observed analog and other archaeologically observable phenomena [L.R. Binford 1967a:9–10]."

What I was advocating derived from my ideas about systems and the organization among elements integrated systemically. I had in mind the investigation of the degree to which hide smoking was, for instance, conducted at the same time as skin scraping, the degree to which it was always a fall activity, the degree to which it was in the hands of specialists—in short, how hide smoking was organized within a wider array of related activities. I thought that if we knew such things we could specify a new set of relationships (I called them hypotheses) at a higher level of organization than that of the feature itself. Such expectations would specify how hide-smoking pits should covary with other classes of archaeological remains. Looking back on these suggestions now, I might claim that I then had an idea of theory building, an idea that we needed to be able to anticipate when hide-smoking pits should occur and with what other independent archaeological materials they should be associated. More realistically, however, at the time I was thinking mostly in terms of empirical generalizations from ethnographic and historical documents. I was suggesting a set of tactics designed to expand the operational definition of a hide-smoking pit to include properties of the wider system within which such features were organizationally integrated. Hill, in turn, was suggesting the expansion of the operational definition for a class of features, the storage room, at the level of organization of the feature class itself. Both of us were exploring tactics that sought expanded definitions for the concepts with which we were working and trying to use in giving meaning to phenomena observed archaeologically.[7] *What neither of us faced squarely at the time was that we could not use the archaeological record to test the accuracy of meanings assigned to archaeological facts by these tactics.*[8]

I had been trained in traditional archaeology, as had most of the new archaeologists. We never questioned the premise that the archaeological record was the empirical domain that had to serve as the arbiter for our ideas about the past. We were not arguing about the past in this historical sense; rather, we were arguing about the causal dynamics responsible for the archaeological record. What empirical domain serves as the arbiter for our ideas about those causal dynamics? Both Hill and I initially answered this question incorrectly, of course, assuming as we had been taught that the arbiter was the archaeological record. It was in this context that I had urged the use of a set of deductive tactics for evaluating the ideas we set forth about the meaning of archaeological facts. If we had a set of interpretative principles and wanted to evaluate them, then clearly we had to reason from them to a set of empirical expectations (different from those properties being interpreted) and see if our expectations were met. It seemed to me that the symmetry of the covering law model of explanation was uniquely appropriate to the particular problem of explanation that archaeologists face. Using the covering law model, the archaeological observations would remain as "symptoms" or forms of circumstantial evidence implicating the operation of the past dynamics that produced them. If we could state a set of laws regarding the operation of causal dynamics in general—that is, laws regarding the dynamic conditions that brought into being the symptoms—then we should be very secure in inferring the dynamics (causal conditions in the past) from the symptoms themselves. In short, the symptoms would be explained by the inferred causes. The laws would render secure the linkage between cause and effect.

The only problems seemed to be, first, how to obtain the needed laws, and, second, how to test their accuracy. Leaving aside for the moment the problem of obtaining the laws, the problem of testing seemed particularly sticky for archaeologists, since the need to specify the circumstances or the initial conditions surrounding the events where "laws" could be said to have operated always permitted the archaeologist to immunize the theory. That is, the lack of correspondence between deduced expectations and observed patterning in specified archaeological facts could always be dismissed by postulating particular initial conditions or the operation of additional variables that would accommodate the facts without challenging the theory.

I thought of this as a problem of relevance.[9] Were the general interpretative principles relevant to the situation? Only with a very strong argument warranting the relevance of the principle to the situation could the accuracy of the principle be implicated by the facts of the archaeological record.

> At each juncture of explaining observations from the archaeological record, we must question anew to what variables operative in the past our observations refer. Any explanatory proposition must be reasoned in terms of relevance to the operation of the cultural system under study [L.R. Binford 1968a:25].

The ambiguity of whether the arguments attempting to warrant the relevance of an interpretative principle to the "symptoms" seen archaeologically versus the need for a correspondence test between expectations deduced from a set of principles and the facts deemed appropriate from the archaeological record presented us with a dilemma. Judging the relevance independently of the implications as to accuracy seemed to me to render impossible the testing of interpretative principles with the facts of the archaeological record. To test the validity of an assertion that a set of observations unambiguously implicates a set of past conditions, we must study the linkage between the observations (symptoms) and the particular causes said to be implicated. This *cannot* be done through a study of the archaeological record, since all the characteristics of the archaeological record are static and contemporary and the past is inferentially known and was dynamic. The causes in a dynamic sense are long gone and not directly knowable.

I was already acutely aware of this frustrating situation in 1966 when I wrote,

> The validity of the interpretive principle itself can never be independently tested since its accuracy is tested only by reference to the empirical generalization it is said to cover. Extension of the generalization to cover new cases simply provides more instances for which the principle might be relevant, it in no way tests the principle itself [L.R. Binford 1968b:2].

To update this statement, I would now say that one can never reason correctly to a conclusion that contradicts the premises with which one starts. In fact, the power of deductive reasoning is just that: If done correctly, the linkage between conclusions and initial premise is direct and unambiguous. The deduced propositions are logically dependent in every way on the accuracy of the premises. Using the archaeological record as the empirical arbiter, if one starts with premises regarding causal dynamics and then reasons deductively to a set of expected static properties, and the deduced expectations do not correspond to the archaeologically observed facts, the most obvious conclusion is that the premises were irrelevant to the empirical case being investigated. The accuracy of the initial premises is not necessarily implicated, because the initial conditions (additional characteristics of the past) are not known and are not therefore unambiguously specifiable.

Ironically, this was the very situation that provided security for all the interpretative conventions used by traditional archaeologists. One investigated the archaeological record, judged which interpretative principle applied (was relevant), and then reconstructed a past using the interpretative conventions judged appropriate.

I came to the simple conclusion that this use of deductive reasoning was of little utility when the empirical domain was the archaeological record. I did recognize that if one were arguing about historical dynamics or causal processes operating in history, then deductive reasoning might be very important and the archaeological record could be used as the arbiter. This would be true, however, only if the variables cited in one's explanatory argument could be unambiguously operationalized to facts recoverable from the archaeological record. Of course this ability rests with the demonstration of unambiguous cause-and-effect relationships between the causal dynamics and the derivative statics that would be cited to warrant the use of chosen static facts as measures for the variables in question. In short, only if middle-range research had justified the meanings assigned to archaeological observations as measures for the variables cited could such testing proceed.

As I have already suggested, these assignments of meaning cannot be evaluated with "test implications" reasoned directly from the archaeological record, where all conclusions regarding past dynamics are in fact inferences. By late 1969 I had come to the position outlined here. In addition, I had concluded that our methods for inference could only be tested actualistically; that is, in situations where the dynamics of archaeological formation processes could be examined experimentally and directly. Given these conclusions I viewed two publishing events of the early 1970s as setbacks in my attempt to develop a sound archaeological methodology.

The first of these events was the appearance in 1970 of an article by John Fritz and Fred Plog titled "The Nature of Archaeological Explanation." This paper represented the combination of two papers delivered at the 1968 annual meeting of the Society for American Archaeology in Santa Fe, New Mexico. The part I consider most misleading—regrettably, one of the more influential pieces written during the 1970s—was titled "The Explanatory Research Design." It was most likely the work of Plog, and has been reprinted in a number of his subsequent works (see, e.g., Plog 1974). Ironically, it has been cited as the basic epistemological position of the new archaeology.

Plog opposed the strict inductivists' research design and presented a new form, one that he believed would place archaeological research in its proper "new" posture. This research design may be summarized as (a) acquisition of a hypothesis, (b) formulation of test implications, (c) formulation of a research strategy, (d) acquisition of data, (e) analysis of data, (f) testing of the hypothesis, and (g) evaluation of research.

This sequence of tactics appears to be a rational method for testing a hypothesis, but in the case of archaeological research we may reasonably ask where one acquires the "data" for testing, and how one formulates test implications. As I have already suggested, if one is testing an interpretative principle linking static residues to causal or conditioning dynamics, one cannot test such a hypothesis against archaeological data where only static material exists empirically. Nevertheless, Fritz and Plog have focused on the testing of interpretative propositions about the meanings to be assigned to archaeological observations. In later works by Plog (1974), the same research design is again advocated; however, here Plog is interested in testing propositions about the way culture change proceeded in the past. In such a case a true deductive–nomological approach would begin with a hypothesis deduced from a body of theory regarding the causes of culture change. Instead Plog (1974:55) begins with a definition of growth and proceeds to justify the definition as a useful statement or concept. He summarizes what is considered to be an essential definition of growth, which entails increases in a system conceptualized in four dimensions: population, differentiation, integration, and energy or resource use. *As I see it he presents a definition of growth,* and no hypotheses. The next section focuses on the combinations and permutations of potential interaction among the various dimensions said to define growth by their magnitude changes. Then follows a chapter titled "Test Implications." The discussion is an attempt to warrant the use of certain archaeological facts as indicators of the four dimensions outlined in the definition of growth. The number of dwelling units in the study area is taken as a measure of population, and the number of different kinds of activity sites is taken as a measure of differentiation, whereas integration is said to be measured by the kinds of groups inhabiting a settlement, differential treatment of persons within burial populations, and the appearance of new kinds of "integrative structures." What we see in all these cases are inductively reasoned arguments assigning meaning to properties of the archaeological record. They constitute an operational definition of growth stipulated for use by the archaeologist. Plog then argues that the technological changes commonly noted by others for the Basketmaker–Pueblo transition in the Southwest should be accounted for by the "growth model" (Plog 1974:80). As I read it, the idea is that there are determinant interactions between a system's condition of growth and patterns of formal change in technology as have been measured by others. This is at best a vague "functional" model that says that changes in one section of a system will affect other components of the system. How this happens is not specified, and certainly the basic statistical approach used is simply an inductive search procedure aimed at uncovering patterning. No details of the patterning were specified as expectations beyond the "functional" expectation. All the test implications are inductively reasoned stipulations of meaning. *There is no argued theoretical position, nor are there any hypotheses deduced for testing.* Test implications become expanded operational definitions. No consideration is given to the problem of using the archaeological record as meaningful fact, and there is no recognition of the differences between researching the character of the archaeological record and the historical processes of the past. Nevertheless, Plog's work has served as a model for many as to how the "new archaeology" should be done.

The second event was the appearance of Watson, LeBlanc, and Redman's (1971) *Explanation in Archaeology.* When the book appeared I found it very frustrating in a number of ways. First, unlike Plog, these authors recognized that there were major differences imposed on archaeologists' tactics by the nature of the data base. For instance, in recognition of the points I have developed here, that one cannot readily test an argument relating statics to dynamics when all one has are static facts, Watson *et al.* (1971) state,

> Ordinarily, accepted or confirmed laws are used to formulate hypothetical explanations for a given case. The laws themselves are usually neither formulated nor explicitly tested by the archaeologist; his primary concern is almost always with the formulating and testing of explanations of given cases [p. 26].

This is a very telling argument. If it is correct, and I think it is, then the major challenge for archaeologists using strictly archaeological facts is not testing laws,[10] which serve as the covering propositions for explanations of past processes of culture change, but instead justifying the linkage of a causal dynamic (the relevant and unambiguous conditions for production of archaeological properties) to the facts used in constructing the past. As I have already pointed out, the linkage between the conceptual world of conditioning dynamics and the conceptual world of derivative statics is neither direct nor self-evident. Ideas about this linkage must be justified through the citation of well-developed diagnostic criteria establishing the unambiguous relevance of certain observations to the conceptualization of those facts as an accurate statement about past conditions. Unfortunately, the authors seem to forget this basic point, and proceed to outline the Hempel–Oppenheim scheme of deductive–nomological or covering law mode of explanatory argument. Given this, they move directly into the discussion of the works of Bill Longacre and James Hill as examples of this approach. This simply is not accurate. These two pieces of research were never conceived or executed in terms of the deductive–nomological model. (In the case of Longacre's work, this is well demonstrated by a fine analytical piece of work by Morgan [1973].) Look at what happened to James Hill's work when it was translated by Watson *et al.* (1971) into their idea of the deductive–nomological model:

> Hill then deduces a series of sixteen test implications utilizing his knowledge of activities in contemporary pueblos. His reasoning is as follows in terms of the logical framework established in the preceding part of this chapter. . . . On the basis of the general considerations described above Hill infers that the rooms at the archaeological site of Broken K Pueblo were functionally similar to those in contemporary pueblos. This inference can be stated in the form of a hypothetical general law, although the law is of limited scope because of the specificity of the circumstances [p. 39].

To my way of thinking, this is nonsense. Hill was performing a classic inductive argument from ethnographic analogy where he sought to strengthen the inductive inference by expanding the positive analogy through further ethnographic study.

As a result of the wide circulation and great attention given both the Fritz and Plog (1970) article and the Watson *et al.* (1971) book, there arose a view of the new archaeology as a school dedicated exclusively to the testing of propositions within a deductive–nomological framework using a covering law model of explanation. Ironically, the failure to analyze the particular problems of inference that archaeologists have to face ensured that this is the very thing that archaeologists can not do as long as they sought to use the archaeological record as their empirical domain for testing. As I have pointed out, there is no way to achieve the program laid out by Plog or by Watson, LeBlanc, and Redman as long as the archaeological record is seen as the source of information for use in testing propositions about dynamics. When any proposition links the dynamics of the past to the static derivatives remaining in the present, there is no way of testing such a linkage with only static facts. Similarly, when an argument is advanced citing two or more variables operating in mutually determinate ways as accounting for the dynamics of systems change occurring in the past, such an argument can only be made by linking past dynamics to contemporary statics. As long as the science treating relationships between statics and dynamics is nonexistent, all such argument will remain intuitive, impressionistic, and unevaluated.

Some persons seemed to sense the dilemma and have suggested that archaeologists are only "law users." That is, we justify the laws we use in explanations by citing research justifications in the works of scientists operating in other fields. The only problem with this position is that no *other* science seeks to explain the statics of the archaeological record. Others have operated as if we had a science capable of testing propositions about dynamics but have used conventions and stipulated meanings assigned quite intuitively to archaeological observations. The growth of a science of archaeology that I and others envisioned in the early days of the new archaeology was effectively retarded by the failure to appreciate the interesting epistemological problems presented to us by the static character of our primary data base.

Notes

1. The traditional view regarding the meaning of similarities is still very much a part of the contemporary literature (see, e.g., Sackett 1982). Ironically, the view that Sackett attributes to me is the view that I was arguing *against* as expressed by Bordes. (See my discussion of the "old world view" in Chapters 24 and 28.) Sackett also mistakenly suggested that I was advocating a "lithic sociology" because of the success of "ceramic sociology." I have never advocated a "ceramic sociology." In fact, the very demonstration of within-site variability in style was a challenge to the standard approach, or what Sackett calls the isochrestic model (Sackett 1982:96). If the arguments of Longacre and Hill are correct as a general condition, then the association between place and ethnic identity as normally conceived is clearly challenged.

2. One of the most interesting properties of culture is that it makes possible the expedient assignment of meaning to experience. This is as true today as it was in the past, and as true for persons reading essays in archaeology as for any other type of experience.

Perhaps the most mistaken reading of my work (particularly my essay "Archaeology as Anthropology"), as well as some of the works of Longacre and Hill, was that we were advocating the elimination of the difference between archaeology and ethnography. For instance, Eggert (1976) equates my statement about recovering the "fossilized structure of the total cultural system" with the ethnographer's ability to "produce data about almost every aspect of life of the group he is dealing with [Eggert 1976:58]." He then points out that the archaeological record does not yield data on an equal range of phenomena. I never suggested that the archaeological record would yield the same kinds of facts as an ethnographic study. What I sought to demonstrate in the early 1960s was that (a) all statements about the past were inferences, and (b) there was sufficient information already presented in ethnographic descriptions to illustrate the complex interrelationships between material things and the organizations of a cultural system. These descriptions were sufficient to illustrate that most of the then current interpretative conventions (diffusion, migration, independent invention, progressive growth, and cultural decline) were inadequate to account for the patterning demonstrable in the archaeological record.

The claim that we advocated a kind of ethnography of the past was a favorite polemic of the strict empiricists. Their position was that we were limited to generalizing from the facts as given in the record. The quantity and quality of these facts were clearly limited, and we should not try to go beyond our data base and engage in inferential argument. This is what I have come to think of as the Yale position (see, e.g., Coe 1978; Dunnell 1978, 1980; Eggert 1976). Yale has not been the only seat of such views, however. The most distorted idea of what was going on, for instance, is perhaps best illustrated by the following passage:

Not all anthropology is appropriate to the aims of archaeology, and, what is perhaps even more important, we cannot allow archaeology to be presented as a kind of imperfect anthropology of the past.

Archaeology sailed perilously close to this particular intellectual iceberg during the 1960s when it set out to discover matrilineal pottery and other "signatures" of prehistoric social organization. I concur with Roland Fletcher's recent argument that such efforts created false expectations for archaeologists while at the same time [they] demeaned the discipline of archaeology [R.A. Gould 1980:250].

3. For a very honest and revealing reaction to the developments during the early years of the new archaeology, see Bayard's article (1969). If the reader follows all of this rhetoric, then he or she understands the viewpoint that the new archaeologists were criticizing—a strict inductive approach. Bayard's article illustrates, as did most of the writings of the traditional archaeologists, a strong belief that the archaeological record could not be directly "translated" into statements about the past: "The archaeologist's laboratory does not consist of a cultural system; it consists of a severely limited sample of remains of the material manifestations of cultural systems [Bayard 1969:337]."

This point was a basic tenet of traditional archaeology and was taken for granted by the new archaeologists of the early 1960s. We had all been trained as traditionalists and had all been instructed in the "dangers" of inference and the speculative ("theoretical," as it was then called) character of attempting to make inferences from archaeological observations.

Informational attrition is great in our discipline. Ten to 15 years after "Archaeology as Anthropology" was written, Michael Schiffer (1972, 1976a) felt called upon to rediscover the fact that we should keep straight the distinction between *archaeological context* (facts of the archaeological record) and *systemic context* (dynamic conditions that existed in the past).

4. The first point to be emphasized is that I never presented the "Smudge pits" article as a deductively reasoned argument. I simply do not know where the myth was started that this paper was intended to illustrate deductive argument. For instance, R.H. Thompson wrote, "his 'Hide Smoking' paper (Binford 1967a) is an excellent example of inductive reasoning . . . despite the fact that Binford presents it as an example of the deductive approach [1972:37]." I wish to emphasize that I presented it as an inductive argument and then tried to illustrate why such an argument was of limited utility. Sabloff *et al.* (1973:110–111) cite the paper as a case study of "Hempel's deductive–nomological model"! Then they note its "failure" in these terms as evidence that it is "impossible to construct a hypothetico-deductive structure that does not ultimately rest on inductive confirmation." I suppose the ultimate irony came when Ruth Tringham (1978) pointed out that the failure of my argument was simply that it was an argument from analogy!

"Having found a 'convincing' correspondence between the formal attributes of the archaeological features and the ethnographic features . . . Binford makes a leap and assumes that the function is also the same [Tringham 1978:187]." Of course, that was the point I was illustrating. It's nice that after so many years someone finally got the point.

5. Some confusion exists regarding the use of the term middle-range research and the source of its introduction into the archaeological literature. In 1972–1973 I conducted an advanced seminar at the University of New Mexico, which was locally known among the students as the "middle-range theory seminar." This was during the time that I was developing some of my Nunamiut material and trying to get students to accept the challenge of theory building. I had previously discussed archaeological theory (see Chapter 2), but it became clear that the strategies appropriate to both the development and the testing of archaeological theory did not apply to the development and testing of general theory. As this contrast was clarified the term archaeological theory seemed increasingly ambiguous, and so I adopted the phrase middle-range theory, or middle-range research. In the spring of 1974 three students who had been in my seminar delivered a paper to the Society of American Archaeology entitled "Middle-Range Theory in Archaeology." In it they discussed the need for more attention to be given to *linking* arguments, arguments that gave meaning to the archaeological record.

Independently of this event Mark Raab and Al Goodyear developed a paper entitled "On the Value of Middle-Range Theory in Archaeological Research Strategies." As I recall, I first heard of this paper after James Ebert, Robert Hitchcock, and Richard Taylor returned from the Washington meetings where someone had told them about it. In the paper the authors suggested that archaeology should adopt a position advocated by Merton (1968) for sociology—as I understand it, that high-level theory is very abstract and therefore not amenable to discussion in empirical terms, so a middle ground, a kind of theory with empirical content, is advocated (see Goodyear *et al.* 1978).

My idea of middle-range research is not so much concerned with levels of abstraction as with the tactics of both theory generation and testing using different types of data and serving different ends in research. (See Chapter 27, and the discussion in *Bones* [L.R. Binford 1981b].)

6. The dates of publication for some of the works mentioned may be somewhat misleading with regard to the actual integration of others' ideas and arguments into my thinking during the late 1960s. For instance, my reply to Willey and Sabloff (Binford 1968c) was delivered at the annual meeting of the Society for American Archaeology in Santa Fe in May 1968. At this same meeting John Fritz and Fred Plog delivered their papers, which when combined would not appear in print until 1970. (See "Society for American Archaeology" in *American Antiquity* **34** (1): 105–112, particularly page 107.) I was aware of the arguments they were developing in 1966, certainly, and probably earlier. Similarly, Patty Jo Watson and her husband, Red, visited my former wife, Sally, and I while we were still teaching at UCLA. (I think it was the summer of 1967.) At that time I became familiar with the major thrust of the Watsons' thought as it would appear much later (Watson *et al.* 1971).

7. The degree to which the later works of Watson *et al.* (1971) as well as the earlier paper by Fritz and Plog (1970) presented a distorted picture of the new archaeology is perhaps nowhere better illustrated than in Mike Schiffer's review of the book I edited under the title *For Theory Building in Archaeology*. He suggested that when I pointed out that Jim Hill's storage room argument was not an example of deductive–nomological reasoning I was repudiating "for the wrong reasons contributions made by colleagues and former students [Schiffer 1980:377]." Schiffer clearly believed what others had said about Hill's work.

8. The important article by Pat Munson (1969) pointed to even further problems with the use of arguments from analogy. I was fascinated by Munson's article and tried to find ways around the seeming ambiguity of the case he presented. His work appeared to me to be just the type of constructive exploration into our problems of inference that would move us toward a better understanding of our methods.

I wrote most of my reply in the spring of 1969 and submitted it about a year later to *American Antiquity* for publication. The new editor had just started a policy of peer review. My article was sent out for review and returned with a rejection notice plus copies of the comments by my "peers." One reviewer went on and on about how I was only motivated to prove myself right, concluding that my discussion had no intellectual merit. Another said that "finally" someone had put me in my place and that I was just trying to wiggle my way out of a "clear intellectual defeat." I appealed to the editor but to no avail, I thought it clearly unfair to publish an answer to my article but to refuse to publish my reply. I became angry and dropped my subscription to *American Antiquity*, that is, my membership in the society. I remained a nonmember until my levelheaded friend Jerry Sabloff persuaded me to rejoin in 1978.

My reply was published in *An Archaeological Perspective* L.R. Binford (1972a:52–58). It was there that I first presented the idea that we needed to demonstrate a "necessary relationship" between the properties cited in a positive analogy and the conditions inferred. My whole argument in that reply was a classic example of what C.G. Morgan (1973:271–272) would consider "an attempt to support a hypothesis by making a plausible (but not deductively valid) chain of reasoning from the hypothesis to observationally available data." This is a far cry from the general belief that my "Smudge pits" arguments were examples of deductively drawn arguments.

9. I have written a description of the events surrounding my facing the issue of testing interpretative principles with archaeological data (see L.R. Binford 1983, and Chapters 5 and 8, this volume). It was my work with the Mousterian and the problem of interassemblage variability that was my best teacher. (This is treated in Chapters 8 and 12 of this book.)

10. Schiffer's suggestions seemed to me to miss the mark in a number of important ways. Traditional archaeology had operated with an inadequate array of interpretive conventions. Schiffer (1976a:17–22) seemed to be saying that we should invest time in testing the interpretive principles and propositions

then in current use within the field. I was of the opinion that we had a great deal to learn about the archaeological record and needed to get on with the investigation of formation processes through direct field study. On this issue I was in agreement with Tuggle *et al.* (1972).

> While it is true that archaeological research is often carried to the point of testing and then not followed through [Binford 1968a:14] it may be that the major problem behind this *is the lack of propositions worth testing*. This in turn is probably related to both the lack of explicitness in research designs as well as to the general weakness of archaeological explanatory frameworks. All of these areas of difficulty—explicitness in research systems—*may be related to the general lack of concern for logical and methodological theory*. In sum, a research design which is concerned with explanation in archaeology should devote as much attention to the problem of hypothesis formulation as to other problem areas [p. 6; emphasis mine].

2   1968

Archeological Theory and Method

> Archeology is neither history nor anthropology. As an autonomous
> discipline, it consists of a method and a set of specialized techniques
> for the gathering or "production" of cultural information [Taylor, 1948,
> p. 44].

It has been said that archaeology, while providing data and generalizations in such fields as history
and general anthropology, lacks a systematic body of concepts and premises constituting archaeological theory. According to this view, the archaeologist must borrow his theoretical underpinning
from the field of study his work happens to serve, or do without. Whether the latter alternative
be an admissible one does not seem to be an arguable point. Acceptable field work can perhaps
be done in a theoretical vacuum, but integration and interpretation without theory is incon-
ceivable. . . . It seems to us that American archaeology stands in a particularly close and, so far
as theory is concerned, dependent relationship to anthropology [Willey and Phillips, 1958, p. 1].

These quotations voice a common opinion regarding the degree to which archeology can be said to make use of a body of theory which is unique or even specific to
itself. Taylor defines archeology as a method and set of specialized techniques; Willey
and Phillips accept this view, at least in part, in stating that it is possible to do field
work in a vacuum, but they add that interpretation is dependent upon theory, in this
case anthropological theory. In the papers that follow it will be argued that scientific
methods and techniques can be developed only when they are relevant to certain aims
and only with regard to the properties of the empirical data utilized. A. C. Spaulding
has stated:

Archaeology can be defined minimally as the study of the interrelationships of form, temporal
locus, and spatial locus exhibited by artifacts. In other words, archaeologists are always concerned
with these interrelationships, whatever broader interests they may have, and these interrelationships
are the special business of archaeology (1960a, p. 439).

Accepting Spaulding's minimal definition of what archeology is, we can go a step
further and specify its aims as the explanation of the observed interrelationships; in

Originally appeared in *New Perspectives in Archaeology,* edited by Sally R. Binford and Lewis R. Binford, published by
Aldine Publishing, Hawthorne, New York, pp. 1–4, © 1968.

other words, as an explanation of the order we observe in the archeological record. Archeological theory consists of propositions and assumptions regarding the archeological record itself—its origins, its sources of variability, the determinants of differences and similarities in the formal, spatial, and temporal characteristics of artifacts, and features and their interrelationships. It is in the context of this theory that archeological methods and techniques are developed.

Since artifacts are cultural data and since they once functioned as elements of a cultural system, many of the explanations we might offer for observations made on the archeological record will refer to organizational features of past cultural systems. On the other hand, the archeologist might explain an observed pattern in his data by citing sampling error. The former situation is no more justification for saying the archeologist is a technician in the service of anthropology than is the latter for calling him a technician in the service of probability statistics. The archeologist *is* an anthropological scientist, but this does not imply that there is no body of theory specific to his specialty. On the contrary, advances in archeological theory are prerequisite to the achievement of broader anthropological goals. It is through theoretical advances and sound arguments of relevance that we can link our observations on the archeological record to particular questions on the operation of past cultural systems.

Archeology shares with other anthropological sciences the aim of explaining differences and similarities among cultural systems. We are, therefore, concerned with cultural theory and processual arguments which treat problems of the interrelationship of cultural (and any other relevant class of) variables which have explanatory value.

If archeological theory attempts to develop arguments of relevance for archeological data to past conditions, then it should develop arguments on the explanatory relevance of cultural and ecological variables to differences and similarities among cultural systems. Archeological anthropologists must try to advance both of these complementary areas. We might be able to demonstrate the relevance of our observations to certain past conditions, but if these conditions are irrelevant for measuring either cultural change or variability, then our accomplishments would be (as Deetz cautions) "sterile methodological virtuosity." On the other hand, advances in cultural theory which place crucial explanatory value on variables not previously considered challenge the archeologist to develop arguments of relevance so that he may make use of these advances. In such a case the hope would be that archeological data could be used in testing hypotheses drawn from theories of general anthropological interest. The ability of archeologists to maximize advances in culture theory depends on the existence of a viable and progressive body of archeological theory and method.

3 1975

Sampling, Judgment, and the Archaeological Record

Introduction

In Part One of this book very little discussion has been devoted to sampling. Discontent about the bias in the archaeological record is one nonsampling theme common to several chapters.[1] Such a discussion seems to stem from the naive notion that the archaeological record is directly observable as "meaningful" information about the past; it is not, never has been and never will be.

The archaeological record is a contemporary phenomenon. It is above all a static phenomenon. It is what remains in static form of dynamics which occurred in the past as well as dynamics occurring up until present observations are made. The only meaningful statements we can make about the past are dynamic statements. The only statements we can make directly from the archaeological record are some form of descriptive statics. Getting to the past is then a process in which the archaeologist gives meaning to static phenomena in dynamic terms. This is a cultural process, the assignation of meaning to experience engaged in by the archaeologist. To point out continuously that data do not speak for themselves and that meanings assigned to archaeological observations may be wrong should not be surprising to anyone. Scientists particularly should appreciate that the scientific method was developed to cope with this problem in the first place.

That the archaeologist is surprised or just coming to the realization that data do not speak for themselves tells me something about the lack of scientific development in the field, but nothing about "limitations" on our potential understanding of the past. The limitations on our knowledge of the past derive from our lack of imagination as to how best to operationalize archaeological observations for permitting an evaluation of the meanings which we have given to archaeological facts. Gaining an evaluation of our ideas about the past through the use of archaeological observations of specified relevance is a scientific approach.

Originally appeared in *Sampling in Archaeology*, edited by James W. Mueller, published by University of Arizona Press, Tucson, pp. 251–257, © 1975.

Raising objections that the archaeological record may be "biased" seems to stem from some strange expectation that the archaeological record is some kind of fossilized picture remaining to us from the past with built-in and self-evident meanings upon which "times arrow" has played disturbing tricks. No such meaningful picture exists complete with semantic directions as to how properly to read the record. All meanings come from us. All evaluations as to the reliability of those meanings as statements about the past must be made against facts operationalized as relevant and organized so as to permit an evaluation of our ideas about the past. Telling me that the archaeological record cannot be translated mechanically into statements about the past according to some set of rules for assigning meaning does not surprise me or depress me as to our potential for gaining understanding about the past. That only depresses nonscientists.

One general sampling point that has been raised in a contemporaneous publication concerns anatomy and physiology (Jelks 1975). What can you learn about an organized structure from a random spatial sample? My impression is that little can be learned using conventional archaeological grid units (three-meter squares, five-foot squares, etc.). If I am attempting to obtain an unbiased, representative sample of the population of pottery sherds on a site, or flint chips etc., I might come fairly close with a 10-30 percent spatial random sampling in conventional grid units. However, if my target population is the population of houses on a site, I would recover none if my grid units were conventional units, unless of course they were exceptionally small houses! Finally if my concern is with the internal organization of a site, what could I learn from a 10-30 percent random spatial sample? Nothing, or very little. I might be able to define the problem in that I could demonstrate differences and similarities between the sample units. However, the necessary spatial structure of proximity, association with features, and patterns of continuous variation, which provide the linking warrants in the definition of a structure, would still be buried (Jelks 1975). At last we are dealing with a sampling problem. Population biologists have faced similar problems and some knowledge has been gained and some solutions have been suggested. First, a sampling strategy must be evaluated with regard to the character of the target population to be sampled, not in absolute terms. A given strategy may work well for supplying information about the population of small movable items on a site, but not very well for houses. Secondly, to recover data on a number of target populations simultaneously may require a variety of sampling strategies executed in series; this is the reason that long ago I suggested *stage excavations*.

Some anti-sampling discussions set up a straw man, a sampling problem, and an inappropriate sampling procedure. Discussions which attempt to argue that sampling has no role or is a cookbook technique to be used by nonexperts have no place in archaeology. Such discussion betrays a naivety about what archaeologists are doing. The demonstration that one procedure does not do what an archaeologist wishes simply indicates that the archaeologist used an inappropriate strategy; it in no way argues that an appropriate sampling strategy could not have been used by an archaeologist who understood sampling and the problem to be solved. The same answer could be made to the person who smilingly objects that the archaeologist using sampling procedures is somehow not using good judgment. For instance, I once heard an objection that if the sampling procedure suggested by me was employed, the crew would have to dig a 10 × 10 out in the middle of Saginaw Bay. Another time it was laughingly said that Binford couldn't dig a particular burial mound because it had been excluded from the area gridded for sampling. Such objections are silly. For instance, one of the assumptions of a sampling strategy is that one can enumerate all those units in the frame from which a sample is to be drawn. If the investigator missed a burial mound, or suggested that some area under water was within the frame, it may well betray a real problem about the archaeologist's competence; it is not, however, a comment on the utility or lack thereof of a sampling strategy. This is one of the largest problems in archaeology—the inadequacy of the archaeologist. Sampling can help the archaeologist overcome these human limitations and uniquenesses which bias his ability to see clearly that the archaeological record is an aid. This is one of the roles of sampling, aiding our judgment.

Specific Comments

After this general discussion, I would like to review each of the individual chapters. The major thrust of chapter 2, by Michael B. Collins is about confusion, confusion between the character of static data, and explanations for the character of that data. All archaeological data are static and importantly *contemporary*. Our observations on the archaeological record are contemporary phenomena, and it is only with these contemporary facts that we learn something either about the character of the archaeological record or in turn what static archaeological facts can do to inform us about the accuracy of our ideas about the dynamics of the past. Any statements about the dynamics of the past or event sequences, which have occurred up until the time the archaeologist makes his observations and which might alter the archaeological facts as seen. Sampling is a procedure which is concerned with providing a representative and unbiased view of the archaeological record as it exists at the time the archaeologists begin making observations. All the problems of erosion, disturbance by rodents, attrition through decay, subsequent destruction by man, etc., which may contribute to the complexity of the archaeological record as it exists at the time the archaeologist begins making observations are potential explanations for the observations which the archaeologist makes. They are in no way relevant to strategy decisions made by the archaeologist as to how best to obtain a representative and unbiased set of observations on the archaeological deposit as it exists. Sampling is concerned with getting as clear a picture as possible, within the limits of stated budget, labor investments, and research goals of the archaeological record as it exists. Discussion of all the factors, which may contribute to distortions in the record between the time of observation and the target time in the past of interest to the archaeologist, do not affect in any way the desirability of obtaining a representative and unbiased view of the archaeological remains as they in fact exist. Viewed from this perspective most of what Collins has to say is of no interest whatsoever to a discussion of sampling. Perhaps his arguments are more relevant to the questions of whether we should even attempt to use archaeological facts in evaluating our ideas about past dynamics or whether it is worthwhile to even do archaeology of any kind!

James W. Mueller's chapter 3 is an argument of "misplaced concreteness." I am suggesting, regardless of the unit specified in the sampling frame, that that unit is known through some idea of a cluster of attributes. Thus, regardless of the units in the sampling frame, one can argue that at least semantically one is cluster sampling. Stated another way, any entity can be analyzed into some set of properties, a cluster of attributes, and if this is done one is cluster sampling, as long as the entity is the unit in the frame. Viewed this way all sampling events are either clusters or not, depending upon the analytical level at which one is working.

Chapter 4, by Dwight W. Read, is fine and requires no comment.

David H. Thomas' chapter 5 appears to be beating a straw man. He seems to be proclaiming that archaeologists have been all wrong, and he has data to prove such a contention. He seems to be saying archaeologists have considered that basic units of meaning in the archaeological record came in site packages. He looked and couldn't find such packages; therefore archaeologists have been wrong all along. Although archaeologists continually speak of sites, this does not mean that they assume sites as basic units of organization. To my knowledge, K.C. Chang and his students, and perhaps Bruce Trigger, are the only archaeologists I know of to whom Thomas' arguments are directed. Chang proposed, as an alleged revolutionary idea, that archaeologists abandon the artifact as the basic unit of observation, and treat the site as such. He never understood, even after I forcefully pointed it out, that the site is a unit of synthesis. One cannot demonstrate the existence of a site until one can demonstrate some spatial clustering of artifacts, which are the units of observation necessary to the definition of a site. As Thomas points out, if one cannot demonstrate a clustering of artifacts, one does not have sites. Only Chang would be distressed to find that archaeology could not be conducted in Thomas' area since the basic units of archaeological observation did not exist! Thomas seems to think his data would somehow distress other archaeologists and demands that they change their ways. That expectation, in my view, could only arise if Thomas felt that K.C. Chang spoke for the field of archaeology. Chang is wrong in his arguments and I think most archaeologists appreciate this, except perhaps Thomas.

Charles L. Redman was kind enough to point out that it is over ten years ago that I read my first paper at a Society for American Archaeology meeting on sampling (Binford 1964). At that time I had a message for archaeologists and they did not like it; I was telling them that their judgments were bad. I suggested that they did not know as much about the archaeological record as they thought they did; it was not as simple as they thought, and that we might try to generate some procedures which would help us learn, rather than assume we knew it all while we were destroying the archaeological record in the meantime. Since that time there have been a number of studies made in which the archaeological record was viewed as a potential set of organized relationships. Applied to its investigation were procedures largely designed to permit the evaluation of one's "judgment" and the traditional "judgment" of archaeologists. The result has been that we have learned some interesting things about the character of the archaeological record, and the inadequacies of our own or traditional judgments for guiding archaeological data collection.

In informal discussions and in the literature, one frequently hears the criticism or suggestion that sampling procedure is a method for idiots, and any archaeologist worth his salt would instead use "good judgment." Such a statement, as I see it is a paradox, since in my view the archaeologist must be continually using good judgment with respect to two sides of an equation. First, he must attempt to use good judgment about the nature of the archaeological record and what he hopes to gain from its investigation. Second, he *must* use good judgment as regards his potential ignorance of the archaeological record. Only when both are considered is "good judgment" evident; if only one or the other is evident, we have naivety or arrogance, but not good judgment. I would say I am in favor of good judgment on all grounds. We must continuously remind ourselves of our ignorance, and if we ever conclude that no ignorance exists, then we are not scientists. Science has the interesting characteristic of being cumulative, and hopefully what we are ignorant about today, we can use good judgment about tomorrow. To argue that having good judgment about the nature of the archaeological record is justification for abandoning good judgment about our potential ignorance of the archaeological record is a fallacy. Sampling is a procedure addressed to the latter; it cannot be abandoned in favor of arrogance. As we learn more of both the archaeological record and our ignorance, we may begin to elaborate and make more complex the techniques based on good judgment.

My findings with respect to feature and artifact distributions at Hatchery West were confirmed by data from the Gilliland Site in Southwestern Colorado (Rohn n.d.). These sites help illustrate my discussion of good judgment in the preceding paragraph. Once we begin to see that there are redundancies between places as widely separated as central Illinois and southwestern Colorado or Upper Paleolithic sites of France and those of contemporary Eskimos, we have the basis for beginning the development of middle-range theory dealing with the human use of space, resources, etc.; in short, theory building. As such progress is made and we understand more— have more detailed expectations of the archaeological record—we may use better judgment in the design of excavation strategies. For instance, I am confident that there are certain features and variables common to occupation in rock shelters, regardless of their specific locations and periods of occupancy. Comparative studies of rock shelter occupations from Australia, Southeast Asia, Southern France, the American Southwest etc., would almost certainly uncover much redundancy in the way in which man has made use of such bounded life-space. In short, we might expect certain common solutions to common contingencies, such as drip lines, limits of natural light, areas of natural heat radiation, etc. If we know such things, we certainly could excavate rock shelters from a more informed position, with more specific expectations and problems in mind; in short, our excavations could be guided by better judgment. Regardless, we would still be constrained to take precaution so as to insure that the exercise of our good judgment did not bias our results in directions unwarranted by the archaeological realities. No matter how informed we become, no matter how skilled and "expert" as archaeologists we become, we must continue to approach the archaeological record with humility and take steps to insure that our actions do not distort the character of the data we recover. That is one of the primary goals of sampling, particularly when total excavations are out of the question and we must make use of "partial" data.

Chapter 9, by James A. Brown, is a fine example of good judgment. In developing a procedure Brown seeks to use as judiciously as possible our accumulated knowledge and expectations about the archaeological record while also providing for a sampling-based strategy that will permit us to evaluate how good our judgment has been.

Chapter 10, by David L. Asch, provides us with an example of relative use of judgment, and it in no way negates the need for sampling strategies. For instance, Asch makes the point that sampling made little sense in the context of asking questions about a large population of deer represented on his site, and yet he had only 52 mandibles for evaluation as to age. Here is an example of the use of judgment in the context of limited knowledge; expand the knowledge, and the use of good judgment leads to different conclusions. For instance, instead of attempting to obtain information on relative ages of deer from mandibles which are minimally represented, why not examine the abundant remains of long bone articulator ends for an epiphyseal union series and obtain age data on the population in that manner? Good judgment would dictate epiphyseal union studies rather than tooth eruption studies to obtain the desired information. In the latter case if one was convinced that articulator ends were not biased in their presence or preservation, a sampling strategy might well save much time and effort without diminishing the accuracy of one's age estimates of the deer population present. In such a situation we see good judgment used in conjunction with sampling strategies to obtain desired results in the context of both economy of effort and goals of accuracy. Good judgment is always relative to our secure knowledge and understanding; if we have some humility about the latter, then the need for implementing strategies for obtaining some evaluative control over our alleged good judgment is always a necessary part of archaeological strategy—sampling strategies play such a role.

Robert Benfer's chapter 13 is interesting, although it might have been used more profitably elsewhere. His concern is obviously with pattern recognition in data already collected. Stratification is a process of analysis carried out by an investigator in terms of domains of information or areas of concern which the investigator deems important to gather information. The way one stratifies is a function of the assumptions or tentative hypothesis one generates as to the relative independence, dependence, or explanatory potential of dimensions of variation. How one goes about this task is related to how one does theory, and warrants for one method over another are gained from arguing down from theory, or more commonly, poorly formulated biased hunches as to what is important. Once again, no sampling for the latter is the approach used to obtain a representative and unbiased body of empirical material already specified as to its relevance.

The remaining chapters, by Judge, Ebert, and Hitchcock; Matson and Lipe; Morris; and Reid, Schiffer, and Neff (chap. 6, 7, 11, and 12), suggest means to improve and make more flexible sampling strategies. These things we need to know; we don't need to know in graphic terms that some archaeologists are poorly trained in how to do archaeology and the inherent problems associated with that task. Any archaeologist who is going to perform even at minimal acceptable levels in modern archaeology must be concerned with sampling procedures and how best to make use of them. The days of argument about whether sampling is appropriate in archaeology are over, and those engaged in such discussions are in my opinion fossils of a past era—an era in which archaeologists thought of themselves as knowledgeable experts applying their skills and expertise, totally naive about the responsibilities of the scientist. The scientist is continually worrying about his alleged knowledge and understanding. He worries about developing new means of using empirical materials for evaluating his alleged knowledge and understanding, and developing rules for giving meaning to things observed. Sampling plays a role, an important role, in this endeavor to increase the accuracy and breadth of our understanding about the past.

Note

1. All references to other parts and chapters refer to *Sampling in Archaeology*, the volume in which this originally appeared.

4   1977

General Introduction

Much has been written regarding the claims for a "New Archaeology," and there are arguments that attempt to assess the successes or failures of this alleged "movement." As far as I am concerned, however, much argumentative literature obscures the issues, at least those issues that I have tried to stress over a substantial period of time involving thought, research, writing, and teaching. I will not offer here an exhaustive critique of current debates, but I will point to certain differences between my views of archaeological science and the views of some of those who are generally lumped together with me as "New Archaeologists." In so doing, I will attempt to show that understanding is difficult to achieve, and that misunderstanding and confusion are common in the hands of struggling scientists.

The most commonly cited and debated point I have tried to emphasize is that to be productive, a scientist must operate with a self-conscious awareness of the ideas and assumptions by which he proceeds. I have suggested that facts do not speak for themselves; alleged inductivist approaches, which seek empirical generalizations, will not move us in the direction of explanation, and therefore understanding, of the facts observed. I have suggested that a self-conscious use of deductive methods is a prerequisite for scientific achievement. Since these suggestions appeared, there have been many attempted demonstrations and programmatic discussions of them. It is my impression that most of these have been misleading or simply plain distortions of scientific method. Allow me to emphasize the point that scientific methods are designed to evaluate ideas. Science seeks to employ empirical materials in such evaluations. Thus, the problem that any scientist must understand is how one moves from ideas to facts or observations, and, in turn, how one may then relate the empirical findings back to ideas in an evaluative manner. Many who have been confused about these points tend to view empirical materials as sources or inspirations for ideas. This may be true in many cases, but the sources for ideas are not the concern of science directly; the primary concern is *only the evaluation of ideas once they have been advanced.*

Originally appeared in *For Theory Building in Archaeology: Essays on Faunal Remains, Aquatic Resources, Spatial Analysis, and Systemic Modeling,* edited by Lewis R. Binford, published by Academic Press, New York, pp. 1–13, 1977. Copyright © 1977 by Academic Press, Inc. All rights of reproduction in any form reserved.

At this point, the reader may justifiably ask questions regarding the kind of ideas that scientists seek to evaluate. Are all ideas and concepts proper targets for scientific investigation? In one sense, the answer is yes, but in many important ways, it is no! The scientific method addresses itself to the evaluation of *theory*. The introduction of this term implies that all ideas and concepts are not aspects of theory, although all theory is essentially ideational and conceptual in character.

In moving between ideas about the world we live in and empirical observations of this world, the scientist must face a major problem: namely, what meaning is to be attributed to empirical observations? Only when observations have been given meaning can we discuss the nature of their relevance to ideas. That is, we can use only relevant empirical observations to argue the utility of our ideas. Relevance is established through arguments attempting to warrant that particular observations reliably and unambiguously inform us about certain conditions or states of systems or variables. Such arguments are always phrased in terms of the meanings given to observations and not simply in terms of the character of the observations themselves.

For instance, if we have the idea of a variable—for example, population pressure—we may immediately ask what empirical observations reliably and unambiguously inform us regarding the condition of this variable in different settings. Do we count numbers of archaeological sites, numbers of burials, numbers of broken pots, and so on, per unit of time? If we can advance a strong argument to support the contention that some class of empirical material reliably and unambiguously informs us about population pressure, we have provided meaning to that material through an operational definition of population pressure. In turn, we have simultaneously advanced a *convention* for assigning meaning to a specified class of empirical material. *A definition is not an hypothesis.* A definition specifies the relationship between a concept, word, or phrase, and a class of empirical or observational experience. On the other hand, an hypothesis asserts a relationship between two or more independently monitored variables said to be operative in the empirical world. When testing an hypothesis, the scientist must employ independent instruments to measure the multiple variables. He must have operational definitions of the variables stated in the hypothesis and, in turn, must specify the character of the anticipated interaction between the two or more classes of *defined* observational materials. Was the character of the observed interaction anticipated accurately by the hypothesis? If so, the ideas about the way in which the world works, from which the particular hypothesis was argued or deduced, can be said to have some utility.

Science is a method or procedure that directly addresses itself to the evaluation of cultural forms. That is, if we view culture as at least referring to the particularly human ability to give meaning expediently to experience, to symbol, and, in turn, view experience through this conceptual idiom, science is then concerned with evaluating the utility of the cultural tools produced.

Under these conditions, there is a paradox in that the scientist must use conceptual tools to evaluate alternative conceptual tools that have been advanced regarding the ways in which the world works. He never uses meaningless empirical material, only observations with alleged, and hopefully specific, attached meanings. There is no way out of this paradox: an evaluation of one set of ideas is dependent upon the accuracy of an assumed set of meanings, not currently under investigation, about what our observations meaningfully imply! This paradox is at the heart of the so-called "uncertainty principle," which asserts that we cannot prove anything positively; we may only negate hypothetical propositions. In any scientific argument, there are at least two types of tentative propositions: *hypotheses* deduced from ideas which we seek to evaluate, and *definitions* advanced as part of the argument that seeks to warrant the assertion that certain empirical materials may justifiably be used in evaluating the hypothesis. There is much confusion in the literature regarding different types of propositions and how they may be evaluated. Much of the recent discussion regarding scientific methods has failed to cope with this crucial paradox and has confused operational definitions with hypotheses.

For instance, James Hill's (1968) work is frequently cited as an example of hypothesis testing (see Watson, LeBlanc, and Redman (1971:37–45) and, therefore, as an example of the hypothetico-deductive method. I have not been able to find a single hypothesis in his work. (In all fairness, Hill does not make this error, only those who write about this work do so; he faithfully uses the term "proposition.") He addresses himself to a problem of identity. How do I archaeologically identify a storage room? He is concerned with warranting an *operational definition* for the concept "storage room." He is in no way testing an hypothesis regarding the expected forms of interaction between two or more variables, each operationalized independently for observational purposes. Hill's work is an excellent example of a strongly warranted argument that when certain observations are made and found to be congruent in rooms in sites of the American Southwest, one is justified in assertings that the room was used as a storage room in the past. The argument specifies the definiens of the concept "storage room." When one's experience matches the definiens, one is, by *convention,* justified in asserting that the room in question was a *storage room* in the past. Hill provides us with an operational definition for a concept that is useful in a restricted geographical and temporal frame. His work in no way allows us to understand (a) why he thinks such an operational definition is needed, (b) what ideas about dynamics would require the identification of storage rooms, or (c) how identifications, once they have been made, would be used in hypothesis testing.

In contrast, I might state as an example of an hypothesis that, other things being equal, dependence upon stored food will increase as the diversity of the subsistence base decreases in environments with less than 365-day growing seasons. Alternatively, other things being equal, dependence upon stored food will increase as the size of the consumer population increases in environments of less than 365 days of growing season. I will not attempt to argue the theory from which these hypotheses have been deduced; rather, they are simply cited as examples. Given these aforementioned hypotheses, we might view Hill's work as an attempt to operationalize an instrument for measuring dependency upon stored food. Some might argue that his operationalization—namely, the identification of storage rooms and perhaps the counting or measuring of storage room volume—is inadequate or ambiguous in that there are possibly other modes of storage or that things other than food may be stored in storage rooms. What I am suggesting is that, although one may offer strong support for the meaningful identification of some observed phenomena, this must remain merely an exercise or, at worst, a trivial endeavor, since the context of relevance in science for such attempts derives from the problem of operationalizing variables stated in hypotheses. Hill's work does not provide us with such a scientific context of relevance beyond some functional "understanding" of pattern variability in the archaeological record. Here Hill's work becomes unclear, since "understanding" is sought in the absence of theoretical relevance.

Aside from the confusion about hypotheses and definitions, there is a more general confusion about propositions and hypotheses. All propositions are not hypotheses. Many propositions are related to the evaluation of the adequacy and unambiguous nature of definitions. A classical, logical form of such a proposition is that all swans are white. Observations of black swans in Australia refutes the proposition. Has an hypothesis been tested? The answer is emphatically *NO*. Implied here is that the concept "swan" may be defined by criteria other than color, and, at one stage of our knowledge, we believed that white color was a powerful defining criterion of the concept "swan." Further observation shows that this is an unwarranted defining characteristic. Has such an observation refuted some theory regarding the pattern of interaction between color variables and other morphological or physiological variables? No, it has simply been shown that a particular incomplete definition of the concept "swan" is inadequate or ambiguous!

Let me draw another example from the recent literature, a work by Steven A. LeBlanc (1973:199–214). LeBlanc asserts that the logic used to evaluate a proposition has a basic form, and persons employing the proper form of logic, regardless of the content of the proposition, should not be subject to criticism, such as that of Flannery (1973:47:47–53). He also attacks the work of Tuggle, Townsend, and Riley (1972) and indirectly the work of Meehan (1968) as characterized by confusion concerning "models" and "laws." In my opinion, neither understands the differences between definitions and hypotheses, and LeBlanc is far from such an understanding. LeBlanc further confuses the issue by attempting to argue that good science is dependent on the adherence to the proper logical form of evaluation regardless of the character of the proposition or its role in scientific argument! One does not advance science by spending one's time evaluating definitions simply because they exist. Who cares whether they are accurate or inaccurate if they are irrelevant? Relevance in science derives from the relationships between theory and hypotheses; propositions in hypothetical form generated in a theoretical void remain at best some form of empirical generalization. If our work misses this point, regardless of how well our procedures meet certain criteria of formal logic, we are not scientists. We may be logicians, Jesuits, or "law and order archaeologists," but we are not productive scientists simply because we adhere to a formal paradigm of reasoning. If we work only with existential propositions, such as "the size of a Bushman site is directly proportional to the number of houses on it"—an observation inductively summarized from direct experience— rephrasing it to read "the size of an archaeological site is directly proportional to the number of houses on it" does not constitute theory building. If we then proceed with good logic and method to evaluate the general accuracy of the statement, what has been evaluated beyond the existential accuracy of the proposition? Nothing necessarily has been evaluated. In short, we have perhaps proven a universal fact, but we have in no way validated any theoretical proposition. One does not build theory by accumulating universal facts or empirical generalizations, no matter how complex they may be. This is not to say that knowledge of such empirical relationships or forms of patterning may not be useful, but that their utility can be evaluated only with regard to (a) the degree to which they serve to inspire questions as to why the world is the way it appears to be and (b) the degree to which they may be useful in arguments of relevance attempting to relate concepts of theoretical interest to facts of the empirical world. Both of these criteria ask how they stimulate theory building, not how they help to evaluate theory or to provide us with theory directly. What I am suggesting is that polemic assertions that one is working "hypothetico-deductively" are meaningless when only propositions of an existential or definitional character are involved. Such a stance is a misguided inductive strategy. It results in, as Flannery (1973:51) has aptly phrased it, "Mickey Mouse laws."

It has been suggested that there is a procedure or third "paradigm" consisting of the evolutionary-systems "package" with a statistical-probabilistic wrapping (Willey and Sabloff (1974:196) that may prove useful in archaeology. This, of course, is not a new suggestion, and it is one that has met with crowning failure whenever it has been attempted—as, for example, in sociology. Statistical or probabilistic statements as to relationships among things are simply complex empirical facts. The only assumption one needs to make in order to project from such facts is that the system will remain unchanged, that things will stay as they are. These are *projections*, not *predictions*, since the latter require the specification of the conditions under which both stability and change will be manifest. Predictions require understanding of dynamics, not merely simple comprehension of patterning. In my opinion, evolution refers to the processes responsible for changes and diversification in organization; it does not refer to the products of evolution and the patterning that we may observe in these products when they are viewed temporally or spatially. The products, including patterning, are what we must explain with evolutionary theory. Statistical summaries and probabilistic statements about the patterning do not explain; they simply describe.

This form of criticism brings us to a discussion of what I view as an interesting phase of archaeological history: Archaeology–1976. I have argued, perhaps with some effectiveness, that the traditional paradigms of archaeology were inadequate, misleading, and essentially, a set of conventions for accommodating archaeological observations to a given cognitive map of man, the past, and cultural dynamics. By opening Pandora's box, by questioning the accuracy of meanings traditionally assigned to observations, and by insisting that we concern ourselves with the scientific task of evaluating ideas and concepts used in archaeology, the field was placed in a self-evaluative posture. Reactions have been varied but of essentially three forms. (a) There has been a rejection of the entire argument and an adherence (with tenacity) to traditional views (Flannery's [1973] old and new fogies). (b) There have been impatient and enthusiastic excurions into the application of "scientific" methods and rhetoric in the absence of any substitutive or original theory. Here we see an overemphasis on method or logic coupled with an apparent faith that the application of logical methods will result in the generation of theory (the law-and-order people of Flannery [1973]). In my opinion, this has been a return to an inductive strategy. (c)

Finally, there are some who view the development of theory as the primary concern. This is a creative process for which there are no methodological rules to insure success. Given a theoretical vacuum left by the shaking of traditional archaeological ideas and conventions, we must seek new ideas, concepts, and their theoretical integration with reference to how the world works, why man behaves the way he does at different times and places, and how we may understand recognized patterns of changes and diversity in organized human behavior. Only to such theories may the scientific method be properly addressed. Thus, today's challenge is in theory building, and thus far little progress has been made, although many persons have seen the challenge and accepted it.

As I currently view this challenge, there are urgent needs for theory building on at least two levels. One level is what I refer to as *middle-range theory*. If one accepts observations made on the archaeological record as contemporary facts along with the idea that such facts are static, then clearly basic problems for the archaeologist include (a) how we get from contemporary facts to statements about the past, and (b) how we convert the observationally static facts of the archaeological record to statements of dynamics. Both of these problems pose the question of meaning. What meaning may we justifiably give to contemporary static facts regarding past dynamics? What conditions of dynamics, not available for observation, produce the forms and structures observable as static patterning in the archaeological record? In approaching this problem, we must develop ideas and theories (middle-range theory) regarding the formation processes of the archaeological record. Only through an accurate understanding of such processes can we reliably give meaning to the facts that appear, from the past, in the contemporary era.

It is interesting that, in the early days of the development of the science of geology, the focus of study was directed toward the elucidation of formation processes. What dynamic conditions produce what kinds of static effects? What remains in a geologic section can be reliably viewed as deriving from the operation of erosional processes in the past? Clearly such questions must be investigated through the study of contemporary facts, both dynamic and static. Early arguments in the field of geology centered around the validity of assumptions of uniformitarianism—that the same dynamic processes operative in the past are operative today. Obviously, such an assumption must be warranted to a high degree, since it is central to the development of meaningful arguments about the past that are deduced from contemporary observations on the geological or archaeological records. Without the development of a body of theory treating the relationships between statics and dynamics, and, also important, approaching this development with a deep concern for the degree to which uniformitarian assumptions may be justified, no real progress will be forthcoming.

I consider this the challenge to develop "middle-range theory"; I consider it middle range because I believe that we seek to make statements about the past in order to evaluate ideas we may hold about the conditions that brought about change and modification in the organization of dynamics occurring in past living systems. We seek understanding of the *processes* responsible for change and diversification in the organizational properties of living systems. In approaching this problem, we seek the development of general theory. The archaeologist must seek parallel development in theory relating to determined change and variability in processes resulting in the static facts remaining for our observation. Only with developments in both general and middle-range theory can the "scientific" method be appropriately employed. In the absence of theories and ideas for evaluation, discussion of appropriate scientific methods seems strangely misplaced.

Why do I suggest that the development of general and middle-range theory must proceed hand in hand? Simply because, in the absence of criteria of relevance, we may waste much time in developing middle-range theory concerning the dynamic significance of certain static facts that prove to be irrelevant to the evaluation of our ideas about the general determinant processes that promote change and diversification in living systems. The field must advance as a whole. Advances in middle-range theory divorced from general theory may prove to be a waste of time; similarly, advances in observational techniques or "field methods" may prove irrelevant once we have some idea of the kinds of data needed for evaluating our ideas.

In the following essays,[1] we present (a) a variety of attempts to explicate, not so much scientific methods conceived of as a set of procedures, but the particular functions that scientific methods play in seeking understanding and explanation; (b) a number of provocative discussions aimed at the development of middle-range theory—namely, suggestions concerning the relationships between dynamics and their static by-products remaining for the archaeologist to observe; (c) papers treating a further complication arising from the operation of noncultural dynamics on archaeological remains that modify the statics away from their original patterns as derived exclusively from the dynamics of cultural system—in Schiffer's (1972) terms, "N-transforms"; and finally (d) a number of papers that address more general issues relating to both the evaluation of ideas advanced, as well as provocative suggestions concerning ideas not previously considered in seeking to understand the processes responsible for changes in dynamics of cultural systems.

The chapters in this book are the products of students and faculty of the University of New Mexico. Most of the papers grew out of an advanced seminar I conducted with graduate students and colleagues, which focused on the contemporary state of archaeology. Our aim in so doing was, hopefully, to isolate areas of research critical for advancing the field. The papers represent specific endeavors in that direction. We have attempted to integrate the diverse papers by means of cross referencing and in discussions of relevance as to how and why we viewed the subject covered as important and in need of study.

The organization of the book implies some opinions and convictions that may not be directly apparent in the context of the chapters. As has been suggested, most theory is at some point dependent upon the accuracy of uniformitarian assumptions—namely, that things were in the past as they remain in the present as far as conditions or processes are concerned. As far as man is concerned, such an assumption cannot be supported over the span of time with which archaeologists are concerned. Certainly, early populations of *Australopithecus* were not the same kind of creatures as modern man and, in turn, were probably not even capable of the kinds of behavior that we take for granted among ourselves. As I have pointed out many times, this means that *interpretations* of behavior from the products of early man (tools and artifacts) is likely to be a very risky business indeed. We may reasonably ask ourselves whether or not there are other classes of data remaining from the past which might better support *uniformitarian* assumptions. In short, are there not classes of data available to us for which a more reliable set of conditions might be projected into the past than for projections of human behavior per se? I answer with a resounding *yes*. I further reason that there are at least three domains of data that are archaeologically recoverable which, if developed theoretically, well might serve as excellent reference dimensions against which to view and evaluate different examples of hominid behavior relative to one another and to behavior of modern man as documented ethnographically. The first domain is ecological and is with respect to the species with which man interacted in the past. For many species, examples are still available for direct observation concerning their behavior and qualities that might have been useful to ancient populations. Some of the species of aquatic shellfish, fish, and even some terrestrial example are cases in point. We may evaluate these species today in order to determine their periods of availability, abundance, and utility to man under different conditions. Given such knowledge, we may then evaluate the actual patterns of use employed by ancient populations and the conditions under which we might expect variable usage. Such arguments are developed or alluded to in the chapters in both Parts I and II of this book. Additionally, I reasoned that, since most animals can be known anatomically, that is, we may know quite accurately the numbers of different bones in an animal of a given species from the past, we may study the frequencies of parts actually used, transported, or abandoned by ancient people as a direct measure of their economic and logistical sophistication and appropriate variable behavior in different settings. The first steps in our efforts toward a middle-range theory with emphasis on anatomical part frequencies is introduced in the chapter by Bertram and myself. Thus, the ecological and anatomical domains are emphasized in the chapters of Parts I and II in this book.

The third domain that I envisioned as having potential for theoretical development was that of space use. My original thoughts were simple. Human or hominid behavior always takes place in a spatial theater. The way in which this behavior is organized must be conditioned by certain relationships between the properties of alternative spatial organizations and the labor and social pressures operative during periods of organized behavior. If we could isolate even some of the constraints that are operative, within a dynamic system, on the character of spatial usage, we might well be able to analyze at least some aspects of past behavioral systems in structural terms rather than the more commonly emphasized formal or content categories of tool frequencies, types, and so on. The two chapters in Part III address themselves to this problem. One deals with the recognition of structural properties in the archaeological record, and the other treats the problem of middle-range theory building in the spatial domain.

In Part IV are three papers which seek to relate some aspects of systems organization meaningful to the static facts of the archaeological record or, conversely, some patterning in such facts to variables or states characteristic of past ecological interactions or systems functioning. These are important concerns, and much more work is needed in this area of archaeological theory building.

The term "new archaeology" has been much used. In the absence of progress toward usable theory, there is no new archaeology, only an antitraditional archaeology at best. I look forward to a "new archaeology," but what has thus far been presented under the term is an anarchy of uncertainty, optimism, and products of extremely variable quality.

In my opinion, the new archaeology was something of a rebellion against what was considered sterile and nonproductive endeavors by archaeologists. Rebellion cannot continue simply for rebellion's sake. The "stir" created in the 1960s has not resulted in many substantial gains. If we are to benefit from the freedom of nonparadigmatic thought that has perhaps resulted from our little rebellion, such benefits must be in the form of substantial new theory and knowledge of both the archaeological record and the relationship between statics and dynamics—archaeological formations processes. This book is an attempt to move in this direction. As such, we hope that some advance in the field has been accomplished and that, with this volume available, others will be stimulated to address the difficult task of theory building and methodological development. If the argumentative environment of the 1960s stimulates only further argument, then the "new archaeology" will have been a failure, providing only social excitement in a relatively dull field.

Note

1. References to other chapters refer to *For Theory Building in Archaeology,* the volume in which this orginally appeared.

5

On Covering Law and Theories in Archaeology

I find Read and LeBlanc's (CA 1978:307–17) article frustrating. I agree with the thrust of the presentation and even with what I perceive as its goals. I disagree with the style of presentation, the description of the field, and the use of both vocabulary and examples.

Stylistically the article would have been more stimulating and certainly less ambiguous if it had included examples of authors who have committed the errors of logic or emphasis said to characterize some of the "new archaeologists." I want to know which contemporary authors and which papers Read and LeBlanc view as subject to their criticisms. As it stands, identification is left up to the readers, and I am sure that the persons and works believed to be targets of criticism will vary greatly. I believe that one needs to take the time for analysis and cite the literature which is being criticized rather than adopt an "if the shoe fits, wear it" approach. Strangely, in my experience, one never finds shoe-wearers.

As is frequently the case, "criticism" is often offered for positions or arguments which have been formulated clearly only in the minds of the critics. For instance, the authors state (pp. 308–9):

> Implicitly, if not explicitly, the "new archaeologists" have incorrectly suggested that somehow confirmation of covering laws comes through using the hypothetico-deductive form of argumentation. By thus emphasizing the deductive aspects of the covering-law model and rejecting the inductive arguments (Binford 1968:18, 1977:1) the "new archaeologists" are forced to presume that in some manner confirmation is contained within the framework of the covering-law model of explanation.

With the first sentence I can only agree. As a "new archaeologist," I have suggested that confirmation of covering laws only comes through the use of the hypothetico-deductive form of argumentation. The next sentence makes no sense to me, but I will try to give meaning to it in terms of what I think are the confusions of the authors: *If I assume that they believe that there are laws to be discovered and developed through*

Originally published in *Current Anthropology* 19(3):631–632, 1978. Reprinted by permission of the University of Chicago Press. © 1978 by the Wenner-Gren Foundation for Anthropological Research.

inductive arguments, then I may be able to understand the second part of their state-ment, that "'new archaeologists' are forced to presume that in some manner confir-mation is contained within the framework of the covering-law model of explanation." I do not believe laws of relevance to explanation can be discovered and evaluated through inductive arguments, nor do I presume that confirmation is "contained within the framework of the covering-law model of explanation." The authors' seeming acceptance of empirical "laws" or, as I would term them, "empirical generalizations" as playing a role in explanation is at the base of their confusion, as well as the confusion in the contemporary literature to which they appear to be objecting. This is certainly an error made by Sabloff, Beale, and Kurland (1973:113). It is a mistake made by Yellen (1977b) and is at the root of my recent criticism (1977b) of many "new archaeologists."

The basic points of my earlier arguments advocating a goal of *explanation* and the conscious use of hypothetico-deductive methods in seeking confirmation for ideas used in explanations are as follows: As scientists we seek explanations for observations we have made. The most powerful and successful form of explanation is one which has been described as the "covering-law model." This presupposes the development of theoretical laws—theory itself and a history of confirmation. Clearly, if the field can boast no theoretical laws and no confirmed theory (the theory that was around at the time I began these arguments has been, in my opinion, largely falsified), then clearly no explanations in covering-law form can be offered. If we accept the goal of explaining our observations, then what is needed? We clearly need theory and, by implication, *laws*. The current confusion among both "new" and "other" kinds of archaeologists is how one proceeds in the development of theory, and for some "new archaeologists" this has taken the form of searching for laws as if they could be discovered. I have always cited Hempel and others to the effect that laws are invented, not discovered. For instance, Hempel (1966:15) states: "The transition from data to theory requires creative imagination. Scientific hypotheses and theories are not derived from observed facts, but are invented in order to account for them." Apparently some of the authors' confusion, as well as that of many of the persons they intend to criticize, stems from a failure to appreciate this point. One needs to distinguish clearly between theoretical laws and empirical generalizations, which Nagel (1961) calls "experimental laws" and Hempel (1966:70) "empirical laws."

Empirical generalizations are observationally based summaries of experience. Con-firmation is exclusively in terms of inductive criteria. Good examples of the search for such generalizations are found in Schiffer (1976a:20; compare the examples given by Schiffer with those offered by Salmon 1963:14 as a model of inductive argument). Empirical generalizations are all potential premises for an inductive argument. For instance, if I assert that all residential sites which I and others have observed are characterized by the presence of centrally located hearths, I have offered an inductive argument. Inductive arguments are amenable to easy conversion into conventions of identity. It is easy to offer inductive arguments as justifications for giving meaning to observations. The premises for inductive arguments are always empirical gener-alizations, statements about the way the world "is" or "appears to be." One need not know, or understand, anything about why the world is the way it appears to be in order to offer strong inductive arguments. Nevertheless, one cannot build theory from empirical "laws," and one cannot evaluate theory with inductive arguments. This point is forcefully made by Hempel (1965:57–58):

> Thus, whether a statement of universal form counts as a law will depend in part upon the scientific theories accepted at the time. This is not to say that "empirical generalizations"—statements of universal form that are empirically well-confirmed but have no basis in theory—never qualify as laws. Galileo's, Kepler's and Boyle's laws, for example, were accepted as such before they received theoretical grounding. The relevance of theory is rather this; a statement of universal form, whether empirically confirmed or as yet untested, will quality as a law if it is implied by an accepted theory (statements of this kind are often referred to as atheoretical laws).

Stated another way, the empirical facts may assume theoretical relevance if they are the deduced consequences of a set of theoretical propositions. Under such conditions, the empirical generalization functions as a confirmation for a hypothesis deduced from the theory. In short, the world is the way it is anticipated to be given the theory regarding how it works. *One does not build theory with confirmed propositions; one evaluates theory with confirmational strategies.* In turn, explanation as a scientific goal is not a confirmational strategy. Further, one cannot explain by reference to an empirical generalization, regardless of how "universal" the fact may be. For example, most would agree with the statement that the sun rises in the east. This is a fairly secure universal fact or empirical generalization. The inductive argument that the sun will always rise in the east would be accepted by most. If I observed that early-morning shadows were long and oriented in a westerly direction and asked why, how satisfied would I be with the answer that they are that way because the sun rises in the east every morning? Clearly, shadows are produced by light sources other than the sun, items in many settings do not cast shadows in the morning, etc. A satisfactory explanation for the phenomena is not to be gained by the simple citation of an empirical generalization, no matter how secure that generalization may be. What is needed is a theory, a means of anticipating the phenomena of shadows in all their various manifestations, not simply the citation of a correlation or coincidence between one set of empirical observations and another.

Much of the confusion in current debate about the "new archaeology" and in the critique of confusion by Read and LeBlanc derives from a basic confusion over empirical generalization, laws, and how one builds theory. The "covering-law model" of explanation implies the existence of theory, not empirical generalizations.

The dictum that one may start with false premises and arrive at useful conclusions is well demonstrated in this article. The authors conclude that we need to build theories. With this I am in complete agreement.

Objectivity—Explanation—
Archaeology—1981

Albert Spaulding once said that archaeologists reminded him of a stately minuet with lots of twirling and pirouetting and nobody going anywhere. This impression of archaeology is nowhere more evident than at conferences where individuals posture and present their paradigmatic suggestions in strongly polemical phrases.

For instance, Hodder stated at a recent meeting that "the dangers of the ecological functionalism rife in prehistoric archaeology are first that ranking in, for example burial, is seen as directly reflecting social hierarchy, whereas, in fact, burial patterns are meaningful transformations of social differentiation."

Another charged statement was recently issued by Gledhill and Rowlands (1982:144): "Over the past few years a growing number of archaeologists have begun to move away from explanations derived from functional ecology, system theory, and the more naive forms of cultural materialism towards a focus on specific social and political processes and their economic functioning within defined historical circumstances.

These are statements of posture or paradigmatic bias. They advocate the wearing of a particular pair of glasses through which to view the world. The implication is clear that one pair of "glasses" will permit us to see the world more clearly than when we wear, for instance, "naive-materialists'" or even "ecological-functionalists'" glasses. Such statements have their place, and it is acknowledged that change of paradigm is one source of change within scientific disciplines. However, such statements do not fulfill functions other than purely sociological ones within the discipline to which they are addressed, unless they are coupled with rather fundamental ideas concerning the nature of science and with a full acceptance of the responsibility that we have to evaluate ideas scientifically once they are proposed.

Paradigms Are Not Explanations

You may think of our cognitive frame of reference or paradigm as forming the ideas and concepts that give meaning to experience. These condition what one considers relevant to describe or what one chooses to discuss as of interest. One's cognitive

Originally appeared in *Theory and Explanation in Archaeology*, edited by C. Renfrew, M. J. Rowlands, and B. A. Segraves, published by Academic Press, London and New York, pp. 125–138, 1982. Copyright © 1982 by Academic Press, Inc. All rights of reproduction in any form reserved.

frame of reference may be thought of as the culture of science. It consists of the concepts or terms in which experience is intellectually assimilated. In spite of the definitional controversy (see Masterman 1970), I follow Kuhn (1977) in viewing a paradigm as the intellectual terms upon which one meets experience. In short, it is what we expect the world to be like. Things become complicated when we recognize that we cannot gain a direct knowledge of the essential properties of the world. Our cognition is not direct nor objective, but it may be indirect and subjective relative to our beliefs about the world, i.e., our paradigm.

We generally defend our knowledge claims about the world with inferential arguments. I prefer to call these *warranting arguments:* They are arguments advanced that tend to *warrant to others* the beliefs that one has about the world. If done in a robust manner, they make one's knowledge claims appear plausible and acceptable to others. Rarely are such arguments formalized in that the premises are rarely explicit, so conclusions are warranted by appeal to a "common body of knowledge or belief." The more comprehensive the alleged knowledge or widespread the belief serving as the intellectual context for a warranting argument, the more plausible it appears and therefore the greater likelihood it has of being accepted.

Working within a frame of reference is similar to participation in any other culture: We accommodate experience through our shared cognitive devices. The fact that they facilitate this accommodation appears to us as proof that the world is in fact the way we expect it to be. We may be astonished that others don't see the world the way we do. Cultural man has for all the time felt that his beliefs were given by "reality" and were therefore "right," while those of other cultures were clearly misguided or "stupid" for not having seen the "truth" inherent in experience.

Everyday arguments of accommodation—where models of the world are merely fitted to experiences through conceptual devices—form the normal method whereby individuals are enculturated to varying points of view or differing cultural conventions for seeing the world. Contrasting paradigmatic understanding is the basis for all forms of conflicting belief. It is the form of reasoning used to justify or warrant every belief system that man has ever invented outside of the culture of science. The criteria used for justifying one's belief are generally that: (*a*) it accommodates experience in terms of a broader, more comprehensive view of nature; and (*b*) it appears plausible. These are the criteria that cultural man has used ever since he has enjoyed a reasoning capacity. These are the criteria around which argument centers when the pros and cons of contrasting religions, political views, or other culturally variable systems of belief and value are discussed.

There is an unfortunate misconception regarding explanation that is current today, namely that a paradigm provides a useful explanation. Science has been an experiment in developing ways of going beyond the epistemologically unsatisfactory approaches and forms of evaluation already outlined. The history of science describes a long series of investigations in search of criteria for evaluating ideas that go beyond the everyday cultural bias of whether a proposal appears to be a "good or satisfying idea to think." I discussed this problem previously in the following manner (Binford 1977, 3);

Science is a method or procedure that directly addresses itself to the evaluation of cultural forms. That is, if we view culture as at least referring to the particularly human ability to give meaning expediently to experience, to symbol, and, in turn, view experience through this conceptual idiom, science is then concerned with evaluating the utility of the cultural tools produced.

What is being asserted is that the production of a paradigm with the accompanying warranting arguments may be sufficient to justify its serious consideration, but the warranting arguments—citing a close accommodation between the argument and experience, numerous, seemingly convincing arguments from example, as well as the subjective criteria that it appears to be a good and satisfying idea to think—are unsatisfactory epistemological criteria in any endeavor that seeks to evaluate cultural forms of thought.

Objective Evaluation

Scientific investigation is the conscious and designed attempt to obtain an *objective* evaluation of the utility and accuracy of proposed ideas and propositions. The reader will immediately recognize that the crucial word in the above sentence is *objective*. What constitutes objectivity? How can we achieve it, given the recognition that *we* in fact design the scientific procedures? Perhaps the first place to begin is to say what objectivity is not. It is not the view of an "outsider" seeing nature in its true form from some privileged observation platform outside of nature. It is not the "pure observer" frequently discussed during the nascent days of science. This change in perspective has been well summarized by Amsterdamski (1975, 169, italics added):

> Characterizing by one, shortened formula the intellectual revolution of the 16th and 17th centuries, *it is possible to state that God, as the measure of all things, was replaced by man.* Man, however, as a knowing subject was provided with at least some divine attributes. *He was to be an ideal observer external to the universe under study, and he was to be capable of achieving the absolute truth about this universe.* Beginning with Descartes and Bacon, and ending with Kant and Hegel, this concept of man, variously justified in all philosophical terms as being capable of cognitive procedures, co-determined the style of thinking of modern science. This may be discerned within both empiricists' as well as rationalists' epistemology. . . . By including the knowing subject more and more into the world of nature, by depriving it of its privileged, outside status within nature, modern science steadily undermined its own epistemological basis. *Now not God, not man standing beyond nature and confronting it as a perfect knowing subject, but nature itself was to become the measure of all things.*

In short, man as the creator of his own destiny and man as the observer, outside of nature, capable of *seeing* truth directly, has fallen. We have turned to the study of the causes of human action itself and the evaluation of the effects of our own ideas and actions on how we view the world and what appear to be "facts." Man, both as a subject of study and as observer, has been returned to nature instead of being seen as standing above or outside it.

As suggested above, the growth of knowledge within science gradually under-mined early ideas about the world and about the epistemology used. This does not mean that science had rendered itself obsolete, as many alleged social scientists would like to suggest. Quite to the contrary, another and more useful view of "objectivity" developed within the sciences. That was the view that it was not the status of the observer that yielded objectivity *but the status of logical or intellectual independence between the ideas being evaluated on the one hand and the intellectual tools employed in the evaluated investigations on the other.* Under this view, objectivity now rested with the design characteristics of a methodology and the procedures of its implementation rather than with the characteristics of a particular observer. It was something that could be differentially achieved and could be evaluated quite independently of ad hominem arguments or allusions to subjective manipulations by different observers. This linkage between ideas and observations, which suggests that ideas be evaluated by objective means, pinpoints the need in any science for developing such means and further emphasizes the *fact* that the testing of theory is dependent upon the availability of robust methods. I have designated development of such means as "middle range research." It is not middle range because it is unimportant. Quite to the contrary, it is middle range because it links observations and experiences as to what the world is like to ideas—theories (if you will) that seek to tell us why the world is the way it appears to be.

Middle Range Research

Middle range research results in the production of knowledge and understanding that may grow, serving as the research-based paradigmatic underpinning of a science. This point has been well-presented by Amsterdamski (1975, 86) with regard to developed sciences.

> The distinction between "empirical" and "theoretical" . . . may be only a relative one. It is relative historically. A scientist who undertakes the study of a particular problem, for example of a biological one, and who uses various scientific instruments constructed on the grounds of different physical theories, is quite aware of the fact that together with the equipment he uses he accepts also these theories. In spite of this fact, however, he will treat the statements he will formulate by means of these instruments as observational. The observational language is, for him, something already present and historically given by the development of science and common knowledge.

Archaeology is perhaps in a fortunate position in that while there is much contemporary "culture" or paradigmatic bias regarding the nature of man or concerning the causes of history, there is very little folk "knowledge" regarding the formation of the archaeological record. This means that there is little explicit prior development of cognitive devices and frames of reference—paradigmatic development—regarding archaeological phenomena in the literal, "static" sense of the word. For the further development of archaeology, the growth of a paradigm that develops cognitive means for identifying properties of the past or diagnoses the archaeological record and thereby gives meaning in terms of the past is crucial.

An observational language is at present essentially nonexistent in archaeology. I believe the concepts and hence paradigmatic characteristics of traditional archaeology are essentially useless for modern archaeology. As was suggested in the preceding quotation, the instruments that permit and facilitate unambiguous, meaningful observations must be developed, demonstrated, and tested, using scientific means. Later, as the science of archaeology becomes more mature, these "instruments for measurement" may be taken for granted, and the results of their utilization treated as direct observations on the past. We are a long way from this level of maturity today. We need to recognize very explicitly the current "state of the art" and address the growth of a scientific paradigm as basic and fundamental.

What we are seeking through middle-range research are accurate means of identification and good instruments for measuring specified properties of past cultural systems. We are seeking reliable cognitive devices. We are looking for "Rosetta Stones" that permit the accurate conversion from observations on statics to statements about dynamics. Put another way, we are seeking to build a paradigmatic frame of reference for giving meaning to selected characteristics of the archaeological record through a theoretically grounded body of research, rather than accepting "folk" knowledge— let alone implicit folk knowledge—as the basis for describing the past.

My view is that we cannot know the past until we first address the problem of how we go about giving meaning to the archaeological record (see Binford 1968b). *Meanings are carried by concepts and arguments, and the archaeological record contains only arrangements of matter.* We assign concepts to different arrangements of matter or offer arguments regarding the sources or conditions that brought into being particular arrangements of matter. All such propositions are inferences from static to dynamic states that are no longer available for observation.

Given that we have made observations on the archaeological record, offered some generalizations about its properties, and have gained considerable experience with the record, we must now ask the question that is crucial to paradigmatic growth: Why is the archaeological record constructed and patterned the way it appears to be?

The Archaeological Record

The direction of attention to the archaeological record itself, rather than the continuation of the self-deceit that we study the past directly, seems central to progress. We not only have to seek knowledge of the archaeological record, we have to seek explanations for its many forms. Explanations (Hempel 1977, 244, italics added) presuppose theories or statements as to why the world is the way it appears to be.

> Theories are the key to the scientific understanding of empirical phenomena, *and they are normally developed only when previous research has yielded a body of information, including empirical generalizations about the phenomena in question.* A theory is then intended to provide deeper understanding by presenting those phenomena as manifestations of certain underlying processes.

During the early 1970s it became clear that my views on archaeological theory were not generally shared. For instance, one view (Watson, LeBlanc, and Redman (1971, 164) equated "theory" with arguments about the explanations for "what happened in history": "There is in a sense an 'archaeological theory' although it might be better characterized as evolutionary anthropology . . . human and cultural evolution is of such scientific and intrinsic interest that there is certainly an essential nomothetic role to be played by archaeologists."

I saw the development of archaeological theory as necessary for the making of reliable statements about the past. Others seemed to see this task as a simple matter of paradigm growth where "constructing" the past was assumed to "flow" naturally from the interaction between a good archaeologist and his experience with the archaeological record. We "did" archaeology, it was felt, to investigate interesting problems, such as the origins of the state, the shift to agriculture, and so forth. Under the latter approach, "doing" archaeology was viewed as the experimental phase of investigating the causes of the past. In my view, we had to conduct another type of experimental research in order to use our observations on the archaeological record for making statements about the past. As stated earlier, *the principles used in making inferences from observations on the archaeological record could not be adopted from other "sciences" since no other science addressed itself to the study of the properties of the archaeological record.* Second, in the absence of reliable inferential procedures for describing the past, there was no way of using the archaeological record either to explicate the past or as "data" for evaluating models or arguments as to why the past was the way it appeared to be.

I saw as a necessity the development of the science of the archaeological record—theoretically independent of the "science of cultural evolution" or other nomothetic approaches that made use of the history constructed by archaeologists. This view addresses directly what Michael Schiffer (1972) has called the formation processes of the archaeological record. We seek to understand the dynamic conditions that brought into being the static forms and arrangements of matter remaining for us to observe. To be useful for developing a picture of the past that is accurate and germane to our curiosity and to ideas about the past, we must develop a theoretical understanding of certain properties of the archaeological record that will *have unambiguous referents in the past and will be uniformly relevant to the past.* If the conditions that brought into being a particular fact are unique and restricted to a particular time period, we cannot make meaningful statements about such phenomena directly. We must derive meaning with reference to some sets of facts that we do not understand. This implies that the intellectual means that serve the functions of a paradigm within a science must largely refer to the unchanging characteristics of human sociocultural organizations of behavior. We must be able to establish intellectual "anchors" in the past before we can explore characteristics that may differ from our current understandings of our current ideas of the past. We can only evaluate differences with reference to some known and stable factors. The latter must be developed for use in inference before we can make meaningful statements about the character of the past. Researching such uniform and regular patterns of relationships between static and dynamic conditions is research directed toward the elucidation of *functional relationships*.

The study of functional relationships is central to the development of well-grounded middle range understanding of the archaeological record, and hence it constitutes the very basis for making statements about the past. From this point of view I find it difficult to understand critics who decry "functionalist" propositions (see Hodder 1982b). Basically I subscribe to many of the criticisms of functionalism as it was practiced in the social sciences. I fully concur that functional arguments cannot offer explanations for differences between systems, nor explain a system's change, although they may be essential to its useful description. On the other hand, they must, in my opinion, be the basic form of argument used by us in the development of methods for inferentially referring observations on the contemporary archaeological record to active dynamic conditions in the past. Any statement that confers meaning in historical terms to observations made on the archaeological record is an inference. The justifications for such an inference must be robust arguments that link the properties (*static matter*) to the properties inferred (*dynamic conditions*). These linkages refer to organizational properties within sociocultural systems, and by definition they are therefore functional arguments. Those who discourage research of such linkages would have us remain wallowing in opinionated paradigmatic debate forever.

Some Misunderstandings

While addressing criticism I cannot fail to mention those critics who decry the reconstruction of the past! Those who seek some knowledge of the past from the archaeological record are labeled "reconstructionists" (Dunnell 1978:194–195), or berated with the claim that their approach is the *"fallacy of prehistoric archaeology as cultural anthropology* (Eggert 1976, 57). Such critics fail to realize the central role that methodology must play in our field. We seek to know the past through the investigation of contemporary phenomena, and we seek to describe the past in dynamic terms, having only "statics" to provide the clues.

For instance, critics frequently attempt to characterize the methodological challenge associated with gaining a knowledge of the past as misguided reconstructionism (see Dunnell 1978, 194–195)—overly influenced by "cultural anthropology." These critics suggest that those who seek reliable means for making inferences from the archaeological record to the past are attempting to "reconstruct" an ethnography as might be done by some half-cocked, contemporary ethnologist or even by a more traditional one, for that matter. There has never been any suggestion by myself or my colleagues that we should seek to reconstruct prehistoric "lifeways" in terms of criteria dictated by cultural anthropology. I did suggest that there seemed to me to be every reason to suspect that we could develop ways of extracting from the archaeological record information regarding properties of cultural systems, including social and ideological components, since they were organizationally integrated with the matter remaining in the archaeological record—the relic of an ongoing system in the past. I never proposed or seriously considered the idea that we should attempt to use the archaeological record to investigate limited subject interests as dictated by various cultural anthropologists. I did maintain that insofar as we sought to know something about the past based on our observations in the present, then we shared with cultural anthropology a common subject matter—the dynamics of cultural systems.

I further suggested that the causes of variability observable in the archaeological record could be expected to refer to the dynamics—both functional and evolutionary—of past cultural systems. I saw no reason to expect that the statics remaining could be understood solely in terms of coincidentally preserved components of the archaeological record. The archaeological record was conditioned in its completeness by largely postdepositional processes of decay, displacement, and mixing. The properties surviving are, quite literally, remnants relative to the dynamics of the past and could have been conditioned both in their form and patterns of association by many factors that have not left direct material by-products. Stated another way, the reality of the present archaeological record cannot be viewed as limiting the reality of past dynamics or the realities of history. Because something was not preserved does not mean that it may not have been a crucial factor in the operation of a past system. It was this situation that prompted me to encourage students to seek operational means for monitoring aspects of social organization or ideology through the study of archaeological remains.

Those offering the reconstructionist criticism appear to deny the need for inferences to the past and to be willing to take the archaeological record at face value. This is an old apologist's view held by traditional archaeologists. In 1968 I (1968a, 15) wrote:

> Rouse (1964, 1965) has offered archaeologists an "out" and his ideas undoubtedly have great appeal for those who would like to study cultural processes but lack the methods for doing so. He states that since we recognize a difference between the processes of evolution and the products of evolution, that the study of process should properly be the domain of ethnologists, "who are able to observe change as it is still going on" (Rouse 1964:465). He suggests further that the archaeologists might more appropriately study the products of evolution in systematic terms—by descriptive taxonomic and distributional schemes.

Rouse is not alone in this perspective, and it certainly represents the view of many dedicated and thoughtful archaeologists. For example, Wauchope (1966, 19) has written:

> One reason for archaeology's continued lag as a contributor to culture theory, in spite of great strides in the last ten years, is that we continue to see our main goal as the reconstruction of ancient ethnology. Since we have so great a handicap to begin with here, where speculation and inference mix too confusingly for the students who likes to keep his lines of reasoning clean cut, most archaeologists, if they are concerned, are fighting a very uphill battle indeed. I think we are overlooking another order of interpretation which is in some ways much better suited to our data, for it is less dependent on inference; one can manipulate the artifacts statistically without much concern whether one understands precisely what they originally were, exactly how they were used, and just what they meant to the ancients.

This rather dismal view seems to be the very basis of recent criticism by Dunnell (1978, 195). He states:

> Two general notions . . . have prevented . . . development . . . (2) a belief that the appropriate subject matter is behavior rather than the hard phenomena of the archaeological record. This belief, inherited from the reconstructionists, forces us to manipulate inferences instead of phenomena, and thereby deprives us of the full use of performance standards.

While some, like these critics, would have us manipulate the archaeological "phenomena" directly, others would have us treat archaeological remains as manifestations of unseen, past-mental phenomena. Since mental conditions are only "reflected" in material things, they are knowable only by accommodative post hoc arguments as to what appears consistent with material patterning. A defense of argument through accommodation is often presented, alongside a quest for labored exceptions to more substantial arguments, as the justification for the mentalist paradigm. In fact the strict empiricist view and the strict mentalist view both neatly sidestep the basic issues: How do we justify the relationship of empirical materials to ideas? The empiricists claim that our paradigm derives from common sense and is drawn "in an unstructured fashion from common experience" (Dunnell 1978, 196). Advocates of a "contextual approach" require a concern with the "implementation and reconstitution of beliefs in practices, the ideological manipulation of beliefs . . . and the development of models concerning such inter-relationships" (Hodder in press).

In one case the link between ideas and empirical properties of the archaeological record is taken as direct and unambiguous, while in the other the link is simply viewed as one of plausible accommodation. Both deny the need for scientific objectivity and hence for a battery of robust middle range means for making inferences to the past. But posturing gets us nowhere. Even good ideas, which could explain or provide explanations for many basic questions about the past and about the central issues of why things happen as they do, will remain in the area of opinionated debate until we develop the methodology for evaluating ideas in objective terms. *Objective* is here used in the sense introduced earlier—namely, that the arguments used for warranting the meanings given to observations must be intellectually independent of the arguments being evaluated through an appeal to the meanings of observation.

The Linking Process

Radiocarbon methods provide a good example of what is meant by scientific objectivity. We can all recognize the importance of knowing the "date" of events indicated archaeologically. We may for instance have some theory regarding the rates of change in agricultural intensification relative to political growth. Clearly, one way of obtaining a partial evaluation of such a proposal would be by measurement of the rates of change by dating sequent archaeological materials, referable to both agricultural and political growth. In order to achieve objectivity, our methods of dating must be intellectually independent of the arguments being evaluated. Radiocarbon techniques are admirably suited to the task, since the justification for inferring a period of elapsed time—from observations of radioactive emissions as measured by some device similar to a Geiger counter—derive from observations regarding the distribution of radiocarbon relative to stable nonradioactive isotopes in nature, from a knowledge of decay rates of radiocarbon, as well as from a knowledge of processes that lead to the fixing of radiocarbon in living tissue. In short, the theory that permits the inference of elapsed time treats the interaction between biological and physical processes, processes that are in no sense dependent for their characteristics or patterns of interaction upon interactions between agricultural intensification or political growth.

Since the warranting arguments for inferring elapsed time from archaeological charcoal or other organic debris refer to causal or interactive conditions totally independent of the arguments being evaluated with the method of inference, it constitutes an objective measure relative to the argument being evaluated by dating methods. We must generate such methods, and only with the growth of objective paradigmatic means can we proceed realistically to the task of evaluating alternative explanations and ideas advanced as to why the world is the way it appears to be. Why is there patterning in history? Why are there apparently regular sequences of events leading up to the development of agriculture. Why do power-based sociopolitical forms in the history of culture change differentially in different regions? We all may have ideas—some may even be good ideas—but we will never know until we have objective means for linking the conceptual domains, which we are so skilled at creating, to the existential characteristics of the world of nature in an evaluative manner. The linking process is the true foundation of science, and we must seek to develop the skills required.

Those who do not place critical emphasis upon the development of middle range theory are forced into the strange position of generating theories with pitifully few objective means to use in their evaluation, or conversely, into making many observations on the archaeological record that are naive to the possible conditions in the past that were responsible for the properties observed. Theories generated about the past in the absence of middle range theory have little hope of being related to relevant observations on the archaeological record in a reliable manner. Discussions of the past in such a situation remain idle speculations, and suggestions regarding the meanings to be attached to observed archaeological phenomena likewise remain intuitive insights to be accepted or rejected in terms of one's subjective biases. In short, given an absence of a robust body of well-founded middle range knowledge and understanding, general theory remains in the air, adrift from the empirical phenomena with which it could be profitably evaluated. Similarly, observations of patterning within sets of the empirical materials serve only as stimuli for intuitive insight, itself remaining in the domain of opinion and subjective evaluation and guided by generally inconclusive inductive argument.

The social sciences have generally failed to develop a robust body of principles serving the methodological needs of the fields in question. This failure has doomed those alleged sciences to endless paradigmatic debate and endless stylistic replacements of one "theory" by another, largely in response to sociological characteristics within the discipline and in step with simple rates of generational replacement within the academic community. The result of these conditions is pseudoscience, operating with exactly the same intellectual tools that cultural man used in ethnocentric debate since the beginning of conceptual thought. I use the term *pseudo* because the practitioners of simple paradigmatic debate in the modern academic world, while commonly denying the epistemological basis of science, claim to be generating knowledge of general utility! Science is the only strategy thus far developed for evaluating the general utility of ideas generated in a paradigmatic context. It is the search for ways of using experience as the arbiter of ideas that renders some measure of utility. As we achieve increased understanding, that is, as we develop theories as to why the world is the way it appears to be and seek objective means for evaluating such ideas, we stand in the exciting position of contributing to the growth of knowledge. This position has reference both to our theories as to why the world is the way it appears to be and to our paradigms that condition for us the way the world appears. Progress must proceed through both growth of theoretical understanding and paradigmatic accuracy.

Thomas Kuhn (1977) argued that the very process of scientific growth was the patterned replacement of one paradigm by another. I take strong exception to such a view, while fully recognizing the paradigmatic character of our conceptualizations of experience. Science grows as a consequence of the development of means for objectively monitoring experience in its myriad forms. As our skill at objective evaluation of ideas grows, there is a growth with continuity, or pattern of accumulative development of knowledge. Kuhn's view of change by paradigm replacement could only be true in the absence of objective means of evaluating experience. It may be the normal pattern for prescientific intellectual change, but within science orderly growth and accumulative development of knowledge are the patterns to which the scientific method is dedicated. Paradigm change may give the appearance of revolutionary change when poorly developed areas of a science become increasingly developed and there is a shift from the general cultural paradigm to a more objective, scientific one. Such realities of life are in no way valid justifications for abandoning scientific goals and returning to prescientific forms of debate. Similarly, the argument against the logical positivist's position, questioning the role of theory testing, is misguided.

For instance, we may all acknowledge that if our paradigm leads us to consider the earth as flat, we may nevertheless proceed to ask the question, Why is the earth flat? We may then develop a body of theory that seeks to explain our "observation" of a flat earth. It should be clear that given that the earth is round, we could waste considerable time and energy in testing our theories as to why the earth is flat. More likely, however, we could just as well learn, through our search for objective means of evaluating our ideas, that the world was round. We would therefore gain knowledge and simultaneously a good reason to modify our paradigm. Paradigms are routinely modified as a consequence of scientific research. It is true that they may be modified or conditioned by factors outside the domain of science per se, but it is the regular growth of knowledge, and modification of both paradigm and theories, toward which scientific effort is directed. The recognition that science can be affected by extrinsic factors or even fail to succeed at times is not justification for abandoning the goal of achieving an orderly pattern of accumulative growth in knowledge and understanding through scientific endeavors.

As long as our reasoning remains "paradigmatic" in character, we are doomed to the endless polemical debate, laced with emotionalism, that also typifies other arguments about alternative cultural beliefs or values. The self-deceit that social scientists can observe cause and therefore study directly why the world is the way it appears to be (see Leach 1973) lies at the root of the ill-founded belief that man is too complex and that human sociocultural phenomena are by nature unsuited for study by scientific means. It is a false paradigm that treats as extranatural the human sociocultural experience and that already claims as a failure those scientific methods that, in general, have never been implemented or indeed in most cases have not yet been developed.

7   1982

Meaning, Inference and the Material Record

The papers assembled here represent a major shift in interests from what we might
have heard from a similar group ten to fifteen years ago.[1] Most of the papers address
a body of data which the authors believe in one way or another reflects on the ideas
they are using to 'understand' processes which operated to bring about transformations in ancient society. Emphasis is generally placed on the appearance of ranking
and/or other institutional forms of social inequality.

These are, of course, interests in process, in dynamics, the active characteristics
of living systems. Archaeologists dig up static mute things, mere arrangements of
matter: how may such things realistically speak to such issues?

I tend to think of what archaeologists do when engaged in intellectual activity as
largely understandable in terms of relatively few operations. I will present these
conceptual guides to viewing archaeologists' activity and see how the papers tend to
group when viewed from these perspectives.

The first major distinction I make is between *what the world is like and why it is
that way*. When we are engaged in making statements as to what the world is like we
are using a paradigm or an observational language to relate how the world appears
to us. For us as archaeologists there is a kind of dual challenge since what the world
is like takes two forms: one is an orientation toward the archaeological record which
is contemporary and with us in the here-and-now. We frequently wish to describe
the characteristics of this 'world'. On the other hand, being archaeologists, we wish
to talk about the world of the past, we wish to say what that world was like. Both
of these are descriptive tasks but tasks which place very different intellectual demands
upon us. In the former case we may use an observational language which appeals to
general experiences with the world of everyday experience. We may talk of colour,
size, shape, number of items, association, covariation, and all manner of other properties of the archaeological record. The utility of the descriptive devices which we use
are evaluated through the interaction which occurs between the world of experience

Originally appeared in *Ranking, Resource and Exchange,* edited by C. Renfrew and S. Shennan, published by Cambridge
University Press, Cambridge, © 1982.

and the words we use to assimilate these experiences meaningfully. Things are not so simple when we face the task of describing the past. The observational language which we use quite literally falls on deaf ears as far as permitting us to interact with experience is concerned: the past is gone, mute and only recognizable as such through inference. We cannot use a 'direct' strategy of describing the past. All our experience is in the present and all the normal ways of evaluating our observational language or our cognitive devices for giving meaning to experience are also restricted to the present: the past cannot cry out and protest against our descriptions. It cannot intrude itself on our ways of thinking since it is passive and mute. Quite literally, our descriptions of the past are constructions. The accuracy of such inventions can only be evaluated by evaluating our 'observational language', our intellectual tools for inference—in short, our methods.

In addition to these descriptive interests we as archaeologists are interested in understanding, in seeking answers to the 'why' questions of why the world is the way it appears to be. When we ask such questions we are seeking explanations, we are seeking a kind of understanding which goes beyond an unweighted description of the world; we want to know what makes the world work the way it appears to. When we address such questions we are demanding of ourselves a different kind of intellectual endeavour. We are demanding the use of our creative powers to imagine the links of determinant interaction, the 'causal' links if you will, which glue together the dynamics of experience and render it both understandable and capable of being anticipated. This concern with causation, determinacy, is the context of *theory building*.

The reader will recognise that I have not yet used a word which is quite current in archaeology and other social sciences, that is, *model*. In archaeology, this word refers to a wide variety of intellectual products. Much of its ambiguous usage derives from a failure to recognise some of the distinctions which I have suggested thus far. For instance in archaeology, a model is frequently built of what the past was like. This is a speculative description of the past. This is frequently accomplished by using certain, largely implicit, assumptions as to how the world is in general. Such conceptualisations of the past are at least minimally based on some conditions in the present, some properties of experience which can be assumed also to have characterised the past. In a more technical sense these are frequently characterised as uniformitarian assumptions. That is, at least with respect to some properties, the past is considered to be similar to the present. (See Binford 1981b for a more detailed discussion of such assumptions.) I would suggest that the accuracy with which we can infer the past is directly related to the degree that our uniformitarian assumptions are justifiable. Concern with the justification of such assumptions and with the development of strongly warranted means for giving meaning to our contemporary observations made on the archaeological record is what I have called middle range research. I detect very little concern with this area of archaeological research in these papers. More are engaged in building models of the past which if 'true' would accommodate the particular 'facts' of each author's case as described. No methods for inferring past conditions independently of the nascent theories of dynamics are evident. In short no operational objectivity (see Binford 1982b) seems to have been achieved.

This is not unique to those concerned with complex societies, nor to the British, but I find it interesting that there appears to be little recognition of the problems which are strictly speaking archaeological and revolve around our use of archaeological observations either for gaining a knowledge of the past or for rendering the past accessible for testing ideas we might have regarding the way the world works.

As state-of-the-art type comments, many of these papers seek to build models of the past for accommodating certain 'cases' which are summarised as currently archaeologically described; yet there is little concern with the actual methods of inference which permit one to move from descriptive statements about the archaeological record to descriptive statements about the past. About the only hints of concern in this regard have to do with the 'interpretation' of mortuary data. The inference of ranking and various social inequalities is seemingly linked almost exclusively to mortuary arguments.

Most of these papers are models in the sense of 'pictures' of the past where the methods for 'viewing' have not yet been seriously addressed.

In situations where 'model' building is common, I have found that those building the model feel that the internal 'logic' of the presentation is compelling, and hence their position appears 'self-evident' and clear. Such a view is generally derived from having adopted a methodology, yet being totally innocent or unselfconscious relative to the assumptions inherent in the methods used in such situations.

I have found that one of the most revealing diagnostic tactics for looking at theories and models is to examine the character of the uniformitarian assumptions inherent in the arguments, in spite of the suggestions by some archaeologists that we must avoid such assumptions (Gould, R. 1980). Avoidance is methodologically impossible in any situation of inference. We must have what A.N. Whitehead (1932, 188) has termed the 'eternal objects', the common points of reference between our experience and the 'past', if we are to reason to the past in any realistic sense.

From the perspective of the types of uniformitarian assumptions which are well represented in these papers I find them very 'historical' in character. When I use the term 'historical' I am not referring to their concern with the past nor to their emphasis on chronicle, nor even to the degree to which they are particularlistic or exhibit more generalising interests (see Carr 1961 for a debunking of such ideas). Such characteristics are not unique to history, for instance, as distinct from anthropology etc. In general what I find most common to historians is the character of their uniformitarian assumptions. Most often historians treat 'human' events and the 'human' past, and consequently they make the assumption of a common and constant human mentality. The uniformitarian assumptions which historians make most commonly are about the 'nature' of man.

> . . . the ordinary historian . . . according to him, all history properly so called is the history of human affairs . . . The archaeologist's use of his stratified relics depends on his conceiving them as artifacts serving human purposes and then expressing a particular way in which men have thought about their own life. . . . (Collingwood (1956, 212)

Under this view the past is a 'human' past and the only way that we could make inferences to the past from the products of human behaviour would be through an understanding of 'human nature' itself.

When a man thinks historically, he has before him certain documents or relics of the past. His business is to discover what the past was which has left these relics behind . . . this means discovering the thought (in the widest sense of that word . . .) which is expressed by them. To discover what this thought was, the historian must think it again for himself. (Collingwood 1956, 282–3)

This approach has been called the method of empathetic understanding, and it should be clear that the uniformitarian assumptions being made are about our own psychic propensities under differing conditions.

This seems to be the major methodology when giving meaning to many of the mortuary 'facts' cited in many of the papers in this volume. We hear appeals to prestige, rivalry, display, conspicuous consumption, etc., all of which in the long run postulate a kind of universalistic psychological response to social conditions. Similarly, there is a variety of arguments which range between strict 'formalist' and 'substantivist' views on economics, both of which rest in the final analysis on assumptions about the behavioural playing out of 'human' motives through economising decisions. On the more formalist side there are what appear as rather direct appeals to the 'profit motive' and the entrepreneurs' world view. These are all variously disguised statements about 'human nature' or what a 'reasonable man' might be expected to do under various conditions.

These approaches are in direct conflict with views commonly associated with the 'anthropological' position. Under arguments advanced which might be associated with a more traditional anthropological viewpoint was the view that our feelings, our ways of thinking, our ways of responding to the world were conditioned by *our cultural context;* therefore, we could not project *our* responses onto actors in different cultures at different times or under changes in cultural conditions. According to the anthropological view, the use of the methods of 'empathetic understanding' was an ethnocentric approach and not defensible. As I read Hodder's paper this seems to be his message. He appears to have noted the same thing that I have, namely that much of the discussion regarding the meaning to be given to the past as seen through the archaeological record is proceeding with a 'historian's bias as rendered plausible through the use of the methods of empathetic understanding. He is insisting on the positions argued by Franz Boas (1940) and other leaders of the anthropological reaction against ethnocentrism and racism.

Hodder's version is of course 'culturally' updated and drips with Parsonian idealism. In fact, Hodder appears to adopt for archaeology a British view of social anthropology.

The anthropologist is concerned with a systematic understanding of what he sees . . . He learns the culture, as he learns the language of the people . . . The first step is to find out . . . the meaning which people themselves attach to what they do . . . In short, the work of the social anthropologist may be regarded as an . . . act of translation in which the author and translator collaborate. (Pocock 1961, 85–8)

As Hodder realises, the 'authors' are long since gone, so the character of the 'translation' rests solely with the translator. This 'realisation' leads inevitably to his denial of objectivity, to the claim that we practice an art, and the assertion that all insight into the past is subjective.

This, of course, is not even logical unless one accepts the proposition that:

> All archaeological data are expressions of human thoughts and purposes and are valued only as revelations thereof. (Childe 1962:10–11)
> It is the mediate agency of a mind that brings about the cultural relationships between cultural products. (Taylor 1948, 143)

Hodder's appeals for the consideration of cultural context are surprisingly reminiscent of Taylor's analogous appeals (see Taylor 1948, 1972). They both seem to derive from a complete acceptance of the Parsonian equations of culture with ideas (see Harris (1979, 279) for a discussion of this issue). Of course, once such a position is adopted, *no* methodology of inference appears possible which does not adopt the method of 'empathetic understanding'. If this is rejected all science also must be rejected.

While Hodder's criticism of much that is presented in contemporary archaeology is valid, since it is uncommonly lucid with respect to ethnographic analogy and empathetic assumptions, I should hope that no one would be misled into following Hodder's 'remedial' suggestion. *We do not have to try to study mental phenomena. In fact we study material phenomena.* We study material things, matter in various forms and arrangements. To equate these forms, distributions and patterns of association with an ideational 'system' seems to be strange at best. Systems of adaptation are material systems composed of matter and energy sources. Information may be important in organising and integrating a system, but it is not the system. Culturally organised systems of adaptation are no less concrete and materialistic. They are composed of things, places, persons, resources, communication channels, energy pipelines, etc. We do not find 'fossilised' ideas, we find the arrangements of material which derive from the operation of a system of adaptation culturally integrated at some level. I don't have to know how the participants thought about the system to investigate it as a system of adaptation in a knowable natural world. That is, I fully recognise that we are not observing a purely 'practical' system given in terms of some universalistic assumptions of reason or practicality deriving from a 'rational' human nature. Only when we can view culturally organised phenomena against a backdrop of phenomena not subject to culturally organised variability can we gain an appreciation for cultural properties themselves. I do not have to know how the participants thought about the system to investigate those very properties.

Only when you insist that the sole uniformitarian principle which can link the present and the past is 'human nature' do you get into the relativists' trap which Hodder is inviting archaeologists to enter (see Habermas 1971). On the other hand, most archaeologists have not shed the idealist baggage they inherited from the last century. The methods of empathetic understanding will not work in seeking explanations for cultural differences and similarities. I simply don't know what it was like to think like a Neanderthal man, in spite of Hodder's implied claim that he could perhaps achieve such contextual empathy. Fortunately this is not necessary. We can study properties of adaptation, properties of organisations involving energy demands for maintenance, reproduction and growth. The appearance of complex systems was among other things a growth process: it was a process of internal differentiation. We need to get down to the task of studying material systems.

While doing so we must become much more self-aware and face quite squarely the methodological problems of inference from which the silly equation of artefacts with fossilised ideas protected us in blissful naivety for so many years. Truly archaeologists must lose their 'innocence' (Clarke 1973).

I commented in Philadelphia after listening to these papers that this is a 'long way from Beaker Folk'. I have suggested here that clearly the concern with social evolution and a desire for explanations of major transformations, such as the appearance of ranking, are new domains of discourse for archaeologists. There is some indication, as in Hodder's appeals for a 'new' cultural relativism, and in some of the arguments which appear to be rather straightforward 'formalist' economic positions, that we need to do some catching up with events which have already been argued in anthropology and the social sciences in general. Fortunately, in our ontogeny we don't have to recapitulate phylogeny. We don't have to make all of those old mistakes with 'wide-eyed' enthusiasm. Clearly in moving away from discussions of the 'Beaker Folk' to considerations of why ranking or stratification came into being we have lost some innocence: we now need to lose much more if we are going to use the archaeological record to the fullest in furthering the evaluation of our explanatory ideas and in providing the only truly important body of relevant facts regarding long-term evolutionary processes. We need to abandon the idealist view, we need to stop trying to reconstruct the past largely by using historical methods of empathetic understanding.

These papers represent a kind of intellectual push–pull where Hodder seeks to draw the field off into subjectivism and idealism, while Rowlands and Gledhill are beckoning with a very cautious materialistic call (see Friedman 1974). In between these poles are almost all the intellectual legacies of western economics; we heard a full-blown Adam Smith approach to economics where land is viewed as the source of wealth and power. Similarly we saw the idea of sharing risk developed into a near Hobbesian contract in the 'social storage' argument. At the other end of the economic spectrum that old standby of the west, the 'free enterprise' system, was clearly on centre stage in many of the models presented. Most of these arguments lack the level of sophistication currently evident in debate in much of social science (Sahlins 1976; Harris 1979; Godelier 1977).

Nevertheless, there is no question but that we are now 'participating' in the discussions of central interest to social scientists. We need to 'clean up our act' so that the wealth of past experience can realistically be brought to bear in evaluating some of the ideas we heard used in these papers. Archaeology seems to be in the middle of a major set of changes in which 'learning to do science' is a painful process. I am of the opinion that the rewards will be well worth the struggle.

Note

1. All references to other papers refer to *Ranking, Resource and Exchange*, the volume in which this originally appeared. British spellings and punctuation have been preserved, wherever possible.

PART II

Interassemblage Variability: The Mousterian Problem

8

Working at Archaeology:
The Mousterian Problem—
Learning How to Learn

The chapters that follow were developed in the context of learning how to learn about the archaeological record. Similarly, the focus of research has consistently been the problem I address in Chapter 9, namely the meaning to be attached to the patterning isolated by François Bordes within the archaeological record of the Middle Paleolithic (see L.R. Binford 1983:Chapter 5).

Beginning in the early 1960s (L.R. Binford 1962) I argued that the archaeological record was the organized product of the operation of cultural systems, and that such systems were internally differentiated in terms of actors, energy sources, places, and institutions. Put another way, the organizational properties most likely to condition the form, structure, and content of the archaeological record were thought to be the repetitive, ongoing internal dynamics of a cultural system. One may think of this suggestion in terms of the differential tempo of systems dynamics. The time frame of normal systems operations is rapid and repetitive relative to the tempo of systems' evolution, which is directional, not strikingly repetitive, and most likely punctuated, or occurring in spurts. In addition, the punctuations are apt to be relatively short-lived and hence documented within the archaelogical record (see Harpending and Bertram 1975). If we recognize that cultural systems are differentially localized in different places and are internally differentiated, then we must expect some of the more visible archaeological patterning to refer to these internal differentiations and their differential disposition in space, not systems change or differences in the identity of systems per se. Although a culture might be relatively stable and unchanging, the archaeological record generated by such a system might well be variable and differentiated (see Chapters 19–25). Similarity does not necessarily indicate systems identity, as traditional conventions assumed. Only through an understanding of systems functioning (dynamics) as manifest archaeologically (statics) can we understand the meaning of patterns that we might isolate within the archaeological record. Bordes had isolated impressive patterning. I challenged the use of traditional interpretative conventions to give meaning to the recognized patterns. From the very first exchange of views, there was little question that the Mousterian controversy was about the meaning to be attached to the observations that we as archaeologists might make.

It is interesting that most who read the literature of this controversy saw the argument in terms of a specific interpretation for a specific data set, the Mousterian. I always saw this as the key test case for learning about the limitations of our methodologies. It also provided the provocative "anomaly"[1] described by Bordes, the investigation of which had the potential of increasing not only our skill as archaeologists but also our knowledge of the past.

In 1967 my former wife, Sally, and I addressed a research proposal to the National Science Foundation seeking to test our views about the meaning of Mousterian interassemblage variability (Chapter 10). True to the beliefs of the times we thought we could test our ideas against the archaeological record at the Mousterian sites that Bordes had studied and from which he had the provocative patterning. Our ideas for testing were deceivingly straightforward. We had argued that the Mousterian assemblages were organized compounds made up of "tool kits,"[2] and that these tool kits varied in their relative contribution to different assemblages as a function of the differential frequency with which certain tool-kit-using actions had been carried out on one site versus another. We reasoned that we should be able to discover patterned associations and correlations between key tool types and other indicators of differing activities, such as faunal remains. In addition, we reasoned that there should be some patterned spatial clustering of tool kits within the sites; it seemed reasonable to expect that there would be at least some relationship between the organization of an activity as seen in patterns of tool covariation and its differential execution in space.[3]

Sally and I spent the summer and fall of 1968 in France laboriously studying the Würm Mousterian levels (55 separate geologic units of deposition) as excavated by Bordes from the site of Combe Grenal. First, catalogues had to be generated for each of the levels, because Bordes's records were by square, not by level. After this, inventories for the fauna had to be generated in terms of anatomical part, breakage pattern, and butchering marks, because these properties had not been observed by the paleontologists making the original identifications. Distribution maps of tools from each level had to be generated, inasmuch as the data had never been previously summarized in this fashion. Finally, information on lithic debris as well as features had to be recovered from the records, because the levels had never been described as such; only the assemblage composition from the levels had been reported. We did all this work getting data into the form needed to conduct our studies of site structure and item and class covariational patterning.

After the tools and features were plotted, and maps generated of the surfaces for each level, and after all the other classes of data (debris, anatomical parts, broken quartz pebbles, and so on) had been summarized and studied statistically, what we had was an absolute profusion of new facts—an embarrassment of recognizable patterning, and more correlations between things than anyone had ever imagined. We started out with some observed patterning among tool type frequencies studied across assemblages. We sought understanding for this patterning by reasoning to test implications regarding additional patterning. We investigated and found the world to be characterized by much more complicated patterning than we had expected.

More important, we had no Rosetta stone, no way of translating the wealth of patterns into meaningful statements about past conditions. In short, our knowledge of the dynamics of technological organization and the organization of tools and work was inadequate for the development of a theory of site formation. We had no idea what "other things" had to be equal. We had no idea what other variables and initial conditions would influence archaeologically visible patterning. We had little understanding of the relationships between an organized work force and the patterns of tool production, use, and discard. Our ignorance quite clearly rested at the interface between dynamics, as causes and conditioners, and statics, as consequences and effects. *No amount of studying the statics would yield the information necessary to both model and test arguments about the relationships between dynamics and statics.* The static patterns lay mute as to the nature of their causal dynamics.

The only source of statements on dynamics at that time rested with our imaginations. We could imagine certain organizational determinants and conditions producing the patterning, but whether our imaginations were correct could not be evaluated, except in terms of the degree to which our imagined past accommodated the static present of the archaeological record. Of course we were generally smart enough to imagine conditions that would accommodate the statics as known. We were literally locked into a very weak form of argument, the post hoc accommodative argument. The only test is the "goodness of fit" between our imagined past and the empirical archaeological present. This is the very form of argument that I and others had argued was inadequate, where the important step of "testing" had not been performed (see Chapter 12, this volume; also L.R. Binford 1981b:238–292).

The new archaeology began with a double approach. First, because it was a child of the computer, ^{14}C, and funding for large-scale field projects, we were seeking new facts, as well as new ways to discover properties of the archaeological record. Second, we were questioning the accuracy and adequacy of traditional conventions for interpreting archaeological facts. As pointed out earlier, we were seeking ways of evaluating the interpretative principles in use for converting contemporary observations into accurate statements about the past. Results from these paired strategies converged at the end of the 1960s. The use of new techniques in both data recovery and analysis resulted in so many new types of facts that the inadequacy of the traditional interpretative principles became obvious even without formal testing. For instance, in the 1950s the observation and reporting of the relative frequencies of different anatomical parts in a faunal assemblage began to be regularly carried out. Using traditional interpretative principles, differences and similarities were thought to reflect differences and similarities in butchering practices, which were thought to be interpretable in the same way any other cultural practice could be interpreted. Similar patterns meant similar cultures; different patterns meant different cultures (see Dibble and Lorraine 1968; Wood 1962). As more observations were made it became clear that the distribution of differences and similarities was nothing like the patterning seen when differences and similarities in projectile points, ceramics, or other cultural traits were studied comparatively. The cultures one would identify from faunal assemblages would be very different from the cultures recognized through studying other classes of things. Either these different things were informing us about different facets of the past, or the civilizations of the past were truly a "planless hodgepodge."

> To that planless hodgepodge, that thing of shreds and patches called civilization, its historian can
> no longer yield superstitious reverence. He will realize better than others the obstacles to infusing
> design into the amorphous product; but in thought at least he will not grovel before it in fatalistic
> acquiescence but dream of a rational scheme to supplant the chaotic jumble [Lowie 1920:441].

I accepted Lowie's challenge. We had to develop a "rational scheme to supplant the chaotic jumble." Our knowledge and understanding were clearly inadequate; further testing of the traditional conventions would only continue to tell us what already seemed apparent, that our interpretative principles were inadequate.

The realization flooded in on me as I tried to come to grips with the enormous quantity of new facts gleaned from the excavation record and the materials recovered during excavations at Combe Grenal. There was little help from traditional interpretative conventions. It was also clear that I could not learn what the facts meant in dynamic terms by studying the static archaeological record; all that was yielded by such tactics were more static facts. All experiences led unrelentingly to the same conclusion: If we wished to study the relationships between dynamics and statics, either (a) for testing ideas about the nature of these relationships or (b) as an educational strategy for seeking new insights, making discoveries, or inventing ideas, *then we must in fact study situations where organized dynamics were taking place and where patterned statics were a natural by-product of the dynamics.* In order either to test or to invent ideas, we had to study the subject of interest, the formation processes of the archaeological record. These conclusions were reached during the winter of 1968–1969. In the spring of 1969 I went to the Arctic to begin my studies of archaeological formation processes among a living group of caribou hunters, the Nunamiut Eskimo.

Ironically, at the very time that Fritz and Plog, as well as Watson, LeBlanc, and Redman, were working on their programmatic statements as to what archaeology should be, I had decided that most of their suggestions were untimely (see D.L. Clark 1972).[4] They were concerned with testing theories, doing "normal science" in Thomas Kuhn's terms, whereas I had decided that we needed a new paradigm. I could not find any prepackaged guidelines for achieving that goal.

Notes

1. The idea that seeming anomalies are clues to potential areas in need of investigation is very old indeed (see, e.g., L.R. Binford 1972b:119–127). In fact, it has long been maintained that our very desire for an explanation arises from the recognition of an anomaly, a surprise. This surprise results from a conflict between our expectation and the reality of a situation. When this occurs we want to know why; in short, we want an explanation (see Harvey 1969:11). Richard Gould (1980) has rediscovered this principle, but instead of seeing it as a way of isolating a problem he has proposed that the method of anomaly be substituted for the methods of reasoning by analogy. Most will recognize that as utter nonsense, inasmuch as one is a procedure for inference and the other is a tactic of discovery at best.

2. There have been a number of confusions generated regarding the idea of tool kit. Part of this is certainly my fault, stemming directly from the examples I gave in the original argument (Chapter 9). I did not mean to imply that I thought that the only units of organization "between the tool type and the assemblage" were activity specific in their constitution; that is, activity specific in the sense of "things used

for scraping hides" or "things used for killing animals." It is true that this type of organized association among tool types was an obvious form of tool kit. I also expected that there could be and almost certainly were other bases for organizing a technology. These factors could result in the regular association of different classes of things at different places, and could ensure that different combinations of such "sub-units" could be seen as contributing to the total assemblage that might occur at one site versus another. The main point being made was once again that a cultural system was internally differentiated and that there were regular and repetitive organized units of things within the system. These units of organization may vary independently, or at least partially independently, of one another among different places produced by the same cultural system. I never claimed that I knew all the various ways a system might be internally differentiated, only that we should expect differentiation and we should make some attempts to learn how differing systems were internally organized. In Part IV of this book I present basic research articles aimed at a beginning understanding of how technologies can be organized (at least among mobile peoples) and in turn how statics are differentially conditioned as a function of such organizations.

3. Under traditional normative assumptions it was common to deny that it mattered where on a site one collected a sample for use in seriation studies. The argument normally given was naturally in terms of normative ideas, namely that any variability was referable to the relative popularity of contemporary styles, and that differing combinations of things simply indicated slightly different periods of occupation. For those who adhered to strict normative views, the idea that sites were both structured and internally differentiated into functionally different locales and areas was a very troublesome challenge. Some, such as Bordes, acknowledged that there might be "horizontal" variation within a site but that it was minimal and never sufficient to confuse the excavator as to the "culture type" he or she was dealing with. It must appear strange to many contemporary archaeologists, but we then felt it necessary to demonstrate that sites were internally differentiated; that is, organized into differentiated spaces used for different purposes. This was the motivation behind the study by Longacre and Ayres (1968). We simply wanted to demonstrate that the idea of a spatially differentiated site was realistic. Many accepted this for complex sites such as Hatchery West, but tended to dismiss the idea for simpler mobile hunter–gatherer sites.

4. I had come to agree almost completely with David Clark's (1972) reaction to the Watson, *et al.* (1971) book:

> There are many related forms and many linked ideals of explanation at many levels, all of which refer to the particular logic, epistemology and metaphysics of particular disciplines. What is currently required is the internal analysis (with external aid) and explicit development of valid principles of archaeological reasoning (archaeological logic), the specification of the general nature and special qualities of archaeological information (archaeological epistemology) and the careful clarification of archaeological concepts and their limitations (archaeological metaphysics) [p. 239].

A Preliminary Analysis of Functional Variability in the Mousterian of Levallois Facies

Lewis R. Binford and Sally R. Binford

Ever since the discovery, more than 100 years ago, of the remains of Neanderthal man, there has been great interest in the cultural status of this hominid. We have come a long way in our understanding of the problem since the first outraged reactions to the suggestions that this "brutish" creature might represent our ancestral population.

In 1869 de Mortillet defined the Mousterian as the culture associated with Neanderthal man, the culture taking its name from a rockshelter in southwestern France, Le Moustier (de Mortillet 1885:252). According to this early definition the Mousterian culture was characterized by the presence of points, side-scrapers, and a few handaxes that were thinner than those of the preceding Acheulian stage; also noted by de Mortillet was unifacial treatment of tools and the absence of end-scrapers. The development of the Mousterian was seen as following a unilinear development from early types with handaxes, a middle type with no handaxes, to a late manifestation characterized by special kinds of retouch.

The first step toward a more realistic understanding of the complexity of the Mousterian was taken by Denis Peyrony (1930) in his investigations of Le Moustier where he found that this tidy order of development simply did not occur. But it is the monumental work of François Bordes in systematizing Mousterian typology and in defining the complexity of occurrences of different types of Mousterian assemblages that has advanced our knowledge most remarkably.

Bordes has introduced into the methodology of archeological analysis standards of description and comparison previously unknown, and has made possible for the first time objective comparison between Mousterian assemblages. Such comparison has led Bordes to recognize four basic types of Mousterian assemblages; these are expressed quantitatively and are objectively definable. These Mousterian assemblage types have been fully described (Bordes 1953a) and summarized (1961a) and the typological units which comprise the assemblages have been defined (1961b).

The four kinds of Mousterian assemblage are:

Originally appeared in *American Anthropologist*, **68**(2), Part 2, Recent Studies in Paleoanthropology, edited by J. D. Clark and F. C. Howell, pp. 238–295, © 1966.

1. *The Mousterian of Acheulian Tradition,* characterized by the presence of hand-axes, numerous side-scrapers, denticulates, and particularly, backed knives. There are two subtypes of this kind of Mousterian that appear to have temporal significance—Type A has higher frequencies of handaxes and occurs during the first half of the Mousterian time range (Würm I and the succeeding interstadial); Type B (Würm II) has many fewer handaxes and those that are present are of a different type, and Bordes also notes an increase in backed knives and a decrease in side-scrapers.

2. *Typical Mousterian* differs from the preceding type principally in sharply reduced frequencies of handaxes and knives.

3. *Denticulate Mousterian* contains up to 80 percent denticulates and notched tools; there are no handaxes or backed knives, and the percentage of the assemblage not accounted for by the denticulates and notched tools consists of end-scrapers, side-scrapers, burins, borers, etc.

4. *Charentian Mousterian* is subdivided into two types—*Quina* and *Ferrassie*. Both are characterized by having few or no handaxes or backed knives, as well as by very high frequencies of side-scrapers. Tool types contained in the other assemblages appear here also, but the Charentian is notable for the numerous side-scrapers, often made with a distinctive kind of scalar retouch. Quina and Ferrassie assemblages are distinguished by the absence in the former and the presence in the latter of a special technique of core preparation—the Levallois technique.

The Levallois technique cross-cuts the other three types of assemblages in a complicated way. When the percentage of tools made by Levallois technique exceeds 30, the industry is defined as being *Mousterian of Levallois facies* (Bordes 1953a, 1953b). Since the Levallois technique is so prevalent in the later Mousterian of the Near East and since for a long time prehistorians thought Levallois represented a distinct cultural tradition rather than a technique, the later Mousterian in this area is often called Levalloiso-Mousterian. Actually, the superimposed levels in the rockshelters and caves of the Near East exhibit the same kind of alternation of industries which Bordes has demonstrated for Europe. This alternation of the subtypes of assemblages does not seem to have any pattern that could be said to be directional through time.

For example, at Combe Grenal, a deeply stratified site in Dordogne, France, Bordes has described a sequence beginning with Denticulate Mousterian, overlain by layers of Typical, Ferrassie, Typical, Ferrassie, followed by a long sequence of Quina layers. Overlying these are less patterned alternations of Denticulate, Ferrassie, and Mousterian of Acheulian Tradition (Bordes 1961a).

Three major hypotheses have been offered to explain the well-documented alternation of industries in the Mousterian (Bordes 1961a):

1. The different types of Mousterian are associated with a seasonal pattern of living, each type representing the remains of activities carried out at different seasons of the year.

2. Each assemblage represents a slightly different adaptation to a different environment, the alternation of industries being determined by environmental variations through time.

3. Each type of Mousterian represents the remains of a different group of people, each group characterized by its own traditional way of making tools.

Bordes (1961a:4) has amassed data which suggest that within any one type of Mousterian assemblage all seasons of the year are represented; evidence that negates the first hypothesis. The second interpretation is contradicted by the presence of more than one type of Mousterian within a single geological horizon, suggesting that assemblage type varies independently of environment. This inference is further supported by the identification of the various types of Mousterian from sites in Spain, North Africa, the Near East, and China. These areas are widely enough separated to have represented a great variety of environments but still yield the alternation of industries within a single deposit. The very distribution of the known types of Mousterian argues against a strict environmental explanation, no matter how sophisticated the terms in which it is presented.

Because of the evidence refuting the first two hypotheses, Bordes has tentatively accepted the third—that the four types of Mousterian assemblages are associated with different Neanderthal "tribes" (Bordes 1961a). Good arguments can be presented against such an explanation, based on our knowledge of formal variation in material remains of populations of *Homo sapiens*. Nevertheless, such arguments remain opinion, for as yet no one has proposed a means of testing Bordes' hypothesis. If a means of testing were developed and the hypothesis confirmed, a major contribution would be made since we would then be forced to conclude that the social behavior of Neanderthal populations was vastly different from that of *Homo sapiens*.

Studies in many parts of the world have shown that formal variation in material items that is inexplicable in terms of function or raw materials can be termed *stylistic* variation (Binford, L. R., 1963); these stylistic variations tend to cluster spatially in direct relationship to the amount of social distance maintained between societies. Spatial clusterings of the various Mousterian assemblages are not demonstrable; in fact, in the Dordogne region of France the four types of Mousterian assemblage occur interdigitated at several localities.

In view of the demonstrated alternation of industries, one must envision a perpetual movement of culturally distinct peoples, never reacting to or coping with their neighbors. Nor do they exhibit the typically human characteristics of mutual influence and borrowing. Such a situation is totally foreign, in terms of our knowledge of *sapiens* behavior.

The purpose of this paper is to present an alternative set of testable hypotheses as possible explanations for the observed variation and alternation of Mousterian industries demonstrated by Bordes. Another purpose is to introduce certain analytical techniques that we feel are particularly useful for the interpretation of archeological materials.

The Method

There has recently been a burst of activity in the investigation of multivariate causality of social phenomena and an elaboration of general field theory (Cartwright 1964), ecological theory (Duncan 1959), and general systems theory (see *Journal of General Systems Theory*.) These represent different but compatible ways of conceptualizing multivariate causation. The phrase "multivariate causation" implies that the determinants of any given situation are multiple and may by linked, and that some determinants may contribute in different ways to different situations.

If we assume that variation in the structure and content of an archeological assemblage is directly related to the form, nature, and spatial arrangement of human activities, several steps follow logically. We are forced to seek explanations for the composition of assemblages in terms of variations in human activities. The factors determining the range and form of human activities conducted by any group at a single location (the site) may vary in terms of a large number of possible "causes" in various combinations. The broader among these may be seasonally regulated phenomena, environmental conditions, ethnic composition of the group, size and structure of the group, regardless of ethnic affiliation. Other determining variables might be the particular situation of the group with respect to food, shelter, supply of tools on hand, etc. In short, the units of "causation" of assemblage variability are separate activities, each of which may be related to both the physical and social environment, as well as interrelated in different ways.

Since a summary description of a given assemblage represents a blending of activity units and their determinants, it becomes essential to partition assemblages of artifacts into groups of artifacts that vary together, reflecting activities.

If techniques were available to isolate artifact groups reflecting activities within assemblages, then the ways in which they are combined at various localities could be analyzed. We therefore seek a unit of comparison between the single artifact type and the total assemblage—a unit that will, we believe, correspond to the basic units responsible for the observable variation within assemblages.

The major methodological problem is the isolation of these units and a comparison between them, utilizing multivariate techniques. *Factor analysis* seemed the most appropriate method (Harmann 1961). This technique, although widely used in other scientific fields, has not been commonly applied in prehistory. Its application here is one step of a continuing program of research in the investigation and development of analytical methods. Much of the preliminary work was conducted over the past four years by the senior author in collaboration with students at the University of Chicago.[1]

The basic set of statistics necessary for the beginning of a factor analysis is a matrix of correlation coefficients. Correlation coefficients are expressions on a scale from -1 to $+1$ of the degree of correlation between two variables. A value of $+1$ signifies that there is a perfect one-to-one correlation between two variables; as one increases in number, the other increases in perfect proportion. A value of 0 indicates that the variables are unrelated. A value of -1 indicates that as one variable increases in number, the other decreases proportionally. Correlation coefficients must be obtained for all possible combinations of pairs of variables to be included in the study.

Another essential in a factor analysis is the concept of types of variance. The total variance squared of a variable may be subdivided into three general classes—common, specific, and error variance. Common variance is that portion of the total variance which correlates with other variables. Specific variance is that portion of the total variance which does not correlate with any other variable. Error variance is the chance variance, due to errors of sampling, measurement, etc. The latter is assumed to be uncorrelated with the reliable variance (common and specific) and other error variance.

A basic assumption of factor analysis is that a battery of intercorrelated variables has common factors running through it, and that the scores of any individual variable can be represented more economically in terms of these reference factors. The number and nature of these common reference factors is measured in terms of the configuration of *common variance* demonstrable between the numerous variables.

This assumption is essentially in perfect correspondence with the reasoning concerning the composition of an archeological assemblage. For example, if a group of people occupy a location and are engaged in a specific activity, such as hide-working, they would employ a number of different tools—knives, scrapers, and possibly pins for pinning down the hides or stretching them. The number of tools used in hide-processing will be directly related to the number of individuals engaged in the activity and the number of hides processed. Regardless of these variations, we would expect that the proportions of the tools used in the activity would remain essentially constant. In other words, they would share a high degree of common variance and would be positively correlated.

If, after the eposide of hide-working, the group began to manufacture clothing, a different set of tools might be employed, along with some of the same tools used in hide-working—knives, abraders, piercing implements, etc. Once again, the relative proportions of the tools used in this activity would vary directly with the number of persons engaged in the work and the number of articles being manufactured. Therefore, there would be a high proportion of common variance between the tools used in this particular activity.

Through factor analysis of many assemblages from sites where these activities were performed, the configuration of common variance would be observable, and the analysis would result in the recognition of two *factors*. These factors express the configurations of common variance between the tools used in hide-working on the one hand and clothing manufacture on the other.

It will be recalled that one type of tool (knives) was used in both activities and would consequently be expected to exhibit some common variance with tools in both kinds of activities. In addition, if there were any relationship between the number of hides processed and the number worked into clothing, given a constant size of work force, then tools in both activities would exhibit some common variance; this common variance would be less, however, than that which would be shown among other tools used in a single activity.

Through such an analysis of the configuration of shared or common variance exhibited by a number of variables (artifact types, in this case), we hope to derive objectively defined *factors* which are summary statements of common variance. Our analysis does not provide information as to the particular activity represented by a factor; it simply allows us to identify a regular relationship between a number of artifact types. Our identification of the function of a factor depends on analogy with the tools of living peoples, tool wear, and associations with refuse. Whether or not our interpretation of a factor in terms of function is correct, this does not affect the demonstrable relationship between the variables analyzed.

The actual methods and mathematical procedures involved in factor analysis are rather complex, and for this information the reader is referred to Fruchter (1954) and Harmann (1961).

The Sample

The data used in this study come from two sites in the Near East and from one site in northern France. A number of considerations entered into the selection of these particular data. One such consideration was the need for typological consistency; we had to be sure that "scrapers," "points," "knives," etc. meant the same thing in all assemblages. The open-air station of Houppeville (near Rouen, France) was excavated and analyzed by Bordes (1952). The shelter of Jabrud (near Damascus, Syria) was excavated by Rust (1950) and the lithic assemblages were re-analyzed by Bordes (1955). The cave site in our sample, Mugharet es-Shubbabiq (Wadi Amud, Israel), was excavated by the junior author and the lithic material analyzed under Bordes' supervision at the Laboratoire de Préhistoire, Université de Bordeaux (S. R. Binford 1966).

In addition to being able to control for typological consistency, Jabrud Shelter I (Levels 2–8) was selected since it is the only other Near Eastern site yielding Mousterian of Levallois facies which was analyzed in comparable units. Houppeville was chosen since the *série claire* assemblage exhibited a marked similarity in total assemblage with Shubbabiq. One of the things we wished to test was whether total assemblages that are similar when expressed in Bordes' cumulative percentage graphs would remain similar under factor analysis. Do assemblages identified as Typical Mousterian, for example, exhibit the same configuration of factors?[2]

The Variables

A total of 40 variables was used in this study. Some of the 63 Mousterian artifact types isolated by Bordes were not included because of their absence, or near absence, in the samples under study. Variables such as cores, introduced rocks, cracked rock, and worked bone were not used since they were not present in the counts from Jabrud and since they did not occur in primary archeological context at Shubbabiq.

Table 9.1 presents the list of variables used in this study together with the number they represent in Bordes' type list. We have included a priori judgments as to the mechanical task for which the implements would have been utilized. When we felt our judgment was shaky or that there was ambiguity in the morphology of the tool, an alternative suggestion is offered.

Results of Analysis

The computer output expresses summary information in several stages of analysis. The final summary consists of the delineation of *factors* (five, in this case); a factor is the quantitative expression of the configuration of common variance in the matrix

TABLE 9.1

Functional Suggestions for Tool Type Used in Bordes' Type List

No. in Bordes' Type List	Variable Number	Variable Name	Functional Interpretation	
			First	Second
1	1.	Typical Levallois flake	Delicate cutting	
2	2.	Atypical Levallois flake	Delicate cutting	
3	3.	Levallois point	Spear point	
4	4.	Retouched Levallois point	Spear point	
5	5.	Pseudo-Levallois point	Perforating (?)	
6	6.	Mousterian point	Spear point	
7	7.	Elongated Mousterian point	Spear point	
9	8.	Simple straight side-scraper	Cutting-scrap. Nonyielding Surface	
10	9.	Simple convex side-scraper	Cutting-scrap. Nonyielding Surface	
11	10.	Simple concave side-scraper	Scraping cylindrical objects	
12–17	11.	Double side-scrapers		
18–20	12.	Convergent side-scrapers[a]		
22–24	13.	Transverse side-scrapers		
25	14.	Scrapers on the ventral surface	Push Plane	
26	15.	Scrapers with abrupt retouch		
30	16.	Typical end-scrapers		
31	17.	Atypical end-scrapers		
32	18.	Typical burin	Deep incising	Perforating
33	19.	Atypical burin	Heavy cutting	
34	20.	Typical borer	Perforating	
35	21.	Atypical borer	Perforating	
36	22.	Typical backed knife	Heavy cutting	
37	23.	Atypical backed knife	Heavy cutting	
38	24.	Naturally backed knife	Heavy cutting	
39	25.	Raclette		
40	26.	Truncated flake		
42	27.	Notched piece	Gut-stropper (small obj.)	
43	28.	Denticulate	Sawing	
44	29.	Bec	Perforating	Deep incising
45	30.	Ventrally retouched piece	?	
48–49	31.	Utilized flakes		
50	32.	Pieces with bifacial retouch		
54	33.	End-notched piece	Scraping cylindrical objects	
56	34.	*Rabot* (push plane)	Planing	
61	35.	Chopping tool	Heavy duty cleaving	
62	36.	Miscellaneous[b]		
—	37.	Disc		
—	38.	Unretouched flake	Delicate cutting	Unused debris
—	39.	Unretouched blade	Delicate cutting	Unused debris
—	40.	Waste flake (Trimming flake)	None	Index of flint work

[a] The various types of convergent and double scrapers recognized by Bordes were represented in such small numbers that they were lumped for the purposes of this analysis into two classes, convergent and double.

[b] This category includes not only unclassifiable tools but also those which have received some kind of special treatment (= Bordes' type No. 62—"divers").

of variables and samples under study. The factors are described in terms of factor loadings (the square roots of the percentages of variance accounted for by each factor). Factor loadings are expressed on a scale from -1 to $+1$ and may be read as positive and negative percentages of common variance.

The five factors define clusters of artifacts that exhibit internally consistent patterns of mutual covariation; these are independent of each other with respect to the determinants of variation. It should be reemphasized that in this method there is no built-in technique for interpreting the particular "meaning" of the factors. The computer end-product is simply a statement of configurations of common variance. The interpretation of the factors—i.e., the type of unit activities they represent—must be offered in terms of hypotheses for testing.

In general there are two types of formal differences between artifacts that can reflect human activities and social context: *functional* and *stylistic*. These may be fixed along two axes—time and space. In this context, when we ask "What kinds of activities do our factors represent?" we must consider three kinds of information:

1. the formal content of a factor—i.e., the kinds of artifacts that exhibit a high degree of mutual covariation;
2. the relative value of the factor scores among the artifact types with paired factors;
3. the relative significance of the factors within a single assemblage and their temporal and geographical occurrence.

Figure 9.1 shows four hypothetical cases in which two factors are plotted on a Cartesian graph; the discussion that follows is to illustrate the application of the principles of interpretation outlined above.

In Pattern A we compare two factors that are functionally distinct but which share specific tasks performed with specific tools. Such a situation might arise if, for example, one factor were associated with butchering and the other with hide-working. Cutting and scraping tools would be common to both activities, but each activity would also employ artifacts not used in the other. Both might require scrapers, but butchering might require cleavers, while hide-processing might demand heavy-duty choppers. In Pattern A there are many diagnostics of the two factors clustering on the individual factor axes but with several types aligned along the diagonal. These latter would be the types exhibiting equal factor loadings within both factors (in the case cited, these would be scrapers).

The distribution shown in Pattern B, where the great proportion of artifacts cluster along the diagonal, is interpreted as representing two factors that are similarly determined and therefore inferred as being functionally equivalent. The few tools that occur outside the diagonal cluster would, if we were comparing factors at the same site on different time horizons, represent a stylistic shift through time—a change in preference for similar tools within one functional class. If the two factors occurred on the same time horizon at different localities, it might be interpreted as reflecting regional style preferences.

Pattern C bears general resemblances to Pattern B but with the following exceptions:

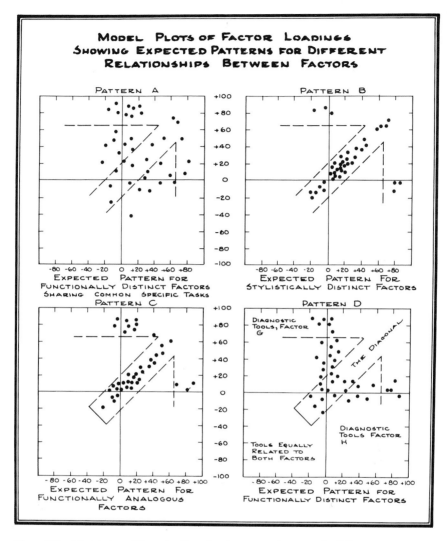

Figure 9.1   Model plots of factor loadings showing expected patterns for different relationships between factors.

1. The numbers of tools falling outside the diagonal are not equal in both factors.
2. Within the diagonal, some tools positive on one axis are negative on the other.
3. Some of the artifacts in the larger cluster outside the diagonal have functional equivalents in the smaller cluster, but some do not.

Pattern C would express a situation where the two factors reflect very similar activities, but the tool kit in one factor is more complex than in the other. If this pattern occurred with respect to two factors at the same location but on different time levels, we might infer an adaptive shift as the result of minor differences in a specific activity—

e.g., a change in type of animal being hunted. If the pattern obtained between two factors from different localities on the same time horizon, we could infer that we have represented different adaptations to varying local conditions. This type of pattern is potentially very informative and provocative for the framing of hypotheses.

Pattern D represents two factors that are mutually exclusive, exhibiting nothing in common in the determinants of variability. It is inferred that in this situation we have totally different activities involved.

We will examine the artifact samples studied by factor analysis to see which factors occur in combination in the assemblages, and analyze these combinations in terms of the temporal controls offered by the stratified site of Jabrud and the geographical controls provided by having samples from three spatially distinct regions.

Factor I

Table 9.2 presents the list of variables arranged according to a descending order of mutual determinancy as they occur in Factor I. The table is divided into six major groupings of variables, the groups having been defined by the angle of a line described when the factor loadings were plotted on a Cartesian graph in order of descending value. The tools in each group not only share the same kind of mutual determinacy but also exhibit the same relationship to the first two groups, which are the diagnostics for this factor.

These diagnostics—the first two groups in the table—exhibit a consistent pattern of proportional variation with respect to each other, and each shows a similar kind of frequency variation with respect to all other varables. Not only do they show positive correlations between themselves, but they also behave as a group with respect to all other variables.

The variables in the bottom two classes have no tendency to vary in the same ways as the variables within the top two groups. This does not mean that they are negatively correlated; on the contrary, their presence is being *independently* determined by other elements not operative for Factor I.

The variables listed in the two middle groups have some tendency to vary with those in the first two classes, but they also vary independently of them. Stated another way, their frequency in any assemblage of which Factor I is a major determinant would be expected to display variability which could not be explained by a unique relationship to the determinant of the first two classes. Variation might occur which would not be proportional to the variation of the tools within the diagnostic group.

Since the artifacts within the first two classes in Table 9.2 share determinants and behave as a unit with respect to other tools in the assemblage and since archeological assemblages are the fossil remains of human activities, we postulate that the variables diagnostic for a factor represent a functionally related set of tools.

In the case of Factor I there is a high frequency among the diagnostics of tools with working edges oriented transversely to the longitudinal axis of the piece, as well as borers, becs, and burins. Nothing in this list of tools suggests hunting or butchering; many of the points and scrapers occur toward the bottom of the list, indicating that they tend to vary independently of the diagnostics of Factor I. We suggest that the diagnostic group of Factor I represents maintaining the technology—i.e., secondary

TABLE 9.2

List of Variables Arranged According to a Descending Order of Factor Loading—Factor I

No. in Bordes' Type List	Variable Name	Factor Loading	Percentage in Bordes' Essential Graph
35	Atypical borer	.925[a]	1.11
44	Bec	.912[a]	1.64
30	Typical end-scraper	.834[a]	1.79
11	Simple concave scraper	.830[a]	3.27
62	Misc. Tools	.809[a]	12.29
31	Atypical end-scraper	.785[a]	2.69
33	Atypical burin	.772[a]	5.96
45	Ventrally retouched piece	.770[a]	—
42	Notches	.745[a]	15.49
40	Truncated flake	.739[a]	5.09
34	Typical borer	.719[a]	.42
38	Naturally backed knife	.705[a]	9.73
2	Atypical Levallois flake	.630	—
54	End-notched piece	.625	1.18
50	Bifacially retouched piece	.582	—
43	Denticulate	.555	18.09
22–24	Transverse scrapers	.524[a]	.72
12–17	Double scrapers	.488	3.59
48–49	Utilized flakes	.480	—
32	Typical burins	.454	3.70
—	Unretouched flakes	.445	—
9	Simple straight scraper	.389	5.17
5	Pseudo-Levallois point	.308	.89
1	Typical Levallois flake	.265	—
10	Simple convex scraper	.212	6.09
36	Typical backed knife	.212	.31
61	Chopping tool	.137[a]	.03
6	Mousterian point	.094	.31
—	Waste flakes	.084	—
7	Elongated Mousterian point	.070	.18
37	Atypical backed knife	.030	.09
—	Unretouched blade	.026	—
56	Rabot	.017	.01
3	Levallois point	− .007	—
18–20	Convergent scrapers	− .016	—
—	Disc	− .032	—
25	Scrapers retouched on the ventral surface	− .041	—
39	Raclettes	− .071	—
26	Scraper with abrupt retouch	− .091	—
4	Retouched Levallois point	− .097	—

[a] Indicates that the variable exhibits the highest factor loadings with respect to this factor and can be considered diagnostic of the factor.

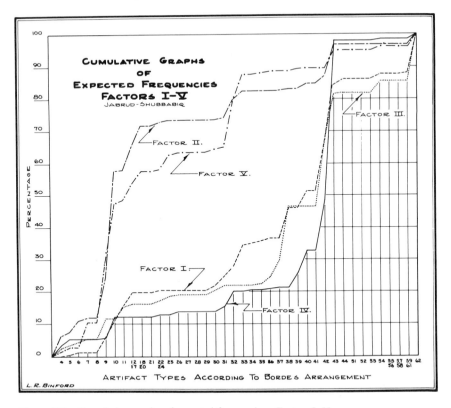

Figure 9.2   Cumulative graphs of expected frequencies—Factors I–V.

tool manufacture activities—perhaps the processing of bone and wood into shafts or hafts, as well as possibly the working of skins for cordage.

Another striking fact about this group of tools is the high proportion of "Upper Paleolithic" types (Bordes 1961b). This suggests that the activities represented have much in common with activities represented by many Upper Paleolithic assemblages. Our interpretation of this set of implements as a tool-manufacturing and maintenance factor may be the clue to its "Upper Paleolithic" flavor.

If we wish to express graphically the expected frequencies of artifact types if a single factor were the sole determinant of an assemblage, the following operation is performed. A single-tailed index is derived by multiplying the factor loading by the mean for each variable. These variable indices are summed for the entire list of variables. Each variable index is then divided by the sum of all indices. The resulting figure is a percentage, to be thought of as the expected relative frequency of each variable under the assumption that only one factor was determinant.

The expected percentages for all factors are given in Figure 9.2. The graph for Factor I is similar to the kind of curve defined by Bordes (1953) as characterizing the Typical Mousterian.

Factor II

As in the case of Factor I, the variables are arranged in the table form (Table 9.3) in a descending order of factor loading values. The first two groups of variables are taken as diagnostic of Factor II; these are remarkably consistent in that they contain all of the point forms, with the exception of the elongated Mousterian point. In addition, convergent scrapers are high on the list, and these have a number of features of gross morphology in common with points. Scrapers are also significantly present in the diagnostic groups. Unretouched flakes, blades, and Levallois points also have high factor loadings and can be seen as a class of blanks used in the production of points and scrapers.

The composition of the diagnostics for Factor II contrasts sharply with Factor I, and many of the diagnostics for Factor I are not correlated with diagnostics for this factor. The nature of the diagnostic group of tools for Factor II strongly implies hunting and butchering as the major activities represented. Further, practically all of the small tools that are diagnostic for Factor I show negative loadings with respect to Factor II (see Table 9.3), while most of the points and convergent scrapers were negative for Factor I.

If we plot the two factors on a Cartesian graph, the pattern produced essentially duplicates Pattern D (Figure 9.1), a pattern which is expected when two mutually exclusive activities are represented. The only divergence from the anticipated pattern occurs with respect to three types which fall along the diagonal in the moderate range of factor loadings. These types are bifacially retouched pieces, typical burins, and unretouched flakes. As a group, these appear to have little in common, and their positioning probably should not be interpreted as indicating a major overlap in the activities represented by the two factors. Rather, these three tools are probably multipurpose implements.

In general we can say that the difference between Factor I and Factor II is that they are representative of two major types of distinct activities. Factor I is interpreted as associated with maintenance activities of the group, while Factor II represents the implements used for hunting and butchering. From the very nature of these two activities, we might expect them frequently to be conducted at different locations. The maintenance activities would be carried out most often at locations selected as suitable for habitation of the group as a whole; requirements of space, protection, etc., would be important. Hunting and butchering sites, on the other hand, would be chosen in relation to distribution and habits of game as well as to the temporary maintenance requirements of a hunting group.

Factor III

The results of the factor analysis are presented in Table 9.4 with the variables arranged in descending order of factor loading. The first two classes of artifacts are diagnostic of this factor. With the exception of end-notched pieces, all of these artifacts have in common edges suitable for fine cutting. The specific context of this activity can be suggested by a comparison of Factors I and III, and the relationship both bear to Factor II.

TABLE 9.3

List of Variables Arranged According to a Descending Order of Factor Loading—Factor II

Number in Bordes' List	Variable Name	Factor Loading	Percentage in Bordes' Essential Graph
3	Levallois point	.893[a]	—
18–20	Convergent scrapers	883[a]	6.22
10	Simple convex scrapers	860[a]	32.72
4	Retouched Levallois point	.855[a]	6.31
6	Mousterian point	.834[a]	3.56
12–17	Double scrapers	.785[a]	7.76
9	Simple straight scrapers	.720[a]	12.67
50	Bifacially retouched piece	.651[a]	—
—	Unretouched blade	.591[a]	—
1	Typical Levallois flake	.531[a]	—
32	Typical burin	.517[a]	5.58
—	Unretouched flake	.465[a]	—
22–24	Transverse scrapers	.373	.68
2	Atypical Levallois flake	.355	—
25	Scraper retouched on ventral surface	.304	.79
7	Elongated Mousterian point	.303	1.07
5	Pseudo-Levallois point	.248	.96
43	Denticulate	.225	9.71
33	Atypical burin	.225	2.30
40	Truncated flake	.161	1.48
62	Misc. tools	.134	2.69
11	Simple concave scraper	.113	.59
45	Ventrally retouched piece	.103	—
42	Notch	.094	2.59
30	Atypical end-scraper	.078	.13
54	End-notched piece	.071	.18
—	Disc	.061	—
37	Atypical backed knife	.047	.18
31	Typical end-scraper	.046	.90
38	Naturally backed knife	.037	.67
36	Typical backed knife	.037	.07
39	Raclette	.032	.09
26	Scrapers with abrupt retouch	.031	.03
44	Bec	.025	.06
—	Utilized flakes	.024	—
35	Atypical borer	− .029	0.00
—	Waste flake	− .078	0.00
34	Typical borer	− .189	0.00
61	Chopping tool	− .336	0.00
56	Rabot	− .486	0.00

[a] Indicates that the variable exhibits the highest factor loadings with respect to this factor and can be considered diagnostic of the factor.

TABLE 9.4
List of Variables Arranged According to a Descending Order of Factor Loading—Factor III

Number in Bordes' List	Variable Name	Factor Loading[a]	Percentage in Bordes' Essential Graph
37	Atypical backed knife	− .976[b]	5.35
36	Typical backed knife	− .938[b]	2.57
1	Typical Levallois flake	− .752[b]	—
54	End-notched piece	− .704[b]	2.49
—	Unretouched flake	− .697[b]	—
2	Atypical Levallois flake	− .664[a]	—
38	Naturally backed knife	− .638[b]	16.55
42	Notch	− .534	20.91
—	Unretouched blade	− .532	—
62	Miscellaneous	− .520	14.82
45	Ventrally retouched piece	− .466	—
26	Scraper with abrupt retouch	− .413	.46
22–24	Transverse scrapers	− .412	1.06
25	Scraper with retouch on ventral surface	− .381	1.41
11	Simple concave scraper	− .341	2.53
9	Simple straight scraper	− .290	7.24
7	Elongated Mousterian point	− .261	1.30
31	Atypical end-scraper	− .259	1.67
43	Denticulate	− .247	15.12
4	Retouched Levallois point	− .237	2.48
30	Typical end-scraper	− .223	.90
5	Pseudo-Levallois point	− .213	1.17
3	Levallois point	− .169	—
6	Mousterian point	− .106	.65
—	Waste flake	− .106	—
12–17	Double scrapers	− .074	1.03
48–49	Utilized flakes	− .056	—
35	Atypical borer	− .054	.12
44	Bec	− .049	.16
	Tools showing positive loading on Factor III		
39	Raclette	.011	0.00
10	Simple convex scrapers	.019	0.00
18–20	Convergent scrapers	.030	0.00
34	Typical borers	.048	0.00
31	Atypical burins	.102	0.00
50	Bifacially retouched piece	.104	0.00
56	Rabot	.136	0.00
61	Chopping tool	.141	0.00
40	Truncated flake	.174	0.00
—	Disc	.180	0.00
32	Typical burin	.246	0.00

[a] The variance is the square root of the standard deviation. Variance may, therefore, be expressed positively or negatively. For purposes of clarity the factor loadings may be expressed either positively or negatively for different factors. The square of the factor loading is the percentage of common variance accounted for by a single factor. Therefore, the sign of the factor loading itself is irrelevant.

[b] Indicates that the variable exhibits the highest factor loadings with respect to this factor and can be considered diagnostic of the factor.

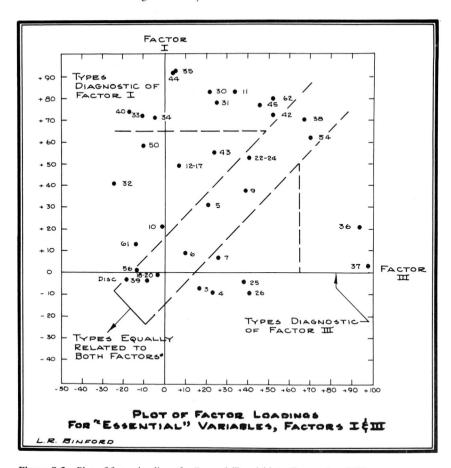

Figure 9.3 Plot of factor loadings for "essential" variables—Factors I and III.

When Factors I and III are plotted against one another on a Cartesian graph (Figure 9.3), the distribution which results is like Pattern A, in Figure 9.1. It will be recalled that this pattern suggests distinct activities with certain mechanical tasks in common; these common elements are ranged along the diagonal. In this case, the tools on the diagonal (from low to high loadings) are: Mousterian points, pseudo-Levallois points, simple straight scrapers, transverse scrapers, and naturally backed knives. All of these types are diagnostic for Factor II, suggesting that Factors I and III stand in a similar relation to Factor II, the hunting and butchering factor.

Since points are not a major diagnostic of Factor III, we suggest that the particular cutting and incising tasks represented by this factor are related not to butchering at kill sites but to the processing of animal products for consumption. If this inference is correct, we would expect to find Factor III as a consistent component in base-camp sites and to be associated with hearths.

If we tentatively identify this factor as primarily related to food processing, versus food procurement (Factor II) and maintenance activities (Factor I), the association of Factors I and III with base-camp activities and with different aspects of maintenance can be seen in the similar curves for these factors as they have been plotted in Figure 9.2. It should be noted that the curve for Factor III in Figure 9.2 is very like the curve for the Mousterian of Acheulian Tradition (Type B) of Pech de l'Azé (Bordes 1954). Unfortunately, bifaces were not included in our variables, since they occurred in low frequency in three of the samples and were absent from the others.

Factor IV

Table 9.5 presents the variables arranged in descending order of determinancy by Factor IV. This factor differs from the others in that there is a very sharp break in the value loadings between the diagnostics for the factor and those variables related in a minor way (see the factor loadings for the fourth and fifth items in Table 9.5). A percentage plot of expected frequencies of Factor IV according to Bordes' type list Figure 9.2 reveals a curve strikingly similar to that for Denticulate Mousterian (Bordes 1953a, 1962).

Comparisons between Factor IV and all other factors reveal some interesting relationships. It will be recalled that Factor II was identified as a hunting and butchering factor, and Factor V is similarly identified. If Factor IV is plotted against Factors II and V on a Cartesian graph, a pattern is obtained which strongly resembles Pattern D (Figure 9.1). This pattern is interpreted as representing mutually exclusive activities.

A Cartesian graph comparison of Factor IV with Factors I and III reveals distributions like those shown in Pattern A (Figure 9.1), where, it was argued, there existed distinct activities with analagous mechanical tasks in common. The types which exhibit mutual variation in both Factors I and IV are: denticulates, retouched flakes, truncated flakes, typical borers, notches, and atypical end-scrapers. Many of these can easily be seen as implements for sawing, fine scraping, and planing. Bordes (1962:47) has suggested that Denticulate Mousterian might be associated with the processing of plant material, a suggestion which is borne out by our analysis.

Comparison of Factors III and IV shows a pattern of greater exclusiveness of function for the two factors; nevertheless, there is common determinancy exhibited with respect to notches, denticulates, and scrapers with abrupt retouch. If Factor III represents food processing as we have suggested above, we might see in these tools common functions in preparing plants and possibly scraping bones.

Factor V

The variables are arranged in descending order of determinacy by Factor V in Table 9.6; the first six variables in the list are the diagnostics for this factor. The cumulative percentages of types when Factor V determines the assemblage can be seen in Figure 9.2; the curve closely resembles that for Ferrassie Mousterian, according to Bordes' system (1953a).

Comparison between Factor V and the other factors on a Cartesian graph yields the following results. Factors IV and V when paired exhibit mutual exclusiveness of

TABLE 9.5

List of Variables Arranged According to a Descending Order of Factor Loading—Factor IV

Number in Bordes' List	Variable Name	Factor Loading	Percentage in Bordes' Essential Graph
39	Raclette	.905[a]	4.36
48–49	Utilized flakes	.824[a]	—
26	Scrapers with abrupt retouch	.792[a]	1.03
43	Denticulates	.707[a]	49.79
40	Truncated flakes	.477	7.15
34	Typical borers	.381	.49
42	Notches	.347	15.63
5	Pseudo-Levallois points	.326	2.05
4	Retouched Levallois point	.296	3.56
—	Disc	.268	—
31	Atypical end-scraper	.254	1.88
—	Unretouched flake	.242	—
22–24	Transverse scrapers	.236	.70
32	Typical burins	.230	4.05
—	Unretouched blade	.227	—
3	Levallois point	.218	—
54	End-notched piece	.120	.49
36	Typical backed knife	.119	.37
2	Atypical Levallois flake	.117	—
50	Bifacially retouched piece	.102	—
10	Simple convex scrapers	.101	6.26
62	Miscellaneous tools	.043	1.41
37	Atypical backed knife	.039	.24
9	Simple straight scraper	.018	.52
1	Typical Levallois flake	.015	—
3	Atypical burin	−.002	0.00
44	Bec	−.020	0.00
30	Typical end-scraper	−.046	0.00
6	Mousterian point	−.059	0.00
12–17	Double scrapers	−.095	0.00
7	Elongated Mousterian point	−.107	0.00
38	Naturally backed knife	−.117	0.00
33	Atypical borer	−.135	0.00
45	Ventrally retouched piece	−.165	0.00
25	Scraper with retouch on ventral surface	−.187	0.00
11	Simple convex scraper	−.190	0.00
—	Waste flake	−.192	0.00
18–20	Convergent scrapers	−.200	0.00
61	Chopping tool	−.242	0.00
56	Rabot	−.352	0.00

[a] Indicates that the variable exhibits the highest factor loadings with respect to this factor and can be considered diagnostic of the factor.

TABLE 9.6

List of Variables Arranged According to a Descending Order of Factor Loading—Factor V

Number in Bordes' List	Variable Name	Factor Loading	Percentage in Bordes' Essential Graph
7	Elongated Mousterian point	.869[a]	7.29
—	Disc	.749[a]	—
25	Scraper with retouch on ventral surface	.744[a]	4.64
32	Typical burin	.569[a]	14.67
—	Unretouched blade	.517[a]	—
9	Simple straight scrapers	.461[a]	19.41
10	Simple convex scrapers	.368	17.48
33	Atypical burin	.339	8.27
56	Rabot	.293	.39
12–17	Double scrapers	.241	5.62
22–24	Transverse scrapers	.217	.94
18–20	Convergent scrapers	.205	3.45
30	Typical end-scrapers	.204	1.38
5	Pseudo-Levallois point	.166	1.53
1	Typical Levallois flake	.164	—
36	Typical backed knife	.142	.66
3	Levallois point	.129	—
26	Scraper with abrupt retouch	.111	.21
54	End-notched piece	.102	.61
39	Raclette	.096	.68
4	Retouched Levallois point	.084	1.48
11	Simple concave scrapers	.082	1.02
—	Waste flake	.077	—
62	Miscellaneous tools	.073	3.50
2	Atypical Levallois points	.072	—
43	Denticulate	.057	5.88
50	Bifacially retouched piece	.052	—
31	Atypical end-scraper	.037	.40
40	Truncated flake	.021	.46
—	Unretouched flake	.009	—
35	Atypical borer	− .007	0.00
37	Atypical backed knife	− .012	0.00
48–49	Utilized flakes	− .026	0.00
45	Ventrally retouched piece	− .051	0.00
44	Bec	− .059	0.00
6	Mousterian point	− .084	0.00
61	Chopping tool	− .102	0.00
42	Notch	− .128	0.00
38	Naturally backed knife	− .237	0.00
34	Typical borer	− .290	0.00

[a] Indicates that the variable exhibits the highest factor loadings with respect to this factor and can be considered diagnostic of the factor.

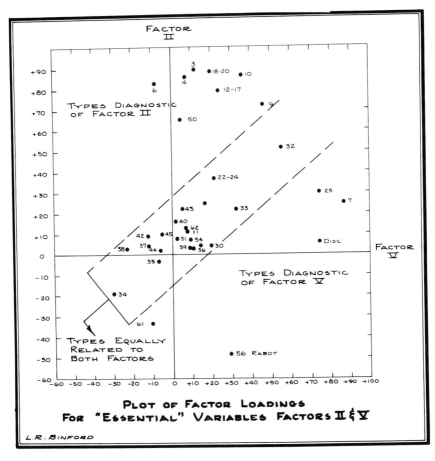

Figure 9.4 Plot of factor loadings for "essential" variables—Factors II and V.

the two activities represented (Pattern D, Figure 9.1). When Factor IV is plotted against Factors I and III, a distribution like that in Pattern A (Figure 9.1) is obtained, suggesting distinct activities with minor overlap of the kinds of tools used in both. In the comparison with Factor I, simple straight scrapers and typical burins are shared; in the case of Factor III, the tools shared with Factor IV are simple straight scrapers, scrapers with retouch on the ventral surface, and utilized blades. In both instances, cutting and scraping tasks appear to be involved.

The most instructive comparison, however, is that between Factor II and Factor V (Figure 9.4), where the pattern closely resembles that of Pattern C (Figure 9.1). This configuration would be expected if there were represented two very similar activities, one being more complex in terms of tool differentiation. In Figure 9.4 the majority of the variables are aligned along the diagonal, indicating that most of the implements were being employed in the same way. However, in the diagnostic cluster for Factor II there are artifacts that have no functional counterparts in the diagnostics of Factor V. These tools are various scrapers—convergent, double, simple straight, and convex forms. This distribution suggests the presence of component tasks as part of the activities represented by Factor II which do not characterize those of Factor V. Points and cutting–scraping tools are diagnostic for both factors, leading us to conclude that both Factors II and V are related to hunting and butchering.

The functional analogy between Factors II and V together with the greater complexity in the diagnostics for Factor II, suggest several interpretive questions. Does this situation represent

1. change through time in hunting activities?
2. differentiation of hunting methods in terms of kinds of game exploited by contemporaneous groups?
3. regional variability in hunting practices?
4. increasing specialization of tools in performing essentially the same tasks?

These questions can be answered only by analyzing the temporal and spatial correlates of the materials at the sites; such an analysis is attempted in the following section.

Redesign of the Cumulative Graph in Light of the Factor Analysis

Five groups of artifacts have been isolated that differ in the determinant of the relative percentages of artifacts occurring with each group. We wished to present this information in graphic form, along with information pertaining to the percentages of individual tool types in each assemblage sample. The artifacts most diagnostic of each factor were grouped and arranged in a descending order of relative frequency in the population studied. A curvilinear plot was then drawn which, when placed in series with the other factor diagnostics, has five different steps or plateaus, corresponding to the five factors. In designing the arrangement of factor groups on the horizontal coordinate, those factors sharing the greatest number of artifact forms were placed next to each other, while the most discrete factors were separated.

The cumulative percentage graph presented here (Figure 9.5) also differs from the conventional Bordean graph in that several artifact forms omitted from Bordes' "essential" counts have been included—Levallois points, ventrally retouched pieces, and bifacially retouched pieces. We have included them since in our analysis they showed regular modes of variation and because they are highly diagnostic of some factors.

Artifacts not included in the graph but included in the study are: typical and atypical Levallois flakes, utilized flakes, unretouched flakes and blades, and waste flakes. These seem to be associated with flint-working, a discussion of which follows in the next section.

Table 9.8 shows the proposed arrangement of the artifacts for Figure 9.5 and provides the expected percentages of each factor block of artifacts if a single factor were the only determinant of the composition of an assemblage. In addition, the expected percentages of the "nonessential" artifact classes are given, together with the expected ratios of essential to "nonessential" artifacts.

TABLE 9.7

Summary of Factors

Factor Number	Diagnostic Variables	Suggested Activity	Type of Activity	Analogy to Bordes' Types
I	Typical borer Atypical borer Bec Atypical burin Typical end-scraper Truncated flake Notches Miscellaneous tools Simple concave scraper Ventrally retouched piece Naturally backed knife	Manufacture of tools from non-flint materials	Maintenance tasks	Typical Mousterian (concave graph)
II	Levallois point Retouched Levallois point Mousterian point Convergent scrapers Double scrapers Simple convex scrapers Simple straight scrapers Bifacially retouched piece Typical Levallois flake Unretouched blade	Killing and Butchering	Extractive tasks	Ferrassie (convex graph)
III	Typical backed knife Atypical backed knife Naturally backed knife End-notched piece Typical Levallois flake Atypical Levallois flake Unretouched flake	Cutting and incising (food processing)	Maintenance tasks	Mousterian of Acheulian Tradition (concave graph)
IV	Utilized flakes Scrapers with abrupt retouch Raclettes Denticulates	Shredding and cutting (of plant materials?)	Extractive tasks	Denticulate (concave graph)
V	Elongated Mousterian point Simple straight scrapers Unretouched blade Scraper with retouch on ventral surface Typical burin Disc	Killing and butchering	Extractive tasks	Ferrassie (convex graph)

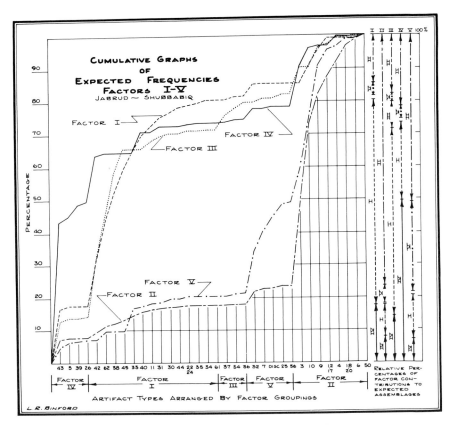

Figure 9.5   Cumulative graphs of expected frequencies—Factors I–V.

The general order of artifacts in Figure 9.5 is the reverse of that in a normal Bordean graph; scrapers and points are at the end of the type list rather than at the beginning. The result of this reversal is that curves that are concave in Bordes' system will, in this arrangement, generally be convex.

Inspection of the graphs in Figure 9.5 shows that there are three types of graph: first, that represented by Factors II and V which yield a concave curve; second, Factors I and III, which form a low-stepped convex curve; and third, the high-stepped convex curve of Factor IV. The relationships between the factors can be seen in Figure 9.6, where the percentages of the total assemblage contributed by the diagnostics for each factor are presented. It is evident from Figure 9.6 that Factors I and III represent very similar assemblages which differ in detail rather than in the general class of artifacts represented. We have suggested that these two factors are related to maintenance activities conducted in a relatively permanent location—activities involving the preparation of food and the manufacture of tools for the processing of nonflint raw materials.

Factor IV diagnostic artifact percentages are higher in Factors I and III than in Factors II and V. The frequency of Factor I diagnostics is higher in Factor IV than

TABLE 9.8

Expected Percentages for Variables Included in This Study Arranged According to the Revised Ordering of Types Suggested by the Factor Analysis

Factor	No. in Bordes' List	Variable Name	IV %	I %	III %	V %	II %
I. *Essential Graph*							
	43	Denticulate	43.28	16.69	12.75	4.98	7.03
	5	Pseudo-Levallois Point	1.79	.82	.98	1.29	.69
IV	39	Raclette	3.81	.00	.00	.57	.06
	26	Scraper-abrupt retouch	.89	.00	.39	.17	.01
	42	Notches	13.65	14.32	17.63	.00	1.87
	62	Misc. Tools	1.23	11.33	12.50	2.96	1.95
	38	Naturally backed knife	.00	8.97	13.95	.00	.48
	45	Ventrally retouched piece	.00	7.25	7.53	.00	1.00
	33	Atypical burin	.00	5.50	.00	7.01	1.66
	40	Truncated flake	6.24	4.76	.00	.38	1.07
I	11	Simple concave scraper	.00	3.02	2.13	.86	.42
	31	Atypical end-scraper	1.64	2.48	1.40	.35	.65
	30	Typical end-scraper	.00	1.65	.76	1.16	.09
	44	Bec	.00	1.51	.13	.00	.04
	22–24	Transverse scrapers	.60	.66	.89	.79	.49
	35	Atypical borer	.00	1.02	.10	.00	.00
	34	Typical borer	.43	.39	.00	.00	.00
	61	Chopping tool	.00	.03	.00	.00	.00
	37	Atypical backed knife	.20	.08	4.51	.00	.13
III	54	End-notched piece	.42	1.09	2.10	.51	.12
	36	Typical backed knife	.32	.28	2.16	.55	.05
	32	Typical burin	3.53	3.41	.00	12.42	4.04
	7	Elongated Mousterian point	.00	.17	1.09	6.18	.77
V	—	Disc	.27	.00	.00	4.63	.13
	25	Scraper with ventral retouch	.00	.00	1.18	3.93	.57
	56	Rabot	.00	.01	.00	.33	.00
	3	Levallois point	12.46	.00	8.11	10.48	25.92
	10	Simple convex scraper	5.47	5.61	.00	14.80	23.69
	9	Simple straight scraper	.45	4.76	6.10	16.44	9.17
II	12–17	Double scrapers	.00	3.31	.87	4.76	5.63
	4	Retouched Levallois point	3.11	.00	2.09	1.25	4.57
	18–20	Convergent scrapers	.00	.00	.00	2.92	4.50
	6	Mousterian point	.00	.28	.54	.00	2.57
	50	Bifacially retouched piece	.21	.55	.00	.14	.64
			99.99	99.99	99.99	99.99	99.99

TABLE 9.8, *(Continued)*

Factor	No. in Bordes' List	Variable Name	IV %	I %	III %	V %	II %
II. *"Nonessential" percentages*							
	2	Atypical Levallois flake	9.19	28.66	20.82	14.50	16.70
	1	Typical Levallois flake	1.04	10.63	20.79	29.09	22.02
	48–49	Utilized flake	39.83	13.42	1.07	0.00	.69
	—	Unretouched flakes	42.21	44.92	48.49	4.00	48.55
	—	Waste flakes	0.00	1.83	1.59	7.42	0.00
	—	Unretouched blades	7.72	.51	7.20	44.98	12.02
III. *Ratios of essential to "nonessential"*							
		Percentage of total essential	27.29	30.78	15.14	40.36	30.67
		Percentage of total nonessential	72.71	69.22	84.86	59.64	69.33
		Index of Essential/nonessential	.37	.44	.18	.69	.44

in Factors II or V (see Figure 9.6). This pattern suggests that the activities represented by Factor IV are related more to Factors I and III than they are to Factors II and V. Nevertheless, Factor IV exhibits a higher frequency of Factor II diagnostics than does Factor I or III, suggesting a minor overlap of activities not appearing in Factors I and III.

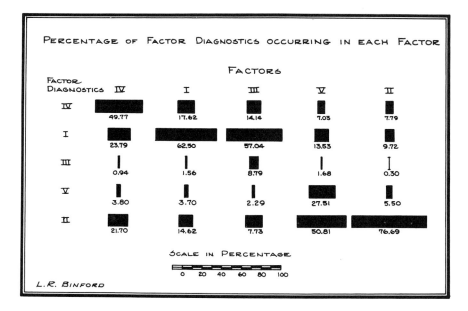

Figure 9.6 Percentage of factor diagnostics occurring in each factor.

If we are correct in inferring that Factor IV represents the procurement and processing of plant products, then it, along with Factors II and V, can be said to have a primary extractive function. On the other hand, if such activities were conducted by women, on the assumption of a primary division of labor by sex, then the correlations with Factors I and III (the maintenance factors) is not surprising. The division of labor would have involved women preparing food and working in the immediate area of the settlement, while the men hunted at more distant locations and did not engage much in the gathering and processing of plant materials. If we could isolate variability in Mousterian assemblages that reflected a basic sexual division of labor, we would have a powerful tool for considering problems of marriage and residence patterns (for example, see Longacre 1963).

Another major point to be noted in Figure 9.5 is that none of the curves describes a "diagonal" pattern (this is also true of Figure 9.2). The "diagonal" form of cumulative graph is characteristic of assemblages classified by Bordes as Typical Mousterian. None of the factors is identifiable as typical, suggesting that these assemblages may possibly be composed of tool kits (factors) which separately would describe convex and concave curves; their combined result would be a "diagonal" graph. This point will be treated more fully in the section dealing with the analysis of site samples.

Flint-Working

Artifact forms not included in Bordes' essential graph and believed to be associated with flint-working are of five general classes:

1. pieces made by Levallois technique, believed to represent blanks intended for eventual modification or use as tools (typical and atypical Levallois flakes);
2. pieces made by non-Levallois technique which probably also represent blanks (unretouched flakes and blades);
3. cores, or prepared forms from which blanks and incidental by-products were derived;
4. waste flakes, or those by-products believed to be primarily derived from shaping cores;
5. utilized flakes.

Members of the last group were excluded from the essential graph because they are not diagnostic and because their quantity is such that they tend to distort the graph. All of the other groups were included in the factor analysis (see Table 9.8) with the exception of cores, which were excluded because of possible typological inconsistencies. The data on cores from Jabrud were obtained from Rust's report, while those from Shubbabiq were typed by the junior author under Bordes' direction.

The internal variability of groups of artifacts that we believe to be associated with flint-working is quite probably different from the variability discernible in the factors clusters. The latter represent, in our opinion, unit activities, and their determinants are of a different order than those that condition flint-working, which cannot really be thought of as a unit activity. What is suggested by our study is that flint-working was broadly related to the logistics of tool production; the conditions affecting the presence or absence of flint-working may be generalized as follows:

1. location and disposition of available raw material;
2. location and spatial distribution of loci of tool use;
3. the necessity of transporting products of flint-working from locations of manufacture to locations where they will be used.

The combination of these conditions may vary greatly at any given habitation site and in conjunction with activities related to group maintenance or extraction of subsistence products. Thus we envision flint-working as a series of production steps which may or may not be carried out at a single location. For this reason the by-products of flint-working vary more in terms of the five factors than they do mutually (see Table 9.8).

Since we are interested in flint-working as an index of economizing behavior and as a clue to site utilization on the part of Neanderthal populations, the "nonessential" artifacts have been analyzed by means of ratios which hopefully inform about the degree to which several independent phases of tool production were executed at a single location.

Table 9.9 presents the expected ratios for the following pairs of items:

1. *Ratio of cores to Levallois blanks:* This is obtained by dividing the total number of cores by the total number of Levallois blanks (typical and atypical Levallois flakes).

2. *Ratio of cores to non-Levallois blanks and/or by-products:* This is obtained by dividing the total number of cores by the combined counts for unretouched flakes and blades. In assemblages of Levallois facies, this ratio is probably primarily a measure of the amount of core preparation, independent of the degree to which Levallois blanks were removed from the site (see Bordes 1953a:478–479). In non-Levallois assemblages, this ratio probably more closely approximates the ratio of blanks to cores.

3. *Ratio of cores to finished tools:* This is obtained by dividing the total number or cores by the total number of tools in the "essential" category. A low value indicates

TABLE 9.9

Expected Values for Technical Ratios

Factors	Expected Ratios					
	(1) C/LB	(2) C/By	(3) C/T	(4) LB/T	(5) LB/By	(6) By-non LB/T
I	?	?	?	.88	.86	1.02
II	?	?	?	.87	.63	1.04
III	?	?	?	2.33	.74	3.12
IV	?	?	?	.28	.21	1.32
V	?	?	?	.64	.89	.72

that activities other than flint-working were dominant; a high value signifies that the knapping of cores was a major activity.

4. *Ratio of Levallois blanks to tools:* This value is obtained by dividing the sum of typical and atypical Levallois flakes by the sum of the tools in the "essential" category. A low value would reflect a primary emphasis on tool use as opposed to tool production. This situation could result from either the modification on the site of blanks into tools (resulting in there being more tools than blanks), or the removal of blanks from the site for subsequent modification elsewhere. A high value signifies either on-the-spot production of Levallois blanks or their introduction into the site from another flint-working locality.

Another useful element to measure the degree to which blanks were modified into tools in any given site would be the relative quantity of secondary and tertiary chipping debris. This element was not included in our study since we had no way of knowing how much of this class of material was kept at Jabrud.

5. *Ratio of Levallois blanks to by-products of core modification:* This ratio is particularly important in assemblages of Levallois facies. It is obtained by dividing the sum of typical and atypical Levallois flakes by the sum of unretouched non-Levallois flakes and blades. This ratio should measure the degree to which cores were being worked on the location for the production of Levallois blanks. A low value would indicate that Levallois blanks were being produced on-the-spot; a high ratio would mean that blanks produced elsewhere were introduced into the site.

6. *Ratio of non-Levallois blanks and/or core by-products to tools:* This ratio is obtained by dividing the sum of unretouched flakes and blades by the sum of tools in the "essential" group. A low value would indicate that the use of already manufactured tools dominated the activities at the site, to the general exclusion of the production of Levallois blanks from cores. This interpretation is predicated on the relatively high frequency of Levallois over non-Levallois cores. Where non-Levallois cores are much more numerous, the production of non-Levallois blanks might as easily be inferred. A high ratio value would suggest that on-the-spot processing and production of both Levallois and non-Levallois blanks from cores was a major activity.

Table 9.9 presents the expected values of the ratios for assemblages that were determined solely by the activities indicated by the five recognized factors.

Inspection of Table 9.9 reveals that there is a great difference between the factors with respect to flint working and its various phases. Factors I, II, and V are quite similar in the ratio of Levallois blanks to tools (ratio #4), suggesting that the Levallois technique was important in the production of tools used in all three sets of activities. Factor III is strikingly different in the very high value of ratio #4; this could indicate that the production of Levallois blanks was an important component of the activity we infer for Factor III. Factor IV is remarkably low in the value exhibited for ratio #4; this could mean either that Levallois technique was relatively unimportant in the production of tools utilized, or that the production of Levallois blanks was not a component of the activity represented by Factor IV.

With respect to ratio #5, Factor IV is again distinctive. The ratio has a very low value, suggesting that the manufacture of Levallois blanks was unimportant but that the working of cores was a major component. The other factors are fairly similar in the proportion of Levallois blanks to unretouched flakes and blades.

Ratio #6 shows that Factors I, II, and IV are similar in the frequencies of non-Levallois blanks and/or flint-working by-products as compared to tools. Factor II has a high ratio value, indicating that flint-working (as opposed to tool use) was probably a major component of the activities. On the other hand, the low value of the ratio in Factor V suggests that flint-working was not generally associated with the activities defined by that factor.

Analysis of Sites and Site Samples

Five factors have been recognized, each of which represents a different set of conditions which determined the mutual frequency variation of the variables included in the study. Comparisons were made between the factors in terms of:

1. the configuration of mutual co-variation between the variables;
2. the general appearance of a factor when expressed in terms of the expected percentages for an assemblage inventory;
3. the pattern of distribution of determinacy among the variables when the two factors were compared.

Functional interpretations of the factors were based on tool morphology and on the similarities in levels of mutual determinacy for classes of artifacts. Two kinds of interpretations were made: first, the kinds of activities inferred for each factor; second, the social context in which the suggested activities would be most likely to have occurred.

The following expansion of the interpretive framework is formulated to aid in the development of an explanatory model for understanding the observed variation. We are restating, and in some cases slightly modifying, the useful material presented by Philip Wagner in *The Human Use of the Earth* (1960).

All known groups of hunters and gatherers live in societies composed of local groups, regardless of the way they may be internally organized (Steward 1955, Service 1962). The local group is invariably partitioned into subgroups which function to carry out different tasks. Sex and age criteria frequently are the basis for the partitioning of the local group, with subunits generally composed of individuals of the same age or sex who cooperate in work forces. For example, young male adults often cooperate in hunting, while women may work together in gathering plant materials and preparing food.

At other times the group breaks up along different lines in order to form reproductive and/or residence units—i.e., family groups—which are, unlike the work groups, more permanent and self-sustaining.

Although we have no idea about the specific ways in which Neanderthal groups were socially partitioned and segmented, it is reasonable to assume that their societies were organized flexibly and included both work and family subgroups. If this assumption is granted, we would expect this organization to be reflected in the variability both among assemblages at a given site and among different sites.

Geographical or spatial variability would be expected since the total sum of activities engaged in by a given society is not conducted at a single location. This is the result of differential distribution in the environment of game, plant material, appropriate living space, and raw materials for tool manufacture. We would anticipate that certain locations in the territory of a society would be occupied for the performance of certain tasks, while other tasks would be carried out in other parts of the territory. Spatial variability would also be affected by the kinds of organizational principles outlined above. For example, one site might be a favorable hunting location where groups of young males killed and partially butchered animals before returning to the site where the local group was living. Another site might have been used by a group of females while gathering and partially processing plant materials while away from the location where the larger group was "housed."

Thus, we might generalize that the composition of archeological assemblages from various locations will be determined by (a) the kinds of tasks performed, and (b) the size and composition of the social unit performing the tasks.

The form of the archeological remains of a stable society might vary temporally for several reasons. Differential availability of plant and animal resources in the annual climatic cycle is primary and results from the correlated reproductive cycle of the plants and animals themselves. In addition, the society itself varies throughout the course of an annual cycle and goes through a number of *structural poses* (see Gearing 1962). The ways in which various members of a society are organized and how they cooperate at different times of the year vary with the characteristics of activities performed at different times of the year. Other considerations which modify the group's behavior during a yearly cycle concern the integrative problems the society must solve as a result of maturation of the young, death of members, relations with other groups, etc.

Temporal variation (within an annual cycle) within the archeological remains of a stable society is determined by: (a) the kinds of tasks performed, and (b) the size and composition of the social units performing the tasks.

In addition to the factors discussed above which can affect the spatial and temporal variability of archeological assemblages, there exist other determinants which profoundly modify site utilization. The kinds of locations utilized for different activities and the way these specialized locations are related are referred to respectively as *settlement type* and *settlement system*. (An excellent example of these concepts as applied to the data of North American prehistory can be found in H.D. Winters' *Survey of the Wabash Valley* [1963]).

For technologically simple societies we can distinguish between two broad classes of activities: extraction and maintenance. Extractive activities are those that center around the direct procurement of subsistence items or of raw materials to be used in the manufacture of artifacts. Maintenance activities are related to the preparation and distribution of subsistence goods already on hand and to the processing of on-hand raw materials in the production of tools. The distribution of resources in the environment bears no necessary relation to the distribution of locations affording adequate life-space and protection, and we would therefore expect differential distribution in the territory of a group of locations for extractive and maintenance activities. We would expect there to be *base camps* selected primarily in terms of adequate life-space, protection from the elements, and central location with respect to the distribution of resources. The archeological assemblages of base camps should reflect maintenance tasks—the preparation and consumption of food as well as the manufacture of tools for use in other locations.

Another settlement type would be a *work camp,* a location occupied while subgroups were carrying out extractive tasks—e.g., kill sites, collection stations, and quarries for usable flint. In these locations we would expect the archeological assemblages to be dominated by the tools used in the specific extractive tasks. The degree to which maintenance activities may be represented at work camps would be a direct function of the length of time a given social unit was there and of the size of that unit.

The way in which these two general classes of camps are utilized by a single society defines the settlement system. In the settlement system of hunters and gatherers who are relatively sedentary, base camps would exhibit little discrete seasonal variability since we would expect them to have been occupied for a longer period and over a greater span of the seasonal cycle. If, on the other hand, the society went through a sequence of structural poses common to many hunters and gathers—i.e., living in relatively large aggregates part of the year and dispersing into smaller familial units during other parts of the year—we might expect to find more than one type of base camp for a given society, and these types should exhibit some seasonal correlates.

We would anticipate a greater variety in the types of work camps of a given society since each location would have been occupied for a shorter time, and the activities conducted there would have been more specifically correlated with the kinds of resources being exploited. Further variability in the composition of work camp assemblages would be related to the degree to which resources exploited there could be transported. For example, in the case of the killing of very large mammals or the successful hunting of large numbers of animals, the local group might come to the kill site to partially consume and process the animals. In such a case we would expect to find large numbers of artifacts related to processing and consumption at the work camp, although the variety of tasks represented would be less than would be associated with a base camp.

We might also suggest that the degree to which maintenance tasks are represented at work camps will be directly related to the distance between the work and base camps. If the work camp and the base camp are close together, we would not normally expect to find evidence of maintenance activities at the work camp. However, as the distance between the work and base camp increases, an increase in maintenance activities could be anticipated in the work camp assemblages.

This consideration of the mobility of groups and their travel through the territory leads us to suggest another type of settlement we might expect to find: the *transient camp.* At such a location we would have the remains of the minimal maintenance activities of a travelling group, possibly representing no more than an overnight stay.

We have discussed certain minimal types of spatial and temporal variability which we might expect to occur in the archeological remains of a simple group of hunters and gatherers whose social organization was based on principles of internal partitioning and segmentation. These models, together with our postulates as to the functional significance of clusters of artifacts isolated by the factor analysis, led to our suggestions as to the possibility of relating types of activities to types of settlement. We turn now to the more specific discussion of the sites and assemblages in this study.

In our study there were three different sites from three different geographical regions. Two of these sites provide slightly different types of control with regard to variability within assemblages. Jabrud provides data on a sequence of occupations, while Shubbabiq provides data on a number of samples from what is believed to represent a single kind of occupation. By studying the patterns of variation between the samples from the three locations we hope to determine the following:

1. Does the composition of assemblages from different occupations correspond to unit factors, or do they represent various combinations of factors?

2. Do the types of Mousterian industries defined by Bordes always correspond to the same assemblage composition defined by factor analysis?

3. Is there any regularity in the composition of assemblages at a given location which can be interpreted in terms of regular patterns of past human behavior?

4. Is there directional change through time evidenced in assemblages from a single location which suggests evolutionary or situational changes in human behavior?

These four questions will guide the analysis of the separate samples from the several sites.

In comparing the results from the several sites we hope to determine to what degree the assumptions and postulates set forth in the preceding arguments have been supported, and what testable hypotheses can be offered on the basis of our analysis and comparison.

Jabrud

The Jabrud shelters are located on the eastern edge of the anti-Lebanon range, near Damascus (Syria). Two of the shelters were excavated by Rust during the 1930s and reported several years later (Rust 1950). The samples included in this study are from the upper 2 meters of the deposits in Shelter I. This rockshelter is on the side of a small valley and at a considerable elevation above the valley floor; it is approximately 35 meters long and is oriented in a north–south direction, opening to the east. At the time of excavation, there was a heavy rockfall in the center of the shelter, leaving only the north and south ends available for entry. It could not be determined from Rust's report if the rockfall had been present during the full span of occupation of the shelter. However, Dr. Ralph Solecki's (1964) recent findings indicate that it was in fact present during the occupations represented in our samples and can therefore be taken as a boundary on the space available within the shelter.[3]

Rust's excavations exposed approximately 22.5 meters along the shelter wall, roughly centered with respect to the total length of the shelter. The excavation was, on the average, 3 meters wide. Judging from Rust's report, the excavated area would represent about half of the living space available in the shelter at the time of the occupations of Levels 2–8.

The artifactual remains were originally published by Rust (1950) and subsequently analyzed by Bordes (1955). Our study has made use of Bordes' analysis of the artifacts but also includes the totals for cores as reported by Rust.

Level 8 (Shelter I)

This level occurred between 1.5 and 1.7 meters below the surface, and was continuous over the entire portion of the excavated area. The recovered materials came from a matrix of approximately 13.5 cubic meters of deposit, and included 784 artifacts reported by Bordes plus 19 cores reported by Rust. This represents a density of 59.4 artifacts per cubic meter of matrix.

In the original report Rust (1950:49) interpreted the assemblage as a culture derived from a mixture or blending of Jabrudian and Acheulian, and he termed it "Upper Jabrudo-Mousterian." Bordes (1955:494) compared this level with Level 10 of the same shelter (not included in this study) and identified it as the Ferrassie type of Charentian Mousterian.

Figure 9.7 is a summary cumulative graph of Levels 2–8 with the artifacts arranged by factor groupings. Figure 9.8 is a cumulative graph of expected and observed frequencies for three levels of Shelter 1, with the expected frequencies based on varying assumptions about the composition of the assemblages. With respect to Level 8, the expected frequency curve is on the assumption that 33 per cent of the determinance of the assemblage was controlled by Factor I, and 67 per cent by Factor V. This assumption on the nature of the controlling determinants allows us to reproduce the observed frequencies with remarkable accuracy.

Thus, we interpret the assemblage from Level 8 as representing a combination of artifact groups utilized in two major activities: maintenance and secondary tool manufacture (Factor I) and rather specialized hunting and butchering (Factor V).

Inspection of the ratios of "nonessential" artifacts shows that, while the correspondences between observed and expected frequencies in the essential category are very close, they are much less so in this case. It appears that the discrepancies are primarily a function of the amount of flint-working as compared to other activities.

The lowest ratio values of any level studied from Jabrud were with the first three ratios (see Table 9.10), suggesting that cores were relatively rare and that, once introduced, they were reduced to blanks and waste. Such an interpretation is supported by ratios #4 and #5. The expected index for the essential to nonessential components of the assemblage is 0.60; the observed index is 0.44, indicating that flint-working was more frequently carried out than would have been predicted from the range of variation in the total population of artifacts.

We may conclude that Level 8 at Jabrud was an example of an occupation representing mainly hunting and butchering (extractive tasks) and secondarily flint-working. We suggest, in terms of our discussion of settlement types, that this is a *work camp*.

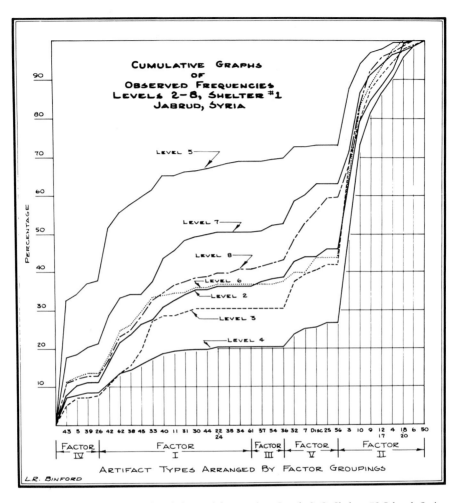

Figure 9.7 Cumulative graphs of observed frequencies—Levels 2–8. Shelter #1 Jabrud, Syria.

Level 7 (Shelter I)

This occupation occurred between 1.3 and 1.5 meters below the surface and was continuous over the entire excavated portion of the shelter. 774 artifacts were reported by Bordes (1955) and 64 cores by Rust (1950), representing a density of 62.1 artifacts per cubic meter of matrix. This is only slightly greater density than in Level 8. In his original analysis, Rust interpreted the Level 7 assemblage as being derived historically from the "pre-Aurignacian" but blended with the local Mousterian tradition of the region. The size of the implements is somewhat smaller than the average for the site; for this reason Rust related this assemblage to that of Level 5 which also yielded some implements of reduced size. He therefore designated these materials "pre-micro-Mousterian."

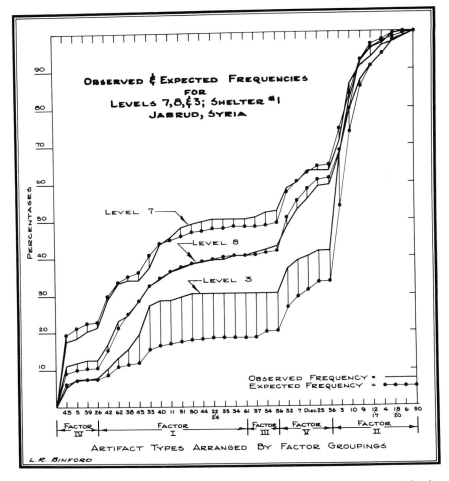

Figure 9.8 Observed and expected frequencies for Levels 7, 8, and 3. Shelter #1 Jabrud, Syria.

Bordes (1955:494) comments thhhat while the assemblage from Level 7 is identifiable as Typical Mousterian as known in France, that this sample contains more blades, burins, and denticulates than are normally found.

Of all the levels analyzed from Jabrud, our analysis indicates that this is the most complex. The cumulative graph for the assemblage can be duplicated only by postulating that three distinct factors determined the composition—50 per cent Factor V, 33 per cent Factor IV, and 17 per cent Factor I (see Figure 9.8). The fact that in combination the factors yield a graph identifiable as Typical Mousterian can be understood in terms of the individual graphs of each component factor. One half of the assemblage is determined by Factors I and IV together (convex graph) and the other half by Factor V (concave graph). When combined these yield a cumulative graph roughly halfway between the two, approximating a diagonal with, as Bordes noted, more denticulates, burins, and blades.

TABLE 9.10

Observed and Expected Ratios for Samples in the Study—Technical Characteristics[a]

	(1) C/LB	(2) C/By	(3) C/T	(4) LB/T		(5) LB/By		(6) By/T		Ess–Non		Density (CuM.)
				o	e	o	e	o	e	o	e	
Jabrud Levels												
2	.21	.18	.21	1.02	1.36	.87	.66	1.17	1.73	.43	.35	52.7
3	.29	.27	.25	.87	.73	.93	.78	.93	.85	.48	.58	93.0
4	.18	.09	.11	.64	.87	.54	.63	1.20	1.04	.50	.44	149.9
5	.82	.34	.41	.50	.68	.41	.32	1.22	1.27	.33	.39	511.0
6	.20	.12	.17	.83	.70	.62	.59	1.34	1.01	.39	.48	44.2
7	.39	.24	.28	.73	.56	.62	.66	1.18	.97	.41	.54	62.1
8	.10	.08	.07	.76	.72	.76	.88	1.00	.82	.44	.60	59.4
Shubbabig												
Units												
100	.51	.31	.34	.81	1.17	.73	.79	1.11	1.44	.42	.39	•
100A	1.01	1.15	.58	.57	1.17	1.13	.79	.50	1.44	.79	.39	•
103–109	.37	.20	.27	1.42	1.17	1.05	.79	1.35	1.44	.32	.39	•
113–	1.14	.50	.37	.33	1.17	.44	.79	.74	1.44	.75	.39	•
115–116	.65	.45	.47	1.10	1.09	1.05	.72	1.05	1.38	.39	.38	•
117	1.04	2.08	.72	.70	1.07	2.00	.71	.34	1.36	.76	.38	•
300–10	.42	.29	.39	1.00	1.17	.76	.79	1.31	1.44	.31	.39	•
200–8	.28	.24	1.47	4.95	2.11	.74	.72	6.00	2.81	.05	.21	•
Houppeville												
1	•?	•?	•?	1.28	1.71	.65	.64	1.95	2.33	.29	.27	•

[a] o = observed ratio; e = expected ratio.

Factor V, accounting for half the assemblage, is interpreted as a specialized hunting and scraping factor. Contributing 17 per cent and 33 per cent respectively were activities believed to be related to the production of nonflint artifacts (Factor I) and to the as yet poorly understood activity represented by the denticulate factor (Factor IV), presumably related to scraping and shredding and to the procurement and processing of plant materials.

As was pointed out above, Level 7 (along with Level 5) is distinctive in the small size of some tools and in the raw material used for tool manufacture. Rust (1950:50) reported that the material used was a brown patinated flint available at the site but of poor quality. It is probably more than coincidence that both Levels 5 and 7 are distinctive in (a) the size of some tools, (b) the raw material used, and (c) the representation of the denticulate factor (Factor IV). We therefore suggest that the expedient use of relatively poor raw material in these levels is associated with Factor IV. We are *not* implying that the morphology and size of the artifacts were *determined* by the nature of the raw material, but that this particular raw material was expediently utilized for the manufacture of these implements.

Turning to the "nonessential" ratios, we note that this level is quite similar to Level 8 except that there are more cores and slightly greater number of core-working by-products and/or non-Levallois blanks as compared to finished tools (see Table 9.10).

We suggest that this level represents an occupation of the same general type we inferred for Level 8—a work camp specifically related to hunting tasks sufficiently distant from the base camp that tools for tunting were prepared here. In addition, in this assemblage there are represented the activities related to Factor IV, possibly the procurement and processing of plants.

If we wish to put ourselves further out on an interpretive limb, we might ask if the differences in raw materials and technique associated with Factor IV represent a basic sexual division of labor—with men making and using the hunting tools while women made and used the tools for processing plant materials.

Level 7 exemplifies one of the significant findings of our study. The assemblage was identified as Typical Mousterian by univariate statistical analysis, but multivariate analysis indicates that the assemblage might well be understood in terms of the operation of three distinct factors which, in combination, determine the form of the assemblage.

Level 6 (Shelter I)

This occupation occurred at between 1.00 m. and 1.20 m. below the surface and was continuous over the entire excavated portion of the shelter. The recovered artifacts were in a matrix of approximately 13.5 cubic meters of soil. A total of 570 artifacts are reported by Bordes (1955) plus 27 cores by Rust (1950), representing a density of 44.2 artifacts per cubic meter of matrix. This density is considerably lower than that calculated for Levels 7 and 8.

Rust (1950:53–54) described this assemblage as composed of unusually large implements that were strongly Levallois, and added that the raw materials were of high quality and available in adjacent valleys but not on the site itself.

In his analysis of the lithic materials Bordes (1955:494) found this assemblage comparable to those of Levels 8 and 10 (the latter not included in this study) and found it analogous to the Ferrassie type of Mousterian in France.

According to our analysis, this assemblage is the result of three determining factors, one of which (Factor V) also is related to the assemblage from Level 8. If we assume 60 per cent determinacy by Factor II and 20 per cent each for Factors IV and V, the cumulative graph which results is almost identical to that observed for Level 6 (see Figure 9.9). The differences between the observed and expected frequencies are in three types diagnostic of Factor I—miscellaneous tools (#62), naturally backed knives (#38), and ventrally retouched pieces (#45).

The three factors that determine this assemblage have been interpreted as representing hunting and butchering (Factors II and V) and possibly procurement and processing of plants (Factor IV). All of these factors are believed to be related to extractive tasks, and this assemblage does not reflect the maintenance tasks inferred for Levels 7 and 8.

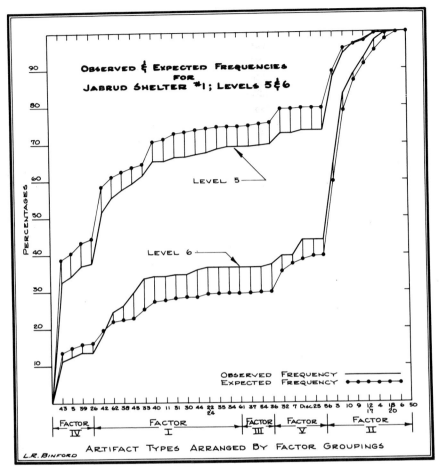

Figure 9.9   Observed and expected frequencies for Jabrud Shelter #1. Levels 5 and 6.

Examination of the "nonessential" ratios shows that there is a lower relative frequency of cores than in Levels 7 and 8. For those ratios whose expected values could be calculated, the observed exceed the expected in all cases. This means that there were more Levallois blanks and by-products and/or non-Levallois blanks than expected, and further, there were more Levallois blanks than non-Levallois blanks or by-products. This suggests that Levallois blanks were introduced and that for the number of finished tools observed there was more evidence of flint-working than expected. This observation is also supported by the fact that the ratio of essential to nonessential classes of artifacts is lower than expected.

This situation might be interpreted as reflecting expediency in tool production because of either poor advanced preparation of tools or loss or discarding of tools at another location. In any event, the indications are that the flint-working was related to the production of tools used directly in the extractive tasks represented. Rust observed that the flint materials in this level were introduced into the site but that the material was available in neighboring valleys. This, taken together with the fact that the density of artifacts is lower for this level than for the two previously discussed, forms a picture of a small group of people primarily engaged in hunting and in making tools for the hunt. The absence of factors related to maintenance, together with the relatively low density of artifacts, suggests that the length of occupation was shorter than those in Levels 7 and 8.

Level 5 (Shelter I)

This occupation occurred between 0.8 and 1.0 meters below the surface. Unlike the other levels, this assemblage was concentrated in a very restricted area of not more than 10 square meters of horizontal distribution at the south end of the rockshelter (Rust 1950:54–56). Bordes (1955) reports 946 artifacts, and Rust's core count is 98, making a total of 1,044 artifacts in about 10 cubic meters. The density here is enormously higher than in any of the other levels—511 artifacts per cubic meter. This unique concentration makes comparisons with other levels very difficult. Taken together with the horizontal concentration, all we can say is that it represents exceedingly intensive use of a small area of the shelter.

Rust noted that this assemblage was quite distinctive in the small size of the implements, which averaged between 2 and 4 cms in length. In addition, they were manufactured of the rather poor quality brown flint that we described for Level 7.

Rust termed this assemblage "micro-Mousterian." Bordes (1955:494–496, 1962:48) saw similarities between this assemblage and the Denticulate Mousterian of France.

We can best reproduce the observed frequencies of this assemblage on the assumption that its composition was determined by two factors—83 per cent by Factor IV and 17 percent by Factor I (see Figure 9.9). In terms of activities, this would represent scraping and shredding possibly of plant material (Factor IV) and some secondary tool manufacture (Factor I).

Inspection of the "nonessential" artifacts (see Table 9.10) shows that cores were common when compared to Levallois blanks (ratio #1) and that the ratio of tools to by-products and/or non-Levallois blanks is high, suggesting an economical use of flint. This interpretation is supported by other ratios—those of tools to Levallois blanks (#4), of Levallois blanks to by-products and/or non-Levallois blanks (#5), and of by-products and/or non-Levallois blanks to tools (#6).

This occupation appears to represent a very short-term but intensive use of part of the shelter by a small group engaged in a restricted range of extractive activities, possibly the procurement and processing of plant materials. The economical and expedient use of local flint suggests a situation in which the group was apparently poorly equipped in advance. Because of the distinctive nature of the tasks represented by this assemblage and the use made of immediately available flint, we tentatively suggest that the composition of the social unit responsible for this assemblage might have been somewhat different from that of the groups occupying Levels 6 and 8.

Level 4 (Shelter I)

This occupation occurred between .6 and .7 meters below the surface and was presumably distributed over the entire excavated portion of the shelter with a slightly higher concentration in the south section (Rust 1950:61). The recovered artifacts came from a matrix of approximately 6.8 cubic meters of deposit. Bordes (1955) analyzed a total of 977 artifacts, and 36 cores were reported by Rust (1950), yielding a density of 148.9 artifacts per cubic meter, making the density in this level second only to that of Level 5.

Rust (1950:57) viewed this assemblage as representing a cultural break with preceding assemblages, noting that it was as a whole somewhat smaller. He suggested further that many of the points present were intended for further modification into more "specialized" tools. The raw material used was a fine quality flint available in the neighboring valley and was introduced into the site.

Although our analysis does not make use of any of the specific data cited by Rust in support of his suggested cultural break, our results also indicate that Level 4 marks a general change in the nature of the occupations (see Figure 9.10).

Bordes (1955:496) sees likenesses between this assemblage and those of Levels 10, 8, and 6 but with a much greater number of side-scrapers. He adds that the assemblage resembles that from the site of La Ferrassie and Aïn Métherchem (Tunisia).

According to our analysis, this is the only one of the levels analyzed from Jabrud which can be accounted for by a single factor. On the assumption that Factor II determined the composition of the assemblage, there is a strong correspondence between the observed and expected frequencies (see Figure 9.10). This factor is believed to represent hunting and butchering.

In comparing the ratios of the "nonessential" artifacts, a basic difference is seen between this assemblage and the others previously discussed (see Table 9.10). In Levels 8 through 5 the observed ratios of essential to nonessential classes were less than expected, suggesting a greater amount of flint-working than expected, given the activities represented. The case in this level is the reverse—less evidence of flint-working than expected.

In addition, in both the ratios of Levallois blanks to tools (#4) and of Levallois blanks to by-products and/or non-Levallois blanks (#5) the values are lower then expected, suggesting that Levallois blanks are being deleted from the assemblage, possibly lost at other locations or being taken away by the occupants. Another possible interpretation is that more of the Levallois blanks are being modified into tools.

On the other hand, the observed ratio of by-products and/or non-Levallois blanks to tools (#6) is higher than expected. This lends support to the idea that tools were being removed from this site. The ratio of essential to nonessential components is greater than expected (*N.B.:* Levallois blanks are categorized here within the essential class), suggesting also that there are more tools than by-products and/or non-Levallois blanks than could be expected for the inferred activity.

The picture from these varying lines of evidence is one of a relatively small group of well-equipped hunters (i.e., equipped with blanks for points and scrapers) occupying the site while carrying out a highly restricted range of extractive tasks (hunting

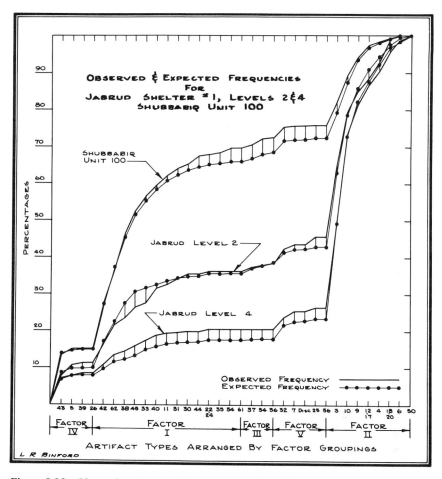

Figure 9.10   Observed and expected frequencies for Jabrud Shelter #1, Levels 2 and 4 and for Shubbabiq, Unit 100.

and butchering of game). In addition, some tools were manufactured here which were either lost at other locations or carried away when the group moved on. This level is interpreted as a *work camp* of a more specific type than those represented in Levels 7 and 8 and functionally very different from those in Levels 5 and 6.

Level 3 (Shelter I)

This occupation occurred at a depth of .4 meters below the surface and was apparently more concentrated near the south end of the shelter (Rust 1950:61). Although the exact depth of the layer is not clear from the report, we estimate that the density of artifacts was probably about 93 per cubic meter. Rust reports that the raw material was a low-grade reddish-brown transparent flint available in deposits in the plateau and around the site. Rust compares this assemblage with that of Level 4 but notes that the burins are larger and cruder (1950:59).

Bordes (1955:496) interprets the assemblage as belonging to the same series as those from Levels 10, 8, 6, and 4, exhibiting analogous typological and technical characteristics, despite the greatly higher burin count.

We were best able to reproduce the observed frequencies by assuming 40 per cent determination by Factor II and 60 per cent by Factor V (see Figure 8). Both of these factors are interpreted as representing hunting and butchering, with Factor II employing rather specialized tools. The discrepancies between observed and expected frequencies are associated with miscellaneous, naturally backed knives, ventrally retouched pieces, and atypical burins.

Inspection of the "nonessential" ratios (Table 9.10) indicates that this level is similar to Levels 6 and 8 in that there is more flint-working present than would be expected for the activities. In addition, the greatest discrepancy between observed and expected ratios occurs in ratio #5, or in a higher frequency of Levallois blanks.

The density of the artifacts, their restricted distribution, the lack of maintenance activities all suggest a *work camp* occupation specifically concentrating on hunting and butchering.

Level 2 (Shelter I)

This level occurs between .2 and .3 meters below the surface at the south end of the shelter; however, it rises to the north end and has been partially eroded. This deposit is a breccia which can be traced by fragments adhering to the wall in the north end. Despite this lack of continuity, the artifacts were observed to be more concentrated in the northern portion of the shelter—a fact which distinguishes this level from the others studied.

Estimation of artifact density is difficult for this layer since no longitudinal sections were given by Rust; however, it seems likely that the density did not exceed 52.7 artifacts per cubic meter of matrix. This figure is most like those obtained for Levels 8 and 6, and these are the levels said by Rust to be most like this one. His comparison was based on the size of the artifacts, the presence of handaxes, and on the relatively large size of cores (1950:61).

Bordes (1955:496) finds strong similarities between this assemblage and that of Level 3, except for the reduced frequencies of burins and the presence of handaxes.

The best correspondence between observed and expected artifacts frequencies in the assemblages is obtained on the assumption that Factors II and III determine the composition, by 67 per cent and 33 per cent respectively (see Figure 9.10). We have suggested that these factors are associated with Ferrassie and Mousterian of Acheulian Tradition, and presumably the handaxes in this level are related to the latter. It should be noted that the discrepancy between the observed and expected graphs is due to the counts of naturally backed knives, ventrally retouched pieces, and atypical burins—types that behaved the same way in the assemblages from Levels 3, 5, and 6.

Factors II and III probably bear some functional relationship to one another, since the former is believed to be related to hunting and the latter to the preparation of meat. In the case of Factor III, the interpretation is supported by the occurrence of fire lenses in this layer, the only one in which Factor III plays a role.

In examining the "nonessential" component of the assemblage (Table 9.10) we find that there were in general fewer Levallois blanks and by-products and/or non-Levallois blanks than expected from the range of activities represented. Nevertheless, there are more Levallois blanks observed per tool than in any other level studied. This suggests that blanks might have been introduced into the site.

The presence of Factor III as a determinant singles this assemblage out as distinct from all the others. However, it is still identified as a work camp with primary emphasis on hunting with some consumption of game on the spot.

Summary of Analysis: Levels 2–8

In our analysis we hoped to gain information on four questions posed above (see p. 102). We will therefore summarize the results in terms of these questions.

1. *Does the composition of the observed assemblages correspond to unit factors as isolated by the factor analysis?* We may answer this question in the negative. Six of the seven levels analyzed were *compounds* of two or more factors; that is, the gross behavior represented by any given assemblage generally represents varying combinations of demonstrable subgroups of artifacts. This implies that we must be able to isolate the factors (subgroups of artifacts) in order to make regular inferences as to past behavior.

2. *Do the types of Mousterian assemblages isolated by Bordes always correspond to the same combination of factors?* Once again, we may answer in the negative. Five assemblages classified as Ferrassie appear to be composed of different combinations of factors. Levels 3, 4, and 6 all have in common a dominance of Factor II or V as determinants along with an absence of Factors I or III. Although there is internal variability between these three assemblages, they all appear to be distinct from those of Levels 2 and 8 (also classified as Ferrassie). These latter two are alike in the presence of Factors I or III, which, as seen in Figure 9.6, are quite different from Factors II and V. Thus, we find that the five assemblages classified as Ferrassie display a considerable range of variability with respect to the groups of artifacts (factors) present in each, and that these five can be said to represent two generic types of assemblage on the basis of the presence or absence of Factors I or III.

With respect to Level 5 (classified as Denticulate) and Level 7 (classified as Typical), there is less variability in the factor contributions of these two assemblages than there is between the assemblages classified as Ferrassie. For example, Level 7 (classified as Denticulate) is more like Level 8 in factor determinants than Level 8 is like Level 2 (also classified as Ferrassie).

We therefore conclude that the use of multivariate analysis allows us to discriminate between assemblages which, with the use of univariate statistics, appear to be similar, as well as allowing us to recognize common factors in assemblages thought to be different. This should allow us to re-examine the problem of correlations between seasonal phenomena, types of game represented, and environmental variables and to formulate new hypotheses about past behavior.

3. *Is there regularity in the composition and form of assemblages at a given location which can be interpreted in terms of regular patterns of past human behavior?* We may answer this question affirmatively. First, it should be noted that all the assemblages were dominated by Factors II, IV, or V, all of which have been interpreted as reflecting extractive activities. In only one case (Level 5) was Factor IV dominant, all the others being determined principally by Factors II or V, the hunting and butchering factors. We may therefore generalize that all seven levels studied reflect extractive tasks, principally hunting and butchering, and on this basis we interpret the occupations as representing work camps.

In addition to this overall regularity in site use, we would like to point out certain provocative patterns of association between factors. In levels where Factor IV is a major contributor (Levels 5 and 7) exploitation of similar raw material was observed. Immediately available flint was used, whereas in all the "hunting" levels flint was obtained from a broader geographical area. This observation coincides with that of Freeman (1964), who observed that in the northern Spanish Mousterian assemblages denticulates were characterized by an inordinately high frequency of medium grades of quartzite. Bordes (1962:44) also notes that the workmanship in denticulate assemblages is "often mediocre." Our observations, taken in conjunction with those of Bordes and Freeman, suggest that there is something special about the raw materials and techniques employed for production of Factor IV diagnostics. There is apparently an expedient use of local material, as well as an areal limitation of the sources exploited. Could it be that what is being reflected is a primary difference in terms of social division of labor between males and females? The model we have in mind is that of women carrying out restricted tasks close to the site, making use of local flint sources, and making tools by slightly different techniques than did the men. The men, in this scheme of things, are envisioned as engaging in more far-ranging tasks like hunting, and working flint with techniques better suited to the production of points, scrapers, and knives.

Another regularity in these assemblages is the fact that in no case were Factors I and II observed to co-occur as determinants, whereas all other possible combinations of the factors were observed. When Factor I was present, Factors IV and/or V were associated. Keeping in mind that Factor I has been interpreted as representing maintenance activities, the following hypothesis are offered:

a. Factor V represents a special kind of hunting of particular game which necessitates a longer stay away from the base camp, and hence more maintenance tasks in the work camp.
b. The differences between Factors II and V reflect differences in the logistics of hunting—i.e., whether or not the game was butchered before returning to the base camp. Such an interpretation fits the major observable differences between Factors II and V but would not explain the association of Factors V and I, since it is Factor II which has the greater number of artifacts which can be inferred as butchering tools. We must, therefore, also assume that there were differences in the number of animals taken at one time. If they were being taken singly and were also small, we might anticipate the need for more maintenance activities to cover a longer period of hunting.

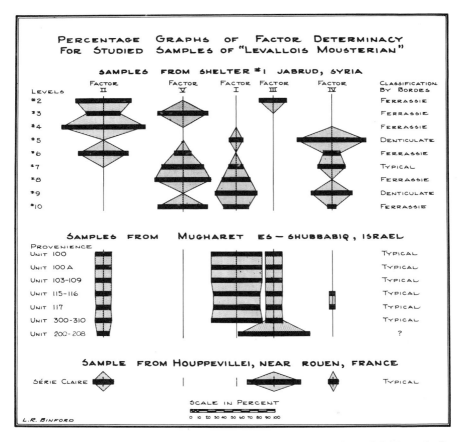

Figure 9.11 Percentage graphs of factor determinacy for studied samples of "Levallois Mousterian."

c. The third alternative is that the sample from Jabrud is not representative of the kinds of sites included in the settlement systems of the late Typical Mousterian and that the failure to observe coincidence between Factors II and I is due to sampling error.

4. *Is there regular change through time in the assemblages that might indicate either general evolutionary or specific situational changes in the activities of the occupants?* With a number of qualifications, we may answer this question in the affirmative. It has been demonstrated that Factor II tends to replace Factor V through the Jabrud sequence (see Figure 9.11). We may ask if this replacement of one hunting assemblage by another is a function of (a) general culture change, or (b) a shift in the way this specific location was utilized through time. Since Factors II and V are differently related to Factor I, we tend to favor the latter interpretation. The total configuration of variability of the levels suggests essentially different types of occupations. Those of the lower levels are interpreted as work camps, some distance from the base camp of the local group, involving the exploitation of local resources. The occupations of

the upper levels, on the other hand, suggest more specific work groups occupying the shelter for shorter periods of time. These observations do not rule out the possibility of there having been a major change in the cultural systems represented; however, given these data alone, such a change cannot be demonstrated.

We may summarize the findings from Jabrud as follows:

1. The Mousterian assemblages represented are not made up of single factors; on the contrary, they are generally composites of two or more factors.
2. The use of multivariate statistics in analyzing assemblages allows us to distinguish between types of assemblage which appeared similar when univariate statistics were used.
3. There is apparent regularity in the utilization of the shelter of Jabrud in that:

   a. all the occupations appear to have been work camps;
   b. the major activity represented seems to have been hunting;
   c. Factor IV appears to be associated with an expedient use of immediately available sources of flint. We have further tentatively suggested that the activities represented by Factor IV may reflect a primary (sexual) division of labor.

4. There was a regular shift in the activities in the occupations of the shelter—from work camps with a minor element of maintenance tasks to hunting and butchering without maintenance activities being represented.

Mugharet Es-Shubbabiq

This site was excavated by the junior author in 1962 (S. R. Binford 1966); it is located in the Wadi Amud, a few kilometers northwest of the Sea of Galilee, Israel. The site is a cave in a dolomitic limestone cliff, and its opening stands approximately 40 meters above the present level of the wadi. The cave is a large one (ca. 295 square meters of floor space within the limits of natural light, with an additional 53 square meters in the rear chamber beyond the limits of natural light). The roof of the cave is a domed vault, about 20 meters above the cave floor over much of the area within the limits of natural light.

Although the exact floor space of Shelter I at Jabrud is not known, it is estimated from the published floor plan to have been approximately 178 square meters (Rust 1950; plate 3). Both the shelter of Jabrud and the cave of Shubbabiq face east and are lightest in the morning hours. In Shubbabiq the light inside the cave is sufficient for reading until about 3 p.m., after which the light diminishes rather rapidly. Presumably at Jabrud more light would have been available later in the day, because of the open nature of the site.

The main chamber of Shubbabiq is well protected from both wind and rain; even during the height of the rainy season in 1962, this portion of the cave remained completely dry. In short, the cave provides excellent living space with ample requirements of light and protection from the elements.

Unfortunately the archeological deposits in the main chamber of Shubbabiq were removed by later inhabitants; the only traces remaining are in crevices in the bedrock and in semiconsolidated deposits just outside the cave entrance. Undisturbed deposits, highly brecciated, did occur in the rear chamber; these most certainly represent a dump or midden deposit rather than living-floors. Eight samples from the site were used in this analysis; they are

Unit 100: disturbed soft deposits, about an average of 1.4 meters thick, in the rear chamber.

Unit 100A: undisturbed soft deposits, directly underlying 100 in most places.

Unit 103–9: the first 5 cm of depth of the undisturbed breccia in the rear chamber, 50–54 m. line.

Unit 113: the first 3–5 cms. of depth of the undisturbed breccia in the rear chamber, 55–57 m. line.

Unit 115–116: material from a lateral cut (N–S) in the breccia of the rear chamber, from the top to bedrock (1.3 m. thick), across the 1 m. test trench.

Unit 117: material from a section in the breccia at right angles to the one described above (E–W), along the side of trench from the 57–58.80 m. line.

Unit 300–310: material from an unconsolidated, undisturbed deposit which lay between the breccia and a fault crevice formed by the floor and the north wall of the cave, along an area 1.2 m. long and averaging .75 m. wide.

Unit 200–208: material from the semiconsolidated remnant deposit several meters to the east of the cave entrance.

Analysis of the factor content of the samples from Shubbabiq (Figure 9.11) shows that there are only three recognizably different kinds of assemblages present. The material from Unit 115–116 and Unit 117 exhibited some variation from the others in that Factor IV was represented. Since these two samples were derived from vertical cuts in the breccia and included artifacts from stratigraphically lower levels than did the other samples from the rear chamber, we may possibly have reflected here a differential in tools through time—i.e., there might have been a heavier use of denticulates in the earlier occupation period. However, the variation seen in the factor analysis is not great enough to suggest a major change in occupation type.

The sample from Unit 200–208, from the remnant deposit outside the cave entrance, does differ markedly from the other samples. Due to the small size of the sample, it was not possible to partition it as reliably into the factors contributing to its composition. But it is evident (Figure 9.11 that Factor III contributes over 50 per cent of its determinacy. This area was the only one at Shubbabiq that yielded traces of fire lenses; it will be recalled that Level 2 at Jabrud in which Factor III was present also had evidence of fires. The most reasonable interpretation of the distinctive nature of this sample is that it represents a localization of activity on the site.

The remaining samples are all essentially alike. They were originally analyzed using

Bordes' methods and checked by Chi Square tests (S. R. Binford 1966) and were identified as Typical Mousterian of Levallois facies. The factor analysis indicates that these samples are composed of three major components, each factor representing a set of activities. Factor I is the dominant one at the site, with 60 per cent of the variability accounted for by the activities represented by this factor. Factors II and III each contribute 20 per cent to the total determinacy of the assemblage composition.

Factor I is believed to be associated primarily with maintenance activities—the manufacture of tools and processing nonflint raw materials into usable items. Factor II is interpreted as a tool kit used in the killing and butchering of animals, and Factor III is seen as a specialized group of implements used for cutting and incising, possibly related to the preparation and consumption of food. This particular set of factors is very different from the combinations observed in the samples from Jabrud. In none of the levels studied from Jabrud did Factors I and III occur together; in none of the Jabrud levels was either Factor I or III a prime determinant of an assemblage. It seems that the occupation at Shubbabiq is well outside of the range of settlement types represented at Jabrud.

The nature of the factors and their inferred activities at Shubbabiq suggests that the occupation here represents a central and more permanently occupied location. The major activities represented (Factor I) appear to be associated with maintenance, rather than extractive, tasks. The assemblages at Jabrud, on the other hand, suggest occupations of differentially constituted social groups primarily engaged in exploiting local resources. The character of the Shubbabiq assemblage suggests the site might have served as a *base camp* for work groups analogous to those responsible for the occupations at Jabrud.

Further support for the hypothesis that Shubbabiq represents a base camp settlement type in a more complex settlement system is found in our growing understanding of the minimum numbers of persons capable of maintaining a self-sustaining human society. It has been suggested that the minimum size of a local group within such a population is of the order of 20 to 24 individuals (Howells 1960:179–180). Such an estimate does not imply that a group of this size would necessarily remain together throughout an entire seasonal cycle; rather, that only during certain phases of a cycle would the aggregation live together. If we take this observation as a point of reference, we may then propose that the site where the larger social unit was localized during the annual period of aggregation must have had sufficient life space to allow for daily living of a group composed minimally of 20 to 24 individuals. A recent study suggests that there is a constant in the numbers of people living together and the amount of necessary sheltered space, the minimum being of the order of 10 square meters per individual (Naroll 1962).

Given this figure, we can argue that the 178 square meters of floor space estimated for Levels 2–8 at Jabrud could not have accommodated more than 18 people for any extended period of time. On the other hand, Shubbabiq with its 295 square meters of floor space could have provided adequate living space for about 25 persons, and possibly for as many as 30. This argument, taken together with the demonstrable differences in the composition of the assemblages from the two sites, leads us to conclude that we are dealing with two basically different types of locations in a differentiated settlement system.

There are also interesting differences in the "nonessential" artifact ratios for the two sites. Table 9.10 presents the summary indices for the "nonessential" artifacts from the various provenience units at Shubbabiq. Units 100A, 113, and 117 all have a large number of cores, with no indication of their having been worked on the spot; blanks also appear to have been introduced. The ratios involving completed tools indicate a primary emphasis on tool use rather than on tool production. These three units are interpreted as derived from areas where tool use, rather than tool production, was primary.

Units 100, 103–9, 115–16, and 300–10 suggest a different situation, one in which there are a great many blanks and by-products from flint working and fewer tools. It is suggested that these samples were derived from areas where blanks and tools were being produced in higher frequencies than were finished tools.

Unit 200–8 is distinctive in that it is exceedingly high in those indices reflecting primary flint-working. It will be recalled that this deposit lies outside the present cave entrance and toward the south wall, an area which would have been both well-lighted and yet away from the center of living activities.

These samples demonstrate that the various phases of tool manufacture were conducted at different locations and independently of the particular tool-using activities conducted in the same locations.

In summarizing our findings from Shubabbiq, we again return to the four questions for which we originally sought answers:

1. *Does the composition of the observed assemblages correspond to unit factors as isolated by the factor analysis?* As in the findings from Jabrud, our answer is negative. The samples from Shubbabiq are minimally constituted of two factors and maximally of four.

2. *Do the types of Mousterian assemblages isolated by Bordes always correspond to the same combination of factors?* Our response here is also in the negative. The total assemblage from Shubbabiq was classified by Bordes's techniques as Typical Mousterian and was found to have strong resemblances to Level 7 of Jabrud. However, when the two assemblages are analyzed in terms of factor content, they are seen to be quite distinct. The material from Shubbabiq is dominated by Factor I, with Factors II and III as minor contributors, while Level 7 from Jabrud was primarily controlled by Factor V, with minor determinacy by Factors I and IV.

3. *Is there regularity in the composition and form of assemblages at a given location which can be interpreted in terms of regular patterns of past human behavior?* This question can be answered affirmatively. The overall similarity between seven of the eight samples from Shubbabiq suggests that although the occupation of the cave may have spanned a considerable period of time, the location was utilized in essentially the same way by its occupants. The data specifically indicate use of the cave as a base camp.

4. *Is there regular change through time in the assemblage which might indicate either general evolutionary or specific situational changes in the activities of the occupants?* This

question must be answered negatively. The slightly larger loading on denticulates in the two samples certainly is not of an order to suggest any major difference in occupation type.

By comparing our results from Shubbabiq and Jabrud, a number of testable hypotheses can be offered:

Base camps, identifiable by a major determinacy of the statistical form of the assemblage by Factors I or III, will have the following characteristics:

   a. they will offer good shelter and protection from the elements;
   b. they will be relatively large locations and, if they are caves or bounded areas, will have at least 250 square meters of floor space;
   c. there will probably be a wider range of activities represented than at work camps, as indicated by the number of factors contributing to the assemblages;
   d. the fauna will probably exhibit a wider range of forms available over a longer period of the seasonal cycle.

Houppeville

The material from Houppeville is not directly relevant to a study of the Mousterian of the Near East; Houppeville is a quarry in the Seine basin, near Rouen, France (Bordes 1952:431). This assemblage was included in the computer run for two reasons: first, to increase our sample size; and second, because there appeared to be strong resemblances between this material and that from Shubbabiq when analyzed by Bordes' methods.

When studied by factor analysis, the assemblage appears to be the result of a combination of determinants (see Figure 9.12). Factor III was dominant, with an appreciable amount of variance accounted for by Factor II, and a minor role played by Factor IV. In terms of the activities represented, based on our interpretation of the factors, we have represented at Houppeville food preparation, hunting and butchering, and processing of plant material. The ratios derived from the "nonessential" flint materials suggest that tool production was also an important activity at this site (see Table 9.10).

In view of the difference in environmental setting from the other sites analyzed plus the fact that this was an open-air location, we do not feel it possible to make an interpretation as to the type of settlement represented nor the nature of the settlement system, on the basis of this one site.

Summary and Conclusions

The purpose of this paper was the presentation of alternative testable hypotheses for the observed variation and alternation of Mousterian industries demonstrated by Bordes. The value of our results lies chiefly in the realm of methodology, and these methodological developments are inextricably predicated on a theoretical position, which we summarize here.

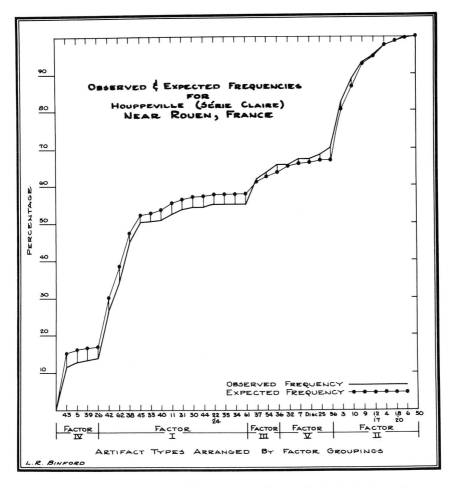

Figure 9.12 Observed and expected frequencies for Houppeville (série claire) near Rouen, France.

We argue that culture is most usefully defined as man's extrasomatic means of adaptation (White 1959:8) and that a major component of man's adaptive success has been his ability to behave rationally. We would therefore expect differences and similarities in cultural remains to be relatable, at least in part, to the rational use of cultural means for the maintenance and perpetuation of human groups. We suggest that variability in archeological assemblages should be investigated from this point of view, that such variability presents analytical problems which the prehistorian must solve before he can make inferences concerning behavior in the past. This research has been directed toward the development of techniques which make possible the explanation of differences and similarities, without reference to "migrations" or unalterable "traditions," and expressed as hypotheses which can be tested by future work.

Our analytical methods must allow us to determine (a) when variability does in fact reflect past behavior and is not simply the product of sampling error, and (b) what differences and similarities in archeological assemblages signify in terms of past behavior. The first problem can be solved by the use of research designs planned to control sampling error (L. R. Binford 1964a) and by the use of standard statistical tests (Spaulding 1960a). It is toward the solution of the second problem that the methods developed here have been directed.

Our approach to the solution of this problem involves certain assumptions and postulates concerning the nature of human activities and their relation to (a) the composition of any given archeological assemblage, and (b) the cultural systems which were the context of these activities. The basic assumption allowing us to deal rationally with archeological assemblages is: *The form and composition of assemblages recovered from geologically undisturbed context are directly related to the form and composition of human activities at a given location.*

A second assumption we make is that: *The minimal social process and organizational principles exhibited by human groups today were operative in the past.*[4] Given these assumptions we can advance the following propositions:

1. An undifferentiated mass of archeological data can, by the use of methods designed to reveal patterns of covariation, be partitioned into sub-units of artifacts which we can infer were used in a related set of activities.

2. These groupings of artifacts that exhibit mutual determinacy should also share morphological characteristics which, on the basis of simple mechanics, can be reasonably inferred to have been used in a set of related mechanical tasks.

The first step in the study was the application of factor analysis to a series of Mousterian assemblages that had been summarized as counts of various artifact types using identical typological methods. The factor analysis yielded five *factors*—groups of artifacts that exhibited a high order of mutual covariance—which shared common determinants for the relative quantitative variability of the included artifacts. These findings supported our first proposition. Further, there was a high degree of consistency in the form of artifacts diagnostic of each factor, a finding that lent support to our second proposition.

The second step in the study was the analysis of the various samples of artifacts from the sites of Jabrud, Shubbabiq, and Houppeville. On the basis of the two major assumptions stated above, we suggested that we would expect assemblages, as the product of human activity, to vary in terms of (a) the form of the social unit—e.g., social segments or cooperating groups organized along age and/or sex lines, and (b) the specific tasks performed. It was argued that the differential distribution of resources and advantageous living sites would lead us to expect both spatial and temporal variability in both the form of the social unit and the specific tasks performed by a given group.

A distinction was made between *maintenance* and *extractive* tasks, the former involving activities related primarily to the nutritional and technological requirements of the group, and the latter activities related to the direct exploitation of environmental resources. It was suggested that these two types of activities were not isomorphic in their distribution, extractive tasks more commonly being performed by work groups and minimal segments of the society at locations determined by the distributions of resources within a territory. Maintenance activities, on the other hand, would tend to occur at locations selected principally in terms of space and shelter requirements of the residence group. We proposed that, on the basis of these arguments, we should be able to distinguish *base camps* and *work camps*, as two settlement types within a settlement system.

The detailed analysis of the samples from Levels 2–8 at Jabrud (Shelter I) in terms of the models suggested above shows that all of the levels appear to represent work camps, and primarily hunting camps. Variability was noted between the several levels in both the combinations of factors present and the relative presence or absence of those factors which were interpreted as reflecting maintenance activities. This variability was interpreted as related to (a) the length and intensity of occupation, and (b) the range and nature of tasks represented. Kinds of data not available for our study such as animal bone, features, pollen and plant remains, etc., might be profitably investigated and should provide confirmation or refutation of our interpretive hypotheses.

The analysis of samples from Shubbabiq revealed a very different situation. The factors contributing to the variability of the assemblage suggest a dominance of activities related to maintenance, and the composition of the various samples indicate the consistent use of the site for similar purposes—for use as a base camp. (No settlement type interpretation was offered for Houppeville.)

Our findings suggest that a great deal of the variability in Mousterian assemblages can be interpreted as *functional variability*. Further, the nature of this functional variability strongly suggests that the social systems represented were culturally based and that the principles of organization of these social systems were similar to those known from contemporary hunters and gatherers.

Our findings also suggest some possible solutions to the problem of interpreting the alternation of Mousterian assemblages demonstrated by Bordes. The following points are relevant:

1. The use of multivariate statistics allows us to partition Mousterian assemblages into subunits of artifacts which can reasonably be interpreted as representing tool-kits for the performance of different sets of tasks.
2. These subunits of artifacts vary independently of one another and may be combined in numerous ways.

The significance of these findings is that correlations must be sought not for total assemblages but for these independently varying factors. This can be implemented in the field by the following methods of data collection:

1. Excavation of sites to reveal their internal structure (e.g., digging wide, contiguous areas), thus allowing us to study the spatial clustering of activities at a given location.
2. Excavation of as wide a range as possible of different forms of sites (e.g., open-air stations, caves, and rockshelters) to obtain information on the relationship between settlement type and range of activities.

3. Excavation of sites from different environmental zones to test the relationship between extractive tasks and the differential distribution of resources in a region.

4. Observation of a number of attributes not generally studied in detail:

    a. the degree of correlation between kinds of raw materials and groups of artifacts to evaluate the differential use of local and distant flint sources for artifacts used in various activities,

    b. the degree of correlation between different sets of activities (as defined by factors) and the form and composition of faunal assemblages;

    c. degree of correlation between types of activities and the form and composition of floral assemblages (pollen and macroplant remains).

    d. degree of correlation between kinds of activities and the physical characteristics of sites (extent of living area, degree of protection, etc.).

The provocative results of our study suggest to us that the methods of analysis used here are potentially useful for formulating testable hypotheses about social organization and evolutionary culture change within prehistoric communities.

Notes

1. An early attempt to develop analytical means for the isolation of functional variability is exemplified by the work of James Brown and Leslie Freeman (1964) in their use of linear regression models in the analysis of ceramics from a site excavated under the direction of Dr. Paul Martin of the Chicago Natural History Museum.

William Longacre conducted the pioneer study using multiple regression techniques in his study of ceramic design elements from materials obtained from the same site, Carter Ranch (Longacre 1963). The first application of multivariate analysis to Old World Paleolithic data was done by Robert C. Whallon (1963) as a Master's thesis.

Leslie Freeman (1964) used a factor analysis model in his study of Mousterian materials from Cantabrian Spain, his results serving as the major portion of his doctoral dissertation at the University of Chicago. At the same time James Hill conducted a more elaborate factor analysis study of ceramics, design elements, stone and bone tools, and animal bones recovered from the Broken K site in Eastern Arizona (Hill 1965). This analysis constitutes a large portion of his doctoral thesis, submitted to the faculty of the University of Chicago in spring 1965.

2. Prof. Bordes graciously provided us with copies of his work-sheets on Houppeville and Jabrud. The data from Shubbabiq were obtained during the tenure of a Postdoctoral National Science Foundation Fellowship by the junior author. The factor analysis was conducted at the Institute for Computer Research, University of Chicago, whose facilities were made available through the kindness of Professor Allan Addleman and through the consistent encouragement and assistance of Prof. Benjamin Wright, Advisor for the Social Sciences, at the computer center. The actual calculations were performed on the 7090 IBM computer, using a University of California program (Mesa 83) modified at the University of Chicago (Mesa 84); the program was supplied through the Social Science Computer Program Library at the University of Chicago.

3. At the time this study was undertaken, Dr. Solecki's first season of work at Jabrud was just beginning. At this writing the first season's work is completed but the results have not been completely analyzed. These new data should make possible the testing of some interpretive hypotheses we have offered here, based on Rust's data.

4. This is not to say that we believe that social units of the Lower and Middle Pleistocene were organized along the same lines as are living social units; rather, we take these units as baselines against which to compare social units of the past.

10

Comment on "Culture Traditions and Environment of Early Man," by Desmond Collins

Collins' paper presents arguments relative to a number of important and controversial points in contemporary paleoanthropology. I have selected for comment what appear to me to be two of the central points made by Collins with regard to the understanding of variability among archaeological assemblages: (a) variability in form and content among archaeological assemblages is appropriately viewed as a sufficient and adequate measure of a single variable—culture; and (b) variability among archaeological assemblages to be used as the empirical basis for the construction of a two-dimensional systematics with traditions and stages as the basic units. I shall also address some comments to the manner in which Collins operationalizes his views.

Collins offers a number of poorly drawn analogies based on his misunderstandings of arguments set forth by my wife and myself (see comments of S. R. Binford) and then proceeds to the following statement (p. 268):

> If the culture-tradition theory were entirely wrong, I feel sure that the archaeological data would not pattern as neatly as it does into traditions and stages.

He concludes this argument with the following statement (p. 270):

> It is indeed fortunate that the study of culture traditions does not necessarily involve knowing the functions of artefacts, since we can rarely do more than guess at these. I suggest that we are justified in proceeding on the hypothesis that similarity of style and content in assemblages is an indicator of common cultural tradition.

In short, Collins makes an assumption as to the significance of interassemblage variability. He proposes to test the validity of this assumption by the degree to which empirical materials can be arranged systematically into taxa. The criteria for assignment into taxa are logically consistent with the original assumption, plus others, regarding the nature of information flow in cultural systems (see p. 277). They are as follows: (a) Two independent traditions are established when contemporary assemblages exhibit contrasts in their form and content (p. 270). (b) Two independent traditions

Originally published in *Current Anthropology* 10(4):297–299, 1969. (The Collins article appeared in the same issue with this article.) Reprinted by permission of the University of Chicago Press. Copyright 1969 by the Wenner-Gren Foundation for Anthropological Research.

are established when two or more assemblages are non-contemporary but close to overlapping temporally and exhibit sharp contrasts in their form and content (p. 270). (c) Two evolutionary stages are established when two or more assemblages are non-contemporary but close to overlapping temporally and exhibit "some overlapping of traits" [p. 270]. I suggest that by following these proposals, one will inevitably be successful in generating patterned stages and traditions, simply because the criteria are exhaustive, given the formal and temporal dimensions employed for discrimination. This patterning in no way tests the validity of the assumptions standing behind the taxonomy; it only tests the degree to which the criteria for discrimination are sufficient for the generation of mutually exclusive and exhaustive taxa. This fallacy is one that has retarded archaeology for a long time.

A similar confusion of the empirical data relevant to the operation of past cultural systems and the criteria used for the generation of scales for measurement is well demonstrated in Collins' discussion of hypotheses. He begins with the astonishing statement: "I know of virtually no archaeological research in which hypotheses have been specifically formulated" [p. 278]. He then proceeds to offer a number of "hypotheses"; for example, ". . . that the assemblages from Choukoutien 1 and Vértesszöllös belong to a single assemblage type, ancestral to the Clactonian." This is not a hypothesis. It is an anticipatory proposition asserting that when his criteria for discriminating stages and traditions are applied to these data, they will stand in the suggested taxonomic relationship to each other. This is analogous to saying that when I measure with a ruler the height of this table it will be 32 inches high and will be shorter than the dressing table on my right and taller than the footstool on my left. A hypothesis is a statement of anticipated relationships between two or more variables, each of which is measured by independent instruments for measurement. What Collins calls a hypothesis is an anticipatory proposition regarding the "value" of a variable characteristic of one or more independent populations, and the relative position of these values in a nominal scale (traditions) or an ordinal scale (stages) of these values. This is not a hypothesis in any scientific sense of the word.

Another "hypothesis" offered by Collins is that the Acheulian and Clactonian were contemporary in Mindel times. This is an existential proposition and has none of the properties of a hypothesis. It is analogous to the assertion that in this box on this table there are a red ball and a black ball. The truth or falsity of the proposition tells us nothing about either the balls or the box; it only informs us on the accuracy of the judgment regarding the distribution of entities. This is not to say that an accurate distributional knowledge is unimportant. Quite the contrary; knowledge of the distributional facts is essential to the generation of explanatory propositions and hypotheses. Nevertheless, Collin's "hypotheses" are not hypotheses, and the demonstration of their truth or falsity would in no way increase our understanding of cultural differences and similarities.

I could continue through the entire list of so-called hypotheses; not a single one is a hypothesis in the scientific sense of the word. Further, even if all the propositions offered by Collins were either confirmed or refuted, the results would be irrelevant as tests of the validity of his basic assumption in interpreting interassemblage variability (i.e., that it is an adequate and sufficient measure of cultural affinity) or of his criteria for taxonomic discrimination. The only result of testing his propositions would be a possible modification in the temporal–spatial distributions of taxa, whose patterns would then be differently read in the reconstruction of "culture history." The logic used by Collins is an excellent example of the prescientific epistemology that has dominated the work of archaeologists in the past.

In operationalizing his suggestions, Collins first attempts to establish the validity of the recognition of two separate traditions in Europe and Asia from Mindel through Eem times. In order to do this, he must, according to his own criteria, demonstrate rough contemporaneity of assemblages which are contrastive in content. Table 1 compares five assemblages—two Clactonian and three Acheulian—demonstrating that these two sets of assemblages are contrastive in a number of characteristics. Examination of Collins' chronological assignments for the assemblages compared in Table 1 reveals that the two Clactonian assemblages are assigned to the lower and lower-middle Holstein Interglacial (Tables 9 and 10), while two of the Acheulian assemblages are assigned to the middle-upper Holstein (Table 8). The third Acheulian site is not included in his tables, but we are told in the text (p. 274) that the Hundisburg assemblage belongs to the "Northfleet II stage" which is assigned to the "proto-Riss" period. In short, the assemblages in Table 1 span approximately 230,000 years, and the two sets—Clactonian and Acheulian—are not contemporary but sequential in nature.

One can only assume, then, that the criterion for establishing two traditions here is the second one—namely, that two traditions are established when two or more assemblages are not contemporary but close to overlapping temporally and exhibit sharp contrast in their form and content. If this was the criterion, however, a comparison between the Acheulian at Hoxne and the Clactonian from the freshwater bed at Clacton would according to Collins' own criteria, have been suffcient (see Collins' discussion of this point on p. 270). The presentation of Table 1 must have been motivated by other concerns, perhaps by a concern to provide a data base for the formal contrasts that would allow new or unstudied assemblages to be assigned to one or the other of his two traditions.

Having concluded to his satisfaction that there are two traditions, Collins proceeds to the consideration of "Cultural Variation and Evolution." Through a series of cross-correlations—the basis for which is far from clear—Collins produces a seriation of Acheulian assemblages. (For example, in Table 6 assemblage Ca LCQ is shown as earlier than Sw UL, yet in Table 8 it is placed later than Sw UL.) The data on which his "stages" of the Acheulian are based are represented in Table 8. Examination of this table reveals that of the seven indices, all but two deal with handaxes, and both of these (one of Levallois flakes and the other on side- and end-scrapers) are expressed in proportion to handaxes. Collins has argued strongly for the use of the *assemblage* as the basic comparative unit, stating that "The inclusion of all the artefacts is important if any significance is to be attached to the presence or absence of particular features" [p. 267]. He has informed us, using the analogy of Ferrassie preceding Quina Mousterian, that stages are recognized when *assemblages* are non-contemporary but close to overlapping and exhibit "some overlapping of traits" [p. 270]. (I might point out that the analogy is false, since well-documented Quina assemblages are known to predate many known Ferrassie assemblages; for example, Pech de l'Azé compared with Combe Grenal.) Here, however, we see Collins establishing stages of the Acheulian primarily on the basis of different frequencies in the shapes of handaxes, and his confidence in this method is sufficient to permit him to include undated assemblages (Dovercourt and Tillet blanche) and give them temporal assignment on this basis.

Having produced this table with a total of 14 samples that, according to Collins' dating, span approximately 150,000 years (10 samples from Great Britain and 4 from France, with two of the British samples chronologically placed on the basis of their handaxe shapes), he summarizes that handaxes with straight or concave sides decrease in frequency relative to those with convex sides through time; handaxes of limande shape increase at the expense of ovate and cordiform shapes; there is an increase through time in Levallois flakes relative to handaxes and a similar increase in scrapers. Handaxes with the S-twist and cleaver tips also increase in frequency through time. One can only wonder what would happen to this picture of regular change if, for example, the Abbeville assemblage had been included, or the Cagney assemblage. (Cagny is roughly contemporary with St. Acheul Sable Rouge, but 271 of 300 handaxes are limande and the S-twist is quite common [Bordes 1968:59]). One could enumerate many empirical cases to the contrary, particularly the early Würm layer 6 of La Micoque, where straight- or concave-sided handaxes are the most common forms; but this seems unnecessary, since the very idea that a small and geographically biased sample of handaxes could be used to establish reliable empirical generalizations for the cultural succession of all of Europe is highly unlikely.

Essentially the same general types of criticism apply to Collin's treatment of the Clactonian. Rather than continue with further specific criticism, I would like to pose certain questions which should help to point up some of the general problems which have been ignored by Collins in his work. For example, if he had compared Acheulian assemblages through time with respect to the same characteristics which were used in differentiating the Acheulian from the Clactonian, what kind of stages would he have generated? It would appear that many of the characteristics would exhibit independent patterns of variability. His own work suggests that handaxes become less numerous and scrapers more numerous through time, and we are even told that there are during the Eem ". . . new assemblage-types with distinctive Acheulian traits, such as backed knives, denticulates, and well-made Levallois flakes. In these there are few or no handaxes" [p. 277]. Similarly, Clactonian assemblages are known in which Levallois technique is strong (Bordes 1968:137). For practically any trait used by Collins in his original demonstration of contrasts between the Acheulian and the Clactonian, we find instances in which it crosses over or varies within a tradition as much as between traditions. This situation has been observed by prehistorians many times in the past, and the normal interpretation offered is the one that Collins himself offers—acculturation, diffusion, and the taxonomic parallel of these interpretations, "hybrid cultures."

Collins himself seems to question that all the traits or characteristics with which he works are equal and specific measures of cultural affinity. For instance, in his discussion of the Northfleet stage, in which handaxes are said to be rare and Levallois flakes abundant, he attributes this to the differential availability of large flint nodules during periods of high sea levels (p. 290); but in discussing the late-Riss "Charentian levels of Peyrards and Baume Bonne," he suggests that their differentation into Levallois and non-Levallois facies "may indicate cultural bifurcation in the Charentian" (p. 276). What, then, is the significance of varying frequencies or presence or absence of Levallois technique? Is it a measure of sea level, or of cultural preference, or of differential distribution of sizes of raw materials? If it could be all or some of the above how reliable are traditions and stages that are said to represent some kind of bounded cultural unit defined by the analysis of this trait? What do we know of the determinants of the differential distribution and frequency variation of handaxes, scrapers, etc.? Probably even less than we know about Levallois technique! Any taxonomy is an instrument for measurement, and unless we know what it is we are measuring, any statements concerning the meaning of the various groupings of empirical data produced by the taxonomy remains sheer guesswork. Arranging archaeological data according to a taxonomy can contribute nothing to our knowledge of the past. It may permit some systematic observations at the descriptive level regarding the character of the archaeological record; but describing the archaeological record only increased our knowledge of the past when the significance of the record to events in the past can be established with some confidence. Proceeding as Collins has allows us only to test the efficacy of our taxonomies as adequate instruments for measurement, never the significance of what is being measured.

Collins' research is based on unacceptable scientific theory and method. It is rationalized in terms of an epistemological tautology and is implemented without regard to his own criteria for analysis or reasonable concern for sampling problems. The suggested correlations offered between traditions and environment and between traditions and races can all be questioned on empirical as well as on methodological grounds.

11

Interassemblage Variability:
The Mousterian
and the 'Functional Argument'

Since the initial publication of my preliminary results (Binford and Binford 1966 and 1969), designed to explore the character of inter-assemblage variability in the Mousterian, a number of objections have been raised to the view expressed and the results obtained. I will attempt to clarify several points which I think have served to confuse the issue and attempt to answer a number of the objections which have been raised to the arguments thus far set forth.

Central to the issues are what I consider to be rather limited notions about culture itself and the manner in which it serves man as a clearly successful adaptive basis for the organization of behaviour.[1] Possibly the best way to make my point is to contrast what I might refer to as an archaeologist's and an ethnologist's perspective of culture. Let us imagine ourselves as ethnologists placed in the situation of evaluating the degree that two neighbouring communities are culturally alike or culturally different. From a traditional point of view they are culturally alike if they have similar cultural repertoires regarding the behaviours appropriate to similar sets of recognized situational stimuli. As ethnologists we may investigate this problem by attempting to observe the behaviour of the members of each group in the contexts of similar stimulus situations. If members of both groups respond to these control stimuli with identical or similar ranges of behaviour, then we have to conclude that both brought to the situation similar repertoires of culture, both in terms of the cognitive structure for the analysis of the stimuli and in terms of a learned pattern of appropriate response. For the purposes of ethnographic investigation we may not be concerned with whether or not one group exhibits behaviours in response to uncontrolled stimuli that distinguish it from the other. Clearly these behavioural differences refer to the differential distribution of stimuli and their relative frequencies of occurrence in the environments of the two groups. We might then say that behaviour variation is the byproduct of the interaction between the kinds and frequencies of environmental stimulus and the kinds of cultural repertoire which persons bring to these stimulus situations.

Originally appeared in *The Explanation of Culture Change: Models in Prehistory*, edited by Colin Renfrew, published by Duckworth, London, pp. 227–254, © 1973.

The archaeologist is in the position of being limited to the observation of the byproducts of behaviour itself. When we observe varying frequencies in the association of conventionally recognized forms of tool or forms of modification in the environment, we are directly seeing the results of behaviour. I have pointed out that behavioural variability is the result of the interaction between the stimuli and the learned and traditional responses considered appropriate to the stimuli. We are therefore inevitably faced with the problem of determining whether the behavioural differences result from differences in the response repertoire of the actors or to the differences in the character and distribution of stimuli presented differentially to varying segments of a culturally homogeneous population.

My original research was directed towards the solution of this problem. It was argued that if similar or identical patterns of co-variation among similar tool classes could be shown to cross-cut recognizably different assemblage 'types', then the probability would be high that the assemblage types derive their consistent associational patterning from the organized distribution of stimuli, and not from the differential distribution of distinct cultural repertoires among population segments. I was successful in the original preliminary work and have been more successful since in the demonstration that there are consistent organizational properties which cross-cut consistent patterns of association (assemblage types). The organizational properties to which I refer are consistent patterns of mutual co-variation between sets of tools, regardless of whether they occur in assemblages which are considered similar or different in terms of associational patterning—e.g. Quina versus Typical Mousterian.

The debate which has followed the presentation of these ideas is largely reducible to a number of misunderstandings, irrelevant arguments, and points about which there is no contention. I will treat the arguments offered by the three authors of major critical works.

Arguments of Desmond Collins

In a paper treating the problem of Clactonian and Acheulian assemblage variability (1969), Collins presents an interesting distortion of my ideas and an irrelevant argument against them. He argues that, 'it is a mistake to contrast cultural and functional explanations of an artifact form' (1969: 268), justifying this position by pointing out that 'every illustrated ethnographic book is a corpus of refutations of the notion that knives, spearheads, and scrapers take the same form everywhere so long as they are used for the same purpose' (1969: 268). In these points I concur, but I see no possible relationship between them and the views which I have expressed. In the first place I never addressed myself to the problem of explaining differences between different forms of tools. My concern was with differences in proportional frequencies of typologically identical forms of tools as they occur in distinctive assemblage forms.

In a more recent article (1970), Collins continues to argue against a straw man; the 'functional hypothesis' presumably refers to my work though he does not cite it. He states:

Functional hypotheses conflict with cultural hypotheses only when they insist that the close similarities which recur between assemblages are caused or determined by function, and they will recur without the factor of culture tradition. Such 'pure' functional hypotheses are both more recent and less carefully developed than the culture view of Childe and Warren. In particular they offer no explanation of how function can determine the similarities, and accordingly they can be tested only in a partial and unsatisfactory way, as the two examples below show. (Collins 1970: 18)

Collins proceeds to offer his devastating evidence, pointing out that if two different assemblages were to be found in such similar contexts as kill sites, such evidence would disprove the 'functional' argument. I fail to see how this argument relates in any way to those which I have set forth. I have made no arguments against the existence of culture; I have never suggested that culture is not manifest in the archaeological record or that observable differences in the archaeological record might not have cultural significance. What I have suggested, however, is that behaviour is the byproduct of the interaction of a cultural repertoire with the environment. The archaeological record is the direct result of behaviour. Variations in the frequency with which certain culturally patterned behaviours will be executed is referable to the character of the environmental and adaptive situations in which cultural man finds himself at different points in time and space. To equate the archaeological record directly with the cultural repertoire of culture bearers is to ignore the reality of their adaptive behaviour and the advantages which a culturally based form of adaptation offers.

Collins has offered yet another argument against, as he phrases it 'the functional explanation of assemblage types' (1970:17). He points out that there are ethnographic and behavioural precedents for recognizing the differential distributions of behaviour both temporally and spatially for members of a 'single community'. However, he argues that this should not be manifest in the archaeological record because 'each type (assemblage with reference to differentiated behaviour) would have been left somewhere within the confines of their territory over a similar period of time. But as time passed one would expect that the assemblage types would often come to be left at the same site. The overall distributions of the assemblage types would inevitably remain similar' (Collins 1969:268). This argument makes a number of unwarranted assumptions. First, it assumes that environment for adaptive purposes is homogeneous and that human groups randomly distribute in the environment; this implies that, given a sufficient sample of events and sufficient passage of time, all behaviours are equally likely to occur at any location. This is demonstrably not the case. The environment is a complex ecological organization in which the energy and materials needed to maintain a human group are differentially distributed; it follows that all the activities necessary to the group's successful survival will not be performed at any one location. This differential distribution of matter and energy in the habitat insures that during a stable environmental episode the probabilities of different activities clustering at different locations is quite high. In the context of unstable environmental conditions it insures that a single location may offer very different advantages to a group in direct relation to the degree and character of environment change. In regard to the differential distribution of assemblage types over broad geographical provinces, such differential clustering may well be expected since the environment may be expected to vary across such regions. It is a matter for investigation to what degree there is a correspondence between behavioural variation across environmental zones and differences in the cultural repertoires of the persons so distributed; the simplistic equation of behaviour with culture is not an answer.

Arguments of Paul Mellars

The criticisms of Paul Mellars have been very different in character. His work has been concerned with a refinement in the recognition of patterning in the archaeo-logical record and a demand that this patterning be explained. He has further inves-tigated some of the apparent lack of correlation between the patterns of assemblage variation and the variation exhibited by environmental indictors as published. I will try to consider Mellars' scepticism in a very different manner since it is obviously presented in a sincere attempt to increase our understanding of the past.

> By far the strongest argument against a purely functional interpretation of Mousterian industries in Southwest France is provided by evidence from the relative chronology of three of the major industrial variants—the Ferrassie, Quina and M.A.T. groupings of Bordes' Taxonomy. The evi-dence suggests that in the area under consideration industries belonging to each of these groupings may well be confined to a single, relatively brief span of time, and that contrary to earlier beliefs, the time ranges occupied by these variants may not have overlapped to any appreciable degree. (Mellars 1970:76)

Mellars, then, has pointed out that the variants of the Mousterian are not randomly distributed temporally; and Bordes has shown that they are not randomly distributed spatially (1970:73). These demonstrations mark the beginning of the recognition of some patterning in the bewildering array of Mousterian variability. My impression is that a clustering of cases of Typical Mousterian is demonstrable for much of Würm I in the French sequence. Mellars may be correct in suggesting that, at least on the basis of the sample available, a clustering of Ferrassie followed by Quina variants is demonstrable for the first half of the Würm II oscillation. Of all the variants, Den-ticulate seems to exhibit the least tendency of temporal cluster. Bordes has long recognized some temporal significance in variations in the M.A.T. (Mousterian of Acheulean Tradition), and further noted its clustering at the beginning and the end of Würm I, II sequence. The statistical clustering of assemblage types against a temporal reference dimension does not, however, necessitate an evolutionary argu-ment that one form of assemblage was the 'ancester' of another. Similarly, it does not necessarily affect my arguments to any appreciable extent. I anticipate some patterning in the assemblage variability, although I do not anticipate the same patterns to be demonstrable from different regions, and I do not anticipate an exclusive sequential arrangement of all the variability. The clustering of Charentian—like Mousterian—in the early phases of the Near Eastern sequence as opposed to its generalized place-ment in the Southwestern French sequence is a case in point. The lack of apparent temporal patterning currently demonstrable in the Denticulate variant is another relevant case in point. Why do I anticipate some temporal patterning? Because there was a rather significant amount of environmental change occurring during the course of time represented by the Mousterian assemblages in question. I would clearly anticipate some behavioural accommodations. To what degree behavioural change is to be equated with cultural change is as I have pointed out previously something to be investigated, not simply assumed.

The second major point of argument made by Mellars is stated as follows:

> By analogy with the behaviour of recent hunting and gathering societies one might expect that the specialized activities which led to the production of contrasting forms of assemblage would be undertaken at distinct types of settlement location, suited to the exploitation of differing environmental resources . . . In fact, the existing data from Southwest France provide very little evidence for patterning of this kind; not only are the overall geographical distributions of the different Mousterian variants broadly similar, but horizons representing two or more of these variants have frequently been encountered on precisely the same sites . . . The outstanding example of this is provided by the sequence at Combe-Grenal in which all five of the major Mousterian groupings . . . occur within a single stratigraphic column. (Mellars 1970:77)

There are seemingly two points to be discussed in answer to this argument. First, Mellars is incorrect in asserting that the overall distribution of Mousterian assemblage types as recognized by Bordes exhibit the same 'overall geographical distributions'. My own experience contradicts this point and certainly Bordes has amassed data which are directly contrary to this position.

> Some territories seem to have been occupied for very long times by the same type of Mousterian. In Charente, the M.A.T. is not quite unknown, but rare, while the Charentien seems to be almost the absolute master. The Combe-Grenal region seems to have been occupied throughout Würm I by Typical Mousterian, with the exception of a very brief incursion of Denticulate Mousterian . . . . In Provence . . . territorial continuities seem very strong, and the M.A.T. is unknown. (Bordes and Bordes 1970:73)

I might add that on the Paris plain, Typical, Denticulate and Ferrassie are most abundant with Quina all but absent. Other cases of the differential distribution of the recognized types could be cited which are contrary to Mellars' assertion. Secondly, Mellars appears to ignore the evidence of environmental changes when asserting that single sites yield stratigraphically arranged examples of the different variants. By citing Combe-Grenal Mellars leaves himself open; my analysis of that stratigraphic sequence will show a remarkable association between marked changes in the environment and changes in the composition of assemblages. In general there is a good correspondence between the stabililty of the environment and the stability of the assemblage form. I do not wish to imply that there is a casual relationship between the form of the environment and the form of the assemblage, only that the utility of a given location for particular forms of human use is modified with changes in the environment. During periods of roughly similar environments, a given location is utilized in roughly similar ways, although other contemporary locations in the same area may be utilized in different ways depending upon the particular characteristics of the location in the context of the economic geography of the groups represented.

I conclude that Mellars' second set of arguments is undermined by misinformation about the character of geographical variation in the frequency of occurrence of recognized Mousterian variants, and by his failure to consider the dynamics of environment as a conditioning factor in the occurrence of different Mousterian variants.

The third argument presented by Mellars against a 'functional' view of assemblage variability has to do with the flaking techniques used in the manufacture of tools. Mellars argues that there is a correspondence between the forms of the assemblage and the techniques used in production, suggesting that such a correspondence is 'more suggestive of stylistic than functional patterning within the material' (1970:80). I question whether this type of correspondence can be demonstrated.

Bordes long ago pointed out that the Denticulate variant was known in four different forms with regard to the index of Levallois debitage, index of faceting, and variations between real and essential indexes. At that time Bordes recognized a Denticulate Mousterian of Levalloisian facies and with Levallois debitage; one with non-Levallois debitage but with a high index of faceted platforms; and a non-Levallois, non-faceted variant (Bordes 1963:45–6). Such variability clearly indicates that at least for the Denticulate Mousterian there is no necessary correspondence between the type of Mousterian as described by the content of the assemblage and the degree of faceting on the butt of flakes or the degree that Levallois technique was being used.

Bordes further contradicts Mellar's arguments directly:

> It is interesting to note that some assemblages, Quina by their Quina index, are assigned to Ferrassie because of their debitage (very Levallois) and conversely some assemblages, Quina by their debitage, have a Quina index which puts them in the Ferrassie type. [1970:71]

Thus I must conclude that Mellars' third argument is presented on the basis of a poor understanding of the character of variability exhibited by Mousterian materials. In way of further comment I must point out that my original work and the work currently under way (which attempts to test the degree that properties can be anticipated to exist if some behavioural model of the past is employed) are in no way directed toward the explanation of variation in technique. I have been working almost exclusively with the content of assemblages as measured by Bordes' type list; my attention has not been directed toward understanding the patterns of variation in technique which clearly cross-cut the recognized Mousterian variants as opposed to corresponding with them as Mellars has argued.

The fourth major point presented as evidence against the utility of my approaches is a very fascinating one and one to which I will return with some additional comments later.

Mellars points out that

> It is important to remember that an exclusively functional interpretation of Southwest French Mousterian industries would carry with it the implication that the behaviour of the Middle Palaeolithic communities who occupied this region was substantially different from that of the succeeding Upper Palaeolithic populations in the same area. [1970:80]

This argument is documented by asserting that research has failed to reveal 'any appreciable variations with the Upper Palaeolithic assemblages of this region which demonstrably reflect functional variability of the "interlocational" form' (1970:80). He goes on to suggest that all recognized variability is 'unquestionably of chronological and/or "cultural" significance.'

I don't know exactly how to answer this point since I find it self-contradictory.

For instance, alterations between Aurignacian and Lower Perigordian are now clearly documented in the Dordogne. If Mellars is referring to the properties of industrial alternation seen in the Musterian as the criteria for recognizing 'functional variability of the "inter-locational" form', than he is clearly in error. Similarly I might point out that the once supposedly clear chronological succession of Perigordian Va, b and c has been challenged by well-documented excavations at Flageolet (Rigaud 1971). I do not wish necessarily to suggest that such variability may ultimately be referable to 'functional variation' although it is a possibility. I only wish to point out that Mellars' generalizations regarding the character of variability in the upper palaeolithic may be questioned on empirical grounds.

Now to the more important question and the one to which I feel Mellars is referring. I would agree that there is a much greater degree of temporal patterning demonstrable in the upper palaeolithic than is currently demonstrable for the Mousterian, in spite of Mellars' arguments to the contrary. Secondly, I am of the opinion that this contrast does point to major organizational differences between middle and upper palaeolithic cultural systems. At present I am confident that at least part of the contrast derives from the character of the typologies utilized for evaluating variability in the two periods. Bordes' tool typology for the middle palaeolithic is demonstrably of wide applicability. It is equally useful for summarizing materials from North Africa, the Near East, Central Europe, and even China, as Bordes has demonstrated. By way of contrast, when the standard 'type list' used for upper palaeolithic materials in the southwest of France is applied to materials from areas distant from the region itself, substantial modifications are necessary to accommodate its typological features to areas outside of southwestern France. One might conclude from this that (a) the middle and upper palaeolithic typologies are measuring substantially different kinds of variability, or (b) there is a contrast in the character of variability between the middle and upper palaeolithic. Regardless of the position taken, the upper palaeolithic and the middle palaeolithic are clearly different as they are currently known through typological valuations. Thus, this difference is in no way an argument against explanatory attempts which demand that a difference be recognized. At best it is an excellent argument against an attempt to argue that variability in both is to be understood in the same terms (the position of those favouring a 'cultural' interpretation of the variability in both).

It is my personal opinion that the upper palaeolithic typology is a compound instrument for measurement which incorporates as equal units characteristics reflecting stylistic as well as functional features. Since taxonomic priority is generally given to features believed to be most discriminating temporally, as in the case of the old Perigordian V sequence, we more often see a temporal patterning in the taxonomic variants. In the middle palaeolithic such monitors of temporal variation are difficult to identify and priority for taxonomic purposes is given to numerical superiority as in the distinction between Denticulate vs. Charentian, etc. I suggest that the middle palaeolithic typology incorporates few if any stylistically significant characteristics and is therefore a better instrument for monitoring pure behavioural variation; whereas the upper palaeolithic typology incorporates both and therefore monitors simultaneously behavioural and organizational variation at the ethnic level. This position leads us back to the original question: does our difficulty in identifying characteristics which exhibit clear temporal clustering for the middle palaeolithic reflect major differences between the middle palaeolithic and the upper palaeolithic? My opinion is that it does and thus far I have been unconvinced that patterned 'stylistic' variability has been demonstrated in the archaeological record prior to the upper palaeolithic. This is not to say that variability does not exist in the particular characteristics of shape, size and manufacturing procedure, which we have learned are frequently of stylistic significance; nevertheless, the demonstration that this variability exhibits any directional patterning is thus far lacking to my satisfaction.

I would argue contrary to Mellars and suggest that there are major differences between the middle and upper palaeolithic as currently known and that these differences demand explanation.

The final argument which Mellars offers has to do with the recognition that marked environmental changes occurred during the course of Mousterian occupation of southwestern France. He further suggests that because of this, one would expect on purely *a priori* grounds that some chronological patterning might be demonstrable. This is exactly the point which I made in answer to his second argument. Here we agree, but to what degree this expectation is an argument against a 'functional' interpretation of interassemblage variability is quite unclear to me.

After Mellars discusses the problem of Mousterian variability in southwest France, he more specifically addresses himself to the published results of my students and myself on the problem of interassemblage variability in the Near East and Spain. Mellars' criticisms of these published works will be taken up point by point.

1. *In the first place one may challenge the initial assumption that the groupings of total types which constitute the different factors represent functional 'tool kits'* (Mellars 1970:83).

Mellars goes on to argue that an alternative interpretation might be that they represent 'associated [tools] for cultural rather than functional reasons.' He then proceeds to suggest that if a factor analysis were done of upper palaeolithic assemblages the results would be factors which grouped the tools most diagnostic of each recognized phase of cultural systematics in the region. He concludes that to interpret such 'factors' as tool kits would not accord with our understanding of the assemblages in question. With this I totally agree. The point at issue is whether or not this is a relevant argument. I would say that it is not. Clearly if one were to perform a factor analysis and the factor scores for a given factor were to exhibit substantial temporal clustering, one might reasonably investigate the proposition that the factor isolated was of cultural chronological significance. However, the actual results of the Near Eastern analysis, of the Spanish analysis, and of my unpublished analysis of the Combe-Grenal materials from southwestern France *do not* demonstrate any discrete temporal clustering for the factors isolated. On the other hand, there is some statistical clustering of factors corresponding nicely with directional changes in the environment, particularly in the southwest data. To account for the factor groupings in cultural terms would demand (a) equating each factor with an independent cultural tradition of which there are fourteen represented in the materials from Combe-Grenal, and (b) visualizing a situation in which these cultural traditions blended and hybridized in a manner unrelated directly to the time sequence or to the demonstrated changes in the environment. In short, the temporal patterning envisioned for the hypothetical upper paleolithic factors is clearly not demonstrable in the analysed cases of the Mousterian, nor is it demonstrable for the correspondence between their presence and the currently recognized types of Mousterian. I fail then to find any support of Mellars' position.

2. If one accepts . . . that the factors do represent tool-kits . . . the essential problem here is to decide how far the separate factors represent different, and how far similar activities.

This problem—that of imparting significance to observations made on the archaeological record—is the essential problem of archaeology and is not unique to the use of any given technique. Pointing it out as a problem is in no way a criticism of any given technique used for looking at the archaeological record. I can only paraphrase Mellars' conclusions as follows: until more reliable evidence is available concerning the particular functions for which Mousterian tools were intended, the problem of deciding how far the different 'tool-kits' represent similar and how far dissimilar *cultures* will remain without any satisfactory solution.

The final point of Mellars' arguments to which I will address myself is a curious one in which he makes the major point of my argument and then tries to use it against me! He argues:

> If it could be demonstrated by factor analysis or other means that all of the variability displayed by assemblages can be accounted for entirely by variations in the activities undertaken in the different horizons, it is difficult to see why this should rule out the possibility that the different types of assemblage were manufactured by distinct ethnic groups. All that one could logically infer would be that this particular line of inquiry had failed to reveal evidence for such ethnic differentiation . . . . To infer that because two assemblages appear to reflect rather different economic activities they must have been produced by the same human group would seem a curious non-sequitur. (1970:84)

With which argument I concur. I defy Mellars or anyone else to produce a reference documenting any opinion offered by me as to the nature of the ethnic organization of human groups responsible for the variability in the Mousterian. I have only asserted that the typology, an instrument for measurement, was monitoring primarily activity variation and not stylistic variability. In the absence of any instrument for measuring ethnic affinity, there is no way of evaluating the ethnic character of the groups responsible for the behavioural variability documented. On the other hand, the ability to demonstrate a strong identity in the patterns of covariation between identical sets of tools among diverse sets of assemblage types seems to me to be strong evidence that the patterns of use for the mutually covariant tool forms were similar in a variety of associated contexts. That does appear to me to be clear evidence that at least in this aspect of culture the units represented were very similar. The degree that they thought of themselves as members of a consciously recognized community is something which I cannot see any evidence for or against at the present time. In short, the variability documented in the archaeological record prior to the upper palaeolithic appears to lack any significance whatsoever with regard to the ethnic composition of groups. Could it be that ethnicity as we think of it was not yet a part of the cultural environment of man?

Arguments of François Bordes

In attempting to answer the criticisms of Bordes I am dealing with a very different kind of opponent. If Desmond Collins argues from a position of ignorance as to the character of my arguments and Mellars argues from a position lacking a clear understanding of the character of variability in the Mousterian itself, François Bordes argues from a position of strength. He has an unquestionable knowledge of the Mousterian and a well-informed understanding of my argument. Disagreements may then take us into very different and more profitable fields of discussion.

I will try to clarify some of the differences between Bordes and myself. I once stated that:

> in view of the demonstrated alternation of industries, one must envision a perpetual movement of culturally distinct peoples, never reacting to our coping with their neighbours. Nor do they exhibit the typically human characteristics of mutual influence and borrowing. Such a situation is totally foreign, in terms of our knowledge of *sapiens* behaviour. (Binford and Binford 1966:240)

Bordes answers this point by referring to demonstrated 'traditions' defined currently as having great integrity over long periods of time. If one accepts the demonstrated differences between assemblages as of ethic significance, then he is correct in pointing out that contemporary assemblages of different form are documented. The crucial point not faced by Bordes is whether documented stability and/or contemporaneous variability refer to ethnic distinctions. In his answers, Bordes clearly assumes that they do. I make no such assumption. Our difference then is over the *assumed* significance of variability, a point to which I will return.

In further arguing against the proposition I have set forth, Bordes makes an impressive case against one of my assumptions as to the character of life during middle palaeolithic times. Crucial to my model of the past is the proposition that man relied strongly on mobility as a major strategy in his subsistence practices. This mobility would have insured that activities were differentially performed not only in space, but through a seasonal cycle in varying combinations. This differential performance would insure that a complicated set of associations of tools related to the spatially and temporally differentiated activities performed would remain. Bordes points out that Bouchud's (1966) study of reindeer teeth and antlers from a number of Mousterian locations leads him to conclude that the sites were occupied in many cases on a year-round basis. If this finding were upheld my position would clearly be damaged. On the basis of the data available to him, Bordes is clearly justified in rejecting my position. At this point I must either accept defeat or offer very powerful evidence that the conclusions of Bouchud might be reasonably doubted.

I would like first to point out that for purposes of evaluating the season of death for the reindeer studied, Bouchud relied exclusively on the data from teeth. Antlers were not systematically considered. Bouchud makes use of two kinds of information for purposes of determining month of death of the reindeer represented in the Mousterian levels which he studied. First, Bouchud found from his study of a large sample of archaeologically recovered mandibles that the overall configuration in the increasing evidence of wear on teeth was amenable to arrangement into a continuum. He was able to correlate certain patterns of increasing attrition on teeth with the sequence of permanent tooth eruption. In order to convert these demonstrable properties of teeth into a usable scale for evaluating the month of death several facts are necessary and one very important assumption.

First it is necessary to know whether all reindeer are born at the same time, and second when birth is likely to occur. On the basis of available data drawn from studies of Siberian animals, one can clearly state that these animals exhibit a definite birth cycle, such that the vast majority of the births occur about the same time and this is generally during the latter part of May and the early part of June. Already we have introduced a problem of population statistics. All births are not simultaneous, and there is variability from year to year in the exact period of birth. Bouchud assumes for purposes of his analysis that *all* births are simultaneous, and regular from year to year. The next crucial point in Bouchud's analysis is the maturational dating of the period of permanent tooth eruption. For instance, Bouchud adopts an estimate of 27 months as the elapsed maturational time for the completed eruption of the pre-molars. Recent studies of Alaskan Caribou show that complete eruption may occur as early as 22 months after birth, and as late as 26 months with an average completed eruption time of 24 months (Skoog 1968, 74). Two points are of significance: (a) actual field sampling revealed a span of four months over which eruption might occur, and Bouchud assumed that it was simultaneous for all individuals; (b) Bouchud was off three months in his estimate of mean eruption time ensuring that teeth from the same animal killed on the same date would be tabulated in two different months since his estimates of eruption time for the second molar were accurate. Further com-pounding the problem are his estimates for the first and third molar. He estimated three months for the first molar where current data shows that four months is the best mean estimate with a range of two months. The third molar has a mean completed eruption age of twenty-five months from birth with a range of six months. Bouchud again estimated 24 months and assumed a simultaneous eruption date for all indi-viduals. These errors insure that a single animal (two and a half yers old) killed in November would be tabulated on Bouchud's scales as evidence for animals killed by premolars in September, third molar in October, second molar in November, and first molar in December. Since Bouchud was tabulating isolated teeth, in the main, and not mandibles, quite clearly his errors in eruption time for the different teeth ensure that 'evidence' for continuous occupation will be accumulated. Each diagnostic tooth group from a single individual will yield a different estimate of the month of death spanning the three months before and one month after the actual death. Add to the above error the error arising from the fact of demonstrable individual variability in eruption time and we are further assured of a continuous distribution.

To complicate the picture further, Bouchud made the assumption, since he could demonstrate a continuous sequence of attrition on teeth, that attrition proceeded at a constant rate. It was this assumption which made it possible for him to assign a month of death to fully erupted permanent teeth. Two facts are of importance here: (a) current research shows that rates of attrition are not constant throughout the year, varying particularly with the character of the diet. Most attrition occurs when sedges are a major component of the diet, which among the animals currently under study is during the late summer and fall. Attrition seems to be all but absent during the winter months as does growth in teeth (Skoog 1968, p. 70). Although attrition may appear as a morphological continuum, the assumption that it proceeds at a continuous and constant rate is not justified. This unjustified assumption stands behind Bouchud's ageing scale for tooth wear. Thus, we may anticipate that these age estimates for month of death based on that scale are certain to be inaccurate. This would be particularly true for animals dated to the winter months since both degree of tooth development and the character of attrition is arrested during the winter. Animals in early March appear very much as they did in late October. The compounding of all this error, and its differential distribution, ensured by the fact Bouchud was independently estimating the month of death from premolars, 1st, 2nd and 3rd molars, as well as the attrition on premolar milk teeth, with all five scales then being summed and a mean presented, ensures that the data will be continuously distributed around the year except in cases where near identical individuals make up a very small sample.

Thus I feel quite confident in dismissing Bouchud's analysis as conclusive that the Mousterian sites studied were occupied on a year-round basis. In fact I am confident that a re-analysis, making use of populational approaches and the refined data now available on periods of tooth eruption and the character of the attrition process, would demonstrate conclusively that they were indeed occupied exclusively on a short-term basis.

Bordes likes to point out that many of the layers are thick and frequently appear to have accumulated over a long period of time. He argues: 'We should then presuppose a kind of covenant between Mousterian tribes, reserving such and such a cave for summer activities and some other one for winter activities' (Bordes and de Sonneville-Bordes 1970:66). This is an old idea between Bordes and me and was expressed in jest in the cartoon on p.xi, presented to me in good humour in 1968. The difficulty is that I have never argued that each of the four types of Mousterian as known in Bordes' assemblage typology was either a single activity or a single and consistent combination of activities. I anticipate some differentiation in behaviour and hence in assemblage forms which should show seasonal correlates, yet I am not at all convinced that such correlations would be with the most frequent forms such as scrapers and denticulates, which currently tend to serve for discriminating between the different types of Mousterian assemblage. Secondly, the consistent utilization of a single location over a long period of time for essentially the same purposes does not seem to me to require 'covenant', since unlike Bordes I do not picture the territory utilized differentially to the advantage of the occupants. That there should be a consistency in the way it is utilized sometimes spanning a long period of time does not appear surprising, and I would expect such consistency to be disrupted only in the face of environmental change which would tend to modify the utility of locations for particular use.

Bordes has pointed out, and quite justifiably, that many of the kinds of location among which we might expect some differentiation in activities on strictly *a priori* grounds are rare or unknown in southwestern France for the Mousterian. He has further pointed out that there are documented cases where very similar assemblage forms are known from open as well as cave locations (Bordes and de Sonneville-

Bordes 1970:68). He argues that 'the difference of type of site, and therefore, the-oretically at least, of activities, does not transform one type of Mousterian into another.' This is very true; however, I have no way of knowing at this time what the determinants of different activities were during the Mousterian and therefore no way of evaluating the degree that the difference between cave and open locations might be correlated in a consistent manner with activity differentiation. If this is true for the same general geographic area, it is certainly true for locations as topographically and ecologically different as the areas around Sarlat and Bergerac.

Bordes has warned against the dangers of ethnographic comparisons pointing out that the Mousterian peoples of southwestern France were not Eskimos or Australian Aborigines. This is a point worthy of comment and one in the context of which Bordes himself has offered some interesting arguments. I have recently been studying the hunting strategies of the Nunamiut Eskimos[2] as a means of learning something about what it is like to live in a tundra environment—the degree that different problems present themselves for solution as a function of seasonal changes and the particular strategies followed in hunting caribou. My motive for undertaking this research were directly related to my work on the Mousterian, particularly that of the climax of the Würm II cold period as recorded in the pollen profiles from Combe-Grenal. These Eskimos are currently sedentary, a condition postulated by Bordes to have characterized the Mousterian peoples.

Without going into all the fascinating details of this research, I would like to point out some interesting facts. I have accompanied the Nunamiut hunters on practically all of their different kinds of hunting and subsistence activities. I have noted what they in fact do on these locations and in turn what debris remains for the archaeologist. The most striking fact to emerge from this research is that with regard to artifacts *per se* there is little correlation between what is done and the artifacts remaining. Their technology is what I will call an almost exclusively *curated* technology, in which a tool once produced or purchased is carefully curated and transported to and from locations in direct relationship to the anticipated performance of different activities. Under such an efficient system of technoeconomy the archaeological record is more properly considered a record of the organization of entropy as opposed to the orga-nization of the ongoing activity structure of the group. Almost any item has a different life expectancy and will be discarded more in terms of its estimated utility for future use than as any direct reflection of its context of use or importance in the ongoing technology. Over time there is an accumulation of archaeologically relevant debris on sites which are clearly different in terms of observed activities. Nevertheless, taking a strict archaeological perspective the contents of these sites are grossly similar in that the most common items on all are generally similar and are those items most expend-able, of least importance is the ongoing technological system. Plotting these assem-blages by means of cumulative graphs shows that they exhibit, in general, less variability in content that might be currently demonstrable between many different assemblages from the upper palaeolithic assignable to a given 'cultural phase'. Loca-tions which are demonstrably very different from the behavioural standpoint are only differentiated archaeologically by items which are rare and almost always broken and modified heavily through use. The other context of differentiation is the erratic occurrence of rare items in mint condition which were cached in anticipation of future use and as a result of unanticipated events were never recovered. These generalizations apply to the fabricated tools; however, they do not apply to the immediate byproducts of the activities performed, such as parts of animals differentially discarded, or consumed as a function of the logistics of hunting. The differences in the sites are clearly reflected and very marked in the differential remains of consumption and the processing of animals in the context of the logistics of getting the animal from its location of kill to its location of consumption.

Returning to the patterns of variation in tools for a moment, it is clear that the character of the archaeological record and the degree that it is a direct reflection of the activities performed at any given location will vary inversely with the degree that there is an efficient economizing techno-logistics system in operation. The more that tools are curated, transported, and preserved for future use, the less correspondence there will be between the behavioural context of their use and their associated occurrence in the archaeological record. Similarly, there will be an inverse relationship between their importance in the ongoing behavioural system and their frequency in the archaeological record. Differential frequencies between archaeologically observable classes of artifacts, all of which are curated and maintained as a continuous part of the technological tool kit of individuals or groups, will reflect directly the different replacement rates between the various tool classes and not their importance in the ongoing behavioural system. There may be some correlation between replacement rates and the frequency with which things are used; however, this would be greatly modified by the degree that different raw materials with different stress properties were employed in their manufacture.

Another observation made among the Nunamiut which may be of some significance is that the degree that conscious stylistic variation occurs in the products of craft production appears to vary inversely with the degree that the item produced is considered expendable. Items produced expediently and discarded in the immediate context of use exhibit less investment from the individual standpoint and hence have less of the identity of the manufacturer expressed through individualized and group conscious 'stylistic' characteristics. On the other hand, items which are produced with the clear anticipation of long-term use and long-term association between the manufacturer or others for whom he is serving as the producer, exhibit a greater tendency to range in patterned stylistic expression and formal diversity. Thus I would anticipate that the best material markers of ethnic identity might well be found in items curated and preserved for relatively long periods of utilitarian life within the technological system. These of course would be items which were relatively rare in assemblages for the reasons outlined above.

Bordes has pointed out that the analysis by Carmel White and Nicholas Peterson (1969) of materials from Australia has revealed a dichotomy between sites linked to seasonal occupation of the plateau and coastal plain. Bordes correctly points out their findings as follows:

> The main tool types present at Tyimede are similar to the range found in the plain sites, including points, small scraper-adzes, utilized flakes and edge ground axes, but the Tyimede assemblages

differ in one major way from their plain counterparts, for many of the stone tools here seem to have been manufactured in situ; the overall ratio of tools to waste flakes is 1 to 25 (in the plain sites, the ratio is 1 to 5). (Bordes and de Sonneville-Bordes 1970:72, quoting from White and Peterson 1969)

Bordes continues to argue as follows:

> Roughly speaking, we have to do with two sites belonging to the same culture, one in which tools were frequently made on the spot, and in the other less so. In our graphs, where we do not count flakes, even utilized, with the 'true' tool, the two sites, following what the authors say, would very probably yield comparable diagrams, and we would never interpret them as different industries. Completely different is the case of the Mousterian facies, where, in the first place, we have to do with semi-sedentary people present all the year round at the site, and, in the second place, we are concerned with differences in the tool types and their proportions, which are sometimes very strong. (Bordes and de Sonneville-Bordes 1970:72)

In this argument I fear Bordes has violated his own warning against the use of ethnographic comparisons. He has cited the Australian data and the apparent lack of differentiation in the archaeological record among differentiated locations as evidence that the differentiation noted in the Mousterian could not refer to differentiated activities. Any student of Australian technology will readily characterize their technology as a highly efficient system in which tools are curated, transported, and preserved. As White and Paterson found, the only items directly to reflect differentiated activities are the immediate byproducts of those activities—manufacturing debris—not the tools used. This is of course what we observed among the Nunamiut. Bordes in another argument points out a most important point offering strong support for my contentions. He states: 'In the caves or shelters, as well as on the open-air sites, one usually finds not only the tools, but also the cores, flakes, chips, etc., which indicate that fabrication and *utilization* of the tools took place in the same area.' In short, Bordes argues that the Mousterian tools were in the main expediently manufactured and used. This is clearly not the case among the Australians or the Nunamiut where their tools are curated, preserved and transported. Clearly then, under conditions of expedient tool production and use, we would expect the variations in tools more directly to reflect differences in the activities performed. Bordes in his citation of the Australian data has failed to consider the big differences between the Australian Aborigines and the Mousterian.

Conclusions and a Summary of the 'Functional Argument'

In the discussion of Mellars' criticisms, I introduced the idea that ethnicity may not have always been a component of the cultural environment of man. This suggestion is in need of further clarification since it bears directly on one of the assumptions which served operationally in the context of the original statement of the 'Functional Argument'. In the context of the history of the development of the approaches and arguments being discussed under the rubric of the Functional Argument the initial question which I asked myself was, what is Bordes' taxonomy measuring? It is quite easy to defend the position, since any taxonomy is an instrument for measurement, that the answer to the question, what does a given taxonomy measure? is central to prehistory. Bordes in personal conversation and in a discussion of the principles employed in the development of his middle palaeolithic 'type list' refers to (a) variations in the orientation, and (b) variations in the form of the working edge, as being the two major dimensions along which variants are grouped into tool types. It seems reasonable to proceed as if such variation may bear some relationship to the way tools were used and the particular technical acts which they enhanced. In short the middle palaeolithic typology was designed to differentiate fabricated stone forms into taxa on the basis of properties potentially related directly to their differential design as implements employed to enhance the transfer of energy from a source—a human— to some other object upon which work was being performed. A reasonable suggestion as to what Bordes' taxonomy is measuring is the character of differentiation in the design of tools as such. If true then one might reasonably expect that variations in their frequency and patterns of association might be referable to the character of the work being performed and hence the context of the activities in the course of which they were used. Archaeologists and the layman alike have long been aware that the character of the morphology and the distribution of material items among contemporary peoples varied also in terms of social variables. It has been this observation that has led archaeologists to make use of variability in material items as a clue to the social arrangements of persons in the past. I was led to reject the relevance of this observation to the tools of the middle palaeolithic for a number of reasons. First, the character of variability as documented for the Mousterian was manifest in different proportional frequencies between similar tool forms in different locational contexts. Among contemporary peoples ethnicity is more frequently directly demonstrable through morphological variations between different localized groups with respect to roughly anologous functional classes of tools. It is difficult to see how a denticulate is a functional equivalent of a Quina scraper.

More important however is the recognition that for variability in tools and other material items to be of direct cultural significance in the sense of having recognized symbolic significance, this variability must be cognitively recognizable. If an item is to serve to express conscious ethnic, or individual identity, it must be something which is immediately and directly perceived. I find it difficult to imagine that something as remote from reality as a scraper index could have direct ethnic or social symoblic significance.

The argument, as generally presented, in which variability in the Mousterian is viewed as 'cultural', and hence indicative of different traditions, must make an interesting assumption, namely that the cultural background and hence tradition which refers to the design of tools is essentially identical for all recognized 'cultural traditions'. This is necessary in that the morphological variants of tools, the types, are for purposes of the taxonomy identical in the different traditions. It is variability in the proportional frequencies of these similar morphological forms which is said to distinguish the traditions. One must envision a pattern of behaviour culturally transmitted which ensures that once a site is occupied the occupants busy themselves with producing and discarding a wide variety of tool forms in a set and traditional pattern of proportional frequencies. Such an expectation must either deny any relationship between these items and the character and magnitude of work performed in the context of which they would be used—or a lack of variability in the work performed by members of a similar tradition. The latter proposition, when pushed, seems to be that preferred by traditional archaeologists. They argue that tradition A preferred to do one thing or tradition B preferred to do something else if some demonstration of a relationship seems forthcoming between frequencies of tools and the character of work performed. The specificity of the ecological niche which one would have to imagine if the tools were in fact tools and yet there was no variation in the character of work performed by persons representative of the different traditions would directly militate against these traditions exhibiting any long duration in the face of environmental change or any common distribution across a variety of environmental zones viewed geographically. Of course we know that just the reverse is demonstrable. Since we have already shown that we would have to postulate similar cultural traditions for the context of tool design but different ones for the context of tool association, it seems more reasonable to recognize that social and ethnic considerations do not seem to be operative at the level of tool design, since typologically identical forms are demonstrably distributed over half the inhabited world during the middle palaeolithic. To demand that they are being expressed in a form which is not cognitively apparent, e.g. proportional frequencies varying between locations in identical tool forms, clearly goes beyond any understanding of the functions of culture and its dependence upon cognitively recognizable expediently assigned meanings to form—i.e. symbols.

Thus I made the operational assumption that Bordes' typology was discriminating fabricated forms with respect to their properties as tools, and that explanations as to their variations in frequency must be referable to differences in the character of work performed with their aid. Insofar as I may be successful in demonstrating this, I will have demonstrated that ethnicity and other social considerations are not being monitored at all by our current instruments for measurement, our taxonomies of the middle palaeolithic.

The objection may be raised—There are differences in the morphology of tools, in their shape as among handaxes, or their metrical properties, etc. How can you say there is not stylistic variability of social significance? I am not saying that there is no variability or that there is no variability which from a modern perspective we might expect to have social significance. I am saying that the variability demonstrable for the earlier time ranges has not been demonstrated to pattern in such a way as to be suggestive of its having social significance. Even if spatial clustering at a contemporary time period in these morphological properties, or even some limited directionality through time in patterns of morphological variability were recognizable, patterning may well be referable directly to the operation of stochastic processes such as 'drift' (Binford 1963), or others not thus far explored. Such patterning may well inform us about the degrees of isolation between population segments but in no way informs us as to their being partitioned into consciously recognized ethnic units or culturally bounded social units. My original hypothesis was then offered regarding the character of the middle palaeolithic typology. It was proposed that it was measuring formal variability that reflected exclusively tool design. In order to test this proposition a number of test implications had to be deduced and a series of bridging arguments offered. These were developed as follows:

If Bordes' typology is measuring varying degrees of functional differentiation among tools, then assemblages defined in terms of summary tool frequencies must be compounds resulting from the various differentiated work units—activities—in the context of which the functionally differentiated tools were used.

If this is true, then we should be able to identify organized units–clusters of mutually co-variant tools, which maintain the same pattern of organization across a variety of assemblage types.

This was essentially as far as my basic reasoning had gone at the time of the analysis of the Mousterian material from the Near East (Binford and Binford 1966).

The results of these preliminary studies were rewarding in that in experimenting with techniques which would allow us to isolate units of organization within and among assemblages, multivariate analytical techniques seemed to provide the appropriate tools. The application of these techniques did in fact result in the recognition of mutually co-variant groups of tools which maintained their organizational integrity across the recognized types of Mousterian assemblage as defined by Bordes. Two important points were established in these preliminary studies. The first has been demonstrated in print and I am prepared to demonstrate even more forcefully in a forthcoming publication, that the assemblage types as defined currently for the Mousterian are *not* homogeneous units when analyzed into components of mutually covariant sets of tools. I quote from my original results:

> Do the types of the Mousterian assemblages isolated by Bordes always correspond to the same combinations of factors? Our response here is negative. The total assemblage from Shubbabiq was classified by Bordes' techniques as Typical Mousterian and was found to have strong resemblances to Level 7 of Jabrud. However, when the two assemblages are analyzed in terms of factor content, they are seen to be quite distinct. The material from Shubbabiq is dominated by Factor I, with Factors II and III as minor contributors, while Level 7 from Jabrud was primarily controlled by Factor V, with minor conributions from Factors I and IV. (Binford and Binford 1966:287)

It is this failure of correspondence between the assemblage taxonomy when total assemblages are compared, using discriminatory criteria weighted in favour of commonly occurring forms such as denticulates, scrapers, etc., versus discrimination based on the common presence of tool classes demonstrably related to one another in covariant fashion, which has, I feel, contributed to the failure of researchers to uncover any strong correlations between assemblage types as defined by Bordes and environmental characteristics such as seasonal variation, character of the fauna studied etc. Thus 'tests' of my arguments which are alleged to demonstrate an absence of expected relationships between assemblage variability and the enviornment conducted with the current taxonomy of assemblages are clearly irrelevant to my arguments. I have never said that I had such expectations, only that those sets of tools exhibiting strong patterns of mutual co-variation *across* assemblage variants should be related to consistent features of the environment playing conditioning roles in human behaviour.

The second major point and one to which none of the critics have addressed themselves, is simply that consistent patterns of mutual co-variation as demonstrable between tool classes, crosscut the recognized forms of assemblage variation. This is a fact and not an inference or an interpretation. It is clearly as much a fact as are the summary proportional frequencies of the various tool classes. No critic, other than Bordes, has even acknowledged this fact. Any criticism of the approaches I have taken must seek to destroy the factual character of this observation, and/or offer an alternative explanatory argument with clear test implications. No critic has yet done either, and most have ignored the factual character of my findings.

These factual findings provided me with the confidence to pursue as potentially productive further research aimed at specifying in behavioural terms the contexts in which the observed patterns of mutual co-variation were generated. The obvious place to start was with further study of the Mousterian. With the aid of a grant from the National Science Foundation and the hospitality of François Bordes, I began to study and organize the data from Bordes' excavations at Combe-Grenal with particular emphasis on the fauna, the character of the raw materials used in tool production, the character of the debris, and the data on features such as hearths, etc. These were studied with an eye to the possibility of demonstrating correlations between the components of assemblages shown to vary independently of one another and to crosscut the recognized assemblage types, and indicators of behaviour and the activities related to the subsistence and maintenance of human groups. Quite early in this research it became clear that there was tremendous variability in the nature of the faunal remains present as viewed in terms of anatomical parts as well as in the species present. It was with the aim of gaining some insight into the behavioural contexts within which differential associations of anatomical parts are produced at different locations that I began my research among the Nunamiut Eskimos. Simultaneously a number of critics began to bombard me with arguments drawn largely from upper palaeolithic data or modern ethnographically documented cases. I was uneasy with such arguments, having clearly the intuitive impression that the upper palaeolithic was different in a very relevant manner. I asked myself to what degree is the upper palaeolithic typology apt to be measuring the same thing as the middle palaeolithic typology? My conclusions were that the probability was slight and that stylistic features of cultural significance were being monitored at least in part by the upper palaeolithic typology. However, this answer was not completely satisfying since there were other differences, particularly in the degree that marked variations among assemblages could be demonstrated even if one eliminated from consideration those tool types which apparently were more informative of stylistic or social differences as opposed to those having more direct functional reference. The solution to this problem presented itself in the data obtained from the Nunamiut. A clear relationship exists between the efficiency of the technology (as measured in terms of the utility derived from a tool expressed in terms of the energy expended in its production) and the degree that archaeological remains will reflect the organized entropy of the system versus the organized activities executed in the context of ongoing behaviour. Clearly we can reasonably expect the efficiency of the technology as defined above to exhibit marked variation among different cultural systems and exhibit changes through time, in the direction of increasing efficiency. We can well expect that the very early use of technological means was relatively inefficient and probably characterized by the total expedient manufacture and use of tools. Under such conditions we would expect great variety in assemblage composition which would be directly referable to the activity variation performed at different locations. Systems of the modern era are generally characterized by rather efficient techno-systems such as those of the Nunamiut and the Australian Aborigines. The recognition that technological efficiency as conceived above was a variable phenomenon which might well be expected to exhibit some directional trends in the history of cultural evolution, and that differences in such efficiency might well have profound effects on the character of the archaeological record itself, was a very exciting idea. Taking the implications further, we can deduce a series of consequences for the character of the archaeological record. If technological efficiency is increasing then there should be a concomitant decrease through time in the magnitude of intersite variability at the regional level. Conversely, as technologies become more efficient there should be an increase in inter-regional diversification as manifest in items relatively rare in the total assemblage. These expectations seem to be strikingly realized in the overall character of the palaeolithic.

Almost every time we get new data on living floors of the very early time ranges, we find that they are relatively distinctive and that the growing body of interassemblage comparisons requires more and more complicated forms of systematics to accommodate the variability (for instance, see Mary Leakey, 1967) when summarized in terms of proportional frequencies of tools. Similarly, we find that frequently analogous comparisons take us to locations rarely located in contiguous geographic zones. As we approach more closely the contemporary era, we find more correlation between particular regions and the frequency with which similar tool forms are manifest in assemblage types. Yet consistent associational groupings are seen among areas widely separated geographically where the same forms of tools are being manufactured and used. A good example might be the Mousterian of North Africa versus the Mousterian of southwestern France or Central Europe. Not until the upper palaeolithic, and then probably the later phrases of it, do we find a reduction in intersite variability within a region as measured by proportional frequencies of tools, and increasing regional differentiation as marked by unique tool forms and stylistic variants of analogous tools. The situation of the palaeolithic is well reflected in the character of the archaeologist's systematics. For the early time ranges, more and more argumentation requiring the postulation of 'parallel phyla', and complicated arguments of cultural blending accounting for the variability documented regionally and in broadly contemporary time periods, is the order of the day. My guess is that as more work is done in the Rissian levels and the Acheulean proper, more and more facies will be recognized and more and more parallel phyla will be postulated. On the other hand the systematics of the upper palaeolithic have a very different character. Variability as summarized by proportional frequencies tends to exhibit both temporal and spatial clustering. We must learn numerous regional sequences as we find the systematics of one region rarely applicable to that of another without substantial modification. This same contrast is becoming evident in New World studies as we push back further in time. It has recently been proposed that in South America at the threshold of a knowledge of human occupancy there were seven major traditions, the Edge-Retouched tradition, Burin tradition, Biface tradition, Side Scraper tradition, Fluted Point tradition, Blade tradition and Bi-Point tradition (Lanning 1970). These traditions are recognizable by comparisons in the proportional frequencies of tools between locations and frequently from the same general regions. Needless to say there are many cases of hybrid cultures.

These contrasts seem to cry out for explanation, and at present the only attempts are in the direction of postulating much greater migration and movement of isolated peoples for the earlier time ranges. I suggest that much of this contrast derives from differences in the degree that tools were expediently manufactured or alternatively curated and preserved in anticipation of future use. A corollary of this is the suggestion that the degree of stylistic and artisan investment manifest in products varies directly with the degree that tools are curated and are considered constant parts of a person's equipment for carrying out his roles.

What started out as an unrecognized necessary assumption—namely that the Mousterian tools were expediently used and manufactured, the assertion that organized relationships between tools were directly referable to the ongoing activity structure of the social system represented—turns out with greater understanding to be a variable phenomenon. It is in need of explication before reliable assertions can be made regarding the significance to be attached to variations in inter-locational associational patterns.

Returning then to the specifics of my progress on the 'Mousterian' problem, I am currently working up my data from the Nunamiut on the logistics of hunting and the behavioural contexts in which anatomical parts of animals are directly disposed of at different junctures of the logistics process, from procurement to the final steps of consumption. Since this is a direct disposal process not modified by curating except in a minor way relating to the effectiveness of food preservation techniques, my results should have some direct applicability to the past. I am sufficiently aware of the patterns of variation in the Combe-Grenal data and similar patterns in the Nunamiut data to anticipate (a) that I will be largely successful in specifying with some reliability the behavioural context responsible for the differential frequencies of anatomical parts in the Combe-Grenal assemblages, and (b) that many of the sets of co-variantly related tools will be shown to vary directly with variations in anatomical parts understood from a behavioural perspective. I clearly anticipate that demonstration of tool frequency variation in correlation with other variables referable to the environments as conditioners of behaviour.

To what degree these demonstrations once available for evaluation and criticism will convince my colleagues of the value inherent in the 'functional approach' I cannot predict. Nevertheless, I would like to offer a few general comments on the nature of our science. My arguments have already touched off what I consider to be a healthy and in many ways colourful discussion which goes directly to the basic issues of archaeological science. The current discussion revolves around the problem of *what significance can we as prehistorians justifiably attach to our contemporary observations on the archaeological record.* All our observations are contemporary, only by attaching significance to certain observations can we succeed in referring these observations reliably to the past. If successful at this stage we go on to offer certain propositions about the character of the past by attributing significance to our archaeological observations. The traditional archaeologist made this attribution of significance in terms of conventions which equated measurable differences in the properties of the archaeological record with ethnic differences between peoples in the past. If this were justified, then any taxonomy which consistently employed whatever criteria should yield comparable results varying only in the possible levels of discrimination. Clearly, on this view, the use of different taxonomic devices should never yield incompatible results, since they are all presumably measuring the same thing, possibly varying only in their discriminatory powers. I can clearly demonstrate, however, that a taxonomy generated on the basis of grouping assemblages as alike in terms of their similar organizational properties as measured by demonstrably different sets of co-variantly related tools will be *incompatible* with the taxonomy which groups assemblages on the basis of gross similarities in the proportional frequencies of tools with priority given to frequently occurring forms. Which taxonomy is correct? That is the wrong question to ask, we should concern ourselves with the question of what each is measuring. Both are valid; clearly the differences derive from the different properties of the archaeological record being systematically monitored and hence measured. The demonstration of the valid derivation of incompatible taxonomic evaluations of the archaeological record should make obsolete the glib assumption that we know what significance to attach to taxonomically recognized properties of the archaeological record.

How then do we go about the task of reliably attributing significance to our observations on the archaeological record? The scientific basis for the confident assignation of significance to observations made is the degree that we can refer to law-like propositions for justification. Thus the use of C-14 tests, principles of stratigraphy, etc., all are justifiable by reference to law-like statements in which we may confidently assume the principle of uniformitarianism—the laws operative in the past were the same as those operative at the present. Only when archaeologists address themselves to the difficult task of formulating and testing laws will we be able confidently to ascribe significance to our observations on the archaeological record. I have in this paper offered for testing such a hypothesis of law-like potential regarding the economizing character of the technology and the character of variability in the archaeological record. Operationalizing and verifying this hypothesis would make possible the simultaneous explanation of certain properties of the 'living archaeology' of the Nunamiut and the Australian Aborigines as well as the Mousterian peoples of southwestern France. In addition it would make possible a much greater understanding of the demonstrable contrasts in the lifeways as recorded archaeologically for the peoples of the lower-middle and upper palaeolithic and provide us with explanatory understanding of some of the directional trends demonstrable through this vast span of time.

I would like to suggest that what has been summarized by my critics as the 'functional argument' is really an appeal to archaeologists to explain their observations. This means addressing themselves to the difficult task of determining what our taxonomies are measuring and what demonstrated patterning refers to in the organization of past human systems of adaptation out of which these patterns derive. I never opposed a 'functional' interpretation against a 'cultural' interpretation. I have been attempting to develop and oppose an explanatory against an *interpretation* strategy as to the significance of variability observed in the archaeological record.

Notes

1. British spellings and punctuation have been preserved thoughout, as much as possible.
2. Research supported by the Wenner-Gren Foundation for Anthropological Research and the National Science Foundation.

PART III

The Mousterian Problem: How to Research the Issue

12

1983

Working at Archaeology:
The Debate, Arguments of Relevance,
and the Generation Gap

As was pointed out in Chapters 1 and 8, in the late 1960s I came to the conclusion that we could not test the validity of our dynamic models, our ideas about the details of the dynamic process standing behind patterning in the archaeological record, by investigating the archaeological record. We have seen how this put me in basic disagreement with the popularist literature on "scientific" archaeology.

In one very real sense this conclusion presented an additional problem. Traditional archaeologists had always argued about their models of the past by appeals to primarily archaeological facts. In most cases their arguments appeared quite rational—how could this be? Similarly, the debate and the response of the field to my proposals regarding the meaning to be attached to the forms of Mousterian patterning (see Chapter 9) appeared for the most part rational and in many cases had to be taken seriously. Yet they were frequently arguments about facts of the archaeological record! If we could not test the validity of an argument about dynamics by appeal to statics (in the absence of a prior understanding of the causes for the static—that is, we could not argue post hoc to the meanings of statics), how was it that these arguments appeared rational?

Although there was an early reaction (de Sonneville-Bordes 1966) to the functional argument, most of the debate[1] did not surface in print until the early 1970s, more or less concurrently with the programmatic appeals for the acceptance of a logico-deductive set of tactics in the context of a covering law model of explanation, as discussed earlier.

The Debate and Arguments of Relevance

Two important articles appeared in 1970 (Bordes and de Sonneville-Bordes 1970; Mellars 1970). The main point of Mellars's argument was that the forms of interassemblage variability isolated by Bordes were not generally (a) alternating (see Chapter 24 for a discussion of this property) and (b) tenacious. In short, they were not surprising (see L.R. Binford [1972a] for a discussion of the big and little surprises), but sequent; that is, they chronologically followed one another. If this view could be sustained, then a necessary condition for the function model to be relevant to these facts would not be met. Clearly, if the functional view postulates an internally differentiated system, then the variability thought to refer to such organizational differentiations *within a system* must appear in the archaeological record as essentially contemporary variants, or at least greatly overlapping forms in time. Mellars was arguing that one of the necessary conditions for the relevant application of the interpretative argument was not met by the archaeological facts.

> The remarks made in the preceding sections are *in no sense intended as a general criticism of functional variability in Palaeolithic and Mesolithic assemblages.* . . . It may well be that certain industrial groupings which are at present regarded as distinct "cultures" will eventually prove to be simply economically specialized "facies" of a single culture.
> Nevertheless, the data outlined in the earlier part of this paper *indicate that the application of functional interpretations to lithic assemblages needs to be approached with caution* [Mellars 1970:84-85; emphasis mine].

Mellars went on to point to certain vague characteristics of legitimate problems with the functional argument, not the least of which was this:

> Attention should be drawn to the difficulty of testing hypotheses concerning functional variability in lithic assemblages. In fact, hypotheses expressed in the simple form "assemblages of types A and B were manufactured by a single social group" are virtually incapable of being positively refuted by any kind of archaeological evidence [Mellars 1970:86].

This was a very astute observation, and one with which I was in complete agreement.[2] I might add, however, that it could in my view equally apply to the traditional views of what archaeological observations might mean. We could paraphrase Mellars's comment as follows: A hypothesis that links assemblages of similar form from sites A and B as manufactured by a single culture group is "virtually incapable of being positively refuted by any kind of archaeological evidence." As I saw it, this was the essential challenge to archaeologists. How could we develop a sufficient understanding of archaeological evidence so that we could test and evaluate our ideas about the past as rooted in observations made archaeologically?

As in Mellars's case, Bordes's main criticism was in the form of an argument of relevance. The arguments Bordes gave were somewhat more difficult to see in this form but nonetheless they were of this type. They hinged on the role of ethnographic facts in arguing about the past. Bordes acknowledged, as all traditional archaeologists did, that the patterning in the archaeological record is subject to interpretation. He was aware that it is an act of inference from archaeological observations to statements about the character of the past (Bordes and de Sonneville-Bordes 1970:67).

Relevance refers to the reasoned relationship between one set of ideas and another, or one set of ideas and observations said to implicate or reflect on those ideas. Bordes and de Sonneville-Bordes were arguing more about the relevance of my model of a spatially differentiated cultural system to the data of the Lower and Middle Paleolithic. For instance, they pointed out that kill sites and specialized workshops were generally unknown for the Middle Paleolithic, noting that the "fabrication and utilization of tools" occurred at the same place.

This was a major point made early by Bordes—in his view there was no differentiation between workshops and places where tools were used. He said many times that when we find tool manufacturing debris, we also find the tools that were made. He would then puff on his pipe and say, "They had to use the tools in the same places where they made them. Strange." Bordes saw this as a telling observation relative to my arguments that technologies were organized so that different things were done in different places.[3]

A second point made by Bordes was that in his view culture is emergent, particularly in terms of complexity. He noted that for the Paleolithic a site (a basic cultural unit) was a single place (cave, shelter, open station), whereas such a basic cultural unit in Neolithic times was "more complicated, being a village or hamlet," and in the modern world[4] a cultural unit would be a nation (see Bordes and de Sonneville-Bordes 1970:66-67).

Bordes's third major point was that if organized Paleolithic life was as internally differentiated and responsive to situational conditions as I had suggested, then there was a truly "strange" internal consistency to the deposits in many Mousterian levels (Bordes and de Sonneville-Bordes 1970:68). I had noted this in working with Sally Binford's data from the Near East (L. R. Binford 1972a:188): in thick deposits, there was commonly no difference in composition between lower and upper segments of the deposits (see Chapter 28).

In all cases, the critical observations offered questioned the relevance of my view of the past to the facts I had suggested they covered—specifically, the arguments questioned the relevance of my argument to the data of the Mousterian. They did not question either the reality or the accuracy of my characterization of a cultural system—only the relevance of such a view to the archaeological facts under consideration.

There are several points illustrated by these early debates.

1. Appeal to the archaeological record was not done in the context of testing the accuracy or validity of the explanatory argument itself. Instead such appeals were cast in the form of arguments of relevance, which questioned the degree to which the explanation could be justified as covering the facts or case at issue.[5]

2. In many cases these arguments served as a stimulus to subsequent research and did in fact point to serious and important points in need of investigation.

3. At a more particular level, the challenges of Bordes regarding the relevance of my arguments drawn from contemporary societies and his general skepticism regarding the use of ethnographically warranted arguments underscored the problem of how to use knowledge from the present to illuminate the past.

My response to these debates was to initiate research in the hope of resolving some of the issues raised by the critics. This was not, however, the general reaction of the field.

The reaction among Americanists to the early as well as subsequent argumentative literature was to listen, discuss the points made by the disputants in a kind of high-school debate team frame of reference, and then decide who was right. Little reaction beyond this kind of "choosing up sides" actually took place. Many conventionalists were uninterested, as they perceived my arguments to be light-years away from their data. For them it was simple: Artifacts reflect culture; differences in artifacts therefore reflect differences in culture, and similarities in artifacts reflect similarities in culture. This was thought to be an unassailable truth and statements about the past made in these terms were rooted in the data. My ideas appeared as wild speculations unsupported by the data as they saw it.

> The way French archaeologists reacted to the American New Archaeology is typical of the superficial penetration of foreign ideas. Though many of them had read the writings of L. and S. R. Binford there were no written reactions before 1973. No one expressed the commonly shared feeling of defiance in front of the gap which existed between the theoretical models and the available data [Audouze and Leroi-Gourhan 1981:182].

Others with leanings toward a less conventionalist and a more empiricist view also saw my arguments as wildly divorced from the data. For the more empirically inclined, inference was considered to be a very risky business.

> One reason for archaeology's continued lag as a contributor to culture theory, in spite of great strides in the last ten years, is that we continue to see our *main goal the reconstruction of ancient ethnology*. Since we have so great a handicap to begin with here, *where speculation and inference mix too confusingly for the student who likes to keep his lines of reasoning clear-cut, most archaeologists, if they are concerned with* such matters at all, are fighting a very uphill battle indeed. I think we are overlooking another order of interpretation which is in some ways *much better suited to our data for it is less dependent upon inference*: one can manipulate the artifacts statistically without much concern whether one understands precisely what they originally were, exactly how they were used, and just what they meant to the ancients [Wauchope 1966:19: Emphasis mine].

I was not surprised by many of the "dismissal" reactions. I fully expected them, given the views then current in archaeology. For me, however, the early debates forced an issue that I had not really faced earlier when thinking about testing ideas. My early thoughts had been concerned with testing explanations phrased in the dynamic mode. I had thought about the problems of justifying a particular view of the world (the systemic view) and testing the utility and accuracy about cause and effect as modeled in the context of a dynamic view of the operation of a system. Clearly, there was more to the problem. I was engaged in constructive debate regarding the relevance of my ideas to the facts they were said to explain. I was not arguing about whether my explanatory arguments were accurate or correct, *only whether they were appropriate*. I had begun to consider the problem of relevance as very important by the late 1960s.

> Intuitively established analytical units, whose significance is not specified, can at best be of limited utility in testing hypotheses. For in hypothesis testing we must always be able to justify our observations as relevant measures of the variable identified in the propositions we have formulated [L. R. Binford 1968a:24].

Arguments of the type seen here, arguments of relevance, were a type archaeologists had always mounted. It occurred to me that Raymond Thompson's suggestion that our knowledge of the past rests primarily on an assessment of "the professional competence" (R. H. Thompson 1956:331) of the archaeologist making the reconstruction appeared particularly germane to arguments of relevance. For instance, most of the arguments or criticisms offered against the functional view pointed to facts that I had not discussed or had seemingly failed to consider. In short, they were pointing out the negative analogy between my view of dynamics and the statics implied by that view.

In my previous discussions of analogy, and in most other discussions (see, e.g., R. H. Thompson 1956), emphasis had been placed on the justification of inferences through the citation of positive analogies between ethnographic descriptions and archaeological observations. Here we see the opposite face of the same logic, arguments about the strengths of the *negative analogy*, things that were being suggested as not the same between the cases being compared. If many properties considered critical to the case could be shown to be dissimilar, then the argument from analogy could not be sustained. Viewed in this way, the argument of the Boas group simply asserted that no arguments from ethnographic analogy were justified, because *a critically relevant variable—history*—could not be the same in an ethnographic case and an archaeological case. After all, history separated the two cases! Looking back over the literature of traditional archaeology, it was probably the skill with which various archaeologists had been able to present convincing arguments of relevance that was particularly important for establishing their competence. Most of the time arguments of relevance took the form of pointing out to opponents critically important facts they had overlooked. (I did this in dealing with D. Collins; see Chapter 10.) If this was done well, then the strength of such a presentation reflects directly upon the competence of the opponent, because, after all, they should have known such things! *Here we were involved in an old fashioned archaeological argument.* Was there any way of taking this problem—establishing the relevance of observations to ideas—outside of the logical context of arguments from analogy in which they seemed to be rooted? This particular analysis rendered the problem of the use of ethnographic information in seeking understanding of the past central, in that we not only mounted positive warranting arguments from analogy, but also evaluated arguments once advanced by arguing about the critical relevance of properties in the negative analogy. It was success or failure in this forum that built or diminished professional reputations. *There must be better ways to learn about the past.*

The Generation Gap

The reader might well appreciate my surprise when in the mid-1970s I read the following:

> The early years of the new archaeology witnessed the frequent and unquestioning repetition of major methodological principles. One such principle was enunciated by Binford [1964a:425] in perhaps its most explicit form:
>> The loss, breakage, and abandonment of implements and facilities at different locations, where groups of variable structure performed different tasks, leaves a "fossil" record of the actual operation of an extinct society.
> . . . Under the aegis of this principle, new archaeologists have approached the remains of the past

in bold and exciting ways, seeking with sophisticated techniques assorted patterns in artifact distributions and *interpreting them directly in terms of past behavior and social organization. As often happens in times of normal science, few investigators have noticed that the principle is false* [Schiffer 1976a:11].

If this claim could be sustained in all its aspects, then essentially every idea and piece of research I have done would be rendered obsolete and valueless. There is no question that central to my ideas was the proposition that cultural systems were internally differentiated. By virtue of this we would expect different things to occur at different places and at different times as a function of the degree and character of the organizational differentiations within the system. In turn, I expect there to be archaeological consequences of such a past reality. If Schiffer's view could be sustained, then we were truly in need of a "revisionist's" new archaeology.

Looking back over earlier discussion it should be clear to the reader that the principle to which Schiffer refers makes assertions about the interface between the dynamics of an ongoing system and its static derivatives. In order to test this principle, Schiffer would have to study in a dynamic context.[6] That is, he would have to show that normal functioning of a cultural system *did not* leave "a 'fossil' record of the actual operation of an extinct society," which could only be done in an actualistic context. This is not, however, what Schiffer does or even suggests. It would appear that the principle he alleges to be false is in fact not being questioned!

What then is Schiffer questioning? *He is questioning the procedures of researchers working under such a principle.* He claims that the researchers being criticized interpret artifact distributions *"directly in terms of past behavior and social organization,"* and it is the "direct interpretation" to which Schiffer appears to object. In fact, his early discussions were directed toward two examples, the arguments of Longacre and Hill regarding evidence for matrilocal residence at southwestern pueblos, and the research aimed at the recognition of activity areas by Paleolithic archaeologists.[7] In both cases the context of *relevance* was already established, namely a model of past dynamics that was being suggested as relevant in various forms of archaeological patterning. Schiffer was not questioning whether the "models" or explanatory arguments were accurate or correct, *only whether they were appropriately related to archaeological facts.* Schiffer sees formation processes as potentially distorting the relationship between the dynamics of systemic context and the statics of archaeological context. He questions the degree to which the cited facts of the archaeological record are unambiguously relevant to the explanatory models being proposed to cover the facts. Schiffer continually points to the operation of processes that intervene between the systemic context targeted in an explanatory hypothesis, and the archaeological facts said to be covered by the explanation. These pesky processes serve to increase the negative analogy between the static conditions anticipated by a formation model and the actual structure of statics observed archaeologically. That is, other things are *not* equal; the archaeological record results from processes not included in the original explanatory model, so the explanatory model does not explain the record. Neither does the record necessarily "directly" inform us about *past dynamics of interest.*

Although it is quite true that traditional archaeologists regularly engaged in arguments of relevance, as is illustrated here, it is also true that as we changed the character of the arguments advanced to explain archaeological patterning, new contexts of relevance were established. The old points that commonly engaged traditional archaeologists in arguments "faded away" in favor of new forms, as a new appreciation grew for new boundary conditions relative to the character, diversity, and newness of the explanatory arguments being explored. I pointed this out as early as 1968:

> During the past thirty years archaeologists have warned against the mixing of levels and inaccurate partitioning of archaeological deposits; the warning offered here is against the analytical mixing of variables and against the partitioning of our observational universe into irrelevant analytical units [L. R. Binford 1968a:25].

So it was quite true that as new explanations were proposed we had to learn how to use the archaeological record differently. We had to control for different kinds of ambiguities and different kinds of boundary conditions; in short, those other things that had to be equal for our explanation to apply. In this sense the explorations by Schiffer and colleagues were both appropriate and potentially of great interest and importance. In one very real sense they had hit upon the only concrete way that we can use the archaeological record in evaluating our ideas about the past. As pointed out, we cannot use the record to evaluate our ideas of causal dynamics in any direct sense. We can, however, use the properties of the archaeological record to make *a judgment* whether a particular idea regarding dynamics may or may not apply to a given archaeological case. This was clearly the thrust of Schiffer's early work.

Sadly, Schiffer's writings drifted in another direction, one where it was gradually assumed that there were "formation processes" in the absolute sense. He conceived of formation processes as intervening between the discovery context of the record as found and recorded, and the past of interest. This view has a hidden assumption, that *the target context in the past is known or has been specified.* To be between, something must have at least two reference points, two points that bound it. One of these reference points is obviously the point of archaeological observation, the facts of the archaeological context, or the "discovery context." What then is the reference point in the past? Clearly, at least for Schiffer, this point was initially taken up by the various models that had been proposed by my generation of researchers as potential alternatives to the traditionalists' view of how the archaeological record was structured dynamically in the past. In short, Schiffer's arguments were classic arguments of relevance, which sought to show that a necessary condition for the relevant application of an interpretative argument had or had not been met by the archaeological facts. (Compare Schiffer's arguments to those illustrated here from the "debate".) One can only wonder why Schiffer feels he has established a revisionist's form of new archaeology, when men such as Mellars and Bordes making the same kind of argument saw themselves as participating in the *normal business of working at archaeology.*

I think part of this at least is referable to a shift in perspective that occurred between the archaeologists of the 1960s, who sought to change the directions of the field, and the following generation of the 1970s. I generally began with the facts of the archaeological record. This was the way I had been trained. One starts with patterning, as in the case of the Mousterian problem, and moves to interpretation. My strategy had always been to use knowledge of dynamics, basically the ethnographic literature, to develop a model of relationships between material things and forms of dynamics known to exist. It would then be argued that such "realistic" situations would be unrecognized if the archaeologists used traditional interpretative conventions. This was a kind of reality testing for the traditional conventions. A justifiable form of dynamics, which could certainly implicate facts analogous to types known from the archaeological record, was explored. If it was therefore admitted that conditions such as I described could account for the archaeological facts as known, then the limitations of traditional interpretative conventions were clearly exposed. At least initially, I was not so interested in whether the alternatives proposed were appropriate; I asked only that they be realistic. If they were, then the inability of traditional approaches to uncover such a reality, as well as the distortion of appropriate facts that the use of traditional conventions would ensure, was demonstrated.

For the generation of archaeologists coming on the scene in the 1970s, a very different intellectual context existed. A number of models had been built, dealing with the relationship of material things to systems properties in general, and a number of arguments had been advanced as alternatives to traditional interpretations. The problem of testing that we had stressed while developing our tactics of falsification rested heavily on the shoulders of the young people entering the discipline in the 1970s. But they accepted the challenge. They addressed the models built during the 1960s with critical arguments of relevance developed in terms of the data said to have been covered by the models. Of course this was, in their view, dependent on there being an appropriate fit between the data and the arguments said to explain them. They were not concerned with the accuracy of the theoretical propositions per se, but with the justifications for citing the propositions as explanations for a given body of fact.[8] Engaged as they were in this type of activity, it is not difficult to see how they continued to think that one could test archaeological theories by "deducing test implications" from facts of the archaeological record. They were testing, not theories, but the prudence with which theories had been used. As long as the literature rested at this stage, it appeared legitimate and potentially useful, although I must admit that I had always thought that I knew how to tell a dump from a house floor. Michael Schiffer and his colleagues were not content, however, to be engaged in constructive arguments of relevance; they wanted to be uncovering the "laws" of formation processes. It will be recalled that in the view of Schiffer and his associates these were the dynamics of "the transformation problem," the distortions occurring *between* the archaeological record as discovered and the target point for inference in the past. In the absence of a specific proposal, or a trial explanation, how does one establish a target for inference in the past that could serve as a general reference point for the "between" where formation processes are said to operate? For Schiffer the target seems to have become a reconstructionist's picture.

The above . . . presents a framework for describing the interrelations between behavioral and-spatial-material aspects of activity performance with reference to the life-history of cultural elements. This orientation demands that the description of activities performed at an archaeological site be expressed in terms of highly specific hypotheses on an empirical, behavioral level [Schiffer 1975a:112].

It should be clear that the goal of these suggestions is the descriptive reconstruction of the *activities performed at the site,* that is, life as an ethnographer might have seen it. If this is what we seek to infer and the archaeological record is what we have to work from, then getting from one to the other is only possible through an understanding of the formation processes, the acts and interactions that structure and distort the archaeological record away from the "day in the life of" picture that is sought.

Basically, I do not agree that this is our primary goal. I do not think a generic study of formation processes relative to a discussion of all past activities will yield much insight into either the nature of cultural systems or archaeological methodology, because our methods have to serve broader experimental goals than acknowledged in "behavioral Archaeology" as it has been proposed.

In the changed intellectual context of the 1970s, arguments of relevance went beyond the particular explanatory contexts in which relevance could be specified, to the offering of programmatic statements presented in absolutist terms. Relativity was lost and a specific, inflexible reconstructionist target for inference became the framework for relevance. There is truly a generation gap between my views and these.

Yet another generation gap surfaced during the 1970s, and this had to do with the ethnoarchaeological study of living peoples. I had always thought that (a) the literary ethnographic record, although provocative, was essentially inadequate to inform us about the potential relationships between statics and dynamics, and (b) given a demonstration of inadequacy for the traditionalists' conventions, the real challenge was to develop new, better, and more accurate understandings for this natural system we call cultural, in the context of which humans live their lives and the archaeological record is created. This meant that we needed a theory of cultural statics, a theory that treated the relationships between statics and dynamics. As argued earlier, this could only be studied actualistically—in a living systems context. Theory building was and is in the main dependent ethnoarchaeological experiences. Most of the justification for a theory has to be done in situations where dynamics and statics could both be monitored, and the archaeological record per se is of little utility for this.

It was my understanding that the justifications for theories are dependent exclusively on inductive forms of reasoning. That is, theories were always more than the experiences cited to justify thinking them. One cannot "deduce" a theory from the experiences that prompted one to conceive of it. Here rests perhaps some of the irony for the 1970s. As pointed out, during the 1960s when my students and I were attempting to demonstrate the inaccuracy of traditional interpretative conventions, we were pursuing a falsificationist's set of tactics. In that context exploration of the role of deductive reasoning seemed germane. Once we had moved beyond disproving the old and had faced the challenge of inventing the new, the relevance of deductive forms of argument diminished, and we had to learn how to use skillful inductive tactics, for purposes quite different than those of the traditionalists. Thus, while many archaeologists of the 1970s were discussing arguments of relevance as if there was an absolute context for such discussions, and seeking to test their arguments deductively, I was trying to learn how to develop theories, and seeking to perfect my inductive skills to achieve such ends.

Perhaps better than many other examples, this dynamic view of the discipline illustrates what is meant by a processual perspective. Those who were looking for a "right" way of doing archaeology sought a normative set of rules for working. However, the actual situation was dynamic and the notion of how to do things was changing according to what one sought to accomplish. As we learn the character of the productive questions to be asked, we must in turn learn how to do new things in search of new understanding.

Notes

1. One of the first challenges to the functional argument was published by Desmond Collins. In it he tried to test my arguments, particularly concerning the dynamic view of culture. It was in following up the lines of argument laid down in my answer to Collins that many of the ideas later developed rather extensively were initially presented.

2. Compare this conclusion with that drawn by C. G. Morgan (1973:270-271) in his analysis of Longacre's thesis regarding matrilocal residence. Almost everyone who had thought about the problem came to the same conclusion about testing.

3. I came back at Bordes with this point at the Sheffield conference (1971) where I discussed my ideas on curation (Chapter 11) for the first time. This point was critical and it has served as the stimulus to considerable research (see Chapters 19 and 20).

4. Perhaps it should be pointed out that in attempting to explain to Bordes my ideas about the internal organization of cultural systems I frequently used examples from the modern world, because he was not very familiar with the ethnographic literature on hunter-gatherer peoples. I pointed to the differences in artifact content between Bordes's kitchen and his bedroom, his lab, and his house as examples of systems differentiation. (This idea is illustrated as perceived by Bordes in the cartoon published in Renfrew [1973:xi].)

5. That this is a characteristic form of argument presented by archaeologists has been recognized by others:

> While archaeologists often talk of testing laws, most often they are testing explanations based on accepted laws, so the disconfirmation of the explanation should not necessarily lead to reject the law, but merely to reject it as the basis for an explanation of the case in hand [P. J. Watson *et al.* 1971:18].

6. It was of course this principle that I sought to evaluate in my studies of the Nunamiut system. Chapters 13 and 14 are germane to this issue, as are some of my conclusions presented in Chapter 22.

7. I think it is clear that early criticism focused on how a "floor" had been defined in the excavations that had provided the data for Hill and Longacre's arguments. Many times I have heard Schiffer and Jefferson Ried argue that the samples used to monitor the occupants of rooms were probably contaminated by secondary refuse and that arguments about the character of the occupants were therefore unjustified because of the ambiguity of the provenience units studied. The best illustration of such an argument is provided by Schiffer (1975b). Schiffer tried to make a similar argument against the work of Bob Whallon (see Schiffer 1974; Whallon 1973, 1974). Whallon was aware of the situation, as were most of the 1960s generation, as is illustrated by the following statement (emphasis added):

> Criticisms are all aimed at the details of *how I applied the method of dimensional analysis of variance to some specific data.* I agree fully that my application and interpretations can be questioned on these and many other grounds (some of which are also raised by Schiffer). *The analysis of Guila Naquitz was not the point of my article, however, beyond providing a brief demonstration that the method of dimensional analysis of variance could lead to results which might be meaningful in one way or another in the analysis of archaeological data* [Whallon 1974:494].

It is perhaps interesting that still another kind of "generation gap" misunderstanding surrounded the work of Whallon. For instance, John Yellen (1977:134) argues that Whallon proposed that each activity had to be located in a different place! I have tried to deal with this type of distortion elsewhere (L. R. Binford 1983: Chapter 7, n. 10).

8. I must admit that the generation gap took me by surprise. I can recall an oral presentation of a doctoral proposal given before the Department of Anthropology at the University of New Mexico in the mid-1970s. The student, counseled by a thesis adviser (a 1970s generation person), proposed to study the stylistic variation among floor samples from a locally excavated pueblo. The purpose was to determine if the proto Rio Grande pueblos were organized matrilocally like the more western Anasazi! I was amazed. I could not understand how anyone could think that Hill and Longacre's work had established the utility of a method for inference. The generation of the 1970s started with the models; some were willing to accept the models as warranted methods for inference. At the time of the proposal hearing, I was beginning to make to my students the arguments that later appeared in the *Bones* book—that adopting post hoc accommodative arguments as methods for inference without their prior evaluation resulted in myths about the past.

Another generation gap idea of the 1970s was that one could test the explanatory model by another application, by "duplicating the experiment," as I have heard it described. Several things happen when this is done. By mounting different arguments of relevance, a judgment is passed about the relevance of the model to the new situation, but of course no test of the explanatory argument between the two cases is controlled. Also, a judgment that the explanation does not apply to the new case does not implicate the previous case in any way. For instance, I have heard it said that excavations were planned in the Midwest to test my successional model as used to interpret the archaeological record at Hatchery West! (See L. R. Binford 1972a:314-326.) This is silly, because the specific successional argument was developed post hoc to accommodate all the *specific facts* of the archaeological record as known at Hatchery West. Only if one found another site identical in all relevant properties could one even consider the idea that my specific interpretation applied to the other site.

9. Glynn Isaac likes to talk about "multiple working hypotheses," and tries to identify the "most likely working hypphesis" at the present time, and so on. These were not new ideas to me but the tactics for inference seemed to present some interesting contrasts with those commonly employed by Americanists. Most of the time what Isaac is calling a hypothesis is a special kind of argument of relevance. The question being asked is whether a particular meaning is appropriate for a given body of data. In most cases the meanings are concepts such as "base camp," and "hunting," conditions or activities that we are not sure characterized the past. The question is whether one can apply such concepts to certain archaeological facts or sets of facts. We may, for instance, note bones in association with stone tools. At question is the significance of the facts to the past. We might in Isaac's terms propose multiple working hypotheses—that animals introduced the bones to the site, that the bones were washed together with stone tools and both came to rest in a stream deposit, and so on. We would like to have unambiguous operational definitions for such situational concepts. Given the lack of unambiguous markers permiting discrimination of one situation from another, we tabulate the criteria that might implicate each of the alternatives, and then we accept as the most likely working hypothesis the alternative with the most positive and least ambiguous criteria. This is a procedure where one conducts simultaneous arguments of relevance. I will have more to say about such approaches in Part IV.

13

Historical Archaeology:
Is It Historical or Archaeological?

It's New Years Day 1975. I am trying to prepare a paper for presentation at a conference on historical archaeology. Do I have anything to say?

This was the setting and my thoughts as I began preparation of this paper. Then I began to think along the following lines. If this was a conference on archaeology I would have no problem. I have unpublished material relevant to many subjects of general archaeological interest. Obviously my problem arose from the "historical" orientation of the conference. Why? Why should I be uncomfortable and indecisive as to an appropriate subject or way of treating a problem. I continued to be uneasy with "historical." Clearly I felt that persons doing "historical" archaeology were different from myself with different interests. Why? Certainly it is not because of specially relevant or technical information which is part of the "information pool" of persons working in sites of relatively recent age in North America. I can talk creamware and kaolin pipes with the best of them. Why? That word "historical" again! What does it mean? Well, it means that there is information available from the past in addition to the archaeological record. It means that the past may be investigated with resources other than those provided solely by archaeological investigation. Great—wonderful— that should mean historic archaeologists should be more sophisticated and better informed. Specialists in this field should provide the most informative tests or evaluations of ideas set forth by archaeologists in general. They should be in the forefront in theory building. Why in god's name am I hesitant—I should be jumping up and down with anticipation. I was not. Back to that word "historical" again.

It must mean more than just having nonarchaeological information surviving from the past. Yes, sadly it does mean more—it implies a philosophy, an epistemology, and a value system in operation among the adherents. How does a Unitarian say anything of relevance to a congregation of fundamentalists, or a chiropractor excite the assembled American Medical Association? On the other hand, are my conceptions of historical archaeologists incorrect? This is a conference, and presumably its advan-

Originally appeared in *Historical Archaeology and the Importance of Material Things*, edited by L. Ferguson, published by the Society for Historical Archaeology, Special Publications No. 2, pp. 13–22, © 1977.

tage stems from discussion and interaction ideally aimed at understanding. Okay, instead of delivering a paper on how to do science perhaps based on an incorrect appreciation of the audience, I have decided on another approach. I will relate some relatively recent experiences which I consider revealing and informative about the process of attempting to do archaeological science. Perhaps these experiences, when discussed, will promote a more constructive conference on how to advance archaeology regardless of the adjectives preceding the word.

One hundred and thirty six Eskimos are settled in a permanent village at Anaktuvuk Pass, Alaska. One steps off the commercial plane which currently delivers mail twice a week and is immediately struck with a number of very deceiving features. Used oil drums, some rusting, others with the distinctive State of Alaska blue paint seem to dominate the land. A visitor remarked "I had the feeling I was entering a migrant workers' camp in central California." The people around the plane are dressed in a wide variety of clothes, some donated by missionaries, some abandoned by visitors, others freshly arrived from the mail-order houses of the "lower 48." The visitor arriving as I did in 1969 to learn about the Eskimos' way of relating to their treeless tundra world seize upon certain features for reassurance. Some wear "traditional" parkas in spite of their being made of mail-order cloth. There were racks for drying and storing meat scattered throughout the village. Roughly fifty percent of the visible houses were "traditional." These were hard to see because of the new boxes made of plywood and painted in a variety of blues and yellows which obscured the low lying houses built of earth and blending with the colors of the land. My disappointment must have shown. I had read of the Nunamiut, the Caribou hunters of the central Brooks range. I had carefully planned to live and work with these people in order to learn which strategies must be followed to cope successfully with their tundra world. Some ninety miles north of the arctic circle, two hundred miles from the nearest community, these facts seemed irrelevant. The modern world had engulfed the most remote part of the rugged sawtooth mountains in Alaska's arctic. I noted the younger teenagers wearing Beatle boots and the first undercut suggestions led me to predict that when I came again the boys would be wearing long hair.

I walked up into the village with the children pulling at me asking, "What's your name?" Then coming down the path a man "late for the plane" said with a shy smile "my name is Johnny Rulland." He wore a dingy pair of Air Force dress blue pants, a torn and greasy "ski jacket," and a small baseball cap. This was the man I was to contact, the man whom I had arranged to work with for learning about hunting strategies! I offered a kind of forced smile, trying to hide from him and myself my disappointment. I know this world of "poverty," this world of donated clothes, and the absence of waste disposal collectors. I felt oddly at home when I had anticipated a world about which I knew nothing!

We pitched our tents on the east side of the airstrip and began to unpack. The children were all around, pulling on our arms, "come see the nest over here." "You want to fish?" "You got hooks?" "I'll catch fish for you." I looked at my watch, two thirty in the morning! My god, these kids should be in bed. I should be in bed! Yet the sun was still shining and one would judge from a New Mexico summer perspective that it was about eight o'clock in the evening. The environment hadn't changed. I tried to sleep with the light coming through the tent walls; instead I thought about why I had come and what I had hoped to accomplish.

I had become excited by the prospects of doing "living archaeology" with this group of people when Nicholas Gubser's book (1965) on his experiences here in 1962 was published. At that time I was deeply involved in research on the Mousterian materials from southern France. Some two years later I became convinced that if we were going to make sense out of the Mousterian and its remarkable forms of variability, we needed some reliable behavioral context in terms of which variability in stone tools could be studied. I had summarized this interest in a research proposal as follows:

A number of challenges have recently been offered to the views which have traditionally guided archaeological interpretation. For instance, François Bordes has convincingly demonstrated that lithic assemblages of the Middle Paleolithic, of Mousterian, do not exhibit regular directional trends through time (Bordes 1961), the pattern which archaeologists have come to expect as "normal." Rather, through a sequence of deposits from a single location, variations in the artifact composition from discrete occupational episodes often exhibit an alternating pattern so that tool frequencies from a level in the middle of the deposit might resemble most closely those from the bottom or top of the site, rather than resembling most closely the depositionally adjacent assemblages. In addition to demonstrating a lack of directional change, Bordes has also been able to show that there are four basic forms of Mousterian assemblage, as measured by the relative frequencies of tool types. Three major propositions were advanced to explain this well-documented and apparently unpatterned alternation of types of Mousterian assemblage through sequences of occupations:

1. The different types of Mousterian assemblage are the result of seasonal patterns of living, with each type representing different seasonal remains.

2. Each kind of assemblage represents a slightly different adaptation to a different environment, the forms of the assemblage being directly determined by climatic alternations through time.

3. Each type of assemblage represents the remains of different groups of people, each group characterized by its own distinctive complement of tools. The alternation of industries reflects the variations in the spatial distribution of these groups through time.

Bordes has been able to argue convincingly that the data do not support the first two arguments; he therefore tentatively accepted the third—that the four types of Mousterian assemblage were associated with different Neanderthal "tribes" (Bordes (1961). I have argued (Binford and Binford 1966) that some variability among assemblages is ignored in Bordes' classification of assemblage types and secondly that much of the interassemblage variability is to be understood as the by-product of different activities having been conducted at various locations in the context of an essentially nonsedentary hunting and gathering adaptation. I have further suggested that much of the variability can be understood as expected differences between base camps versus hunting and gathering stations, kill sites, and other functionally specific locations related to extractive versus maintenance tasks. Contrary to these views Bordes (1968:144) argued, based largely on the thickness of some archaeological deposits and the consistency of assemblage form in many thick deposits, that the sites were relatively permanent and group sizes were large.

I reasoned that if activity variability and its logistics were the proper context for understanding interassemblage variability documented by Bordes, then this should certainly be manifest in the faunal materials preserved. Following this lead, funds were sought from the National Science Foundation in 1968 for a complete study of the fauna from the deeply stratified site of Combe Grenal. Funds were granted and Sally Binford and I spent eleven months studying the fauna, tools, and other related phenomena of the uniquely varying Mousterian assemblages excavated by Bordes. Preliminary analysis revealed a number of interesting patterns. . . .

Yet in spite of the demonstrable variety in patterning noted among anatomical parts, and correlations between tools and fauna or faunal elements, these remain facts in need of explanation as did the original observations on stone tool variability. It is clear that without an understanding of the causes of archaeological variation in faunal elements, I am unable to suggest the behavioral contexts in which stone tools were used when correlations are demonstrated between tools and fauna; in short, without an explanation facts remain facts. Regardless of the accuracy of Bordes' "historical" interpretation, here were facts not easily accommodated and clearly sources of potential information about the past. Could they be understood in processual terms?

My original thoughts had been that the Nunamiut were primarily dependent upon a single terrestrial mammal—caribou. They had been, until around 1950, a fully mobile hunting and gathering band. They lived in the broken mountainous tundra. The Neanderthals who had occupied the site of Combe Grenal for part of its occupational span had lived in a full tundra in a broken, low mountainous setting. They had been heavily dependent upon reindeer—the European form of the New World caribou. They were also most probably mobile hunters. The Nunamiut provided the closest analogue to the conditions envisioned for the Neanderthals of any known contemporary society. I wanted therefore to observe behavior under conditions as closely analogous to the Neanderthal situation as possible. Clearly, the old men who could remember that way of life were the ones for me to concentrate upon. I had to do classic "salvage ethnography." I had to collect as much "memory culture" as possible. Finally, I went to sleep.

The June sun on the tent woke me around eleven o'clock the next morning. I crawled out, went down to the stream for water while the students prepared breakfast. While eating, we talked of the "old men." I recalled a picture in Helge Ingstad's book *Nunamiut* (1954). It was a magnificent picture of a smiling Eskimo with the wind whipping the long guard hairs of the wolf ruff around the hood of his parka. The caption had read "The Eskimo Paniaq, a matchless hunter and splendid story-teller" (p. 17). Simon Paneack is a famous man, practically every anthropologist to live with or visit the Nunamiut has obtained a large share of their information from him. I wondered if he would remember the locations where he had lived year by year, the details of hunting, caching, food preparation, and processing which I wanted to know in order to "understand" the variability in anatomical parts anticipated on the sites where he had lived before he became sedentary.

Coming through the low willows toward our camp was a man of medium height, walking slowly as he swished a green willow stick to drive off the morning crop of mosquitoes. He wore a pair of very baggy "oxford grey" pants and a pair of black "street shoes" like one associates with formal social occasions. He spoke first, "Do you fellows plan to stay very long?" I remember thinking how "good" his English was. I explained that we were "anthropologists" and wanted to learn about how his people had lived "before they settled at Anaktuvuk village." He said, "I'm Simon Paneack, what's your name." I felt faintly embarrased, like one feels on meeting a famous man who has fallen, or become an alcoholic. Paneack pulled up an empty Blazo can and we talked for some time. He drew us maps of where he had lived on various occasions at Tulugak Lake some miles north. He said he had killed his first bird while camped there in 1906. He said his parents had seen their first flour, obtained in trade from the Kobuk, while they were camped on the Killik River in 1892. All this was noted in my small brown surveyors' notebook.

I was unable to make an appointment with Paneack for further questions in the afternoon. I had noted from the plane that there were caribou bones scattered on the tundra all around the village. I would walk out and examine these and record the parts abandoned in the field by hunters. A good sample of data from "kill sites" would come in handy to give me some idea of the parts of the animals given preferential treatment.

Once out of the village the environment began to scream its presence to my senses. Looking north across the tundra there was no discernible evidence that man had ever been there. Lakes were discovered behind almost every knoll, the mountains were magnificent giants standing mute with snowcaps around their high shoulders and cloud shrouded heads. It was easy to imagine groups of Neanderthal men in such a setting; it was easier to see Paneack as a young man with his dogs moving amongst these valley pathways in search of game. It was exciting. The kill sites were very reassuring, the bones lying around were identical to those that I had spent hours counting while at the archaeology laboratory at Bordeaux, France. I began to take the recording of kills seriously and became fascinated by the obvious differences between one and another.

I returned late that night to the village encouraged and began to ask questions of the younger men whom I was meeting gradually. I had met Noah Ahgook. My notebook records the following: "Noah is the Postmaster—I asked him about the unbutchered cows that I had seen and he replied that they were left on the tundra because too many were killed." He didn't want to talk about hunting and just smiled when I asked why some animals were represented by only heads, others by heads and lower legs, and others by many different combinations of parts. He said, "Sometimes we do it one way, other times another way—if you want to know about 'old timers' you will have to ask the old men." I hadn't said anything to Noah about "old timers." He of course knew I was an anthropologist since the word on new arrivals to Anaktuvuk travels fast. As one of my younger Eskimo friends later explained it, "we know what anthropologists want to know—they come here to talk to the old men about the ways of the 'old timers.'" I recalled a class I had had in "Ethnographic Field Methods" at the University of North Carolina. As a class project each student was to study a nearby local community. I had selected a Church congregation in the small community of Union Grove, North Carolina. I had been counseled to tell the people I was an historian "because if they hear you are an anthropologist they may shy away thinking you want to learn about their sex practices." Clearly the Eskimos had a different notion of the anthropologist, but nevertheless one I had to cope with.

Finally I explained that I was going to Tulugak Lake to map and excavate the locations that the young men had lived in during the seasonal rounds of 1947–48, the year Ingstad had lived with them, the year for which there was good "historical documentation." My plan was simple. Ingstad had visited the Nunamiut while they were still fully mobile hunters. He had described his experiences with these people. I wanted to view them archaeologically for the same time period so that some equations could be made between what a group looks like when viewed archaeologically and ethnographically. The almost universal response to my plan is typified by a response from Ben Ahgook, "Ingstad is not all true—he made some of it up." I pressed for clarification—"Oh he made it sound too much like 'old timers.'" I questioned on the subject of Ingstad's book many times and gradually a pattern emerged. The men agreed that Ingstad's writings made "it sound too much like old timers," and he had overdramatized the uncertainty of the hunting way of life. A frequent response was "Ingstad made it sound like the caribou didn't come—they did and things weren't so bad that winter as he said." Was it true that I couldn't trust the most relevant historical source?

Living in the village those first weeks convinced me that although the old men had remarkable memories for certain features of their past, my questions on the details of processing and disposal of caribou parts generally prompted responses such as "Eskimos use all the parts of the caribou." My best strategy would be to excavate the sites documented for the 1947–48 seasonal cycle so I could question them from a perspective of known characteristics of their sites. The archaeological data would provide the basis for the best interrogation strategy. If I could show them the concrete results of their behavior they would certainly be able to tell me what that behavior had been. Moving from the village to Tulugak Lake where we would begin archaeological investigations became a goal with a "promised land" kind of aura. We moved to Tulugak.

Johnny Rulland had gone with us as our guide and informant since he had lived at Tulugak in 1948. As I grew to know him better, his baseball cap and cast off military pants disturbed me less.

We worked hard recording and mapping the locations where the Nunamiut had lived during the summer of 1947 and summer and fall of 1948. Johnny remembered where every house had been, who had lived there, how long they had stayed and many other details. Working with him was a pleasure and he was a remarkable man when it came to memory of the terrrain, locations of things, and the details of manufacturing different items. However, questioning him on the significance of variability in anatomical parts was rather unsatisfactory. He never seemed to understand what I was trying to learn. We worked hard, Johnny and I, and began the tedious job of collecting bone samples from the many houses we had mapped.

As this work proceeded and I learned more about methods of food preparation, little suggestive tidbits about drying meat, making rawhide rope, etc. I began to be anxious—there were so many things that seemed relevant as contributors to differing bone frequencies. How could I possibly get adequate control data?

As Johnny and I were collecting bones from around the telltale ring of stones where he and his father had camped in 1948, I noticed on an exposed rocky area a dense concentration of very tiny bone fragments. I asked Johnny what they had been doing that resulted in such a pile of tiny bones. He said "nothing—they must be from 'old timers.'" By this time knowledge about the "old timers" had become a goal since the contemporary setting was "so modern." We began to dig and with each tuft of tundra moss removed more bones in fascinating combinations and concentrations were exposed. A few flint chips appeared and we searched for the house we knew had to be there—all indications were that it was a winter occupation of some duration. We found the house and worked long hours on a site that was something of an archaeologist's dream. With every artifact discovered Johnny's eyes would light up and a detailed silent examination would follow with a statement, "This is a bird arrow, my father made one just like this for me when I was seven years old." He was interested and fascinated by what we were uncovering. This enthusiasm didn't extend, however, to my interest in the bones. I would ask, "Why are there nothing but metapodials in this pile?" Johnny's face would be almost a blank and finally he would say "I guess somebody was making akatuk." I quickly realized that Johnny, an Eskimo of forty years experience, who admittedly had seen or participated in practically every activity possibly represented on the site, was in the position of a very experienced archaeologist; he was making informed inferences. He was never willing to say for certain what the behavioral context had been for the patterns we observed. At best he would offer informed guesses. I was certainly glad to have his opinions; in most cases I think he was correct, but this was a far cry from the kind of "control" data I wanted to "explain" the observed variability in anatomical parts. While in the field I didn't let this stop me; we excavated with fascination and enthusiasm. Everything was recorded, plotted, measured—archaeologically the site and its documentation was truly extraordinary. There was a high yield of artifacts, nothing had been disturbed, and the fauna was magnificent.

I returned to the village carrying protectively the collection of artifacts, bones, and the crucial distribution maps of the bones. The most obvious forms of patterning at the site were in the bones; almost each artifact was unique and analogous forms were rarely present. The word about our work had preceded us and the old men were clearly fascinated and interested in seeing what we had found. Interviews were set up and I began interrogations of the old men in terms of the concrete archaeological facts. The results were fascinating. Arctic John, Paneack, or Kakinya would sit with a bone arrow in their hands, a smile on their faces, and sometimes point out the most minute detail, talking of its meaning and frequently relating a series of personal experiences or experiences related to them by their fathers, relevant to the particular artifact which they held almost reverently. Such interest was not however uniformly expressed with respect to all the artifacts. They would paw through the box ignoring some, picking them up and tossing them back finally selecting one and smiling. This behavior annoyed me since each artifact was of equal value to me. Each artifact represented to me potentially new and different kinds of information about the past; each was a component of an assemblage. To understand the assemblage as a whole I needed information of equal detail on each different form.

I changed the manner of interviewing, keeping the assemblage hidden and producing an artifact at a time. This procedure worked better but still it was clear that the old men became bored quickly with some artifacts putting them down during my questioning and leaning over toward the box asking. "What else you got in there?" My disillusionment reached its highest peak when I attempted to question them about the most common item on the site—the bones. The men would look at the maps discussing in some detail the house remains, the hearth, and even spotting such details as where the dogs must have been, but when questioned about the patterning exhibited by the bones and different anatomical parts the common response was "I don't know, I guess they just put them that way." They were as surprised and more baffled by the bone data than I was, yet it was a way of life that they had experienced that had produced the distributions—why weren't they aware of them? I would press with more information about the bones and they would sit listening to some detail of association of frequency variation and respond "crazy Eskimoes."

Some said they would ask their wives, because after all the women did the cooking and taking out of trash. I set up interviews with two of the older women in the community. I went through the artifacts with them and noticed immediately a very different pattern of response. When showed the assemblage they would choose very different artifacts and express the same kind of nostalgic reminiscences over items which in many cases the men had largely ignored except when prompted by me. Clearly what was being played out in front of me was a different "value system" but it was not to be understood by the mere recognition of it in those terms. What I was witnessing was the expression of differential meaning being attached to the same objects clearly as a differential extension of self identities. I was administering a kind of artifactual Rorschach test. I was fascinated and spent much time trying to isolate the characteristics in terms of which common evaluations were being manifest by the choice sequences. In this I think I have been fairly successful. In spite of the fascination with the artifacts I shifted my work with the women onto the subject of the bones with high hopes. They saw different things in the patterning, asked questions of me, but were in general no more informative than the men.

I returned to New Mexico excited by the site, the knowledge gained about the artifacts, and impressed with the "old people." Charles Amsden remained in the village to collect information about group composition and settlement patterns from the old men. He had the additional charge to record in detail the activities of the hunting during the fall migration of caribou. As his data were mailed down to me piece by piece, my disappointment with the modern conditions in the village faded into the background. He was describing hunting, butchering, caching, and transporting of caribou parts. His statistics on the killing of males versus females matched almost exactly my statistics from the kill site survey. I was excited again about the bone data. It was not until over a year later that I had the opportunity of revisiting the Nunamiut.

I left New Mexico in April of 1971 excited by the prospects of observing them during the spring hunt and collecting data comparable to that already on hand for the fall hunt of 1969. As I stepped off the plane into the forty-two below zero temperature I WAS SHOCKED ANEW. The same people were there to meet the plane but this time the modern world seemed remote. Caribou skin parkas were everywhere, the baggy caribou skin pants on some of the men seemed to roll and flair to the sides making them appear rounded and capable of bouncing if dropped. A sled and dog team were at the plane to carry the mail to the post office. In addition to the seeming remoteness of the modern world compared to my summer experience there were other surprises. Trails through the village familiar from my summer experiences were covered or blocked by huge snow drifts and winter sled trails wove through the village in a very different network.

There were marked differences in the social atmosphere. During summer the young men had hung around the village seemingly bored and idling away their time. Now they were so active it was difficult to find them. Everyday they were out with the dog team or snow-mobile "checking traps"—"looking for caribou"—"bringing in firewood"—"hauling water." On the other hand the women who had been so obvious during summer, as well as the old men, were rarely seen outside. In summer, the complaints commonly voiced were about how hot it was, the mosquitoes, and the behavior of the young people. Now all one heard from the women and aged was how bored they were and how they looked forward to summer. The hunters on the other hand complained of the absence of game, the fact that the caribou were late and the behavior of their dog teams or snow machines. How different things were. Suppose I had only records of a summer experience!

I stayed with Johnny and told him from the start that I didn't really want to talk to the old men; I wanted to do as many things with him and his age mates as possible so I could get some idea of what it was like hunting and trapping. He reacted with great enthusiasm and most of my time with the Nunamiut during that short experience was spent on a sled in temperatures which never got above eighteen degrees below zero.

It was during this period that I realized the information I wanted was right before my eyes in the form of the contemporary patterns of land use and variability in the activities at numerous locations still regularly used by the Nunamiut. They were still hunting caribou, still setting up hunting camps, still differentially treating caribou in terms of numerous conditions of temperature, number killed at once, location of kill, distance of transport, etc. My experience in winter hunting camp verified that the elusive differential distributions of parts of caribou were still being produced by the Nunamiut although they were not totally aware of it themselves. In this setting Johnny observed with me the high frequency of lower front leg bones on the winter hunting camp; he along with me became fascinated to discover how many different patterns there were and why they were different. His interest was never as intense as mine, but he recognized the problem and frequently guided me into situations which I would never have thought to investigate.

When I returned the following June with a large crew of students I saw in them surprise at the "modern" character of the village. They voiced their lack of understanding for my interest in the modern sites by tactfully pointing out the "really interesting" old timers' site nearby. That summer I collected a body of control data which began to yield the secrets of the patterning observable among anatomical parts. It was collected from the contemporary activities of the Nunamiut using guns, snowmobiles, etc. and they were much more surprised by its presence than I was. The dimensions, in terms of which contingent behavior operates, must be relevant to my Neanderthal data although the concrete behavior was certainly different.

Perhaps my initial disdain of the appearance of modernity reflects a bias by archaeologists as to the "relevance" of historically recent case material. Similarly my "discovery" of its "relevance" is something which "historical archaeologists" need to discover.

This was historical archaeology in the best sense of the word since I had available the best possible sources of information in addition to the archaeological record regarding past behavior—in many cases the persons who in fact had been responsible for the production of the archaeological record. Further, I had written documentation by both Ingsted and Gubser surviving about the past which I wished to investigate. Why were the details of this research not presented at a conference on "historical archaeology?" Was it because I was not interested in reconstructing the sites I had worked? Perhaps it was because persons living in the sites or the events occurring there were not considered historically "important" by contemporary American standards? Or maybe the questions I was asking and the approaches I used to gain answers would not be considered interesting or appropriate. After all, my interest in the Nunamiut did not stem from some abiding commitment to Eskimos or even their history. It arose out of a concern with explaining observed variability in the archaeological record as observed in Mousterian materials a continent away and separated from the Nunamiut by at least 60,000 years. I was interested in controlling variables so that their operation in determining observed distributions in the archaeological record could be evaluated, and meaning in processual terms could be given to what was observed. In short I chose to work with the Nunamiut because of the relevance of their situation for furthering the science of archaeology—not because of their "historical importance." Finally my primary interest was in a class of material—bones—about which historical accounts were mute and even the men who produced the patterns were unaware of their existence and meaning. This was an archaeological problem.

If we in discussion can answer the question as to why the results of my Nunamiut research were not considered by me to be appropriate to a conference on "historical archaeology," we may each gain a better understanding of the potential information to be gained from research by archaeologists on historically documented materials.

14 1978

Introduction to Nunamiut
Ethnoarchaeology

Before I delve into the details of my work among the Nunamiut, I want to set forth
the ideas that prompted the study. These are very basic ideas, indeed—they focus on
the question of precisely what archaeologists do.

Archaeologists attempt to make systematic observations on the remains of past
human behavior; that is, they investigate the archaeological record. The archaeological
record, however, is contemporary, and any observations that I, as an archaeologist,
make through the excavation of an archaeological site are contemporary observations.
My interest is in the past but my observations are on the present.

To pursue my interests I must accomplish two quite separate kinds of acts: (a)
I must project my contemporary observations accurately into the past and (b) I must
assign meaning to my observations. I accomplish the first through methods of dating.
I may then examine these projected and temporally arranged observations for forms
of patterning. If I find variability in patterned configurations, I have some evidence
for dynamics, changes that occurred in the past. I know that something happened,
that some dynamics were operative, but I do not know why the changes occurred;
neither do I know anything about the character of the changes. To make a statement
about the character of changes I must first *assign meaning* to the contemporary facts
of the archaeological record.

Suppose I observe that a metal tool is present in a particular archaeological site.
Examining additional sites, I may note that metal tools are present in some but not
all of the sites. Accurate dating tells me that all the sites without metal tools are older
than the sites with metal tools. I may assert that this pattern reflects the events of the
invention of metallurgy. If I also discover metal tools in archaeological sites in adjacent
regions at time periods increasingly more recent as a function of their distance from
the region initially observed, I may assert that this pattern reflects the spread of
metallurgy to other places. The definition of such patterns in no way tells me *why*
they exist. My assertions are descriptions of the world as known and do not provide
answers to the questions of why the world is the way it appears.

Originally appeared in *Nunamiut Ethnoarchaeology*, published by Academic Press, New York, pp. 1–14, 1978. Copyright
© 1978 by Academic Press, Inc. All rights of reproduction in any form reserved.

Let's take another example. If I (a) observe a series of small, molded objects in the form of a human female, (b) assert that each object is a mother goddess, (c) project into the past a series of archaeological assemblages, some of which yield mother goddesses, (d) recognize a patterned distribution both temporally and spatially, and (e) ask the question, "Why were mother goddesses invented and increasingly distributed over wider geographical areas?" I have already restricted my thinking to a particular context involving religion, cults, ritual behavior, and the like. I may then seek to understand the distribution and the context of appearance of these little female effigies in terms of arguments about the role of religion in human life, the symbolic importance of females and fertility, and so on. But suppose I had a time machine and was able to determine that the objects are not mother goddesses but toys, or perhaps magical devices used to divine the sex of children before birth. Under these ascriptions of "meaning" I would be directed to pursue very different lines of thought seeking an explanation for the effigies' appearance and geographical spread. If I am to make accurate statements about the past or even to engage in relevant forms of thought I must have a relatively accurate understanding of the context in which the facts of the archaeological record came into being.

The relevant past to a set of static facts of the contemporary archaeological record can only be the conditions that brought the observed facts into existence. Much of the history of archaeological work has been characterized by changing views as to the conditions producing archaeological facts. For many years—and even today in many places—the dynamic standing behind an archaeological fact was thought to be simply the maker of the artifact. Thus, the archaeologist might view a recovered artifact and make judgments as to the skill of the maker, his artistic sense, and the degree that he seemed to share certain artistic values of the archaeologist's culture. The meaning archaeological remains carried became a statement on the character and quality of the maker. If artifacts were crude by the archaeologist's standards then the makers were crude. If artifacts were "beautiful" then the makers were advanced and had "advanced" aesthetic senses.

Gradually, this paradigm for giving meaning to the contemporary facts gave way to other arguments. It was reasoned that a person's overall intelligence or capacity of "humanness" is not necessarily directly translatable into accomplishments, and that many intelligent men can produce crude products. Factors other than those intrinsic to the artifact's maker condition his behavior, so we can not legitimately use the human products recovered archaeologically as a statement on the "quality" of the producers; rather the products are to be seen as a statement on the "culture" of the makers. For instance, according to a commonly cited statement, cultures are "historically created designs for living, explicit and implicit, rational, irrational, and nonrational, which exist at any given time as potential guides for the behavior of man [Kroeber and Kluckhohn 1952:97]." Built into this definition of culture are the rules for its own explanation. Culture is said to be historically created. Thus it is not surprising that, viewing human products as reflections of the culture carried by the makers, we can hope to convert contemporary observations into statements about past culture. We can compare the contemprary facts uncovered as a result of excavation with other, similarly recovered remains, evaluate the differences and similarities, and arrange them taxonomically to express the degree to which they indicate shared culture. When a temporal assessment can be made, we can trace, through our assessments of similarities and differences, the history of cultural development.

This view proposes that culture, the ideas or "ideational guides for living" held in the minds of men, is simply projected into their products. The products can thus be viewed as accurate reflections of mental templates, so culture in turn can be seen as a model of past dynamics normally discussed in the context of artifact production. Few would disagree that planning is characteristic of acts of fabrication and that fabrication plans are guided by some ideas regarding the desired outcomes. This "fabrication model" comes into question when we ask whether it is relevant to all facts and patterns observable in the archaeological record. Is it an adequate and accurate dynamic model that accounts for the frequency variability in an archaeological assemblage? Do makers arrive on a site and proceed to fabricate an assemblage of tools relative to a mental template of what an appropriate "assemblage" should look like? Is it reasonable to expect that men carry in their heads fabrication plans for what archaeological sites should look like after they leave? An uneasiness with the basic model linking the dynamic past to the static facts of the contemporary archaeological record leads me to question the relevance of this linking model.

Under the "traditionalist" paradigm, the composition of an assemblage is measured by relative frequencies of recognized classes of artifacts. Redundancy is accepted as "patterning" and hence a manifestation of the "cultural norms" of behavior transmitted and shared among the people represented. The assemblage is equated with the community. The expectation is that if we are dealing with the remains of identical or related groups of people the composition of the assemblages should be similar since they share a common body of culture. I challenged this paradigm:

> The behavioral model recognizes that behavior is the dynamics of adaptation. People draw upon a repertoire of cultural background and experience to meet changing or variable conditions in their environment, both social and physical. Our expectations, then, are for variability in the archaeological record to reflect a variety of different kinds of coping situations. Activities will vary with the particular adaptive situation of the group and the character of tasks being performed. We would therefore expect variability in the archaeological record to reflect these different situations.

> Assemblages may therefore be expected to exhibit variability concomitant with the various "structural poses" (Gearing 1962) of a community through its annual adaptive cycle. In addition, many assemblages may be expected to vary directly with the degree to which the community may be partitioned into specific kinds of task groupings for performing work at different locations. In short, assemblage variability may be expected to exhibit or reflect a variety of segments of community life and cannot always be expected to exhibit similarities as a direct reflection of the continuities among the persons performing the acts. Similarities may equally reflect continuities in the character of the acts performed. Differences may arise when the organization of activities varies temporally and/or spatially, resulting in a variety of assemblage types characteristic of the life of a given community [Binford 1972:132].

At the time I wrote the foregoing statement there was no direct empirical support for the argument. It represented a plausible view of archaeological formation processes, but there were no empirical studies to demonstrate that what was plausible was indeed realistic.

In addition to questioning the character of the linkage between past dynamics and present static data, I was issuing another challenge to the then prevailing view of the past. Under the fabrication model, characteristics of the archaeological record were linked directly to differing mental templates, which in turn were tabulated and summarized as a "trait list" of enumerated culture. I was suggesting not only that the archaeological record derives from an adaptation but also *that adaptations have all the properties of a system* in which various components are responsive to one another in their ongoing operation. The basic elements or components of the system are units of organization rather than discrete elements as viewed by us in the contemporary world. One cannot understand the workings of an automobile through a strategy that enumerates all the screws, nuts, springs, and other parts. One must first develop some way of recognizing basic functional components, such as carburetors, distributors, and voltage regulators, and then seek to understand how these units articulate with one another and interact under differing conditions external to the system to which they are responsive. Ways of developing a realistic appreciation for the characteristics of a system of adaptation must be sought, since the model of an automobile or other handy mechanical system is apt to mislead us if we attempt to use it to appreciate the organizational properties of a flexible behavioral system. Such flexibility can be thought of as deriving from responsive modifications through the use of alternative strategies and variable means to accomplish similar ends.

Under this systematic view of past dynamics we might anticipate much variability in the archaeological record that is directly referable not to differences between systems, but to *differing states of a single system*. We might also imagine that systems differing in overall organization could well share very similar strategies of adaptation. Sites that actually represent analogous situational states might be grouped, under the traditional methods of analysis, as similar systems. Such arguments are plausible, but as with the basic challenge to the fabrication model itself there was no empirical demonstration supporting them.

While such "processual" views of the nature of the linkage between static archaeological facts and past dynamics were being developed, argued, and made available in the literature, I was engaged in research and controversy primarily with François Bordes regarding the appropriate meaning to be given to certain archaeological facts regarding Mousterian material from both Europe and the Near East (see Binford 1972b; Binford and Binford 1966, 1969). These arguments were not related to the character of processes responsible for culture change, evolution, and the like; they were a direct confrontation regarding the assumed linkage between contemporary archaeological facts and past dynamics. We differed on the character of the dynamics believed responsible for observed archaeological facts and therefore on the meanings that could be rationally assigned to them.

In a more basic sense, we were arguing about the relevance of concepts and in turn the operational definitions associated with these concepts. Definitions are basic tools used to give meaning to what we see. They provide the links between concepts, our tools for thinking about the world, and observable properties of the world. It is the operation of translating perceptions into cognitive units that provides the meaning for sensory experiences. The concepts are the conventions that give the "paradigmatic" character to any field of endeavor. If we question the utility either of concepts or of the definitions associated with them, we are questioning the basic "culture" of a science. At this point we are not questioning a theory about the way the world works, since such theories are always phrased in terms of understandings about the way the world is. Theories attempt to answer the question, "Why is the world the way it appears to be?" Of course the way the world "appears to be" is conditioned quite directly by our paradigm or set of conventions for giving meaning to experience. We may question the usefulness of theories and still operate in terms of what Kuhn (1964) has called *normal science*. That is, although we may be skeptical about a given explanation for the world as known, such skepticism in no way questions our tools for knowing. We do not challenge the conventions whereby we give meaning to experience.

On the other hand, if we do question these conventions—the utility of our concepts and the rules for their appropriate use—we are questioning the very character of our alleged knowing, the character of our understanding of the way the world is, not simply ideas as to why it is that way. Normal science in Kuhn's (1964) terms proceeds in the context of an assumed paradigm. Normal science is concerned with evaluating the usefulness of explanations offered in answer to the question of why the world is the way it appears to be. The methods of hypothesis testing, deductive reasoning, and so on that characterize an epistemology based on scientific methods in no way address themselves directly to the problem of knowing what the world is like; they are part of a procedure for evaluating propositions as to why it is the way it appears.

When we do question our conventions for knowing we are questioning quite directly our view of the world, the meanings we give to experience. This questioning produces what Kuhn (1964) has called a *crisis period*—a period during which the conventions for knowing are uncertain and no one knows how to give meaning to what he sees. During such a period, therefore, there is no agreement on problem, procedure, or aims of science.

> In such times of crisis this conflict over the aims of science will become acute. We and those who share our attitude will hope to make new discoveries; and we shall hope to be helped in this by a newly erected scientific system. Thus, we shall take the greatest interest in the falsifying experiment. We shall hail it as a success, for it has opened up new vistas into a world of new experience. And we shall hail it even if these new experiences should furnish us with new arguments against our own most recent theories. But the newly rising structure, the boldness of which we admire, is seen by the conventionalist as a monument to the total collapse of science. . . . In the eyes of the conventionalist one principle only can help us to select a system as the chosen one from among all other possible systems, it is the principle of selecting the simplest system—*the simplest system of implicit definition*, which of course means in practice the "classical" system of the day [Popper 1959: 80–81].

During times when the paradigm has been questioned, when the definitional conventions for giving meaning to experience are under attack, there is great confusion. Some seek to evaluate "new" concepts and definitions through the methods of normal science—the use of deductive reasoning, hypothesis testing, and the like. These methods do not work. They were designed as methods for evaluating ideas about the way the world works. Under crisis conditions we must evaluate our rules for knowing, not proposals for understanding what is known. To my knowledge there are no procedures that are clear-cut when a paradigm is questioned. At such times we can only attempt to demonstrate that the world is different from the picture we would obtain had the conventions previously assumed been applied to given experiences. We must attempt to invent new conventions more appropriate to our experience and seek to eliminate ambiguities that might plague the use of these new conventions. This is a problem of developing new concepts and associated "operational definitions," new links between experience and our tools for meaningfully describing it. We may seek to justify both the concepts and their definitions to our colleagues. Such justification normally consists of arguments as to the reality basis for the concept, and in turn the utility of the concept for thinking about experience.

Science is based on the premise that the external world is knowable, and knowable *directly*; that is, it is accessible. When our tools for apprehending the world are questioned there is but one recourse: *to seek experiences in the world*, experiences that can elucidate the usefulness and accuracy of our tools for apprehending and describing reality. In turn we follow a strategy that, it is hoped, will prompt our inventiveness such that new concepts will result, new tools for describing more accurately the properties of nature. As Francis Bacon suggested (in Commins and Linscott 1947: 78–85),

> Man, being the servant and interpreter of nature, can do and understand so much and so much only as he has observed in fact or in thought of the course of nature; beyond this he neither knows anything nor can do anything. . . .
> . . . we must lead men to the particulars themselves, and their series and order; while men on their side must force themselves for a while to lay their notions by and begin to familiarize themselves with facts.

The search for certain, relevant experience is the concern of this book. I am not directly involved in hypothesis testing. I am not involved in a direct way with the problem of explanations. I am concerned with sharing a series of concrete experiences sought in the hope of uncovering some of the links between an ongoing living system and the static archaeological products resulting from the dynamics of the situation.

On the other hand, this is not a blind appeal for empiricism. Nor is it a contradiction of my earlier arguments in favor of the use of logico-deductive stategies in the important task of seeking verification for our ideas as to how the world works. Here, however, we face the serious problem of what the world is like.

In seeking experience, the problem of relevance and relevant experience is crucial. The paths that led me to decide in favor of the experiences reported here as relevant are perhaps informative.

In this book I discuss in some detail my observations on animal anatomy and the ways the Nunamiut Eskimo behaved toward animals. Why have I focused on fauna, and why have I chosen to study the Nunamiut Eskimo? Several lines of reasoning led me to concentrate my studies in these two areas. In 1966 my former wife and I argued that:

if we assume that variation in the structure and content of an archaeological assemblage is directly related to the form, nature, and spatial arrangement of human activities, several steps follow logically. We are forced to seek explanations for the composition of assemblages in terms of variations in human activities. The factors determining the range and form of human activities conducted by any group at a single location (the site) may vary in terms of a large number of possible "causes" in various combinations. The broader among these may be seasonally regulated phenomena, environmental conditions, ethnic composition of the group, size and structure of the group regardless of ethnic affiliation. Other determining variables might be the particular situation of the group with respect to food, shelter, supply of tools on hand, etc. In short, the units of "causation" of assemblage variability are separate activities, each of which may be related to both the physical and social environment, as well as interrelated in different ways [Binford and Binford 1966: 241].

This "assumed" view questioned the relevance of the previously discussed fabrication model and the linked additive or enumerative view of an adaptation. We were suggesting that the dynamics out of which the properties of an assemblage were derived were different from the dynamics traditionally argued for the production of an artifact. In short, what we questioned was the relevance and utility of the concept of culture to the facts of assemblage composition when viewed in terms of a fabrication dynamic. In the case of the mother goddess, if we accepted the equating of assemblage composition with "mental template" or "design for living" or "culture," then an explanation for the patterning demonstrated by Bordes among assemblage types would rest with arguments as to what would condition the differential presence of different cultures in certain regions of France during the Mousterian era. On the other hand, if we rejected the relevance of the concept of culture to the facts observed by Bordes such an explanation would not be acceptable. The solution to such a dilemma does not rest in hypothesis testing; it remains in the domain of evaluation the utility of a concept and in this case its linked model of dynamics. Throughout the 1966 study we sought to justify as plausible such a view of the dynamics standing behind the facts of assemblage composition. At that time, since the targets of controversy were stone tools and archaeologically observed variations in the relative frequencies of similar tool classes, we thought we might be able to demonstrate certain organizational facts about tool assemblages that would support our view that assemblages were composed of organized sets of tools and that assemblage variability derived from the varying degrees in which these sets were represented. We acknowledged that we had no way of reliably giving behavioral meaning to the tools themselves; however, this did not stop us from offering certain guesses.

Although I was "impressed" with the results of the 1966 study I was very uncomfortable with the situation. I was proposing that tool frequencies varied with activity differences. Clearly what was needed was some way of identifying activities, some concepts with linked definitions that would permit me to recognize a past activity from empirical properties of sites, assemblages, or the tools themselves. I first thought that detailed studies of wear patterns on the tool might permit the identification of function. However, results of lithic studies overwhelmingly demonstrated that wear-pattern analysis yielded ambiguous results. A variety of activities could generate similar wear patterns, and, conversely, similar activities could generate different wear patterns.

I became discouraged with this avenue of research and turned to the problem of developing techniques that could be used for isolating activity areas. I hoped that if we could see such areas then we might be able to develop concepts and definitions sufficient to identify activities. I hoped to be able to give meaning to archaeological facts in terms of past behavior.

In 1967 I began to develop another line of argument. Activities are investments of labor in modifying resources for use. If I could relate patterns of tool association, and spatial ordering on living floors, to certain kinds of resources then I might be able to make statements from the static facts of the archaeological record about the behaviors that generated the facts. Under a National Science Foundation grant, I began the detailed observation of the faunal remains and the horizontal distributions of fauna and tools recovered from the deeply stratified Mousterian site of Combe Grenal. A year spent in France recording the bones and laboriously developing the distribution maps of the different levels of Combe Grenal generated a wealth of new data about the site. I found variability among the levels in the species present, and some correlations between species frequencies and tool frequencies. Distribution patterns of tools and fauna varied from level to level, and in turn there was some correlation between pattern differences, tool frequencies, and environmental variables. I was able to make the following summary statements:

A. The number of animals represented in any one occupation zone is relatively small. It is therefore reasonable to suggest that the occupations at Combe Grenal were of relatively short duration, and that group sizes, although variable, were generally small.

B. There are clear differences in the relative frequencies of anatomical parts of various animal species.

   1. *Bovids and horses* are represented by analogous anatomical parts and are clearly differentiated from reindeer and deer in the parts present.

      a. Bovids are primarily represented by mandibular fragments, lower teeth, fragments of the tibia, femur, humerus, and radio-cubitus. Ribs, vertebrae, pelvis parts, skull fragments, metapodials, and phalanges are rare.

      b. Horses are primarily represented by mandibular fragments, lower teeth, and fragments of the tibia, femur, humerus, and radio-cubitus. In contrast to the bovids there is much greater variability in the frequency of maxillary teeth. In some levels there are more maxillary teeth than mandibular teeth. The latter generally occur in levels where numerous horses are represented. Ribs, vertebrae, pelvis parts, skull fragments, metapodials, and phalanges are rare, as they are for bovids.

   2. *Deer and reindeer* bone remains are not as similar as the remains of bovids and horses. However, the similarities are such that they can consider in a grouping seperate from bovids and horses.

      a. There is much greater variability between different occupations in the anatomical parts of deer and reindeer represented than is the case for either bovids or horses.

b. All previously published patterns of variation in anatomical parts are represented among the deer and reindeer remains from the occupations of Combe Grenal. Frequencies analogous to those noted on kill sites (Dibble and Lorrain 1968; Kehoe 1967; White 1954) are represented. Similarly, frequencies analogous to two recognized patterns documented for semipermanent settlements on the Plains of North America (Wood 1962) are also represented, and there are other patterns of variation not previously documented.

C. There are marked and contrasting patterns of variability in the anatomical parts represented from a single species recovered from different occupational zones in Combe Grenal.

D. There are no bone samples from Combe Grenal in which all the anatomical parts of any animal are represented in expected proportional frequencies based on their frequency in the skeleton of the animal.

E. There are clear correlations crosscutting the recognized types of assemblages between some tool types and the pounds of meat represented by certain species. In addition, there are correlations crosscutting the recognized types of assemblages between some tools and the total amount of meat represented regardless of species

F. There are correlations crosscutting recognized types of assemblages between some tool types and particular parts of certain species.

G. There is no demonstrable directional change in the patterns of variation among anatomical parts from the bottom to the top of the deposit.

H. There are some correlations between faunal components and the four types of Mousterian assemblage recognized by Bordes.

Despite this new knowledge, the facts did not speak for themselves; I had no way of reliably giving meaning to what I had seen, of relating my observations to the dynamics of the past from which they derived. I was frustrated. There seemed to be no unambiguous way of demonstrating the inadequacy of the fabrication model of dynamics as an explanation for the facts of assemblage composition.

One of the findings that emerged during the Combe Grenal study was the existence of considerable interspecies and intraspecies variability in the relative frequencies of anatomical parts among the several archaeological levels. Other investigators had attempted to give meaning to such differential frequencies. Theodore E. White was one of the first to do so. In general, White viewed frequency variations as resulting from varying butchering practices and considered that these practices might well differ between societies (White 1952).

Working independently of White, Raymond Dart investigated over 7000 animal bones associated with *Australopithecus*. Dart found serious disproportions in the skeletal parts preserved as fossils. Certain parts were common in the assemblage, whereas others were generally missing. Dart interpreted these differences as the result of australopithecine hunting and tool-using behavior:

The disappearance of tails was probably due to their use as signals and whips in hunting outside the cavern. Caudal and other vertebrae may also have disappeared because of the potential value of their bodies as projectiles and their processes as levers and points . . . femora and tibiae would be the heaviest clubs to use outside the cavern, that is probably why these bones are the least common. Humeri are the commonest of the long bones; probably because they would be the most convenient clubs for the women-folk and children to use at home [Dart 1957:85].

In 1968, Dexter Perkins and Patricia Daly reported on the fauna from a "Neolithic" village excavated in Turkey. They investigated the relative frequencies of anatomical parts recovered for several species. They observed that, among the bovids, bones of the upper legs were strongly underrepresented compared to the bones of the lower legs. The argued that

> the missing leg bones indicated that the cattle were slaughtered near the village. . . .
>
> When a . . . hunting party killed a wild ox, they apparently butchered it on the spot and used the animals own hide as a container for carrying the meat home. They evidently stripped the fore-quarters and hindquarters of meat and threw the leg bones away. They apparently left the feet attached to the hide, perhaps because the feet made convenient handles for dragging the meat filled hide [Perkins and Daly 1968:104].

R. E. Chaplin discussed the low frequency of sheep upper-leg bones compared to the frequency of lower-leg bones at a Saxon site near London. He concluded that this discrepancy resulted from the "export" of the meat joints from the site and was therefore indicative of trade (Chaplin 1969:233–244).

White (1954) suggested that low frequencies of the upper-leg bones at the site studied from the Plains was the result of their destruction beyond recognition during the aboriginal manufacture of bone grease (White 1954:256). Underrepresentation of the bones of the lower leg at living sites was a result of their having been abandoned at the kill site (White 1954:256). The latter suggestion was borne out by the higher frequencies of lower limbs on demonstrated kill sites (Dibble and Lorrain 1968:100; Kehoe 1967:107).

In these examples the same phenomena—high frequencies of lower limbs and low frequencies of upper limbs—are interpreted as indicative of (a) use of the upper limbs as clubs away from the site, (b) abandonment of upper limbs at kill sites and intro-duction of lower limbs into living sites, (c) removal of upper limbs from the living site through trade in meat, (d) destruction of upper limbs at living sites through the manufacture of bone grease, and (e) abandonment of lower limbs at kill sites and the removal of meat bones to living sites. The only interpretation that appears to be borne out through comparative study of documented cases is the last one, which is directly opposite to the interpretation placed on the same phenomena by Perkins and Daly (b).

The complexities of the problem can be further demonstrated by a summary of the suggestions offered in the literature to account for observed frequency patterning:

A. Suggestions offered to account for differing proportional frequencies observed at a single site between anatomical parts of a single species:
   1. Removal or destruction of some parts as a function of their use as tools or as raw materials for tools (Dart 1957:85; Kitching 1963:49–53; White 1953b:162; 1954:177)

2. The differential destruction of parts during butchering (Kehoe 1967:72; White 1952:338)
3. The differential transport of anatomical parts from kill sites to sites of consumption (Dibble and Lorrain 1968:103; Kehoe 1967:72; Perkins and Daly 1968:104; White 1952:162)
4. The differential transport of parts away from sites of consumption in the context of trade (Chaplin 1969:223)
5. The differential destruction of anatomical parts during consumption by man
   a. Direct eating of soft bone parts (Brain 1969:15–16; White 1954:171)
   b. Destruction of bone parts as a result of marrow extraction (Brain 1969:15, Kehoe 1967:72; White 1954:258)
   c. Destruction of bone parts as a result of pounding of bones for the extraction of bone grease (Kehoe 1967:72; White 1953b:162)
6. The differential destruction of bone parts on sites of consumption by domesticated dogs (Brain 1969:15; Dibble and Lorrain 1968:93; Guilday n.d.:7; White 1954:256)
7. The differential destruction of anatomical parts on kill sites or abandoned living sites by carrion feeders (Brian 1969; Kitching 1963:22–23; Voorhies 1969:20)

B. Suggestions offered to account for differences noted between species in the proportional frequencies of anatomical parts represented within a single deposit:
   1. The differential degree of butchering of different species at kill sites as a function of their size and portability (White 1953b:160, 1954:255)
   2. Differences between domesticated and wild forms being butchered at the site of consumption and wild forms being butchered at kill sites (Perkins and Daly 1968:104; White 1954:172)
   3. Differential destruction of parts from different species as a function of differences in the size and strength of analogous anatomical parts (White 1954:256)
   4. Differential food preferences for analogous anatomical parts from different species (White 1952:337)

C. Suggestions offered to account for differences noted between proportional frequencies of anatomical parts from a single species recovered from different archaeological sites:
   1. Functional differences between the sites, notably kill sites versus village sites (Clark and Haynes 1970; Dibble and Lorrain 1968:102; Kehoe 1967:72; White 1952:337)
   2. Ethnic differences in food preferences and butchering practice between the social groups represented at different sites (Dibble and Lorrain 1968:102; Kehoe 1967:72; White 1954:254; Wood 1962:203)

Most if not all of these suggestions have some basis in ethnographically known behavior. Many are specifically documented as affecting the differential introduction or destruction of anatomical parts at archaeological sites. What is clearly lacking from our current understanding is a *specific knowledge* of the particular effects that might be expected to result from any of the activities mentioned.

The picture is further complicated by the research of C. K. Brain (1969). Largely stimulated by the work of Dart, Brain investigated the remains of goats found in recently abandoned Hottentot villages. In a situation where the animals had been slaughtered in the village and no meat traded, he found that there was still a marked discrepancy in the frequencies of anatomical parts recovered. In an attempt to account for the missing parts, Brain conducted preliminary studies of the specific gravity of the different bones and the differential fusion time of articulator ends of long bones. He demonstrated that the survival of identifiable bones varied directly with the specific gravity of the part and inversely with the fusion time of the articulator end. On the basis of these findings, he suggested that most if not all the discrepancies observed by Dart in the Makapansgat fauna could be understood solely as a function of the differential durability of bones subjected to destructive natural agencies. Thus, Brain's data appear to be a major challenge to those who see behavioral or cultural significance in differential bone frequencies. Brain's conclusions are supported by the observed differential frequencies of anatomical parts observed in pre-Pleistocene fauna from North America. Voorhies (1969) has reported in detail on the frequencies of parts of animals preserved in an early Pliocene deposit in Nebraska. The animals represented in this deposit lived in North America long before man was present, so human behavior and cultural practices could not possibly have contributed to the observed discrepancies in anatomical part frequencies. Voorhies concluded that the activity of carrion feeders, differential sorting by natural agents, and the differential breakdown of parts as a function of their strength all contributed to the observed frequencies.

Clearly this is a provocative set of findings and one that is of great importance to the archaeologist. I have followed up on these suggestions and my findings regarding processes of natural attrition have been published elsewhere (Binford and Bertram 1977).

In spite of the ambiguities and the clear lack of any reliable procedures for giving meaning to faunal facts, I reasoned that research in this area might provide the needed context for evaluating the models of past dynamics and therefore the general relevance of the concept of culture to facts of assemblage composition.

The obvious advantage of research with fauna is that there is no question about the irrelevance of the fabrication model with regard to the character and formal properties of the bones. Man did not make the bones; their form is not a product of any mental templates or designs for living. Therefore it becomes possible to set forth a completely culture-free taxonomy of bones. Any variability observed in the relative frequencies of anatomical parts among archaeological sites must derive from the dynamics of their use. Man's role is only one of partitioning, segmenting, and differentially distributing the segments of animal anatomy during the course of his exploitation of the animal. Little question could exist that any patterning derived from the faunal remains reflected use.

In spite of these obvious advantages, I still could not see how to demonstrate that the activities of use were inappropriate to a fabrication model for the formation processes of the archaeological record. Such a situation had frequently been pointed out by my critics. It had been asserted that activites are also cultural—that is, the fabrication model of dynamics applies equally to activities of use as it does to the activity of tool production. To this assertion there is no appeal except to the empirical world. Do people behave this way? Do people conduct their ongoing activities in terms of invariant mental templates as to the appropriate strategies regardless of the setting in which they find themselves? Do members of a given cultural unit, equal participants in a tradition, fabricate tools for use in their activities in terms of a shared ideal as to what their assemblage should look like in terms of the relative frequencies of tools or other elements? Are the results of actually coping with the world isomorphic with the traditionally passed on ideas as to means for coping? Are the cultural means independent of the problems presented to a group for solution?

To obtain answers to such questions about the way the world is, one must investigate the relevant world. What is relevant here? Would seeking additional empirical experience through the excavation and subsequent analysis of additional archaeological facts provide the relevant experience? The answer must be no. The relevant experience is one where we can directly experience the character of the linkage between the archaeological by-products and behavior. At the same time we must be able to evaluate the behavior relative to the degree to which it is differentially responsive to situational variables, the degree to which individuals sharing a common tradition or body of common knowledge use this shared culture differentially in dealing with situational differences arising from the dynamics of their environment, and the character of the adaptive interaction between persons and their environment. It is necessary to experience directly the process of adaptation and in turn the archaeological products of this process. Relevance is achieved when we can examine variability in the archaeological products and hold culture a constant. In this situation, we could directly evaluate the utility of the fabrication model of behavior as the assumed link between the dynamics of behavior and the static facts remaining for us to observe.

Such experience can never be obtained from empirical work with archaeological remains. We must therefore proceed along the research path forged quite eloquently by our sister discipline geology in its adoption of the proposition of uniformitarianism. Is the formation of archaeological remains as a by-product of adaptive behavior a process that is operative in the contemporary world? Can we directly experience this process relative to a domain of facts that are observable in the archaeological remains for the past? If so, we may experience this crucial linkage of behavioral dynamics and statics. If we find our assumptions about the nature of this linkage to be inadequate, we are perfectly justified in rejecting these assumptions, since their general adequacy must be demonstrable if they are to be used universally to give meaning to the archaeological record.

My conclusion was that the formation processes of archaeological remains were indeed common to both contemporary and past eras. Many of the animal species present in assemblages are still extant, and the processes of exploitation and use operative in the past are still operative today.

The study of fauna offers another advantage: Since we can assume that earlier populations used animals primarily as food we can evaluate the food utility of various anatomical parts by studying representatives of modern species. This would permit the objective assignment of "utility" values to anatomical parts thereby providing a meaningful reference dimension for our taxonomy of bones. Such an assignment of utility seemed impossible to work out for stone tools. How could we develop a procedure for giving utility values to stone tools relative to different potential uses? Using fauna we could not only employ a culture-free taxonomy for tabulating relative frequencies of faunal elements in different sites, but we could develop a reference dimension of food value for the taxonomy. We could display patterns of assemblage variability against scales of resource utility as a basis for evaluating the degree to which the patterning reflected consistent strategies relative to the use of the animals. Patterning in faunal frequencies might then be reasonably viewed as resulting from variable strategies in the use of food sources.

Although the advantages evident in working with fauna were exciting, it was recognized that following up these advantages in whatever detail would not directly solve the problem of relevance. What was needed was a set of concrete descriptions of the dynamics of behavior resulting in static patterning in the archaeological record. The static patterning had then to be related to the behavioral dynamics so that we might evaluate whether differences in culture were or were not manifest in the patterning. It was deemed desirable to seek an opportunity to observe such dynamics with respect to the genesis of faunal assemblages. If we could elucidate the models of dynamics standing behind faunal variability we might then use such understanding as a reference dimension for evaluating variability in stone tools.

To achieve these ends I chose to conduct ethnographic work among the Nunamiut Eskimo of the central Brooks Range in Alaska. These people are hunters, reported to be over 80% dependent for their subsistence on a single species, *Rangifer tarandus* or caribou. If there was any place in the world where I could learn about the problems presented by a strong dependence on hunted food, how these problems are solved, and how such solutions are manifest archaeologically in faunal remains, it would be with the Nunamiut.

My aims at the time of initiating fieldwork were simple: to learn as much as possible about all aspects of the procurement, processing, and consumption strategies of the Nunamiut Eskimo and in turn relate these behaviors directly to their faunal consequences. I hoped to accomplish this for most if not all of the locations used by the Eskimo throughout a full seasonal cycle of their subsistence-settlement round.

The Nunamiut are inland Eskimo, currently localized in a sedentary community at Anaktuvuk Pass, at the drainage divide of the Brooks Range. (See Figure 14.1 for the location of Anaktuvuk Pass and its relationship to the caribou migration routes.) The contemporary community is composed of two amalgamated bands, the Tulu-gakmiut and the Killikmiut, plus two attached families of the Ulumiut, a local band that broke up in 1942.

During the month of August 1969, the village of Anaktuvuk was composed of 126 permanent residents and 4 visiting Eskimos. The population was segmented into 21 households, 17 of which were composed of nuclear families (a husband and wife and their offspring only). Two househlds were composed of extended families—the nuclear family plus a widowed parent of the husband. The remaining 2 households

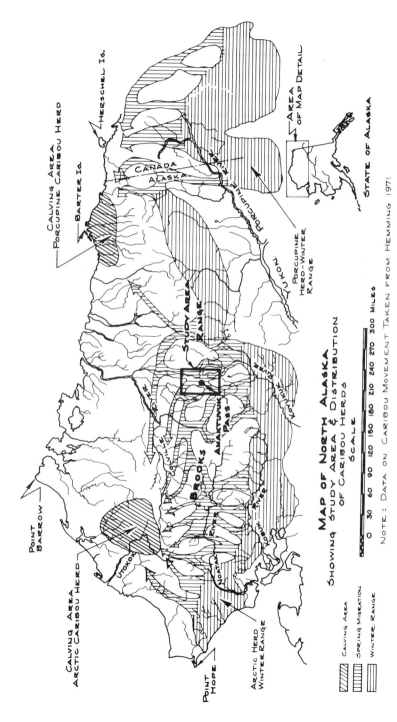

Figure 14.1 Map of North Alaska showing location of research area.

were composed of unmarried adults with their offspring in one case and adult unmarried brothers in the other.

The Nunamiut have been studied previously and a considerable literature covering various aspects of their society and patterns of adaptation is available (Binford 1975a, 1976; Binford and Chasko 1976; Campbell 1968, 1970; Gubser 1965; Ingsted 1951; Pospisil 1964; Rausch 1951). Other researchers have summarized various aspects of Nunamiut life or conducted short-term interviews with some of the more famous "old men" at Anaktuvuk (Burch 1972b; Solecki 1950; Spencer 1959; these are just a few).

This book[1] reports the results of the study of the economic anatomy of sheep and caribou, and my experiences with the Nunamiut Eskimo. Throughout I have described the faunal materials collected from the sites of known behavioral contexts among the Nunamiut. These assemblages have then been referred to anatomical scales of value developed through the study of animals, as a means to the evaluation of the Eskimos' behavior and their adaptive strategies.

Note

1. The book referred to here is *Nunamiut Ethnoarchaeology*, the book in which this originally appeared.

Olorgesailie Deserves More Than the Usual Book Review

Olorgesailie: Archaeological Studies of a Middle Pleistocene Lake Basin in Kenya. Glynn Ll. Isaac, Assisted by Barbara Isaac. *University of Chicago Press, 1977. 272 pp., $7.00.*

The appearance of this report has been long awaited by persons interested in man's evolutionary history. Data from this site have been cited by practically every person writing on African prehistory since the immediate postwar years.

Active excavation was carried out at Olorgesailie between 1941 and 1965 and at least seven different archaeologists conducted major excavations at the location during this interval. One can only marvel at the relative success which Isaac has had in "reconstructing" the archaeological record from the records of so many investigators. While the number of investigators certainly contributed to the variable quality of the archaeological data remaining from the excavations, another set of conditions further complicated the picture. The period of time during which investigations were conducted at Olorgesailie spans major changes in the field of African archaeology. Aims, methods and the overall support for research in the area changed drastically during the period of active investigation at Olorgesailie. These factors—change in the field, and a high "turn-over-rate" among investigating archaeologists—contributed to the accumulation of a body of information highly variable in quality. For instance, information on the horizontal position of artifacts in the excavations is only available for five of the seventeen major excavation units and all of these were the result of excavations by Isaac after 1961. Similarly, what was considered a potential source of information clearly changed during the course of excavation at Olorgesailie. Of the 19 samples from the 17 excavation locations three show no record of the frequency of angular fragments, while seven have counts for the category, but there is no certainty that all such items were collected. Only nine of the 19 samples reliably tabulate this category of worked stone. Such differences in the quality of available

Originally published in *Journal of Anthropological Research* 33(4):493–502, © 1977.

data condition what can be done with these materials as well as render the site less important from the perspective of 1977 than it was during the years when it was yielding primary data relative to the issues of the day.

I do not mean to imply that the site is no longer important. Any such assertion would be far from true. It is a location yielding some of the best information available regarding the long span of time between the lower Acheulian of Bed II at Olduvai Gorge and the late Acheulian of Kalambo Falls. Although inconclusive, a date for the Olorgesailie formation of around 400,000 years is cited by Isaac as reasonable. The possible range of time represented is from 700,000 to 60,000 years ago.

Isaac's report is separated into two basic parts corresponding to what Isaac recognizes as two basic research concerns. Part one (Chapters 1-4) represents "research operations designed to provide elucidation of the subsistence economy, land use pattern, and the socioeconomic configuration of early prehistory hominids." The second part (Chapters 5-8) "is focused on the collections of artifacts themselves." In this section Isaac is concerned with patterning in morphological properties of artifacts and in turn how morphological variation may be patterned in relation to temporal and compositional variations among assemblages.

In the area of subsistence economy there has been an increasing solidification of two very opposite points of view relative to the subsistence behavior of early hominids. The first set of ideas to achieve widespread recognition was the so-called "hunting hypothesis." The basic ideas were articulated by Raymond Dart (1957) and then popularized by Robert Ardrey (1961, 1976). These ideas held that strong behavioral selection was associated with a shift to predation and that the latter shift largely brought into being basic conditions of human nature. For Dart and Ardrey man was viewed as aggressive, even bloodthirsty, and such traits were seen as naturally stemming from our predatory background. Empirically this view was challenged by Louis Leakey, based upon his finds at Olduvai Gorge. A more sophisticated challenge to the hunting hypothesis has gradually developed in the writings of Glynn Isaac. Two ideas are central to Isaac's position. (a) Man's early subsistence strategy was a mixed one in which the early role of predation was not well established, and (b) one of the major features distinguishing the behavior of early man from his primate relatives was his "home base" oriented subsistence strategy. It is argued that linked to a home base strategy was the cooperative sharing of food. Increasingly, Isaac has emphasized "sharing behavior" as a major evolutionary conditioner of "human nature" in opposition to the "the hunting hypothesis" and its linked emphasis upon aggression.

In the Olorgesailie report these issues are skirted in a direct sense. Nevertheless, there is a hidden dimension of concern for evaluating the relationship of the archaeological facts to past events. In the work of extreme advocates of the "hunting hypothesis" there was a tendency to directly translate the archaeological record into past behavior. If bones of animals were found associated with the remains of early hominids, it was assumed that this association could only result from the dynamics of hominid behavior. Hominids killed the animals, accumulated the bones, and consumed the meat, activities which resulted in the associations observed archaeologically!

Perhaps the most insightful innovation in this book is the direct confrontation which Isaac has offered to all those who would uncritically accept all archaeologically recovered facts as inevitably relevant to past hominid behavior. For instance, of the nineteen basic assemblages recovered from Olorgesailie seven are characterized as almost certainly reorganized by post depositional phenomena being described as "disturbed" (MFS), "transported and possibly sorted" (Tr. M10, Meng, Mid, H/9AM), "derived and rearranged" (H/9A), "disturbed and abraded" (DE/89A), as well as three not previously mentioned (MPS, DE/9B, and Fr. Bed HL). Six of the above are additionally described as occupationally "composite," that is being mixtures of more than one occupation. In addition to these nine "composite" assemblages, an additional six (LHS, Hog, H/9A Cat, I_3 and BBA) are described as "very composite" meaning that they are most likely mixtures of many separate occupations dispersed over a considerable period of time. Only three samples, H/6A, DE/89C, and Friday Bed are described as "localizations" with no clear estimate of the amount of post-depositional modification. The final sample, BBB, is basically undocumented and no knowledge of its context is indicated. What these conditions mean is that these are not "sites" in the sense of locations of spatially and temporally discrete hominid behavior. They are *localizations* of artifacts and other remains. We do not know specifically (a) the origins of the elements occurring in these localizations, or (b) the degree that associations and patterns of demonstrable co-variation among the localizations derive from hominid behavioral processes rather than post-depositional processes. This uncertainty was attacked quite directly by Isaac. He has explored the possibility that many if not all the "localizations," but particularly those associated with sand deposits, could be understood as the result of a "kinematic wave effect" which has been argued to result in concentrations of coarse particles in ephemeral streams. Commonly, such concentrations are on top of sand lens. This is the most common situation where there are major localizations within the Olorgesailie deposits.

The kind of on-and-off skepticism which pervades Isaac's work is well illustrated in his discussion of diet. He seemingly accepts the argument that the high frequency of *Pelorovis* (a kind of African goat) at the Olduvai location of BK II represents a game drive. Leakey originally observed that at least one of these goats was stuck in the mud with the legs vertically placed in the deposit and the remains of the torso scattered around the legs. Given that this was a general condition, and it appears likely, then the inference that the herd of goats got stuck in the mud seems clear. One can only marvel at the hominid that had enough sense to drive the goats into the mud but not enough sense to remove them from their sticky matrix for butchering? In going over the data from the BK location as published (M. D. Leakey 1971, 197–222), I see no convincing patterns of association between the tools and the *Pelorovis* remains at the locality. Why is Isaac willing to accept the localizations of artifacts at Olduvai as "living floors"? This type of variable use of data characterizes almost all of Isaac's summarizing and concluding sections (see particularly Chapters 4 and 9).

I will attempt to demonstrate that these varying postures are not "determined" by the facts. They represent some intellectual biases on the part of the author. For instance, if natural processes were largely responsible for the localizations of materials recovered at Olorgesailie, there are important implications. First, Isaac argues that the aggregation of tools in ephemeral stream beds would be a very local phenomena. That is, the movement of tools from their original position would be over a relatively short distance. It is also likely that there would be little sorting under the proposed

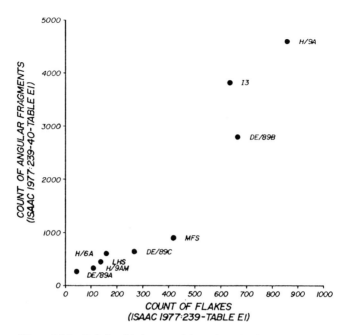

Figure 15.1   Relationship between flake and angular fragment counts—
Olorgesailie.

kinematic wave effect. Although the patterns of spatial positioning among tools and
other solid objects would be referable to natural agents, Isaac maintains that the
patterns of *association* or co-occurrence among various classes of artifacts would in
general reflect actual patterns that had existed in their primary depositional context.
This means that in Isaac's view facts of *site structure* were destroyed at Olorgesailie,
but facts of *assemblage composition* are believed to be essentially preserved. By extension,
facts of *association between artifacts and fauna* are also accepted as meaningfully preserved. The uncertainty, however, of the latter assumptions contribute to a kind of
wishy-washy interpretive posture on Isaac's part. A conservative no comment posture
is spread among what appears to me to be a wide eyed naivete where associations
between tools and fauna or the content of assemblages are accepted as directly referable
to hominid behavior. They may be in reality so referable but these links need to be
established. Isaac does not address such questions analytically. I consider this to be
a major weakness of this report and most of the current reports coming from the
earlier time periods of African research.

To show that this "lack" is not due to the character of the data but instead reflects
bias on the part of Isaac and certainly less rigorous African archaeologists (see Leakey
and Lewin 1977, for instance), I have conducted a few analytical exercises using data
presented by Isaac.

Figure 15.1 illustrates the relationship between the frequency of flakes and the
frequency of artifactual rubble for those assemblages where the both sets of data are
available. Clearly there is a strong positive and slightly curvilinear relationship between

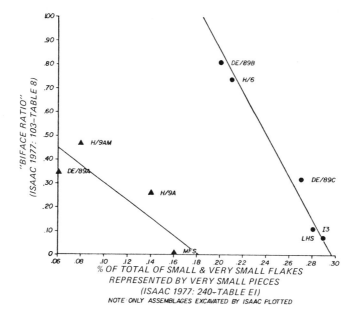

Figure 15.2   Relationship between "biface ratio" and the percentage of flakes represented by very small pieces—Olorgesailie.

these two classes of material, both presumably the byproduct of raw material processing for tool manufacture. It is truly difficult to imagine that such a tight relationship would be preserved among two classes of material for which there is good reason to suspect a strong correlation if the facts of *assemblage composition* had been vastly distorted by stream sorting and other natural agents. On the other hand, if one examines the data in a more detailed manner, one's confidence in the facts of assemblage composition is not nearly so strong. For instance, one would expect that modifications in assemblage composition deriving from hydrological processes would most likely modify the numerical relationships between elements differing primarily in size. In order to gain some perspective on the likelihood that processes modifying assemblage content did go on at Olorgesailie, I examined some of the detailed morphological information supplied by Isaac on assemblages which he excavated or has judged roughly comparable to his excavation procedure. As a good control over size-related modifications I calculated the proportion of the total for small and very small flakes which were represented by very small flakes as given by Isaac in Table E1 on page 240. These values were then plotted against the "biface" index as given by Isaac in Table 8 (p. 103) (See Figure 15.2). The result is most illuminating. As can be seen, there are two distributions roughly paralleling one another. The outermost distribution demonstrates an inverse linear relationship between the biface index and the percentage of very small flakes present in the flake component of the assemblage. Stated very simply, this shows that as bifaces increase in an assemblage, very small flakes decrease within the flake component of the assemblage. This means that there is a size-related correlation between biface frequencies and the other elements of the assemblage. This is even more strikingly demonstrated in a second and paralleled distribution. What one must realize is that the asssemblages occurring in the "internal" scatter were designated by Isaac as disturbed, transported, sorted, derived, rearranged, or clearly modified as evaluated by the condition of the elements making up the assemblage. The important point to be made, however, is that two parallel distributions were observed. One is exclusively made up of cases which were independently evaluated as very disturbed. They exhibit about one half as many "very small" flakes relative to "small" flakes as do the assemblages in the "outer distribution" which were judged to have been less disturbed. Nevertheless, there is an inverse relationship between the biface index and very small flakes to small flakes in the flake component of the assemblage. This demonstrates that among the heavily disturbed assemblages there is a systematic relationship between bifaces and other large items. Looking at the assemblages which were judged to be less disturbed we see that this same condition is indicated by the independent but parallel distribution. There are about twice as many "very small" flakes relative to other complete flakes than was true for the disturbed assemblages. Nevertheless, the reduction in proportions of "very small" flakes is systematic with increases in the biface component of the assemblage. This is taken as evidence that these assemblages are *also* modified in their proportional content particularly in size variable items. I would conclude from these simple studies that there are *no* assemblages at Olorgesailie which are not modified away from the facts of content which characterized them at the time of deposition by hominids. Isaac does not face this issue squarely.

Similarly, when one plots the relationship between certain facts of assemblage composition and the character of associated fauna, simple associations are not as evident. Table 15.1 summarizes data taken from Isaac regarding the general conditions of faunal material associated with the stone tool components at the recognized sites. The list of sites is arranged in order of increasing index values (taken from Isaac p. 103). Higher values indicate increasing dominance of the assemblage by large tools (bifaces) relative to small flake tools. What is provocative is that all sites where some documentation of fauna existed and with index values less than .30, faunal remains were numerically dominated by long bone splinters and fragmented bone, while teeth represented a numerically minor part of the faunal assemblage. Fauna documented with all assemblages where the index value for bifaces was greater than .30 was numerically documented by teeth except at locations where remains of complete animals were indicated. Ignoring for the moment those sites where the remains of complete animals were indicated, the observed degree of separation between the types of faunal remains and the sites with low-biface index values versus sites with high biface index values could be expected to arise under chance conditions less than one in a hundred times. It seems likely then that there are "real" differences between sites in the relative preservation of faunal materials. It is generally recognized that teeth are the most dense elements in the osteological anatomy of animals. My studies (see Binford and Bertram 1977) showed that long bone splinters were the second most dense elements of a bone assemblage with articulator ends almost always being less dense than the splinters of bone shaft. Given our current understanding regarding the preservation of bone, assemblages subjected to the most intense action by attri-

TABLE 15.1

Summary Data on Faunal Information From Olorgesailie
(Taken from Isaac 1977: 34–79)

	Assemblage Designation	Biface Index (Table 8 page 103)	Modal Faunal Elements
Scraper-Dominated Assemblages	MFS	.000	splinters
	BBB	.013	n.d.[a]
	LHS	.086	splinters
	Hog	.097	n.d. –(Hippo)[b]
	Friday	.115	n.d.
	I$_3$	.121	splinters
	MPS	.133	splinters
	BBA	.216	n.d. –(Hippo)
	H/9A	.262	splinters
Intermediate Set	DE/89C	.328	Teeth
	DE/89A	.358	Teeth
	Tr M10	.386	n.d. –(Hippo)
	H/9 AM	.482	n.d.
Biface = Dominated Set	Meng	.742	n.d.
	H/6A	.742	Teeth
	DE/89B	.810	? [c]–(Baboons)
	Mid	.946	n.d.

[a] n.d. = no data were systematically collected.
[b] Sites where at least major segments of complete animals were.
[c] Other species are reported but parts represented are not identified.

	Splinters	Teeth	Totals
Index less than .30	5	0	5
Index greater than .30	0	3	3
Totals	5	3	8

$X^2 = 7.824$
d.f. = 1
Expected X^2, .01 level of probability, 6.635

tional agents would be represented only by teeth. Less intensive action by attritional agents would insure the association of teeth and long bone splinters with increasing frequencies of articulator ends and a graded series of frequencies of other anatomical parts numerically varying as a function of bone density. Given these expectations it would appear that among the Olorgesailie samples there is some relationship between the degree of faunal preservation and the composition of the associated tool assemblage. It is hard to imagine how such a relationship could arise except as a result of post-depositional phenomena, processes which were equally responsible for bringing into being some of the facts of the faunal assemblage. Another interesting point regarding fauna is that locations cited as yielding evidence of faunal remains of complete or near complete animals appear to exhibit no pattern of correlation with the differences between "splinter" assemblages and "tooth" assemblages. This condition makes a great deal of sense given that post-depositional processes as suggested by Isaac have destroyed facts of the internal site structure. Although limited, the data from faunal material summarized here suggests that these post-depositional processes may well have modified the "content" of both tool and faunal assemblages. Any complete or near complete skeletons occurring in the deposits must therefore have been deposited *after* the events which resulted in the production of the basic tool and faunal assemblages as defined by the excavations. If this is the case then there is *no* association between such skeletons and the artifacts which had been subjected to post-depositional processes of "localization." This point is particularly important for an assemblage which has yielded a sample of bones from about 44 adult and between 6 and 17 juvenile baboons found at DE/89B. This is the assemblage from Olorgesailie which Isaac attempts to interpret regarding hominid hunting behavior and diet.

> A killing pattern such as is observed at the DE/89B might have been achieved if the baboons had been driven against a hazard or if their waterhole had been poisoned. But driving baboons or geladas against a hazard is almost inconceivable, since the species shows such guile and agility. Poisoning of waterholes, while a possible explanation for the killing pattern, would have resulted in a much broader spectrum of species in the refusal.
>
> An ethnographic analogy provided the inspiration for a plausible if untestable reconstruction . . . (p. 91).

Isaac goes on to suggest that "perhaps" the hominids intruded on a baboon nesting area at night driving them from their trees and killing some in the confusion.

The first point to be made in considering the relationship between the tools and the fauna is an interesting one. What makes Isaac think that the fauna present is informative regarding hominid behavior? Clearly because the fauna was found in association with the tools. Let's look at this relationship first. There are approximately 1250 identifiable elements of baboon skeleton (1000 of which are teeth) and an additional 12.5 Kg of bone splinters (approximately 13,000 small fragments) all this presumably representing 40–50 adult and 5–20 juvenile baboons, let's say 60 individuals. Found with these 60 animals were 4,429 worked artifacts and 433 manuports. Of the worked pieces there were 581 shaped tools of which 245 were picklike handaxes and 148 were cleavers. If the association between tools and baboons is directly meaningful, this would mean that there were 4.08 picklike handaxes, 2.47 cleavers, or 73.8 pieces of worked stone used in the killing and processing of each baboon! I find this highly unlikely. Now, if the facts of assemblage composition are not derived from the same events which resulted in the presence of the baboon remains, then where is the evidence for the role of man in accounting for their presence?

I do not wish to go further with this type of analysis. I hope that I have offered sufficient reasons for doubting the patterns of assemblage composition as well as the patterns of association between tools and fauna. This doubt must render easy "interpretations" of past hunting behavior, settlement pattern and the like highly suspect at best.

Isaac concluded that facts of site structure were not preserved at Olorgesailie, but tentatively accepted the facts of assemblage composition and faunal association as referable directly to past hominid behavior. I have questioned such assumptions and feel that Isaac's failure to address the latter two problem areas represents a major weakness of the book. I do not wish to engage in speculations on Isaac's motives for this lack of analytical involvement; however, certain facts are interesting. Isaac has increasingly presented the "home base"–"sharing" argument in opposition to the "hunting hypothesis." Isaac has summarized this position as follows:

> The archaeological evidence seems to indicate that by about 2 million years ago or earlier in Africa the behavior of some primate had undergone changes that greatly enlarged the importance of patterns fundamental to the repertoire of man . . . (1) tool making and a degree of tool dependence are documented at an intensity outside the known range of any ape; (2) meat eating was regularly practiced and persistent hunting almost certainly took place, and (3) localities at which both discarded tools and bone refuse accumulated are most readily explained as home bases in the distinctive human sense . . . the consumption of food at home base involves transporting that food from the place where it was obtained. The quantities that can be estimated suggest that far more food was transported than was needed for feeding infants; thus, extensive foodsharing seems an inevitable conclusion . . . (Isaac and Isaac 1975, p. 17).

Crucial to this argument is the assumption that (a) man hunted, (b) localizations of tools derive from localizations of behavior with high loss rates over relatively short periods of time, and (c) associations between fauna and tools must represent behavioral relationships given the above two conditions. Let's pretend for the moment that (a) hominids did not hunt, and (b) that localizations result primarily from post-depositional aggregation processes for non-localized items with low loss rates over long periods of time. Under such conditions the associations between fauna and tools could derive from the aggregational processes and not necessarily from any behavioral integration between tools and fauna. Add to this condition the possibility of sorting as indicated by my study of flake size and the neat little reconstructions of early hominid behavior fade away very quickly. Similarly, the basis for the "home base" sharing argument also goes down the drain.

I have said many times that one cannot reconstruct the past in ignorance of the processes which operated to bring the archaeological facts into being. Isaac has made major moves in the direction of understanding some of these processes. *A frontal attack is now needed on assemblage composition and tool–faunal associations for the earlier ranges of time. We need to know more of the formation processes for the archaeological record.*

The second section of Isaac's book is a detailed description of certain morphological attributes of the artifacts recovered from Olorgesailie. Many of these facts are presented by Isaac as being useful for comparing Olorgesailie with other middle Pleistocene sites and many such comparisons are made. In addition, there is always the question of the degree that patterns of variability in assemblage content observed between differing sites is referable to (a) different "cultures" or whether (b) they result from the differential compounding of sets of tools used primarily in differing behavioral contexts, or (c) as Isaac suggests they have no systematic meaning. Isaac offers many opinions as to the proper context of referral for the facts from Olorgesailie but never attempts to make use of the archaeological facts to evaluate competing ideas directly. In short, he never deduces consequences of these ideas for the archaeological record. He seems content to offer opinions. This is not exactly science.

Most people would not question the relationship between facts of tool morphology and hominid behavior. In spite of this near certainty of behavioral relevance there is very little behavioral discussion centered around the facts documented by Isaac. Most discussion centers around questions of the significance of interassemblage variability, and the degree that directional patterning could be demonstrated across time or over space. One area given little analytical attention was relationships between various morphological attributes within assemblages. For instance, my perusal of the data suggests a rather strong correlation between degrees of denticulation (Table 22) on flake tools and high values for the "biface index" (Table 8) except three cases which are themselves tightly clustered. This must mean something—carry some information about the past. It is even consistent with a pattern known from more recent times where denticulation and notches are the numerically dominant tools in assemblages called "Mousterian of Acheulian tradition" and typified by the presence of handaxes!

What is taken for granted, what is dwelled upon in analysis and what is discussed in the idiom of opinion all betray something of the "state of the art" as archaeology is practiced. Isaac is in the forefront of research on "early man" in Africa. He has been a leader in both methodology and interpretation in the past and continues to hold a dominant position. This position can be evaluated somewhat by the degree that his ideas are adopted by others without citation. (See, for instance, Leakey and Lewin 1977 as well as G. Clark 1977). A major work by a major figure in the field deserves some special attention and I have tried to give just that to the Olorgesailie report. I have tried to use the report as a barometer of things to come in Africanist's studies. I have tried to find "weaknesses" which in my opinion will be given increasing attention in progressive Africanist's studies in the future. The "weaknesses" which I have singled out are certainly not exclusively recognized by me. In fact, Isaac himself has been in the forefront in both studying and stimulating study in the processes whereby animal's bones become included in deposits which may be investigated archaeologically. Similarly, more work on the consequences of natural agencies operative on tool distributions, a research area also pioneered by Isaac, can also be expected.

I have suggested that as we know more of these things our ideas about the behavior of early man may be significantly altered.

This book is important. It provides a systematic body of archaeological observations on materials believed to be relevant to hominid behavior in Africa over an extended period of the Middle Pleistocene. The mass data were collected under differing conditions and biases regarding both ideas as to how to do archaeology in the field and what to do with the facts once observations had been made. Isaac is to be commended for making available much useful information. The level of analysis and the varying degrees to which Isaac is willing to push the analytical question of meaning is sometimes frustrating. When discussing the "localizations" he proceeds with an analytical caution which is to be commended. However, when discussing faunal associations he treats the facts as if their meanings were self-evident thereby permitting the "easy" reconstruction of past lifeways. After years of sensationalism, African archaeology needs methodological rigor. Isaac has moved the field in that direction, but we can look forward to still many more successes in the future.

On Arguments for the "Butchering"
of Giant Geladas

Lewis R. Binford and Lawrence C. Todd

The question that Shipman, Bosler, and Davis (*Current Anthropology* 22:257–64) claim to address is an important one: "Is it possible to identify the agent responsible for bone breakage directly from the evidence of the bones themselves? Unfortunately, the procedures they use in attempting to justify the identification of hominids as the agents responsible for the breakage of gelada bones at the Olorgesailie location of DE/89 B are totally inadequate. In the opening sentence we are told that systematic butchering of giant gelada baboons is documented. This "documentation" consists of basically two types of "evidence": (a) an unexpectedly high concentration of *Theropithecus oswaldi* remains at DE/89 B, most of them broken, and (b) the association with these bones of large quantities of stone tools. The opinion, very weakly supported, is then offered that the pattern of breakage observed among the gelada bones was produced by hominids.

As an alternative to their view, Shipman et al. discuss the possibility that the demonstrated fluvial activity at this locality may have been a cause of concentration and breakage, but they summarily dismiss it (p. 257) because "all body parts of *Theropithecus* are represented." The work of Voorhies (1969) and Behrensmeyer (1975) is cited as support for this conclusion. The investigations of both Voorhies and Behrensmeyer were based on the proportional representation rather than presence or absence of skeletal elements. In fact, if the criterion used by Shipman et al. were applied to Voorhies's *Merycodus* sample, we would be forced to conclude that he was incorrect in seeing fluvial activity as primarily responsible for the creation of the Verdigre quarry; all skeletal elements of this genus were represented (Voorhies 1969:table 2). It is the relative abundance of elements that was seen by Voorhies and others as being of interest. This focus on proportional representation is nicely illustrated by the following statements by Badgley and Behrensmeyer (1980:145) concerning assemblages from northern Pakistan:

> Localities occurring in the Type 1 channel facies generally contain a wide variety of taxa and skeletal parts. Skeletal part composition is altered from the proportions present in average complete

Originally published with Lawrence C. Todd in *Current Anthropology* 23(1):108–110, 1982. Reprinted by permission of University of Chicago Press. © 1982 by The Wenner-Gren Foundation for Anthropological Research.

skeletons by a relative increase in teeth, long bones, metapodials, and mandibles, and a decrease in scapulae, skulls, vertebrae, podials (including astragali, calcanea), and phalanges. The condition of fossils varies from very weathered and abraded to fresh and complete. Many bones are broken.

The question is not whether all elements are present, but rather in what proportions they occur. Obviously, there are differences in the proportions of elements present at DE/89 B; otherwise there would be no differential patterning to interpret. Such proportional data are not, however, presented. Discounting one of the potential major sources of patterning (fluvial activity) without evaluating its possible significance is the first analytical error of this paper.

This omission is especially disquieting in light of the striking general similarity between the composition of the DE/89 B assemblage and that of the fluvially modified assemblages described by Badgley and Behrensmeyer. Examination of Shipman et al.'s figure 5 indicates patterning of element representation quite similar to that noted by Badgley and Behrensmeyer. Although it is not stressed by Shipman et al., a wide variety of taxa is found at the DE/89 B locality: elephant, hippopotamus, rhinoceros, giraffe, large bovid, various antelope, equids, suids, and "a few small rodent, frog, and fish bones and crocodile teeth, which may not be specifically associated with the occupation" (Isaac 1977:57). In addition, "the bone remains show marked variation in degree of weathering" (Isaac 1977:57). This is not to suggest that exactly the same processes that produced the Middle Siwalik faunal assemblages were responsible for the patterning at Olorgesailie, but to point out that the information presented by Shipman et al. is ambiguous. Without realistic evaluation, the conclusion that fluvial activity was not responsible for the accumulation remains a poorly informed opinion.

Regarding characteristics of the gelada skeletal materials which could perhaps be made to yield some clue to the agents responsible, the authors have chosen to look at two basic sets of properties, the age and sex structures of the animals represented and the patterns of bone breakage/preservation characteristic of anatomical parts represented in the deposit.

The authors conclude that the observed age structure is more consistent with an accumulation of remains from attritional death occurring on a natural population than with the more spectacular catastrophic mass killing suggested by Isaac. While we are in sympathy with such an interpretation, we find little to support it. Most commonly the pattern of attritional mortality is cited as indicative of natural death— that is, what one would expect from a normal mortality profile for a wild population. Remarkably, Shipman et al. conclude (p. 251) that "the cause of death was probably hunting" rather than natural causes. We are not presented with any supporting arguments as to why hunting should be assumed over scavenging or predation by a nonhominid or the differential actions of disease or starvation (their Hypothesis 3). Any of these could well have had a "hand" in the creation of the type of death assemblage found at DE/89 B. Although the recognition of an attritional pattern as opposed to a catastrophic one has dislodged one "hunting hypothesis," is has failed to lead even to the consideration of a nonhunting explanation. The "anthropocentric program" of research illustrated by this investigation has quite the same effect on anthropology that the "adoptionist program" is characterized as having had on biology: "It has led to a reliance on speculative storytelling in preference to the analysis of form and its constraints; and if wrong, in any case, it is virtually impossible to dislodge because the failure of one story leads to the invention of another rather than abandonment of the enterprise" (Gould, S. J. 1980:128). Just such speculative story-telling predominates throughout this article and reaches the heights of imagination in the discussion of the "butchering patterns" observed at DE/89 B.

The authors assert (p. 261) that "a distinctive pattern of breakage and skeletal representation was found in the Olorgesailie *Theropithecus* material that was strongly suggestive of butchery by hominids." If this were true, it would clearly be of great importance, so we must first ask what the "distinctive" properties of the Olorgesailie fauna are and, importantly, how these observed patterns may be unambiguously referred to hominids.

The distinctiveness of the DE/89 B materials is recognizable in comparison with an amalgamation of assemblages for which the taphonomic agents have not been isolated. Basic to Shipman et al.'s approach is the comparison of the Olorgesailie materials with several ancient assemblages. The rationale for the selection of the faunas used as "controls" (i.e., the "nonarcheological sites from East Turkana" and "several campsites and living floors at Olduvai Gorge") is not made clear. Controlled comparison is a valid research tool, but there is no control here. Although procedures such as comparison of like with like, the use of a standardized classification, and the consideration of overall patterns indeed play a role in controlled comparison, a major factor is overlooked. Essential to a valid controlled comparision is an understanding of the causes of the patterning of assemblages we wish to use as "controls." It is not at all surprising that any specific assemblage will exhibit differences when compared with a "control" assemblage which is in all probability the result of the actions and interactions of a very wide array of agents. Comparison such as is attempted by Shipman et al., in which assemblages of uncontrolled origin are compared with other uncontrolled assemblages, can only lead to confusion.

The method of analysis is to attempt to demonstrate formal differences between the Olorgesailie fauna and the population of bones observed from Turkana and Olduvai. If differences can be demonstrated, it is assumed by the authors that the agent responsible must have been hominids. In short, there is no analysis of the observed differences designed to evaluate the degree that there is any reason beyond the existence of the "difference" for believing that hominids may have been the modifying agents.

In the Olorgesailie case, for example, even if we were to accept the assumption that the baboon materials had been originally collected and modified by a hominid agent, how would we go about distinguishing the remains of the "hominid pattern"? Shipman et al. would seem to believe that we can take the archaeological patterning at face value and read the results of hominid action directly from it. If we take the minimum number of individuals of 57 based on canines, then the number of each set of paired elements expected in the assemblage, barring differential preservation, would be 114. This indicates that the best-represented element used by Shipman et al. (calcanea: $N = 39$) accounts for only 34% of the expected elements, while the least well-represented element used in the comparisons (tibiae; $N = 16$) accounts for only 14% of the expected value. The assumption seems to be made that such biased representations can point *directly* to the actions of an agent presumed to have operated on the assemblage prior to the agents of differential destruction which have led to the present recovered sample. There is no consideration of the ways in which intervening agents can alter the patterning in an assemblage.

The observations considered by the investigators to distinguish the Olorgesailie materials from the other unknown samples are largely concerned with the pattern of destruction of anatomical parts and features on bones. According to the authors (p. 261), nine characteristics are "so different from those at the other sites . . . [that they] are judged to have been in all probability caused by hominids." When we plotted the percentage frequencies given by the authors in table 2 for the nine characteristics at Olorgesailie versus their grouped data, the resulting distribution described a positive curvilinear relationship, showing that exactly the same pattern of destruction is present in both populations, only in Olorgesailie it is more pronounced. Postulating the action of different agents is not warranted when the difference in pattern is only one of degree. All of the properties cited by the authors are well-known properties of ravaged assemblages of bones (see Binford and Bertram 1977; Brain 1969; Binford 1981b:183–241). In most animals the proximal humerus is the least dense bone and is almost always the most poorly represented when the assemblage has suffered destruction from attritional agents such as gnawing animals, the action of soil acid, or exposure. We can see no evidence of a "distinctive pattern" in the differential preservation cited by the authors.

In this regard, the authors' tabulation of formal properties of broken bones is quite revealing. They note that there are high frequencies at Olorgesailie of perpendicular fractures of humeri and tibiae. This is not conclusive, but is more common in dried and exposed bone. That the Olorgesailie material was broken when dry is further supported by the lower frequencies of spiral fractures among the Olorgesailie bones than in the Olduvai or East Turkana samples. While many have taken the presence of spiral fractures as indicative of human activity (see Dart 1959, Bonnichsen 1979), this is certainly incorrect (see Binford 1981b:37–42). Spiral fractures are, as the authors recognize, most common in fresh bone. Both the low frequency of spiral fracture and the high frequency of perpendicular fracture indicate that much breakage of the Olorgesailie bones occurred after they had been exposed, stripped of meat, and desiccated. In short, there was breakage of old degreased bones, possibly during transport by stream action or as a result of trampling or other mechanical "experiences" suffered by the bones long after their deposition in the context of natural deaths or consumption by predator–scavengers. At least some of the "distinctiveness" of the Olorgesailie bone material almost certainly had nothing to do with any biological agent, man or beast.

Finally, there is an additional set of provocative observations reported by the authors. The gelada femora from Olorgesailie exhibit significantly more "flaking" on breaks than femora from the other sites. Although "flaking" is not described, their figure 2*d* shows a bone with a short pair of "flakes" originating at a break coupled with a "puncture" on the distal end of the bone. It is not clear if these two properties were regularly observed together, but we would not be surprised if they were, since both are properties which, in our experience, result from gnawing, typically by canids (see Binford 1981b:figs. 3.10, 3.11, 3.12). This observation becomes perhaps more interesting in light of the observations by the authors of the repeated occurrence of an oval pitted area on the anterior surface of the proximal femur at the level of the greater trochanter. This is not described or illustrated, but it seems possible that this is the same type of pitting which has frequently been mistaken for evidence of the use of "compressors" by many analysts (see Binford 1981b:figs. 3.04, 3.05). Such oval concentrations of pitting commonly occur when there is repeated gnawing by an animal too small or weak to collapse or shear the bone in question. At least partial dismemberment of an animal as large as the giant gelada by a much smaller predator carnivore may be indicated.

From the materials presented, the case could be made that the giant geladas were initially preyed upon or at least scavenged by a relatively small predator–scavenger with well-developed canine-carnassial teeth. Later, the bones of the geladas were subjected to considerable attritional breakage by nonbiological agents or simply by trampling. No properties are cited which are not understandable in terms of action by nonhominid agents.

The authors have consistently chosen the speculative–storytelling approach rather than approaching the important problems of early hominid behavior through scientific analysis. With the exception of the information on the age and sex structures of the sample, we are presented with neither useful data nor productive analysis. The story-telling is, however, excellent; not only are the Olorgesailie hominids now seen as "regularly and systematically" killing and butchering the giant geladas, but this trait may have been the "exclusive practice of a few bands of individuals that had mastered the technique," perhaps as part of a ceremonial rite de passage, or simply with the impetus of an "acquired taste for *Theropithecus* flesh." Given the nature of Shipman et al.'s arguments, we cannot even verify that the hominids responsible for the production of the stone tools had anything to do with the recovered fauna, much less infer aspects of ceremonial behavior. The industry and imagination of the stories presented is not, unfortunately, matched by the logic or rigor of the investigation.

Researching
Formation Processes:
My Style

Working at Archaeology:
The Generation Gap—Reactionary
Arguments and Theory Building

As suggested in Chapter 12, the generation gap idea of productive research captured the focus of the field during the 1970s. Attention shifted to testing the applicability of the early systemic models, which in my view had not even been proposed as serious acts of theory building. Rather, they had been presented in terms of the following logic: If certain organized relationships between past dynamics and potential patterning in the archaeological record could be defended as realistic—that is, they could have obtained somewhere, someplace—then it should be clear that traditional methods of archaeological inference would not recognize them, and the properties produced under the imagined conditions would most certainly be misinterpreted using traditional approaches to inference. This was the context in which I saw the importance of the Longacre–Hill arguments, my own arguments about interassemblage variability and organizational variability both within and among sites produced by a single cultural system, and some of my interpretations of mortuary practices.

During the 1970s the work of both the supporters of our early views and the opponents—the defenders of the traditional view—was aimed at demonstrating that the application of these models was inappropriate or not justified. That is, as I have suggested (see Chapter 12), almost all the arguments were arguments of relevance, not tests of the degree to which the modeled dynamics were accurate or evaluations of the suggested relationship between statics and dynamics.[1] I would have been amazed if the first models of systems organization had turned out to be both correct and unequivocally relevant to the data on which they were tried.

Several things conspired to deceive the opposition into thinking that they were testing the validity of the arguments basic to the new archaeology. For example, everyone believed that we could test arguments about the nature of dynamics with archaeological facts. As I have already suggested, this is simply not the case. Given such a belief, various arguments of relevance were seized upon as tests of our arguments about dynamics and the nature of culturally organized systems. For instance, I have heard people say that because Dumond (1977) has "shown" that Hill's factor analysis was not correct, or that because the dating of the site at Broken K correlates with the ceramic variability, the position of the new archaeologists was disproven. *This is simply not correct.*[2] I have already illustrated how arguments of relevance do not implicate the validity or the accuracy of the theory or perspective being used, only its fits to a particular data set. Whether there is a fit or not relates solely to the relevance of the argument to the data.

Given that I and my associates were trained in traditional archaeology, in which there was never any concern for how the organized properties of a cultural system conditioned forms of static patterning, I would not be surprised if *all* our initial guesses about these relationships turned out to be wrong or naïvely simple (see Chapter 28 for my current views on the Mousterian problem.) We needed to be engaged in theory building. We needed to learn of the relationship between forms of dynamics and forms of statics. All of our trial theories regarding this relationship did not have to be correct in order to justify as worthwhile the search for accurate theories. Traditionalists and others who wished to be left alone to investigate the archaeological record empirically tried to discredit the new archaeology, as a justification for continuing to do things as they had in the past. From the very beginning, the thrust of the new archaeology was not that we knew everything, or even that we knew how to accomplish our goals. Rather, we were arguing that we did *not* know what the archaeological record meant, and that we must accept the challenge to reduce this ignorance as much as possible. Illustrations that in fact we did not know what things meant were certainly not sufficient reasons for concluding that we therefore did not need to investigate further! This was essentially the argument advanced by those who accepted all the negative arguments of relevance (regardless of their validity) as evidence that the new archaeology approach should be rejected. The new archaeology was first and foremost about what we thought the world was like, what we thought the general relationships were between statics and dynamics. In short, we were offering a contrastive paradigm, or set of expectations, as to the general way that archaeological observations implicated the past. We were dealing with paradigmatic expectation and moving in the direction of theory development in the context of our paradigmatic views. In order to evaluate the utility of the basic new archaeology, we also had to evaluate paradigmatic suggestions and dynamic theories about how static patterning was generated (see Chapter 3). In order to achieve the goals of the new archaeology, we had to be engaged in the refinement of a new paradigm, and the invention of theories designed to explain static patterns of a variety of types. All the little argumentative exercises cast in the form of arguments of relevance did not affect these concerns.

One way of thinking about theories is to consider them as a kind of definition of a natural system. Such a "definition" consists of the laws and the particular theoretical terms that specify how the system works. Systems that work in fundamentally different ways from the theoretical specifications of one theory require theories differing in their "rules" of dynamics. Part of our job as scientists is to identify systems characterized by fundamentally different determinant and conditioning properties, which can be expected to be understandable in terms of differing theories. For instance, a Mendelian theory can be said to cover those real-world systems where sexual reproduction is the mode of inheritance and the laws of segregation and dominance regulate the inheritance pattern. Clearly there are forms of inheritance which occur among sexually reproducing forms where there are relevant laws. Under such conditions those real-world cases could not be considered instances where a strict Mendelian theory was applicable. It has been said that a theoretical hypothesis is one that asserts that a particular real-world system is of the type defined by a particular theory. We can think of this as a kind of mega-argument of relevance.

It should be clear that if we have only vague and poorly developed theories then complicated and almost metaphysical arguments may take the place of the relatively "clean" theoretical hypotheses proposed by practitioners in more advanced fields.[3] In fact, in fields with poorly developed theories theoretical hypotheses are more akin to what have been termed *explanation sketches*. Here the variables cannot be identified yet but the domains are suggested and some poorly specified "directions" may be explored regarding the patterns of conditioning interaction among the domains. It is a hunchy and vague view as to how the system works, not yet specific enough to be formalized into a theory. When we discuss the appropriate domains to be investigated for clues to theory building, we are working with sketchy ideas of a theory and in turn sketchy ideas about which real-world phenomena might be explained once it is developed.[4] If we are consciously trying to develop theory we generally offer vague justifications for looking at a particular segment of the real world as potentially understandable in terms of a unitary theory. That is, we believe that there is something integrated or organizationally cohesive rendering it likely that a unitary theory covers the domain singled out for study. This is a judgment conditioned by our knowledge of other natural systems and the workings of the world in general. The guiding ideas conditioning our ways of looking at the world constitute our paradigm (see Chapter 28 for a good example).

Perhaps the most recurrent paradigmatic suggestion in our field is the argument that it is people who do things and people who are the causes of "their doings." This is as common today (in the work of Schiffer, Speiss, and Jochim, to mention only a few) as it has been throughout the recent history of anthropology, despite the lack of new, productive theories of human behavior. There is a "faith" that humans mold their own life systems. Anthropologists have had to deal with this idea for a very long time. For instance,

> Opposition to the science of culture expresses itself variously, but one theme runs fairly consistently through most if not all of it. This is the objection that it is not culture but people who do things. Again to quote Lynd's pointed and apt phrase, "Culture does not enamel its fingernails, vote, or believe in capitalism but people do." This observation is no doubt meant to express scientific realism as well as common sense. Anyone can see for himself that it is human beings that mark ballots and drop them into a box.
>
> "Realism" of this sort is simply pathetic. As a matter of fact, it is not realism at all but anthropocentric, an inability to interpret a chain of events except in terms of man as the prime mover [L. A. White 1949b:143].

My views on this issue were voiced in a review of A. E. Spiess's book *Reindeer and Caribou Hunters* (L. R. Binford 1980a):

The Paradigm—or What He Expects the World to Look Like

Beginning from what appears as a very limited understanding of the arguments which have taken place in the Americanist literature over the past 20 years, Spiess summarizes contemporary archaeology as suffering from an "80 year old schizophrenia" (p. 2). This malady is conceived as a situation where diachronic and synchronic viewpoints are assimilated to a contrast between "science" and "history" which in turn is characterized as "generalizing" and "particularizing" orientation. Spiess sagely suggests that an "integrative viewpoint" is needed and proceeds to offer his solution to the field of archaeology. His suggestion is to adopt the "ecological" perspective of John Bennett . . . which views the organism as playing a game with the environment. In this game the organism is "endeavoring to learn, manipulate, or change the rules in order to realize goals, satisfy needs, or maintain a degree of freedom of choice and action" (Bennett 1976:848). In other words, the adaptive process is seen as the evolutionary process and the explanation for evolutionary changes rests with modification in the adaptive process which derives from goal-seeking behavior guided by man's free will. Spiess cites with approval the following statement from Bennett (1976:848): ". . . how can one speak of material causation of human actions when the unpredictable and creative powers of the human mind are at work in nearly every situation?"

This question has been asked by practically every idealist since the beginning of scientific studies. For instance, David Bidney [1946] writes "man . . . controls his own cultural destiny and is free to choose and realize the ends we would achieve." Commenting on this view, Leslie White states in *The Science of Culture* [1949b:142–143]:

> Opposition to the science of culture expresses itself variously, but one theme runs fairly consistently through most if not all of it, this is the objection that it is not culture but people who do things . . . the culturologist knows who does the drinking quite as well as his "realistic" opponents. The question is "Why does one people prize milk as a nutritious and tasty beverage while another regards it with loathing?"
>
> To the culturologist the reasoning that says that one people drinks milk because "they like it," another does not because "they loathe it," is senseless; it explains nothing at all. Why does one people like, another loathe, milk? This is that we want to know.

By adopting the idealistic and antiscientific posture that man has free will and behaves variously because of choice, Spiess essentially denies that we can understand or explain cultural variability. At best differences in complexity of cultural system and fullness of culture content must simply reflect differences in the "taste" of the participants. This leads us either back to a racist position or a position where the "accidents of history" account for the differences in "taste." We want to understand cultural differences, not deny that they can be understood.

The "integrative viewpoint" which Spiess proposes to save us from our "80 year schizophrenia" is best summarized by Spiess himself:

> I would like to reaffirm that human behavior and human choice is the causality behind what is recovered in the archaeological record. . . . there are two levels of explanation that can be attempted with adaptation theory; they fit well into the categories of generalizing and particularizing explanation.
>
> Particularizing explanation deals with a historic incident, a particular incidence of choice or group of choices. . . . Explanation on the general level can be had when similar choices are made many times over given similar preconditions, and these choices result in similar or convergent systemic changes. . . . Many anthropologists strive for explanation on the generalizing level only, equating the concepts of explanation and generalization. However, I am content with explanation at either level because both add to our knowledge of past human adaptations (pp. 14–16).

In the above quotations we have an excellent statement of idealistic positivism. The position is one in which directly perceived experience is all that is admitted in "explanation." This position is one in which the place of reason is denied in explanation. The latter is seen as some form of accurate description of an empirical experience. Science as "generalizing" therefore consists of offering empirical generalizations which remain "abstractions" from a series of analogous experiences. I am surprised that Spiess has not taken the next step and denied the utility of generalizing as this would be consistent with his idealist position. No one has stated the idealist position better than Collingwood in *The Idea of History* (1956:223) and his conclusion on generalizing is worth quoting:

> . . . the task of mental science could be to detect types or patterns of activity, repeated over

and over again in history itself. . . . the historian, when he is ready to hand over such a fact to the mental scientist as a datum for generalization, has already understood it in this way from within. If he has not done so, the fact is being used as a datum for generalization before it has been properly "ascertained." But if he has done so, nothing of value is left for generalization to do. If by historical thinking we already understand how and why Napoleon established his ascendance in revolutionary France, nothing is added to our understanding of that process by the statement (however true) that similar things have happened elsewhere.

Adhering to a strict positivist position and at the same time adopting an idealistic assumption of determinacy leads to greater weakness in both positions. While there are many idealistic positions current today, there are few if any defended positions which espouse a strict positivist viewpoint. Such a position where empirical descriptions are all that is admitted in explanation is a position which was argued in the context of Newtonian physics and has been totally obsolete in modern science and philosophy since the latter part of the 19th century. Spiess needs to catch up to the 20th century [Binford 1980a:630–631].

Although these discussions clearly indicate that there is disagreement over the domains considered appropriate for study in seeking to formulate theories of relevance for archaeologists, the polemics are not enough. I will try to justify my paradigm, my views, regarding cultural systems by taking the reader through some background materials from the history of anthropology. This background will tend to place in a broader perspective my opinions and views as to what is appropriate to study and what we might seek to learn if we wish to build theories of importance to archaeologists.

During the nineteenth century explanations were sought for why different peoples behaved in vastly different ways. One explanation placed the differences on a scale of qualitative judgment; there was acceptable behavior because there were acceptable people and savage behavior because there were savage people. In essence it was argued that there was a fit between the essential properties of the actors and the quality of the behavior. Today we would call this a form of racism—inferior peoples behave in inferior and unacceptable ways whereas superior peoples behave in progressive, superior, and proper ways. *Anthropology challenged this view.* Anthropologists pointed out that patterns of behavior were learned. Nunamiut Eskimos behave the way they do because they learned how to behave from their parents, who were also Nunamiut Eskimos. In short, there are learned traditions of behavior, and behavioral diversity at any one time is thought to be referable to the diversity in traditions standing historically behind the present. Gradually the questions dawned: Where do behavioral traditions come from? How is culture differentially generated? Various models of causation were developed and one appealing early argument was that the diversity among traditions was a function of an inner dynamic, a vital process of unfolding or emergence inherent in culture itself. It was the idea of progressive and retarded races simply translated into terms of culture. Some cultures were primitive and underdeveloped and others were progressive and advanced. This differential was sometimes viewed as a difference in the rates of change.

Once a tradition starts down a "change" trajectory, the changes generate new problems in a regular sequence, which in solution result in more change; hence some systems are progressive and others are stagnant. All the latter needs is a boost (an initial kick) and they too will start down the "progressive" road (a view still common in treating Third World nations). Attempting to counter this position demanded a slight shift in perspective focusing more on the "kickers," and away from a strict introspective view. We needed to know the particular event that altered the continuity within learned traditions. These historical events were seen as the cause of diversity.

Traditions come from previous traditions, but accidents of history may interrupt continuities between generations and among bearers of differing traditions, resulting in the complex blending of learned behavioral modes (this was the general theory of traditional archaeology). This idea of cultural transmission was well summarized in the contrasts between the "tree of life" and the "tree of culture" models popularized by A. L. Kroeber.

Various models of historical causation were developed. One of great interest was the work of American ethnographers. (I have summarized some of this in Chapter 9.) The results of these studies suggested that there was a clear and interesting relationship between forms of culture and forms of environment. The implication was that ecological interaction might be that mechanism. The more historically minded countered that the environment was passive and only differentially "permitted" certain forms of culture, but in no way conditioned the mix of cultural alternatives; this mix was a function of accidents of history, those specific events that altered the flow of culture both between generations and among contemporary social segments.

Many of the early attempts at integration, theory building, or codifying a view of culture were made by persons who received their information from explorers, missionaries, travelers, and "informants." Even when fieldwork was done by many of the early ethnographers they were inteviewing persons about life "back in the old days," and so never had to face directly the challenge of fitting into the sociocultural system being studied. Given this investigator perspective, the invention of a comparative language and the discussion of the information obtained in *our* terms (that is, in our language and in terms of problems as we saw them) were clearly "natural." This has been called the *etic approach* (see Harris 1968:568–592).

On the other hand, the ethnographer who goes out to live as a participant observer, even if he or she hopes to reconstruct what a past culture was like, has to be able to cope with the other participants in the system on their terms—in terms of their beliefs, values, codes of ethics, and so on. The field-worker may not want to "go native," but he or she certainly wants to know at least how to interact inoffensively and at best how to translate one cultural viewpoint to members of another culture. All this investment in studying the cultural viewpoint from the perspective of how a participant views the culture is a necessary part of doing effective fieldwork among culturally different peoples.

> Cultures . . . have become recognized . . . as phenomena of the natural order, they are not to be understood through mechanical or biological analogies or through an analysis which the scientist can make from outside by confidently appealing to sociological or psychological laws. Rather, this inner world is to be entered with humility, the passport a readiness to listen while the native himself speaks [de Leguna 1960:792].

A good ethnographer is one who can go to an alien group and learn how to be a participant in their culture. In so doing he or she learns at least something of what it is to view the world through their eyes, how behavior is justified and participation motivated for the participants. The challenge to the ethnographer is quite literally to understand an alien culture from the point of view of a participant, and at some level the *ethnographer must participate*. In similar fashion, to reconstruct what an extinct culture was like from the memories of an informant the ethnographer must be able to imagine what it would have been like to have participated. "Boas conceived of his main task as the adoption of an informant's mode of thought while retaining full use of his own critical faculties [Mead 1959:58]." Such an approach has been termed an *emic approach* and has been frequently championed as the only "realistic" approach to the study of anthropological subject matter.[5]

What I am emphasizing here is that one's *perspective* is particularly important as a conditioner of what one considers reality. Viewing cultural variability from the perspective of the participant comes down to appreciating how different one must feel, think, and perform if one is going to participate successfully in a different culture. The task of learning these differences generally consists of assimilating the differing rationales each culture has for the actions, the particular behavioral expectations or role prescriptions that are *assumed of participants* within the system. From a participant's point of view, humans within a culture behave the way they do quite literally because they have learned both the behaviors and the motivational conditions for those behaviors (the ideas, the values, ideals, rules of conduct, and so on characteristic of the system in which they participate).

Anthropology already knew this. Anthropology had maintained for a very long time that people behaved differently in different cultures because they had learned to behave that way. Exploring the world of cultural diversity from the perspective of the participant, although informative of how complicated it is to view the same reality through the eyes of different culturally "programmed" individuals, *in no way helps us explain why there are different cultures*.

Many who have thought about this question doggedly hold to the perspective of the participant. They have continued to contemplate this question with the commonsense view derived from the participant perspective (which is, of course, the way all of us "naturally" view experience within our own culture) that they can explain cultural diversity in terms of the characteristics of humanity, for after all it is "people who do things." There are a wide variety of "decision theory" approaches, which seek to guide us in understanding why men make decisions the way they do. There are those who seek to understand in terms of the "laws of the mind" or the "laws of behavior." In short, they seek to build theories about the characteristics of people, as the basis for understanding why people behave in culturally distinct ways.

There are problems with such approaches. *I do not understand how constant properties can guide us to understand and explain cultural diversity*. Those who seek to establish laws of human behavior, or laws of the mind, presumably see such characteristics as referable to all of humanity. This type of approach is generally explained to the skeptical in this way: If we know how humans will behave, and if we know the differences in the situations in which they find themselves—the environment of decision making—we can predict or anticipate their behavior. Such approaches as that of optimal foraging theory (see, e.g., O'Connell and Hawkes 1981) or a number of arguments that assume a "maximizing" or "risk reduction" law of human behavior are examples (Gould 1980; Sanders *et al.* 1979; Wiessner 1982; Winterhalder and

Smith 1981). Because we "know" how humans behave, all we need to do in order to anticipate their behavior is to establish the systems state conditions just prior to decision making.

Anthropologists should know better than this. If there is one principle that anthropological field studies have affirmed over and over again, it is that the intellectual contexts of behavior in different cultures renders rationality a relative phenomenon. Similarly, the goals of behavior cannot be considered constant. Let's take optimal foraging theory, in which the consumer demand of different individuals is roughly considered a constant. Animals feed themselves, hence the demand curve for food is relatively stable and related to the species in a generic sense. In short, the demand for food is a biologically controlled demand curve for any given species. Given this constancy, the choice of foods by a species consists of matching up this constant demand curve to a slightly variable production regime characteristic of an environment. Does man behave in this manner? The best answer is "perhaps sometimes"! Some cultural systems are organized so the demand curve is relatively constant, as among many hunter–gatherers where the reproductive family is also most commonly the basic unit of food production. In like fashion, the food-getting tactics might well be encounter tactics, and extremely pragmatic. Such societies are frequently called *flexible* in character.[6] With such a culturally organized system an optimal foraging theory might allow us to anticipate the foods taken or the proportions of different species making up the diet. On the other hand, the demand curve may vary seasonally among some groups, with daily feeding of essentially family units being characteristic of part of the seasonal round, but a very different demand curve being characteristic of the season of the year when cooperative labor units are exploiting aggregated resources for purposes of putting up stores. This shift in both the food-getting labor force and the demand for food is not related to the species or a set of species contrasts, but to culturally organized strategies; these must be established in cultural terms *before* optimal foraging models may be modified for use. Man's organization of a food-getting labor force with particular food demands which are neither a simple arithmetic function of the daily food demands of the persons being served, nor a simple arithmetic function of the time frame of food availability renders theories that assume "species" constants inappropriate. Culturally organized properties must be understood before optimal foraging theory can be used to anticipate the dietary mix of different foods available to a given group. In this case the rationality of the tactics is relative to the size of the culturally organized units of production and consumption, and to the goals of the labor force. None of these properties could be assumed by simply knowing that we were dealing with "humans" in the biological sense of the word, or knowing the quantitative and qualitative mix of foods available. *Humans may behave as differently in different cultural settings as different species.* The one thing that must be known in order to work with optimal foraging models is the *nature* of the species of interest. The variable cultural systems of humans permit them to occupy many different niches in the ecosystem, and to shift the niche seasonally, and under other contingencies. This kind of variability is not considered when we slap onto the archaeological record or other "human" data the models developed for dealing with a species with behavioral properties that must be considered constant. If one adopts the anthropological perspective, namely that human behavior is variable relative to the culture within which individuals are participants, then the noncultural arguments about human behavior are of little aid in understanding the cultural variability itself. (This is the basic issue of the "sociobiology" debates now being conducted.)

Those who adopt the participant perspective and also acknowledge the cultural conditioning of human behavior frequently choose to seek an understanding of variability by appeals to free will and human choice. Cultural behavior is different among different segments of humanity because some people choose to behave one way and other people choose to behave another way. Under such a paradigm culture is the patterned consequence of the creative acts of genius, and human individuality. From this perspective, there are no explanations for culture other than the accidents of history, the particular coincidences of people with inventiveness and style in given places and times is thought to influence the behavior of others. Culture is considered the serpendipitous result of history, and remains without explanations beyond its own patterning.

I happen to believe that both of the preceding participant-based paradigms are of little utility and fly in the face of what anthropologists have learned over many years of study. It should be clear that one's perspective is a major determinant or conditioner of one's paradigm, or what one expects the world to be like. If we look at culture more as the archaeologist might see it, we see nothing of the individual's motives or of the ideas and values that rendered a participant's life meaningful and valued by others. Instead, what we see are places used over and over in the same way and continuities in the way things were done at these places. We see repetitive patterns in the forms and kinds of material items as well as modified places used by different groups. These are the cultural contexts in terms of which peoples of the past must have both learned and carried out their culturally distinctive forms of behavior (regardless of the justifications for them). We see duration of form and continuity in design and placement, as well as associations between things that betray durations of organized ways of doing things that greatly exceed the life spans of human participants. Cultural systems have a scale of both temporal and spatial organization that transcends the individual's life span and role space. The molding of individual participants is basic and necessary to this scale of organization and the continuation of the cultural system beyond the life spans of individuals. Institutions and cultural forms must be thought of as having a life independent of their participants, inasmuch as they are the conditioners of the participants' behavior. Culturally organized information is transmitted accurately if each successive generation of participants is to behave like its predecessors. The degree to which near-exact *cultural reproduction* occurs is a function of the culturally organized structures of information transmission and the rigidity of the role structures that recruit new individuals into the system. If these new individuals perform as their prececessors did, then the cultural system lives on unchanged, spanning numerous generations of human participants. It has always seemed strange to me that the field that has stressed the importance of learning as an alternative to genetic forms of information transmission should never have really studied the mechanisms and organized contexts in which learned information is passed on, and what ensures faithfulness in cultural reproduction.

If we ask informants why they do something, they normally tell us about the ideology that inspired them to learn and to execute the particular behaviors being discussed. The entire ideological, institutional, and sociological framework that renders actions rational and necessary are seen in terms of views of the world learned within their culture. This view, that of the participant, is an orientation affected by the institutions of cultural reproduction.

We can think of these as institutions and organizations serving enculturative or educational ends. Most if not all of the world's religions, and most ritualized behaviors commonly thought of as expressions of "ideology," are basic mechanisms of cultural transmission. Ritual is the basic aid to memory. Among peoples without literature, ritual is the fundamental mnemonic technique ensuring accurate *descent without modification*. Archaeologists work with the facilities and gear used in the ancient rituals of complex societies, which are very visible archaeologically and generally occupy central places in our taxonomies and ideas of stability and change (think, for instance, of the Maya collapse). Such parts of a system must respond to conditioning variables different from those affecting materials that functioned in the more subsistence oriented activities. In contrast, many hunter–gatherers leave little material evidence of their enculturative institutions and strategies (mostly some graphics). Why are there such differences in the stability and visibility of the material accoutrements of learning one's culture? Why are there such obvious investment differentials between one system and another? I think that there is much to be learned here. We need theories and actual studies of variability, yet most archaeologists have been content to see such differences as part of the cultural style not understandable in terms of explanatory arguments.

If we acknowledge that a cultural system is a system of extrasomatic transmission for behaviorally relevant information from one generation to the next, then a cultural tradition in its *reproductive mode* would be most effective if the transmission of information from one generation to the next is exact and unchanged in the process. On the other hand, the advantage to the culture bearers is that culturally transmitted information can be modified to make possible rapid responsive adjustments to changed conditions or contingencies in the environment of the cultural system. Here we discuss the cultural system in its *adaptive mode,* where the potential for very responsive descent with modification is possible. The energy requirements of the participants and the cultural organization itself ensure that the cultural system is subject to conditioning interactions with its environment. There will be selection for and against certain culturally organized means of articulating with the environment. These points of articulation provide the *determinant dynamics for descent with modification.* I think it should be clear that discussing a cultural system in terms of the participant view, which is after all the view of the dynamics of cultural reproduction, is not likely to help us understand the dynamics of descent with modification.

As archaeologists seeking to build theory of interest to us, we are not concerned with how it might feel to participate in a past system or even what it might be like to learn to be a member of the culturally organized social unit. Instead we are concerned with the organized internal relationships within the cultural system: how the system works, and particularly how the normal functioning of the system generates patterned static material by-products. We are interested in the production of statics so that we may identify diagnostic properties, which when seen archaeologically would permit the accurate *identification* of the dynamic conditions responsible for the statics. If we are successful in building well-founded methods for inference, we may be able to identify the kinds of cultural systems (in overall systems terms) manifest in the statics of archaeological facts. These things cannot be learned by adopting inappropriate perspectives and paradigms such as the participant-centered idealistic views that many find appealing. If we are successful in this area of systems diagnosis, then we can realistically turn to the fascinating task of seeking understanding for systems change and evolution.

I hope that I have succeeded in making the point that a detailed knowledge of the internal operations of cultural systems is crucial for understanding patterning observable in the archaeological record. We need sophisticated knowledge of the functioning of as many different types of system as possible, for it is such understanding that must stand behind the development of diagnostic criteria for identifying organizational properties of past systems, and in turn recognizing kinds of systems.

This is the challenge of middle-range theory development in general (see Chapter 27 for more on middle-range theory). More specifically, it should be clear that a functional approach seeks understanding of how the operation of different system types generate diagnostically different statics. A functional approach, viewed in systems, not psychological, terms, is thought to be the most productive form of middle-range research for archaeologists.

My basic research, stimulated by the Mousterian problem, has been concerned with investigating organizational properties of cultural systems—organizational properties that condition different forms of archaeological statics. I have been exclusively concerned with researching middle-range issues—in short, solving the problem of what the fascinating variability in the Mousterian remains might mean. The chapters that follow represent some facets of this work.

To return to the debate mentioned in Chapter 12, it will be recalled that François Bordes observed that, on Mousterian sites, tools were made and used in the same places. I was well aware that most ethnographic literature commonly reported people making tools in one place and using them in a variety of other places. I accepted Bordes's challenge as I saw it, namely to determine what conditioning effects different organizations of technology have on patterning in the archaeological record. How can we recognize differing organizations, and what if anything do they imply about other systems state conditions? It should be noted that these are all questions about systems functions, or the effects of one aspect of a system on others. All of our really important discoveries about the meanings of most static patterns will be functional statements, relating material statics to forms of dynamics.

In Chapters 19 and 20, I explore some of my ethnographic experiences to prompt a greater understanding and appreciation for the role of organization within the cultural system in conditioning various patterns (e.g., numerical frequency, spatial associations, and formal diversity—interassemblage variability) among static archaeological remains. This is what I mean by information dynamics responsible for conditioning different or variable static patterns.[7] Without such knowledge we can never diagnose the character of the past from the static present.

In Chapter 21 I look at how a set of organized systems properties moves "across" a place. The place is well established and its properties well known to the users. These are learned by each new generation. The location of the place represents the traditional wisdom regarding the best spot to look for caribou in the vicinity of Anaktuvuk village after spring cow migration. It also must be considered more than just a good environmental setting for doing what Eskimo hunters do during spring straggler hunting. It is very much a part of the cultural geography of the region. Men plan ahead in terms of the use of the place. They know generally what is on the site and this enters into their planning as to what they need to take with them when they go there. They are also very much aware of the archaeological remains there. They know what they can expect to find there if there is an emergency or other need for tools. I tried to indicate again something of the basis for organizing gear among the Nunamiut, as I did in the two preceding chapters. We see here dimensions of planning that are place-centered, as well as planned units of gear that regularly pass through the place but are rarely used or discarded there.

In Chapter 21 I also treat some more generation gap kinds of misunderstanding and misrepresentation. (See L. R. Binford 1979b; Larson 1979; Schiffer 1981; Yellen 1977:132–136; also Chapter 21, this volume.)

Chapter 22 is a section out of my conclusions to the *Nunamiut Ethnoarchaeology* book (L. R. Binford 1978b). I have reproduced some of my observations on the organization of the Nunamiut system of land use as seen in terms of kinds of differentiated use of places coupled with the types of socially organized units using such places. In addition I argue that (a) the patterns of mobility and (b) the organization of mobile groups are the major conditioners for properties that would be seen archaeologically as inter- and intrasite differences generated within a single system.

Chapter 23 explores some of the ecological conditioners for hunter–gatherer systems variables in both mobility and labor organization. This study has clear implications for major regional or macrogeographical patterns of variability in remains generated by mobile hunter–gatherer groups.[8]

In Chapters 24 and 25, focus is back on places, particular localizations of systems functions. Against a backdrop of my experiences with the Nunamiut I explore what a system "looks like" from the perspective of a single place. I have already suggested that the perspective of the individual participant is inappropriate to the task of the archaeologist. I have strongly urged that we adopt the etic perspective of an overall system within which humans participated. We can rarely hope to be able to see a complete system. A complete inventory of places used, and a knowledge of the organizational dimensions that might crosscut the dynamics at all such places, are an unlikely data base for us to expect to uncover. Most of the time we have one or a very few sites that must guide our appreciation for the types of systems that once existed. If we are to use site information we must learn how to see a past system from a site perspective. I have likened this perspective to that of a "rock with eyes" down in a deep hole. What such a rock would see are little glimpses or segments of a system that passes over its hole. In addition, our rock's vision would be biased in terms of the matter that happened to fall into its hole as the living system passes overhead.[9] Our job is to learn how to (a) identify the segment or part of the whole that passed over each particular hole or site, (b) understand the implications of these

Figure 17.1 The rock with eyes.

identified parts for the kinds of total systems represented, and finally (c) understand what conditions the biases in the system parts represented from site to site. Why are some parts repeatedly seen in some places and still other segments seen consistently in other places? If we knew such things we could use site data much more skillfully in understanding the past.

Chapter 25 describes a land use pattern that in geographic scale and tempo has almost certainly not been considered as a potential form standing behind at least some archaeological records produced by hunter–gatherer systems.

All of these studies are middle-range research (except Chapter 23, which reaches out for an understanding of systems variability). They are concerned with functional problems, problems of the organized relationships among aspects of a living dynamic system and still further with the relationships between the ongoing dynamics and derivative structured statics. All of these studies have implications for archaeological methods. Certainly assumptions about provenience units and the geographic scale of mobile systems are clear in Chapters 22, 24, and 25. All of these studies are incomplete in that they point to causal areas or domains of systems functioning that may condition static patterning. Only Chapter 23 addresses the question of the ranges of variability or changed relations in systems of different types. Other researchers must take up the study and add to our understanding of how differences of dynamic organization condition diagnostic differences in static patterning.

Notes

1. The few studies aimed at evaluating theories were without exception ethnoarchaeological studies (Hayden 1976, 1978; Stanislawski (1969a, 1969b, 1977; Yellen 1977). They are important because they illustrate some interesting problems within the field. Yellen, for instance, thinking that new archaeologists were looking for universal laws, noted that in his experience all activities were not localized in different areas unique to each, therefore spoiling the alleged law that he thought someone had proposed. Leaving his confusion aside, the idea that we should be looking for universal laws—by definition timeless and spaceless in their relevance—is most often linked to those who seek to understand human behavior or the workings of the human mind or some other universalistic phenomenon. Archaeologists are faced with the material remains of many different types of systems organized in different ways. By virtue of these organizational differences, these systems almost certainly generate *different kinds of archaeological records*. This is true at the organizational functional level and maybe at the stylistic level as well. If we are to be successful at diagnosing the kinds of system we are dealing with, we must not follow the tactic that Hayden and Yellen have attempted, in which they cite "their people" or their data as disproving others' observations regarding the relationship between organized dynamics and derivative statics in another system. We must seek to understand dynamic–static linkages, and there is no reason in the world why they should be the same in all systems. Our task is to build up an understanding of the range of variability and try to understand what is conditioning that range. This type of approach is seen particularly in Chapter 23.

2. I have always been somewhat amused by those critics who offer a negative statement presented as an argument of relevance but do not see that their criticism is clearly not relevant. For instance, Jelinek (1976) offers a near-complete page of such statements. After presenting a through-the-looking-glass set of arguments noting that we were seeking an alternative way of viewing the variability that Bordes attributed to cultures, Jelinek then points out that our explanation has "little to do with an explanation of variation observed in Mousterian culture by Bordes [p. 30]." That is correct; we were seeking an alternative way of viewing the sources of just that variability. Jelinek continues his criticism by pointing out that we ignored "such possibly functionally significant variables as Bordes' Quina retouch." That is absolutely true. There were no Quina retouched pieces or only counts of one or two in the assemblages studied. We had stated that we were studying Levallois Mousterian, which is defined by the lack of Quina! Given this criterion, our study was also "weak" because we ignored "such possibly functionally significant variables as site structure," site size, and hundreds of other attributes one could think of that our assemblages did not have! Jelinek goes on to note that the layers "may be geological and not cultural" and could contain mixed cultural deposits that "average out" as one of the Bordes cultural types. If that was the case, then how could one argue that the Bordes cultural types unambiguously represented cultures? Would it not be nice to have a method of partitioning the independent contributors? That is what we were doing. Jelinek continues with other observations: "The functional categories based on Bordes' type list which were used to define different kinds of activities are open to question." This one is wonderful. First, Bordes's types, not our functional categories, were being analyzed. Second, our functional guesses about his types in no way affect the validity of the covariant groupings revealed in our analysis. Finally, *all* interpretations about

the past are open to question. The question is, however, this: Are there good reasons to doubt the arguments? Are we to believe that Jelinek is capable of producing inferences about the past that are not open to question? Jelinek (1976, 30) tells us that "since no data were presented with the study, it is not possible either to confirm the results of the analysis or to carry out comparable studies with any certainty of duplicating the methodology employed by the Binfords." The fact is that we analyzed the data—every scrap previously published by Bordes or analyzed under his direction and published—so as to ensure controlled comparability in the tabulation of types in his type list. Why on earth should we republish already published material? It is perhaps true that in the early days of computer work—before there were standard programs—almost every center had its own software and even in some cases its own language. For this reason the programs we used in the early 1960s could rarely be duplicated in the computational sense of the word without the binary decks used. I have these decks, by the way, and could have duplicated them for anyone interested in the way we did things in the old days. In most cases, though, having the decks would not have been sufficient to give an operational program without some modifications to accommodate the system at the investigator's center. All this history does not alter the fact that any researcher could get the raw data and experiment with alternative analyses all he or she wished. I would bet that an objective researcher would get results comparable to ours, albeit differing in minor details. I have run literally hundreds of analyses on many different data sets and in general always get a denticulate cluster, a point-convergent scraper cluster, a Quina transverse scraper cluster, a large tool cluster, or whatever. There is some organizational regularity in the assemblages of the early time periods despite complaints of reactionary critics.

It is perhaps not without significance that in the same volume as the Jelinek article, there is a discussion (Speth & Johnson 1976) that makes it sound as though the dangers of doing an analysis are so great that it may not be worth the effort! There are no *certain* and foolproof ways of gaining a knowledge of the past. Continuously pointing to the fact that it is difficult is no evidence that those *who try have not also worried about such things*.

3. Thus far most of our theoretical hypotheses have been on the order of whether we are looking at the archaeological remains of a state or of a chiefdom. However, more penetrating arguments have appeared (see Lamberg-Karlovsky 1975).

4. We as archaeologists should be forever concerned with dignaosing the organizational properties of the systems that generated our archaeological remains. This is what is usually meant by the statement that many different types of causes could stand behind some of the facts of the archaeological record.

5. There are many advocates of this position among archaeologists. Some are explicit advocates (Hodder 1982; Kushner 1970; Renfrew 1969, 1972). Others speak in vague terms, sometimes saying they are students of human behavior in general (see Rathje and Schiffer [1982], where the participant view is assumed even in speaking about artifacts).

6. "Flexibility" began to be considered as a result of discussions at the Man the Hunter Conference (see Lee and DeVore 1968:9).

7. The behavioral archaeologists use this term in a very different way. See Rathje and Schiffer (1982) for their views.

8. Polly Wiessner (1982) has commented on this paper from the perspective of risk-reduction arguments where different tactics, storage, sharing, mobility, and so on are viewed as stylistic equivalents for reducing risk, and the choice of the one followed is a matter of culture. This is opting for nonexplanation of cultural variability in terms of a postulated behavioral characteristic believed universal to humans—risk reduction. But how they do it is epiphenomenal! This is a more materialist expression of the same type of logic used by those who advocate the study of deep structure, where the differing cultural forms of behavior are merely thought to be epiphenomenal expressions of deeper properties of the human mind. Nonexplanation of the variability is a wonderful way of noncoping with the basic problem of anthropology—how to explain cultural variability.

9. Jeremy Sabloff and I used the rock-with-eyes metaphor in a course we taught during the spring semester of 1982 at the University of New Mexico. At the end of the course the students presented each of us with such a rock. Jeremy's had potsherds and wall plaster on top and mine had gnawed bones and lithics. This treasured gift is shown in Figure 17.1.

18

Behavioral Archaeology and the "Pompeii Premise"

It is argued that "behavioral archaeology," as it has been advocated by M.B. Schiffer, represents a series of partially misguided postures relative to some important points of debate common in the 1960s. Due to failures to understand some points at issue, behavioral archaeologists appear to embrace many of the methods and goals of traditional archaeology, and thereby present a "reactionary" position rather than a "revisionist" position, as it has claimed. The issues upon which behavioral archaeology appears most reactionary are points most urgently in need of change, if archaeology is to progress as a discipline contributing both to our knowledge of the past and to our understanding of historical trends.

Walter Taylor's (1948) Call for more attention to "context" and "affinities" stimulated a healthy series of discussions concerning "interpretation" in archaeology. In general, however, archaeologists reacted with skepticism to Taylor's slate of interpretive goals. Most considered the achievement of the "conjunctive" approach to be primarily conditioned by the preservation manifest in the archaeological record. Stated another way, most archaeologists of the time were strict inductivists, and considered that one's ability to construct "cultural" contexts was a function of the relative preservation of associations with clear "indicative" properties. In short, the degree to which the archaeological record preserved what were perceived as clear and directly "meaningful" associations and patterned structure was seen as the factor limiting the attainment of Walter Taylor's goals for archaeology. Skepticism born of an inductivist's approach was voiced by Hawkes (1954) and supported in the writings of many, including Robert Ascher (1962:368), who stated:

> The foregoing example is designed as a paradigm to illustrate how observations on ongoing cultures might be adapted to the problems of archaeological reconstruction. . . . Unlike endeavors which exclusively emphasize those aspects of culture *which archaeologists cannot learn about* [e.g. *Thompson 1939*], *it directs attention toward the archaeologically possible* [emphasis added].

Originally published in *Journal of Anthropological Research* 37(3):195–208, © 1981.

Asher's reference to Thompson (1939) is to the provocative paper in which he discusses seasonal behavioral changes which he believes would mislead many archaeologists, given then current interpretative conventions:

> The camps and the house types, the weapons and the utensils are of a specialized type and related to the seasonal life, so that viewing these independently at different periods of the year, and seeing the people engaged in occupations so diverse, an onlooker might be pardoned for concluding that they were different peoples (1939:209).

This exchange is typical of the time. A claim is made regarding the nature of living systems, with clear implications for the patterning found in the archaeological record. The archaeologist replies that the cited characteristics are aspects of culture "which archaeologists cannot learn about" (Ascher 1962:368).

It was in the context of further elaborating this skeptical point about our ability to reconstruct the past that Robert Ascher began developing a point of great interest— I have in mind his very early and in many ways pioneering ethnoarchaeological studies (Ascher 1962, 1968)—and his discussions of what Schiffer (1972) would later term "formation processes":

> Every living community is in the process of continuous change with respect to the materials which it utilizes. At any point in its existence some proportion of materials are falling into disuse and decomposing, while new materials are being added as replacement. In a certain sense a part of every community is becoming, but is not yet, archaeological data . . . (Ascher 1961:324)

Ascher's arguments regarding formation processes were extremely insightful. He argued that the archaeological record is some combination of interruptions in an entropy-linked process, and that it is therefore limited in its information potential. He cited the disorganizing effect of the operation of past systems, as well as the disorganizing processes associated with subsequent modifications of the archaeological record, as the sources of "distortion" in the archaeological record as seen by an archaeologist. In short, as he put it, what the archaeologist digs up is not "the remains of a once living community stopped, as it were, at a point in time"; such an "erroneous notion, often implicit in archaeological literature, might be called the Pompeii premise" (Ascher 1961:324). Ascher argued rather that the archaeological record is the disorganized arrangement of matter regularly generated after the point in time which would be of interest to a "reconstructionist." Ascher was attempting to force archaeologists to realize that the archaeological record is ravaged by "time's arrow," and should be treated as such, rather than as a preserved "past." In this important point I agreed with Ascher.

On the other hand, the implications of this empirical point as it reflects upon the aims and goals of archaeology was a point of contention between Ascher and myself. In his view, the archaeological record, viewed from a strict inductivist position, does not generally contain information regarding "cultural context," "social behavior," and other aspects of interest to those who seek to understand the past as it existed. His reasoning was simply that since the Pompeii premise was erroneous, then most reconstructionist goals, as advocated by Taylor (1948) and others, were equally unrealistic. In his view, we should restrict our discussions to subjects which are archaeologically possible.[1]

From this perspective, it follows that those who advocate the discussion of "cultural context" are really only advocating speculation and "theorizing":

> One reason for archaeology's continued lag as a contributor to culture theory . . . is that we continue to see our main goal as the reconstruction of ancient ethnology. Since we have so great a handicap to begin with here, where speculation and inference mix too confusingly . . . I think we are overlooking another order of interpretation . . . one can manipulate the artifacts statistically without much concern whether one understands precisely what they originally were, exactly how they were used, and just what they meant to the ancients (Wauchope 1966:19).

Clearly what was advocated was a "realistic" appraisal of the "limitations of the archaeological record," with the understanding that this would guide us to an appreciation of "realistic" goals for archaeological research.

My approach to the situation was different, and took exception to both points of view being discussed; I disagreed with Taylor's reconstructionist goals, as well as with inductivist skepticism regarding our ability to learn about the past.

I have never viewed the reconstruction of prehistoric lifeways in the form of prehistoric ethnographies to be an appropriate goal for archaeology in general. It has been clear to me that the time frame of ethnography is largely inappropriate for archaeological research. Rates of deposition are much slower than the rapid sequencing of events which characterizes the daily lives of living peoples; even under the best of circumstances, the archaeological record represents a massive palimpsest of derivatives from many separate episodes. Any structure and repetitive patterns of association and covariation must derive from the operation of "systemic events," or dynamics, with a much longer term, more rigidly determined organization than is true of those observed in the lives of persons and groups which embody the ethnographers' perception of time and human systems. My view was that we should be seeking to understand cultural *systems,* in terms of organizational properties, and in turn, to explain differences and similarities among these cultural systems, rather than to generate set pieces of descriptive history. This means, however, that those "things" of interest from the past are organizational properties, which cannot be dug up directly. Stated another way:

> Granted we cannot excavate a kinship terminology or a philosophy, but we can and do excavate the material items which functioned together with these more behavioral elements within the approriate cultural subsystems (Binford 1962:218-19).

In this view, a strict inductivist approach to inference is clearly impossible, since we need to have an understanding as to how living systems functioned in order to make inferences from their static by-products; in short, we need to link our observations of the archaeological record to an understanding of systems dynamics, in order to make reliable inferences about the past. They way in which I diagnosed the situation regarding Taylor and his critics was that while I did not necessarily agree with Taylor's goals, the relevance of his critics' arguments depended on a strict inductivist approach to inference.

From the beginning of my professional career, I have considered the archaeological record to be an ordered consequence of levels of adaptive organization which are difficult to appreciate directly through the observation of events and episodes in the "quick time" perspective of the ethnographer or the participant in a cultural system. Nor have I been surprised or alarmed to find that the archaeological record does not generally carry the intuitively obvious information regarding the "quick time" events and "human episodes" which one would expect from an ethnographer or a preserved Pompeii. I have considered it necessary for archaeologists to investigate the archaeological record as a different order of reality, the patterned structure of which represents not a simple accumulation of little events, but rather some of the basic organizational constraints and determinants operating on the events or episodes of daily living. The archaeological record is therefore not a poor or distorted manifestation of ethnographic "reality," but most likely a structured consequence of the operation of a level of organization difficult, if not impossible, for an ethnographer to observe directly. This level of organization is in turn likely to be the unit upon which ecological–evolutionary selection operates, rather than the level of the specific event.

Consistent with such a viewpoint, I criticized the idealized view of culture (Binford 1962), and suggested that the meanings of artifacts derive from their function in living systems, not from some manufacturer's "ideas" as translated by our classifications for things that archaeologists have found. More directly, my view was that the "Pompeii premise" is important only if one adopts a strict inductivist approach to the archaeological record, expecting to uncover archaeological "facts" with self-evident meaning for the past. I reasoned that if our methods of inference were so faulty that the "realities" of an organized system as reported by Donald Thompson (1939) had to be considered something that "archaeologists cannot learn about" (Ascher 1962:368), then clearly we needed a change in our methods.

In the context of arguing that cultural systems are internally differentiated (Binford 1962), rather than internally homogeneous (the idea threatened by Thompson's descriptions), and that such organizational differences would be manifested in the archaeological record, I wrote (Binford 1964:425) that

> The loss, breakage, and abandonment of implements and facilities at different locations, where groups of variable structure performed different tasks, leaves a 'fossil' record of the actual operation of an extinct society.

Some years later (Binford 1968a:23) I addressed quite directly the problem of the "limitations of the archaeological record," and amplified my views on its information potential:

> The practical limitations on our knowledge of the past are not inherent in the nature of the archaeological record; the limitations lie in our methodological naivete, in our lack of principles determining the relevance of archaeological remains to propositions regarding processes and events of the past.[2]

The degree of preservation of the archaeological record has never been considered limiting in a practical sense, since it has also been maintained that "facts do not speak for themselves," and that all arguments from the archaeological record as to the character of the past are inferences. These in turn are only as good as our understanding of the linkages between dynamics and statics, the causes in the past and the consequences remaining for us to observe archaeologically.

The reader cannot imagine my surprise when Michael Schiffer (1976a) years later announced to the world his discovery that the "new archaeology" had been laboring under a false principle—the Pompeii premise!

> The early years of the new archaeology witnessed the frequent and unquestioning repetition of major methodological principles. One such principle was enunciated by Binford (1964:425) in perhaps its most explicit form:
>
>> The loss, breakage, and abandonment of implements and facilities at different locations, where groups of variable structure performed different tasks, leaves a 'fossil' record the actual operation of an extinct society.
>
> As often happens . . . few investigators have noticed that the principle is false. It is false because archaeological remains are not in any sense a fossilized cultural system. Between the time artifacts were manufactured and used in the past and the time these same objects are unearthed by the archaeologist, they have been subjected to a series of cultural and noncultural processes which have transformed them spatially, quantitatively, formally and relationally. . . . If we desire to reconstruct the past from archaeological remains, these processes must be taken into account, and a more generally applicable methodological principle substituted for the one that asserts that there is an equivalence between a past cultural system and its archaeological record. The principle I offer is that archaeological remains are a distorted reflection of a past behavioral system (Schiffer 1976a:11-12).

This is exactly the point which Ascher had made years earlier; namely, that the archaeological record is a distortion of the Pompeii that he claimed we thought we were finding. Schiffer (1976a:14) describes his Pompeii premise as follows:

> If the human participants and all other energy sources completely halt their actions, the activities cease, as does the operation of the behavioral system, what remains (assuming no modification by other processes) is the closest conceivable approximation of a 'fossil' of a cultural system—its material elements in a system-relevant spatial matrix.

Ascher had discredited the Pompeii premise as a means of discrediting the reconstructionist goals of Walter Taylor. I had rejected these same goals as unrealistic and wasteful relative to the processes which were likely to be responsible for the archaeological record, i.e., the long-term structure and evolutionary dynamics of a cultural system. In turn, Ascher's arguments against Taylor were beside the point.

> Archaeological theory consists of propositions and assumptions regarding the archaeological record itself—its origins, its sources of variability, the determinants of differences and similarities in the formal, spatial, and temporal characteristics of artifacts and features and their interrelationships. It is in the context of this theory that archaeological methods and techniques are developed (Binford 1968b:2).

When Schiffer, years later, claimed that my approaches presuppose the Pompeii premise, my initial response was to ignore his misunderstanding.[3] However, I have come to realize that instead of minor misunderstandings, there are substantive points of disagreement between Schiffer and myself.

Was Distortion Going on at Pompeii?

Schiffer proposed that in order to grasp fully the inferential challenges facing the archaeologist, we have to understand in some detail the sources of, or causes for, the properties remaining in the archaeological record. In this I agree. He further proposed that we must always keep clearly in mind the difference between *systemic context*, or the dynamics within which matter "participated" in the past, and *archaeological* context, or the static form in which we find culturally generated matter in the archaeological record; with this I also agree. According to Schiffer it is the "transformation" of matter from the systemic context into the archaeological context that should receive our focused attention. He called these transformational conditions formation processes, and recognized two basic types: C-*transforms*, or cultural formation processes, and N-*transforms*, or noncultural formation processes. The question now is why does Schiffer consider the archaeological record distorted?

I am quite comfortable with the idea that there may be natural, or noncultural, processes which condition the character of the archaeological record so as to "distort" the organization as it was generated in the "systemic" context. I am somewhat at a loss, however, to understand why events which modified the formal properties of matter during the operation of a cultural system should be considered distorting.

> The principle I offer is that archaeological remains are a distorted reflection of a past behavioral system. However, *because the cultural and non-cultural processes responsible for these distortions are regular,* there are systematic (but seldom direct) relationships between archaeological remains and past cultural systems (Schiffer 1976a:12; emphasis added).

It is clear from Schiffer's statement that he considers C-transforms potentially distorting. From my perspective, archaeologists must understand formation processes—the dynamics of cultural systems which yield derivative residues both in properties of form and spatial distribution—while from Schiffer's perspective, archaeologists must identify distortions between the "systemic" and the "archaeological" contexts.

For instance, Schiffer would view the event of a young boy cleaning out a hearth, taking the ash and other unwanted contents out of the house, and tossing it to one side as a C-transform distorting the juxtaposition of hearth and ashes which obtained during the period of active fire in the hearth. From the perspective of the occupants of the site, it was cleaning up. We may reasonably ask how cleaning up should distort the relationship between the archaeological record and the cultural system from which it derives; some might even argue that cleaning up was essential for the continued use of the location. Similarly, one might argue that adding fuel to the fire was essential to maintaining the fire, but alas, it was also "distorting" the prior relationship between the hearth and the adjacent pile of firewood.

Thus, I totally disagree with Schiffer's idea that the archaeological record is a distortion of a past cultural system. Such a position could only be true if the archaeological record as produced in the past were destroyed or modified by post–depositional events. The archaeological record is a normal consequence of the operation of living systems, all of which are dynamic, "flow through" systems, in which energy is captured and its potential reduced. Entropy is the inevitable product of a living system, *and it is generated continuously.* The archaeological record must therefore be viewed as matter transposed and organized during the *process* of energy use and entropy production. It is the functional linkages between the organization of a system and its energy-capturing tactics, together with its patterned residues (entropy), that yield information about the organization of past systems.

Our inferences from the archaeological record to the past may be wrong or unjustified, not because the archaeological record is a distortion of the past, but because we do not accurately understand the relationship between statics and dynamics. The archaeological record can only be considered a distortion relative to some a priori set of expectations; certainly is is not a distortion of its own reality. It is a faithful remnant of the causal conditions operative in the past, and our task is to understand those causal conditions. Put another way, a pattern or arrangement among artifacts at an archaeological site can only be viewed as distorted if one is not interested in the cultural system as manifest, but rather in some property of a cultural system chosen a priori to receive special inferential attention. Cleaning up is distorting only if it destroys some patterned association in which one might have a research interest.

Paradigm Conflict: Describing Past Cultural Systems versus Reconstructing the Past

I have argued that the idea of the archaeological record as "distorted" by C-transforms makes sense only if we imagine a set of past conditions which would be "optimal," or ideal, for us to find. The archaeological record is not distorted with respect to its own reality, but only relative to an archaeologist's preexisting expectations. The latter will of course be derived from a specific paradigm, or what we expect the world to be like (see Binford 1981b).

What would Schiffer like to find? In the answer to this question rests the clue to the really major differences between our views of the archaeologist's challenge. Schiffer wants to find Pompeii.

> Let us begin by visualizing an ongoing cultural system. . . . What one pictures is a system of action. . . . If the human participants and all other energy sources completely halt their actions, the activities cease, as does the operation of the behavioral system, what remains (assuming no modifications by other processes) is the closest conceivable approximation to a 'fossil' of a cultural system . . . (Schiffer 1976a:12-13)

What Schiffer has described is as close as one can come to the ethnographer's notion of the "ethnographic present"—a synchronic cross-section of all the events or actions transpiring at a given time. It is not a picture of a cultural system, but a slice of "history" in the literal sense of the word. A cultural system is not a summation of all the events, behaviors, or other transactional phenomena going on at a given time, but rather the conditioning organizational framework within which all these events transpire. This organizational framework includes all the places, things, and characteristic social relationships and intellectual conventions in terms of which events are played out. It is true that a cultural system has dynamic properties; it is not true that is is completely dynamic and transitory, as is implied by Schiffer's writings.

Given Schiffer's view of a cultural system, placing trash in a dump is a C-transform; as such, it is a distorting action, marking the transition between systemic context and archaeological context for the items discarded. They were in fact "used" at another place, at a prior time, and as such the presence of the item in the dump is a distortion of such a prior state. But is it also true that it is a distortion of the cultural system? Only if the cultural system is equated with specific actions or the "context of use" for the items in question. However, if one considers the maintenance of life-space part of the cultural system, the act of cleaning up and disposal itself as a part of the cultural system, even the presence of a dump as a component of the cultural system, how are things distorted? *Answer: they are not distorted.* What is distorted is Schiffer's view of a cultural system, and his ideas as to how to understand one.

The history of anthropology follows research oriented toward offering some answer to the question of why different "peoples" consistently behave differently; in short, why their behaviors are so frequently variable in the face of seemingly similar stimuli. Early answers to this question cited "race" differences as the causes of behavioral differences; to counter this position anthropologists pointed to "culture" as the cause of patterned, long-lasting behavioral differences among "peoples." In this context there was a conflict between those who saw differences in culture as referable to differences in individual psychology, which then would feed back to reinforce such populational differences; and those who sought the explanation for different cultures, not from the properties of the participants, but from the ecological history of the system itself, seen in interaction with its environment. The psychologically oriented view sees cultural systems as abstractions or generalizations of all the specific behaviors considered "cultural" in character. Change reflected through such a normative view is the result of microfactors, which push and pull the frequencies with which specific behaviors are executed.[4] In turn, change is seen in an almost Lamarckian framework, where

> most changes result from attempts to cope with the unanticipated consequences of previous decisions" (Schiffer 1979a:366).

I wish to understand in organizational terms the frameworks within which behaviors were carried out, the structural properties of systems within which the dynamic functioning we see as behavior occurred. In turn, I wish to understand in Darwinian terms the pressures on such systems, which result in their structural change, diversification, and evolution.[5]

Consistent with this contrast between the systems and the interactionist views, Reid and Schiffer state (1973:2) that:

> It seems appropriate that archaeologists recognize that culture is knowledge—a system of learned information and the rules for processing and transforming that information into action or behavior. Strictly speaking culture is not behavior.

Here we see another fundamental point of disagreement between processualists and Schiffer and his colleagues. For the latter, not only is a cultural system considered to be behavioral in the literal sense of the word, but culture itself is considered to be mental phenomena—a system of learned information. Culture is then manifest in things and behavior, but is not a material phenomenon itself. *This is traditional archaeology.* Culture provided a mentalist explanation for variability in behavior and manufactured items for the traditionalist; it is again cast in that role in Schiffer's thought. The only difference is that culture is extended to include more than mental templates for producing things, to include plans for "living," manifested behaviorally and transactionally.

Ironically, instead of viewing his ideas as conflicting with those advocated by myself and others in the 1960s, Schiffer saw them contributing to harmony in the field:

> Although the debates of the past decade have resulted in significant advances in archaeological method and theory, they have also led to a fragmentation of the discipline and to overt and covert hostility between rival sub-paradigms and between traditional and processual archaeologists. Thus, before we treat some of the important issues that contribute to the revisionist version of processual archaeology, we offer a scheme for reintegrating the divergent aims and interests of all archaeologists (Reid and Schiffer 1973:2-3).

The intellectual peacemaking which Reid and Schiffer were engaged in would have constituted an intellectual capitulation of processualist views to major components of the traditionalist position. This is neither compromise nor evaluative scientific judgment; it is simple paradigmatic bias.

In addition, there are real contrasts between myself and Schiffer regarding the characteristics of evolution—Darwinian versus Lamarckian—and hence the appropriate types of facts needed to understand cultural change. There are paradigmatic differences regarding the concept of culture, and there are also major contrasts in our views on how to do science: Schiffer is primarily an inductivist, seeking to elevate empirical generalizations to the status of "laws," and worrying about the probabilistic "value" of such propositions. Nevertheless, we agree on the basic need for increasing the power of our inferential strategies, and we agree that this depends on giving priority attention to understanding the archaeological record. Since his major work had been in this latter area, we may justifiably ask if his call for a "revisionist" new archaeology should be taken seriously. Has Schiffer illustrated any methodological gains which would back his call for a "revisionist" perspective?

Behavioral Archaeology at the Joint Site

In Schiffer's model of site formation there are three modes of deposition, resulting in primary refuse, secondary refuse, and de facto refuse. Matter discarded or dropped in the immediate context of use is primary refuse; secondary refuse is matter which has been moved from its primary location, generally through maintenance or clean-up operations; and de facto refuse consists of items lost or abandoned during the abandonment of a site. By definition, de facto refuse is usable items occurring in the context of "late" or terminal use of the site. We may ask how Schiffer would distinguish de facto refuse, deriving from the abandonment by sedentary residents, from site furniture (see Binford 1979b) maintained and regularly used in the residentially abandoned rooms by hunting parties or other logistically organized groups who use the "ruin" as a camping spot. The ruin would, of course, offer shelter and raw materials, and water would necessarily have been nearby, since it was once a residential site. The answer seems to be that Schiffer could not recognize such differences, since he never included the successional alternative in his "paradigm" of possibilities for interpreting pueblo "formation processes."

In this regard it is interesting that in studying debris associated with what Schiffer considers to be deposits accumulated at the Joint Site during the main occupation, as contrasted with associations developed during the "abandonment," he finds that "the flow rate of chalcedony increases by a factor of two during the abandonment period" (Schiffer 1976a:170). Schiffer rightfully seeks an understanding of this interesting observation, by adopting a form of argument from elimination (see Binford 1981a:83), proposing four "hypotheses" and seeking to "test" each of them. After rejecting three, he is left with hypothesis number four, namely, that "chalcedony was used for the same tasks, but the rate of task performance increased" (Schiffer 1976a:173). He then suggests that a biased use of chalcedony is most likely to have arisen in hunting. In evaluating this suggestion Schiffer (1976a:175) argues that:

> The ratio of food species to total chipped stone tools should increase appreciably between the main occupation and abandonment periods. In Table 12.6 the ratio of the total number of identifiable bones (of the five most common food species) to the total number of stone tools is presented for the two periods. Quite clearly, the ratio increases by a factor of at least 10 for all species.

Schiffer's (1976a:177) "historical" scenario is as follows:

> It seems as though the environmental conditions conducive to subsistence agriculture in the Hay Hollow Valley deteriorated considerably during the second half of the thirteenth century. In response to the stresses created by a high rate of crop failure or by reductions in available agricultural products, the inhabitants of the Joint Site diversified their procurement strategies to include more species of wild foods, and greater dependence on the wild foods ordinarily consumed. The heavier emphasis on hunting brought with it a greater demand for arrow points and other hunting and butchering tools. Because the increased rate of hunting by groups of males resulted in more trips to the vicinity of Point of the Mountain, chalcedony, a material favored for manufacture of arrow points, was retrieved more frequently . . .

We have here a fine example of a set of untested conventions used as a method of inference. Given the use of a limited set of formation conventions, we are led to a set of conclusions about the past which, at least in my view, are truly bizarre.

We may reasonably ask: (a) If game density was sufficient to support the local group in the immediate area, why did they practice agriculture in the first place? (b) Wild resources are normally increasingly depleted in the immediate area of a sedentary site as a function of increasing occupational duration. If this was the case here, how were the people able to compensate for "crop failure" at the end of their occupation by shifting to the exploitation of wild foods? (c) In general, the speed of game depletion is inversely related to body size; larger body-sized animals are overexploited first, so that there is an increasing trend toward animals of smaller body size during the tenure of a sedentary occupation. We note that there is a relative increase in mule deer relative to antelope between the "main occupation" and the "abandonment phase" assemblages. This proportional shift is also true with respect to the smaller animals; there is an absolute increase in mule deer relative to other animals. I find this pattern almost impossible to imagine as characteristic of the closing phases of a permanent settlement. *On the other hand, it is perfectly consistent with the post-aban-*

donment utilization of the ruin by hunting parties operating out of another residential base.
Presumably, some years after abandonment, the local flora and fauna would recover,
and the site of the old sedentary village would make a perfect camping spot for
hunting parties exploiting what may well have been a temporary, localized abundance
of game. This abundance would be due to the patterns of recovery within the floral
community, providing more forage for animals than with climax vegetation.

Such an argument might well account for the "de facto garbage" on the floors
(this is site furniture), as well as the presence of quantities of fire-cracked rock on the
"floors" (see Schiffer's Table 11.2, 1976a:150) of these "abandonment phase" rooms.
It is hard to imagine the use of roasting techniques or stone boiling inside the
habitation rooms of an ongoing sedentary site, with the fire-cracked rock not cleaned
up and disposed of as secondary refuse. On the other hand, fire-cracked rock as
primary refuse in hunting camps is quite common, in my experience.

Do We Need a "Revisionist" Behavioral Archaeology?

First, if we view Schiffer's work through the same critical eyes he has turned on the
work of many of the "new archaeologists," then we would have to conclude that
Schiffer, too, has failed because of the pesky problem of the Pompeii premise. He has
assumed a direct relationship between his unit of observation (the site) and a unit
of systemic context (a single occupation, both ethnically and functionally conceived).
The possibility that Schiffer has completely distorted the past rests with his failure
to appreciate an important formation process (successional use) as a possible contributor to his "recovery context" materials (see Binford 1972a:314-26). Using Schiffer's own criteria, then, we are clearly in need of a "revisionist" behavioral archaeology.

I think that the reader would agree that this would be an unwarranted conclusion
to draw from Schiffer's quite probable failure, yet this is the type of conclusion which
Schiffer draws from his critical evaluation of other archaeologists. The "new archaeology" has primarily involved a claim that we did not know all the sources of variability
contributing to the archaeological record. Given this condition, new archaeologists
have argued that it is premature to offer an a priori evaluation as to the "limitations"
of the archaeological record for yielding up information:

> There has been as yet no attempt to assess the limitations of the archaeological record for yielding
> different kinds of information, nor does there seem to be the means of accurately determining
> these limits short of total knowledge of all the systematic relationships which characterize past
> cultural systems. Thus, present discussions of limitations . . . are inappropriate and are based on
> speculation (Binford 1968a:22).

Schiffer distorted this posture into a claim that we know all the sources, and
therefore any failure to recognize, say, a particular "formation process," would be
clear evidence of a false principle (the "Pompeii premise") at work. Schiffer's position
is very close to sophistry.

Pompeii is only an ideal for one interested in events, specific behaviors, and event-
centered "history." For Schiffer, who obviously has a reconstructionist goal in mind,

Pompeii is the most desirable condition of the archaeological record.[6] Sadly, after encountering the archaeological record he became disillusioned; it was not a series of little Pompeiis only in need of "dusting off" in order to yield "ethnographies," or complete pictures of the past.

Just because Schiffer was disillusioned because of his own false expectations, it is unfair for him to blame that disillusionment on the new archaeology; such behavior can only result in the silly posturing visible in Schiffer's 1978 paper (Schiffer 1981). For instance, in striking out against the "Pompeii premise," Schiffer claims that the new archaeologists believe that a complete cultural system is capable of being "seen" at a single site, and that any site contains meaningful information on any subject (Schiffer and House 1977:250):[7]

> While the new archaeologists can be applauded for their desire to promote . . . verifiability in archaeology, they must be faulted for not going far enough and especially for obscuring the fact that . . . not all sites are equal in research potential (Sullivan (1976).

I can only respond with Flannery's words "Leaping lizards, Mister Science!"

Although presented as a "straw man," this little example of disillusionment points to a major flaw in even the positive aspects of Schiffer's work, namely, his search for "precise moments in the remote past" (Roe 1980:107). Paradigmatic growth is crucial to the growth of science, providing as it does the concepts which may in turn be transformed into an observational language for the science. If we dismiss most of the archaeological record as distorted, mixed, or disturbed, and seek only those provenience units which appear to represent little capsules of human behavior, we will continue to have an impoverished, unrealistic view of the past. We must seek rather to understand the archaeological record in the state in which it is available to us. In most cases, the greater the apparent disorganization, the more intense the use of the place in the past; it is these disturbances we must understand, instead of seeing them as conditions which render the site "insignificant" and the past unknowable. Disturbed deposits, such as mixed "plow zone" aggregates of tools, are the most common remains we encounter; if we hold out for the very few sites where we may "recognize" undistorted "analytical units," then we will have very few remains from the past with which to work.[8] The challenge is how to use the "distorted" stuff, not how to discover the rare and unusual Pompeiis. It is clearly impossible to understand the settlement system of a group of mobile hunter-gatherers when you demand, as Schiffer has, "undisturbed deposits made by the same group in different locations in the environment" (Schiffer and House 1977:252).

Holding up the Pompeii premise as an ideal insures that the imperfect world of "dirt archaeology" will almost always be a frustrating one. Perhaps herein lies a clue to Schiffer's recent statements that archaeology is not "prehistory," and that many archaeologists are "not concerned with objects at all and some do not even dig! (Schiffer 1976b:9).

It is particularly crucial to have an adequate and realistic observational language for treating properties of the archaeological record as it is; it is the very act of conceptualizing archaeological observations that conveys meaning to them, and in turn implies conditions in the past. If our conceptual inventory is impoverished, relative to the processes which could be responsible for the objects remaining for us to see, then our views of the past will be correspondingly impoverished and unrealistic.

It is perhaps ironic that Schiffer, who for many has played the role of the master critic, taking many to task for having "failed" to appreciate the complexities of "formation processes," is at the same time content to view so much processual evidence as distortions.[9] Not only is the Pompeii premise rarely justified by the archaeological record, but seeking a reconstructed Pompeii is an unrealistic and unprofitable goal in the light of the knowledge we have and the data available to us in that record.

Notes

1. See Rouse (1964:465) and Wauchope (1966:19) for strong statements supporting Ascher's position on this point.

2. In the minds of many, my claims that we could learn about conditions in the past which were not "directly" recoverable seemed to be a continuation of Taylor's position, and many authors have offered skeptical arguments in the form of "cautionary tales," largely drawn from ethnography, to demonstrate how limited archaeologists' data actually are! Richard Lee's (1966) "lesson" on how limited archaeological remains are when compared to the "richness" of the actual life that left them was amplified in the writings of Carl Heider, who demonstrated how "spurious" associations between things could be generated, and how the dynamics of an actual system would "tend to mislead the archaeologist" (Heider 1967:57). These "cautionary tales" generally assumed a strict inductivist approach to inference, and were usually offered as a skeptical note on some of the goals of archaeological inference, as they were discussed during the 1960's. They were all arguments against a "direct" linkage between the facts of the archaeological record and the past, challenges to the "Pompeii premise."

3. After listening to a major statement of the position presented by M. Collins (1975) in a symposium in San Francisco in 1973, and later championed by Schiffer, I replied as follows (Binford 1975b:252):

> Raising objections that the archaeological record may be "baised" seems to stem from some strange expectation that the archaeological record is some kind of fossilized picture remaining to us from the past with built-in and self-evident meanings upon which 'time's arrow' has played disturbing tricks. No such meaningful picture exists complete with semantic directions as to how to properly read the record. All meaning comes from us. . . . telling me that the archaeological record cannot be translated mechanically into statements about the past according to some set of rules for assigning meaning does not surprise or depress me . . .

4. Such a perspective is certainly not unique to Schiffer (see Jochim 1979:83; Spiess 1979: 1–5).

5. The very practical consequences of these contrastive points of view are well illustrated by comparing Schiffer 1979b with Binford 1979 for vastly different approaches to lithic studies. Similarly, Schiffer's (1976a:56–57) discussion of curation should be compared to my discussion (Binford 1976) for a graphic example of the differences between a search for systems properties and a concern with specific behaviours and their cumulative result.

6. See Dunnell 1980 for his opinion on "reconstructionism."

7. This is also true of other recent critics, who have suggested that I believe that the archaeological record contains information about all past events (Coe 1978), or that I consider there to be an isomorphism between past behavior and the archaeological record (DeBoer and Lathrap 1979:103, 134). Similarly, see Gould's (1980:6–28) "revelation" that sites are multicomponental and behaviorally stark. Cautionary tales continue to demonstrate, again and again, the fallacy of the Pompeii premise.

8. Perhaps the popularity of Schiffer's position with Cultural Resource Management archaeologists arises from its use as a basis for writing off most of the archaeological record as "insignificant," since it does not approach the idea of little prepackaged Pompeiis. This approach renders it impossible even to begin to see something of the organization of past cultural systems.

9. See, for example, Schiffer 1975c and Sullivan and Schiffer 1978.

19

Forty-seven Trips:
A Case Study in the Character of
Archaeological Formation Process

One of my motives for initiating ethno-archaeological work among the contemporary Nunamiut Eskimos was the recognition that they were one of the few remaining groups of people still largely dependent upon hunting for their subsistence. It was possible to study the dynamics of an ongoing technological system in the context of an essentially self-sufficient subsistence economy. To many, the Nunamiut may appear uninteresting since most of the tools currently in use are no longer manufactured locally, but are purchased through mail order houses or obtained through a variety of other commercial means. These conditions fascinated me. If archaeology is to achieve the status of a science it must seek to establish law-like propositions. If law-like, such propositions should cover contemporary as well as past organizational situations. Too long have anthropologists sought the unique, or singled out as 'exceptional' specific features of a case as justification for abandoning the goal of law-like propositions.

The purpose of this paper is to examine the dynamics of behaviour in the context of which archaeological remains are generated: the aim being the specification of some behavioural characteristics which may regularly condition the content and forms of patterning observed by the archaeologist.

The data to be discussed is derived primarily from observations of 47 trips made by Eskimo males out of the village of Anaktuvuk between 4 and 17 April 1971. The following information was obtained regarding each trip: (a) the time of departure, (b) the composition of the party leaving the village, (c) the expressed purpose of the trip, (d) the anticipated destination, (e) an inventory of all gear carried by the party members, and (f) the mode of transportation to be used. When the party returned (or in some cases when I was on the trip and could make a journal) the following information was obtained: (a) the route travelled, (b) the location of all stops, (c) the activities performed at each stop, (d) the duration of each stop, (e) the total distance travelled, (f) the duration of the trip, and (g) an inventory of all gear returned

Originally appeared in *Stone Tools as Cultural Markers,* edited by R. V. S. Wright, published by the Australian Institute of Aboriginal Studies, Canberra, pp. 24–36, © 1977. Reprinted by permission of Humanities Press, Inc., Atlantic Highlands, New Jersey 07716.

to the village. Subsequently, interviews were conducted with the participants of the trips regarding their ideas and cognitive organisation of the gear used.

Information was sought regarding the reasons for discrepancies between the list of gear leaving the village and that which returned. No attempt was made to inventory the items carried in pockets. Cigarettes, sun glasses, a wad of toilet paper, a small screwdriver for adjusting gun sights, and a sharpening stone are the items which most hunters have on their person at any time, and these items can generally be assumed on all of the trips.

Table 19.1 presents the 47 trips arranged left to right in order of decreasing round trip distances from the village at Anaktuvuk. The inventory of items is grouped into three major categories. Group I is all items which are specific to the use of the snow-mobile for transport. Group II is all items which might be termed the hunter's basic spring equipment, arranged in a descending order of occurrence on the trips inventoried. Group III is items considered 'optional' by the hunters, and represents items carried more frequently on longer trips.

Group I (The Snow-mobile)

There is a perfect association between the presence of Group I items and the use of the snow-mobile for transport. The use of the snow-mobile by the Nunamiut is interesting in terms of its recent introduction. The first snow-mobile to be purchased was delivered to the village during the winter of 1967–68. It was bought by Simon Paneack. Quickly most families worked toward the purchase of a snow-mobile, and by the spring of 1971 there were 23 functional (running) snow-mobiles in the village and 5 working dog teams, averaging 7.2 dogs per team. By 1971, snow-mobiles represented 82.1% of the operational winter and spring transportation means. Interviews on the use of the snow-mobile and its advantages over the dog team brought forth a number of comments. Almost universally, the response of the hunters was that the speed of the snow-mobile made it possible to range further without the need for extended overnight camping. In addition, they claimed that the snow-mobile permitted the pursuit hunting of wolves, which they saw as a clear advantage. 'It is fast enough to run them right down.' The disadvantages were clearly recognised to be of two types: (a) frequent breakdown in the field, and (b) difficulty in maintenance due to lack of parts, expense of spare parts, and difficulty in repairing the machines in cold weather.

Of the 33 snow-mobile trips recorded in Table 19.1, 6 were 'breakdown' trips on which the hunters either had to walk back to the village or spend the night in the field awaiting the arrival of other monitors to take them home. This amounts to an impressive 18.1% of the total trips made by snow-mobile. Of the dog team trips recorded, none were 'breakdown' trips. This difference in reliability is fully realised by the hunters, although the risk is tolerated for the added advantage of speed, and the fact that short trips can be made for packing even when the snow is poor or gone.

Although 82.1% of the operational transport means during winter and spring were snow-mobile, only 70.2% of the recorded trips were made with these vehicles. The difference in proportion reflects, to some extent, differences among the active hunters in their willingness to take the risk of breakdown. For instance, during the spring of 1971 I was a member of two parties which experienced snow-mobile breakdowns in the field. The hunter had killed his dogs the previous fall, keeping only three large ones for summer packing. During the summer of 1971 he was very anxious to get puppies to begin training as a team, since he was 'fed up' with snow-mobile breakdowns during the winter. I anticipate a slight increase in the number of functional dog teams among the active hunters during the next several years.

Group II (Hunters' Basic Equipment)

The items listed as Group II, Table 19.1, make up the basic 'trip gear' inventory of the hunters. Most of these items have functional counterparts in the traditional technology of the Nunamiut.

The axe is the most characteristic item which distinguishes the winter and spring equipment from that of summer and autumn. The axe is used for a variety of tasks during the months of freezing weather. Its most common use is to chop out the meat from frozen caches, and to complete any butchering tasks that may be considered necessary at the time of loading meat from caches. In addition, it may be used in cutting down large willows for transport back to the village, and as an ice chisel while in the field if ice fishing is attempted. In case of mishap it may be used to breach the hard crust of the packed snow for making an emergency snow house. I have also observed it being used as a hammer, particularly during attempted snow-mobile or sled repairs, and the handle being used as an expedient snow probe when one is not handy. In extreme cold the axe is frequently used to butcher even unfrozen animals, since the use of the knife generally ensures that the hunter's hands will become covered with blood and therefore more subject to freezing and general discomfort.

The metal axe was one of the first items to be adopted enthusiastically into the traditional Nunamiut technology, once trade with Russian and Euro–American sources was opened up in the last half of the 19th century. However, it was not the first item selected if a maximising choice had to be made. Interestingly, the saw was given selective preference over the axe because 'it could be cut into men's knives and ulus when it was worn out'; the implication being that it was difficult to do much with a broken or worn out axe. In the early trading days the saw was used for many of the tasks for which the axe is used today. The saw was used for secondary and primary winter butchering of frozen meat, and was also used in gathering winter firewood. Traditional ice chisels, generally hafted on the end of a snow probe, spear, or ice shovel, continued to be used for many of the ice chopping and chipping tasks which today are usually performed with the axe.

Prior to the Russian–European trade, highly valued axes were made from Alaskan 'jade'. Although the living informants can remember seeing these items in their youth, they were heirlooms largely used by shamans. By that time metal items obtained in trade had already become an integral part of their technology. Questions directed to the older men regarding the form of the stone axes drew a variety of responses. Most agreed that the 'oldtimers' axes' were not hafted like modern metal ones. Instead, they were hafted with the blade transverse to the handle, which would render the item an adze in our terminology. In addition, they agreed that Alaskan 'jade' was not the only material used for the production of the blade. One informant said he had seen them

TABLE 19.1

Gear Carried by Hunters on 47 Trips

	Trip	28	27	26	25	41	40	42	39	36ª	24	23ª	35	43ª	33	38	21ª	32	34	46	47
Kilometers	(Round trip)	274	274	274	274	203	183	183	183	179	163	158	158	76	76	69	68	63	63	60	60
Group I																					
Pliers		•	•	•	•	•	•	•	•	•		•			•	•		•	•	•	•
Screwdriver		•	•	•	•	•	•	•	•	•		•			•	•		•	•	•	•
Wrench		•	•	•	•	•	•	•	•	•		•			•	•		•	•	•	•
Spark plug		•	•	•	•	•	•	•	•	•		•			•	•		•	•	•	•
Extra gas		•	•	•	•	•	•	•	•	•		•			•			•		•	•
Oil		•	•	•	•	•	•	•	•	•		•			•					•	
Wire		•	•	•	•	•		•	•	•		•			•	•			•	•	
Extra chain		•		•		•	•			•						•					
Hammer		•	•			•	•	•		•											
Group II																					
1 Axe		•	•	•	•	•	•	•	•	•	•	•	•	•	•	•	•	•	•	•	•
2 Sled skin		•	•	•	•	•	•	•	•	•	•	•	•	•	•	•	•	•	•	•	•
3 Matches		•	•	•	•	•	•	•	•	•	•	•	•	•	•	•	•	•	•	•	•
4 Rifle		•	•	•	•	•	•	•	•	•	•	•	•	•	•	•	•	•	•	•	•
5 Ammunition		•	•	•	•	•	•	•	•	•	•	•	•	•	•	•	•	•	•	•	•
6 Pilot bread		•	•	•	•	•	•	•	•	•	•	•	•	•	•	•	•	•	•	•	•
7 Snow probe		•	•	•	•	•	•	•	•	•	•	•	•	•	•	•	•	•	•	•	•
8 Sugar		•	•			•	•	•	•	•	•	•	•	•	•	•	•	•	•	•	•
9 Coffee		•	•	•	•	•	•	•	•	•	•	•	•	•	•	•	•	•	•	•	•
10 Knife		•	•	•	•	•	•	•	•	•	•	•	•	•	•	•	•	•	•	•	•
11 Cup		•	•	•	•	•	•	•	•	•	•	•	•	•	•	•	•	•	•	•	•
12 Coffee can		•	•			•	•	•	•	•	•	•	•	•	•	•	•	•	•	•	•
13 Extra mukluks		•	•	•	•	•	•	•	•	•	•	•	•	•	•	•	•	•	•	•	•
14 Extra socks		•	•	•	•	•	•	•	•	•	•	•	•	•	•	•	•	•	•	•	•
15 Extra line		•	•	•	•	•	•	•	•	•	•	•	•	•	•	•	•	•	•	•	•
16 Extra skin		•	•	•	•	•	•	•	•	•	•	•	•	•	•	•	•	•	•	•	•
17 Glass		•	•	•	•	•	•	•	•	•	•	•	•	•	•	•			•		•
18 Big knife		•	•	•	•	•	•	•	•	•	•	•	•	•	•				•		•
19 Extra parka		•	•	•	•	•	•	•	•	•	•	•	•								
20 Corn meal		•				•	•	•	•	•	•	•	•								
Group III																					
21 Snow shoes		•		•	•			•	•	•			•		•			•			•
22 Dry meat						•		•		•			•		•			•	•		
23 Needle and skin		•		•				•		•			•	•	•						•
24 Rib slab		•		•	•	•	•			•	•		•								
25 Scapula				•						•		•	•								
26 Steel traps						•	•			•											
27 Sardines			•		•	•		•			•		•		•	•					
28 .22 pistol			•		•	•		•													
29 .22 rifle				•		•	•		•												
30 Peanut butter			•		•	•		•													
Gear carried by hunters and not returned																					
Peanut butter jar			•		•	•		•													
Sardine can			•		•	•					•		•		•	•					
.22 shells			•	•		•		•													
Steel traps						•	•			•											
Ribs		•		•		•	•		•	•		•									
Scapula				•			•			•		•									
Cup						•		•			•										
Coffee can						•		•		•					•				•		
Knife		•																			
Snow probe						•															
Rifle shell cases						•															
Axe													•								
Skin						•															
Line										•											

ª Indicates use of dog team on the trip.

TABLE 19.1 *(Continued)*

29	30	20	2ᵃ	6ᵃ	18ᵃ	15	5	44ᵃ	31ᵃ	12	4	17	19ᵃ	37	9ᵃ	46	11ᵃ	13ᵃ	45	14	3	22	10	7	8	1
55	55	50	48	43	42	37	35	34	27	27	27	26	23	21	21	19	19	19	19	19	18	18	18	14	8	

[a] Indicates use of dog team on the trip.

made with flint blades, and offered the interpretation that one of the steeply retouched 'sidescrapers' which I recovered archaeologically in 1971 was like the flint blades hafted in the oldtimers' axes. They all agreed that the blades were hafted into an antler sleeve which was then lashed to a handle. Items recently described by Hall (1971:41) as adzes fit very nicely the descriptions of the informants regarding the 'oldtimers' axes'. In addition, one 'sidescraper' pictured by Hall (1971:90) appears identical to the item which informants identified as a flint axe blade. Informants related that the 'oldtimers' axes were used in cutting up frozen meat, working wood, and chopping antler. They suggested that those with flint blades were better for fine work on wood. I was unable to obtain information from the informants regarding the frequency of jade axes in the past, and the degree that they were consistently used for winter butchering and cache removal tasks as the metal axe is used today. All informants agreed that 'it must have been used that way', since all recognised as a difficult winter task the coping with frozen meat. For this job a knife is considered of little value.

Axes are owned today by each household, and most have more than one. They are rarely stored inside the house, generally being found standing up inside a pile of firewood next to the house, or lying on top of a partially unloaded sled. It is important to note that on every trip made outside of the village during the spring period an axe was included in the equipment.

Matches are today the other item which is considered as essential as the axe in winter and spring field equipment. They have only a single function, unlike the axe. Matches were known through trade as early as the 1890's, but they did not replace the earlier flint and steel set until they were consistently available around 1915. As late as 1946 some old men were still carrying flint and steel sets as part of their regular field equipment. The latter were manufactured from files obtained in trade and a combination of gun flints or locally obtained flints.

Informants, when queried regarding the methods of making fire prior to the availability of trade files, said that the bow drill was used in a wooden hearth. Willow cotton rubbed in charcoal was the preferred tinder. This technique has been used in recent times by hunters with either wet matches or otherwise caught without modern fire making equipment. The young hunters are familiar with the technique and most admit to having used it under emergency conditions sometimes during their lifetime.

Today each hunter has anywhere from two to four rifles, generally varying in size and power. Reloading of spent shells is still common, and new shells are not purchased regularly. Rifles and shells are generally stored in the houses and are rarely left outside. In the field they are carried in a rifle case made of either caribou skin or canvas. The case is sewn so that the rifle is extracted from the butt end. The case is slung over both shoulders so that it hangs across the back with the barrel tip pointing down. Ammunition is generally carried in a small pouch especially made for the purpose, and worn so that it hangs on the right side just above the belt. Sometimes the rifle is packed on the sled, rolled in the 'sled skin' so that the jarring of the sled will not damage the rifle. Nunamiut hunters are not extremely meticulous in the care of their guns. However, I have never seen a hunter load his rifle until game is sighted or he is following very fresh tracks or spoor. Rifles are never stored loaded.

The rifle was first known to the Nunamiut during the time of the great-grand-fathers of the old men living today. The first guns were flintlock rifles obtained in trade. There are many stories which the old men heard from their fathers about the novelty of this gun. Most of the stories relate humorous facts about their exploding, failure to fire, or other inefficiencies. Although such pieces were known and owned by Nunamiut during the last half of the 19th century, they were never numerous or reliable enough to replace the conventional hunting gear, and seem to have had little effect on the traditional hunting practices.

Beginning in the 1890s, rifles obtained from the coast (largely 30–30s) became rather numerous in the interior, and by 1900 had generally replaced the conventional hunting gear, although this was sporadically used until as late as 1946. The combination of the increase of trading activity with the coast and the adoption of the gun somewhat modified the traditional pattern of life in the interior, and had, of course, profound effects on the character of the technology.

The skinning knife, big knife and snow probe all had counterparts in the traditional technology. Today, the most common skinning knife is a small pocket knife. Younger men tend to have larger knives, and the older men comment on how they behave like 'sheep hunters', having a big fancy knife, but not knowing how to use it. Clearly, the small knife is preferred by the skilled hunters. Traditionally, all men carried a 'man's knife', worn in a sheath tied transversely to the belt, directly above the 'belly button'. These knives generally had an additional lashing hole through the antler handle, enabling them to be tied to the belt as insurance against slipping from the sheath. The vertical sheath worn at the hip is an innovation of the late forties, in the mountains, when sheathed knives became available. Prior to that time, most knives were purchased without sheaths, and a sheath was manufactured from the leg skin of caribou.

The big knife is today a large butcher knife, generally of poor quality. Traditionally, these were made of antler, ivory, or whale bone, and were the typical snow knife of earlier ethnography. Today, the big knife is used in several different ways. It is carried as a snow knife, 'in case something happens and you have to build a little snow house'. A more common use is in the preparation of peeled willow sticks for starting fires, or as a small bolo knife for cutting firewood. The back of the blade is also used frequently by the men in the field as a hammer for breaking marrow bones.

The snow probe is used for testing for dangerous overflow waters under snow, or secondarily for locating buried objects. Almost any convenient stick about one metre long can be utilised. Today, men are frequently seen carving a suitable dry willow stick during the summer, which may also be used occasionally as a walking stick in the snowless months. During winter, these will be carried on sled trips and used to test the snow, particularly around lakes and streams that may have overflow water periodically during the winter. These sticks can always be used in an emergency as firewood or as good fuel for starting fires of wet willows or animal bones. The older hunters will rarely go out without such a stick tucked under the sled skin. When dog teams were more prevalent, these sticks were also a source of material for replacing the harness spreader which is a frequent casualty on dog team trips.

Field glasses are common today, and were one of the items sought during the early days of trade, both from Russian sources and the later American sources. Long telescopes of the naval variety were obtained during the early trading years. Field glasses are more recent, and were rare before 1950. There were no functionally equivalent items in traditional technology.

TABLE 19.2

Frequency of Dry Meat and Marrow Bones
Packed by Hunters on 111 Trips

Anatomical part	Dry meat	Marrow bones
Rib slab	68	
Scapula	47	
Belly sheet	27	
Tenderloin	23	
Pelvis	13	
Tibia		73
Metatarsal		57
Radio-cubitus		13
Femur		9
Metacarpal		4

The items remaining in Group II are sugar, coffee, pilot bread, corn meal, coffee can, cup, extra socks, mukluks, skin, parka, and line.

Clothing is generally traditional in design and manufacture except socks, which today are purchased, but formerly were made from caribou fawn skin. The food items are interesting. Customarily, there are three basic kinds of trail foods: dried meats, akutuk, and marrow bones. Hunters generally preferred dried meat which had bones, such as dried rib slabs or a scapula. This preference is directly related to the versatility of bone use. Once the meat had been consumed, the bones could be used as fuel, or pounded up into small chips and boiled to yield a 'bone juice'. This was the only drink besides pure water which hunters customarily consumed in the field. Akutuk was carried as small cakes. These were manufactured by the women from bone marrow and rendered bone grease, sometimes with berries mixed into the marrow, or small strips of dry meat. Akutuk cakes are still occasionally carried by the men, but its manufacture has dropped off considerably since commercial grease has been readily available (since 1953). Marrow bones were carried for the same reason that dried meat containing bones was preferred. They were a ready source of fat, and once the marrow was consumed the bones could be pounded up to produce 'bone juice', or used as fuel.

Statistics accumulated over a four year period from both observation and interview regarding the frequency with which different anatomical parts were carried as trail food are very revealing. Table 19.2 presents the actual frequency of parts carried into the field by members of parties ranging from one to four men, for a total of 111 trips on which either dry meat or marrow bones were packed.

The preferences demonstrated for dry meat is clearly in favour of rib slabs and scapula; next come tenderloins and belly sheets (both parts containing no bones). Least desirable for these purposes is the pelvis. The preferences are not absolute and are relative to season, anticipated activities on the trip, and the regular attrition through a year in the parts remaining in storage.

TABLE 19.3A

Frequency Distribution of Dry Meat Parts Carried by Season

Anatomical part	Spring [a] %	Summer %	Autumn %	Winter %	Total
Rib slab	13 37.14	6 16.66	20 38.46	19 42.22	68
Scapula	11 31.32	0 0.00	14 26.92	22 48.88	47
Belly sheet	0 0.00	19 52.77	8 15.38	0 0.00	27
Tenderloin	2 5.71	11 30.55	10 19.23	0 0.00	23
Pelvis	0 25.71	0 0.00	0 0.00	4 8.88	13
Number of trips on which dry meat was carried:	17	24	23	22	86
Number of items:	35	36	52	45	168
Mean per trip:	2.05	1.50	2.26	2.04	

TABLE 19.3B

Frequency Distribution of Marrow Bones Carried by Season

Anatomical part	Spring [a] %	Summer %	Autumn %	Winter %	Total
Tibia	3 10.00	0 0.00	19 59.37	51 54.25	73
Metatarsal	10 33.33	0 0.00	13 40.62	34 36.17	57
Radio-cubitus	8 26.66	0 0.00	0 0.00	5 5.31	13
Femur	5 16.66	0 0.00	0 0.00	4 4.25	9
Metacarpal	4 13.33	0 0.00	0 0.00	0 0.00	4
Total items	30	0	32	94	156
No. of trips	10	0	21	30	61
Mean per trip	3.0	0.0	1.52	3.13	

[a]Data tabulated here is independent of the data tabulated in Table 1. At the time of collecting the data in Table 1 I did not keep records on marrow bones.

Tables 19.3A and 19.3B present the breakdown of meat and bone parts carried on trips during different seasons.

It is clear that during summer and autumn the boneless dry parts are carried more frequently when fuel is more readily available. Similarly, marrow bones are never carried during summer when marrow spoilage is high and emergency fuels are not a major concern. Another interesting fact is that the femur and metacarpal are more commonly carried during spring when stores are apt to be low. These are the least desirable of the marrow bones listed, the marrow cavities being smaller and the marrow of the femur less fatty than the marrow of the tibia.

TABLE 19.4

Number of Trips on Which Dry Meat, Marrow Bones,
or Both Were Carried by Season

Season	Both	Dry meat only	Marrow bones only	Total
Spring	3	14	7	24
Summer	0	24	0	24
Autumn	14	9	7	30
Winter	19	3	11	33
	36	50	25	111

Table 19.4 shows the seasonal breakdown of the trips recorded with regard to the relative incidence of packing dry meat versus marrow bones.

The clear tendency for increased use of marrow bones during the colder months is obvious. Similarly checking this information against Table 19.2 it is evident that dry meat with bones is more commonly carried in the cold months. Both of these trends reflect the relevance of alternative uses for bones as both fuel and additional nourishment in the form of 'bone juice'.

Group III

The items listed here need little discussion. Today the snowshoes are still manufactured locally in traditional styles. The needle and skin are clothing repair items: mail-order steel needles and small scraps of worked caribou skin. Steel traps are purchased by mail order, as are the .22 pistols, rifles, sardines and peanut butter.

Types of Trips and the Gear Carried

Data obtained from the Eskimos regarding the purpose of the trip fall into two road categories: (a) maintenance trips made for the purpose of recovering meat from caches, and/or trips made for procuring firewood, and (b) monitoring trips made for the purpose of searching for game, frequently coupled with checking traps. Data on distances covered are summarised in Fig. 19.1.

The distances which hunters covered on trips exhibit an interesting distribution. Of the 20 trips made for the express purpose of recovering cached meat or obtaining firewood, the mean round trip distance covered was 23.7 km, with a range between 43.5 km and 8 km. On the other hand, trips made for monitoring purposes exhibited a trimodal distribution. The cluster accounting for 55.5% of the monitoring trips exhibited a mean round trip distance of 53.5 km. This means that the hunters reached an average distance from the village of 26.7 km, or roughly a five to seven hour walk back in the event of mishap. This is a distance that could be covered on the same day the trip was made, depending, of course, on wind and weather conditions. No trips

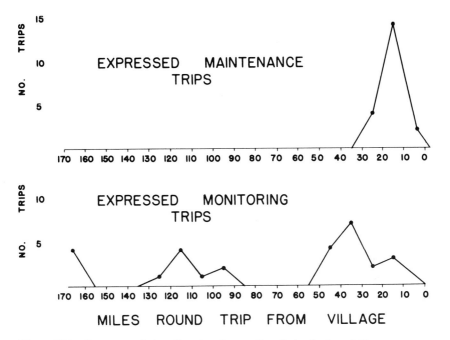

Figure 19.1 Frequency of trips of varying distance (in miles)—Anaktuvuk Pass.

were recorded which were between 76 km and 158 km round trip distance. Eight trips clustered between 203 and 158 km round trip, for a mean trip distance of 192.5 km. Hunters on such trips reached an average distance from the village of 96.2 km. If mishaps occurred, or much time was spent in hunting, an overnight stay would be almost imperative, since the walk home would require upwards of 20 hours. Trips of this distance can, however, be easily made in a single day, barring mishap, since the snow-mobiles can average just slightly under 16 km per hour. A dog team is slower, averaging only about 9.5 km per hour on such a trip (this figure assumes a good trail as is generally present by spring). Hunters using dog teams normally prepare for an overnight stop, while snow-mobile drivers make such preparations but plan to return the same day, barring mishap. Hunters making trips of this distance follow two strategies. The first is for two men to arrange to go out on sequential days along the same general route. This ensures that in case of mishap, aid and transport back to the village will be available. The other strategy is to go out in a party of two or more men. All trips of this distance were handled in this manner, while trips averaging 53 km were all made by single individuals, except for one on which two men went together. The trips recorded which exceed 203 km were made by a monitoring party, and they clearly anticipated staying overnight. We might summarise the monitoring trips as (a) one day trips regardless of mishap, (b) one day trips with provision for overnight camping in case of mishap, and (c) two or more day trips.

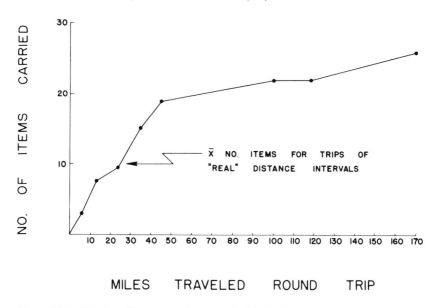

Figure 19.2   Number of items carried compared with the distance (in miles) covered for all trips—Anaktuvuk Pass.

Relationship between Distance Anticipated and the Quantity of Gear Carried

Since the trip distance shows a multimodal distribution along one dimension—monitoring and a single normal distribution for the maintenance trips—we might anticipate some correlation between the trip distances and the quantity and kinds of gear carried. Upon investigation, a clear relationship is demonstrable, but it is not a linar correlation with distance. Fig. 19.2 plots the mean number of items carried exclusive of Group I (snow-mobile gear) for trips falling into 16 km round trip distance intervals up to 80 km, and then the means for the trip distance clusters up to 274 km round trip. A curvilinear relationship exists in which there is a rapid and regular increase in the numbers of items carried until a 80 km round trip distance is reached; then the graph levels off with only a slight increase in numbers of items out to trips of a mean round trip distance of 274 km. This particular pattern is to be understood in terms of the hunters' anticipation of possibly having to remain in the field overnight. As the anticipated round trip distance increases between 16 and 80 km the possibility of returning to the village in case of mishap regularly decreases; therefore, the men tend to carry more emergency gear as a direct function of the anticipated distance. After the overnight threshold is passed, however, few items are added to the gear inventory in anticipation of greater distances.

TABLE 19.5

Hunters' Categorisation of the 'Basic Trip' Gear

Group II A Things—tools	Group II B Food	Group II C Clothes
Dog team or ski-doo	Sugar	Big knife
Axe	Coffee	Extra line
Sled skin	Cup	Socks
Matches	Pilot bread	Mukluks
Rifle	Coffee can	Extra skin
Ammunition	Corn meal	Parka
Skinning knife		
Field glasses		
Snow probe		
(9 items or 42.8% of the list)	(6 items or 28.5% of the list)	(6 items or 28.5% of the list)

The Hunters' Conception of the Gear

Many archaeologists continue to insist that patterning observed in the archaeological record is a direct reflection of the shared ideas and values of a group of people (Rouse, 1972:164–68; Dunnell, 1971:123). I was interested in investigating the nature of the relationship between the way hunters thought about their gear and what, in fact, they did with it. I interviewed seven hunters regarding their ways of viewing the items on the total inventory list of the items carried on the 47 trips. The procedure was to make up a pile of gear representing all the items on the list exclusive of Group I and ask the informants to divide the pile into separate piles in terms of the way they thought about the gear when they were anticipating a trip. Items listed in Group II, Table 19.1, were all singled out by the seven men as constituting the basic inventory of field items which hunters carried. This is the 'trip gear'. Items listed in Group III of Table 19.1 were all singled out as 'optional gear'. Within the inventory list of 'trip gear' the hunters consistently recognised three categories: (1) 'tools and things', (2) food, and (3) clothing. Table 19.5 presents the inventories of the items segregated by the hunters into their three categories.

The archaeologist will immediately recognise that this categorisation is inconsistent. Items which we would include under the heading of 'tools and things', such as the coffee cup or the big knife, are listed under 'food' and 'clothes' respectively. Repeated questions, and queries aimed at pointing out alternative categorisations, including those likely to be employed by archaeologists, resulted in the gradual recognition of the cognitive principles standing behind the way the Nunamiut viewed their gear. For instance, when queried about the cup and coffee can as being 'tools and things', the following response was common, 'Yes, but I carry them when I think about myself and how I will feel, not when I think about what I may have to do out there.' The inclusion of extra line and big knife under 'clothes' brought forth the following explanation: 'They are in that pile because I'm thinking about what may happen to me out there; suppose the dog team lead broke or I had to build a snow shelter'. Quite clearly, the three categories represent three cognitive dimensions of contingency planning: (a) what I will have to do in terms of the goals of the expedition, (b) how I may feel in terms of hunger, and (c) what may happen to me in terms of mishaps. The Nunamiut, in this context, think of their gear in terms of the analogous functions of the items in regard to their dimension of contingency planning, and not in terms of analogous formal properties of the items themselves.

I turn now to an examination of the three recognised categories of gear as they relate to one another. Do they represent independent dimensions in terms of actual association and variation? The frequencies of items falling in the three Nunamiut categories have been arranged according to the four types of recognised trips. These data are presented in Table 19.6.

The above data permits us to examine the degree that these three categories actually represent independent dimensions in terms of behavioural dynamics. The summary percentages in each column for each class of gear express the relative proportions of each class of gear taken on trips of varying distances. These relationships are summarised in Fig. 19.3.

Each of the three categories seemingly behaves somewhat independently of one another. 'Tools and things' and 'food' appear as inverse parabolic curves, while 'clothes' represents a low sigmoid curve. Nevertheless, it is clear that 'clothes' and 'food' are strongly correlated and this is, of course, what we would expect since 'how I may feel' and 'what may happen to me' are not necessarily independent. As expected, these interact in a closely correlated manner. We might summarise the situation as follows: (a) when gear is being assembled for each of the recognised cognitive categories, different consequences of sometimes similar contingencies are being considered; (b) this situation ensures that there will be strong correlations between components of the different cognitive categories; and (c) there are slightly different thresholds for the consideration of varying consequences, correlated with anticipated distance to be travelled, eg. a mishap within return walking distance eliminates the consequence of having to stay overnight, but not the consequence that I may get hungry. These facts ensure that there will not be a perfect correlation, and that there will be some partial independence between the categories as is indicated on Fig. 19.3.

I turn now to a more complicated problem, changing our perspective, and assuming that of the archaeologist beginning the analysis of four samples of gear (the four trip distance samples) as if these were four assemblages remaining from different sites. The analytical task would be to isolate those patterns of association and co-variation characteristic of the items represented in the four samples. In concrete situations, one might elect to perform some 'data reducing' operation such as factor analysis or cluster analysis. This would permit the recognition of sets of items which exhibited strong patterns of co-variation among themselves and analogous patterns with respect to all other items. (See, for instance, Binford and Binford, 1966, and Binford, 1972b. The number of cases is too small for the actual performance of such an analysis; however, some hint as to the likely results can be obtained from a graphic display of the

TABLE 19.6

Frequency of Items in Three Nunamiut Categories
Arranged According to Recognised Trips

Gear categories	Trip categories							
			Monitoring trips					
	Maintenance		Short		Medium		Long	
	#	%	#	%	#	%	#	%
Class I.								
Tools and things								
Axe	20	15.5	15	7.0	8	5.0	4	5.4
Sled skin	20	15.5	15	7.0	8	5.0	4	5.4
Matches	20	15.5	15	7.0	8	5.0	4	5.4
Rifle	11	8.5	15	7.0	8	5.0	4	5.4
Ammunition	11	8.5	15	7.0	8	5.0	4	5.4
Skinning knife	4	3.1	13	6.1	8	5.0	4	5.4
Field glasses	0	0.0	7	3.3	8	5.0	4	5.4
Snow probe	8	6.2	13	6.1	8	5.0	4	5.4
	94	72.8	112	52.8	64	40.0	32	43.2
Class II.								
Food								
Sugar	8	6.2	14	6.6	8	5.0	2	2.7
Coffee	8	6.2	14	6.6	8	5.0	2	2.7
Pilot bread	8	6.2	14	6.6	8	5.0	4	5.4
Corn meal	0	0.0	0	0.0	8	5.0	3	4.1
Cup	3	2.3	13	6.1	8	5.0	4	5.4
Coffee can	2	1.5	12	5.6	8	5.0	2	2.7
	29	22.4	67	31.6	48	30.0	17	23.0
Class III.								
Clothes								
Socks	1	0.8	9	4.2	8	5.0	4	5.4
Mukluks	1	0.8	10	4.7	8	5.0	4	5.4
Extra skin	0	0.0	6	2.8	8	5.0	4	5.4
Parka	0	0.0	0	0.0	8	5.0	4	5.4
Line	4	3.1	8	3.7	8	5.0	4	5.4
Big knife	0	0.0	4	1.8	8	5.0	4	5.4
	6	4.7	37	17.4	48	30.0	24	32.4
Grand total:	129		212		160		73	

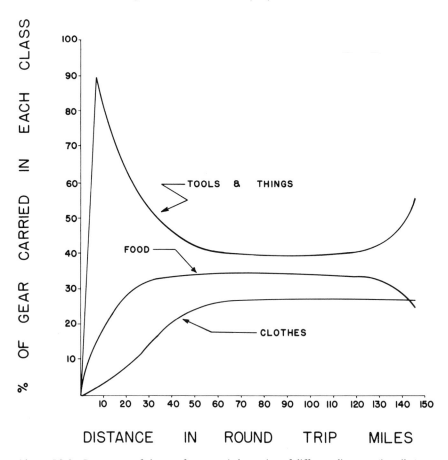

Figure 19.3 Percentage of classes of gear carried on trips of different distances (in miles).

percentage relationships between items across the four samples. This display is presented in Fig. 19.4.

Items depicted in Group I, Fig. 19.4, are highly intercorrelated. These are the axe, sled skin, matches, rifle, and ammunition; all items listed by the Nunamiut as 'tools and things'. Group II consists of pilot bread (food) and a snow probe (tools and things). It is quite likely that sugar and coffee displayed in Group V would exhibit a lower but dominant correlation with Graph II items, the latter being listed as 'food' by the Nunamiut. Here we observe an interesting situation. Items from two of the Nunamiuts' cognitive categories are apparently strongly related co-variantly. Why? The answer is very clear behaviourally. The Nunamiut tend to have various items cached in regularly utilised sites all around their village. These are the normal stopping places for the preparation of field snacks. Sugar, coffee and pilot bread are the normal contents of such snacks, and they can anticipate cups and coffee cans being cached at such locations. Nevertheless, they must find the cached items in the snow—hence

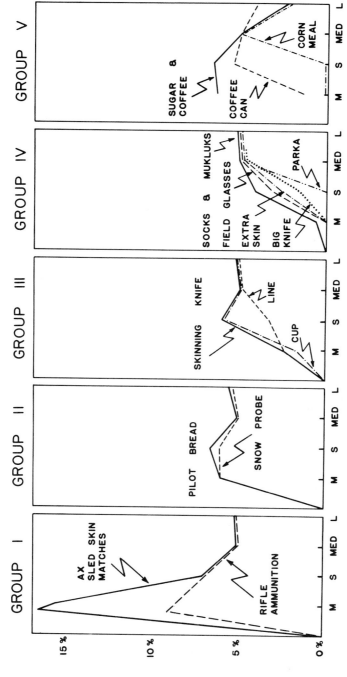

Figure 19.4 Covariation among items carried on trips of different purposes.

the correlation with the snow probe. These correlations reflect contingencies considered by the Nunamiut not made explicit in his cognitive categories. They reflect the actual dynamics of behaviour under a specific set of conditions. Group III is even more interesting in this regard. Extra line (clothes), cup (food), skinning knife (tools and things) make up the highly intercorrelated items with the possible addition of the coffee can from Group V. Here we find a set of correlations between items in all three of the cognitive categories. Why? Once again, in terms of the real behaviour or organised dynamics of gear use, these correlations all make a great deal of sense. The cup and the coffee can are items carried when a stop is anticipated at a place not normally used. Extra line is carried when some mishap is anticipated or feared. Mishaps normally occur at locations not systematically used for the preparation of food—on the trail. The skinning knife is the most versatile item used in repairing dog harness, obtaining firewood from low or minimal willow growth, carving from the snow probe another harness spreader, etc. Thus our correlations group together the gear actually used in case of a mishap. It is, of course, used in conjunction with the sugar, coffee and pilot bread, but those may be used in other situations in the absence of these items. These are the items actually used in the specific and immediate context of a breakdown.

Group V includes socks, mukluk, extra skin, big knife and extra parka, all items listed as clothes, together with field glasses, listed as tools and things, and probably corn meal displayed in Group V. Once again we have a mixed assemblage with regards to the cognitive categories of the Nunamiut. Why? If the previous grouping of items can be summarised as the 'breakdown-stop' assemblage, this represents the 'overnight-stop' assemblage which may or may not be correlated with a breakdown or trail mishap, but may be correlated with a personal mishap such as falling through ice or getting wet in an overflow near a spring, etc. The presence of field glasses and possibly the addition of corn meal is understandable in terms of this type of concrete situation. Corn meal is a more substantial food, and field glasses would aid in locating or spotting a rescue party or emergency game, as well as generally used on long trips.

In summary, from the perspective of the archaeologist, the correlations would betray something of the actual behavioural context of gear use, while the cognitive categories are a convenient planning convention. The contingencies considered in planning, how I feed, what may happen, and what I have to do, are not in reality independent. What may happen may clearly condition how I may feel, etc. *Thus the archaeologist's analysis would not yield direct information relative to the Nunamiut cognitive categories, but would rather faithfully reflect the concrete dynamics of the hunters' behaviour in the field.*

Optional Gear

The third category recognised by the informants was optional gear which they systematically divided into two sub-categories: 'young men's gear' and 'old men's gear'. The items in the two sub-categories are listed below (Table 19.7) together with the mean ages of the hunters carrying each item.

The reader will immediately note that the items categorised as young men's gear

TABLE 19.7

Two Categories of Optional Gear Divided According to Age of Hunters

Young men's gear	Age of hunters	Old men's gear	Age of hunters
.22 pistol	33.4	Dry meat	34.9
.22 rifle	33.7	Snow shoes	35.6
Sardines	33.8	Needle and skin	36.4
Peanut butter	27.0	Steel traps	35.3
		Rib slab	35.5
	31.9 years		35.5 years

represent largely 'store bought' items, while old men's gear includes more traditional items with the exception of steel traps. As is shown, there is a difference between the mean ages of the hunters carrying the two types of gear, although there is not as much as one might anticipate from informants' conversation. It is interesting to note that the range of ages represented by hunters carrying the two categories of gear are identical, the oldest being 43 and the youngest being 26. It is quite clear that there is no neat correlation between the age of the hunter and the type of optional gear he carried. The distinction is not really one of age but one of traditional versus modern orientation of the hunters, and these persuasions are not necessarily a reliable predictor of age.

What conclusions can be drawn regarding the proposition that archaeologically observed patterning reflects the ideas and values or the cognitive characteristics of a culture? The first conclusion which I drew from my interviewing was that Nunamiut have many ways of cognitively structuring their gear, depending upon the behavioural context specified. This observation leads to the suspected proposition that cognitive categorisations vary in terms of the behavioural context specified. We all know this to be true. If asked about my cousins in the context of maternal versus paternal relationship, I will differentiate one way; if asked in terms of how often I interact with them I will differentiate another way. If asked in the context of who I like, I would differentiate still another way, and *ad infinitum*.

Cognition is not a static–formal system, but a dynamic system whose form is partially dependent upon the behavioural or interactive context of discrimination. Such contexts are complicated as in the case of the Nunamiut deciding which gear he will carry. It is convenient for him to think dimensionally in terms of what he will do, how he will feel, and what may happen. In reality, these are not necessarily independent, hence the strong intercorrelation between items considered dimensionally distinct at the cognitive level of trip planning. Based on these data as well as on a general knowledge of behaviour, I must insist that assemblage patterning observed in the archaeological record derives from the dynamics of organised behaviour. In the case of the Nunamiuts' 'assemblages' on trips of different distances, there is no necessary or direct relationship to the cognitive or formal classificatory devices of the people.

The Archaeological Record of the Trips

We turn now to a very interesting body of data, the tabulation and relative frequencies of the items which were not returned to the village by the hunters. Table 19.1 presents the data on non-food items not returned, arranged according to increasing trip distances from right to left. Initially, it is necessary to place the items listed in Table 19.1 in some kind of context. There were 647 trip items carried; regardless of quantity, each unit is counted as a single trip item. Of these, 99 are items which are totally consumed in the course of their use. Most such items are foods: pilot bread, sugar, etc., all items which yield no by-product. Ninety-one of the 99 items were consumed on the trips and not returned to the village. Five hundred and forty-eight of the trip items carried were visible in that there were tangible by-products from their use, or no destruction occurred during their use. Of these items, 53 or only 9.67% of the total visible items were not returned to the village, the items listed in Table 19.1. Of these 53 trip items, 36 are items which are disposable by-products in the context of use, including the peanut butter jar, sardine can, shell cases, ribs from dry meat slabs, scapula from dry meat slabs and rifle shell cases. This is not to say that all of these items could not be reused or recycled, but that in the contemporary setting they are not, and are immediately disposable by-products of use or consumption. Of the remaining 18 items not returned to the village, 14 or 23.3% of the total were cached in the field for future use. Of the remaining four items, three were unintentionally lost on the trail, and *only one was discarded, broken, at the location where it was used*. This is not, however, the only item broken during the course of the 47 trips. Twelve additional items were broken, but were returned to the village for repair. We may summarise that 91.9% of the food carried was consumed, leaving no tangible by-products. Of the 548 items exclusive of food not leaving tangible by-products, only 53 items remained in the field. Of these, 36 were tangible by-products of consumption or use, and only 18 were actual items of gear. Of those 18 items, 14 were cached in the field for future use, leaving only four items lost (three) or discarded (one) in the context of the activities. During this time, however, 12 additional items were broken but returned to the village for repair or recycling into other items.

For the archaeologist who approaches the archaeological record with the expectation that there is necessarily some direct relationship between the importance of the item in the cultural system and importance in the assemblage, and anticipates a neat structure of spatial associations reflecting the behavioural context of use for the items recovered, this is a very grim picture. Let us examine the situation further. From one perspective, the formation processes are one aspect of the organised dynamics in terms of which material items are integrated into a cultural system. All such dynamics must include some organised strategy of procurement, and most archaeologists have given time and thought to this aspect of technological organisation. Equally important is the variability in the organised properties of discharge or entropy. What are the organised ways in which items are discharged or lost to the system? In order to consider systems from the perspective of their efficiency, there must be some balance between these two sides of the dynamics coin. Increases in efficiency may be achieved at either end or in terms of both. For instance, if it takes twenty minutes to manufacture a projectile point, and from that investment of labour I can use the projectile point reliably for four months, this is more efficient than if from the same labour investment I only find the product good for two months' use. I may find that by the additional investment of maintenance and curatorial labour I can increase the life expectancy of an item, and I may, in turn, increase the efficiency of the technology. Thus, maintenance and curatorial investments of labour may achieve increases in the total efficiency of the technological system and, in turn, increase the life expectancies or utilisation time of items. Similarly, by various means of recycling, or using the materials in worn out items for the fabrication of other items, I may substantially cut down on procurement labour investments. *The Nunamiut are a classic case of a system in which the technology is highly organised curatorially, and is frequently characterised by recycling.* For the archaeologist, this means that we cannot expect to find butchering tools at butchering locations, or wood cutting tools at wood collecting locations. Such items are curated, transported, and, if broken in the context of use, frequently transported to residential locations where they may be recycled or repaired for future use.

I recently made a survey of eleven of the more popular books treating the subject of archaeological methods and was unable to find any reference to the organisation of a technology with regard to maintenance and curation of items. Most authors mentioned procuring and manufacturing sequences, but no one mentioned the possible differences between cultural systems in their degrees of maintenance investment or curation of the technology.

Let us consider for a moment the relationships between the relative importance of items in the ongoing technology of the Nunamiut as measured by the frequency with which they were carried on trips, versus the frequency of items remaining as potential archaeological remains at the locations where activities were conducted. The cumulative graphs in Fig. 19.5[1] display these relationships. *It is quite clear that there is an inverse relationship between the importance of the item as measured by the frequency with which it is carried, and its occurrence as an item remaining in the field.* Stated another way, 69.0 percent of the assemblage remaining in the field is composed of trip items which represent only 5.82 percent of the trip items carried into the field. In contrast, 58.2 percent of the trip items carried into the field are represented by only 5.76 percent of trip items remaining in the field. This points out very clearly the character of a curated assemblage. *Important items are maintained and curated, thus their entry into the archaeological record, in terms of frequency, is inversely proportional to the level of maintenance and hence their technological importance, other things being equal.*

This observation coupled with the observation that 67.9 percent of the items remaining in the field were items that were the immediate by-products of consumption, such as bones from dry meat or shell cases from firing guns, provides us with a valuable clue. It tells us that working out analytical means for treating archaeological remains of the immediate by-products of either work or consumption is the most important task. This class of archaeological remains will yield information regarding the tasks performed at varying locations.

Such a suggestion is certainly at variance with general archaeological practice of considering features of secondary importance to tool assemblages as sources of information about activities. Similarly, when faunal remains are given analytical attention it is generally in the context of environmental reconstruction, or as a means to evaluating the character of diet rather than the activities of food procurement. Recently, some attention has been given to patterns of bone breakage, but not with an eye to understanding the activities performed, except as the authors believe them to be related to tool production, and hence as a means to tool recognition. (See Sadek-Kooros, 1972). We need to give more analytical attention to the relationships between features and mundane remains such as fire-cracked rock, bone fragments, chipping debris, and garbage, not as a means to categorical types of generalisation about diet, etc., but as a means to understanding the behavioural context in terms of which the site was produced.

The items remaining in the field which were not the immediate by-products of consumption or work totalled 18 items. Seventeen of these (94.4 percent) remained as unbroken items either cached for future use, or unintentionally lost during the course of the trip. Only 5.6 percent remained in the field as broken or discarded items. Nevertheless, 12 additional items were broken but were returned to the village for repair or recycling.

These observations suggest that we might anticipate certain regular contrasts between archaeological assemblages deriving from highly organised, curated technologies, versus those that are poorly organised and tend toward the expedient manufacture, use, and abandonment of instrumental items in the immediate context of use.

We may now speculate on some of the possible archaeological consequences of cultural systems differing in their degrees of technological organisation on a scale from completely expedient manufacture, use and abandonment of tools, versus a highly curated and maintained technology.

Several major points of contrast stand behind the development of arguments regarding expected forms of patterning in the archaeological record. Most important is the recognition that in non-curated technologies, replacement rates are directly proportional to the frequency of participation in activities in which tools were used. In curated assemblages, replacement rates are directly proportional to the life span or utility of the tool under maintenance care, and may bear no direct relationship to the frequency of activity performance involving tool use.

The second major point of contrast is related to the locational or associational relationships anticipated under the two types of organisation. In non-curated assemblages, the debris from manufacture, and the by-products of the activities in which tools were used should be spatially associated. However, in curated assemblages, where tools are transported and returned to a residential location for repair (as in the case of the Nunamiut), we can expect there to be no necessary regular relationship between the by-products of activities in which tools were used and the numbers of tools themselves. Similarly, we can expect that tool manufacturing debris will only regularly be associated with broken or discarded parts of tools, and not vary with the numbers of tools manufactured 'from scratch' which would have been removed from the location.

We are now in a position to suggest certain expected archaeological consequences of differences in the organisation of a technology.

I. *Relationships between debris and instrumental items*

    A. Under conditions of expedient manufacture and use of tools, other things being equal, we can expect

        1. A regular inverse set of relationships between the number of broken and worn out tools and the number of unbroken unworn tools present.

        2. A regular proportional set of direct relationships between the number of tools present, regardless of condition, and the quantity of debris remaining from tool manufacture.

        3. A regular proportional set of direct relationships between the quantity of debris remaining from food consumption and both the quantity of tools and the quantity of tool-making debris.

    B. *Discussion:* The qualification that other things are equal is very important to these propositions. For instance, in intersite comparisons we might anticipate that quantites of food by-products remaining on a site would vary with the character of the diet represented. An obvious example is variability in the relative dependence upon plants versus animal foods. Such factors would tend to reduce the observed regularities between numbers of tools and the amount of food debris observable archaeologically under normal conditions of preservation. Another consideration is the character of the organisation of the food procurement strategy itself. For instance, if consumers are moved to resources, then we can anticipate the predicted relationship to hold very well; however, if foods are transported to consumers, then we can expect an attrition along the logistics route which may not be proportional to the numbers of persons present, or the intensity of tool using activities performed.

    The same caution holds for the predicted relationship between manufacturing debris and tools, since variability in the character and efficiency of manufacturing techniques would tend to introduce variability in the expected relationships between quantities of debris and numbers of tools.

    Some clarification may be necessary to the first proposition offered. Under conditions of expedient manufacture and use of tools, the numbers of worn or broken tools should relate to the duration and intensity of the activity in which tools were used. Thus, the number of tools in unbroken–unworn condition should be inversely proportional to the number of tools in 'mint' condition.

    C. Under conditions of curated, maintained and portable technological organisation, other things being equal, we can expect:

        1. Proportions of broken to unbroken tools to vary independently of one another.

        2. A regular proportion set of direct relationships between the num-

bers of broken and worn out tools and tool manufacturing debris.

3. A low but regular proportional set of inverse relationships between the numbers of unbroken or unworn tools and tool manufacturing debris.

4. High variability approaching randomness between the total numbers of tools and the quantity of tool manufacturing debris among random site samples. Inverse relationships will dominate comparisons between special purpose locations such as hunting camps, quarries, kill sites, etc., and a tendency toward direct relationships will pervade comparisons between base camps or residential locations, where repairs are more apt to be made.

5. High variability in the relationship between the quantity of debris from food sources and the quantity of debris from tool production or repair among random site samples. Inverse relationships will pervade comparisons between special purpose locations, while low but direct relationships may be anticipated in comparisons between base camp or residential locations.

D. *Discussion:* As previously mentioned, the qualification 'other things being equal' is very important. For instance, I have not considered differences in food procurement strategy. It should be clear that a logistics strategy in which foods are moved to consumers may be expected to be correlated with increases in curation and maintenance of tools, since both are organisational responses to conditions in which increasing efficiency would pay off. Given this expectation, we can anticipate differences in archaeological patterning between tools, tool making debris, and the by-products of food sources. All should vary as a function of the degree that a logistics strategy is correlated with a curatorial technological strategy. Similarly, we may anticipate that composite tools might be expected to occur more commonly in curated assemblages. The degree that this is true may condition the expected relationships between tools used directly in subsistence tasks and tools used in tool-making tasks. Both may well vary in their levels of curation and maintenance, introducing an added complication with regard to debris relationships.

II. *Relationships between different types of tools*

A. Under conditions of expedient manufacture and use of tools, other things being equal, we can expect:

1. Relative frequencies of tool types observed among a sample of site locations will vary directly with the quantities of immediate by-products deriving from the activities in which tools were used.

2. Intersite variability in relative tool frequencies to be high and to vary directly with the seasonal and situational differentiation in the locus of task performance.

B. *Discussion:* These propositions should be clear in that they are the consequences of a technology in which tool use and tool disposal are coincident.

C. Under conditions of curated and maintained technologies, other things being equal, we can expect:
1. Relative frequencies of tool types, observed among a sample of site locations, will vary independently of the quantities of immediate by-products deriving from different activities in which tools were used.
2. Intersite variability in relative tool frequencies to be relatively low and to vary independently of the seasonal and situational differentiation in the locus of task performance.

D. *Discussion:* The contrasts indicated in the above propositions derive from the fact that in non-curated assemblages relative frequencies derive directly from the relative size of the task force and the intensity of the activity involving tool use. On the other hand, in curated assemblages relative frequencies derive directly from the relative life expectancies of a tool under continuous maintenance. In the latter situation we cannot regularly anticipate an association between the tool and the task in which it is used. Associations among tools derive from relative life expectancies in the context of localised maintenance activities.

III. *Implications for temporal patterning*

A. Under conditions of expedient manufacture and use of tools, other things being equal, we can expect:
1. Changing frequencies to vary directly with the importance of the activity in which the tool was used.

B. Under conditions of a curated and maintained technology, other things being equal, we can expect:
1. Decreasing relative frequencies through time to *vary inversely* with the importance of the item in the technology. In short, as curation increases, the relative frequency of technologically important items will decrease.

C. *Discussion:* These propositions are important. For instance, if we observe a decreasing relative frequency for a particular class of item, it may well reflect:
1. Increasing curation and maintenance of the item class.
2. Its prominence in the technology. Remember, in curated assemblages, relative frequencies refer directly to replacement rates and not to incidences of use as in non-curated assemblages. Important items may well be expected to have lower replacement rates than less important items because of the greater utility derived from higher levels of maintenance. This view of the potential significance of frequency trends is directly at variance with the prevailing traditionalists' ideas of the significance attributed to temporal trends in relative frequency. To the traditionalist, decreasing trends mean decreasing popularity, while increasing trends refer to increasing popularity.

In this contrast we see clearly the differences between an approach which has a series of conventions for translating observations into interpretations, rather than attempting to investigate the processes responsible for the observed relationships.

Summary Conclusions

Given the data from the Nunamiut hunters, several conclusions seem warranted— (a) Regardless of the degree of curation and maintenance of the tool assemblage, we can anticipate variability in the immediate by-products of work or consumption to relate to seasonal or situational variation in the activities performed—witness the seasonal variability in the anatomical parts carried by the hunters for food. (This latter point will be demonstrated more forcefully at a later date through the analysis of faunal remains and intersite structure of contemporary Nunamiut sites.) (b) The cognitive categories of the Nunamiut hunters at the assemblage level generally have reference to contingency planning which is treated as if the real world was dimensionally independent. In fact, such dimensional independence is not evident, thus the actual patterns of covariation among gear items derive from the actions performed in the context of various contingencies, and bear little relationship to the cognitive categories used by the hunters for organising their gear. These data demonstrate nicely that archaeological remains refer directly to the organisation of behaviour itself, and not to the cognitive conventions in terms of which behaviour may be expressed or anticipated. (c) The distribution, association between, and relative frequencies of tools are greatly affected by the character of the technological organisation. No simple equation between tool and task, or frequency and popularity is possible. Before one can make meaningful statements as to the significance of patterns of observed variability in the archaeological record, one must consider the causal determinants of the patterning. Processes vary as organisations vary, forms of patterning vary as processes vary. Organisational variability is one of the major characteristics of cultural variation in general. Investigation of the organisational properties of systems and their processual consequences, archaeologically, is the first step toward an accurate attribution of meaning to observed patterning. This must be accomplished through the trial specification and testing of law-like proposition. Implied here is the further investigation of the conditioning relationships implied by the statement 'other things being equal'. I have offered a number of such trial law-like statements. The testing of their validity may take us a long way toward a more accurate understanding of observed forms of patterning in the archaeological record.

I hope this paper serves to prompt greater attention to the formation processes of the archaeological record, for only against such an understanding can we begin to reliably attribute meaning to observed forms of archaeological patterning.

Note

1. The fifth figure in the article was lost in the course of the original publication and never actually appeared in print.

20

Organization and Formation Processes:
Looking at Curated Technologies

This paper draws upon ethnographic experiences among the Nunamiut Eskimo for insights into the effects of technological organization on interassemblage variability. Varying situationally conditioned strategies of raw material procurement, tool design and manufacture, and disposal are described as clues to site function or "placement" in a subsistence-settlement system.

In previous articles I have addressed various organizational properties of Nunamiut Eskimo technology. In one case (Binford 1977a) I explored the problem of site formation processes when gear was highly curated, illustrating the way in which the Nunamiut conceived different types of gear as appropriate to carry on trips of differing purpose, distance and duration. Later (Binford 1978a) I examined factors which conditioned the execution of tasks at a single location, the Mask site. I studied the gear being used or passing through, and that which was finally abandoned on the site. The perspective in that analysis was not person centered, as it had been in the "Forty-Seven Trips" article, but location centered.

In this paper I shift perspective again and view the organization of technology from the perspective of a settlement system. I am here concerned with the organizational characteristics within a technology viewed from a situational perspective. I am concerned with the organizational alternatives within a technology which may be manipulated differently to effect acceptable adaptations to differing situations. What are the technological options for planning and executing tasks in different places? What can we learn about archaeological site formation processes by studying sites which have played different roles in a subsistence-settlement system? As is the case with faunal remains (see Binford 1978b), the content of tool assemblages at different sites studied along logistic, storage, or strategic dimensions must be understandable in terms of strategies that are responsive to concrete situational variables. This paper, therefore, is a discussion of the different modes of procurement, manufacture, use, and discard of tools as these modes are clues to, or correlations with, site functions within a settlement system. I am using my ethnographic experience among the Nunamiut as a basis for this discussion.

It should be pointed out that, in all probability, the Nunamiut are an "extreme" case in both their logistic and storage characteristics, as well as in the seasonal variability of their access to different resources. This is a desirable situation, perhaps,

Originally published in *Journal of Anthropological Research* 35(3):255–273, ©1979.

since it is not empirical generalization which I seek (see Binford 1977b and 1978a for a discussion of this problem). An "extreme" case often facilitates comparison with other "extreme" conditions, and promotes appreciation of variability "between the extremes" better than does an understanding of a "modal" case.

The Nunamiut, for example, obtain more than 70 percent of their yearly food during approximately thirty days: fifteen days during spring caribou migration and fifteen days during fall caribou migration. As can be imagined, they consume food out of storage during much of the year and are faced, therefore, with interesting logistical problems, since it is unusual for the bulk of their food to be obtained in a place where conditions for residential occupation are otherwise optimal. They continually transport either fresh or stored food from one place to another. Because of the bulk involved in stores, there are many logistic locations and special purpose sites where fresh, supplementary foods and other resources can be obtained (see Binford 1978b for a description of the Nunamiut system). Contrast such conditions with those confronted by foragers such as the !Kung and G/wi, or the central desert Australians, or many of the hunters and gatherers of India and of the American southwest, and the Baja sector of California. Such foragers range out into the environment each day, searching for resources, and return to a residential camp each night. Their food is generally procured on a daily basis for more or less immediate consumption. Storage for them plays only a minor and situational role. Since their foods are generally procured in "small packages," their logistic problem is rarely significant (see Binford 1980b for a discussion of Subsistence-Settlement Patterning).

Given very different types of *settlement-subsistence systems* we might expect different types of *"sites"* to result from their different *technological organizations*. Assuming this, some understanding of the factors conditioning different modes of procurement, manufacture, and use of tools should permit the positive functional identification of different sites, and hence their roles as components of specific systems; this in turn should allow us to differentiate and characterize various subsistence-settlement systems. This paper, therefore, is a search for an understanding, in organizational terms, of a technology and how it is *internally* differentiated with regard to the production, use, and maintenance of tools.

Active versus Passive Gear

One important aspect of Nunamiut technology is the change-of-state dynamics certain items undergo. Nunamiut technology is characterized by a well developed storage and caching strategy for gear, such that at any one time some of the gear organized *within* the technology is in storage and not being used: it is *passive gear*. *Active gear* is that which is current, or being used regularly, and this generally means that it is distributed differentially within sites and in different patterns of association. The Eskimo make a conceptual distinction between passive gear, which is seasonal, and *insurance gear*.

The sled and the kayak, considered together, are a good example of complementarily organized seasonal gear. Kayaks are used on lakes, for both fishing and hunting, between approximately June 25 and October 25. In addition, they may be used for stream transport during the same period, although this is rare and very hazardous. Sleds are used between approximately October 10 and June 1. It is clear that sleds are in use when kayaks are not, and that kayaks are in use when sleds are not. The normal pattern is to cache the sled at an early spring settlement when the site is abandoned for the summer. Normally the Nunamiut try to abandon their late winter sites prior to melt so that sleds can be used to transport persons and gear to the early spring settlements, the ones occupied during spring caribou migration; there they are also used to hunt and process animals during the migration. The breakup and following melt of the tundra normally occur immediately afterward, between May 25 and June 10. Any move away from the spring residential site is almost always preceded by the preparation of a cache at the site for items such as sleds, which will not be used again until the following fall: snow shoes and goggles, ice dippers and ice-fishing gear, axes used for butchering frozen meat, winter clothes and sleeping skins, and other winter gear may all be cached at the spring site, entering into a passive state. Similarly, at the end of summer, the kayak, leister, snare elements, fish nets, and summer clothing may be cached at the late summer sites for recovery the following spring. These reciprocal shifts between winter and summer gear, and the transitions from active to passive states for different elements of the gear which they require, determine but one of the ways in which gear may be divided into active and passive states.

Insurance gear is distributed differently from seasonal gear, which is almost always associated with a seasonally occupied residential location. Insurance gear is cached throughout the region, not in terms of specifically anticipated seasonal needs, but in terms of what might generally be needed at the location at some time in the future. Considerations involved are similar to those evaluated in choosing gear for transport on trips (see Binford 1977a:31). Insurance gear is generally distributed throughout the region: as site furniture at locations not in use (see Binford 1978a:329 for a discussion of site furniture), as discrete caches at stream crossings, in well-known caves and rock crevices, in caches adjacent to known archaeological sites, or in deliberately constructed rock cairn caching facilities (see Binford 1978b:241).

As Simon Paneack explained:

Every time men go out for something they have space in the pack or on the sled on the way out. Good men always say "what can I carry that may help someone in the future." Maybe they decide that where they are going there is no firewood, so maybe they take out some extra. Maybe there is no good stone for using with Strike-a-Light, so maybe they take out some extra to leave out there in case somebody needs it later. In the old days, in my father's time and before, fellows always carried out shiny stones for making tools and left them all over the place so if you needed them they would be around. Today men carry out axes, cooking cans, cups, knives, matches, bandages and medicine, and always in winter good food bones for burning, and sometimes stones for sleeping ones feet.[1] I know where there are little secret places all the way from here to Kobuk,[2] to Barrow,[3] to Fort Yukon,[4] and to Barter Island.[5] I could get everything almost a man might need along the way by knowing what people in the past have left as insurance.[6]

Caches are continually being made by the Nunamiut, and in turn stories are continually being told, so that a kind of running inventory of what is in the passive state and where it is located is maintained by most men and boys in the group. I once had the opportunity to accompany a late summer hunting party on the northern tundra some eighty miles north of Anaktuvuk village. Nine caribou were killed, and after butchering the hunters took the metapodials and attached feet of the butchered caribou, made a small slit in the stomachs of the butchered animals and shoved in the feet. The hunters explained to me that the mild stomach acids actually pickle the feet, when left to stand for some time, and commented, "You never know when you may come along here and be real hungry."

The importance of caching strategies is perhaps best summed up in the words of Jessie Ahgook:

> Catch things when you can, if pass good stone for tools, pick 'em up, if pass good wood for sled runner, catch 'em then. Good man never think back and say, 'If I had just pick 'em up last summer!' or something like that. If too much trouble pack 'em, put 'em some place where you catch 'em later. Every dead Eskimo can remember something he not pick up when it was around.. My great uncle broke ankle in winter up around pass at Kongumuvuk. He can't walk to catch firewood, he can't walk to get rocks for making soup, but he remember where man tell him that during summer when sheep hunting, and nothing to do, fellow put willows and cooking rocks, and some extra skin rope in little cave at top of pass. Uncle, he get there and make nice fire, fix food, and pretty soon another fellow see smoke and come to see, find uncle, and take him home on a sled. Good Eskimo always say, 'What might happen to me here during winter or some other time?' then he leave things so later O.K.

In order to obtain some appreciation for the magnitude of the inventory of passive gear, exclusive of seasonal caches, Table 20.1 reports the result of interviewing twenty-one men, who were identified as heads of households in the 1969 census, concerning the disposition of their gear during the first two weeks of June, 1971. The method used to establish the list of gear to be studied was simple: I entered the first house where interviewing was to be conducted and made a list of all items hanging on the walls, exclusive of clothing, or sitting in containers on the table before me. I then interviewed all heads of households regarding that list, making no attempt to enlarge or modify it in terms of subsequent observations in other houses. My goal was not to obtain a complete inventory of all items in use in the village, but rather a sense of the differential distribution of the gear within and outside of the village. Table 20.1 illustrates the situation nicely: 51 percent of all items inventoried were within the houses of Anaktuvuk. The remaining 49 percent were identified as cached: 9 percent within the village, and 40 percent outside the village as distributed caches or as site furniture at locations used in hunting sheep and caribou.

At the time of this interview I was unaware of the distinction which the Eskimo make between active and passive gear. I made no attempt to determine what gear inside the houses or out was considered active or passive. Therefore, relative to this distinction the data of Table 20.1 are ambiguous. I have no measured estimate of the part of the technology which might at any one time be considered active or passive. It is my *guess*, however, that during summer active gear would constitute less than 30 percent, while during winter active gear would be slightly over 40 percent of the total. Stated another way, I estimate that at any one time between 60 and 70 percent of all the gear considered part of the technology might be considered passive. Passive

TABLE 20.1

Disposition of Selected Gear, June 20–30, 1971

Artifact type	Total	In houses within village	In caches within village	Site furniture in various sites	Caches within normal exploitation zones
Fish net	5	1 (20%)	0	0	4 (80%)
Net float	57	9 (16%)	17 (30%)	0	31 (54%)
Pliers	108	34 (31%)	19 (18%)	0	55 (51%)
Net weights	37	6 (16%)	14 (38%)	0	17 (46%)
Fish Lures	150	71 (47%)	19 (13%)	0	60 (40%)
Boiling cans	89	12 (13%)	2 (02%)	44 (49%)	31 (35%)
Fishing poles	47	31 (66%)	0	0	16 (34%)
Cups	139	69 (50%)	3 (02%)	32 (23%)	35 (25%)
Axe	51	27 (53%)	0	13 (25%)	11 (22%)
Big knife	52	34 (65%)	6 (12%)	3 (06%)	9 (17%)
Roast pan	21	16 (76%)	2 (10%)	0 (06%)	3 (14%)
Spoons	267	158 (59%)	22 (08%)	51 (19%)	36 (13%)
Small knife	32	27 (84%)	1 (03%)	2 (05%)	2 (06%)
Kettle	24	20 (83%)	1 (04%)	3 (13%)	0
Rifle	37	36 (97%)	1 (03%)	0	0
.22 Pistol	14	14 (100%)	0	0	0
	1131	566 (51%)	107 (09%)	148 (13%)	310 (27%)

gear would be distributed as site furniture at locations not then in use, in seasonal caches, and in insurance caches. Through this planned activity, the Nunamiut modify their effective environment by distributing resources in terms of anticipated future needs. This is accomplished at very little cost, since the dispersion is made as part of other activities: items are transported when one is moving for other reasons. By these means the Eskimo gain utility in both time and space for their resources, at very little direct cost in mobility or transport (see Binford 1978b:91).

This brings us to the second major characteristic of Nunamiut technological organization.

Embedded versus Direct Procurement Strategies

If everything goes well there are few or no direct costs accountable for the procurement of raw materials used in the manufacture of implements, and only low costs for materials used in the manufacture and repair of facilities.

Raw materials used in the manufacture of implements are normally obtained incidentally to the execution of basic subsistence tasks. Put another way, procurement of raw materials is embedded in basic subsistence schedules. *Very rarely, and then only when things have gone wrong, does one go out into the environment for the express and exclusive purpose of obtaining raw material for tools.* For example: a fishing party moves in to camp at Natvatrauk Lake. The days are very warm and fishing is slow, so some of the men may leave the others at the lake fishing while they visit a quarry on Nassaurak Mountain, 3.75 miles to the southeast. They gather some material there and take it up on top of the mountain to reduce it to transportable cores. While making the cores they watch over a vast area of the Anaktuvuk valley for game. If no game is sighted, they return to the fishing camp with the cores. If fishing remains poor, they return to the residential camp from which the party originated, carrying the cores. Regardless of the distance of Nassaurak Mountain from the residential camp, what was the procurement cost of the cores? Essentially nothing, since the party carried home the lithics in lieu of the fish which they did not catch. They had transport potential, so they made the best use of it; the Eskimo say that only a fool comes home empty handed!

Another example of lithic procurement strategy relative to a primary strategy was related to me during the course of a discussion concerning a particular site at the mouth of Konumuvuk valley, where flakes of pure quartz crystal were the only lithics to be found. My informants, on observing the lithics, launched into an interpretive story about how men must have camped there during the late phases of fall caribou migration while setting deadfall traps for fur bearers in the high mountain passes of Konumuvik! My curiosity was aroused. How could they tell so much from a few flakes? When questioned, they rather condescendingly replied:

> This quartz only comes from little nodules found on the top of the limestone exposures in the highest parts of the mountains. One only goes up there to set deadfall traps for the fur bearers which cross these high upland passes in winter, in going from one valley to the next. The only situation in which one would be up there to pick up this quartz would be while building deadfalls! One only does this in fall after one has put up winter stores of caribou meat, but before substantial snows have fallen in the passes. Nobody would go up there just to get quartz unless a shaman mixed quartz up in his business, but if a shaman messed around with the quartz he would not use it to cut up caribou here (in the site in question, Kakinya No. 2).

This situation reflects nicely an assumption which Eskimo informants always make: that lithic materials obtained in the late 19th century from the Killik or Kobuk rivers were introduced through social mechanisms, primarily as gifts between trading partners, or, at least, that lithic materials from those areas were brought back by persons who had made the trip for some other purpose. The procurement strategy was embedded within some other strategy and, therefore, the cost of procurement was not referrable to the distance between the source location and the location of use, since this distance would have been traveled anyway.

My experience with the Eskimo, and a limited but enlightening experience with the Alyawara of the central desert of Australia, has convinced me that variability in the proportions of raw materials found at a given site is primarily a function of the scale of the habitat which was exploited from the site location, possibly coupled with a founder effect resulting from discard on the site of items which had been manufactured previously at some other location (see Yellen, 1977:73 for an apparently similar observation). This viewpoint yields a very different perspective on relations between locations of discard, archaeological remains, and source locations for raw materials, from that which is commonly assumed. Most analysts of lithic remains *assume* a direct set of procurement strategies for lithic materials; that is, parties going out for the expressed and exclusive purpose of obtaining lithic raw materials. Using this assumption it is reasoned that a minimal "costs" strategy should obtain. The greater the distance between source and anticipated locations of use the greater the attempt to reduce the bulk of materials transported. The greater the distance "traveled" to obtain a material, the greater must be its value to the users! This view is well illustrated by Gould's (1978:288) discussion of lithic source variability at his Puntutjarpa rock shelter:

> Exotic cherts, however, were only the second most efficient raw material for adzing tasks, and they were by far the most difficult to obtain. Was the efficiency of exotic cherts great enough to lead the Aborigines to make the extraordinary efforts needed to obtain them for adze making? I very much doubt that it was, especially in light of the more than adequate supplies of superior white chert at known quarries in the nearby area. Exotic cherts, then, were mechanically efficient enough to be acceptable for adze manufacture, but we can reasonably infer that some other consideration led the ancient Aborigines to make the extra efforts needed to obtain them.

From my perspective, the presence of exotic cherts may simply be a fair measure of the mobility scale of the adaptation appearing as a consequence of the normal functioning of the system, with no extra effort expended in their procurement.

Organization of Gear

Much of the following discussion must be viewed as an ethnographic reconstruction, since the mail-order technology of the Nunamiut at the time of my field work offered little opportunity for studying the organizational consequences of stone tool assemblages.

My interviews regarding traditional strategies and use of gear were basically with four men: Jessie Ahgook, Simon Paneack, Elyjah Kakinya and Arctic John. All of these men learned from their fathers the principles of production and use of the traditional gear of the Nunamiut. All men have made essentially all the bone and wooden tools of the traditional Nunamiut; however, only Jessie Ahgook actually used a "traditional" technology as a young man. Only Simon Paneack and Jessie Ahgook have attempted as adults to use stone tools, and only Jessie was considered "knowledgeable" in this area. All old men basically agreed on the organizational aspects of traditional technology, and most provided situational or anecdotal accounts of the conditions under which various strategies and "mixes" in gear usage might occur.

I approach the problem of technological organization from the perspective of the Nunamiut themselves, that is, how they conceive of their gear with regard to the planned execution of their adaptive strategies. I emphasize the phrase *planned execution,* since my experiences with the Eskimo has convinced me that subsistence-oriented decisions are goal oriented, and are made with definite expectations as to the nature of future conditions. This element of planning in their subsistence behavior is so exacting that anticipating unforeseen events is always present; there is always a "backup strategy" in case the "first priority" does not work. This is perhaps best illustrated by the fact that one old man reports carrying flint cores (we would call this a preform) in a specially made pouch as part of his regular field gear up until about 1930, in spite of the fact that he had *never* had to use stone tools in his life. The core was carried just in case something happened to his metal gear! Three old men in Anaktuvuk village still make and carry flint and steel sets as part of their regular winter personal gear, just in case something happens to the matches. One might view these examples as cases of "conservatism," and in one respect they are. Nevertheless, "back up" strategies and gear are a regular part of young men's field planning.

All the Nunamiut elders agreed that viewed from an organizational perspective, there were three basic types of field gear: *personal gear, site furniture,* and *situational gear.* Both personal gear and site furniture were viewed as *anticipatory* in character, while situational gear was *responsive* in character.

Personal gear

Personal gear was carried by individuals in anticipation of future conditions or activities. In an earlier article (Binford 1977a), I discussed personal gear as it was observed among the Nunamiut during the spring of 1971. They recognize three basic categories of personal gear: gear selected for (a) what I will have to do in terms of the goals of the expedition; (b) how I may feel in terms of hunger and warmth; and (c) what may happen to me in terms of mishaps (see Binford 1977a:31).

My primary concern here was with lithics, so informants were questioned about stone tools which were considered by their fathers to be essential parts of their personal gear. All informants mentioned "bone cutters" (kinnusaak) which were worked (dowel-shaped) pieces of antler with inset side blades, a large one for heavy cutting, and a smaller one for more delicate work. These were used for slotting antler sections from which deer arrows were made, making the barbed sleeves for stone projectiles, and many other antler tools. Informants identified the item illustrated in Murdoch (1892:160, fig. 117) as being similar but not identical to "bone cutters" they had seen as young men. A "crooked knife" was also regularly mentioned, which during the lifetime of the informants had always been set with a metal blade. A very fine example was still in the possession of Elyjah Kakinya in 1972. This is the same one illustrated in Ingstad (1951:112a), and is very similar to the one obtained by Murdoch (1892:158, fig. 114) from an inland Eskimo during his visits to Point Barrow from 1881 to 1883. These knives were worn tied parallel to the belt, which was generally worn over the parka.

Informants always spoke of carrying "cores" into the field; as they put it, you carry a piece that has been worked enough so that all the waste is removed, but that has not been worked so much that you cannot do different things with it. These cores were described as shaped like discs of different sizes; the only item pictured in the books which I had at Anaktuvuk for comparative purposes that were identified as like the "cores" their father carried were the "discoidals" pictured by Giddings (1964:56). That the items being described by the informants were in fact cores, was made clear by many references to the removal of flakes radially around the disc for use in butchering animals, the manufacture of scrapers from flakes struck from the "long side" of the oval, and the fact that once you had reduced the core down to a very small size you had a "round scraper."

In winter, the "old timers" were described as always carrying an "ax" and an ice chisel. The latter was generally mounted on the end of a leister, or an ice dipper used in cleaning ice from fishing holes.

Men always carried flint and steel sets, together with charcoal-rubbed willow cotton for tinder. Before flint and steel, men carried a caribou bone (astragalus) and a strip of hide which could be mounted on almost anything, a caribou rib for instance, to make a fire drill for starting fires. One could always use the men's cutting board, which was generally carried by men into the field, as a hearth for fire making.

Inevitable components of field gear were the bow, arrows of several types, and a quiver and bow case. The bow was the sinew-backed bow so frequently described from the Arctic. The arrows were of three basic types: deer arrows with antler points, bird arrows with rather large blunt points, and bear arrows with stone points. Some extra shafts and points were generally carried. The old men explained that the difference between "deer" and "bear" arrows was not so much that each was exclusively used for the two types of game but that the antler points were used more commonly during the months of freezing weather, and stone when it was warm. Stone points were very easy to break and were unreliable to carry, because they "cracked sometimes from just being rubbed together in the quiver" when it was very cold. Stone points were believed to be better for penetration, and hence better for larger animals; since the bear is a "warm weather animal" they are "bear arrows."

Other items mentioned as components of personal gear for men were extra sinew for sewing and making snares for small animals, needles, extra skin patches in the event clothing repair was needed, a "man's flaker" or pressure flaker used in making stone tools, together with a scraper on the opposite end of the handles used in softening skins. These items, together with flake knives, simple flakes from relatively large cores used in butchering, were carried in a small pouch worn in much the same manner as an ammo pouch is worn today (see photo of Kakinya in Ingstad 1951:96b).

Informants recognized that personal gear was variable, depending upon the purpose of the expedition and the season. For instance, during late spring, summer, and early fall, men always carried a leister as a walking stick. These were used to spear fish in small streams and along lake margins, to support the men while in the field. The poles could be put together to make an emergency drying rack (see Binford 1978b:229). In winter, this item was replaced by an ice dipper with an ice chisel on the opposite end. If men were going hunting at lakes or in well-known ambush areas, a lance would be carried instead of the leister (see the lance in Murdoch 1892:243). Men in winter invariably carried a snow knife, the equivalent of the "big knife" in my 1971 data (see Binford 1977a:28).

Women were said to have had certain distinctive personal gear items; however, I could never get the old men to identify any except the ulu, woman's cutting board, berry bucket, needle, and case for needles.

Men recognized that the gear varied with the mode of transport, as in the 1971 data (see Binford 1977a:31). If the sled was being used, there was always a drill, extra drill bits, preworked wooden and antler pegs, rawhide lashing, extra elements of dog harness, and more "carving tools," including a hafted stone tool used much as a draw knife, with a small stone blade (typologically similar to the raclette of the French typologies).

Personal gear was heavily curated (Binford 1977a:33). Recycling, reuse, and heavy maintenance investments were made in these items. One *never* went into the field with personal gear that was not in good condition and relatively new; informants agreed that personal gear was inspected before going into the field so that worn items or items in need of repair were either repaired first or replaced before leaving for the field. This means that *the discard of personal gear related to the normal wearing out of an item was generally done inside a residential camp, not in the field where the activity in which the item was used occurred.*

Site Furniture

In my discussion of the Mask Site, I noted that there were basically three types of gear introduced to, used at, or carried through the Mask Site. One type was designed *site furniture,* or items which "went with the place" (Binford 1978a:339):

> all the items with low 'use ratios' were most commonly considered to be 'site specific' artifacts that were generally available for use by any occupants of the site. They were considered part of the site in much the same way that facilities such as hearths were considered. These items were generally introduced during the early phases of use, or they were removed from caches at the site, having remained there from a previous period of use. They were thought of as the appropriate 'artifact' furnishings of the site, the site-specific 'hardware.' The best analogy to the way the Eskimo conceived of these items is similar to the way we think of furnishings in a room. They are items that go with the place, not necessarily the persons occupying the place.

The most common items or features of site furniture are hearth stones, hearths, anvils used in pounding bones for broth (see Binford 1978b:163–165 for a discussion of bone juice), and kaotah, used as long tabular hammers and as rather massive "scrapers" for removing the periosteum along long bone shafts before breaking them. Figure 20.1 illustrates several examples of kaotah recovered from Nunamiut sites of the 1940's. Weights for tents and other anchoring functions are very common items of site furniture. Various sticks used in supporting containers over a fire, or antler racks used for the same purpose (see Binford 1978b:183, fig 5.8) are common elements of site furniture. Today, containers, most commonly a Hill's Brothers coffee can with a small wire handle, are found on most sites. In the past, worn wooden "meat dishes" (see Murdoch 1892:99–100, figs. 33, 34), and old "cooking buckets" (see Murdoch 1892:86–89) were frequently "recycled out" to temporary sites as site furniture to be used with a portable skin liner for stone boiling on such locations as hunting stands. Wooden drinking ladles, lithic raw material, repair and emergency parts (such as sled runners, usable sprude wood), and many other items (such as anvils, kaotah, and tent weights) enter the archaeological record only as a function of discontinued site use or natural processes which cover up or otherwise modify the site itself. One process which I have observed with regard to site furniture has been discussed as the "size effect" (House and Schiffer 1975:174; Baker 1978:288–93). Upon arrival at a known site, one generally searches for the "furniture" and pulls it "up" out of its

Figure 20.1 Kaotah from Nunamiut sites.

matrix for reuse. This means that large items of site furniture get continuously translated "upward" if a deposit is forming.

One of the characteristics of many items appearing as components of site furniture, for instance kettles, is that they are items which were previously used in a different context, but for the same purpose, e.g., boiling water. This situation has some of the same characteristics as the "lateral recycling" discussed by Schiffer (1976a). In this example an item is transferred from the context of "household gear," used primarily by women, to "site furniture" on, for instance, a hunting stand where men are the primary uses of the item. On the Mask Site, essentially all of the items shown distributed in the central area among the four hearths (Binford 1978a: fig. 22.17) were items "laterally recycled" from household gear at residential locations. I suspect that this is not unique to the Nunamiut, and that pots introduced into hunting camps, gathering locations, etc. are likely to be well worn but still usable elements of household gear which has been replaced at the household location.

Situational Gear

Situational gear is that which is gathered, produced, or "drafted into use" for purposes of carrying out a specific activity. This is a tool kit "put together" in order to accomplish a specific task. As the Eskimo describe it, situational gear is always in *response* to conditions, rather than put together in anticipation of events or situations. Typical examples of *situational* gear are illustrated by the following statements by informants:

> You know, something like firewood in a hunting camp, when you decide to cook then you look around for wood. I remember one time when I was out on August tundra with my uncle, maybe I was maybe 19. We looked for calves. We came upon hunting wolves; they had run a small herd of mothers and young into a little lake. We run off the wolves and shot many caribou. We dragged all to the side of the lake and then uncle find out he dropped his good knife somewhere. No good, all that caribou and nothing to cut 'em up with! My uncle he not like me always have good knife from taniks (Caucasians); he grow up when they cut 'em up with stone knife. We go around lake looking for shiny stones, and uncle fix little hammer of willow wood and part of old dog harness spreader we find around the lake. Right there he make many good little knives, we cut 'em up good, no sweat. All those little knives he make like what I mean.

Situational gear is expediently designed in terms of the raw material "options" available. One may seek raw material from caches, one may modify elements of personal gear for reuse, one may seek direct sources in the immediate environment as in the above example, or one may scavenge sites for lost or abandoned gear. *The form that such situationally designed and produced gear may take will vary, depending upon the tool demand and the nature of the expediently drafted sources of raw material.* Some of the best examples of situational gear have been described by George Frison (1968), from kill-butchering contexts on the plains of North America (see also Frison 1970, 1974, and Brian Hayden 1977 and 1978 for the Australians).

Looking at Procurement Strategies in Terms of the Organization of Gear

Should we expect the procurement of raw material for site furniture, personal gear, and situational gear to have the same characteristics and therefore to have similar archaeological consequences? In my experience the answer must be an emphatic *NO*. Let us take the situation of the manufacture or replacement of an element of personal gear; where does a hunter go to find the raw material? Regardless of where he is, he attempts to find a piece of suitable material within the camp—regardless of the fact that he may know that the *ultimate* source of the material is far away. Stated another way, among mobile hunters and gatherers raw materials are generally procured as elements of an embedded strategy, and are obtained in anticipation of future needs. Consequently, when one needs raw material one looks around to determine what is on hand. Since the repair and maintenance of gear is also generally embedded in other work schedules (that is, performed in anticipation of future needs) and executed during "off time" relative to other work schedules, if it is concluded that appropriate raw material is not on hand, the word is let out, and it is generally not long before someone introduces the needed materials.

Another aspect of lithic procurement strategies is that, as in most situations I witnessed the amount processed and transported does not vary in terms of "estimated needs." That is, if it is agreed that raw material is needed, then when the opportunity arises, the party with access to it would bring back all it could reasonably carry. This situation is likely to obtain where the availability of raw material in a camp is viewed as a corporate phenomenon, i.e., generally shared throughout the group.

Gear produced for inclusion as "personal gear" or even "household gear" is much more likely to be manufactured according to quality considerations unaffected by constraints on time or immediate availability of appropriate material, since this activity is intended to meet anticipated future needs, rather than immediate needs. I do not mean to imply that procurement is apt to shift to direct strategies, such as making long trips specifically to obtain a given raw material; I am only suggesting that within the range of materials available from normal forays into the hinterland, some will be differentially used because of quality considerations. This situation is apparently well illustrated in the data collected by James O'Connell (1977:277–81).

In direct contrast to procurement strategies for personal or household gear are those for situational gear. In meeting situational contingencies the needs for tools are immediate, so that immediately available materials must be used if the "situation" is to be coped with adequately. As has been pointed out, these materials may be naturally occurring, cached, scavenged, or recycled personal gear. In general there is little investment in the tool-production aspects of "situation gear"; edges are used if appropriate, minimal investment is made in modification, and replacement rates are very high if material is readily available. Under situational conditions practically the only factors conditioning relative investment in maintenance, reuse, and recycling is the quantity of the immediately available material; if it is low, considerable investments may be made in "economizing" so as to ensure the accomplishment of the task immediately before the worker. Quantity is almost invariably "low" if personal gear is being recycled to situationally appropriate forms, so that recycling, reuse, resharpening, and multiple usages for any given form are apt to be most common under situational tool-use conditions. *This is, other things being equal, basically a property of "field" conditions, or special-purpose sites.*

Likewise basic "reduction strategies" for naturally occurring materials may be highly variable in "situational" contexts. If only very small pebble materials are immediately available, for instance, "bipolar" techniques may be used, whereas given larger materials, hand-held percussion techniques may be used. In contrast, one would expect that with "residential locations," where personal and household gear was frequently manufactured and maintained, only larger, higher quality materials would be commonly used, and reduction strategies would be less variable from one site to the next.

Tool Design, Form Function Relations and Tool Use in Terms of Organizational Characteristics

Do I expect the patterns of tool design and use to be the same for site furniture, personal gear, and situational gear when similar tasks are to be performed? As in the previous discussion the answer must be an emphatic *NO*. I would expect elements of personal and household gear to exhibit both maximum design comparability relative to function, and maximum fit between the appropriate "quality" of the raw material and tool design. In addition there should be more design features related to hafting among items manufactured as household and personal gear, while in situational contexts items used for identical functions may exhibit at most only minimal, and perhaps technically different, hafting features.

I would expect that the manufacture of tools for personal and household gear would be executed in a staged manner for many items; that is, the manufacturing process would take place in episodes—certain modifications would be made and then the items would be stored for some time before the next "stage" of manufacture would occur. I would also expect that stage planning, particularly in the production of lithic items, would be manifested both in the logistics of procurement and the context of use. Staging in production may well correspond to transport junctures; that is, items would be partially processed, transported, further processed, and transported again. This expectation derives from the observation that just as the procurement of raw materials is generally embedded in other activity schedules, so is the manufacture of personal and household gear. Staging is at least a partial accommodation to the on-and-off work schedule used in making most tools. In addition, the embedded character of the tool-making schedule ensures that various "phases" of the manufacturing process will be conducted in different places. A good example of this is the craft activity described on the Mask Site (Binford 1978a). I think one can readily imagine that hunters might take lithic items in various "stages of production" to a hunting stand for further modification while watching for game. In fact, this was commonly reported by the older Eskimo as a common activity on "pregun" hunting stands. "Gearing up" locations may well inform us about the intended context of items produced; in one of the earliest detailed studies of lithic production strategies, for instance, Ruthann Knudson (1973:145) describes her understanding of the production sequences indicated at the MacHaffie Site:

> Apparently at least 2 general kinds of chert or chalcedony cores were produced—(1) bihedral or bifacial cores, where the reduced core was the production trajectory goal subsystem B and (2) polyhedral to irregular cores where the flakes or blades were the focus for implement utilization (subsystem C). Blade production is indicated in this assemblage but is not common, subsystem B dominates the technology. This dominance is undoubtedly a function of the fact that MacHaffie appears to have been occupied specifically for lithic provisioning.

By implication the target items of "subsystem B" were removed from the site to be further processed and used in other contexts, resulting in differential debris from staged processing occurring on different sites of the subsistence settlement system.

In the same work Knudson (1973:138) notes that, "As far as is currently known, none of the northern Plains Cody-assigned assemblages includes evidence of significant core/blade production while all the late Paleo-Indian assemblages studied from the southern Plains are characterized by cores with specialized flake production and direct manufacture of bifaces from relatively thin flake blanks." In light of the arguments presented here the reader should be able to appreciate that these differences probably reflect the proportion of situational gear, produced from local materials, as opposed to personal gear, transported for use at a site.

Turning now to consideration of tool design under different forms of intended usage and different organizations of gear, I think it should be clear that the manufacture of situational gear is carried out with a full knowledge of tool needs and replacement potential which is characteristic of the situation. Under such conditions one need only be concerned with design characteristics which facilitate a *specific, known* and *immediate* task; therefore, the tool design may be quire specific or limited, in response to '*short term*' considerations. Planning or designing a tool to be incorporated into personal or household gear is very different, since it will be seen in the context of long-term usage and the requirement that it meet many different types of tool needs. A good example of this is the contrast between spear making by Australian Aborigines as experienced by Brian Hayden and Richard Gould. Hayden asked Aborigines to perform different manufacturing tasks for his enlightenment; since these men were not equipped with traditional gear and were expected to make the tools needed to accomplish a specific task, it should come as no surprise that what Hayden witnessed was almost exclusively the production of situational gear. By way of contrast Gould observed Aborigines who were equipped with traditional gear; when they manufactured many of the same items which Hayden had witnessed, they used different tools! Compare for instance "spear making" reported by Gould (1969:99) with that reported by Hayden (1977:184). In Gould's description a hafted adz (an item of personal gear) was used in working the spear shaft, while in Hayden's what appears to be a hand-held denticulate was for accomplishing the same task. We can expect many such tool-design parallels, that is, tools of very different design being used for identical tasks; but this is not to say that they are functionally iso-morphic, since they are clearly designed for very different *intended roles* within the technology. This context variability is probably illustrated as well by many of the expediently manufactured butchering tools described by Frison (1968, 1970). It is likely that identical butchering tasks would be performed by the same people with different tools in a base camp or other less situational contexts.

Looking at Disposal and Abandonment in Terms of Organizational Characteristics for Gear

Within this context we face quite directly sources of variability among archaeological sites. In a previous discussion (Binford 1977a) I have addressed the issue of expected differences between curated and expediently organized technologies. In that paper I was interested in contrasting site formation processes when the differences were between complete technologies which were expediently produced, and curated tech-nologies where at least some items were produced and then maintained within the technology in anticipation of future usage; I had in mind contrasts between the Mousterian (which I believe to be largely noncurated) and the Upper Paleolithic of Western Europe (which I believe to be curatorially organized). In this paper I have addressed intersite variability which might arise from organizational variability *within* a basically curated technology. What is clear is that as far as actual tool use and production are concerned, the relative roles of household and personal gear (heavily curated) and situational gear (largely noncurated) are variable, and we can expect assemblages which are "curated" in the broad sense to exhibit patterns of interassem-blage variability depending upon the *organization* of the technology as seen in the proportion of situational to more curated types of gear. In seeking such an appreciation we must consider some of the probable consequences of associations between tools of different form, evidence of use, and debris, under different systems conditions within an organized technology. For instance,

1. Items of personal and household gear are apt to be both produced and maintained within residential sites, resulting in an association at such locations of debris from manufacture, repair, and final discard of worn-out items.

2. Items that have relatively long use lives are not likely to be "worn out" on special purpose locations, since pretrip gearing-up operations would result in the replacement of heavily worn items before leaving the residential location.

3. Manufacturing debris from lithic processing is apt to vary in content seasonally (representing different proportions of different sources), since there is very likely to be seasonally variable exploitation of different geographical areas and lithic raw materials would generally be obtained within the context of normal subsistence procurement schedules. Given residential mobility, lithic source variability as indicated in primary debris should be correlated with the geographical position of the residential site.

4. Manufacturing debris occurring on special purpose sites which are intermediate between residential sites and procurement sites (such as hunting stands or camps) may well exhibit considerable lithic debris from work on partially finished or "staged" items. Flakes or bifacial retouch, core reduction, or the use of a "disproportionate" number of tools designed for the modification of other raw material such as wood, antler, bone, or fiber might well be anticipated. On such "intermediate" locations, work scheduling would generally be carried out in "dead time" on items introduced in anticipation of this activity (see Binford 1978a). This means that many "incomplete" items would be further modified on such locations, resulting in "disjunctive" debris to tool relationships.

5. The highest incidence of recycling and reuse of items of personal gear is most likely to occur in special purpose locations. This follows from the observation that personal gear is frequently "drafted for use" as the source of material for situational gear.

6. High incidences of flakes from bifacial "cores" are apt to characterize special purpose sites. Such flakes can be expected to show relatively high use ratios, that is, the number evidencing use should be high.

7. We might expect a general inverse relationship between the proportions of reuse and recycling of personal gear and the abundance of situationally produced gear from immediately available raw materials.

I have made no attempt to compile an exhaustive list of expectations for assemblage variability given differences in the use and differential discard of gear at sites of different function. I have simply listed a few of the more obvious properties we might anticipate given differentially organized gear and a logistically based settlement system.

Implications for Intersite Variability

The discussion in this paper has been directed toward the organization of gear relative to "special purpose" locations. I have not directly discussed the organization and supplying of raw material and gear at residential locations; the emphasis here has been on the way gear is organized in the context of a logistical rather than a foraging set of strategies (see Binford 1980b).

With foraging strategies persons range out into the environment searching for resources and return to a residential location each night; with logistically organized strategies, parties organized specifically for procurement of certain target resources move out of residential locations to temporary camps for their own maintenance while exploiting the resources of a specific location, and range out from these camps in the execution of their procurement strategies. Special purpose locations of relevance here are those which have to do with hunting and trapping activities.

Two major characteristics of systems organized logistically are that raw materials or tools are rarely obtained through direct procurement strategies, and that the logistical operations of the system are supported by a wide-ranging "caching" strategy which insures the dispersion in the habitat of goods and materials which might be needed later. This caching strategy is both anticipatory and logistical in that it seeks to gain spatial utility (see Binford 1978b) from resources. If one adopts systemic expectations for properties of the archaeological record, there are certain methodological challenges which inevitably follow. If we anticipate that past behavior was differentially organized to accomplish different types of tasks, it follows that the "reasons for occupation" as well as the "tasks accomplished" would be variable among sites generated by persons participating in a single system (Binford and Binford 1966); that "functional" differences can be expected is now a demonstrated condition (see Binford 1978b). Given such an empirical warrant for expecting such conditions among at least some prehistoric systems, it becomes necessary to develop a means of identifying generic types of functional differentiation when they are encountered in the archaeological record. It is toward just this end that this paper was prepared. I have been concerned with the differential organization of gear and how this may result in differences in assemblage content, as a clue to the logistical function of sites. I have also suggested that some variability among special purpose locations will be directly attributable to immediate system–state conditions, such as the degree to which tasks were adequately anticipated and the party was "properly" equipped for them. This type of variablity can be expected as a major contributor to frequency variations among assemblages derived from curated technologies; for instance, such conditions may well be responsible for the sometimes high frequency of "Mousterian" tools in upper paleolithic assemblages, i.e., they were "caught short" (see Straus 1978 for a discussion of this problem).

This paper has sought to introduce the idea that tools may be differentially designed, manufactured, used, and discarded, in response to their intended roles in the technology. I have made no attempt to develop actual techniques for the unambiguous analysis of archeological assemblages in these terms; I hope rather that a sufficiently convincing argument has been presented to warrant a "rethinking" of current approaches to the study of lithic assemblage variability. Such "rethinking" especially is needed with regard to "cost/benefit" analysis of lithic source locations and differential relationships between reduction strategies, raw materials, tool design, recycling, reuse, and the relative contributions of each to "assemblage variability." We should expect different designs and reduction strategies for functionally similar tools, depending upon their intended technological roles, given variable situations of tool demand and adequacy of gear provisions. Normative ideas of technically and morphologically "homogeneous" industries should be abandoned as a general set of expectations; rather we should expect that developing situationally reponsive alternative ways of doing things has adaptive significance within most cultural systems.

Whereas the older and largely implicit model of tool design and production was that of a maker producing a tool to perform a task, I have suggested that tool production may be "future oriented," and the manufacturer takes into consideration in the selection of raw material, design, and fabrication of the tool its intended role in the technology. This is a very different set of considerations from that of "simple function," in a task-specific sense. In the case of a hide-scraping tool, to what degree will similar materials, design features, and fabrication methods be used when it is intended for immediate use and discard and when it is intended for incorporation in a portable tool kit for use in a variety of situations in which some scraping of hides may be required? Given that a knapper may well bring his skill to bear in both types of situation, to what degree are the recognizable differences in the products "stylistic" rather than "functional"? Since only one maker is involved, I must conclude that all observed variability would be "functional." This would be true even where use wear would indicate an "identical" task-related "function" for the tool! In this situation researchers might attempt to hold function "constant" by means of use-wear information; observing morphological differences, they would therefore feel justified in asserting that the variation was "stylistic," and so attributable to differences in the identity of the makers—and *they would be wrong*. One cannot "give meaning" to the archaeological record in terms of "conventions," as has been done routinely in the past. The assignment of meaning to properties of the archaeological record must rest on a solid understanding of the processes which operated in the past to generate the patterns remaining for us to observe today.

Notes

1. This reference is to stones for warming, put in the foot of one's sleeping skins.
2. Approximately 175 air miles.
3. Approximately 250 air miles.
4. Approximately 230 air miles.
5. Approximately 175 air miles.
6. These references are to places which form a rough circle around Anaktuvuk Pass, encompassing approximately 135,265 square miles, an area greater than any U.S. states except Montana, California, Texas, or Alaska, and greater than the entire area of the United Kingdom or any countries of Europe except Russia, Spain, Sweden and France. It is an area approximately 70 percent of the size of France. This is the area which the old men of the Nunamiut discuss with ease when remembering the locations of former sites, caches, and resources. By our standards they have a detailed and comprehensive knowledge of an enormous terrain.

21

Dimensional Analysis of Behavior and Site Structure: Learning from an Eskimo Hunting Stand

Detailed behavioral observations permitted the dimensional analysis of formation processes operative on the Mask site, a Nunamiut Eskimo hunting stand. Activity structure, technological organization, disposal mode, and spatial organization were all seen as behavioral dimensions that could each vary, altering the patterns of assemblage content and spatial disposition at an archaeological site.

These ethnoarchaeological experiences were then contrasted with those recently reported by John Yellen (1977), and a critical evaluation of his "conclusions" was conducted from the perspective of the Eskimo experience. It was pointed out that basic differences in philosophy and approach to research largely conditioned the contrasting character of the conclusions drawn from the different experience.

The purpose of this paper is to describe the relationship between characteristic behaviors observed on hunting stands and the structured consequences of these behaviors in the archaeological record.

This article is within the domain of "ethnoarchaeology" in that it describes observations believed to be of interest to archaeologists but experienced in the context of an ongoing living system. All of the observations to be reported were made between 1969 and 1973 during ethnographic work among the Nunamiut Eskimo of north central Alaska. Much of the material resulting from this work has been previously described (Binford 1976, 1978b; Binford and Chasko 1976; Binford and Bertram 1977). This article represents the first of a series that will specifically treat the formation processes and resulting character of the internal site structure for a number of different types of Eskimo sites.

Hunting stands are a type of site commonly produced by the Nunamiut. They are locations where men congregate to watch for game and to plan hunting strategies after game is sighted. They are an integral part of an "intercept" hunting strategy as opposed to an "encounter" strategy (see Binford 1978b). In intercept hunting one employs knowledge of the factors that condition animal behavior to "predict" where animals will be, given the conditions of the moment such as weather, seasons of the year, etc. One positions himself to be able to monitor the surrounding area where

Originally published in *American Antiquity* **43** (3):330–361, © 1978.

game is anticipated. These "stations" from which an area is monitored are hunting stands. They are commonly occupied only by male hunters or hunters and young men. They are rarely occupied overnight, and when they are, there is a continuous monitoring of the area rather than a change of tempo within the site when everyone goes to bed. Sleeping facilities on such locations are always expedient and individual.

Hunting stands provide an interesting situation relative to the assumptions commonly made by archaeologists regarding the relationship between attributes of site location and site content and between the internal pattern of artifact disposition and activities. Frequently an archaeologist may observe that there is some consistent association between features of the physical geography and the presence of archaeological sites in a given area. Upon recognition of such a pattern it is not uncommon to study comparatively the artifactual contents of the sites as a clue to their "function" and hence a basis for understanding their geographical patterning. The assumption is made that what is *in* a site betrays the activities conducted there, and that anticipation of those activities was crucial in selecting the location of the site.

In the case of many Eskimo hunting stands, there is no obvious relationship between what is in the site and the "reasons for its occupancy" and hence the "reasons for its location." The location is chosen because it provides maximum visual coverage for a large area considered a likely place for game to be moving. The location is chosen to maximize the informational input for the occupants. This information is then used to decide upon a hunting strategy. The strategy is normally executed from a series of nearby hunting "blinds" or "ambush" locations. The latter sites are frequently characterized by the presence of facilities such as "fox holes," wind breaks, blinds, and traps. These locations are normally taken up after the hunters have established the game's presence and path of movement. Around a typical hunting stand there may be several alternatively placed "blinds" or "ambushes." A hunting stand is primarily an information-gathering location, and rarely are animals directly killed from such a site, although it sometimes happens. Hunting directly from stands is more common today, given the use of high-powered rifles where "long shots" are more frequent. In the past when the bow and arrow was the only weapon, killing directly from hunting stands was much less feasible, and multiple blinds and ambushes were more commonly located near hunting stands.

The location of the hunting stand, then, is chosen in order to facilitate hunting through the observation of game and the planning that such observational information makes possible. The activities that take place within such stands are, however, largely related to reducing the bordom levels of the occupants during their watch for game. Because the sites are not placed in the environment relative to the major activities conducted within them, we may expect only indirect clues to their function from the inventory of remaining contents. The best way to illustrate this point is by example.

The Mask site is located near the present village of Anaktuvuk (see Binford 1978b). It is commonly used as a hunting stand after the main caribou migration hunting in spring. It is used to monitor stragglers and small postmigration herds of bull caribou in the area to the south and west of the contemporary village. The period of use is from around May 28 through June 19. The general role of this site and its place in the overall spring hunting strategy have been previously described (Binford 1978b).

Our interest is in the facts of its internal organization and how they came into being behaviorally.

I was present on this site for a total of 34 hours spread over the years 1971 and 1972. In 1971 the site was visited several times. Hunting orchestrated from the site was observed, as was the general character of site activities. During a lull in the use of the site by the Nunamiut, the site was mapped and inventoried and then cleaned of all portable items not identified by informants as items "cached" or destined for future use/or retrieval by the users of the site. This was very near the end of the use period in 1971. The site was cleaned so that all items observed there the following year could be referred to behavior occurring on the site during the spring of 1972.

In 1972 the site was visited 3 times during its peak use, and the hunting of bull herds from the site was recorded. Late in the season I was essentially stranded in Anaktuvuk village while waiting for the arrival of my archaeological crew. I used this "dead time" to conduct a rather intensive set of observations on the Mask site (June 4–7, 1972). Within 1 week I spent 23 hours on the site. In addition, the site was inventoried, and all items were mapped according to their exact location. Prior to the start of "systematic" observation I had observed behavior on the site for approximately 11 hours. I attempted to make "behavioral observations" (see Whiting and Whiting 1970; Weick 1968) during the observation periods June 4–7, 1972, but my observations were biased in that no attempt was made to record all action occurring on the hunting stand. I tried to record the times of arrival and departure of persons; I recorded the times at which various individuals initiated activities and when they stopped. For instance, a typical record may note that Johnny Rulland seated himself next to Bob Ahgook around hearth A at 8:50 and began engaging in conversation and the eating of bone marrow. The record may then pick up some time later by noting that Johnny got up from the hearth area and announced that he had "had enough" and was returning to the village. The description would then note the items he collected and carried away with him. Table 21.1 summarizes the census data on the persons present on the site and the manhours of activity that were recorded.

Activities Conducted

My major interest was in actions that resulted in the discard or placement of items as they then entered the archaeological domain. I did, however, as noted above, keep an activity record for the 23 hours of observation. Table 21.2 summarizes these data regarding the numbers of hours in which the occupants of the site were engaged in the several recognized basic activities. There are 7 such activities into which the overall actions of the man were tabulated. Game-watching consisted solely of scanning the area to the south of the site either with the unaided eye or with binoculars. If a man was engaged in carving a wooden mold for a mask and occasionally looked over the area or even picked up binoculars and scanned the area, he was still recorded as engaged in craft or manufacturing tasks; a man was tabulated as engaged in an activity even though he occasionally interrupted his action for other purposes.

The only category of action that might be misleading in Table 21.2 is hunting.

TABLE 21.1
Flow of Men through the Site

Date of observation (1972)	Total hours of observation	No. initially present	Arrived during observation	Left during observation	Total men using site (June 6)
June 4	6	3	4	2	7
June 4	3	5	2	4	7
June 5	3	7	2	3	9
June 5	6	9	4	6	13
June 6	4	5	4	7	9
June 6	1	4	1	1	5
	23				50/16

Date of observation (1972)	Total man hours of on-site activity	Average stay at site per man (hours)	Mean no. men per hour present during observation
June 4	29.0	4.14	5.00
June 4	13.0	1.86	4.33
June 5	19.5	2.17	6.50
June 5	52.3	4.02	8.71
June 6	15.5	1.72	3.88
June 6	4.5	0.90	4.50

TABLE 21.2
Frequency of Activities Conducted on the Mask Site during Controlled Periods of Observation

	Activity						
	Game watching	Off-site hunting	Eating + talking	Target shooting	Playing cards	Crafts	Sleep
Date of observation	No.[a] (%)	No. (%)	No. (%)	No. (%)	No. (%)	No. (%)	No. (%)
June 4	5.5(19.0)	5.5(19.0)	9.5(33.0)	0.0(—)	3.5(12.0)	5.0(17.0)	0.0(—)
June 4	3.0(23.0)	0.0(—)	4.5(35.0)	3.0(23.0)	1.0(8.0)	1.5(12.0)	0.0(—)
June 5	3.0(15.0)	0.0(—)	9.0(46.0)	3.0(15.0)	2.0(10.0)	1.0(5.0)	1.5(8.0)
June 5	12.0(22.96)	5.0(10.0)	21.75(42.0)	2.0(4.0)	9.0(17.0)	1.0(2.0)	1.5(3.0)
June 6	6.5(42.0)	0.0(—)	3.0(19.0)	3.0(19.0)	0.0(—)	3.0(19.0)	0.0(—)
June 6	1.5(33.0)	0.0(—)	1.5(33.0)	0.0(—)	0.0(—)	1.5(33.0)	0.0(—)
Total	31.5	10.5	49.25		15.5	13.0	3.0
Percentage	24.0	8.0	37.0		12.0	10.0	2.0

[a]No. = number of man hours.

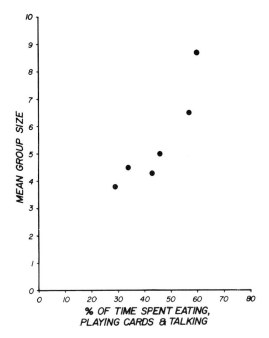

Figure 21.1 Relationship between mean group size and time spent eating, playing cards, and talking—Mask site.

Hunting was never actually conducted on the site; during hunting episodes, all the men (including myself) were off the site. This "hunting" category, then, indicates hours during which the site was abandoned while hunting activities were carried out.

Two other observations regarding the activity categories might be useful. All target shooting was done with guns that were especially introduced for this purpose. That is, the weapons used in hunting were *never* used in shooting targets at the Mask site. It was explained that the powder and shells were too expensive to be wasted on targets. A rimfire .22 was almost always used in target shooting. The craft activities observed on the Mask site were (a) carving of wooden molds for masks, (b) carving of wooden spreaders for a dog harness, (c) carving of a horn spoon to be sold to a collector from Fairbanks, (d) carving of an ivory needle valve for repairing a carburetor on a snowmobile, (e) sewing a small skin pouch for carrying rifle bullets, and (f) repair of caribou skin socks.

The information in Table 21.2 should demonstrate that only the activity of "watching for game" was directly related to the primary function of the site. This represented 24% of the total man-hours of activity recorded; yet there were no recognizable archaeological consequences of this behavior. No tools left on the site were used, and there were no immediate material "byproducts" of the "primary" activity. All of the other activities conducted at the site were essentially boredom reducers.

Figure 21.1 illustrates the relationship between the percentage of the total time spent in the combined activities of eating, playing cards, and talking and the mean

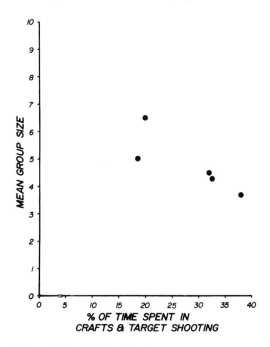

Figure 21.2   Relationship between mean group size and time spent in crafts and target shooting—Mask site.

group size present on the site during observation. What is clear is that the relative proportions of these activities are a function of the size of the group present on the site. The larger the social unit present, the greater the proportion of the total man-hours spent in "socializing" activities. Figure 21.2 illustrates the relationship between the size of the social unit present and the percentage of the total occupation time spent in target shooting and craft activities. The relationship is negatively linear; the fewer men present, the greater the proportion of time spent in target shooting and craft activities. The recognition of these relationships is provocative as regards the problem of interassemblage variability. *Insofar as there are relationships between activities and material items, we could expect that hunting stands which tended to vary in the modal group sizes would also vary in terms of the relative frequencies of activity-related archaeological debris.*

I have described elsewhere (Binford 1978b) a number of different hunting stands, and one of the major differences between them was the modal sizes of the occupying group. Stands used during peak migration hunting are large, with many men frequenting the stand. After main migration, the degree to which individual men continue to hunt is largely a function of the successes during migration hunting. Generally, the less skilled hunters are the ones hunting after migration. Animals tend to be dispersed, hence hunting stands tend to be dispersed and are generally occupied by 2 men at most. We would, therefore, expect the content of such sites to be different from those of migration hunting stands, with a bias in favor of industrial debris, since target shooting is a behavior not generally engaged in when dispersed animals are being hunted. This task-related difference would correlate with "microseasonal" differences.

Individual hunting stands are occupied more commonly after migration, and they would be geographically distributed in a different manner (see Binford 1978b). Hence there would be a correlation between some facts of content and season of occupancy, as well as geographical location. Nevertheless, the relevant explanatory variable would be group size. How could one discover that condition by studying the empirical correlations, spatial patterns, or "typological status" of the assemblages? I do not think the facts of the archaeological record would speak for themselves in this case. Finally, the typological distinctiveness of assemblages from postmigration hunting stands would be illusionary since the same variables conditioning large stands would be operative; the only differences would be the "power" of the different variables as manifest at different locations. This is what is meant by "functional" variability, but more importantly this is what is anticipated by arguments for the multivariable basis of many interassemblage differences. Our analytical tools must be sufficient for recognizing such conditions when they exist and recognizing the effects of such past dynamics or formation processes if we are to achieve accuracy in giving meaning to the archaeological facts we observe. These points will be demonstrated more clearly with the next body of data.

Technological Organization

We have now explored some of the factors that condition the performance of different activities on the Mask site and how these activities relate to the "primary function" of the site. Our next concern is the relationship between the structure of the activities and the organization of the "technology" or material items manipulated in the various activities. Table 21.3 summarizes the data from the 23 hours of observation at the Mask site regarding the material items observed and their relationship to the activities previously described. In addition, the inventory of items is elaborated to include the number of separate items of each type observed together with the number of man-episodes of use for the items. A "man-episode" is indicated (a) for each different man that used the item, (b) for a reuse by the same man during different observational sessions, and (c) if another man had used the item between recorded uses by the same man.

This may sound complicated, and I must admit it was. Working out the conventions for recording was not easy. For instance, a man carrying a skinning knife is observed on the site during observation period number 1. The same man is observed with the skinning knife on the site during observation period number 2. Do we record 2 men and 2 skinning knives? In this case, no, since no observation of "use" was made in either case, and since 1 man and 1 knife had been recorded. Unless some episode of use was observed, no further tabulation was made.

The information in Table 21.3 is supplemented by the data on the number of items observed on the site during the period of behavioral observation and the number

TABLE 21.3

Data from the 23 Hours of Behavioral Observation as Regards the Items Observed and the "Activity" in Which They Were Used.

Activity and items used	A. No. of observations	B. No. of man-episodes of use	$\dfrac{A}{B}$
Eating and talking (18)			
Kaotah	2	4	.50
Meat bones	11	4	2.75
Marrow bones	8	6	1.33
Can of hash	1	1	1.00
Can of sardines	5	5	1.00
Can of pop	2	2	1.00
Sardine can key	5	5	1.00
Pop can tab	2	2	1.00
Coffee cups	6	19	.32
Coffee pot	1	9	.11
Coffee can	2	6	.33
Spoons	2	21	.10
Can of milk	1	9	.11
Stone anvils	5	11	.45
Bottle of instant coffee	1	7	.14
Bag of coffee	4	11	.36
Bag of sugar	12	27	.44
Watching for game (2)			
Binoculars	2	18	.11
Skins	1	18	.06
Playing cards (5)			
Deck of cards	3	22	.14
Can of pop	5	5	1.00
Pop can tab	5	5	1.00
Skins	2	22	.09
Coffee cups	4	9	.44
Crafts (11)			
Abrader	1	1	1.00
Kitchen knife	1	1	1.00
Metal file	1	4	.25
Hone	1	2	.50
Skinning knife	4	4	1.00
Mask mold	1	1	1.00
Scraper (skin)	1	1	1.00
Scissors	1	1	1.00
Screwdriver	1	1	1.00
Dressed skin	1 (sq.)	1	1.00
Skin	1	3	.33
Target shooting (4)			
.22 shells	50 [a]	3	16.67
Pop can (target)	4	13	.31
Milk can (target)	1	6	.17
Skin	1	2	.50

TABLE 21.3 (*Continued*)

Activity and items used	A. No. of observations	B. No. of man-episodes of use	$\dfrac{A}{B}$
Off-site hunting (8)			
Dog packs	3	3	1.00
Rifle	17	17	1.00
Skinning knife	18	18	1.00
Bullets	25	5	5.00
Short ropes	2	1	2.00
Sleds	5	5	1.00
Snowmobiles	7	7	1.00
Binoculars	2	2	1.00
Sleeping (1)			
Skins	1	2	
Other or nonspecific (6)			
Funnel	Not observed	—	
Pair of gloves	Not observed	—	
Soap dish	Not observed	—	
Wolf trap	Not observed	—	
Sheets of canvas	Not observed	—	
Cigarette lighter	Not recorded	—	

[a] An estimate rather than an actual count.

of items observed "archaeologically" at the end of the period of behavioral observation. Several characteristics of the Nunamiut technological system are made explicit in this table. First, all the items with low "use ratios" were most commonly considered to be "site-specific" artifacts that were generally available for use by any occupants of the site. They were considered part of the site in much the same way that facilities such as hearths were considered. These items were generally introduced during the early phases of use, or they were removed from caches at the site, having remained there from a previous period of use. They were thought of as the appropriate "artifact" furnishings of the site, the site-specific "hardware." The best analogy to the way the Eskimo conceived of these items is similar to the way we think of furnishings in a room. They are items that go with the place, not necessarily the persons occupying the place. Items in this category were coffee cups, coffee pot, coffee can, spoons, bottle of instant coffee, bags of coffee and sugar, can of milk, stone anvils, kaotah, sitting skins, and decks of cards. Most of these items were contributed by various occupants for the use by others during the period of occupation. Others were considered to be unowned and simply part of the site, such as the stone anvils and kaotah used in cracking marrow bones. These were collected expediently from immediately available raw materials and are not identified with any contributor as might be the coffee cups or pot.

The other class of items exhibiting low use-ratios were items that were identified as the "property" of an individual but were widely shared at the site. These items include the metal file, the hone, and the binoculars. The metal file and the hone were observed as items cached on the site and in this sense were almost considered in the same category as contributed "furnishings." It was explained that these were not very valuable items, and it would be "impolite" to recover them if someone was using them when the owner decided to leave the site. By convention the person using an item would cache it on the site if the owner was not present when the borrower finished his task. By way of contrast, the binoculars were considered valuable, and therefore it would not be unreasonable for the owner to collect them from persons who might be using them when he decided to leave the site.

A final class of items exhibiting low use-ratios were cans used as shooting targets. In this case they were recycled into this function. This is, they had been introduced to the site for other purposes.

We can see that of all the items exhibiting low use-ratios, only expediently used items such as the anvils and kaotah or recycled items such as the targets went into the archaeological record a manner directly proportional to the number actually used on the site. All of the items having low use-ratios may be thought of as "group" tools or multiple-use containers. These are the items that are apt to occur sporadically on sites if they are curated (Binford 1976) and moved around in cached contexts, or very regularly as in the case of the anvils, if not curated. These are the items that are apt to appear most commonly in the archaeological record as "de facto garbage," in Schiffer's (1976a) terms, if curated.

Among the items exhibiting a use ratio of 1 there are clearly 3 subclasses of items (see Table 21.4): (a) individual serving containers—hash, sardine, and pop cans—all containers for individual servings of food or refreshments, (b) almost all the items used in craft activities, abrader, kitchen knife, etc., and (c) all the items introduced as part of the personal gear of hunters and destined for use at hunting stands, blinds, and butchering locations—dog packs, rifles, skinning knives, etc. Only items in the first category were systematically represented on the site. These were the immediate byproducts of consumption.

What we are seeing are some of the effects of organizational properties on the archaeological record. All items used on the site were not organized within the technology in a similar manner. The particular patterns of technological organization conditioned the degree to which items did or did not go into the archaeological record as a direct consequence of their use. It should not take much imagination to visualize how the archaeological record might vary if the organization of the technology were different with no difference in either the character of the items used or the activity conditions of their use. Suppose for a moment that all the gear listed in Table 21.4, columns III and IV, was introduced to the site as part of "personal gear" and each man had his own cup, spoon, coffee pot, can of milk, coffee can, etc. Clearly the numbers introduced to the site would be very different, approaching the values for rifles and skinning knives in column 2. Let us further suppose that these items were "expendable" as opposed to "curated" (see Binford 1976) or maintained within the technology for considerable periods of time. I think the reader can easily appreciate how vastly different the content of the archaeological record would be given such

TABLE 21.4

Comparison between Numbers of Items Observed Behaviorally and Archaeologically

Column I—Items with values greater than 1			Column II—Items with values of 1		
Item	BO[a]	AO[b]	Item	BO	AO
Marrow bones	8	334			
Meat bones	11	51	Hash can	1	1
			Sardine can	5	7
Shells (ammunition)	25	68	Pop can	7	12
			Can key	5	6
			Can tab	2	12
			Abrader	1	1
			Kitchen knife	1	(1)[c]
			Skinning knife	18	0
			Mask mold	1	0
			Skin scraper	1	0
			Scissors	1	0
			Screw driver	1	0
			Dressed skin	1	0
			Dog packs	3	0
			Rifles	17	0
			Skinning knives	18	0
			Sled	5	0
			Snowmobiles	7	0

Column III—Items with values .99-.25			Column IV—Items with values less than .25		
Item	BO	AO	Item	BO	AO
Coffee cups	6	(6)[c]	Coffee pot	1	(1)[c]
Coffee can	2	1	Spoons	2	(2)
Bag of coffee	4	(2)	Can of milk	1	1
Bag of sugar	12	(1)	Instant coffee	1	(1)
Pop can target	3	4	Milk can target	1	1
Metal File	1	(1)	Binoculars	2	0
Hone	1	(1)	Sitting skin	5	(1)
			Deck of cards	3	(1)
Stone anvils	5	5			
Kaotah	2	2			

[a] Behaviorally observed.
[b] Archaeologically observed.
[c] Note: Values in parentheses indicate that the number of items listed were on the site at the time of mapping but informants were emphatic that these items were only temporarily abandoned and would be used again and eventually returned to the village or moved to another location.

organizational changes, while activities, site functions, identity of occupants, etc., might remain the same.

We can appreciate how systems might vary in their organizational properties; such differences have been explored previously in terms of some of their implications (see Binford 1976). It should be pointed out that organizational properties may vary *within* a system situationally and thereby contribute appreciably to intersite variability within a system. For instance, I have observed situations in which gear normally curated and carried as part of the personal-gear element of the technology may be abandoned or scuttled. We may also appreciate that environmental "contingencies" may well situationally condition how otherwise identical items are organized. For instance, in 1974 I had the rare opportunity to observe tool-making behavior of Alyawara-speaking Australian aborigines at a stone quarry and then later in a base camp. At the quarry, where large quantities of material were immediately available, large flakes were treated as expendable byproducts of flint chipping and discarded essentially where they dropped. On the other hand, in the base camp, where stone working was restricted to the reduction of cores that had been transported over a considerable distance, the large flakes were picked up and circulated among the various families as potential sources of raw material, "blanks" for cores or for further processing into tools. In this case we see how the "organization" of the technology may be situationally responsive to external conditions resulting in within-system differences in the archaeological remains at different locations.

Disposal Modes

Thus far I have discussed factors in the ongoing behavioral system that differentially condition the disposition and use of material items. In this section I am concerned with the important process of the transformation of material items from their "systemic" context (see Schiffer 1976a) to their "archaeological context." I am interested in describing the modes of disposal for items entering the archaeological record at the Mask site. In turn, I am interested in the resulting *structure,* the character of the internal site structure that results from the production of an archaeological record at this site. Given such interests, one can appreciate that my behavioral observations would be biased. I made no attempt to record all observed behavior occurring on the hunting stand, only behavior in the context of which material items were manipulated. Even within this domain I did not record all acts, only those which resulted in the deposition of an item or in the repositioning of an item already placed within the site. The earlier 12 hours of observation were used as the basis for the development of an observational format. I recognized 5 manipulative acts that resulted in items occurring on surfaces within the site: dropping, tossing, resting, positioning, and dumping items.

Dropping

Most of the cases of dropping were cases where elements were detached from an item already held in the hand. The most frequently observed dropping situation was in the context of cracking marrow bones. The bone was commonly held in the hand

and struck with the back of a hunting knife. The impact resulted in detached chips and splinters of bone that *dropped* to the ground directly below the point of impact. Another common situation of dropping was observed during the manufacture of a mold for a mask. The craftsman was carving a piece of wood, and the wood shavings *dropped* to the ground directly below the action. A rare form of *dropping* was "fumble" dropping. That is, an item either held in the hand or in some container such as a pocket was dropped during the course of the action or during the removal of another item from the container.

Tossing

This action was very common and most often occurred upon the completion of some action. For instance, containers such as sardine cans or pop cans were commonly tossed after their contents were consumed. Similarly, articulator ends of bone processed for marrow were tossed away after the marrow was removed. The act is simple, an item held in the hand is tossed aside, effectively removing it from the area of its use.

Resting

Items are set down, normally, in the following contexts: "unpacking" upon entry to the camp, temporary abandonment of a task due to interruptions, or arraying tools that might all be used in accomplishing a general task. Typical behaviors might be the hunter who enters the hunting stand and leans his rifle against a rock or takes off his pack and sets it down beside the rifle. Several men may be sitting around a hearth eating marrow bones and drinking coffee when the "magic word" *caribou* is stage whispered among the men. Almost invariably the coffee cups, partially processed marrow bones, or half-eaten tins of sardines will be set down immediately in front of the man, and he will bolt up seaching for his binoculars, rifle, etc. Such acts result in resting items.

Positioning Items (Placed)

An item was identified as positioned if there was some attempt to (a) aggregate several, (b) unobtrusively place them so they would not interfere with ongoing activites at the location, and (c) insure their easy retrieval at some future date. Formally this is a difficult category because there is an assumed motive—the temporary placement of an item or items in anticipation of future use. This is what the archaeologist would call caching, although some of these "caches" may be very short term.

Dumping

This was an infrequent behavior on hunting stands. It consists of the accumulation of dropped or resting items, normally in a container. The container is then picked up and removed, commonly to the periphery of the site, and dumped. This results in a recognizable high density aggregate distribution.

The above categories were found to adequately accommodate the observed behaviors in which items came to rest in a hunting stand. Obviously this is only a partial picture, since items at rest within a site may be removed and/or reorganized spatially as a result of a variety of actions taking place within the site. The following classification of acts that resulted in the repositioning of items already at rest within the site was found useful:

1. Brushing aside—The action was observed in only four behavioral contexts: (a) before sitting down, (b) in preparation for drawing a map in the dirt, (c) before butchering an animal, and (d) prior to dismantling a snowmobile carburetor. In no case was a special tool used, such as a broom. The hand and arm were used to brush aside litter and to smooth out the surface of the ground in preparation for the performance of the acts listed above.

2. Searching—This action was observed only twice. One of the men would generally ask the group is anyone had picked up his item. In one case the item was a butchering knife and in the other it was a fragment of a broken saw blade used in cutting antler. In camps such as the Mask site, the first assumption normally made when an item is suspected of being missing is that someone else has picked up the item and is using it or has placed it somewhere unknown to the owner. This means that if an individual misses some item that he had at the site he will always query the other men present, "Did anyone see my _____?" If no one acknowledges having seen the item, it is generally assumed that someone no longer present used the item and has left it "around the site somewhere." Most of the time, in the absence of information as to where the item may be found, the men present will get up and begin searching for it. There is a kind of search priority or scale of likelihood about where a lost item may be. First they look on top of prominent rocks and boulders, then around the bases of these rocks and boulders. Next they look under any temporary "ground covers" such as caribou skins, which might have been dragged around and inadvertently covered up an item, or a stack of recently introduced firewood might be poked around in. Finally, there is a ground search centered around the hearth areas of the site. If coverage of these areas fails to turn up the item, the men generally abandon the search, assuming that someone not present has the item and will return it to the owner at a later date. Importantly, during the search there is a moving around of items already present, and almost always some items are picked up to be "recycled" for other purposes. Lost items are "rediscovered" at this time.

Table 21.5 tabulates the items observed on the site and the frequency with which various items were manipulated so that they remained unattended on the site. This does not mean that these items necessarily became part of the archaeological record, for many of them may have been repositioned or removed from the site later. This difference is indicated by the comparison between the items actually inventoried "archaeologically" on the site and the frequency with which items were "positioned" within the site.

Several important facts are illustrated in Table 21.5. There are major differences between the inventories of items dropped, tossed, and dumped. For instance, marrow bone splinters and chips, shell casing, and rib tablets were the items most commonly dropped, while articulator ends of marrow bones, pop cans, and sardine cans were the items most commonly tossed. Dumping exclusively consisted of coffee grounds and rib tablets. On the other hand, many items were rested or placed on the site but never or only rarely did these become part of the archaeological record. Referring the

TABLE 21.5

Comparative Inventories for Items Observed Ethnographically and Archaeologically—Mask Site

Behaviorally observed items		Disposal Modes					Archaeological observations Inventory of site	
Item Observed	Number	Dropped	Tossed	Rested	Placed	Dumped	June 7, 1971	1st week of June 1972
Bullets	(75)[a]	(25)[a]	0	(50)[a]	0	0	123	61 (shells)
Skinning knife	18	0	0	4	1	0	0	0
Rifle	17	0	0	31	0	0	0	0
Bag of sugar	2	0	0	9	6	0	3	1
Meat bones	11							
Ribs	10	(35)	9	4	0	(12)[b]	150	(49)[b]
Scapula	1	0	1	0	0	0	2	2
Marrow bones	8							
Splinters	(60)[a]	90%	10%	0	0	0		85
Chips	(120)[a]	100%	0%	0	0	0	284	223
Ends	16	1	15	2	0	0		26
Pop cans	7	0	7	3	4	0	8	12
Snowmobiles	7	0	0	0	7	0	0	0
Cigarette lighters	7	0	0	3	0	0	0	0
Cups	6	0	0	4	9	0	7	6
Sleds	5	0	0	0	5	0	0	0
Skins	5	0	0	0	5	0	0	1
Deck of cards	3	0	0	8	1	0	1	1
Sardine cans	5	0	5	2	0	0	8	7
Dog packs	3	0	0	3	0	0	0	0
Metal files	3	0	0	6	1	0	1	1
Anvils	5	0	0	0	5	0	3	5
Coffee cans	2	0	1	4	1	0	1	1
Binoculars	2	0	0	6	0	0	0	0
Coffee pot	1	0	0	7	1	(2)[c]	1	1
Mask molds	1	0	0	1	0	0	0	0
Length of rope	1	0	0	1	0	0	2	0
Pop can tabs	204	25	30		42		9	12
Can of hash							0	1
Funnel							0	1
Pair of gloves							1	1
Hone							1	1
Kitchen knife							1	0
Spoon							2	
File							1	
Milk can							1	
Instant coffee bottle							1	
Bag of coffee							11	
Soap dish							1	
Wolf trap							1	
Wool glove							2	
Canvas							3	
Rope fragments							2	

Note: Numbers in italic and underscored indicate items that would have been removed when site was abandoned.

a Estimate of number.

b Fragments.

c Grounds only.

"disposal modes" recognized here to those recognized by Schiffer (1976a: 30–33), both dropping and tossing would result in "primary refuse." Similarly, dumping as it was observed on the Mask site would also result in primary refuse in spite of the fact that Schiffer generally equates dumping with the generation of secondary refuse (see Schiffer 1976a:30). Dumping, as on the Mask site and in other contexts, consists of the disposal of multiple aggregated elements during food processing and/or food preparation activites. Dumping may consist of the disposal of the aggregate immediately adjacent to the locus of use. This is quite different from the situation where aggregates are accumulated during the course of "cleaning up" and removed from the location of primary deposition to a "special area" or specific dumping area. The latter activity was not observed on the Mask site.

As in the previous sections it is hoped that the reader can appreciate the effect that changes in the relationships between item classes and modes of disposal may have on the final form of the archaeological record. For instance, I have described elsewhere (Binford 1978b) the general pattern of disposition of bone elements during the course of a meal within an Eskimo house. Items that are commonly tossed or dropped on the Mask site, such as articulator ends and bone splinters, are most often "placed" in small piles along the edges of hearth rocks, around the stove, or on the edge of serving dishes during eating and talking episodes within an Eskimo house. This behavior is in anticipation of the women of the house "cleaning up" after the meal, accumulating articulator ends in a cache for later processing into bone grease and "dumping" bone splinters in special dump areas. In this example we can see that there may well be very different disposal modes associated with the same item in different site or social contexts.

So far I have discussed 3 basic behavioral categories relative to the "systemic" context (Schiffer 1976a) of the Mask site. Hopefully, I have demonstrated that a location, the actual spatial locus of a site, may be selected relative to criteria for optimizing conditions for a single task. In the case of the Mask site this task was the monitoring of a large area for game movements. The activities conducted within the site were all secondary accommodations to the situational integration of spring straggler hunting at the Mask site into the overall strategy of spring hunting. If migration hunting has been very successful and herds were more mixed than normal, straggler hunting at the Mask site will be conducted by only the most unsuccessful hunters, group sizes will be small compared to the data reported here and activities conducted there while waiting for game will be conditioned by size and length-of-stay considerations.

Similarly, the organization of the technology is at least partially conditioned by the understood or anticipated relationship of the location to use intensity and duration, as well as its actual location relative to other sites in use at the time. For instance, preparation of meals was never observed on the Mask site, because it is located less than a mile from the main village of Anaktuvuk. The only eating observed could best be described as snacking. Only bone marrow and items specifically introduced to contribute to the "picnic" atmosphere of eating (cans of sardines are a good example) were consumed. Meat per se was never cooked, and techniques of boiling and roasting meat were never employed on the site during the periods of controlled observation.

Similarly, the form and numbers of artifactual items that were considered "furnishings" on the site could be expected to vary with the anticipated modal group sizes and anticipated intensity of use. In the example that I offered regarding remote sites, I suggested that gear present on the Mask site as furnishings would be part of personal gear at such a remote location.

Finally, I described the disposal modes observed on the Mask site and pointed out that there was a regular set of relationships between the form and size of items and the modes of disposal. It was further argued that *in other contexts* different disposal modes might well be employed for identical items.

All of the three behavioral dimensions, activity structure, technological organization, and disposal modes interact and contribute to the facts of *site structure,* or the patterning recognizable in the static disposition of cultural features and items at a location.

Organization of Space

Several types of behavioral data were collected during observations on the Mask site. Attempts were made to observe the position of men on the site during the performance of different activities. In addition, I measured the placement of men relative to one another and to basic facilities on the site during the performance of different activities.

The core area of the site is between 3 relatively large glacial boulders. Among these boulders were 5 hearths. Figure 21.3 shows the relationship between the disposition of hearths and the placement of boulders. I never observed all 5 hearths in use at the same time; in fact, I never saw more than 2 in simultaneous use, and that was rare. The differential use of the hearths is basically related to wind direction. When the prevailing winds are from the north, hearths B and E were primarily used; winds blowing from the south prompted the preferential use of hearths A, C, and sometimes D. Prevailing winds from the north tended to carry scent to animals approaching from the south, so large groups of men were never observed at the site when winds were from the north. South winds carried scent away from approaching animals, and more men tended to be in the hunting stand under these conditions. For these reasons hearths A and C were the most commonly used.

I actually measured the placement of men and found that for a sample of 35 men seated in groups of 3 or 4, the mean distance from the left kneecap to the ember edge of the fire was 62 ± 6.8 cm. The mean distance between left and right knees of men seated next to one another was 33 ± 4 cm. When men were seated in groups of 4 they tended to move back from the fire a little to make room if an additional member of the group arrived. Under these conditions I measured 4 groups of 5 (20 measurements) and found the mean distance from the left knee to the ember edge of the fire to be 71 ± 8.2 cm and the mean distance between left and right knees of adjacent men to be 24 ± 3 cm. Figure 22.4 illustrates the mean sitting pattern for groups of 3 men and of 4 men around a fire on the Mask site.

The first thing to be noted is that there is always a vacant side of the hearth, depending upon wind direction. Such a distribution around a hearth, that is, with

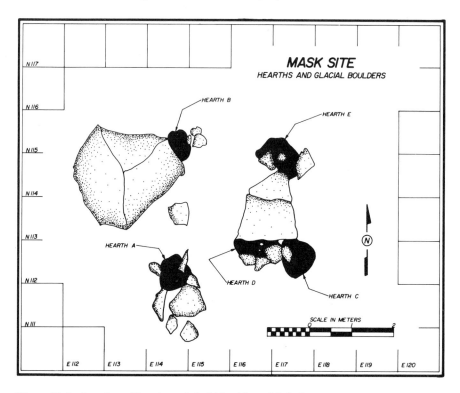

Figure 21.3   Location of hearths and glacial boulders—Mask site.

a side of relatively dense debris and an opposite, low-density side, has frequently been interpreted as deriving from the organization of space within a house; the low-density side is seen as representing the sleeping area (see Leroi-Gourhan and Brezillon 1972) and the high-density side as the area of domestic activity—eating and food preparation. That such a distribution may in fact arise is shown by Yellen (1977). In his case, the low-density side of the hearth relates to the area adjacent to the sheltered sleeping area (Yellen 1977). I have also observed the low/high density pattern of debris around internal hearths, particularly in the case of the Palangana site (see Binford 1978b).

On the Mask site the "seating plan" conditions the dispersion of items that were dropped versus those that were tossed. I did not measure the position of dropped items relative to seated persons. However, I noted that dropped items came to rest within 20 cm of the front of a man sitting cross-legged. They dropped between his legs or fell to the side of his legs within about 20 cm. This means that in the seating plan shown in Figure 21.4 we may add the probable location of the "drop zone," the area within which men seated around the hearth would drop items. While observing on the Mask site, I measured the distance between the knee of the seated man and the resting place of tossed items. Such items were invariably tossed "over the shoulder" and the mean distance from the kneecap of a seated man for tossed articulator ends ($N = 7$) of bones was 1.14 m with a standard deviation of 24 cm. For sardine and

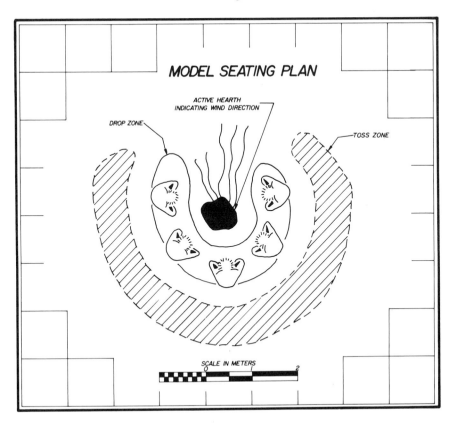

Figure 21.4   Model seating plan.

pop cans ($N = 6$) the mean distance was 2.54 m with a standard deviation of 29 cm. When I asked informants why they tossed cans more vigorously they simply said they were unsightly and got in the way more than bones! Given this information we may add to our model seating plan an additional zone of anticipated debris—tossed items. Figure 21.4 illustrates the anticipated distributional patterning for items disposed of by individuals seated around an outside hearth.

The basic organization or seating plan for individuals around a hearth may not change from a typical "outside" situation as observed on the Mask site to an "inside" situation where there is a hearth in the center of a house. We might anticipate that the seating plan relative to the hearth might be essentially identical, and we may even anticipate a vacant side to the distribution where the sleeping area is adjacent to the hearth. A drop zone could be expected where stone working or marrow cracking was going on adjacent to the hearth. However, in the Nunamiut case we would never observe a "toss zone" around a seated group inside a house. (See Binford 1978b: Chapter 4, for a description of food consumption within the house.) Items normally tossed outside would be *placed* along the hearth stones or along the edges of serving platters so that the woman of the house could easily clean up the large bone debris from meals consumed inside.

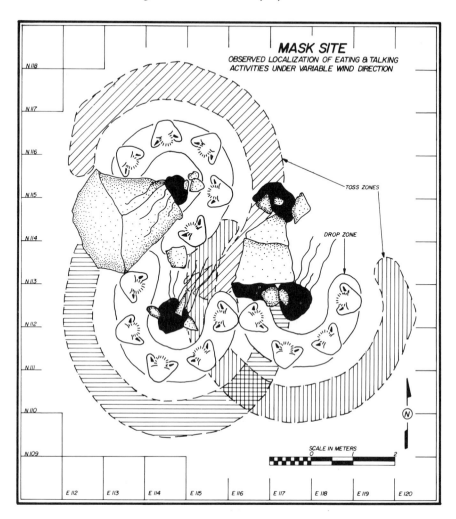

Figure 21.5 Observed localization of eating and talking activities under variable wind directions—Mask site.

Men seated around the hearths of the Mask site in some "size" phase of the pattern illustrated in Figure 21.5 were observed to be engaged in eating and conversation most commonly. Table 21.6 summarizes the proportion of man-hours of activities, as tabulated in Table 21.2, which was spatially organized as men seated in a circular fashion around the hearth.

What is very clear is that the particular pattern of space use characterized as a semicircle of men seated around a hearth was almost exclusively related to the activity of eating and talking. All other activities were characteristically conducted in a different place and in a different pattern of association man-to-man and man-to-facility. *In short, there were different areas associated with the performance of different activities.* The single activity exhibiting the most overlap with eating and talking, in terms of where

TABLE 21.6

Proportion of Man-Hours of Activities Performed by Men Seated in Circular Fashion around the Hearth

Date	Game watching		Off site hunting		Eating + talking		Target shooting		Playing cards		Crafts		Sleep	
	Cir.[a]	Oth.[b]	Cir.	Oth.	Cir.	Oth.	Cir.	Oth.	Cir.	Oth.	Cir.	Oth.	Cir.	Oth.
June 4	0	100%	0	100%	93%	7%	—	—	17%	83%	29%	71%	—	—
June 4	0	100%	0	100%	95%	5%	0	00%	0	100%	50%	50%	—	—
June 5	0	100%	0	100%	100%	0	0	100%	0	100%	17%	83%	0	100%
June 5	0	100%	0	100%	90%	10%	0	100%	11%	89%	0	100%	0	100%
June 6	0	100%	0	100%	95%	5%	0	100%	—	—	36%	64%	—	—
June 6	0	100%	0	100%	100%	0	22%	78%	—	—	25%	75%	—	—
Mask site	0	100%	0	100%	95.5%	4.5%	4.4%	95.6%	7%	93%	26.2%	73.8%	0	100%

[a] Circle
[b] Other

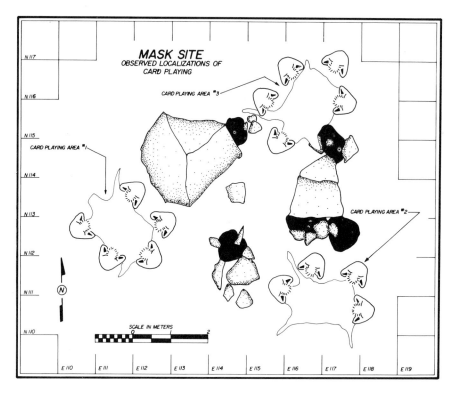

Figure 21.6 Observed localizations of card playing—Mask site.

it was performed, was craft activity. It is shown the 26.2% of the time during which individuals were engaged in craft activity was spent within the circle of men seated around the fire. The actual location and seating plan of men engaged in activities other than eating and talking is best illustrated graphically. Figure 21.6 illustrates the location of card-playing activities. The numbering of the areas roughly coincides with the preferential bias for placement. Area 1 would certainly be preferred for several reasons: (a) Because card playing is an activity of large group sizes, it is almost certain the winds would be blowing from the south and therefore smoke from hearth A (the most likely to be in use) would be drifting in the direction of playing area 3, making it less desirable; (b) Players can see the area to the south of the site from playing area 1, but this is almost impossible from playing area 3 and more difficult from playing area 2 because of slope; (c) The players are less likely to be interrupted by men seeking access to hearths than would be the case in areas 2 and 3.

Craft activities are occasionally conducted by men seated in an "eating and talking" semicircle. Figure 21.7 illustrates the seated postion of all men observed engaged in craft activities. It is clear that the major area independent of men seated in hearth circles is along the large rock where card playing area 1 is also located (craft area 1 in Figure 21.7). An additional craft area is along the east side of the smaller glacial boulder just north of hearth C (designated area 2 in Figure 21.7).

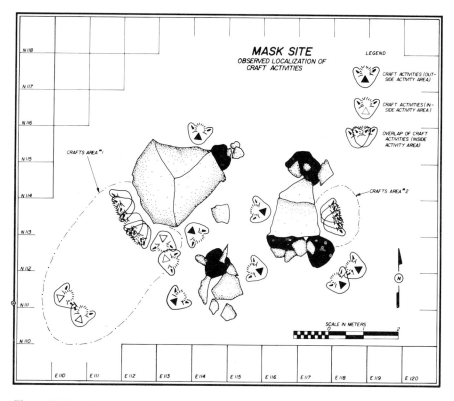

Figure 21.7   Observed localization of craft activities—Mask site.

Less commonly performed activities are perhaps best illustrated by internal site arrangements observed during different occupational episodes. Figure 21.8 illustrates the arrangement of men on the Mask site at the time of my arrival on the site during the afternoon of June 5. Six men were present: 1 sleeping, 1 engaged in carving an antler handle for a "woman's knife" (ulu), 1 watching for game, and 3 engaged in eating and conversation. The wind was from the south, and only hearth A was in use. The sleeping man was in an area otherwise used as an eating and talking area when hearth B is in use. The man working on the antler was in craft area 2, and the man watching for game was seated in the same area where card playing or crafts were also commonly located.

Figure 21.9 illustrates the disposition of men on the Mask site at a point in the early evening of June 6th. Two men are eating and talking around hearth B (the wind was from the north), 1 man was sewing up a rip in a pair of caribou skin socks, and 2 men were target shooting. Target shooting was being conducted from the same area used as a card playing area, a craft area, and an area where men sometimes sit to watch for game. The "craftsman" was sitting on the opposite side of the glacial boulder from craft area 2.

To further illustrate the point that the internal organization of the site is situa-

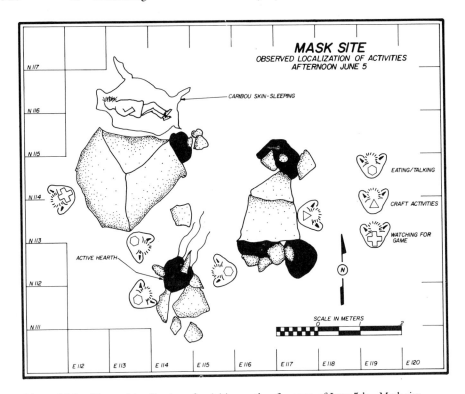

Figure 21.8 Observed localization of activities on the afternoon of June 5th—Mask site.

tionally shifting, Figure 21.10 illustrates the location of men observed at noon on June 5. Three men were eating and talking around hearth A, 1 man was carving the handle of a walking stick while seated next to hearth B which was active, and 4 men were playing cards around a caribou skin in card playing area 1. Two major points are to be emphasized here.

1. At any one time on the site the different activities conducted simultaneously are independently organized in space (see Figures 21.8–21.10).
2. Over time, there is a statistical tendency for given activities to be repeatedly localized in the same places, although these loci would not be reserved exclusively for a single activity.

In order to illustrate these facts, I have organized the observational data from the Mask site in 2 ways. First, based on the cumulative activity maps such as Figures 21.6 and 21.7, I have combined the spatial data from all my episodal maps into a composite map which permits the recognition of 4 basic use areas on the site (Figure 21.11). In this sense a "use area" is a location where activities tend to be localized such that they do not overlap spatially with adjacent areas. The 4 such areas recognized on the Mask site are designated W, X, Y, and Z in Figure 21.11. Returning to my tabulation schedules, I was able to tabulate the man-hours of the various activities

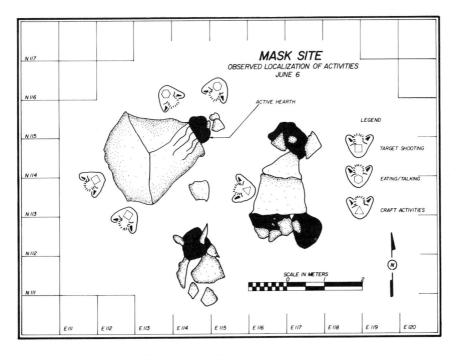

Figure 21.9 Observed localization of activities on June 6th—Mask site.

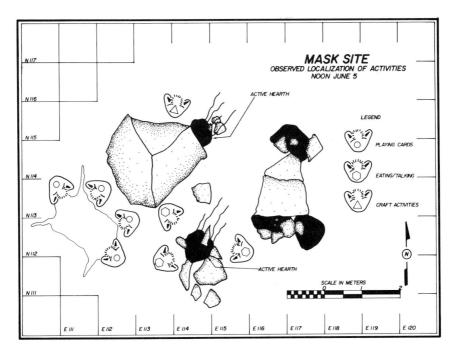

Figure 21.10 Observed localization of activities at noon on June 5th—Mask site.

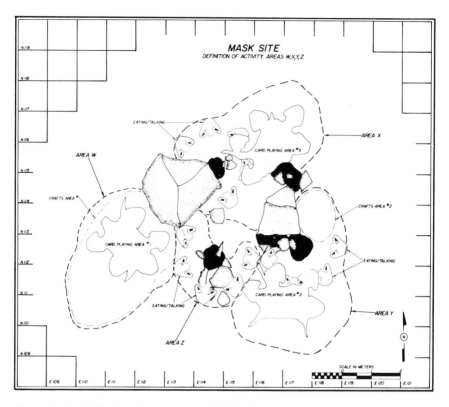

Figure 21.11   Definition of activity areas W, X, Y, Z—Mask site.

which were conducted in each of the 4 recognized "use areas" on the site. Table 21.7 summarizes these data.

Even a casual examination of Table 21.7 illustrates nicely 2 very basic points.

1. The intensity of use was not evenly distributed among the recognized use areas.
2. The various activities were not evenly distributed among the several areas.

The man-hours spent in game watching were 100% localized in area W. The hours spent sleeping were 100% localized in area X. Of the total man-hours spent in eating and talking 80% were localized in area Z. Target shooting man-hours were 95% localized in area W, while 58% of the card playing hours were localized in area Y and 56% of the hours spent in crafts were localized in area W. Quite clearly there is a basis in "reality" for seeking patterns in the archaeological remains which derive from spatial segregation of activities. This is true in spite of the fact that a casual observer seeing the pattern of site use as illustrated in Figures 21.8–21.10 might conclude that there were no special "activity areas" but only a "generalized use of activity space." Such an impressionistic conclusion was reached by John Yellen from his Bushman experience.

TABLE 21.7

Man-Hours of Activity Localized in Different Areas

Areas	Hearths	Game watch	Eating + talking	Target shoot	Playing cards	Crafts	Sleep	Total
W	none	3.0(12%)		10.5(42%)	4.0(16%)	7.25(30%)		24.75
X	B-E		3.75(34%)		2.5(32%)	0.75(7%)	3.0(27%)	10.0
Y	C-D		6.25(32%)	0.5(3%)	9.0(47%)	3.5(18%)		19.25
Z	A		39.25(96%)			1.5(4%)		40.75
Total		3.0 [a]	49.25	11.0	15.5	13.0	3.0	94.75

[a] 28.5 hours of game watching done from boulder area just south of this area, approximately 17 m south of hearth A.

I have suggested that it is unfounded to assume that activities are spatially segregated or arranged by type within a single camp. Most tasks may be carried out in more than one place and in more than one social context; and, conversely, in any single area, one can find the remains of many activities all jumbled together. Unfortunately, many archaeological analyses are based on just such an erroneous assumption, and their resulting conclusions must be called into question (1977:134).

In another place Yellen states:

. . . one may evaluate models archaeologists often use to examine activity patterning within an excavated site. What underlies many of these is the a priori assumption that most activities are performed by special-purpose, job-specific groups, and that individual tasks are spatially segregated from one another. . . . the most misleading aspect of this statement lies not in its overly simplistic nature but its implication that the primary nature of an activity itself rather than its social context uniquely determines the location at which it will be performed . . . (1977:97).

These critical, and to my ears pompous, statements are simply wrong and based on no systematic observation that I can detect. I think that most would agree that it is physically impossible for 2 independent entities to occupy identical spaces simultaneously. Therefore it is impossible for 2 persons to occupy identical spaces simultaneously. Insofar as 2 persons are engaged in different activities simultaneously *they must* be localized in different places. This is clearly illustrated in Figures 21.8–21.10 from the Mask site. As it is impossible to imagine different persons occupying the same space, so it is impossible to imagine activities carried out simultaneously by different persons occurring in the identical space.

Given these conditions, the degree that activities will be spatially separated at any one time can be expected to vary with the number of different activities simultaneously performed by different persons.

The interesting question that arises from this has to do with the degree to which similar activities will be conducted in the same places at different times. Stated another way, we may ask what will be the degree of redundancy in the organization of activities in space? I have illustrated that on the Mask site, Yellen's generalization is correct (see Figures 21.8–21.10), namely:

Most tasks may be carried out in more than one place and in more than one social context and conversely in any single area one can find the remains of many activities all jumbled together (1977:134).

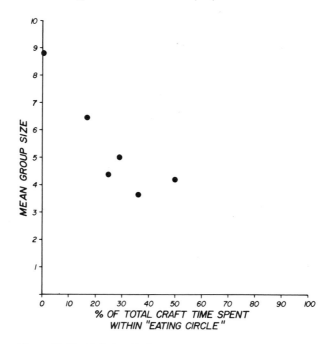

Figure 21.12   Relationship between mean group size and the percent of total craft time spent within an "eating circle."

I have also illustrated that the conclusion drawn from this observation is false. Table 21.7 illustrates that it is not "unfounded to expect activities to be spatially segregated or arranged by type within a single camp." Table 21.7 illustrates nicely that there are meaningful structural facts of spatial association between activities and different places on the Mask site. What conditions these facts? Yellen suggests that the primary conditioner is the social context of performance rather than "the primary nature of the activity itself" (1977:97). Such a generalization makes no sense, and it is contradicted by Yellen himself when discussing head roasting and skin preparation (see Yellen 1977:92, 145). The point is that some activities interfere with others. Similarly, some activities require more or less space, more or less time to completion, and more or less participants. In addition, activities vary in the amount of debris or pollution (noise or odor) produced during the course of performance. They further vary in the relative degree to which the debris or pollution is noxious and thus inhibits or disrupts the performance of other activities. We see very few dances performed inside of active hearths; rarely does a person assemble a complicated craft item in the midst of a group of playing children.

An excellent illustration of this point is provided by the relationship between the modal group size present on the site and the percentage of total activity time spent in craft activities executed in the hearth-centered circles of men. Figure 21.12 illustrates this relationship for the 6 observation periods documented on the Mask site. It is very clear that as group size increases, the percentage of the total activity time spent in craft activities localized in the "eating and talking areas" decreases. This is

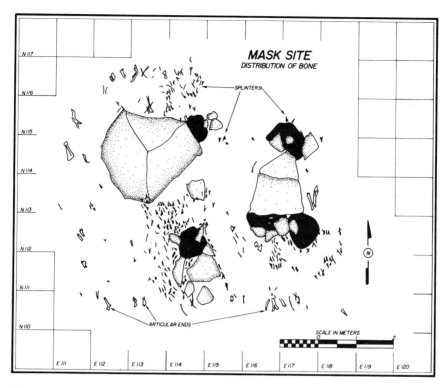

Figure 21.13 Distribution of bone—Mask site.

not to be understood as changes in response to "social context" but simply as a response to the fact that as more men are present and engaged in talking and eating, there is more noise, and craftsmen are less able to concentrate. Noise and distractive activity are cited by the Eskimo as the reasons for abandoning craft-related tasks when many men are present. If they must be performed, a special location away from the talking and eating area is sought by craftsmen, I expect activity differentiation in space to relate to both the anticipated future use of the location and the character of activity incompatibilities. We can build a theory of space use, and we can understand spatial patterning without recourse to vague notions of "social context."

The Archaeological Consequences of All This Behavior

I have tried to illustrate that there were at least 4 basic dimensions of potentially independent variability that interact to contribute to the archaeological facts generated at the Mask site. Figure 21.13 illustrates the observed distribution of animal bone fragments; Figure 21.14 illustrates distribution of wood shavings and shell casings; and Figure 21.15 illustrates the distribution of "artifacts" as observed on the Mask site. It seems to me that little comment is needed here, since most of the facts of the archaeological distribution could be anticipated from the behavioral discussion. Given

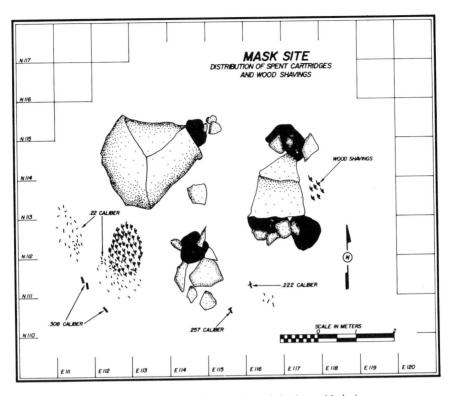

Figure 21.14 Distribution of spent cartridges and wood shavings—Mask site.

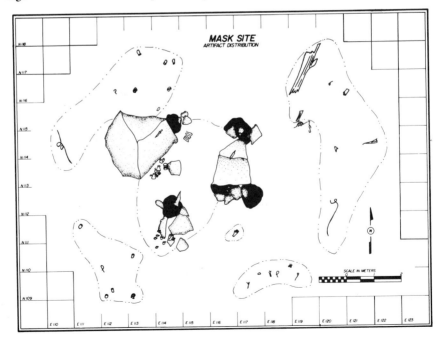

Figure 21.15 Artifact distribution—Mask site.

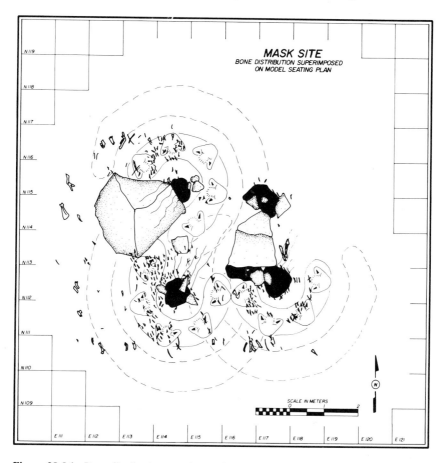

Figure 21.16   Bone distribution superimposed on model seating plan.

the level at which the technology is "curated" by the Nunamiut the archaeological remains at the Mask site relate primarily to the activities of eating and talking. The consequences of the disposal modes is well represented in the site structure. Bone splinters and chips cluster in the "drop zone" and articulator ends cluster in the "toss zone" of a seating plan with men seated in a semicircle around the hearth (see Figure 21.16). The distribution of shell casing faithfully betrays the locations of target shooting, while wood shavings similarly suggest the primary locations of craft activity.

The "artifact" distribution provides us with our only surprise. The items that were actually disposed of on the site—pop cans, sardine cans, segments of rope, worn gloves, etc.—all exhibit a clustered and peripheral distribution to the site as a whole, not just to the areas in which the items were used. In fact there are clusters of such items adjacent to areas that were used least (see Figure 21.17). This pattern implies a biased disposal of items into low use-intensity areas which, of course, presupposes an overall understanding of the use patterns of the site as a whole as opposed to the particular pattern that might be present at the time of disposal acts. Stated another way, disposal patterns result in a distribution that is essentially inversely related to the patterns of use intensity.

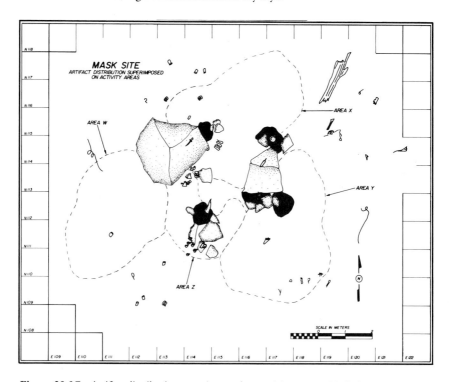

Figure 21.17   Artifact distribution superimposed on activity areas—Mask site.

The consequences of this for different archaeological patterns is most provocative. For instance, let us imagine the Mask site under changed conditions; no marrow bones are being eaten, only dried meat which would contribute no immediate byproduct to the archaeological record. In short, all the chips and splinters seen in Figure 21.13 would be absent. Now the overall structure of the archaeological site would appear quite different; it would consist of an essentially circular "high-density zone" with a central low-density area lacking in any major items except those that might remain as de facto garbage. Under these conditions "high-density zones" would refer almost exclusively to disposal areas and not activity areas. In this case, then, demonstrable associations between items in disposal areas would be more likely to reflect size sorting and would be as likely to reflect relative frequency relations between *activities* as to demonstrate a relationship among items used within given activities. Such a situation suggests that patterns of artifact association from different areas of a site may well refer to different "formation processes" relative to different areas of a site and not necessarily to different areas of primary use on a site. There are strong implications for the analysis of spatial distributions using arbitrary grid units as the basis for summarizing samples. Perhaps techniques of internal stratification based on demonstrable structural properties of a scatter plot are more realistic analytical approaches.

Conclusions

Long ago I questioned (Binford and Binford 1966) the position that variability in the content and internal plan of sites was referable to the single variable "culture." I argued that variability in assemblage composition, site location, and internal site plans could be expected to vary with the activities in which men were engaged. I further suggested that activities were likely to be responsive to seasonal variations, giving rise to archaeological variability which would scale with seasonal monitors. At the same time I suggested that activities could be logically differentiated into extractive and maintenance tasks. I also speculated that it was likely that tasks differing in such a fundamental way would be conducted in identical locations so that some between-site variability may well be referable to differences in site function. Recent investigations into the relationship between site contents and seasonality have been the most discussed, but the complicating problem of site function has not been faced squarely (see for instance Jochim 1976). This has been particularly true in European studies of Paleolithic remains. It appears that almost every investigator concludes that his site was a residential location (see Biette 1977; Delumley 1969; Leroi-Gourhan and Brezillon 1966, 1972; Poplin 1976) and frequently boasts of the former presence of a shelter or house, in spite of there being little if any convincing evidence present.

The most detailed ethnoarchaeological study yet to appear has been that of Yellen (1977), who has strongly criticized these arguments. Yellen suggests that extractive locations, while present among the !Kung, would leave no visible archaeological remains. He further suggests that there are no seasonal correlates to the execution of craft or manufacturing activities. He goes on to argue that although seasonal variability in subsistence activities is documented, since there is also a correlation between season and duration of camps, only large camps would remain archaeologically visible. This situation would render observation of seasonally related variability unlikely in the !Kung case. The only conclusion which one may draw from Yellen's assertions is there are no recognizable differences among !Kung sites that are not simply accommodated by a graded series of variability largely scaling with size of assemblage or site. As Yellen says:

> Any site may be conceived of as a spatial locus containing a sample of the society's total repertoire of activities. . . . I suggest a single scale, ranging from simple to complex, may prove more useful than a typological approach. . . . (1977:135).

The impliction is that if one demonstrates clear and distinct assemblage *types*, arguments for functional variation within systems are inappropriate. The Mask site experience points to the "reality" of functionally specific sites. It indicates sources of variability that may operate independently or in various combinations to result in significant between-site patterns of formal and structural variability within a single system.

I conclude from the experiences at the Mask site that we may expect systems to exist where there are major distinctions between residential and special-purpose sites. I therefore suggest that we must seek methods to permit us to distinguish these functional differences from those which refer to independent systems of organization.

Some of the interesting aspects of "special-purpose" sites are described here. I conclude that we must have means for recognizing such sites and disagree with Yellen's (1977:83) conclusion that a "continuum of variability" is most likely among hunter and gatherer sites.

I also conclude from the experiences reported here that we may anticipate meaningful internal differentiations between items used in different activities even in sites where there are "generalized work areas." In addition, there are likely to be further meaningful differences between disposal modes associated with different items used in similar or different activities, and meaningful associations can be reasonably sought among items by virtue of their spatial positioning. This conclusion is in direct opposition to the conclusions reached by Yellen from his Bushman experiences. He concludes that such expectations are unrealistic: "A corollary of this simple area-activity assumption is that associated remains are functionally related. . . . !Kung data makes this a priori model untenable" (1977:134).

How can 2 people reach such opposite conclusions? In my opinion the major contributor is not the very real differences between Eskimos and Bushman but extreme differences between myself and Yellen in what we consider to be appropriate uses of empirical materials and the role of our thoughts versus our observations. Given such a conflict I caution the reader to read what I have to say and seek an appreciation for what is attempted rather than assuming that he knows what I am doing and why.

This study is an exercise in theory building. The work reported is the justification or a warrant for thinking about some of the ideas that came to me during the course of the fieldwork and the analysis. The ideas are my inventions; they are not in any way summaries of empirical experience. *They are not empirical generalizations. I am not offering inductive arguments or arguments from ethnographic analogy.* I am not saying that all men will conduct the same activities in hunting camps. I am not saying that all men will play cards in sites with glacial boulders in them. I am not saying that all target shooting was normally conducted away from the group because of the noise of rifle fire! I am saying that my study has prompted my imagination. I have been able to imagine patterns of interaction among variables which could result in different patterning in the archaeological record. In turn, I have been able to imagine different patterns in the archaeological record that could be meaningfully interpreted if my imagined understanding of "causal" interaction is correct.

> The transition from data to theory requires creative imagination. Scientific hypothesis and theories are not derived from observed facts, but are invented in order to account for them (Hempel 1966:15).

Basic differences between Yellen and myself in our use of ethnographic experiences are perhaps best illustrated through a criticism of John Yellen's recent work. He has generalized from his data that there is a relationship between the number of occupants of a site and the size of the nuclear area of artifactual scatter, and similarly that there is a regular relationship between the length of occupation and the extension of the artifactual scatter—the area of the "absolute limits of scatter." For instance, Yellen states:

Quantitive analysis indicates that the size of the hut circle, or inner ring, is closely and directly related to group size, while the outer ring, which encompasses special activity areas, reflects length of occupation. On this basis I have offered predictive equations for group size and length of occupation and put them in archaeologically useful form. This constitutes an original piece of research and is perhaps the single most important contribution of this book (1977:134).

Yellen *has observed that there is a relationship between metrical attributes of sites* and the numbers of occupants and the duration of occupancy. He has gone to great lengths to demonstrate that such a relationship exists within the domain of his ethnographic experience. *This is a description of the way the world is or appears.* It is not an explanation as he suggest (Yellen 1977:101). Only in seeking an answer to the question, "Why does such a relationship hold in Yellen's Bushman experience?" does one seek an explanation or understanding of the world. Only with an answer to the explanatory question could we anticipate when the world will differ from Yellen's experience. Yellen ignores this interesting problem and apparently assumes that the number of people and the duration of their stay "causes" the patterning in size among his sites. If this were the case, then the descriptive equations which Yellen presents should allow us to give meaning in a reliable manner to facts of site size when they are observed archaeologically. Clearly this is what Yellen has in mind: "To establish predictive relationships of this nature can provide a valuable tool in archaeological interpretation" (1977:100).

When one has demonstrated an empirical condition, the assumption needed in any warranted projection of the observed condition to situations not previously investigated is simply that there is a causal identity between the 2 situations—that the same causes are active in both situations and that the dynamics of causation are the same. Stated another way, the world stays the way it was, and what we have seen is all there is. We don't have to understand what we have seen, we simply have to believe that what we have seen is "representative of the world in general" and that this world will remain unchanged.

I suggest that theory building is the progressive delineation of the "other things" that must be equal for a given relationship to hold true. In Yellen's case we can reasonably ask what some of those "other things" might be. For instance, according to my calculations of the Mask site there are 73.8 m² in the "ALS" as defined by Yellen (1977:1103), and there are 12.7 m² within the "LMS" limits of most scatter as defined by Yellen (1977:103). Using the formulas given by Yellen, I would draw the following interpretive conclusions from the archaeological remains on the Mask site: (a) It was occupied for 7.89 days (in fact the archaeological scatter measured was accumulated over a period of 21 days); (b) it was occupied by 2.03 nuclear families (no nuclear families were ever present on the site); and (c) the number of occupants present was 9.67 (the mean group size present at any one time was observed to be 5.49 men, but the total number of different men using the location was 34). The latter figure is equivalent, I think, to the way Yellen counted occupants. Clearly some "other things" are causing the Nunamiut case to be so very different from the Bushman cases. For Yellen, my data from the Mask site serve as an empirical case to the contrary, an example of the "spoiler" approach. They exemplify Yellen's suggestion

(1977:113) that, "balloons may be punctured by a single pin." For Yellen, an inductivist, this perception is consistent with his view of investigations, since he seeks patterned regularities or empirical generalizations as an end product of his work. For empiricists working inductively there are only 2 basic conclusions to be drawn from investigating the world: (a) the cases are similar in some way, justifying generalizations or the recognition of a "regularity," or (b) they are different, justifying the definition of a new category or taxonomic unit for subsuming the observed case and any other similar ones discovered in the future. For me, however, the same situation—my data versus Yellen's—simply points to an interesting set of differences between Eskimo and Bushman sites *which are in need of explanation*. The challenge is to build a sufficient body of theory to explain the differences between the cases. Yellen argues that this may be done empirically:

> In an ethnographic situation where the "causes" (answers) are known from the start, one can look at the "effects"—in this case observable remains—and see what techniques offer the best route from the one to the other. . . .
> This is most obvious . . . where a priori knowledge permitted me to devise and evaluate a number of techniques for estimating group size and length of occupation from debris (1977:132).

If Yellen's belief in his ability to see causes directly was justified, I suppose I would have to conclude that all ethnographic work must result in causal arguments which are necessarily accurate, since the causes "spoke for themselves." Ethnography would be a field based on revealed truths in no need of scientific methods since problems of verification and confirmation would be irrelevant! In the light of this "faith" on Yellen's part can we not reasonably ask why his causes did not work in the Eskimo case? The only answer that I can reasonably give is that he never isolated a cause.

Let us examine the situation. Yellen equates numbers of persons and lengths of stay with the size of the distribution of discarded materials. For such a 1-to-1 relationship to exist between numbers of man-days of occupation and scales of debris scatter, we must assume that there is a constant relationship between the consumer demands of individuals and the production rate of debris. Is such a "constant" relationship realistic? I must answer, "no." I have experienced situations where large quantities of foods are procured in a very limited period of time, and then processed for storage. The debris and the size of the area used in processing would bear some relationship to the quantity of materials obtained. For instance, the number of caribou killed in a single day has little if any relationship to the number of men present and the duration of stay. I have also experienced the reverse situation, where consumption of foods was primarily from dry meat stores. Little if any debris results from such a consumption pattern (see Binford 1978b: Chapter 6). What I am suggesting is that the *variables* which interact to cause variations in density and extent of debris are input and entropy variables, not consumer variables directly as "seen" by Yellen.

Among the Bushman, subsistence is essentially a foraging strategy in which inputs of food are largely on a daily basis and proportional to the daily consumer demand. Under such conditions, there is a strong and proportional relationship at any given time between consumer demand and the quantity of input, hence Yellen's results.

(This ignores the problem of debris from other maintenance activities such as tool manufacture and repair, since Yellen argues that among the Bushman this is simply proportional to the length of stay.) This situation does not occur among the Eskimo, where there are seasonal and situational variations in the performance of craft activities. "Gearing up" is the best translation of an Eskimo word referring specifically to the intense craft activity that frequently precedes long expedition hunting trips, typically in summer to the tundra for calf skins or to the mountains for sheep. The constant rate at which food is introduced to the Bushman camps (given a daily foraging strategy) and at which craft activities are performed (as argued by Yellen 1977:82) insures a regular relationship between density and scale of debris scatter and number of man-hours of occupation. This assumes, of course, a fairly regular debris-to-activity ratio, that is, different kinds of consumption or craft activities generating essentially similar quantities of debris. This qualification is one that I find hard to accept as realistic, yet it must be met if Yellen's correlations are to stand. I am not attempting to solve all the problems associated with Yellen's observations versus my own. However, I hope that I have illustrated that Yellen has not "observed" cause, and that he has not been engaged in theory building. More importantly, I have argued that empirical generalizations, no matter how complicated (as, for example, Yellen's observations on site size and group size and occupational duration), are what we seek to understand, and only with understanding can we anticipate how observations will vary under changed conditions. The latter is, of course, what we mean by predictions. Our ability to anticipate variability in the world is in turn a measure of our understanding. I have tried to move in this direction with the Mask-site study.

The Mask site represents a site where activities conducted are "embedded" in another more basic schedule. None of the activities can be considered "primary" to the mission of the occupants. This means that the specifics of the activities will be largely conditioned by factors other than those which prompted the occupation of the site in the first place. I feel that such an "embedded" activity schedule may well be a common phenomenon among hunters and gatherers, who are logistically organized as opposed to foragers. At this point this is simply a hunch. I have demonstrated how at least 4 potentially independent dimensions could interact to result in changed compositon and internal spatial organizations. I have further suggested that these conditioning dimensions are situationally responsive and not simply "normative" or idealized patterns or designs for living. Finally, I have suggested that there are organizational facts to be discovered in distributional data regardless of the degree to which men may have conducted their activities in "generalized work spaces."

I have suggested that the degree to which activities are regularly conducted in different places is at least partially conditioned by the ways in which their execution interferes with other activities. I suggested that scheduling concerns and bulk properties of both items processed and debris produced would condition the degrees of functional specificity among activity areas on a site. These are hints, ideas to be explored in hopes of recognizing or inventing variables that could be used to explore causal relationships between activities and their organization in space. Progress can be made by seeking a processual understanding of the dynamics that produce different forms of archaeological patterning. It will not be achieved by trying to refine empirical generalizations, arguing that someone else is wrong because they have had different experiences, and fooling oneself into viewing empirical descriptions, no matter how complicated they may be, as explanations.

Acknowledgments

Financial support for the fieldwork reported here was provided by grants for the National Science Foundation. Funds from the Department of Anthropology, University of New Mexico, aided in analysis and the preparation of the manuscript. Special thanks are due to Dana Anderson and Tim Seaman, who prepared the illustrations. Lisa Edelhoff translated the text from my unique writing form to finished typescript. Johnny Rulland of Anaktuvuk guided me through this work. Jean-Philippe Rigaud, Peggy Schneider, and Patty Marchiando helped with the original mapping tasks in 1971. Advice on this manuscript was offered by J. Sabloff and L. Straus, and for this I am most grateful.

22

Evidence for Differences between Residential and Special-Purpose Sites

Evidence for Differences in Content Redundancy for Residential versus Special-Purpose Sites

I have described and analyzed approximately 42 archaeologically known locations that related to the pre-sedentary period of Nunamiut adaptation. In addition, I have described many faunal assemblages from the contemporary period. These are not in any way an accurate indication of the number of locations actually visited, or locations on which I participated in ongoing activities with the Eskimo. These locations are those chosen by me for recording in archaeological terms. Factors conditioning my choices were (a) relative development of postoccupational vegetation, (b) relative accuracy with which the location could be documented behaviorally, (c) estimates of the sample sizes of faunal material remaining on the site, and (d) my own logistics. The reported remains, therefore, do not represent an accurate sampling of the entire subsistence settlement system. For instance, there are 14 residential locations, 10 hunting camps, 16 hunting stands, and information from over 200 kill sites reported here. Do these frequencies in any way accurately reflect the actual frequencies with which such locations are generated by the Eskimo during an average year of the pre-sedentary period? Are these locations representative of all the types of locations archaeologically generated? I think the answer must be no to both questions. The normal pattern for groups of hunters or almost any other group traveling is to stop occasionally for rest and snacking. These locations are generally scattered and related to the pace of the traveling party on flat ground. On the other hand, in broken terrain, at river crossings, or in the mountains, such locations tend to be localized and regularly used. They often correspond to change of pace conditions. As an example, a commonly used path from the contemporary village runs north to the mouth of Kongumuvuk Valley, then west up the valley. One enters the valley at a deep V-shaped mouth, but only a few hundred meters farther into the valley there is a dramatic change in the gradient—so much so that along one arm of the stream there is a waterfall. Along the base of this steep grade are the remains of numerous fires, some scattered debris, and a few scattered bones. I have stopped here many times to rest, to eat a snack, and to warm myself beside a small fire before undertaking the much more difficult task of climbing several thousand feet in less than a mile. Such regularly used locations are common in the mountains and at river crossings. These locations generally yield archaeological evidence of having served this purpose over a very long period of time. I have not archaeologically investigated any of these. One reason for this is that the Eskimo still regularly use these sites and they were not overly enthusiastic about my excavating such places. For much the same reason, fish camps are not included in the list of described locations. Archaeological work, of course, is largely limited to the summer and fishing is largely a summer activity. I could not develop much interest among the Eskimo for tearing up a fish camp. In addition, I am completely lacking sites, other than residential, for the winter season. I had underestimated the time needed to obtain a seasonally sampled set of sites. The result was that, on the completion of the project as proposed to the granting agency, I had only looked at spring, summer, and fall locations. I had picked up information on the winter residential locations reported during seasons when the main emphasis was on nonwinter seasonal research. I also determined that in order to investigate the special-purpose locations used during winter I needed to have my own base camp near the forest. An attempt was made to obtain funding and an extension of the research permission for an additional season aimed at collecting the missing winter data. Unfortunately, I was unsuccessful, hence the very short winter chapter. I have, however, visited special-purpose winter locations, and I have even participated in activities in such locations. These experiences lead me to suspect still more variability and even more fascinating patterning in the archaeological record. For instance, there is a particular type of winter logistical location that is best described as a thawing-out site. Animals taken in traps are normally frozen at the time the trapper returns to recover his cache. One cannot skin a frozen animal. In many areas where traps are commonly set—for example, the high passes in the mountains through which furbearers must move in order to go from one valley to another—there are small caves and rockshelters. These have been used for years in winter as thawing-out sites. Here trappers take the bodies of the frozen animals and kindle fires to thaw the bodies sufficiently for skinning. These sites are characterized by substantial hearths, remains from meals (largely from introduced foods carried by the trapper), debris from tool and trap repair, and nearly complete and articulated skeletons of foxes, wolves, and wolverines. Certainly there are many other types of special-purpose locations regularly used by the Nunamiut that are not reported here.

One entire domain of interesting activities that the reader may not appreciate from simply reading about the archaeologically described locations includes the planning strategies that go on prior to an anticipated move, whether it be residential or logistical. In the course of planning a logistical operation there is always a discussion of the route. Anticipating the route permits some judgment to be exercised in selecting the gear needed to move out from the base of operations. The Eskimo know that in almost any logistical situation, the basic problem that they must *anticipate*, if they are to be successful, is simply how they are going to get their kills home.

One of the bulkiest pieces of equipment to transport is shelter. Almost every trip-planning session in which I participated was centered around the question, "Do we have to carry a tent?" Route planning frequently involved selecting a slightly deviating route between the base and the destination of the party in order to take advantage of available sheltering facilities, thus permitting the party to travel without portable shelter. The route would be planned with respect to known locations of abandoned winter houses, rockshelters, and cached sheltering material. Certainly, the role that rockshelters and caves play in the Eskimo system is *exclusively* as a natural shelter that, when proper planning is employed, permits a logistical party to travel without the added bulk of a portable shelter. I consider it a major tragedy that I did not document several caves known to me that were regularly used by the Nunamiut. Archaeologists, particularly those interested in the Paleolithic, tend to view caves and rockshelters as centers of operation. Such a use of these natural facilities is a joke for the Eskimo. When questioned about the potential of such natural facilities for use as "residential locations," they proceeded to cite a truly fascinating list of negative traits that rendered these places useless, in their eyes, as potential residential locations. In winter, they were damp. For the most part because of topography, they are distributed away from fuel. That is, they are in the side valleys and high along the upper talus, but the willows are along the low drainages of the main valleys. Because of this distribution, the caves are lacking the solid ice needed in winter to supply water in any quantity. They are also more common along precipitous rock faces, which are more common in restricted valley systems where the good game trails are. Living where one must hunt ensures that one will not be successful. "Animals are not dumb, they go around and stay away from Eskimo camps." Paleolithic archaeologists commonly expect to find "tents" inside caves and rockshelters. When I suggested this to the Eskimo, they held their sides and laughed. "You go to a cave or rockshelter so you don't have to carry a tent, why go there and climb over the rocks, be away from willows, and have to carry your water if you have a tent?" "If your tent burns up, if somebody breaks a leg and you can't go someplace else, or if you're hiding from Indians maybe you stay in a cave with the women and children like a camp—no other time."

For the Eskimo, caves and rockshelters offer a special advantage for logistically organized hunting and trapping parties and for transient families who may take advantage of the shelter for one or two nights so they do not have to unpack their sled. Because the locations of these natural facilities do not change, and because the locations of certain activities are topographically specialized, the same caves and rockshelters are used repeatedly for essentially the same purpose, that is, as natural shelters for hunting parties exploiting the surrounding area during specified seasons or for specific game. Archaeologically, the caves and rockshelters known to me in the Brooks Range have a characteristic stability to their use that approaches the stability of the intercept hunting locations of Anavik and Anaktiqtauk. Redundancy is the property most likely to characterize the separate episodes of use in such settings unless there is a major change in the environment that could affect the distribution of game and their normal movements. Another comment on the short-term nature of the rockshelters is provided by the very fact that I did not excavate one. To do so would have presented me with a very difficult logistical problem in the maintenance of my own camp. Locating the camp near a cave or rockshelter would have resulted in the camp being very difficult to supply with fuel, water, and other essentials since we, too, were living off the land.

In order to provide the reader with a more realistic view of the relative frequency with which different types of archaeological sites were generated by the Nunamiut, I tried to document, in great detail, the activities of two families during 1948 and 1949. Some of these locations were described here, but many were not investigated archaeologically. Table 22.1 summarizes the number of sites of different types that were recalled by the members of the two families. In addition, I elicited information as to whether the informants considered their use of the location as the establishment of a new site or simply the use of preexisting facilities. The data from Table 22.1 have a number of implications for the character of the archaeological remains that develop at different locations. For instance, we note that in Table 22.1, column 4, hunting camps, fish camps, trapping camps, and hunting stands have a very high incidence of reuse, or occupation of the same location where use of preexisting facilities is anticipated. Rest stops and kill sites follow with a substantial reuse of the same location for the same purpose. In contrast, residential camps and transient camps exhibit no pattern of reuse. Over half of all the locations used during the years 1947–1948 were considered to be reuse of previous facilities for the same purposes. In addition, 40 percent of these locations for one family and 46 percent for the other were known to have been used by others during the same year for the same purposes (column 5). In this system, the production of functionally redundant occupational debris is to be expected most often at fish camps, trapping camps, hunting camps, and hunting stands. Rest stops and kill sites will exhibit less redundancy and reuse. Finally, redundant sequences in the use of a given spot are least likely for residential camps and transient camps. Therefore, given the formation of an archaeological deposit, redundancy among the remains from recognizably distinct occupations is most likely at special-purpose locations and least likely at residential locations. This is consistent with earlier observations regarding centers of residential concentration such as Tulugak Lake, Kongumuvuk, and the present villlage. Around Tulugak Lake, the density of archaeological remains is truly impressive; there are pounds, drive lines, remains of residential camps, special processing locations, caches, and a host of other sites. Nevertheless, one rarely encounters a situation in which one residential camp is directly on top of another. The result is a pattern of almost continuous overlapping multiple occupations of different types. The archaeological view from a single spot is one of great diversity of remains that vary both structurally and in terms of content, depending on which elements of one occupation overlap those of another. In focal locations, such as Tulugak Lake and Kongumuvuk, one may expect to have winter, spring, summer, and fall residential use coupled with migration hunting and seasonally differentiated processing and consumption strategies. Highly variable remains that generally overlap one another result.

A totally different pattern can be expected at the special-purpose locations where there is rarely any overlap in their seasonal use or in the structural role they play in the overall subsistence strategy. Here, redundancy through sequences of recognizable occupations can be expected. If we couple this pattern of location reuse with the data previously summarized about content variability, the situation becomes even more

TABLE 22.1

Frequency of Differentiated Use of Locations by Two Families During the Years 1947–1948[a]

Location	(1) Sites established		(2) Sites used		(3) Total sites		(4) Percentage of total previously used		(5) Number of total occupied by others for same purpose	
	F.R.	S.P.	F.R.	S.P.	F.R.	S.P.	F.R.	S.P.	F.R.	S.P.
Residential camps	9	7	0	0	9	7	0	0	0	0
Hunting camps	1	2	10	8	11	10	91	80	9	6
Fish camps	0	0	2	3	2	3	100	100	1	2
Trapping camps	0	0	3	4	3	4	100	100	1	3
Transient camps[b]	3	4	0	0	3	4	0	0	0	0
Hunting stands	0	0	9	8	9	8	100	100	5	7
Rest stops	17	15	20	25	37	40	54	62	14	19
Kill sites	7	6	4	8	11	14	36	57	4	4
Total sites	37	34	48	56	85	90			34	41
Percentage of total	44	38	56	62					40	46

[a] F.R., Frank Rulland family; S.P., Simon Paneack family.
[b] For familes only, not hunting parties.

impressive. The faunal contents of kill sites, hunting stands, and hunting camps are highly consistent structurally. There are variations, to be sure, but the overall pattern is similar between multiple examples of the same type of site. Contrast this with the faunal remains from the 14 residential sites reported here. The spring sites look quite different from the summer sites. Similarly, the fall and winter sites provide a major contrast to the contents of the spring and summer sites. Not only are the special-purpose locations more regularly located spatially, they are also more redundant in their content. *Residential sites are more flexible in their location and more variable in their content. Special-purpose locations are more discrete in their location and more redundant in their use and contents.* It is into the latter category that the occupation of caves and rockshelters falls within the Nunamiut system. This does not mean, of course, that all peoples would use these natural facilities in the same way. Clearly, there is variability from region to region in the topographic setting of caves and rockshelters. As we have seen, topography is one of the features that conditions the Nunamiut use of these locations. Similarily, there are gross differences among environments in the relative distribution of critical resources such as fuel, water, and food. In environments where fuel and water are widely distributed natural shelters may assume more general roles in the subsistence settlement strategy. Such usage is more likely to increase in environments with increasing biomass and less seasonal fluctuation in resource production. My experience with the Eskimo leads me to make the suggestion that specialized use of caves and rockshelters will increase in relation to residential use as a function of increasing seasonal variance in the environment. This means that, as it gets colder, such shelters are less likely to be used for residential purposes. One can expect increasing correlations between changes in the content and structure of cave–rockshelter occupations and measured environmental change as the use of such locations becomes more specialized. For the Nunamiut, the basic distribution of foods and the seasonal behavior of food animals in their environment is fairly predictable. Thus the location of special-purpose sites is apt to be quite redundant. Any change in the basic structure of the environment that results in changed game distributions and behavior would be the major factor conditioning change in the use of special-purpose locations. As a rough check on these expectations, I surveyed the extant literature on 240 cases of hunters and gatherers and found that there were *no* examples of the residential use of caves and rockshelters by hunters and gatherers occupying environments that are colder than the earth's mean biotemperature. Not one single example could be found for the residential use of caves and rockshelters north or south of roughly 35° north or south latitude. Conversely, there was an increase in the recorded incidence of their residential use as one approached the equator. These observations certainly bring into question our knowledge of the past when this knowledge is largely based on information from caves and rockshelters located primarily in temperate and near-polar settings.

Nunamiut subsistence behavior must be seen as a system. Activities are parts of strategies, and each activity or event represents a judgment that considered not only past experiences and present conditions but future goals as well. Throughout these discussions, I have stressed that some behaviors are accommodated to conditions of the moment. These accommodations are indicators of the systemic character of the adaptation. The various components of a strategy are integrated and may be manipulated to produce a continuing set of compromises between different means to achieve security ends.

What is suggested here is simply that systemic characteristics of an adaptation will condition not only variability among sites in their contents, but *it will also equally condition the pattern of redundancy or variance in the sequence of archaeological remains that accumulate through multiple occupations at a single site.*

Moving to still a more comprehensive view of adaptations, we may appropriately consider the degree to which we may anticipate variable localizations, or use of different areas for different purposes.

Throughout the discussions of faunal assemblages, two aspects of the Nunamiut system of procurement and use of animals as food have dominated. First, the exploitation of animals is a largely logistical problem in that the strategy is to move animals as food from the locations where they are obtained to locations of consumption. Second, there is a heavy dependence on stored foods that results in consumption strategies associated with the long-term removal of food from storage for use. Thus, *we may summarize the Nunamiut system as one characterized by strategies that seek to gain space utility (logistics) and time utility (storage) from resources.* These two basic arms of the Nunamiut subsistence strategy are integrated in such a way that one aspect of the system strongly conditions behaviors in the other. The character of the spring logistical behavior is strongly conditioned by anticipated conditions of the storage component of the system. At present, during spring, labor must be invested immediately to transport meat from kill sites because it is necessary to process for drying the entire amount of meat obtained during spring migration very quickly. If this is not done, the meat will probably spoil before it can be dried and placed into storage. The logistics of the fall–winter system are different in that the transport of meat, when coupled with a caching strategy, can be distributed over an extended period of time since successful storage is more easily accomplished with the decreasing temperatures after fall migration. During fall and winter, the logistical activities may be congruently scheduled with secondary concerns such as the procurement of firewood, trapping, and the procurement of clear ice for drinking water. Thus, during fall and winter the logistical movement of caribou meat may be partially, or completely, submerged or embedded in other logistical operations. In spring, however, it is an activity not accommodated to other logistical concerns.

The patterns of mobility and the shifts in the disposition of consumers in the habitat form one aspect of strategy that seeks to minimize the expenditure of labor in both procurement and consumption activities. Similarly, the organization of work parties may vary considerably in the ways that they are accommodated to the logistical demands, as well as how they are accommodated to the consumer demands relative to anticipated hunting successes. Prior to the use of the gun, according to informants, the largest camp groups were associated with the spring hunting of caribou. This aggregation of social units near the surrounds, pounds, and ambush-hunting locations was a strategy of aggregating labor near the points of procurement. This allowed the quick processing of meat adjacent to the points of procurement prior to transport. Subsequently, the movement of what was essentially stored meat could be accommodated to the dispersion and mobility necessary to procure fresh meat during the summer months. What was transported was the dried meat minus all the parts of marginal utility thereby reducing the transport costs. They also practiced a caching strategy in which the parts with the greatest utility per unit weight were moved with the people and swing populations of parts—that is, those parts with moderate utility as sources of food and with high processing costs—were cached as insurance against lack of summer hunting successes, as well as for emergency food in the area where they anticipated fall hunting activities to be located.

During the period of high mobility, there was an attempt to find topographic settings where successful spring and fall hunting could be conducted in the same general area. It will be recalled that spring hunting was largely done with drive lines, pounds, and ambush strategies associated with the drive lines. These strategies were best accomplished in the wide valleys where there were stands of willows at right angles to the long axis of the valley or where there were topographic features, such as lines of eskers, precipitous talus deposits, or low cliffs, that could be used to direct caribou into ambush settings. Although such settings are more common south of the Brooks Range divide and down near the timberline, during the pre-gun era spring hunting was concentrated on the north slopes of the divide. This can be understood as an attempt to conduct successfully both fall and spring migration hunting in essentially the same place. On the north slope, there are numerous lakes that are not surrounded by deep muskeg as is more commonly the case south of the divide. Fall migration hunting consisted of driving caribou into these lakes and killing them with lances from small inland-style kayaks. Achieving this congruence in the locations of both fall and spring migration hunting made a more extensive caching strategy feasible as is evidenced by the huge stone cairn caches located at Tulugak Lake, near Kongumuvuk, and along the Anaktiqtauk. These locations were the central places around which moves and dispersals and aggregatons centered, once in spring and once in fall. One may think of the pre-gun settlement system as looking something like an asymmetrical bow tie where the spring and fall migration hunting locations are the knot and the summer dispersions are a large loop to the north and winter is a small loop to the south. Summer dispersions were related primarily to food procurement concerns—movement to good fishing lakes, to locations where supplementary summer caribou hunting might be conducted, or, if things got rough, an early return to the knot of the bow tie where caches existed and mountain sheep might be hunted. Winter dispersions were related more to the density of willow growth and the need for firewood in large quantities during winter as well as the need for more substantial forest product materials for construction of winter houses.

In the past, the relative extension of the logistical system was inversely correlated with the bulk of the inputs to the system. When the input bulk was large (e.g., during spring and fall migration) the tendency was to move the consumers near the food, and take advantage of the aggregated labor for cooperative hunting and processing. During seasons when game was dispersed and erratic in movement, logistics might be at maximum extension so that small hunting parties would be covering large distances in search of game, and they would be involved in transporting the relatively small amounts obtained over large distances. This use of specialized hunting parties varied somewhat with the subsistence security afforded by stored meat. If stores were generally sufficient in quantity, but perhaps of low quality, as is characteristic of spring meat dried for summer consumption, hunting parties were the general strategy. On the other hand, if stores were low, supplemental hunting was conducted by highly mobile family groups searching for game. In these situations, both consumers and labor for processing were being moved to the potential sources of food. During late summer, when much hunting was specifically aimed at procuring calf skins for use in the manufacture of winter clothing, the pattern was to move in highly mobile family units. Consumers could thus take advantage of the bonus meat of calves' heads and tongues and could also provide a labor force for field processing hides and then transporting the light but bulky hides to fall locations where clothing was largely manufactured coincidently with fall migration hunting and on into the early winter.

We might view the Nunamiut system as having two arms and a pair of feet. Logistics and storage are the arms, and residential mobility the feet. Each is a potential strategy dimension that is accommodated to the other in any given situation. In the absence of substantial stores, there is a higher probability of a residential move to the general area of procurement resulting in minimal logistical extension. In the presence of substantial stores, there is a lower probability of residential movement to a locus of procurement and, in turn, a higher probability of maximum logistical extension, use of specialized work parties, and transport of procured foods over large distances. Since storage is a planned strategy, the procurement of meat for storage was geared to the spring and fall caribou migrations. This meant that maximum logistical extension was characteristic of the middle of the period of storage dependence, whereas increasing residential mobility and smaller camp groups might characterize the end of the period of storage dependence. Such a schedule was, of course, subject to modification, depending on migration hunting successes or particularly on the nutritional state of the animals. For instance, during the period of critically low caribou density in the Alaskan area between 1890 and 1935, we see increasing residential mobility coupled with a tremendous increase in the total area covered by an average Nunamiut family during the annual cycle. (See Burch 1972; Binford and Chasko 1976.)

The success of a long-term storage strategy is dependent on a reliable and highly aggregated food source. For the Nunamiut, this was provided by the regular, twice-yearly, aggregated movement of caribou between their winter and summer ranges and their passage through the Brooks Range along regular routes dictated by features of the topography. In other topographic settings, the same species offers no such opportunity for integration with a storage strategy. As an example, the farther north one is situated along the upper margins of the summer range of caribou, the greater the probability of hunting being confined to late summer and related to obtaining skins for winter clothing along with some meat; rarely are the scattered animals on the upper summer range present in sufficiently large aggregates to afford the opportunity for accumulating any major stores for winter use on a regular yearly basis. Conversely, the farther south one is in the winter range of caribou, the higher the probability of winter hunting of the scattered animals and the lower the probability of any accumulation of major stores. Only at roughly the border between the winter and summer ranges of caribou is there a sufficient aggregation to make a regular twice-yearly storage strategy feasible. Even there, the degree to which one can rely on the regular aggregation in predictable locations is conditioned by features of the topography. Where topographic relief is at a minimum, so is the predictability of the routes of caribou movement.

This short sketch of Nunamiut adaptive strategies should make it clear that adaptation is always a *local* solution to basically local conditions. Because of this, we can anticipate considerable variability among systems in the character of the adaptation achieved. This will be manifest as geographic variability in the properties of archaeological remains. The form of an achieved adaptation is not necessarily determined by the means, but instead derives from the patterns of use to which means are put in seeking security. We may anticipate, therefore, interregional differences in many aspects of the archaeological record that refer directly to the character of the adaptations achieved, even though the culture or the means known to the people may be similar or identical.

I have thus far demonstrated how the ongoing dynamics of an adaptation may result in considerable variability in the contents of archaeological sites. I have suggested that patterning through archaeological sequences at different sites may be quite different but still referable directly to organizational differences characteristic of a single adaptation. Finally, I have suggested how geographic patterning in the frequency, contents, and forms of sites can be expected to vary as a consequence of the organization of an adaptation in space and the differences in the character of adaptations achieved in different places, whereas the adaptive strategies and factors conditioning decision making may remain constant. I turn now to that almost sacred area of archaeological patterning—temporal variability. What have we learned about archaeological formation processes that might serve to modify the meanings that can be appropriately given to observed stability or patterned changes in the archaeological record?

Evidence for Differential Temporal Patterning from Residential and Special-Purpose Locations

Some of the most provocative findings to be reported by an archaeologist in recent years were those of Robert K. Vierra in his analysis of the archaeological remains from the site of Puente (Ac. 158) located in the riverine subzone of the thorn forest association in the Ayacucho Basis of highland Peru (Vierra 1975). The levels analyzed spanned the Jaywa and Piki phases of the Ayacucho sequence (see MacNeish *et al.* 1975:220). Thus the levels in the Puente sequence spanned the important and critical shift in the highlands from a pure hunting–gathering subsistence pattern to one increasingly dependent on domesticated plants and animals. In short, the sequence spanned the important "agricultural revolution" in highland Peru. Vierra selected 11 stratigraphic samples for comparative study. Chi-square calculations were made for the comparison of general functional categories of lithics, end scrapers, side scrapers, projectile points, and so on, among the assemblages. The result was that the observed differences ranging from top to bottom of the sequence could be understood in terms of sampling variations at the ≥.95 level of probability. In short, there was no demonstrable change in functional character of the assemblage despite the fact that the sequence spanned the critical shift from hunting and gathering to horticulture and the use of domestic animals. Vierra performed a factor analysis of the 11 levels and found that all loaded together on a single factor, demonstrating again that there was little basis for viewing the variability in lithic assemblage content as meaningful in adaptational terms. This was a staggering set of findings. For those who would view lithic assemblages as necessarily responsive to adaptive changes and therefore useful as monitors of systems change these findings must be very disconcerting indeed! Regardless of the interpretation given, *Vierra's findings demonstrate that lithic assemblages may not respond to general systems changes at some sites.* This clearly means that all archaeological sites are not equal as monitors of general systems conditions. It also demonstrates that some remains, in this case lithics, are not equal monitors of general systems conditions. (Vierra demonstrated some changes through time in remains other than lithics.) I am saying that the correct explanations for changes in lithic-assemblage composition at some places may well be inappropriate and even downright wrong when employed for ceramics or other classes of artifacts.

It is my guess that the site of Puente was a special-purpose location (perhaps a hunting camp). I suggest that *during general system changes, the role of a strategy in an overall adaptation may change but the strategy itself does not necessarily change.* Stated another way, hunting deer in the Ayacucho Basin could well present similar problems to hunters regardless of the relative contribution to the diet of deer meat. Change in the cultural system may not change the behavior of deer and the basic hunting strategies may well remain the same. We might expect there to be a change in the success curve for hunting parties since one of the conditions for a shift to agriculture is apt to be decreased reliability of the hunting and gathering strategies. There may even be changes in the social position of hunters and the relationship of persons who hunt to others. Nevertheless, choice hunting locations are apt to remain choice hunting locations, at least for some time. Similarly, the basic hunting strategies and techniques may well remain the same regardless of the changed roles that such strategies played in the overall adaptation. It is not unreasonable to expect the archaeological remains from such special-purpose locations to exhibit very different patterns of variability through time relative to a sequence where there is some compounding of assemblage components that monitor the mix of strategies in an overall adaptation, as one might expect at a residential location with a moderate-grained assemblage.

I think I have achieved a method for giving meaning to faunal assemblages in terms of past behaviors and strategies. In addition, I have demonstrated that many concepts that have been used paradigmatically for giving meaning to assemblage variability are inadequate and generally wrong. I have explored the implications of there being different factors conditioning the processes of archaeological assemblage production at different types of sites. This exploration has led to the argument that patterning in content, spatial distribution, temporal redundancy, and responsiveness to general system conditions are all properties of assemblages and locations that are apt to vary with the function of the site. In short, meanings to be attached to changes observed at a special-purpose location are different than those for a residential location.

I have argued in the past that before archaeologists can give meaning to measured differences and similarities in assemblage content they must understand the processes that brought assemblages into being. I now argue that before archaeologists can give meaning to observed spatial and temporal patterns characteristic of recognizable assemblage forms, they must understand the systems behind the assemblage. Was its generative process an amalgam of components that in their compound condition monitor an overall system, or was the assemblage generated in the context of the execution of a single strategy that may or may not have been successful?

Willow Smoke and Dogs' Tails: Hunter–Gatherer Settlement Systems and Archaeological Site Formation

Hunter-gatherer subsistence-settlement strategies are discussed in terms of differing organizational components, "mapping-on" and "logistics," and the consequences of each for archaeological intersite variability are discussed. It is further suggested that the differing strategies are responsive to different security problems presented by the environments in which hunter-gatherers live. Therefore, given the beginnings of a theory of adaptation, it is possible to anticipate both differences in settlement-subsistence strategies and patterning in the archaeological record through a more detailed knowledge of the distribution of environmental variables.

An old Eskimo man was asked how he would summarize his life; he thought for a moment and said, "Willow smoke and dogs' tails; when we camp it's all willow smoke, and when we move all you see is dogs' tails wagging in front of you. Eskimo life is half of each."

This man was capturing in a few words a way of life now largely vanished from man's experience: mobile man pursuing food, shelter, and satisfaction in different places in his environment. This paper is a discussion of patterns that I have recognized through direct field study as well as long-term research in the historical and ethnographic literature dealing with hunting and gathering adaptations. I am interested in what, if anything, renders differences in man's mobility patterning, and in turn the archaeological "traces" of this behavior in the form of spatial patterning in archaeological sites, both "understandable" and "predictable."

The posture adopted accepts the responsibility for a systemic approach. That is, human systems of adaptation are assumed to be internally differentiated and organized arrangements of formally differentiated elements. Such internal differentiation is expected to characterize the actions performed and the locations of different behaviors. This means that sites are not equal and can be expected to vary in relation to their organizational roles within a system. What kind of variability can we expect to have characterized hunting and gathering adaptations in the past? What types of organizational variability can we expect to be manifest among different archaeological sites? Are there any types of regular or determined variability that can be anticipated among different archaeological sites? Are there any types of regular or determined variability

Originally published in *American Antiquity* 45(1):4–20, © 1980.

that can be anticipated among the archaeological remains of people whose lives might be characterized as "willow smoke and dogs' tails"?

The archaeological record is at best a static pattern of associations and covariations among things distributed in space. Giving meaning to these contemporary patterns is dependent upon an understanding of the processes which operated to bring such patterning into existence. Thus, in order to carry out the task of the archaeologist, we must have a sophisticated knowledge and understanding of the dynamics of cultural adaptations, for it is from such dynamics that the statics which we observe arise. One cannot easily obtain such knowledge and understanding from the study of the archaeological remains themselves. The situation is similar to conditions during the early years of the development of medical science. We wish to be able to cure and prevent disease. Do we obtain such knowledge through the comparative study of the symptoms of disease? The symptoms are the products of the disease. Can they tell us about the causes of disease? In a like manner the archaeological record is the *product* or derivative of a cultural system such that it is symptomatic of the past. We cannot hope to understand the causes of these remains through a formal comparative study of the remains themselves. We must seek a deeper understanding. We must seek to understand the relationships between the dynamics of a living system in the past and the material by-products that contribute to the formation of the archaeological record remaining today. In still more important ways we seek to understand how cultural systems differ and what conditions such differences as a first step toward meaningful explanation for patterns that may be chronologically preserved for us in the archaeological record. As in the earlier analogy with medical science, once we know something of the disease and its causes, we may codify the symptoms to permit accurate diagnosis. Similarly, in the archaeological world when we understand something of the relationship between the character of cultural systems and the character of their by-products, we may codify these derivatives to permit the accurate diagnosis from archaeological traces of the kind of cultural system that stood behind them in the past. These are not easy tasks to accomplish.

It has been my conviction that only through direct exposure to dynamics—the ethnoarchaeological study of living systems—does the archaeologist stand the best chance of gaining sufficient understanding to begin the task of giving meaning to the archaeological record, in short, of developing tools or methods for accurately diagnosing patterned variability.

My most extensive experience with living systems has been among the Nunamiut Eskimo (Inuit) of north-central Alaska. For this reason I will base my discussion of a "diagnostic approach" to settlement pattern on some of my Eskimo experiences. I will compare that understanding with a number of different settlement systems as documented ethnographically by others. I will then proceed to discuss how settlement systems may vary among hunters and gatherers living in different environments. In the course of these discussions, I will consider the types of archaeological sites generated in different environments as well as some of the probable spatial arrangements among such sites. Good diagnosis is "theory dependent." I will therefore be concerned with the factors that condition or "cause" different patterns of intersite variability in the archaeological record.

Collectors and Foragers

In several previous discussions of the Nunamiut I have described them as being "logistically organized." I have frequently contrasted their subsistence-settlement system with that of the San or or "Bushman" peoples, whom, I have designated foragers.

Foragers

Figure 23.1 illustrates some of the characteristics of a foraging system (this figure is largely based on the G/wi San as reported by Silberbauer [1972]). Several points should be made here regarding the characteristics of foragers. My model system as shown in Figure 23.1 illustrates seasonal residential moves among a series of resource "patches." In the example these include the "pans" or standing water sources, melon patches, etc. Foraging strategies may also be applied to largely undifferentiated areas, as is frequently the case in tropical rain forests or in other equatorial settings. One distinctive characteristic of a foraging strategy is that foragers typically do not store foods but gather goods daily. They range out gathering food on an "encounter" basis and return to their residential bases each afternoon or evening. In Figure 23.1, residential bases are represented by solid black dots along tracks indicated by double dashed lines. The circles around each residential base indicate the foraging radius or the distance food procurement parties normally travel out into the bush before turning around and beginning their return trip. Another distinctive characteristic is that there may be considerable variability among foragers in the size of the mobile group as well as in the number of residential moves that are made during an annual cycle. In relatively large or "homogeneous" resource patches, as indicated by cross-hatching on the right of Figure 23.1, the number of residential moves may be increased but the distances between them reduced, resulting in an intensive coverage of the resource "patch." On the other hand, if resources are scarce and dispersed, the size of the mobile group may be reduced and these small units scattered over a large area, each exploiting an extended foraging radius. This situation is indicated by the multiple residential bases on the lower left side of the "seasonal round" shown in Figure 23.1. I might point out that when minimal forager groups (that is 5–10 persons) are dispersed, there is frequently a collapse of the division of labor, and foraging parties will be made up of both male and female members involved in procuring largely identical resources.

Perhaps the use of the desert San as a model for foraging strategies is somewhat misleading, since the most exclusive foragers are best known from equatorial forests. Table 23.1 summarizes some of the information from equatorial groups on numbers of residential moves, average distances between moves, and total distances covered during an annual cycle. What can be seen from Table 23.1 is that there is considerable variability among foragers in the duration of stay at different sites. For some extremely mobile foragers such as the Punam, as reported by Harrisson (1949), residential sites would be extremely ephemeral; one could expect little accumulation of debris and very low archaeological "visibility." There is another characteristic which may vary among foragers to further condition the "visibility" of the archaeological record: that is the relative redundancy of land use from year to year. One gains the impression,

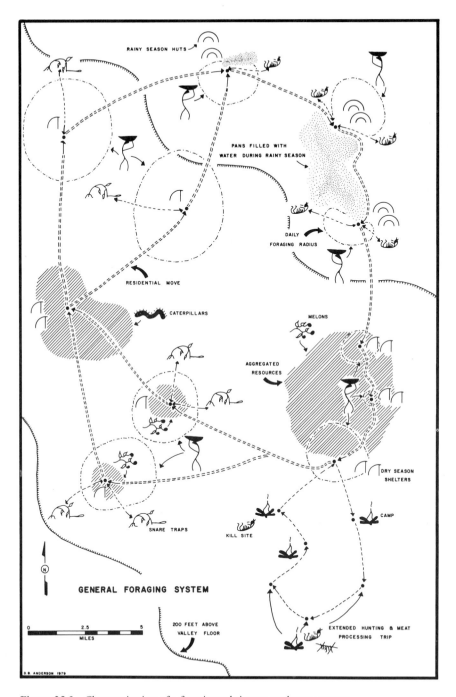

Figure 23.1 Characterization of a foraging subsistence-settlement system.

TABLE 23.1

Summary of Group Sizes and Annual Mobility for a Number of Equatorial and
Subequatorial Groups of Hunter–Gatherers.[a]

Group Name	Modal Group Size	Number of Annual Residential Moves	Mean Distance between Sites (miles)	Total Circuit Distance Covered Annually	References
Penum	65	45	4.2	195	Harrisson 1949:135
Semang	18	21	7.1	150	Schebesta 1929:150
Mbuti	120	12	8.3	100	Bicchieri 1969:149
Siriono	75	26	14.2	370	Holmberg 1950
Guayaki	50–20	50	3.7	220	Clastres 1972:150
Aeta	45	22	8.0	178	Vanoverbergh 1925:432
Hadza	—	31	8.2	256	Woodburn 1972:194
Dobe !Kung	25	5	14.8	75	Lee 1968:35
G/wi	55–18	11–12	16.8	193	Silberbauer 1972:297

[a] These values are estimates from either the observers and interviewers or calculations made by me from indirect information provided by such authors.

from descriptions of such groups as the Punam (Harrisson 1949), the Guayaki (Clastres 1972), and other highly mobile foragers, that camps are not relocated relative to locations of previous use. The resources exploited are scattered but ubiquitous in their distribution and are not clumped or specifically localized as might be the case in deserts where waterholes are limited in number and discretely placed. Under the latter conditions we might expect more year to year redundancy in the occupation of particular places. Extreme examples of limited locations for critical resources may result in what Taylor (1964) has called *tethered nomadism*, indicating extreme redundancy in the reuse of identical places (water sources) over long periods of time. Such spatial discreteness tends to "tie down" the settlement system to specific geographical areas while other areas would be occupied little and rarely used because of their distance from such limited and crucial resources. We might think of a typical forager pattern of land use as looking like a daisy—the center is the residential base, and foraging parties move out, traversing search loops which resemble the petals of the daisy. Figure 23.2 illustrates this actual pattern as recorded by John Yellen (1972) for a mobile group of Dobe !Kung.

In recognition that there is an alternative strategy which may be executed occasionally by peoples who are basically foragers, I have indicated a different pattern in the lower right-hand corner of Figure 23.1. We might think of this as a hunting trip where several men leave a residential base, establishing overnight camps from which they move out in search of game, frequently using what I (Binford 1978b) have termed an encounter of strategy. If they succeed in their hunting endeavors, and if the body size of the animal is large or the distance to camp is great and the temperature

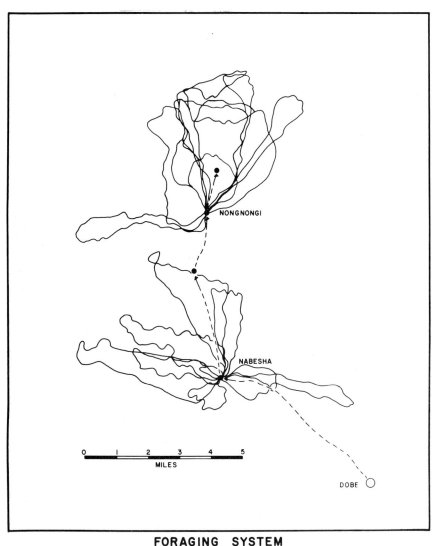

FORAGING SYSTEM

COMPOSITE TAKEN FROM YELLEN 1968

Figure 23.2   Acutal map of foraging trips made by !Kung San around base camps.

is warm, they may elect to dry the meat in the field and transport processed meat back to camp. This possibility is indicated by the little drying rack in the lower right-hand corner. They may then elect to return to the base by the original route or, if more meat is needed, they are more likely to return by a new route where they may even have further success in hunting. This little hunting trip represents a different type of strategy. It is a specialized work party, in this case made up of men, who establish camps for their own maintenance away from the residential base camp where they live. They may conduct special activities which may be only very rarely conducted in the residential base camp. This type of strategy may leave a very different kind of archaeological record and one we will explore in more detail in the next model.

Before going on, however, it may be useful to summarize something of our expectations regarding the archaeological remains of foraging strategies. The first point to be made regarding the archaeological remains of foraging strategies is simply that there are apt to be basically two types of spatial context for the discard or abandonment of artifactual remains. One is in the *residential base,* which is, as we have seen, the hub of subsistence activities, the locus out of which foraging parties originate and where most processing, manufacturing, amd maintenance activities take place. I have indicated that among foragers residential mobility may vary considerably in both duration and the spacing between sites; in addition the size of the group may also vary. These factors would condition the character of the archaeological record generated during a single occupation. I have suggested that foragers may be found in environmental settings with very different incidences and distributions of critical resources. In settings with limited loci of availability for critical resources, patterns of residential mobility may be *tethered* around a series of very restricted locations such as water holes, increasing the year to year *redundancy* in the use of particular locations as residential camps. The greater the redundancy, the greater the potential buildup of archaeological remains, and hence the greater the archaeological visibility. Thus far, I have basically reiterated some of the generalizations Yellen (1977:36–136) formulated from his experiences with the Kalahari Bushman, as well as some of the arguments I (Binford 1978b:451–497) derived from my observations of Nunamiut Eskimo residential camps.

The further characteristics of the *residential base* will become clearer in contrast with the other type of archaeological occurrence that foragers are apt to produce: the *location.* A *location* is a place where extractive tasks are exclusively carried out. Since foragers generally do not stockpile foods or other raw materials, such locations are generally "low bulk" procurement sites. That is to say, only limited quantities are procured there during any one episode, and therefore the site is occupied for only a very short period of time. In addition, since bulk procurement is rare, the use, exhaustion, and abandonment of tools is at a very low rate. In fact, few if any tools may be expected to remain at such places. A good example of a *location* generated by foragers, a wood-procurement site, is described by Hayden (1978:188–191).

> As a rule, they are spatially segregated from base camps and are occupied for short durations (usually only a matter of hours at the most) by task-specific groups; . . . the lithic tools employed are generally very distinctive and the assemblages highly differentiated in terms of proportional frequencies compared to base camp assemblages . . . the tools used are often obtained locally near the procurement site, and are generally left at the site after the activity is accomplished. . . . if one walked extensively among the mulga grove, one could see an occasional chopping implement, usually left at the base of a decaying mulga trunk. Rarely were there more than two chopping implements, and the overall density must have been about one chopping implement per 2500 m² or less.

Under low-bulk extraction or low redundancy in localization, the archaeological remains of *locations* may be scattered over the landscape rather than concentrated in recognizable "sites." Understanding such remains would require data-collecting techniques different from those archaeologists normally employ. So-called "off-site" archaeological strategies are appropriate to such situations. Given that long periods of time are involved and certain resources are redundantly positioned in the environment, we might anticipate considerable palimpsest accumulations that may "look" like sites in that they are aggregates of artifacts; however, such aggregates would commonly lack internal structure and would be characterized by accretional formation histories. Very important research into this type of archaeological distribution was initiated in this country by Thomas (1975). Further provocative investigations of so-called "off-site archaeology" are currently being pursued by Robert Foley (personal communication) of the University of Durham in the Amboseli area of Kenya.

What can be summarized is that foragers generally have high residential mobility, low-bulk inputs, and regular daily food-procurement strategies. The result is that variability in the contents of residential sites will generally reflect the different seasonal scheduling of activities (if any) and the different duration of occupation. The so-called "functionally specific" sites will be relatively few; given low-bulk inputs and short or limited field processing of raw materials such locations will have low visibility though they may well produce considerable "off-site" archaeological remains if long periods of land use are involved. Basically this type of system has received the greatest amount of ethnoarchaeological attention (e.g., Bushmen and central desert Australian Aborigines).

Collectors

In marked contrast to the forager strategy where a group "maps onto" resources through residential moves and adjustments in group size, logistically organized collectors supply themselves with specific resources through specially organized task groups.

Figure 23.3 illustrates some of the distinctive characteristics of a collector strategy. The model is generalized from my experiences with the Nunamiut Eskimo. In contrast to foragers, collectors are characterized by (a) the storage of food for at least part of the year and (b) logistically organized food-procurement parties. The latter situation has direct "site" implications in that special task groups may leave a residential location and establish a field camp or a station from which food-procurement operations may be planned and executed. If such procurement activities are successful, the obtained food may be field processed to facilitate transport and then moved to the consumers in the residential camp.

Logistical strategies are labor accommodations to incongruent distributions of critical resources or conditions which otherwise restrict mobility. Put amother way, they are accommodations to the situation where consumers are near to one critical resource but far from another equally critical resource. Specially constituted labor units—task groups—therefore leave a residential location, generally moving some distance away to specifically selected locations judged most likely to result in the procurement of specific resources. Logistically organized task groups are generally small and composed of skilled and knowledgeable individuals. They are not groups out "searching" for any resource encountered; they are task groups seeking to procure

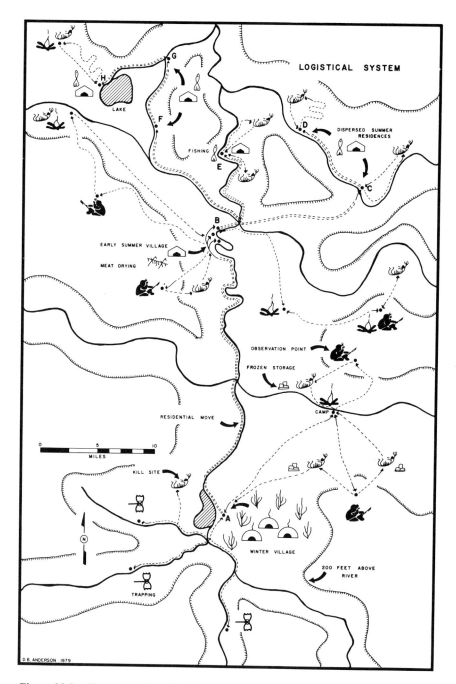

Figure 23.3 Characterization of a collector subsistence-settlement system.

specific resources in specific contexts. Thus we may identify specific procurement goals for most logistically organized groups. They go out to hunt sheep at the salt lick, or pursue big caribou bulls along the upland margins of the glaciers in July. They are fishing for grayling or white fish. They are not just out looking for food on an encounter basis.

This specificity and "specialization" in procurement strategy results in two types of functional specificity for sites produced under logistically organized procurement strategies. Sites are generated relative to the properties of logistical organization itself, but they are also generated with respect to specific types of target resources.

For foragers, I recognized two types of site, the *residential base* and the *location*. Collectors generate at least three additional types of sites by virtue of the logistical character of their procurement strategies. These I have designated the *field camp*, the *station*, and the *cache*. A field camp is a temporary operational center for a task group. It is where a task group sleeps, eats, and otherwise maintains itself while away from the residential base. Field camps may be expected to be further differentiated according to the nature of the target resources, so we may expect sheep-hunting field camps, caribou-hunting field camps, fishing field camps, etc.

Collectors, like foragers, actually procure and/or process raw materials at locations. However, since logistically organized producer parties are generally seeking products for social groups far larger than themselves, the debris generated at different locations may frequently vary considerably, as in the case of group bison kills on the Plains (see Frison [1970] or Wheat [1967]) or spring intercept caribou kill-butchering locations among the Nunamiut such as the site at Anavik (Binford 1978b:171–178). Sites of major fish weirs or camas procurement locations on the Columbia plateau might be examples of locations with high archaeological visibility as opposed to the low-visibility locations commonly generated by foragers. Such large and highly visible sites are also the result of logistically organized groups, who frequently seek goods in very large quantities to serve as stores for consumption over considerable periods of time.

Stations and *caches* are rarely produced by foragers. *Stations* are sites where special-purpose task groups are localized when engaged in information gathering, for instance the observation of game movement (see Binford 1978b) or the observation of other humans. Stations may be ambush locations or hunting stands from which hunting strategy may be planned but not necessarily executed. These are particularly characteristic of logistically organized systems, since specific resource targets are generally identified and since for each target there is a specific strategy which must generally be "informed" as to the behavior of game before it can be executed.

Caches are common components of a logistical strategy in that successful procurement of resources by relatively small groups for relatively large groups generally means large bulk. This bulk must be transported to consumers, although it may on occasion serve as the stimulus for repositioning the consumers. In either case there is commonly a temporary storage phase. Such "field" storage is frequently done in regular facilities, but special facilities may be constructed to deal specifically with the bulk obtained (see Binford 1978a:223–235). From the perspective of the archaeological record, we can expect *residential bases, locations, field camps, stations,* and *caches* as likely types of sites generated by a logistically organized system. Within each class we can expect further variability to relate to season and to the character of the resource targets of logistically organized task groups.

There is still an additional source of variability, since all the logistical functions may not necessarily be independently located. In some situations one might be able to use the field camp as an observation point, in others it may equally serve as a hunting stand. On occasion, kills (*locations*) may be made directly from a hunting stand, and the meat may be processed and temporarily cached there. Many other combinations can be imagined. *The point is simple, the greater the number of generic types of functions a site may serve, the greater the number of possible combinations, and hence the greater the range of intersite variability which we may expect.*

Against this background it is perhaps instructive to follow out some of the conditions modeled in Figure 23.3. Beginning with the winter village (site) at the lower center of the map, several conditions are indicated. The winter village is a cluster of relatively substantial houses located in a stand of willows (winter fuel). To the left of the village a series of expeditions are indicated; these are carried out by special trapping parties for the purpose of obtaining fur for winter clothing. To the right of the village are a series of site types: a *field camp*, where a hunting party is maintained while away from the residential camp; a station, or *observation site*, which is occupied and used basically for collecting information on game presence or movement; and several *locations*, kill sites and cache locations, which might also represent archaeological accumulations. With early summer, a residential move is indicated (site B); this move results in a change in housing and a dependence upon dry rather than frozen meat as was the case in the winter village. From such a site, logistically organized parties may range out considerable distances to hunt such game as caribou or mountain sheep. *Field camps* and *stations,* like observation points and a variety of kill *locations,* might be generated. We see additional complexity caused by the differential combination of functions at different locations. For instance, to the far right of the map is a combined field camp and observation point; in other situations these functions might be spatially separated. In the upper part of the map an additional residential move is suggested. This move is accompanied by a reduction in group size as the local group breaks down into family units, each establishing independent residential camps having slightly different logistical patterning.

It should be clear by now that we are not talking about two polar types of subsistence-settlement systems; instead we are discussing a graded series from simple to complex. Logistically organized systems have all the properties of a forager system and then some. Being a system, when new organizational properties are added, adjustments are made in the components already present such that residential mobility no longer plays the same roles it did when the system had no logistical component, although important residential moves may still be made. Given basically two strategies, "mapping on" and "logistics," systems that employ both are more complex than those employing only one and accordingly have more implications for variability in the archaeological record. It should be clear that, *other things being equal, we can expect greater ranges of intersite variability as a function of increases in the logistical components of the subsistence-settlement system.*

Discussion

Thus far I have been talking about the patterning that I have perceived in the way hunters and gatherers are organized for subsistence purposes. I have been offering certain analytical and descriptive suggestions as to things one might look for in characterizing hunter-gatherer adaptations. I have been attempting to justify a particular way of looking at hunter-gatherers and suggesting that there are some interesting empirical patterns manifested by hunter-gatherers when they are looked at from the perspectives advocated.

Can we now begin the important task of building an explanation for the variability presented? Can we begin to understand the particular adaptive conditions which human groups differentially face by virtue of coping with different environments? Can we understand which conditions would favor "mapping on" versus "logistically organized" strategies? Beginning with a more specific question, are there any clues to the factors that favor or select for a foraging or logistical strategy? If we assume that technological and social characteristics contribute to making up the means and organization of production, we wish to know if there are not some basic "determinants" conditioning the distribution of differing "modes of production" (that is, the characteristic mixes of technology and social organization organized for subsistence purposes). Put another way, since systems of adaptation are energy-capturing systems, the strategies that they employ *must* bear some relationship to the energy or, more important, the entropy structure of the environments in which they seek energy. We may expect some redundancy in the technology or means, as well as the organization (labor organization), of production to arise as a result of "natural selection." That is the historical movement toward an "optima" for the setting. Put another way, technology, in both its "tools" sense as well as the "labor" sense, is invented and reorganized by men to solve certain problems presented by the energy-entropy structure of the environment in which they seek to gain a livelihood.

Given this viewpoint we would expect that a foraging mode of production would serve men well in certain environmental conditions, but not necessarily in all. What might some of these conditions be? Are there any environmental settings where we might expect foraging strategies to offer "optimal" security for groups of hunter-gatherers? I think it is fair to suggest that although most people view seasonal mobility of residential locations as being responsive to differences in food abundance, most have little appreciation for the environmental conditions which structure food abundance from the perspective of the human consumer. Perhaps Hollywood can be blamed for the widespread idea that "jungles" are food rich while deserts and arctic settings are food poor. In turn most laymen and beginning ecology students alike expect the greatest residential mobility in arctic and desert settings and most "sedentism" among non-food-producers in equatorial settings. Simply as a means of provocative demonstration, I have adopted as a basis for further discussion data from Murdock (1967) regarding settlement patterns. Murdock rated 168 cases of hunters and gatherers as to their degree of residential mobility. Each group was scaled from one to four as follows (see Murdock 1967:159): (1) fully migratory or nomadic bands, (2) seminomadic communities whose members wander in bands for at least half of the year but occupy a fixed settlement at some season or seasons; (3) semi-sedentary communities whose members shift from one to another fixed settlement at different seasons or who occupy more or less permanently a single settlement from which a substantial proportion of the population departs seasonally to occupy shifting camps; and (4) compact and relatively permanent settings.

These 168 cases are summarized in Table 23.2 which cross-tabulates Murdock's estimates of residential mobility against a measure of environmental variability developed by Bailey (1960), called "effective temperature" (ET). This measure simultaneously describes both the total amount and yearly distribution of solar radiation characteristic of a given place. Stated another way, ET is a measure of both the length of the growing season and the intensity of solar energy available during the growing season. Since biotic production is primarily a result of solar radiation coupled with sufficient water to sustain photosynthesis, we can expect a general relationship to obtain between ET value and global patterns of biotic activity and hence production. Other things being equal, the higher the ET value, the greater the production of new cells within the plant or producer component of the habitat. This means that in a very simplistic sense we might expect "food rich" environments when ET is high and "food poor" environments when ET is low.

Table 23.2 illustrates some provocative facts. We note that "fully nomadic" strategies characterize 75% of the hunter–gatherer cases located in a fully equatorial environment (ET 25–21); high mobility is also found in 64.2% of the cases in semitropical settings. In warm temperate settings we note a drastic reduction of hunter–gatherers who are "fully nomadic" (only 9.3%), and in cool temperate settings the number is still further reduced (7.5%). Then as we move into boreal environments the number of fully nomadic groups increases slightly (11.1%), and in full arctic settings it increases drastically (reaching 41.6%). Thus we see that mobility, as measured by Murdock's categories, is greatest in equatorial settings, where we have the highest production in the world, and in arctic settings, where we have the most consistently low production. Summarizing the data from Table 23.2 another way, we observe the greatest concentration of sedentary and semi-sedentary hunters and gatherers in the temperate and boreal environmental zones and the least in equatorial and semiequatorial settings. This empirical pattern shows that mobility among hunter–gatherers is responsive to conditions other than gross patterns of "food abundance." This is indicated by the disproportionate occurrence of reduced mobility in the cooler, less productive environments.

I suggest that since mobility is a "positioning" strategy, it may well be most responsive to structural properties of the environment, that is to say the particulars of food distribution that are not directly correlated with the more intuitively appreciated conditions of food abundance.

A clue to the types of problems that different strategies solve is perhaps best sought in the contrasts between the two basic strategies themselves. *Foragers move consumers to goods with frequent residential moves, while collectors move goods to consumers with generally fewer residential moves.* The first strategy, that of "mapping on," would work only if all the critical resources were within foraging range of a residential base. Logistical strategies (by collectors) solve the problem of an incongruous distribution

TABLE 23.2

*Cross Tabulation of Settlement Pattern as Evaluated by Murdock (1967) and ET (Effective Temperature)
Values as Calculated from World Weather Records*

Effective temperature	Fully nomadic (1)	Semi-nomadic (2)	Semi-sedentary (3)	Sedentary (4)	Total	Index Value
25	2	0	0	0	2	
24	1	0	1	0	2	
23	3	1	0	0	4	
22	2	0	0	0	2	
21	1	1	0	0	2	
Subtotal	9 (75.0%)	2 (16.7%)	1 (8.3%)	0	12	1.33
20	1	1	1	0	3	
19	3	1	0	0	4	
18	2	1	0	0	3	
17	1	0	0	0	1	
16	2	1	0	0	3	
Subtotal	9 (64.2%)	4 (28.5%)	1 (7.1%)	0	14	1.42
15	2	11	2	0	15	
14	1	10	1	5	17	
Subtotal	3 (9.3%)	21 (65.6%)	3 (9.3%)	5 (15.6%)	32	2.31
13	3	17	4	4	28	
12	1	15	8	1	25	
Subtotal	4 (7.5%)	32 (60.3%)	12 (22.6%)	5 (9.5%)	53	2.33
11	2	15	9	3	29	
10	3	6	3	4	16	
Subtotal	5 (11.1%)	21 (46.6%)	12 (26.6%)	7 (15.4%)	45	2.46
9	5	3	1	1	10	
8	0	1	1	0	2	
Subtotal	5 (41.6%)	4 (33.3%)	2 (16.6%)	1 (8.3%)	12	1.91
Grand total	35 (20.8%)	84 (50.0%)	31 (18.4%)	18 (10.7%)	168	

among critical resources (i.e., the lack of a reliable supply of a critical resource within
the foraging radius of a residential base camp presumably located with regard to an
equally critical resource). *Under conditions of spatial incongruity it must be appreciated
that a residential move will not solve the problem.* A move toward one location reduces
the access to the other. *It is under this condition that a logistical strategy is favored.*
Hunter–gatherers move near one resource (generally the one with the greatest bulk

demand) and procure the other resource(s) by means of special work groups who move the resource to consumers.

In the case of *temporal incongruity*, a storage strategy is the most likely means of solving the problem. One seeks to extend the time utility for one of the resources beyond its period of availability in the habitat. This is accomplished generally by either drying or freezing. *Storage reduces incongruous temporal phasing of resources, but it may increase the problem of spatial incongruity.* Spatial incongruity may be exacerbated in that storage accumulates considerable bulk in one place, which increases the transport costs of a residential move in favor of other resources that might be "coming in" or located some distance away. With increases in storage dependence there will be an expected increase in the logistical component of a settlement system. Finally, if the argument is made that incongruity among critical resources, whether temporal or spatial, is a condition favoring logistical strategies and a reduction and change in the role of residential mobility, it must also be realized that any condition which either (a) increases the numbers of critical resources and/or (b) increases the climatic variance over an annual cycle will also increase the probability of greater incongruities among critical resources.

Let us consider two logical expectations arising from this postulate. The law of requisite variety states that for maximum stability, the variety of homeostatic responses required in any system is equal to the variety of environmental challenges offered to it. We can expect, therefore, that the more unstable the thermal environment, the greater the number of operative homeostatic mechanisms, and hence the greater the number of critical resources, other things being equal. As the number of critical resources increases, there is a related increase in the probability that a lack of congruence will occur in their distributions. *Therefore, the greater the seasonal variability in temperature, the greater the expected role of logistical mobility in the settlement or "positioning" strategy.*

Given an equatorial environment in which species may exhibit patterns of differential production over an annual cycle, but the interdigitation of differing schedules among species ensures that there will be continuously available foods, a foraging strategy works very well. In temperate and still colder settings, such continuously available food is reduced as a function of decreases in the length of the growing season. Human groups attempting to "make a living" must therefore solve the "over-wintering" problem. Basically three methods are available: (a) exploiting species who have themselves solved the over-wintering problem (that is hunting other animals); (b) storing edible products accumulated largely during the growing season; or (c) storing animal resources accumulated during periods of high density and hence availability. *Although we must recognize that storage may not always be feasible, the degree to which it will be practiced can be expected to vary with decreases in the length of the growing season.* The degree to which storage is practiced will, in turn, increase the likelihood of distributional incongruities and hence condition further increases in logistically organized settlement systems with attendant reductions in residential mobility, at least seasonally. Both of these conditions are related to environmental reductions in the length of the growing season and to the implications of this for man, both in terms of foods and of other temperature-regulated resources. *This means that there is an environmental convergence of conditions acting simultaneously to increase the number of critical resources and to increase the conditions favoring storage.* Given the arguments presented here, we should therefore see a reduction in residential mobility and an increase in storage dependence as the length of the growing season decreases.

It should be pointed out that both of these expectations are supported empirically. As was previously indicated in Table 23.2 there is a marked increase of cases classified as semisedentary and seminomadic in environments with ET less than 16°C. Stated another way, we see increases in seasonal sedentism, with attendant increases in logistically organized food procurement inferred, in such environments.

Figure 23.4 illustrates the relationship between ET and storage dependence as estimated by Murdock and Morrow (1970) for a sample of 31 ethnographically documented hunters and gatherers. Storage dependence is indicated by an ordinal scale distributed from one to six, where six indicates the greatest dependence upon storage. What is interesting in this small sample is that there is a clear curvilinear relationship between increased dependence upon storage and decreasing ET values, measuring decreases in lengths of growing season. It is notable that storage is practiced only among hunters and gatherers in environments with ET values less than 15 (i.e., in environments with growing seasons less than about 200 days). Exceptions to the general trend are interesting and perhaps instructive. In warm environments there are only two exceptions, the Andamanese and the Chenchu. It is my impression that the Andamanese are miscoded while the Chenchu are demonstrably in the process of adopting argiculture. Exceptions on the "cold" end of the distribution are the Yukaghir, Yahgan, Slave, Copper Eskimo, and Ingalik. I believe the Yukaghir to be miscoded, as well as the Ingalik, while the other cases are probably truly exceptional in being more mobile and not putting up stores for winter in appreciable amounts. Additional cases of cold-climate groups who do not put up appreciable stores might be the Micmac, Mistassini Cree, Igloolik and Polar Eskimo, and some groups of Copper and Netsilik Eskimo, as well as some temperate cases like the Tasmanians. Many of these groups might be technically foragers with relatively high residential mobility, nevertheless they are foragers of a different type than most equatorial foragers.

As has been pointed out, equatorial foragers move their residences so as to position labor forces and consumers with respect to food-yielding habitats considered in spatial terms. The cold-environment foragers are what I tend to think of as serial specialists: they execute residential mobility so as to position the group with respect to particular food species that are temporally phased in their availability through a seasonal cycle. Leaving such interesting issues aside for the moment, it should be clear that there are definite geographical patterns to the distribution of environmental conditions that pose particular problems for hunter–gatherers. Some of these specifiable problems may be well solved or at least effectively dealt with through *logistically organized production strategies*. Such strategies answer the problem of incongruous distributions of critical resources. Incongruous distributions may occur spatially and may be further exacerbated by storage strategies. Storage always produces a high bulk accumulation in some place, which then has an increased likelihood of being incongruously distributed with respect to other critical resources such as fuel, water, shelter, etc. High

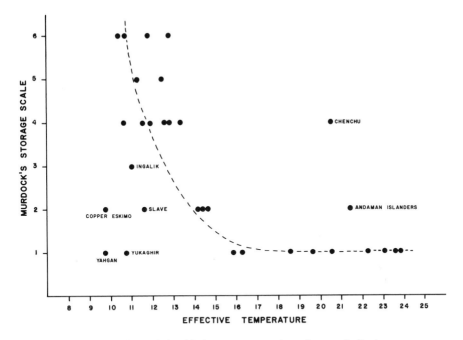

Figure 23.4 Graph of the relationship between storage dependence and effective temperature.

bulk stores necessitate the determination of the relative cost of transporting consumers and stored goods to the loci of other critical resources versus that of introducing these other resources to the storage location through a logistically organized productive labor force.

I should point out that if there are other factors that restrain mobility, such as increased numbers of social units in the area, competition among multiple social units for access to similar resources, etc., then we can expect an accompanying increase in logistically organized production. This is not the place to take up such important issues as the origins of agriculture and other density dependent shifts in both mobility and productive strategy, but I simply wish to point out that *with any condition that restricts residential mobility of either foragers or collectors, we can expect (among other things) a responsive increase in the degree of logistically organized production.*

Conclusions: Settlement Systems and Interassemblage Variability

The above discussion obviously has significant implications for our understanding of archaeological assemblages, their variability, and their patterning. I have argued else-where that we may think of an assemblage as a derivative of "some organized series of events characteristic of a system" (Binford 1978a:483). An assemblage that is the accumulated product of events spanning an entire year is rather gross and may be referred to as *coarse-grained* in that the resolution between archaeological remains and specific events is poor. On the other hand an assemblage accumulated over a short period of time, for instance a two-day camp, represents a *fine-grained* resolution between debris or by-products and events. Having made the above distinctions I previously argued:

1. Insofar as events are serially differentiated, and the composition of assemblages are responsive to event differences, the more fine-grained the assemblage, the greater the probable content variability among assemblages.

2. The factor which regulates the grain of an assemblage is mobility, such that high mobility results in fine-grained assemblages, whereas low mobility results in coarse-grained assemblages. (For further discussion see Binford 1978b:483–495.)

In reference to the initial condition, "the degree to which events are serially differentiated," it was argued that from a subsistence perspective the major conditioner of event differentiation is seasonal variance in the basic climatic variables: rainfall and solar radiation. It was therefore suggested that interassemblage variability *"can be expected to increase with decreases in the length of the growing season" and/or "decreases in the equability of rainfall distribution throughout a seasonal cycle, given moderate to fine-grained assemblages"* (Binford 1978b:484).

The earlier arguments had reference primarily to residential mobility. In this paper I have explored something of the interaction and the determinants for differential degrees of residential versus logistical mobility. I have suggested here that there are two basic principles of organization employed by hunters and gatherers in carrying out their subsistence strategies. They may "map on" by moving consumers to resources, or they may move resources to consumers "logistically." I have suggested that the relative roles played by these two organizational principles in any given subsistance system will also condition the nature and character of archaeological intersite variability generated by the system. Foragers who practice primarily a "mapping on" strategy will generate basically two types of sites: the *residential base* and the *location*. Variability among forager systems will derive primarily from differences in the magnitude of residential mobility and environmental differences conditioning different subsistence activities through a seasonal cycle.

Collectors who tend toward a greater reliance on the logistical strategies can be expected to generate additional types of archaeological sites. That is, in addition to the *residential base* and the *location* we can expect *field camps, stations,* and *caches* to be generated. It was also argued that the character of residential bases, as well as that of locations, may well be expected to change in accordance with the relative degree of logistically organized activity characteristic of a system.

I then turned to the interesting question of what *conditions* the relative roles of "mapping on" versus "logistical" strategies in a subsistence-settlement system? It was argued that logistically based strategies are a direct response to the degree of locational incongruity among critical resources. It was further argued that the number of critical resources increases as climatic severity increases, and that the relative dependence upon stored foods increases as the length of the growing season decreases. It was pointed out that these characteristics are linked, and both tend to vary with geographical variability in the length of the growing season. *Therefore, as the length of the growing season decreases, other things being equal, we can expect increases in the role of logistical strategies within the subsistence-settlement system.* It was also pointed out that any *other conditions that restrict "normal" residential mobility among either foragers or collectors also tend to favor increases in logistically organized procurement strategies.* We would therefore tend to expect some increase associated with shifts toward agricultural production.

I can now integrate my earlier arguments regarding the factors conditioning interassemblage variability at residential bases with the arguments made in this paper regarding variability in the archaeological record stemming from organizational differences in the roles of mapping on and logistical strategies in the subsistence-settlement behavior of groups living in different environments. It was argued earlier that as seasonal variability in solar radiation or rainfall increased, given assemblage responsiveness to event differentiations, there would be an increase in residential interassemblage variability. This is assuming a roughly constant assemblage grain. In this paper it has been argued that under the same conditions increased logistical dependence with an accompanying reduction in residential mobility would be favored. This situation would have the effect of increasing the coarseness of the assemblage grain from such locations. *Increased coarseness, in turn, should have the effect of reducing interassemblage variability among residential sites of a single or closely related system occupied during comparable seasons. It would of course also have the effect of increasing the complexity and "scale" of assemblage content referable to any given uninterrupted occupation, assuming, that is, a responsiveness of assemblage content to event differentiations.*

The overall effect of what appears to be opposing consequences is normally some seasonal differentiation in the relative roles of residential versus logistical mobility. For instance, in some environments we might see high residential mobility in the summer or during the growing season and reduced mobility during the winter, with accompanying increases in logistical mobility. The overall effect from a regional perspective would be extensive interassemblage variability deriving from both conditions. We may also expect minor qualitative difference among assemblages from the winter villages (in the above examples). These are likely to be categorically different from mobile summer residences which would be highly variable and constitute a "noisy" category. Comparisons among winter residences would clearly warrant a categorical distinction of these from summer residences and they would be a "cleaner," less noisy category of greater within-assemblage diversity. Summer sites would be more variable among themselves but also less internally complex.

The point here is that logistical and residential variability are not to be viewed as opposing principles (although trends may be recognized) *but as organizational alternatives which may be employed in varying mixes in different settings.* These organizational mixes provide the basis for extensive variability which may yield very confusing archaeological patterning.

The next step in the arguments presented in this paper treats the production of special-purpose sites. It was suggested that with logistical strategies new types of sites may be expected: *field camps, stations,* and *caches.* It was further argued that the character and visibility at *locations* also changes in the context of increased use of logistical strategies. *We may therefore argue that, other things being equal, we may anticipate regular environmentally correlated patterns of intersite variability deriving from increases in the number and functional character of special-purpose sites with decreases in the length of the growing season.* In addition to such quantitative changes, given the more specialized character of resource "targets" sought under logistical strategies, we can expect an increase in the redundancy of the geographic placement of special-purpose sites and a greater buildup of archaeological debris in restricted sections of the habitat as a function of increasing logistical dependence (for a more extended discussion of this point see Binford 1978b:488-495).

This last point addresses a subject not discussed in depth in this paper, namely, the long-term land-use strategies of hunter–gatherers in differing environmental contexts. This paper has primarily dealt with short-term organizational and strategy differences. "Short-term" here essentially means the dynamic of yearly cycle. I have argued that there are environmental factors conditioning variability in short-term mobility and land-use strategies among hunters and gatherers. I have not seriously considered the possibility that hunters and gatherers would ever remain *sedentary* as a security-seeking strategy unless forced to do so. I am aware of many arguments that essentially appeal to what I term the "Garden of Eden" principle, namely, that things were so "wonderful" at certain places in the environment that there was no need to move. I find that a totally untenable *opinion,* and one which can be countered easily by scholars who understand ecological relationships. This does, however, imply that an understanding of short-term strategies as discussed here is insufficient for treating patterning which derives from variable redundancy in geographical positioning of the total settlement-subsistence systems. A detailed consideration of the factors that differentially condition *long-term* range occupancy or positioning in macrogeographical terms is needed before we can realistically begin to develop a comprehensive theory of hunter–gatherer subsistence-settlement behavior. The latter is of course necessary to an understanding of archaeological site patterning.

Acknowledgments

1. This paper was originally prepared at the request of Peter Bleed, who graciously invited me to participate in the 1979 Montgomery Lecture Series at the University of Nebraska-Lincoln. For both the opportunity and the encouragement to prepare this paper I am most grateful.

My colleague Jeremy Sabloff read and made constructive comments on earlier drafts as did William Morgan and Robert Vierra; for this assistance I am most grateful. Ms. Dana Anderson developed and prepared the illustrations; certainly the quality of her work adds appreciably to this paper.

The field work opportunities which have provided the stimulus for much of the discussion and my appreciation of hunter–gatherer mobility were supported by the National Science Foundation, the Wenner-Gren Foundation, and the Australian Institute of Aboriginal Studies. A grant from the Faculty Research Committee of the University of New Mexico aided in the preparation of the manuscript, particularly the drafting of the illustrations. For this I am most grateful. Colleagues who shared my interest in hunter–gatherer adaptations have provided me with stimulating intellectual environments; I would particularly like to mention Henry Harpending, James O'Connell, Nick Peterson and John Pfeiffer.

24   1982

The Archaeology of Place

It is suggested that if archaeologists are to be successful in understanding the organization of past cultural systems they must understand the organizational relationships among places which are differentially used during the operation of past systems. This point is illustrated by observations made among the Nunamiut Eskimo. Against this background it is demonstrated that the two most common forms of archaeological systematics, "assemblage"- versus "type"-based systematics, are not appropriate for the study of places. In the latter case, it is not possible to analyze places as such, while one cannot see places with different "content" as part of a single system in the former. It is concluded that current archaeological systematics are totally inappropriate for studying past systems of adaptation and their evolutionary modification.

Viewed from the perspective of a living system, an occupation can be defined as the uninterrupted use of a place by participants in a cultural system. The material consequences of an occupation represent a document regarding an organizational aspect or phase of operation of the cultural system under study. The association among different things "falling out" of a system during an occupation may inform about the organization of the human action which occurred at the site. In previous studies I have looked at the way various activities conditioned the internal structure of a site (Binford 1978a) and I have attempted to investigate how a complete system appeared when seen from the perspective of a class of items (bones) deposited during identified occupations (Binford 1978b). In both of these studies I was viewing "the archaeological record" of a living system from the perspective of its known occupations. In this study I assume a more "realistic" perspective, viewing a living system from the perspectives of "sites."

Archaeologists must begin their analyses on materials remaining at archaeological sites. Archaeological sites yield assemblages. Assemblages are sets of artifacts (both items and features) which are found in clustered association (normally defined stratigraphically) at or in archaeological sites. The degree to which such clustered associations may be treated as the results of occupations, or the material derivatives surviving from an uninterrupted use of a single place by participants in a cultural

Originally published in *Journal of Anthropological Archaeology* 1(1):5–31, © 1982.

system, is yet to be clarified (see Dunnell (1971:150-153) for a discussion of assemblage definition). The archaeologist "sees" the past segmentally from the perspective of fixed positions in space. The "fallout" from the events that "moved across" fixed places establishes the character of the archaeological remains on sites. To understand the past we must understand places.

I am interested in sites, the fixed places in the topography where man may periodically pause and carry out actions. I am concerned with *site patterning* both in the frequency with which occupations occur at different places, and in the processes which generate associations among archaeological materials at sites. *Site patterning* in both within-place and between-place contexts is a property of the archaeological record. The accuracy with which we are able to give meaning to the record is dependent upon our understanding of the processes which operated in the past to bring into being the observed patterning. Put another way, our accuracy depends upon our ability to correctly infer causes from observed effects.

The processes which cause site patterning are long-term repetitive patterns in the "positioning" of adaptive systems in geographic space. Site patterning derives from repetition, or lack thereof, in the spatial positioning of systems. It is suggested that the factors which condition the positioning of systems may be somewhat different from the factors which condition the internal operation of a system. In fact, humans may reposition their adaptive strategies in a landscape, a tactic which may generate variability in the archaeological record while serving to foster stability within the ongoing system.

Economic Zonation

I will attempt to demonstrate that there are important consequences for site patterning arising from the interaction between *economic zonation*, which is always relative to specific places, and tactical mobility, which is the accommodation of a system to its broader *environmental geography*. Variability among systems in economic zonation and mobility is expected to result in diagnostic forms of chronological patterning at sites.

One of the more distinctive features of human systems is their spatial focus on a "home base" or a residential camp. At any one time the way in which a group uses its habitat is directly conditioned by the pattern of moving out and then returning to a residential camp. This means that, aside from certain "absolute" characteristics of the biogeography within the region, *there is always a "cultural geography"* which is relative to the location of the residential camp. It is this "relative" character of the cultural geography which prompted the development of "catchment analysis" (Vita-Finzi and Higgs 1970) and the recognition by Lee (1969) and others that there tends to be a regular pattern of land use centered on a residential location. Higgs and Vita-Finzi (1972:30) use the term *site territory* to refer to "the area habitually exploited from a single site." In recognition of the mobility of some adaptations they noted that the overall unit of space exploited during a normal annual cycle represents the accumulative sum of the various site territories. Vita-Finzi and Higgs (1970) refer to this unit as the *annual territory*. I tend to acknowledge the intuitive value of the term territory, but also recognize that the use of the term is ambiguous in anthropology, having had a long history of usage with respect to social relationships linked with conspecific competition (see Stanner (1965), Heinz (1972), and Petersen (1975) for a review of concept usage). For this reason I prefer the more biologically useful term *range*. I will adopt the sense of Vita-Finzi and Higgs's concepts of site territory and annual territory but use instead the terms *camp range* and *annual range*.

I want to outline a particular model of economic zonation around sites drawn largely from my experiences with the Nunamiut Eskimo (Binford 1978b). We can begin to think of zonation in terms of the immediate surroundings of the camp, which are generally quickly overexploited and therefore may provide very little in the way of foods except, of course, in the event there is a highly aggregated, renewable resource near the site. This area is frequently the "campground" for visitors, and the "*play radius*" for children. Beyond the "play radius" there is the "*foraging radius*," which rarely extends beyond 6 miles of the residential camp. This is the area searched and exploited by work parties who leave the camp to exploit the environment and return home in a single day. Archaeological sites produced in this zone are most commonly what I have called "locations" (Binford 1980b:9), although in some circumstances there may be hunting blinds, and other special-use sites within the foraging radius.

Beyond the foraging radius is the *logistical radius*. This is the zone which is exploited by task groups who stay away from the residential camp at least one night before returning. In many cases groups may remain away from residential camps for considerable periods of time. (Among the Nunamiut Eskimo, hunting parties may operate out of a hunting camp for as long as 4 weeks, and trapping parties may operate out of a series of trapping camps for up to 3 months.)

Regardless of the duration of penetrations into the logistical zone, maintenance accommodations including food, shelter, etc., must be provided for the work party while it is away from the residential location. Thus, the remains from exploitation and processing for transport, from consumption, and of creature comfort accommodations of the task group all contribute to the materials remaining at logistical camps. Beyond the logistical range lies an area with which persons are generally familiar, the area about which they attempt to keep informed with respect to resource distributions and changes in production, although they may not be exploiting the area at the time of observation. This area which is regularly monitored will be called the *extended range*.

Among the Nunamiut we could say that beyond the *logistical zone* or the "*extended zone*" is the "*visiting zone*." This is the area contemporaneously occupied by relatives, trading partners, wife-sharing partners, etc., and hence within the foraging radius or logistical zone of another subsistence unit. Exploitation of resources in such a zone generally is dependent upon establishing temporary *residence* at the camp of other persons. Once this is done the "visitor" frequently participates in the exploitative strategies of the host group, joining foraging units and participating on special work groups penetrating the logistical zone for specific reasons. It is not uncommon for visitors to constitute "special work groups" as, for example, an all-male hunting party,

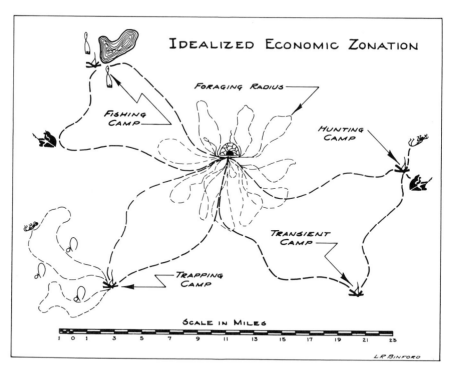

Figure 24.1 Schematic representation of zones of economic activity around a residential camp.

a pair of partners widely ranging over the landscape trapping animals, etc., or a "walkabout" party engaged in teaching young men the characteristics of the environment.

It is unrealistic to view the potential zonation around a residential camp as simply a series of concentric circles where the use which is made of each area is exclusively conditioned by the transport and labor costs of exploiting resources at differing distances from a locus of consumption (see Jochim 1976:51–56). The situation is more realistically visualized as a residential camp at the hub of a *foraging radius* and a *logistical radius* (see Fig. 24.1). The latter is conditioned in scale by concerns for supplying goods to consumers at the residential camp, but it is also conditioned by the need for information regarding a much broader area, the latter being critical for making decisions regarding future moves.

Mobility Patterning

Mobility is the way in which the above economic zones around a residential camp are differentially adjusted relative to the concrete distribution of resources in the habitat. *It is through mobility that a given place may be economically modified relative to the human system.*

I think it should be emphasized that there is an interaction between the degree of development of each zone and the degree of residential mobility characteristic of the group in question. For instance, a highly mobile foraging (see Binford 1980b:5) group like the Punan (see Harrisson 1949) has a pattern of movement which is so rapid that they characteristically cover only half of a foraging radius, with no development of a logistical zone. The residence is then moved to the outer perimeter of the radius previously covered, and through a search of the habitat a new half-foraging-radius "front" is developed from the residence. Once this "front" is covered, another residential move is made. This is what might be called a "half-radius continuous pattern" of movement (Fig. 24.2A). (This is the pattern illustrated by the high mobility of a San hunting party as summarized from Yellen by Binford [1980b:8, Fig. 2]. Another pattern also characteristic of highly mobile hunter–gatherers is the *"complete-radius leapfrog"* pattern of movement (Fig. 24.2B). This is a pattern commonly seen in high-biomass environments. It is frequently linked with a classic encounter strategy (see Binford 1980b) in which resources are exploited in proportion to their encounter frequencies, modified of course by the relative effectiveness of the "capture" techniques.

Much more common in lower-biomass settings is "point-to-point" (Fig. 24.2C) mobility, where a residence is moved from one relatively rare location providing access to food, water, and fuel to another such location within the region. In Australia and in the Kalahari, movement is frequently from one waterhole to another or one specific resource patch to another within the region. Distance between "camps" may be substantial on occasion, and, viewed annually, the distances may exhibit a wide range of variability. This is the pattern of movement most characteristic of residential moves made by the Nunamiut Eskimo. They tend to move camps to specific places prejudged as to the degree that there is an optimal congruence among foods, fuels, and water obtainable from the chosen location. Distances between such point-to-point moves may be many times the foraging radius.

I have observed that the half-radius pattern is exclusive to foragers, while the complete-radium leapfrog pattern and the point-to-point pattern may be found among both foragers and logistically organized groups. It would also appear that point-to-point mobility is more characteristic of logistically organized tactics. The latter makes considerable sense since placement of camps under such an organization is always an accommodation to a prior understanding of resource distributions which are generally incongruent (see Binford 1980b). Residential placement in logistical systems is a compromise strategy relative to already known resource distributions, while forager strategies emphasize tactics aimed at learning about the distribution of resources in a region. Foragers employ coverage tactics, while collector site patterning derives from positioning tactics relative to a prior knowledge of resource distributions.

It can also be shown that many human groups may move through seasonal phases in which their coverage and positioning tactics change. For instance, in some systems people may be dispersed in summer, behaving like foragers by employing a mobility strategy designed for coverage, seeking to maximize the "encounter" with resources, yet during the winter they may be living from stores at a site which was positioned in terms of logistical concerns. Mobility patterning may be both geographically variable and regionally complicated.

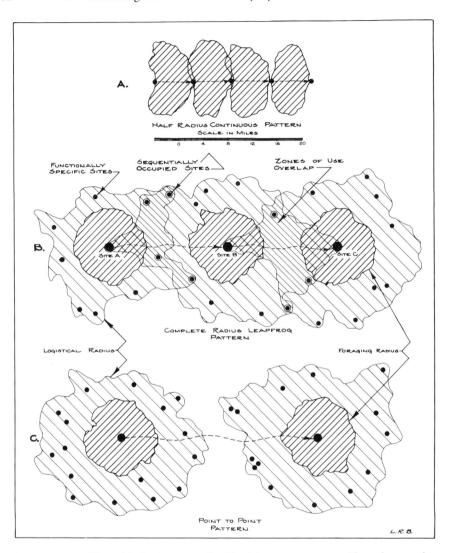

Figure 24.2   Different idealized patterns of residential camp movement, with resultant spacing or overlap of foraging or logistical zones around camps.

Within- and Between-Site Variability

Recognizing that mobility and the tactical aspects of land use may be organizationally complex when viewed from the perspective of a living system, we must now shift to a perspective more appropriate to the archaeologist, the view of a complex living system as seen from the fixed place, the site.

Visualize the complications which may arise from there being a rather fixed radial zonation of land use surrounding a camp but variation in the tactics of camp move-

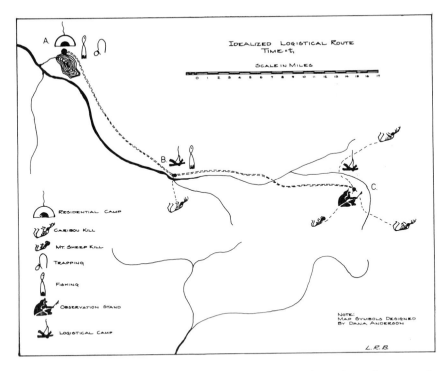

Figure 24.3 Idealized pattern of site use and movement among sites at time t_1 (late summer).

ment. Mobility ensures that the site-centered pattern of land use will be modified relative to absolute geography as a simple function of residential mobility itself. Let me illustrate by way of Fig. 24.3, which shows a situation where at time t_1 a group is living in camp A. From an archaeological perspective we would expect *special use areas* in the play radius, primarily *locations* within the foraging radius, and in the zone of the logistical radius, *field camps, stations,* and *caches* may in fact be the dominant types of sites generated. Now let's imagine that the residential camp is moved sequentially up a valley, as is illustrated in Fig. 24.2B. With each move the land use zonation is centered on the new camp. Several points emerge as important in this example:

1. *The new residential camp is located in what was previously the "logistical zone."*
2. *What was previously the foraging radius with "locations" is now in the logistical zone where camps may be expected, etc.*

What this means is that the same places have different economic potential relative to the sequence of base camp moves. They are different distances from the base camp, and some will be characterized by different use relative to parties coming and going from the sequence of base camps. Figs. 24.3–24.5 illustrate a simplified series of moves for a small group of Eskimo during late summer. In Fig. 24.3 the group was primarily engaged in fishing while male parties were moving out into the logistical zone hunting caribou with the goal of obtaining calves of the year and yearlings for

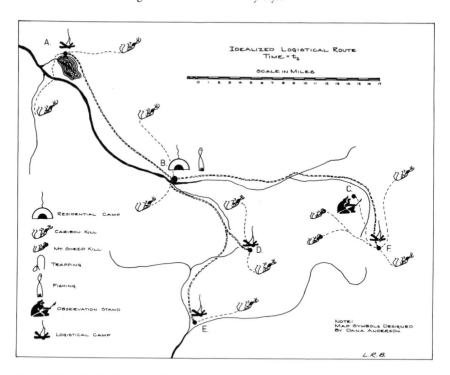

Figure 24.4 Idealized pattern of site use and movement among sites at time t₂ (approximately 1.5 months later than t₁).

their skins to be used as clothing the following winter. The residential camp was located at the junction of the major river and a minor tributary (site A). While living there the women had set numerous traps around the camp for the Arctic ground squirrel; young boys and women carried out extensive fishing for both grayling and white fish that penetrated the stream from the Arctic coast. Male parties were primarily hunting in an open valley at the drainage divide between the Arctic and Yukon drainages (site C). There was a particularly well protected rock shelter in the face of a major limestone bluff at this site. Hunting parties could camp there and also use the mouth of the rock shelter as a hunting stand from which they could observe the movements of game in the valleys below. About halfway between this mountain hunting camp and stand (site C) and the residential site (site A) there was a transient camp and "rest stop" location (site B) at a river crossing. Animals tended to cross the river here so the site was also sometimes used as a nearby overnight hunting camp (meaning that hunting parties rarely took provisions with them to this location since it was very close to the residential site; see Binford (1978b:306–320).

After living in the above situation for approximately 1¹/₂ months, the Eskimo moved their residential camp to site B (Fig. 24.4), where a slightly different pattern of land use developed.

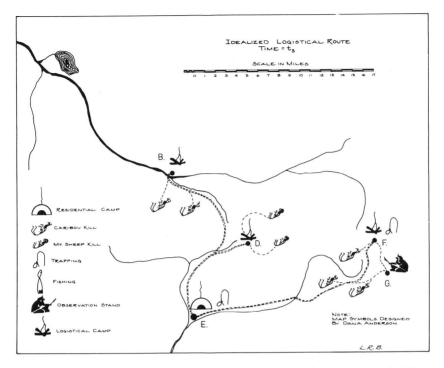

Figure 24.5 Idealized pattern of site use and movement among sites at time t₃ (early fall).

The previous residential site at site A was now used as a hunting camp; the residential site itself was "on top of" the earlier transient stopping place at the river crossing, which had also been used earlier as a nearby hunting camp. The valleys below site C continued to be a favorite hunting ground, but the sun had shifted seasonally so that the rock shelter at C no longer received direct rays of the sun and hence never warmed up during the gradually shortening days of late summer. This meant that the "cost" of dragging fuel up to the shelter was no longer reasonable since it remained cold and damp all the time now. Consequently it was only used as an observation stand, and the hunting camp was located at a much lower location (site F), where fuel was more accessible. Hunting camps were occupied at sites D and E by parties operating out of the residential camp at site B. In early fall, in anticipation of caribou migration, the residential camp was moved across the divide to site E (Fig. 24.5), where there was a continuation of fishing, but sheep hunting and caribou hunting dominated the subsistence activities at this camp. The previous residential camp was now used regularly as a hunting camp since animals in increasing numbers were expected to cross the river at the ford. Hunting activities were concentrated out of site B and out of site F. Although parties camped at site F as when they had been living at site B, they now observed a region from a high ridge (observation stand site G) along a tributary draining ultimately into the Yukon system. Some minor hunting continued from site D but now the target was almost exclusively sheep.

Consequences of Variable Site Utilization

Table 24.1 summarizes the differing uses of the sites discussed in the series of three documented moves. Several points should be clear:

1. *The locations preferred for residential camps can be expected to yield a more complex mix of archaeological remains since they were commonly also utilized logistically when the residential camps were elsewhere.* This is further expected not only because the functional *integrity* of associated remains may be low, given both residential and logistical usage, but, in addition, because the contrasts of residential functions with special purpose sites will contribute to a more complex or at least heterogeneous assemblage at the residentially used sites (see Binford 1978b:486–488).

2. *There may be seasonally correlated shifts in the activities conducted at both residential and logistical sites.* An example is the shift from predominantly fishing activities at the summer residential camp (site A) to the predominantly caribou hunting activities conducted out of the early fall residential camp (site E). An analogous seasonal shift was noted at site D, used initially for taking caribou bulls in late summer, while early fall hunting from the location was almost exclusively for mountain sheep.

3. *There may be seasonal changes in the characteristics of places which conditioned their appropriateness for various uses.* An example is site C, where during one season of the year the rockshelter was warmed by the sun, making it a desirable location for camping. As the sun moved on the horizon relative to the site, however, it became less and less desirable as a camp and was then used only as an observation stand.

4. *The logistically used sites exhibit less functional shifting with each residential move than other sites.* Sites C, D, F and G exhibited minor changes, but all maintained some functional integrity through a series of residential moves.

Occupation and Deposition

Finally, archaeologists must realize that *there is no necessary relationship between depositional episodes and occupational episodes.* Rates and magnitudes of "burial" of archaeological remains are generally consequences of processes operating independently or at least semi-independently of occupational episodes. The primary determinants of the "burial" of archaeological remains are the rates of geological dynamics resulting in surficial deposition of matter. Floods, exfoliation of the walls of a rock shelter, loess deposition, slope wash, etc., are the major determinants of the "provenience" packages in terms of which we "see" archaeological associations.

Only in "high-energy" cultural contexts where the actions of man actually bury artifacts can we relate provenience units which represent unit burial events to unit

TABLE 24.1

Comparative Usage of Place

Time of occupation	Site	Function
Time 1	A	Residential camp—fishing, minor hunting
Time 2	A	Caribou hunting camp
Time 3	A	Transient camp
Time 1	B	River crossing and transient stop and hunting camp
Time 2	B	Residential camp—fishing, moderate hunting
Time 3	B	River crossing and hunting camp
Time 1	C	Hunting camp and observation stand
Time 2	C	Observation stand only
Time 3	C	Not occupied
Time 1	D	Not occupied
Time 2	D	Hunting camp, caribou—sheep
Time 3	D	Hunting camp, sheep only
Time 1	E	Not occupied
Time 2	E	Hunting camp
Time 3	E	Residential camp—hunting with minor fishing
Time 1	F	Kill site
Time 2	F	Hunting camp
Time 3	F	Hunting camp
Time 1	G	Not occupied
Time 2	G	Not occupied
Time 3	G	Observation stand

human actions. Even in such contexts the more likely situation is that the artifacts included in matrix units actually deposited by man were derived from earlier deposits or surficial distributions. (This is a point frequently stressed by Schiffer (1976a). Returning to the condition of interfacing between occupational episodes and processes of burial, I think that it can be appreciated that, given certain depositional dynamics, the *tempo of land use,* or how frequently a place is utilized, conditions how discretely occupational episodes may be buried and therefore preserved as event-specific associations among artifacts. Given relatively intensive use such as site F, which was occupied seven times during the course of 4.5 months (Figs. 24.3, 24.4, 24.5), there seems little likelihood that the different occupational episodes would be discretely buried and hence preserved as occupational units. It is much more likely that the debris from all seven occupations would appear as a single depositional unit. It may even be the situation that several yearly accumulations would be combined to produce a palimpsest "assemblage" occurring as a thin lens on a stabilized land surface which was occupied on numerous occasions over a considerable number of years. This example emphasizes that *the composition of assemblages and their "grain" does not generally derive from the operation and hence organization of a cultural system but instead from the interaction between the cultural system and the processes which are conditioning burial of cultural debris.* Put another way, the burial of cultured debris is not necessarily a cultural process. Since it is the burial processes which strongly condition the character of associations in buried deposits, it should be clear that assemblages defined in terms of depositional criteria (excavated in so-called natural units) are not likely to refer to discrete occupational episodes. Any repetitive patterning which might be demonstrable between depositionally defined "assemblages" is likely to derive from factors conditioning stable repetitive sequences or patterns of place use at the site. In addition, the *associations* among classes of things in depositionally defined "assemblages" would derive from the regular associations among different occupations at the place, and not necessarily from regular performance of sets of activities during any one occupation. In reality, the compositional character of the depositionally associated assemblage would derive from both organizational properties characteristic of given occupations and the particular serial occupational pattern.

For example, let's imagine that the variability in utilization of the different sites listed in Table 24.1 was also accompanied by differences in the debris remaining from each functionally distinct occupation. Let's further imagine that no burial or different occupations occurred during the 4.5-month period so that the accumulations at each site were occupationally undifferentiated in any depositional sense.

A classification of the gross "assemblage" occurring on each site would tend *to group those assemblages which had similar combinations of occupations in a functional sense.* Sites D and F would most likely constitute a group; sites G and C another group; and the "assemblage" from sites A, B, and D a third distinct but internally variable class. These three assemblage types would not refer directly to any specific activities, but instead to the combinational pattern of occupations which occurred at the several locations. It is true that some activities would tend to dominate one or more classes— hunting camp derivatives in the type made up of sites D and F—while "observation stand" derivatives would dominate the assemblage type defined by sites C and G; nevertheless, hunting camp debris would be submerged in the assemblage from site C while kill site activities would be swamped by the hunting camp materials at site F.

It is perhaps shocking to realize that a recurrent pattern of association among artifacts may derive from regularities in the history of site use. *The demonstrably associated things may never have occurred together as an organized body of material during any given occupation.*

If we are to have confidence in our techniques for making inferences regarding the past our techniques should accurately anticipate the dynamics of a system known to have produced patterned statics at archaeological sites. This is not a question of whether the past was like the Nunamiut Eskimo but whether our inferential strategies are adequate to inform about a case like the Nunamiut.

In this paper I have discussed conditions under which we could expect to recover different things at different places which were in fact referrable to a single cultural system. The observations presented, as well as the discussions of land use, have led us to anticipate a number of patterns in the archaeological record.

Summary of Ethnoarchaeological Observations

I. It has been demonstrated that:
   A. In a logistically organized system of exploitation (collectors), different places in the habitat of a single system are used differentially and occupied for different purposes.
   B. There are fundamental organizational differences between residential camps and special purpose sites occupied in the context of a logistically organized system. (See Binford 1978b:483-497.)
   C. Given A and B above, the economic potential of other fixed places within the habitat changes with any change in the placement of the residential hub.

II. It is expected that:
   A. There would be some correspondence between material items entering the archaeological record and the activities and tasks carried out during an occupation.
   B. There would be some correspondence between the economic potential of a place and the character of the activities normally conducted there during any given occupation.
   C. There would be some bias in the environmental characteristics favored for residential usage.

III. Given the conditions and expectations outlined in I and II above we can anticipate some of the following patterns to be generated in the archaeological record:
   A. Different assemblage forms to be recovered from contemporary sites located within the region occupied by a single cultural system.
   B. Chronologically sequential changes in assemblage content occurring at fixed sites within the region. These may be in response to changes in the economic potential of the place relative to mobile residential camps.

IV. If so:
   A. Such sequential changes do not represent organizational change in the system, only shifts in the economic potential of the place itself and as such could result in:
      1. Occasional chronological reversals in the forms of assemblage deposited at different sites as well as different sequences of assemblage forms at different sites within a region.
      2. Occasional nonsequential reoccurrences of similar forms of assemblage at a given site (alternation of industries). (Note: Both conditions could arise from simple vagaries in the relative positioning of different residential sites vis-à-vis the site in question.)
      3. Some potential independence among contemporary assemblage types with regard to their microenvironmental associations within the region. (Simple but different types of assemblages can be expected to show some environmental correlates even within a relatively localized region.)

All of these expected patterns of interassemblage variability, as well as implied regional and chronological patterns, could arise from simple internally differentiated systems of action which were not static in geographic space. The realization that we might see shifts in site function as indicated by assemblage composition in the absence of environmental change or change in the organizational character of the cultural system itself has perhaps not been widely recognized by archaeologists.

By the same token, we can expect that some locations, particularly special purpose sites, may exhibit little if any change in the functional characteristics of site use in spite of organizational change in the cultural system and/or shifts in its regional positioning. This point has been made previously (Vierra 1975; Binford 1978b).

I am proposing that we can regularly expect variability in chronological sequences at different sites within regions. Contemporary "levels" should frequently be different. The sequence of change through a deposit may be related to function and therefore different at different sites as a simple function of use differences which may arise from simple shifts in regional positioning. At the same time the possibility exists for there to be functionally related stability, in that particular places may continue to be used in similar ways in spite of overall organizational change in the system (e.g., a good sheep-hunting camp in the mountains remains such regardless of changes in the role which sheep may play in the overall organization of the settlement subsistence system).

Between-System Variability

If we shift perspective again to that of an observer "high in the sky" capable of "seeing" variability among systems differentially distributed spatially and perhaps in terms of change through time, how might we anticipate the character of changed patterning from the perspective of the "observer" at the bottom of a "site" looking up as the dynamics of human systems passes over, resulting in a "fallout" of matter?

The interesting example of variability or change in the scale of movement practiced by organizationally different systems is a case in point. If the reader has followed the arguments thus far it should be clear that there would be a quantitative scaling in variability with differing magnitudes of movement. The greater the distance between residential camps the greater the likely change in economic potential for any given fixed point in the habitat. Similarly, the more seasonally repetitive the movement of residential sites, the greater the chance for repetitive types of occupations at particular logistical sites. On the other hand if the scale of residential mobility is large and not geographically repetitive, so that the places utilized during one year are not necessarily used again in succeeding years, the pattern of occupational differentiation and hence assemblage heterogeneity might be greater at a given site than if the pattern of seasonal mobility were repetitive or "smaller" in scale.

I expect that the degree of change in the economic potential of particular places will vary with the scale of movement characteristic of the human group making use of the location. We may anticipate increasing repetition in the use of particular places when the system is becoming more sedentary. It should be clear that *when residential mobility is at a minimum the economic potential of fixed places in the surrounding habitat will remain basically the same, other things being equal.* This means that a system changing in the direction of increased sedentism should generate ancillary sites with increasing content homogeneity. This should have the cumulative effect of yielding a regional archaeological record characterized by greater intersite diversity among ancillary or non-residentially used sites but less intrasite diversity arising in the context of multiple occupations.

Stated in a less formal manner we can imagine a group of hunter–gatherers moving about the landscape. A particular place may be used as a hunting camp at one time, a transient camp at another, and a short-term observation stand at still another, depending on the relative placement of the residential camps. As the system changes and a more permanent residential settlement is established such situational variations would be reduced. The relative "economic potential" of different places becomes increasingly stabilized as a function of the increasing permanence of the residential camp. Correspondingly, the use made of ancillary places becomes increasingly repetitive. A given cave might now be used almost exclusively as a hunting camp, while another place in the habitat may become a functionally specific lithic procurement site, etc. By way of contrast, under the more mobile system lithic materials might have been obtained incidentally to the carrying out of hunting and gathering activities (see Binford 1979b), and the site now used exclusively as a hunting camp might have been occupied for multiple purposes, given shifts in the utility of the places relative to the changing locations of residential camps under earlier conditions.

The overall effect of reduced residential mobility among logistically organized hunters and gatherers, from the standpoint of patterning, would be an archaeological record characterized by better defined "types" of sites giving the appearance of greater specialization in functions, when in fact all that may have gone on is that the same activities were increasingly located in the same places.

Implications of This Study

I hopefully have demonstrated that assemblage variability can be expected within deposits and between sites. When viewed from a higher level of organization, differences in both the scale and the actual patterns of mobility between major regions can be expected to be manifest in the form and patterns of both within- and between-site assemblage variability.

Stated another way, the consequences of the dynamics described here would condition patterns of assemblage content, or the overall form of complete inventories recovered from deposits judged to have had some depositional integrity. There is really only one approach in common use, "la Méthode Bordes" (de Sonneville–Bordes 1974–1975), which yields an assemblage-based systematics. With this approach the summary content of a complete assemblage is taken as the unit for comparison.

The use of this method became widely known through F. Bordes' (1950, 1961b) studies of the Mousterian materials from Europe. There he demonstrated a number of patterns which most archaeologists had neither expected nor really "seen" previously. Bordes illustrated new and convincing cases of "parallel phyla," that is, very different assemblage types co-occurring in a similar region over long periods of time. In addition he illustrated for the first time convincing cases of "alternating industries."

That is, through a sequence, sometimes at a single site, the pattern of assemblage variability was *not directional* through the stratigraphic column. Assemblage types might reoccur at various points in the column, with very different assemblages inter-stratified between nearly identical assemblages. Finally, Bordes demonstrated that when stratigraphic sequences from several sites in a region were cross-correlated temporally, that is, when rough contemporaneity could be established between levels from different sites in the same region, contemporary assemblages might be very different in formal content. This has been interpreted as the presence of culturally distinct peoples living side by side and maintaining their cultural distinctiveness either in the absence of interaction or in spite of interaction. I term this the idea of "tenacious cultures."

The reader must realize that these patterns are consistent with the expectations derived from the ethnoarchaeological example from the Nunamiut given here. In this case we saw how different assemblages could occur in a single region, how different assemblage sequencing could occur within sites, and how different assemblage configurations could be contemporary within a region. It would be nice to move directly to the conclusion that the dynamics observed among the Nunamiut were the type responsible for the patterning observed by Bordes in the archaeological remains of the Mousterian. This is not possible. There are several problems which must be cleared up before the relevance of this example to problems of prehistoric interpretation can be assessed.

Problem 1

The example is drawn from an Eskimo system which is certainly a product of modern men. The type of patterning described by Bordes for the Mousterian has not been widely recognized in the remains of demonstrable modern men from the Old World. The patterns which Bordes made so famous are from the Middle Paleolithic of Europe and are referrable to hominid ancestors living before the appearance of fully modern man. If you take this situation at face value, it might appear that the patterns which Bordes discovered were characteristic of the Middle Paleolithic. Such a view would certainly be supported by claims for the absence of such patterns from both the Upper Paleolithic and more recent materials of Europe (de Sonneville-Bordes 1966). I might note that such patterning is not normally recognized in the New World.

The conditions illustrated by the example presented here would lead us to expect the presence of such patterns. Of equal interest are other implications for differing views of the past which this case renders explicit.

This example has been drawn from a subsistence settlement system which I have termed "logistical" (Binford 1978b, 1980b) in its organization. It is recognized that there are other forms of systems largely representing differing tactical mixes of consumer versus producer mobility in a variable setting of temporally and spatially differentiated distributions of resources. In an earlier paper I contrasted the systems organized so as to move consumers to goods rather than, as in the examples given in this paper, to move goods to consumers. (In a logistical system, residential mobility still positions consumers relative to goods in a long-term sense, but the short-term supply is commonly handled with logistical tactics.) Ironically I see no reason to suspect that the Mousterian systems studied by Bordes were logistically organized.

I currently consider the contrasts between the Mousterian and the Upper Paleolithic to be so great that the systems must have been fundamentally different in an organizational sense. In turn the Upper Paleolithic appears to me to represent no greater range of organizational differences than are currently known among contemporary hunter–gatherers. For this reason I consider the details of site formation described here to be of greater relevance to hunter–gatherer societies of fully modern man living in environments with relatively short growing seasons, and organized logistically, at least seasonally, as were the Nunamiut Eskimo.

This means that some form of patterning similar to "parallel phyla," "alternation of industries," and "tenacious cultures" should be manifest in the Upper Paleolithic, that is, given that our methods of arranging observations do not obscure the types of variability expected when an assemblage is the unit of comparison and its classificatory status is evaluated with a procedure similar to Bordes' type list.

Interestingly, everywhere in the Paleolithic world where "la Méthode Bordes" (de Sonneville–Bordes 1974–1975) has been employed over any length of time, regional workers have been forced to the conclusion that there were "parallel phyla," sometimes "alternating industries" and "tenacious cultures." As more work is done, particularly survey, increasingly complex patterns of association are recognized between the "phyla" and local habitat differences. Finally, as still more work is done, particularly more stratigraphic work, it generally develops that similar "assemblages" are not necessarily contemporary and the "classic sequence" as defined from the earliest modern excavations appears not to be robotically repeated in each new site! This situation is apt to produce great consternation among the workers in the region since their expectations for "culture" are normally (a) gradual, continuous directional change, (b) graded variability across geographical regions, and (c) graded transformational change through time, where similar things belong in similar time periods.

> . . . les types et leurs proportions sont stables et constants a l'inérieur d'une même culture pour une période donnée dans une région donnée. . . . (de Sonneville–Bordes 1975:3).

Radical change within a sequence is accommodated by a post hoc argument which tends to "save" the view of culture outlined above, namely, that a migration of different people entered the region, abruptly replacing an earlier population. Alternation of industries is accommodated by the post hoc argument that an earlier population returned to the region. Parallel phyla is a little more difficult, demanding that the above expectation for a graded pattern of cultural variability across a region be abandoned in favor of a different view of "culture."

> . . . man is more ready to exchange his genes than his customs, as the whole history of Europe demonstrates. (Bordes 1968:144)

This is the view of culture which postulates a kind of tenacious holding on to one's way of doing things in spite of the types of social milieus that may be "around" a "people." This is an idea of culture much more consistent with "ethnic" phenomena characteristic of societal segments within complex systems rather than the types of graded regional patterns ethnographically described for small-scale societies (see Wissler 1914; Kroeber 1939; Milke 1949; Hodder 1977). Nevertheless, the conventions commonly used as ad hoc arguments in many cases tend to "save" the view of culture believed by the researcher. Nonsynchronous chronological patterning is the most difficult for most archaeologists to accommodate by ad hoc arguments about "culture." When faced with what appear to be "alternating industries" most are apt to question the accuracy of the "facts"; e.g., the excavator must have mixed levels, the C-14 date must be wrong, etc.

It is suggested that the problems of prehistory as illustrated by the well-documented sites of south-central France are "classic," but not in the sense in which French prehistorians tend to use the word; rather they are classic in the sense of the "predictions" given above.

It was in the pioneer area of research into man's prehistoric past, the Dordogne area of France, that the idea of a "classic sequence" or a basic chrono-stratigraphic sequence became popular. The French prehistorians viewed the stratigraphic sequence as observed in a given site as a document regarding the evolution of culture in general. Situations where there appeared to be no easy transition from one form to another were conventionally interpreted as referrable to historical shifts in the geographic distribution of differing cultural "phyla" or, in layman's terms, in the distribution of different prehistoric "tribes." The view of parallel phyla as originally proposed by Peyrony ("two great industrial traditions which coexisted in the Perigord and which evolved over time through a succession of more or less synchronous . . . stages of development"; Laville et al. (1980:282) has been stated in more popular language by F. Bordes as follows:

> The Aurignacian and Perigordian people seem to have lived 'side by side' during the Wurm III period, without influencing each other to any greater extent than the various Mousterians did during Wurm I and II. (Bordes 1968:157)

The old idea of a "classic" sequence of Paleolithic cultures revealed through careful stratigraphic research at a limited number of sites (de Sonneville–Bordes 1966), is no longer tenable. In fact, as new work is done, the single site–single chronological sequence view of the past is challenged.

> . . . Upper Perigordian systematics can no longer be viewed in terms of a simple linear model of successive assemblage types. (Laville et al. 1980:287)

Similarly, the later Solutrean–Magdalenian sequence is also presenting problems.

> Perhaps it's [the Magdalenian] industries do not belong to a single continuum of change and thus, in reality, there exists no simple succession of tool forms over time. (Laville et al. 1980:340)

While the debates regarding such challenges to the traditional view are quite colorful (see, for instance, F. Bordes' characterization of the dates from Level IX at Flageolet II as forcing us to imagine Charlemagne riding on a motorcycle F. Bordes 1979:81), the fact remains that with almost every new excavation the old "classic" sequence is being challenged in that the newly excavated sites do not exhibit the same sequences (Straus and Clark 1978:456; Straus 1980:625; Laville et al. 1980:312, Fig. 9.8). Nor do typologically similar assemblages appear to be necessarily contemporary as would be "expected" under conventional views (Laville and Rigaud 1973; Montet-White 1973:131–132).

Even more interesting in this regard is the recent "recognition" of multiple phyla among both Middle and Upper Paleolithic materials from the Near East (see Bar-Yosef 1980:115–118 for a summary of the Upper Paleolithic situations) and in North Africa. Needless to say, the archaeologists who "recognized" the different "cultures" were using approaches similar to "la Méthode Bordes" for classifying their materials.

> . . . the Kom Ombo Plain [was] a mosaic of cultures in late Paleolithic times where groups bearing a number of industrial traditions, both indigenous and intrusive frequented the environmental zones of this attractive region. . . . (Smith 1967:150)

> . . . the apparent presence of more than one Upper Paleolithic tradition in the Avdat/Aqev area. This is seen most clearly at Boker, where areas BE and C contain three technologically distinct assemblages which are more or less contemporaneous. (Marks 1977:78)

Almost simultaneously there has developed a series of arguments regarding the possible alternation of assemblages in sequences and the likelihood of parallel phyla as characteristic of the prehistoric past in South Africa (see Parkington 1980)!

It seems that everywhere an assemblage approach to prehistory is used, a past with independent cultures living side by side in the same regions over vast spans of time is created! I feel quite confident that, as "la Méthode Bordes" is being increasingly adopted in both Japanese and Indian research, we can anticipate the "recognition" of parallel phyla in the Paleolithic of both these regions.

Problem 2

The dynamics described here were observed among logistically organized systems of contemporary Eskimo—how does this illuminate the Mousterian, where there is apparently analogous patterning?

The first observation which I ever made with regard to patterning within Mousterian materials was a surprise (Binford 1972a:88). I had been unable to demonstrate a statistically "significant" difference between tool frequencies within samples recovered from the bottom of a deposit approximately 1 m deep and those recovered from arbitrary levels within the deposit, or even differences between the bottom and the top of the deposit. In my experience, that was new. Working with New World materials the reverse situation was generally present, namely that comparison between any combination of recovery units, natural levels or arbitrary levels within a geological deposit generally yielded "significant" differences. Clearly the descriptions of formation dynamics described here are much more consistent with my "New World" experiences than this Mousterian experience. Since my first brush with Mousterian materials I have had many additional opportunities to examine Mousterian assemblages. I have partitioned the deposits from Levels K, L, and M at the site of Combe Grenal and found that there were no "significant" differences between the arbitrarily defined "assemblages" from the bottom of the levels and the top. We have once again the picture of incredible internal homogeneity among the occupational episodes contributing to the buildup of a deposit over a considerable period of time.

This type of internal "couche" homogeneity would seem to be inconsistent with the formation dynamics currently described for foragers (see Yellen 1977:73–84), and it is certainly inconsistent with the formation dynamics as described here and in earlier accounts (Binford 1978b:451–497, 1980b:5–19). Some might argue that the Mousterian situation reflects an increasing repetitiveness in the character of site use conditioned by decreased mobility. Certainly some have thought the Mousterian represented essentially sedentary hunter–gatherer systems (see Bordes 1968:144; Marks and Freidel 1977). At least in terms of characteristics normally associated with high degrees of sedentism, such as regular trash disposal and cleanup of sites, increased investment in facilities, and intensification of subsistence practices—obtaining food from less space than when mobility is high, and an increase in logistical tactics for obtaining widely scattered resources—I find it very hard to view the Mousterian as a system of sedentary hunter–gatherers. We might be able to model some of the intersite variability documented from the Mousterian given the understanding of formation dynamics provided here, but I find it very hard to model the intrasite, or intra-"couche" variability or lack thereof from the perspective of our current understanding of sedentism.

The situation of seeming "I-N-C-O-N-S-I-S-T-E-N-C-Y" between what we think we understand about site formation, and the demonstrable pattern of both within- and between-site variability in the Mousterian is the signal that we still have considerable growth potential as a science. We don't have a comprehensive understanding of the conditions which bring into being patterning in the archaeological record. Mousterian patterning remains a challenge yet to be "decoded." The simple answer is that I don't understand the Mousterian patterning.

Problem 3

This example was drawn from a contemporary group of New World hunters. Why have patterns similar to those described here not been regularly reported from the New World?

The simplest answer to this problem is that in the New World archaeologists rarely describe "assemblages," and, even if they do, New World systematics is not based on "assemblage" units. The type of variability being discussed is reflected in content summaries for artifact inventories recovered from depositionally defined levels or from sites considered to have some minimal degree of occupational integrity. New World archaeologists work with different kinds of units. The basic unit of observation is most commonly the "type" (Krieger 1944; Ford 1954), considered to be a demonstrated cohesion of properties or attributes regularly associated on analogous artifacts recovered from a number of different sites (therefore demonstrating continuity). This approach yields what Dunnell has called nonclassificatory arrangements or, as Hodder (1977:294) has called them, "association groups." Cultures are then conceived as recurrent "bundles" of types. Patterns of repetitive association at different sites of a number of different "types" illustrate a "cohesion" of traits said to represent a "cultural" unit. This is thought to be a meaningful way of conceptualizing the past.

In a limited but growing number of cases where assemblage-based comparisons have been attempted using "type list" approaches analogous to "la Méthode Bordes," patterns of tenacious cultures (Vierra 1975; Irwin and Wormington 1970) and "parallel phyla" (Winters n. d., 1963b, 1969; Judge 1973) have been suggested. These studies illustrate nicely how dependent our views of the past are upon the particular *conventions* which we employ for ordering our observations. Put another way most New World archaeologists did not "see" the patterned variability described in this article *because their analytical conventions render it invisible.*

Conclusions

The conclusions to be drawn from this study reflect directly on the state of the art in archaeology.

1. The types of patterning illustrated here derive from the basic organizational properties of mobile human adaptations. I have suggested how different patterns studied comparatively might well inform us regarding differences in the fundamental organizational properties of past cultural systems.

2. This type of variability is at present only "visible" in terms of inventory differences among assemblages recovered from depositional units at different sites in a region.

3. An assemblage-based systematics is really only common among European Paleolithic archaeologists, and their work does yield patterning of the forms illustrated here. These archaeologists insist that the patterning is telling them about "culture" instead of the organizational functioning of cultural systems. The use made of their observations is, therefore, never directed toward the elucidation of evolutionary processes or the study of systems change and diversification. Their observations are "explained away" with ad hoc arguments which then become their constructed "culture histories."

4. New World archaeologists, by tradition, use a "type" -based systematics which renders it impossible to "see" the kind of variability described here. The result is that, in the main, New World systematic summaries tell us little of interest for studying processes of evolutionary change and diversification.

Among mobile peoples the differentiation of activities among places in both form and frequency of use carries direct information about the organization of a past system of adaptation, as do patterns of occupational redundancy. *The facts of interest are the ways in which places are differentiated* one from another, and how this differentiation is related to patterns of seasonal environmental dynamics as well as to longer-term cycles and shifts in environmental conditions. *All of these facts of interest are facts which differentiate one place from another.*

Until we turn our serious attention to the design of reliable methods for monitoring past conditions of interest, we will never be able to address interesting questions through the investigation of archaeological remains. Our current systematics is rooted in misguided ideas of "inductive objectivity" and is based on limited experiences believed to be informative as to the "nature of culture." These impressionistic ideas then guide our judgments as to how to observe and, in turn, how to interpret observations once they are made. I frequently hear the call for the development of "interesting" theory dealing with the "big" issues of cultural evolution, etc. Given the current state of our "observational language," our classifications and systematics, we simply cannot generate facts of relevance to these issues, much less move to the evaluation of theories designed to explain events of the past which we are unable to accurately recognize. In short we must turn our analytical attention to understanding the role of different places in the organization of past systems.

25

Long-term Land-Use Patterning:
Some Implications for Archaeology

Almost anyone who has studied or analyzed stratigraphic sequences has noted that there are periodicities or "punctuations" in the intensity with which a given place has been used. Commonly one might observe a period of intense use followed by relatively minimal use not uncommonly of a slightly different kind, and then another period of intense use, etc. This pattern is well represented and monitored by the excavators at Sudden Shelter (Jennings et al. 1980), Rodger's rock shelter (McMillan 1977), Hogup Cave (Aikens 1970), and many others. The purpose of this paper is to explore at least one set of conditions which when operative bring into being occupational periodicities at archaeological sites.

Most archaeologists are comfortable with the idea of seasonal mobility as a characteristic of at least some hunter–gatherer adaptations. There is even an increasing acknowledgement of variations in site function which may be generated somewhat independently of seasonal patterns of mobility. There has, however, been essentially no discussion of long term patterns of change in the disposition of a complete system in space.

Obviously long term patterns of land use are not something that an observer resident with a living group of people for the normal tenure of ethnographic fieldwork would have the opportunity to observe. In fact it is my impression that most ethnographers view the situation of the peoples they study in a normative manner and expect that the way they were at the time of study reflects a stable system state. My research among the Nunamiut Eskimo forced me to reject such an idea and to seek ways of gaining at least some temporal perceptions of the Nunamiut system. Clues to the dynamic character of their land use came through questioning aimed at understanding the composition and in turn their conceptualizations of local groups or "bands."

Repeated questioning of informants regarding the cultural specification of rela-

Paper delivered at the 46th Annual Meeting of the Society for American Archaeology, San Diego, California, April 1981.

WORKING AT ARCHAEOLOGY

tionships between persons and geographic or economic space failed to yield any indications that territory or resources were culturally assimilated to social roles.

My conclusions regarding the Nunamiut were that there was *no cultural specification of territoriality.* If there is *no territoriality,* does this mean that there is no regular patterning to the distribution of persons spatially? Certainly not. There are no cultural specifications regarding resources or geographical space among oak trees, deer or any other species yet we find regular patterns of distribution and association with resources. Similarly we find such patterns among hunters and gatherers who have no culturally specified territoriality. *The patterns derive from the interaction between culturally organized social dimensions and the nonculturally organized distribution of resources and life space.*

While this conclusion is interesting and casts some light on a number of problems which have been widely discussed in anthropology regarding "band" structure an additional observation was made which bore more directly on formation processes. The Eskimo expected to be living in one place for a substantial period of time, at least long enough for the young men to learn a regionally specific body of folklore but acknowledge that they would most likely be living elsewhere during much of their life. In order to follow out this hint of a potentially interesting situation I devised a scheme for interviewing elderly Eskimo men regarding the patterns of land use which their parents had trained them to expect during their lifetime. By interviewing informants in this way I hoped to gain a small glimpse of mobile big game hunters prior to the changes related to the intrusions of modern Western life.

In recognition that the Nunamiut case is probably neither unique nor wholly representative of all hunters and gatherers, I will refer to the economic space of an aggregate of persons as their *range* as opposed to territory in cases where their economic space is not culturally specified. In general, nonterritorially organized groups differentially exploit their range so that more intense use is made of some parts than of others. The intensively utilized segments of nonterritorial groups' *ranges* will be referred to as their residential *core areas.*

I have previously described the Nunamiut system as logistically organized (Binford 1978b and 1980b). That is, resources are commonly obtained by task groups moving considerable distances beyond a normal foraging radius where temporary camps may be established during the several days they are away from the residential camp. Given such an organization there is a pattern of economic zonation to the range surrounding any given residential site. This generalized pattern is shown in Figure 24.1. We may think of this zonation in terms of an immediate area surrounding the camp where resources are very quickly exhausted. This area, designated the foraging radius, rarely provides much in the way of foodstuffs unless there is a highly aggregated, renewable, or unearned resource adjacent to the site.

Archaeological sites produced in this zone are commonly what I have called locations (Binford 1980b), although in some circumstances there may be trapping sites, hunting blinds, and some special use sites within the foraging radius. Beyond the foraging radius is the logistical radius. This is the zone which is exploited by parties who stay away from the residential camp at least one night before returning. Beyond the logistical radius are lands unoccupied in the residential sense which are

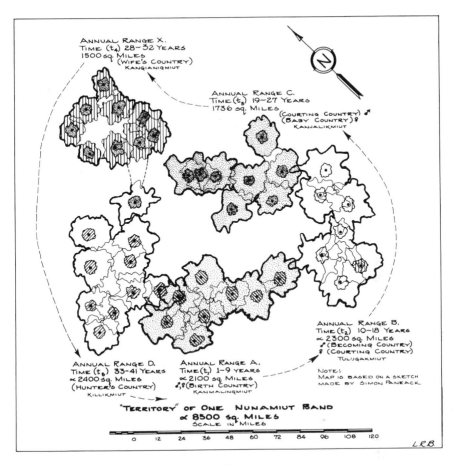

Figure 25.1   Traditional cycle of Nunamiut Eskimo land use.

termed here the *extended range*. In recognition that most hunters and gatherers are annually mobile, that is, they move their residential sites from one place to another during the year, the area regularly used residentially and logistically during an annual seasonal cycle is referred to as the *annual range*.

As suggested earlier, under the ideas of "territorial groups" common in anthropological circles most observers have tended to interview informants regarding their annual range and equate this with their territory. The implication has been that annual ranges did not vary greatly from one year to the next. In my experience with the Nunamiut it was clear that the placement of the *annual range* was not stable over long periods of time. During the mid-1930s their annual range was centered in the Killik River basin, during the early 1940s another range was centered in the Okomelaga Valley, while during the late 1940s the annual range was centered in the Chandlar Lake area. In the late 1940s and early 1950s the annual range was centered in Anaktuvuk Valley. The average size of known annual ranges was about 1650 miles^2

(4273.5 km^2) for a band of approximately 35 people. There was some tendency for there to be overlapping use of areas depending upon which summer "hub" an annual range was centered on. This shifting of the placement of sites within an annual range might be considered one type of "range drift" (see Hill 1969). In contrast *long term range drift is a pattern where a group relocates in space so that there is little if any overlap in area with previous annual ranges.* Among the Nunamiut this generally took the form of shifting the summer hub of the annual range. During the course of my records one band of approximately 35 people utilized 2.5 annual ranges during the course of 22 years or almost 9 years per "annual range." Viewing my data historically the gross range of the Nunamiut for which I have documentation represents 4.46 annual ranges per band. During the period of record, each band of inland Nunamiut had available an *extended territory* equal to approximately 4.5 annual ranges. If a band remains centered in a given annual range for approximately 9 years and moves through 4.46 or realistically 5 such ranges without competing with another band this cycle takes between 40 to 45 years or essentially the active life of a male hunter and the reproductive life of a female.

Figure 25.1 displays the summary information on land use which I recovered from five old Eskimo men regarding what they had "expected" to happen if their lives had not changed drastically from the "traditional" life of inland Caribou hunters.

The old men all started their "model" of expected land use in the home range where they were born—this they called their "birth country." There they expected to live until they were approximately 6–10 years of age. Within this range they expected to move through normal annual rounds of residential movement camping at different places and generally "being mobile" but within a generalized range.

After the *annual range* has been positioned in an area (typically a river valley) for a number of years, the willows—the major and in most cases the only source of firewood—begin to be depleted in the favorable places for winter houses. Similarly, local sheep populations may well be depressed in number since under normal conditions they were heavily hunted during the mid to late summer months (see Binford and Chasko 1976; Campbell 1978). In like fashion the local populations of ground squirrel—particularly around summer residential camping locations—would be diminished and snares would be set at ever-increasing distances from the optimal spots for summer camps. In addition to the unrelenting depletion of the local area around camping spots would be a general increase in what might be called commensal vermin. As residential camp use of locations intensified over time there is an inevitable increase in debris from both human as well as dog consumption and excretion. Associated with this buildup of organic by-products is an inevitable increase in the population of flies. The latter are the biggest threat to the successful storage of dried meat during the summer months (see Binford 1978b—an insecure time for the Nunamiut (see Campbell 1970). Camping in a single area gradually depletes the usable resources around camping spots and enhances the environment for flies and other vermin.

These conditions were frequently verbalized by the old men in terms of changing attitudes among the people. "When we first move into a valley everything is good, people want visitors, people want to see friends, people want to share, but as time goes on, things get used up and the place gets full of flies, then people start to fight. When that happens it's time to move to a place where nobody has lived for a long time." The old men all agreed that between 6 and 10 years was about the duration of occupation in any given annual range.

In short, the sustained use of a given annual range results in (a) reduction in the number of locational options for the placement of residential camps as the willows and local populations of supplementary food species are depleted around residential camps and (b) this tends to intensify the localization of camp groups into the fewer larger and more productive patches in the habitat, where as group sizes tended to increase in camps, the effect of impact is stepped up. The overall result was to increase tension and competition among "band units" and as tension builds the decision to move to a "new area" becomes increasingly inevitable.

As young men, the Nunamiut elders expected to move into what they refer to as "becoming country" not more than 10 years after they were born (Figure 25.1B). The new annual range into which they moved between the ages of 6 to 12 was the area in which they expected to be living when they were learning the adult roles of a hunter, making long trips to other uninhabited regions as well as areas occupied by adjacent groups since they must have detailed knowledge of the "lifetime range" or the area over which they can expect to live during their lifetime. This was the area which provided their "group identity."

After about 7 to 10 years living in this core residential area the "band" would move on to another core residential area, which normally coincided with a major valley or watershed area. This third residential area was called by boys their "courting country" while for girls it was called "birthing country."

On marriage the male leaves his "courting country" (Figure 25.1C) and moved into the area occupied by his wife's people (Figure 25.1X). There he may stay for anywhere between 5 and 6 years. The next move by a male is commonly back to his "band" after his period of "bride service." By this time he expects his "band" to have moved into a new annual range (Figure 25.1D) and it is this area in which he will achieve his maximum notoriety as a hunter ("Hunter's country") and an expert at performing male roles.

After living the average of 9 years in "hunter's country" the band moves back into the annual range occupied at the time the man was born. In this setting he becomes a respected elder in the country in which he had been born.

The picture which I obtained of long term mobility among the Nunamiut implies a number of things relative to patterns of site production and histories of "place" utilization.

Perhaps the first clear consequence for site formation of the long-term patterns of land use indicated here is that we would expect to see clear periodicities in the use of sites. During times that a given site was incorporated into the normal pattern of use with a lifetime range we might expect it to be used relatively frequently as long as the "band" was occupying the annual range where the site was located. It is also true that we might expect some "functional" variability in the way the site was used in response to the movement of residential sites from one place to another within the annual range (see Binford 1982a for a discussion of this process). Nevertheless, we may expect a maximal intensity of use during the period of time that the site was actually incorporated into the active annual range of a group.

On the other hand, when a group shifts annual ranges, the places within the previously occupied area generally change radically in the pattern of occupational utilization. I have shown (Binford 1982a) that with a shift in the position of a residential site there is a related shift in the "use potential" of other places in the region. When a residential site is in one place, another site within the range may be regularly used as a temporary camp or a logistically organized extractive camp. On the other hand, a move in the residential site sets up a new set of spatial relationships relative to the new residence and the use potential of the old sites may be radically altered. The same place may now be inappropriate for its former use because of its changed position relative to the new residential site. The same principle applies to the shifting or the positioning of the entire system within the macroregion. Given a change in the annual range of the system, sites which were previously residential in function may now become logistical in character. Similarly, favorite hunting camps regularly used from the perspective of one annual range may now be only used as transient camping spots, once the annual range is shifted to another segment of the lifetime range.

I think one can appreciate that given variable durations to the use of annual ranges the repetition in use of a place may vary considerably between one phase of regional positioning for the system and another. With such shifts in annual range the tempo of site use almost certainly changes as does at least some functional characteristics of site utilization. This alone is probably sufficient to result in a recognizable difference in the character of a deposit accumulated over a substantial period of time.

We might see a considerable buildup of archaeological material at a site relating to its use during the tenure of placement of one annual range. When the annual range shifts, the same site would be most likely used in a different way and in a different tempo of occupational reuse. This shift would show up differences between the "assemblages" of material, accumulated while the site was within an annual range versus when it was part of the extended range of an annual range centered elsewhere. The magnitude of the contrast might well be considerable. The fidelity of use at a place occupied as a component of one annual range is apt to be high with a corresponding likelihood of considerable internal homogeneity among the remains deposited. On the other hand, the same place utilized by the same people living on a different annual range is quite likely to have served different functions and hence to exhibit considerable assemblage contrasts with the material deposited earlier. This means that "strata" recognizable because of differing anthropogenic conditions would also tend to be more internally homogenous and exhibit marked contrasts with adjacent superimposed strata.

Such a shift could, archaeologically, give the appearance of considerable change. *It would occur, however, not as a consequence of change in the organization of the system, only in its positioning within the region.*

Associated with such a change in site function and hence assemblage content there may well be a correlated change in the occupational tempo and/or intensity of utilization at a site. This would result in changed rates of archaeological accumulation

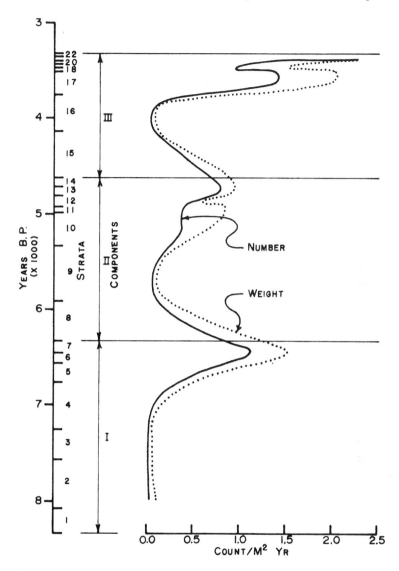

Figure 25.2 Curve of use intensity for Sudden Shelter (total debitage concentration versus time.)

per unit of time and/or natural depositional episodes at the site. This would have the effect of producing a "punctuated" curve of use intensity at the site over time as has been illustrated for sudden shelter by Jennings and his associates (1980) (see Figure 25.2). We might well expect there to be some correlated shifts in assemblage composition and use intensity. Such patterning should be investigated for clues to systems functioning rather than assuming that superpositional changes in the character of archaeological deposits necessarily monitor organizational changes in cultural systems.

In the case of the dynamics I have described, such a change could occur depositionally at a given archaeological site *in the absence of system change*. All that would be needed is a repositioning of the system in space, and there would be formal changes in both content and use intensity chronologically arranged within the deposits at some if not most sites within the geographical area of the systems repositioning. Put in blunt terms, there might well be stratigraphic or at least superpositioned archaeological deposits differing in content and use intensity which would not be a measure of culture change, only systems positioning. Archaeologists have generally never considered such a possibility; in fact, the equation of a change in a deposit with culture change is almost a "basic tenet" of archaeological interpretation.

PART V

Some Current Views

26

Working at Archaeology: Some
Thoughts about the 1970s and Beyond

The articles assembled in this section include a statement on the importance of par-adigms and perspectives (Chapter 27) and my most general statement on middle-range research (Chapter 28). I have ended the book with a review of the Mousterian problem (Chapter 29).

Several of my opinions should be clarified by these chapters. I think that the nature of our intellectual problems as archaeologists is now clear. We have learned how to conduct research fostering theoretical growth, and we are learning how to address the complex problem of specifying the properties of systems for which no modern analogues remain. (This issue is directly addressed in my *Bones* [L. R. Binford 1981b] book.)

The Mousterian problem, still unsolved, has prompted much research. This research has increased our understanding of statics, particularly the statics generated by mobile hunter–gatherers. It has also stimulated a quest for an understanding of cultural systems as manifest by the differentiated components of technology and the organized use of these components at different places. My tactical approach to the study of the Mousterian problem remains productive (see Chapters 4 and 14). In the 1980s I will be working toward the use of faunal facts as an organizational Rosetta stone for examining patterning in assemblage composition as defined by stone tools. I hope to supplement such studies with increased understanding of site structure (see L. R. Binford 1983:Chapter 7). I look forward to writing a global cross-cultural study of hunters and gatherers as documented ethnographically and historically, a study I started during the early 1970s.

The reader should realize that *Working at Archaeology* reports on a personal research program that was developed primarily while I was attempting to solve the Mousterian problem. As I have tried to illustrate, this program was a direct and important part of the new archaeology. I do not claim that my work is the new archaeology of the 1970s; however, it is certainly one of the archaeological perspectives directly linked to the events of the 1960s. When we (S. R. Binford and L. R. Binford 1968) published *New Perspectives in Archaeology,* we were self-conscious about using the plural, *perspectives*. The advantages of having a number of researchers working at archaeology in the contexts of their own research programs is not to be underestimated. We need various views of problems and persons seeking solutions in multiple ways. However, I do have opinions about what will advance the field and what will not. Productive personal research programs depend upon an initial, hardheaded assessment of the state of the art. The researcher then needs to evaluate his or her particular skills, and, against a backdrop of that assessment of what is needed, develop a long-range research program for learning. The thrust of much of my discussions at the beginning of each part of this book has been the scarcity of skillfull assessment of where the field was, what we needed to learn, and how to go about learning the needed information. The productive researcher *must* have a problem, in terms of which he or she recognizes an area of ignorance, and then proceeds to work against this ignorance, trying to gain knowledge to narrow the zone of ignorance and expand the domains of our understanding.

There have been a number of research directions followed by archaeologists during the 1970s. Many of these we may see in retrospect as relatively nonproductive, but that was not necessarily clear at the time they were initiated. For instance, many archaeologists took an approach analogous to that taken by most of the new archaeologists (see L. R. Binford 1964a; Flannery and Coe 1968). A descriptive model of a type of system would be adopted from ethnographers or economists and accommodated to the facts of the archaeological record from some particular region and time period. Widely read examples of this approach are the writings of Sanders and Price (1968), and Renfrew (1973) for European materials. In both cases the evolutionary typology of societal forms proposed by Sahlins and Service (1960; Service 1962) was used to explain the archaeological remains of interest. Many may recognize the methodological bind that these tactics forced on the archaeologist. *All argument from archaeological facts is of necessity an argument of relevance* (see Chapter 12). All that can be judged is the appropriateness of the model to the case in question. Such arguments are of necessity equivocal. The models used were sometimes wrong or misleadingly simple (see for instance Earle 1977), and there was no objective way to translate the model into diagnostic static properties that could unambiguously permit the identification of one type of system rather than another, or signify the presence of a system not described by the models. In short, most were working with a description produced by ethnographers, and then they "deduced test implications" from the models for forms of expected statics that, if observed, would "identify" the suspected system type. Such approaches are doomed because the test implications are not deduced; in fact, inductive logic is needed. One must *guess* in order to argue for linkage between dynamics and statics,[1] and such guesses give inductive conclusions more content than the original premises had. Such links were not studied by the ethnographers and economists who invented the dynamic models; neither were they studied by the archaeologists using the models. In short, there was no middle-range research to provide an unambiguous linkage between statics and dynamics. Without such a link, no relative objectivity (see Chapter 6) could be achieved in the identification procedure, and the logic generally came around to being a poorly disguised tautology.

Perhaps we need to take a lesson from my Nunamiut studies. The facts described in these studies are very different from those an ethnographer would study and report. The reason is very simple: *I was trying both to understand the statics as archaeologists see them and to uncover the dynamics that produced them.* In this context, the dynamic points of interest were relative to the statics and hence very different from facts of interest to an ethnographer. This contrast is illustrated in Richard Gould's frustration with having done his research as an ethnographer,[2] viewing experiences from the perspective of day-to-day dynamics, and then seeking ways of seeing the same experiences in the archaeological remains. He expressed his frustration as follows:

> The case of Tikatika is a powerful example of the futility of trying to draw direct archaeological conclusions from ethnographic observations. Studies of this kind, in which one attempts to compare behaviour with its "archaeological" manifestations, tend in most cases to be cautionary tales. . . . As science lurches on, it sometimes takes paths that lead to dead ends. The case of Tikatika is an example of one such methodological cul de sac, and we are still left with the haunting problem of how to do justice to the richness and complexity of behavior observed in the Western Desert on that day in December 1966, and on many other days while these remarkable people, the desert Aborigines, were still living directly off the land [R. A. Gould 1980:27–28].

Gould recognized the inappropriate character of most ethnographic observations and generalizations (see R. A. Gould 1980:250), but failed, in my opinion, to appreciate the need to begin with the statics and then work toward the recognition of the conditioning effects of *relevant dynamics*.[3] Instead, he started with ideas of dynamics (see R. A. Gould 1980:251) and worked back to statics, seeking "archaeological signatures" for the dynamics "of one's choice." This ensures that as archaeologists we work simply to translate statics into dynamics as viewed by others. If we start from statics, we have a chance to see kinds of dynamics not directly observable by the ethnographer. For instance, no student of hunter–gatherer ethnography has recognized or discussed the organizational properties of mobile systems treated in Part IV of this book!

The fact that my approach was in no way simply a materialist-oriented ethnography is well illustrated by Richard Lee's (1980) review of my *Nunamiut* book.[4]

> I have been asked to review this book from the viewpont of the nonarchaeologist. What is there here for the student of the cultural ecology of hunter–gatherer societies? . . . data of interest to social anthropologists and cultural ecologists are there but you have to have the patience to find them, wedged in between the proximal metatarsals and the distal metatarsals [Lee 1980:632–633].

Lee rightly concludes that my book was for fellow archaeologists (Lee 1980:633). It was not an ethnographic study. Instead, it sought to understand statics, which ethnographers do not study, in the context of those dynamics relevant to the statics. Once again we see a major contrast in perspective and in approaches to research. There is a lesson in these contrasts. Some approaches get us where we need to go, and others lead to dead ends, as R. A. Gould learned.

Adopting ethnographic or economic models and then engaging in endless arguments of relevance, to the extent that we become disenchanted with one set of models and look about in search of new ones,[5] is not going to advance our understanding of the past. In fact, this procedure could well retard the growth of understanding. For instance, as long as archaeologists think they are *testing* a theory as opposed to evaluating its relevance to a specific real-world situation when they engage in arguments of relevance, they will almost certainly discard useful theories. This is not because of the inaccuracy or nonutility of the theories, but because of their inappropriate application by the archaeologists. This is like denying the existence of cancer because a patient thought to have it was later shown to have died of a heart attack! Many ethnographic models have undoubtedly met this fate.

We need to stop this kind of strategy and seek control cases where we know something about specific dimensions—mobility, stratification, and so on—and then we need to study the statics. Once we note patterns in relevant contexts, we may seek through further investigation a knowledge of the causal dynamics. In this fashion we may gradually build up instruments for measuring specified dynamic variables. Controlled research, in which the knowns are demonstrable and statics can be studied as a way to uncovering their dynamic determinants, is needed. This will enable us to build up diagnostic markers for variables of interest to a number of different models, and instruments that are not model specific. Given our current state of knowledge about statics (very little), control study is most economically done actualistically.[6]

Part of the failure of many suggestions for doing ethnoarchaeology rests with the unfortunate belief that we should be studying human behavior. We will not grow, nor will we gain a realistic sense of problem, until we adopt a systemic paradigm. For instance, Schiffer advocates the study of human behavior to understand the relationships between it and material culture (Schiffer 1976:4). Given such a view, it is consistent for him to think he can seek laws through the study of humans whenever they are found.

> Even aspects of Binford's (1973) Nunamiut study can be duplicated in the United States—curate behavior of mobile social units can be studied among modern campers. For archaeologists, such as I, who are reluctant to endure the rigors of the arctic cold, even in the name of science, the study of modern material culture offers an appealing and inexpensive alternative for acquiring and testing laws of human behavior [Schiffer 1976a:193].

We must realize that we are seeking to understand the *systems-specific laws* giving the differing relationships between statics and dynamics among differently organized cultural systems. We cannot simply study phenomena such as mobility just anywhere, and expect to be able to offer an empirical generalization that might be raised to the level of a law through arguments by enumeration (see Schiffer 1976a:4). This simple matching up of things that share a formal analogy and assuming that they all were organized in identical ways—presumably by virtue of the common determinant, human nature—is the ultimate misuse of ethnographic analogy.

I view the 1970s as a time of much wheel spinning. It was a time of rather damning, generation gap kinds of misunderstandings,[7] a time when many perspectives were being followed. This testing of alternatives has served a valuable purpose, and we can now begin to identify productive versus nonproductive approaches. Perhaps the 1980s will see major growth based on the painful, trial-and-error learning of the researchers of the 1970s.

Notes

1. Many of the "model fitters" generated test implications with variables that are categorical, what logicians call analytical statements. These are statements for which the meanings are true by definition, rather than statements that have empirical content and therefore make assertions about properties of the empirical world. A very popular categorical property is *diversity*, which any organization or aggregate of phenomena can be said to have by definition, because diversity is a measure of the number of and/or formal similarity among the elements making up the unit being discussed. The meaning of diversity does not, therefore, derive from an understanding of the external world. Many such categorical concepts are commonly employed in test implications; *integration, efficiency,* and *complexity* are examples. The use of such concepts removes from consideration the problem of the meaning for observations. Because meaning is assigned by definition, the question becomes what value a particular real-world case exhibits, not what meaning it has. Once this is achieved, a "theory" that can account for differing values for these variables is proposed. It is absolutely astonishing how many different theories are said to be supported by varying estimates for these variables. In like fashion, there are numerous arguments that hold that because we are dealing with the same phenomenon, efficiency, for example, or perhaps diversity, there must be a single theory regulating variability in this variable! The problem with this approach is that these categorical concepts are not theoretical terms. They do not take their meanings from theories; rather, they are universalistic concepts applicable to any organization or aggregate of phenomena. Yet there is no universal theory for organizations and aggregates! This is the deceiving aspect of what has been passed off as "general systems theory." It is in reality a collection of categorical statements without integration in a theory. Use of such categorical or analytically defined variables means that one can rationalize any results one obtains to any view one wishes to assume (see for instance, my criticism of M. Conkey in Chapter 29). It is quite likely that very different determinants condition such properties as diversity in different systems. We lack a general theory of how systems vary relative to such properties, and we certainly lack the tools for recognizing differently organized systems. Most of the time we end up with vacuous arguments that appear convincing because anyone can comprehend the "meaning" of the variables being discussed!

2. Gould's basic ethnoarchaeological fieldwork was done in the Gibson Desert during the early to mid-1960s. This is reported in his book *Yiwara: Foragers of the Australian Desert* (1969), which begins, as does the later *Living Archaeology* (1980), with a description of a day (the former gives December 28, 1966; the latter, December 26, 1966). In the *Yiwara* book, the description sets the tone for the remainder of the book, which is essentially ethnographic; only minor departures point to what we used to call "correlates" in the material culture of his people. The fact that this is ethnography is emphasized by the acceptance of Gould's work that is illustrated by Margaret Mead's comments printed on the back cover of the paperback edition. This positive reaction by an ethnographer should be contrasted to Richard Lee's reaction to my book, where there is no doubt that he cannot accept it as ethnography.

3. This is a point that Kent Flannery has made in his review of Coe and Diehl's book on the Olmec (Flannery 1982:446–447).

4. I do not wish to imply that I consider Lee's review either accurate or insightful. For instance, he refers to the Nunamiut book as "an avalanche of undigested computer-generated data [Lee 1980:632]." No computer was ever used on the compilation of the tables in the Nunamiut book, which present raw data tabulated from field observations. That Lee appears to be more concerned about the facts as I present them relative to his generalizations about the role of hunting among hunters–gatherers (see Lee 1968) is clearly seen in the following statement: "The Nunamiut of Anaktuvuk Pass in northern Alaska have been hunting with guns since the turn of the century. So equipped they have turned their inhospitable inland-mountain habitat into a veritable paradise for hunting of caribou, the meat of which forms over 80% of their animal diet [Lee 1980:632]." Here we see Lee trying to dismiss the Nunamiut data by the old "evolutionist's" trick of arguing that they are exceptional because of modern influence. He has ignored the fact that the book included considerable data on the pregun Nunamiut, including faunal counts and frequencies showing essentially no difference in the role of meat pre- and post-gun. Even more important, all data from the fieldwork clearly showed that the gun resulted in the killing of *fewer* caribou, not in an increase in their exploitation. When traditional hunting techniques, such as spearing caribou in lakes, were

used, it was much more difficult to keep track of the number of animals killed. Communication among the hunters in the kayaks was nearly impossible, and frequently the result was overkill. With rifles, hunters can see the animals drop, count the number killed, and communicate with other hunters quite well using raven calls and hand signals. My data from archaeological sites support the view that the rifle resulted in a reduction in the number of caribou killed annually.

5. See, for instance, the section "Processual Models" at the conclusion of *Lowland Maya Settlement Patterns* (Ashmore 1981:408–415) for a good example of model searching. Another example is Upham (1982), and I am sure the reader could add others.

6. I am not implying that this is the only way we may work, only that this seems to be the most productive way now. Later, as the field matures, we may be able to accept some instruments for measurement as accurate and unambiguous. We may then begin the interesting use of archaeological cases as control information relative to specified variables for which we have developed good instruments for measurement (see Chapter 6 for a further discussion of this point).

7. The generation gap is at least in part a failure of our educational institutions to promote *descent without modification*. As I read the generation gap literature, it is clear that we are dealing with culture within a system. In this context Hodder (1982) is absolutely correct. Ideas and symbols cannot be understood without an understanding of the cultural context in which they were used and developed. In Chapter 13 I tried to illustrate how this context shifted between the work of the 1960s generation of new archaeologists and the ambitious young people of the 1970s. What our education system failed to do was to teach these young people the contexts in terms of which we worked in the 1960s.

27 1982

Paradigms, Systematics, and Archaeology

Lewis R. Binford and Jeremy A. Sabloff

The ways archaeologists view the past—their paradigms—directly influence their interpretation of the archaeological record. Paradigm change need not be irrational or undirected; such change can best be accomplished by focusing attention on the various ways that dynamic cultural processes can be linked with the static archaeological record.

The assumption that scientists are capable of clearing their minds and achieving total objectivity is basic to the strict empiricist ideas which dominated early science.[1] Boasian anthropology in the United States, and most of the intellectual background of archaeology in general, was founded on this belief in strict empiricism and in the old, Baconian idea of "psychological" objectivity: one simply cleared one's mind of bias and allowed the great truths of nature to be uncovered through the vehicle of one's "bias-free" mind. Such were the views dominating the "great days" when "discoveries" were considered to be the products of a science whose mission was to accumulate and inventory "natural facts."

But starting in the late nineteenth/early twentieth century, local positivists challenged the idea that an "objective" observer is capable of seeing nature directly and accurately. Instead, these philosophers distinguished between the process of discovery (gathering facts and generating theories) and the process of evaluation (of theories used to account for these "facts"). They therefore sought to develop methods largely dependent upon deductive forms of reasoning for evaluating ideas that were already

Originally published with Jeremy A. Sabloff in *Journal of Anthropological Research,* **38** (2): 137–153, © 1982.

in existence. They also recommended that scientists predict causal occurrences (i.e., if A, then by necessity B) and then test these predictions against the facts.

Anthropology, and more particularly archaeology, was relatively slow in absorbing the implications of logical-positivist thinking. In the 1960s, many archaeologists (often labeled "new archaeologists") reacted to the strict empiricism of their colleagues by suggesting that the field at least catch up with the changes in other sciences, i.e., acknowledge the fallacy of being able to achieve "psychological objectivity." New archaeologists argued that the discipline should adopt logical-positivist methods or develop ones of its own (see Binford 1972a, Spaulding 1968).

At about the same time that these suggestions for updating archaeological epistomology were being made, some interesting ideas were percolating in the philosophy of science. Perhaps the most influential of these was the thesis of Thomas Kuhn (1962a, 1962b) that one should distinguish between *paradigm* and *theory*. A paradigm is one's world view, translating one's experience into meaningful statements. A theory is an argument one makes about why the world is patterned in a particular form. Through arguments involving necessary linkages between classes of data, theory makes prediction possible. Theory is thus derived from one's paradigm: it is a subset of it.

Kuhn's argument amounts to a very explicit recognition of the position that meaning comes from humans, that conceptualizations of experience are our inventions, and that nature does not dictate the meanings we assign to it. It recognizes further that when we seek to explain nature through theories, we are seeking to explain our conceptualization of nature, rather than some objective, "true" nature such as Sir Francis Bacon thought himself capable of seeing directly.

Kuhn's thesis clearly was significant. He implied that while the logical positivists had recognized that the source of ideas was subjective, they had sought to evaluate these admittedly subjective inventions by referral back to experience, through the use of "objective" observational methods. Kuhn's thesis suggested that this was a fallacy. Objectivity is not attainable either inductively or deductively. Rather, one's observational means for conceptualizing experience are rooted in one's paradigm. The testing of theories was thus an illusion, ultimately bound by paradigmatic subjectivity. Falsification and theory testing as advocated by the logical positivists were thus mere puzzle solving, and were not acknowledged as capable of advancing the paradigm. It is in our reading of Kuhn's argument, as well as that of many other critics, that he viewed paradigmatic change as resulting from irrational interaction of one's domain of thought with other domains. He suggested that such change was responsive to "historical" trends in the wider intellectual domains of society. Science thus did not grow through rational progress but through the chance interaction between investigatory games played out inside a paradigm-bound discipline and "noisy" intellectual conditions outside the discipline, which tended to modify the paradigm under scrutiny (see, for example, Kuhn 1962b:77–78, 1970:208).[2]

What is interesting in these developments is that the very paradigmatic distinctions which Kuhn so insightfully introduced were ignored by many who have accepted or elaborated his arguments (see, for example, Feyerabend 1975; Toulmin 1972). These distinctions were (a) his conceptual separation of paradigms from theory, (b) his recognition that science may grow by changes in either, and (c) his assertion that logical positivism had not considered paradigmatic change. Having insisted that paradigms are an intellectual domain capable of being unaffected by debate about theory and that many different theories might be offered within the context of a single paradigm, Kuhn stated that paradigm change is not subject to development by methods of rational change. He linked this idea of "irrationality" to the very conceptual recognition of paradigms, and the argument for existential validity of the concept was then cited as rationale for a belief in the associated theory of irrational paradigm change. Such a linkage does not appear to be necessary at all. The challenge to science is to address directly the problem of developing methodological aids to paradigm change and evaluation, as well as the continued perfection of such aids for the evaluation and production of theories. In short, we may accept Kuhnian insights regarding the importance of paradigms and their impact on our ideas of objectivity without accepting his particular approach to paradigm change. We may profitably explore alternative theories of change and seek to build into scientific procedure methods for encouraging rational paradigm growth.

We believe that archaeologists today are in an excellent position to show how such rational paradigm growth can be achieved. The archaeological literature of the past two decades is replete with arguments which point out that if a major goal of the discipline is to explain culture change, then the traditional ways of looking at the past—the normative paradigms—have not been very productive. A new way of looking at the world, the systems paradigm (see Binford 1962) has been proposed as a potentially more productive means of reaching this explanatory goal. The question is, how should the discipline proceed in developing this (or any other) paradigm? This paper seeks to address the issue both as a first step in the direction of developing rational methods that will foster productive paradigm change and as a means of heightening archaeologists' awareness as to how difficult the challenge of science can be. As the senior author (Binford 1977b:3) notes,

> Science is a method or procedure that directly addresses itself to the evaluation of cultural forms. That is, if we view culture as at least referring to the particularly human ability to give meaning expediently to experience, to symbol, and in turn, view experience through this conceptual idiom, science is then concerned with evaluating the utility of the cultural tools produced.

Two Views of "Culture"

Cultural "Cohesion" in Continuity: A New World Paradigm

Archaeologists are often unaware of how their traditionally held paradigms influence their views of the past. Two such paradigms are presented here to illustrate their effect on archaeological systematics and interpretations.

A view which developed largely in North America focuses on the continuity of culture (as manifest in material objects) over wide geographical areas. The perspective stems largely from early empirical studies of North American Indian culture as developed by Wissler (1914) and elaborated by Kroeber (1939).

On the basis of comparative study of "culture traits" (particularly material aspects of culture) among certain American Indian groups, Wissler (1914:468) noticed that "while many have called attention to the intergradations of culture, few, for example, have considered the significance of the rarity of abrupt breaks in its continuity." He then pointed out that in known cases where identified "ethnic" groups, such as Cheyenne, Plains Cree, etc., moved from one region to another during historic times, they quickly assimilated to the "culture type" characteristic of the area into which they moved. In turn, they "lost" the culture traits not shared with the groups in their new setting. Wissler (1914:469;emphasis added) concluded that:

> What evidence we have seems to indicate that by separating a tribe from a center [of culture area] its material culture is made intermediate [between the form of its parent 'center' and the 'center' toward which it moved] and by joining a tribe to a center its culture is made typical. *Hence, unless we find data to support the wholesale movement of a material culture center, we must assume stability of habitat during its historic life.* We need not, however, assume stability as to its political, linguistic, and somatic unit constituents . . . We have been long familiar with the lack of correlation between culture, language, and somatic type.

Throughout the writings of the founders of American anthropology, we find repeated emphasis that the "essential" feature of culture is that culture traits can be exchanged independently of race, language, or socio-political identity. As Wissler (1914:490) indicated, the one thing culture does not have is "cohesions" among units over time:

> Tribal individuality appears only in decoration and a few inessential features, but even so is rarely restricted to a single tribe and tends toward a geographical rather than a random grouping."

Basically, Wissler's view (which was shared with many other American anthropologists) was that continuities exist across geographical regions and through time as long as the environment stays roughly the same. Traits and complexes are free to move among the social, linguistic, racial, or other types of groups. Any cohesion, or tendency toward a stable association among elements of material culture, is a phenomenon of large geographical regions and relatively long life spans; not a phenomenon of social or ethnic units. The implication was that cultural dynamics must be understood in terms more comprehensive than simple interaction among persons or social units. Although this view was modified in North America and ultimately reduced to a "psychological" point of view, presented in terms of learning theory and ideas of "historical causation," most archaeologists, who clearly recognized that they were studying "material culture," adopted the view that culture must be described in terms of continuities.

It is no accident that the development of observational "tools" by archaeologists, and the growth of archaeological systematics in general, was guided by the above ideas. New World systematics was generated by archaeologists using units (types) which were considered equivalent to the "culture traits" of their ethnographic colleagues. Summing up what was most certainly a view held by a majority of his colleagues, Krieger (1944:272) states that: "The purpose of a type in archaeology must be to provide an organizational tool which will enable the investigator to group specimens into bodies which have *demonstrable historical meaning in terms of behavior patterns.*" He then operationalizes a means of achieving these "bodies": after describing two steps in the sorting of material using judgments of similarity based on morphological criteria, he then discusses the next, crucial step (1944:280–81):

> The third step is a process of recombining the groups obtained in the second step, through the study of their comparative distributions. . . . *Only* in this way can it be determined that certain characters are variations of single underlying plans, while others which do not fall together consistently are not variations but culturally distinct ideas. Those details which do consistently combine through site after site, in the same temporal horizon and in the same culture complex, may thus be safely regrouped into *tentative types. These differ from all other so-called types in that the cohesiveness of their elements has been proved through the use of archaeological data rather than simply supposed through a variety of assumptions.*

For New World analysts, a "culture trait" was something that had "cohesion" among its particular properties (attributes). This cohesion was demonstrable only if the pattern held across a number of spatially distinct cases (sites). In this sense, the criterion of cohesion was used to define a culture trait *qualitatively,* which could only be demonstrated by a pattern of continuity or repetitive association of properties across a number of cases. Culture itself was seen to represent a "cohesion" of demonstrated culture traits, considered to exist at a level of organization transcending the level represented by the social, ethnic, racial, or linguistic "identity" of the participants.

Cultural "Cohesion" in Association: An Old World Paradigm

As far as we can determine, the modern concept of culture commonly used by many Europeans was popularized by V.G. Childe. For example, he (1929:vi) noted that:

> We find certain types of remains—pots, implements, ornaments, burial sites, house forms—constantly recurring together. Such a complex of regularly associated traits we shall term a 'cultural group' or just a 'culture'. We assume that such a complex is the material expression of what would today be called a 'people'.

Childe's idea of culture appears to have been adopted from the Germanic literature, in particular from the works of Kossinna, who used it to express strong racist sentiments (see Trigger 1980). According to Kossinna, differential cultural achievements should be understood in terms of the degree that societies are kept racially "pure." Childe rejected the linkage of social success (judged in terms of cultural "achievements") with racial purity. He did not, however, reject the linkage between society and culture. For Childe, cultures were the material expressions of particular "peoples."

Childe's view, as well as that of many others of the time, represents a poorly analyzed blend of holistic ideas then current in European circles.[3] The idea that a "society" is the basic unit of "cultural variability" is perhaps best illustrated by one of the most influential writers who espoused a holistic viewpoint (Durkheim 1938 [1895]:19–20):

> If we represent historic evolution as impelled by a sort of vital urge which pushes men forward, since a propelling tendency can have but one goal, there can be only one point of reference with relation to which the usefulness or harmfulness of social phenomena is calculated. Consequently, there can, and does, exist only one type of social organization that fits humanity perfectly; and the different historical societies are only approximations of this single model.

He goes on to say that this view is unacceptable for a number of reasons. He then proceeds to develop his argument (1938:120–121).

> If . . . the fitness or unfitness of institutions can only be established in connection with a given milieu, since these milieus are diverse, there is a diversity of points of reference and hence types which, while being qualitatively distinct from one another, are all equally grounded in the nature of social milieus . . . the constitution of the social milieu results from the mode of composition of the social aggregates . . . the considerations just stated lead us back to the idea that the causes of social phenomena are internal to society.

Durkheim's approach to the understanding of "milieus" was based on his view that such social "essences" are formed by coercive forces operating within societies. He states (1938:103–4;emphasis added) that:

> Society is not a mere sum of individuals. Rather, the system formed by their association represents a specific reality which has its own characteristics. Of course, nothing collective can be produced if individual consciousnesses are not assumed; but this necessary condition is by itself insufficient. These consciousnesses must be combined in a certain way; social life results from this combination and is, consequently, explained by it. Individual minds, forming groups by mingling and fusing, give birth to a being, psychological if you will, but *constituting a psychic individuality of a new sort*. It is, then in the nature of this collective individuality, not in that of the associated units, that we must seek the immediate and determining causes of the facts appearing therein.

Such views provide archaeologists with a particularly defined reality to monitor along with their classifications. The seat of both causes and perpetuation of cultural distinctiveness is the internal, "collective" characteristic of each society. It is this inner "milieu" which serves to differentiate and perpetuate societies. In short, any demonstrable cohesion among parts must derive from the operation of internal social factors—the collective. In many places in the Old World, and particularly in France, this view was linked with ideas expressed frequently by the German word *Volk* and the French *esprit*. Both have the suggestion of vitalism, where there was something driving the "esprit de corps." One's public spirit, or devotion to one's society, was seen as driven by an inner vitalism, somehow "natural to man." When this vitalism breaks down, "civilization" begins to flounder. In such a view, "cultures" were seen as differentiated packages, isomorphic with ethnically or nationally differentiated peoples. Blendings and mixings represented the breakdowns of one's very "spirit" and hence a kind of degeneracy similar to that which racists considered to result from "race mixing." As Durkheim (1938:124) states, "The principle we have just expounded would . . . create a sociology which sees in the spirit of discipline the essential condition of all common life."

This emphasis on spirit and the maintenance of distinctiveness through "discipline" is consistent with the frequently expressed view that some measure of a people's worth could be seen in the degree to which *external* factors could not intrude or impinge upon the cultural expressions of their distinctiveness. Such a point is emphasized by de Sonneville-Bordes (1975). Under this view of culture, continuity should be demonstrable among the materials left at different archaeological sites by representatives of the same "people." In a similar manner we should expect conservative patterns of formal change, and we should not expect blended or mixed "traditions," since each people manifests its essential characteristics, its "spirit," in its products.

This view is well stated by Bordes (1968:144): "Man is more ready to exchange his genes than his customs, as the whole history of Europe demonstrates." In sum, culture is expressed in terms of formal distinctiveness of artifacts and cohesion, seen in the repetition of a distinctive formal pattern at different sites.

When this "ethnic" view of culture was popularized in the United States it was characterized as follows (Rouse 1965:6):

> All components that have yielded similar assemblages are grouped together. Each group is defined by listing its distinctive traits and is given the name of a typical site. . . . The name applies not only to the groups of components but also to the traits which characterize it and to the people who lived in the components. The traits constitute a complex which is indicative of the people. Whenever one discovers a new site one can identify the people who lived there simply by determining which complex it contains.

The ethnic view of culture was operationalized by the archaeologist François Bordes. His methods of classification consist of a type list, or a set of categories, generated essentially as a "paradigmatic classification" (see Dunnell 1971). For example, he classified Paleolithic tools as a set of combinations and permutations of forms of working edge and the placement of such forms relative to the axis of percussion used in detaching the flake on which the tool was produced. The basic unit of observation is the assemblage, defined in terms of the principle of association; that is, all those tools found together within a recognizable unit of deposition within a site. The units of observation can then be described by tabulating the items in the assemblage relative to the type list. This quantitative pattern was commonly presented in the form of a cumulative graph. Thus, a culture was represented as a unit of "cohesion" by the repetitive pattern of similar relative frequencies occurring among assemblages from different places. Cohesion was measured by formal similarity, described in quantative terms.

Mixed Paradigms

As one might imagine, there has been some mixing and blending of the Old and New World points of view. There appear to have been two types of mixing or blending—operationally blended views and intellectually blended views.

Operationally Blended Views

"La méthode Bordes" was developed in its pure form to treat lithic assemblages from very early time ranges. In general, lithic industries are all that the very early sites yield, except for occasional animal bones. Analysts are fairly comfortable adding, subtracting, and calculating percentages among an array of things scored according to Bordes's type list. However, all know we should not add apples and goats. As long as we have only lithics, the definition of an assemblage in quantitative terms is acceptable. On the other hand, when in later time periods we recover worked bones, art work, ceramics, ground stone, burials in substantial numbers, etc., the definition of an "assemblage" in quantitative terms appears to violate our sensibilities for dimensional mixing. How can we interpret the statement that an assemblage includes 13 percent laterally retouched scrapers, 14 percent extended burials, and 9 percent interior red-slipped pottery sherds? For the more "domains" of things recovered, the more we develop separate, self-contained classificatory schemes to deal with each independently; we then usually define "cultures" in terms of the particular mix of "types" generated independently in each of our separate classificatory schemes. The approach thus begins to appear like the tactics of New World, or Kriegerian, methodology, discussed above. In short, we may begin with an Old World paradigm but be forced to use a New World methodology because a simple quantitative summarization cannot treat all the things found in association within a single paradigmatic classification. Such a development seems to be the type of "mixed" approach which many Old World archaeologists employ when dealing with materials more complicated than the simple lithic industries of the early time ranges. As Childe (1929:9–10) points out:

> Societies are represented, not by their members' skeletons, but by . . . pots and houseplans, personal ornaments, and burial sites, the materials they fetched from afar. . . . Such remains archaeologists divide and classify into types, and when the same types are repeatedly found together at different sites within a limited region they are grouped together to represent what we term cultures . . . types are repeatedly found together just because the traditions they embody are approved and transmitted by a society of persons. . . . In this sense archaeologists' 'cultures' do really stand for societies.

It should be clear that Childe's statement is consistent with Kriegerian method, but what a cohesion of types is said to represent is very different from what a typical New World archaeologist, familiar with the extensive distribution studies of culture traits, would conclude. Such studies fail to show any "cellular" distribution of culture traits corresponding to the social boundaries between separate societies (see Childe 1940; for more recent confirmatory studies of this problem, see Klimek 1935; Milke 1949; Clarke 1968; Hodder 1977). All these studies confirm that while some traits may tend to be distributed in terms of social units, configurations of traits representing demonstrable "cohesions" tend to exhibit more regionally extensive distributions, confirming Wissler's and Kroeber's earlier findings.

In this case of operationally blended views, we see researchers starting from a paradigm which assumes the perspective of an internal participant (who sees the distinctiveness of "peoples" arising from the "essential" distinctiveness of their social identities). The researchers are forced by the logic of treating different things not easily included in a single quantitative frame of reference to use methods developed from an almost diametrically opposed set of paradigmatic expectations as to what the world of culture is all about. We can expect that when these conditions hold, the cultures developed by such workers for time periods yielding increasingly diverse archaeological remains will begin to take on the character of "New World" cultures, in direct proportion to the numbers of different data sets recognized by the analysts.

Intellectually Blended Views

Unlike the situation above, where incompatibility derives from the limited relevance of "la méthode Bordes" in treating complex archaeological remains, intellectually blended views derive from recombinations of elements in the reasoning used by archaeologists.

It is not uncommon to hear archaeologists from some area of North America talking about archaeological materials, described by largely Kriegerian methods, in terms of ethnic or social dynamics. We can only assume that these archaeologists are ignorant of the many empirical studies which repeatedly illustrate the point that there is no equivalence between culture, conceived in terms of cohesions among traits, and specific ethnically or politically defined units. Perhaps the ease with which the "ethnic identity" view of culture is adopted by many archaeologists simply reflects the fact that most archaeologists are products of complex systems. Few have had much direct experience with small-scale systems, and as a growing number of scholars' knowledge of general anthropology becomes smaller, they probably do not know that among small-scale societies, at least, culture as an expression of "one's identity" is a viewpoint which is very hard to defend.

Projecting Views of Cultures into the Past: Our Observational Languages

The New World and Old World views of the world are paradigms. They summarize our expectations as to what "culture" is like. Comparison of these two paradigms should illustrate just how insightful philosophers have been when they argue that our world view, or paradigm, conditions our observation and description of experience. But a paradigm also directly conditions the classificatory procedures which archaeologists have designed to measure culture. The first, or New World, viewpoint is rooted in empirical generalizations regarding the nature of culture which early ethnographers generated from their comparative study of culture traits (largely material objects) across the named social groups of the American Indian. The second, or Old World, viewpoint is rooted in a less systematically studied, but just as empirically based understanding of European history. As we have seen, the perspective of the New World paradigm is one of outside observers looking at variability across socially organized groups of people. In contrast, the Old World paradigm takes the viewpoint of inside observers looking at themselves, relative to the social world of their experiences. Advocates of this Old World paradigm compare other societies from this egocentric point of view.[4]

These two paradigms are conscious attempts to describe the world of cultural phenomena accurately. Yet they are generalized from very different data bases and described from different observer perspectives; one from relatively small-scale, low-energy societies; the other from complex, power-based societies. It is not surprising, then, that the "reality" each view projects is different. Given that persons "seeing" the world through each of these paradigmatic "eyes" have developed different conventions for converting observations made on the archaeological record into descriptive statements about past cultures, and that past cultures have been treated like ethnographically known cultures, it is not surprising that classificatory techniques and methods have been designed to yield cultural information in terms of what the archaeologists thought culture was like. It also should not be surprising that the picture of the past generated by "Krieger's methods" is very different from the view of the past generated by "Bordes's methods." The Kriegerian, or New World, past is a picture of continuity within regions and through limited time spans, a picture of geographical continuities in culture but with temporal punctuations, or lacks of continuity, punctuating regional sequences. It should be kept in mind that "types" are primarily recognized in terms of the principle of continuity as viewed across spatially distinct samples. Since the number of dated samples is almost always far fewer than undated ones, continuity is demonstrable primarily in a spatial mode. Thus, it is the temporal sequencing which is free to vary somewhat independently of the defining contexts. Approaching the past with the eyes of the New World view, we inevitably see the cultural past as a series of growths, followed by declines or collapses.

It should be realized there are only two types of change which could possibly have been seen when "cohesion as measured by continuity" is the criterion for defining a culture: (a) growth where new culture traits are being added to the cohesive unit, and (b) disintegration where the cohesion breaks down. Any organizational change which reorganizes cultural phenomena will give the appearance of disintegration, since cohesion of disparate culture traits is the criterion for recognition of cultures themselves (cf. Erasmus 1968). It should further be remembered that a cohesion is an association of culture traits, and thus a qualitative phenomenon. Since the culture traits themselves are each qualitatively defined in terms of the criterion of continuity— that is, the same properties tend to "cohere" in items recovered from many different places—it is not surprising that New World cultures tend to exhibit geographical continuities.

In marked contrast is the view of the past generated through the use of "la méthode Bordes." Here we see very different cultures living side by side in the same regions, characterized by a lack of geographical continuity sometimes described as "parallel phyla." We see a past where tenaciously unchanging cultures replace one another in confusing historical patterns within a similar region, and a lack of temporal continuity described as "alternating industries" is sometimes claimed. Although this is sometimes a point of controversy, we see a past in which cultures change less, mix less, and are modified gradually through time, with few cases of collapse or decline. The picture one obtains is of replacement, not decline; gradual transitions, not punctuated change. Under the Old World view one expects cultures to exhibit a branching, diversifying pattern, very similar to that of biological evolution.

Table 27.1 provides a summary in outline form of the points of contrast between "Kriegerian," or "New World," and "la méthode Bordes," or "Old world," approaches to classification. It should be apparent that the *criterion of similarity* has permitted archaeologists using "la méthode Bordes" to judge which materials from different places represent a single culture. On the other hand, it has been recognized that "peoples" used different things, i.e., different artifact types. The *criterion of association* has permitted archaeologists to judge which different things went together within a given "culture." Different things found together (criterion of association) in an archaeological "level" would show what different things a "people" had. Similar

TABLE 27.1

Old World and New World Paradigms

Operations	"La Méthode Bordes"	"The Krieger Method"
A. Framework for	Type List	Selected Attributes
B. Basic Unit of Observation 1. Criterion for recognition	Assemblage Principle of Association	Artifact "Type" Principle of Continuity
2. Observational Framework	Recognizable Depositional Strata	Examples from Multiple Locations in a Region
C. Method of Description	Quantitative Paradigmatic Arrays	Grouping of "types"
1. Method of Presentation	Cumulative graphs	Trait Lists

D. Unit of Synthesis
  1. Criterion for
    Recognition
	"A Culture"
	Principle of Similarity
		"A Culture"
		Principle of Association

2. Observational Framework	Assemblages from Different Sites	Patterned Repetition of Types at Different Sites
	(Case comparisons)	(Matrix comparisons)
E. "Cohesion" Measured by	Similar quantitative patterns seen among similar things.	Qualitatively defined different things regularly associated at different places.
	(Similarity)	(Continuity)

assemblages found in different places (criterion of similarity) would show archaeologists where different "peoples" had been.

It should be recognized that in the Old World view these conventions for interpretation do not admit the possibility that aspects of a single cultural system could appear as different assemblages at different places. This possibility would, by convention, be designated as an indication of cultural differences per se, used for the definition of different cultures borne by different peoples. In the words of de Sonneville-Bordes (1975:3), "les types et leurs proportions sont stables et constants a l'interieur d'une même culture pour une période donnée dans une région donnée, du moins dans certaines limites." If "la méthode Bordes" is followed rigorously, it absolutely prevents us from ever seeing any organizational facts about past systems beyond those which may be manifest within a single occupation or a single level at a site. All units of synthesis beyond the assemblage will be internally homogeneous by convention of interpretation. We could thus never gain an appreciation for the organization of internally differentiated components of a system which might be manifest at different places.

Turning to the "Krieger method," we face a slightly different problem: the characteristics of sites as such are not studied. In this approach the basic unit of observation is the artifact, in a framework of attributes. Types may be recognizable in many different data classes. Every class of items does not yield types, for some may be judged so generalized in their distributions as to be "nondiagnostic," and as such as most often ignored. Items of this kind traditionally would include most lithic material which is not bifacially worked, many kinds of ceramic utility wares, and classes of tools such as hammer stones, choppers, etc. Another characteristic of cultures defined in terms of "cohesions as measured by continuity" is that features such as pits, house forms, and hearths are frequently not considered to be basic cultural diagnostics because, from a pragmatic perspective, it is recognized that these features are not regularly preserved at most sites, or in some cases, are too expensive to recover. In other words, traits which are frequent, not too generalized, and easily recovered from different places are given priority as the defining characteristics of cultures. The only time that "places" are studied is when it is judged that some extraordinary conditions of preservation are present. Then the aim of archaeology is shifted from studying "culture history" to "reconstructing lifeways," and more attention may be given to the excavation of a site as a location that was used and lived in by past peoples. In general, the alternative aim of reconstructing the past is considered to be possible only under conditions of extraordinary preservation, which frees archaeological interpretation from restructions thought to be imposed by the "limitations" of the archaeological record (see Binford 1981a). Thus, one only investigates "places" intensively if they are judged to be little "Pompeiis" which might offer extraordinary "glimpses" of particular past events or conditions. When doing culture-historical research, one normally needs only to recover a sufficient sample of artifacts to permit a "cultural" assessment of the remains. This means that no real understanding of internal differentiations or organizational variability among components of a single system will be revealed by carrying out normal, traditional archaeological work.

In sum:

1. The properties unique to sites are generally ignored or, if described, are not discussed in terms of developing arguments about "culture." This is perhaps most clearly illustrated by citing "features"—hearths, pits, and other structured arrangements of things in sites.
2. Classes of things which are common to many sites over wide areas are often ignored.
3. Frequency variations among classes of things not considered "diagnostic" are frequently ignored. Even more telling is the absence of anything more than impressionistic treatment of frequency variations among different data sets. For example, relationships between bone frequencies and artifact-class frequencies, or feature frequencies and ceramic frequencies, are rarely discussed in describing sites and are almost never discussed when "cultures" and their definition are the subject of discussion.

The implications are clear: the organizational properties of cultural systems as manifest in the differential use of places is logically excluded in "la méthode Bordes" and is ignored (in favor of measures of cohesion and overriding similarities which tend to exhibit temporal or spatial continuities) in the "Krieger method." Only in rare cases where the archaeologist judges a site to be extraordinarily preserved does the perspective shift toward describing the internal relationships among data sets within a site, and even then the purpose has been to reconstruct small segments of the past, not to seek an understanding of the past in general.

Conclusion

When new archaeologists, and most particularly the senior author, began arguing for a change in the way archaeologists analyzed the archaeological record, they did not argue for a particular theory, or propose a new theory as to how the world worked. Instead, they argued for a change in paradigm. They viewed the need for change as a shift in perspective, and further recognized that it was unlikely that archaeologists would invent on the spot any one "new perspective" which would be the most useful for all archaeological research. The discipline needed to try a variety of new perspectives which would permit it to explore the information potential of the archaeological record. It is no accident that *New Perspectives in Archaeology* (Binford and Binford 1968) did not call for new theories in particular, nor did it attempt to develop a monolithic approach. If one examines the list of contributors and the directions which their research took after 1968, it would be very difficult to find a single unifying argument or position other than a general dissatisfaction with the conventions of traditional archaeology.

Under the more traditional approaches, it had been argued that the archaeological record limits the kinds of information which the archaeologist might refer to characteristics of past cultures. The new archaeologists argued that the discipline had not even begun to explore the archaeological record nor assess its potential for yielding information about the past, since all traditional methods for making inferences had been derived from limited paradigmatic expectations regarding culture.

In the mid to late 1960s, some new archaeologists began to discuss the problem of "verification." It was recognized that the "methods," or interpretation, used by traditional archaeologists were simply conventions, not subject to evaluation by reference to the so-called empirical materials with which they worked. Most archaeologists' understanding was that a scientist "took his or her ideas to experience" for evaluation. In other words, science represented a philosophy which sought the growth of knowledge through subjecting ideas ("knowledge") to trial by experience! It was clear to many new archaeologists that under the procedures of traditional archaeology, new experiences never affected archaeologists' alleged knowledge. The latter served to accommodate all new experiences, and the particular tactics of accommodation became the so-called reconstructed history. The discipline was that of "discovering" (Binford 1982b). The problem in the above analysis is that it was assumed that experience could be conceptualized independently of the ideas being evaluated by appeal to it.

However, in our opinion, no objectivity had been achieved in the practice of traditional archaeology. Thus, the challenge today is how to achieve some independence for the experiences to which archaeologists appeal. Most archaeological reasoning has been a classic example of inductive argument from archaeological observations; no wonder the past never argued back! Archaeological interpretations have been inductively argued, and hence experience (the archaeological record) is simply the vehicle for inference. These inferences are logically tautologies in relation to the ideas which have guided the meanings given to the archaeological record.

Initially, new archaeologists argued that the solution to this problem was to adopt another form of reasoning—deductive argument—where the premises were stated, consequences deduced, and these deductively reasoned expectations taken to . . . what? The past, or the archaeological record? Clearly, archaeologists in the late 1960s and early 1970s who argued for the potential of deductive procedures had not fully thought through the problem of the dependent status of their ideas regarding the past. Archaeological knowledge of the past is totally dependent upon the meanings which archaeologists give to observations on the archaeological record. Thus, archaeologically justified views of the past are dependent upon paradigmatic views regarding the significance of archaeological observations. It is this basic point which we have tried to illustrate here.

The challenge to archaeologists is the realization that the archaeological record cannot be used to test propositions about the meaning of archaeological observations in any direct sense. Such a realization inescapably leads to the conclusion that testing and verification of received ideas is really only possible at two basic junctures: (a) in an actualistic context, where archaeologists can evaluate propositions regarding the meaning to be attached to archaeological observations, i.e., middle-range research (see Binford 1981b); and (b) in the context of evaluating general theories regarding the "causes" of history. The latter of course assumes the existence of a body of unambiguous, independently warranted meanings, which can be attached to archaeological observations for evaluating the accuracy of proposed causal interactions operative in the past. In short, the key to either knowing the past accurately or evaluating theories about past processes is recognizing that both are dependent upon research in the *dynamic mode* (actualistic or historical studies which allow archaeologists to assess the necessity of alleged cause-and-effect relationships between static and dynamic states of matter).

In other words, middle-range studies make it feasible for archaeologists to attempt to "know" the past. What guides such studies? The answer is archaeologists' paradigmatic understanding of the archaeological record. This conclusion implies something quite important: namely, that archaeologists must develop ways of increasing the accuracy and utility of their paradigm. Search the literature of science or the philosophy of science on this issue and one finds little aid or comfort. In the very early days of scientific discussion, the strict empiricists addressed the issue of methods for discovery, but the recent literature has tended to relegate this issue to an imponderable corner of "psychological causation" and restrict itself to considerations of evaluating received ideas (ideas already discovered or invented). These approaches are obviously of little aid to archaeologists today, whose task is the production of a useful paradigm, not the testing of theories produced in the context of the extant paradigm.

Unlike skeptics such as Kuhn, we are convinced that we can learn to encourage productive paradigm change through rational means. We are also convinced that we can learn to evaluate competing paradigms objectively in spite of the claims for extreme intellectual relativism and noncomparability of theories and arguments generated in the context of different paradigms (see Binford 1982b). For example, we can look back to the classic empiricist arguments of Francis Bacon for a guide to paradigm evaluation which is of continuing value to scholars today. Bacon's very arguments appear to be paradigmatic in character and not concerned with theories per se. He states (1947 [1620]:154; emphasis added) that:

> I am of opinion that if men had ready at hand a just theory of nature and experience, and labored diligently thereon, and if they could bind themselves to two rules, *the first to lay aside received opinions and notions,* and the second, *to refrain the mind for a time from the highest generalizations* . . . they would be able by the native and genuine force of the mind, without any other art, to fall into my form of interpretation. For interpretation is the true and natural work of the mind.

If archaeologists can gain a healthy skepticism regarding received conceptualizations of nature and seek to place themselves in positions relative to nature and experience where the adequacy and/or ambiguity of the received concepts may be evaluated, then they can hope to gain some objectivity relative to the utility of their concepts.

Paradigm change is brought about and implemented, we believe, by seeking out new perspectives. The shift from a static to a dynamic perspective offers one example where the utility of concepts and the conventions of an observational language may be evaluated. As we have argued, the "observer perspective" is an important conditioner of the world to be seen. We have illustrated how in the Old World view the observer perspective is that of an internal participant looking from an egocentric position within the system. The New World view is that of an observer high above the cultural geography of a region, looking down at variability across previously identified ethnic units. The internal participant versus the aerial observer perspectives condition very different "realities."

Are either of these observer perspectives really appropriate to the observational framework within which archaeologists commonly work? Let us briefly examine this question. In a very real sense, the spatial frames within which we most commonly work are the "site" and the "region." The site provides us with an observational window to the past which may be likened to the perspective of an immovable observer seated at the bottom of a well, looking up. All the observer can "see" from such a perspective is the "fallout" from some part of an organized system which happened to pass over that one stationary well. We would rarely if ever expect a whole culture to pass over or be compressed so as to be seen within the confines of our tiny window. This means that what we see is always some "part" of a larger "whole." Given that the whole is an internally differentiated system, the parts seen from this perspective may be quite different in terms of content, organization, and "role" played in the organized whole—the overall system. The challenge to archaeological methods is how to integrate reliably different assemblages, organizational forms (e.g., site structure), or parts into an accurate picture of the organized whole which existed in the past. It is very clear that the integrating criteria used under older perspectives—association and similarity—are not relevant and yield distortions. The criterion of continuity remains however as a possibility for integrating dissimilar assemblage units when studying noncomplex groups. Linked with the criterion of association at a much larger scale—the region—it at least appears feasible to begin the tentative description of large-scale, organizationally differentiated systems within which mobile hunter–gatherers carried out their lives. Almost certainly such an approach would be only an interim strategy, for once archaeologists learn how to look at systems from the realistic perspective of observer in a well, they will see many new things which can aid in the organizational diagnosis of past systems.

The recognition of the most fruitful perspective to assume when conducting research is part of paradigm growth. For instance, if archaeologists place themselves in a productive research situation where both static and dynamic aspects of a system may be observed (an ethnoarchaeological project, for example) and assume observer perspectives which are unrealistic relative to the archaeological record (as for instance those of internal observer or ethnographer), they will always come away having seen the archaeological record as limited and impoverished (see, for example, R. Gould 1980:27–28). Rather, we must learn to see the dynamics from a perspective appropriate to the archaeological record. Such a viewpoint should be (a) nonparticipating, (b) outside, and (c) partative.

No amount of ethnographic observations will help us understand a system when viewed from the perspective of statics. Static remains are not the watered-down, impoverished "residues" of ethnographers' experiences. They are an existential domain which must be understood in terms of their own properties. Attempts to translate archaeological statics into a reconstruction of interpersonal interaction or forms of mental "deep structure" is akin to translating facts of cell biology into scenarios of predator-prey interactions. We need a science of the archaeological record. To achieve this goal, archaeologists need to continue to experiment with methods for both the production and refinement of a new paradigm appropriate to our science. If we have successes along these lines, then archaeology will begin to achieve the status of "archaeology as anthropology." Under the previous paradigms, archaeologists used culture to explain the archaeological record. We need to be able to reverse the situation and use the archaeological record to help further the anthropological goal of explaining cultural differences and similarities.

Notes

1. We wish to thank the students of our Anthropology 507 (Fall 1981) seminar at the University of New Mexico for their intellectual stimulation; also Paula L.W. Sabloff and Harry Basehart for clarifying our ideas.

2. We are not arguing that Kuhn contends that the logic which individuals may have used in advocating a scientific revolution were irrational. Rather, we are saying that he appears to us to be arguing that their theories do not necessarily follow in a rational, continuous fashion from the previous theories of the earlier, "normal science" phase.

3. Our argument is based on our interpretation of the relationship of ideas—not on historical influences among scholars. That is to say, we are not arguing, for example, that either Childe or Bordes were directly influenced by Durkheim.

4. These paradigms should not be confused with "etic" and "emic" approaches to theory building, because either could be used in terms of both paradigms.

28

1981

Middle-range Research and the Role of Actualistic Studies

In the previous chapter[1] I showed that the assumptions made regarding the conditions under which the archaeological record was formed directly condition the character of inferences about the contents of the archaeological record. I showed that we may be frequently incorrect or at least highly uncertain about our reconstruction of the past. In this chapter I will explore a somewhat more complicated issue—how we might proceed so as to minimize the likelihood of constructing false pictures of the past. I will be directly concerned with research tactics and how we might use secure knowledge to aid in the development of new knowledge or understanding regarding the past. *How do we carve out knowledge from ignorance?*

The challenge to archaeologists is simply this: How do we proceed? How do we unify the world of archaeological things with our ideas as to the character of the past? How may we use the empirical world of archaeological phenomena to stimulate ideas about the past and at the same time use these empirical experiences to evaluate the resulting ideas? How can we proceed so as to develop confidence that our ideas of the past are informative about the actual past? We face the challenge of science itself— how to keep our feet on the "empirical" ground and our heads in the "theoretical" sky. Basic to the development of a science is a recognition of the domain to which scientific procedures might be profitably addressed—empirical with respect to what? Theoretical with respect to what?

Many archaeologists accept the argument that the discipline of archaeology needs to adopt a scientific approach, yet they are not necessarily in agreement as to the domain of experience to which such an approach is to be most profitably addressed:

> there is in a sense an "archaeological theory" although it might be better characterized as evolutionary anthropology . . . human and cultural evolution is of such scientific and intrinsic interest that there is certainly an essential nomothetic role to be played by archaeologists [Watson *et al.* 1971:164].

In the foregoing view, archaeological theory addresses a domain of past events and conditions. It is concerned with explaining why certain events and systems came into being in the past. It addresses the domain that most traditional archaeologists considered to be their target for seeking understanding: such interesting problems as the origins of the state, the shift to agricultural production, or perhaps the origins of culture itself. Under this view of "doing" archaeology, the act of investigating the archaeological record is viewed as the experimental phase or perhaps the archival phase of investigating the past. I have referred to such interests as *general research or general theory building*. By these phrases I refer to the actions of investigators seeking to explain characteristics of cultural systems past and present. The domain of interest is cultural systems, how they vary, and how they may be modified from one form to another. The domain is interactive, generative, and dynamic.

Important, however, is the fact that all knowledge of the dynamics of the past must be inferred:

> To say that historians construct the past so as not to falsify certain theoretical presuppositions is not to point to a defect in historians or in their method. It is to focus upon the means historians use to find out what happened. It is to day, in a somewhat different way, what has been said before: *that we infer the events of the past from the events of the present by linking them in terms of some general principles* [Kitts 1977:67–68].

If we recognize that science is concerned with developing means for increasing our understanding or observations of nature, this implies that science is simultaneously attempting to generate understanding and to sharpen or increase the informational potential of our observations. The archaeologist investigates phenomena that he has reason to believe remain from the past. These investigations are conducted in the present, resulting in all the observational statements generated by archaeologists being contemporary facts. How does the archaeologist convert these contemporary observational statements or facts into meaningful statements about the past? The first thing that must be realized is that this can only be accomplished intellectually or with reason. Thus there is no way of converting observational statements about the past in the absence of a reasoning process.

Insofar as archaeology remains a discipline that searches for an understanding of the past through the use of objects and other organizations of matter believed to have been parts of past situations, archaeologists must operate as historians attempting to give meaning to observations on the particular archaeological record being investigated. The accuracy with which we may accomplish the conversion of contemporary observational statements into meaningful statements about the past is a direct function of the character of the reasoning processes employed and the methodology developed for evaluating the products of this process.

Our problem is then twofold: (a) We must know the past by virtue of inferences drawn from knowledge of how the contemporary world works, the principles mentioned by Kitts, and (b) we must be able to justify the assumption that these principles are relevant—that at least in terms of the properties of the principles, the past was like the present; we must make a uniformitarian assumption.

The point that we must use general principles in giving "historical" meaning to our observations no longer seems at issue:

> History differs from the generalizing social sciences only in that its primary aim is to explain individual situations in all their complexity rather than to formulate general laws for indefinitely repeatable events and processes. That is what is meant by saying that history is idiographic, the social science nomothetic (Nagel 1961:547; Elton 1969:22–24, 41). This does not mean that historians deny the existence of general rules; rather they seek to employ them to gain an understanding of individual (i.e., unique) and non-recurrent situations [Trigger 1978:26–27].

Where do such general principles come from, and how can we be assured of their accuracy and relevance to our activities as archaeologists seeking to explicate the past?

Those who claim that archaeologists should be historians and not scientists most commonly advise that we should "borrow" our general principles from other nomothetic sciences. The trouble with this suggestion is that I know of no nomothetic science attempting to understand the archaeological record! Many other "sciences" may be concerned with various aspects of human behavior, history, and sociocultural change in which the phenomena studied are events, behavior, or patterning in communicated thought. However, the basic phenomena with which we work are (a) static, (b) material, and (c) untranslated into symbols or clues to human "thoughts." No other "science" addresses such phenomena. It was the recognition of this fact that prompted the following statement written in 1966 and published two years later:

> Accepting Spaulding's minimal definition of what archaeology is, we can go a step further and specify its aim as the explanation . . . of the order we observe in the archaeological record. Archaeological theory consists of propositions and assumptions regarding the archaeological record itself—its origins, its sources of variability, the determinants of differences and similarities in the formal, spatial, and temporal characteristics of artifacts and features and their interrelationships [S. R. Binford and L. R. Binford 1968:2].

Directing attention to the archaeological record rather than continuing the self-deceit that we were studying the past seemed central to progress. My view was that we could not reconstruct history until we first addressed the problem of how we give meaning to the archaeological record (see L. R. Binford 1968b). Meanings are carried by concepts and arguments and the archaeological record contains only arrangements of matter. If archaeologists are to know anything of the past, they must develop a science. The domain of this science must be the archaeological record per se.

In seeking to develop a science of the archaeological record, are there not some fundamental characteristics of both science and the archaeological record that we must consider to guide the growth of this science? The answer must of course be yes. One characteristic particularly important to the arguments advocating a science of the archaeological record is that science attempts to evaluate the role and utility of ideas for enhancing understanding. Ideas are of course cultural forms:

> if we view culture as at least referring to the particularly human ability to give meaning expediently to experience, to symbol, and in turn, view experience through this conceptual idiom, science is then concerned with evaluating the utility of the cultural tools produced [L. R. Binford 1977a:3].

The reference to the "cultural tools" produced is of course to the concepts and ideas in terms of which we conceive the world of experience. If we gain a "knowledge" of the world through the use of cognitive devices, words, concepts, and ideas, and the world is described in these terms, we must face the problem of the accuracy, utility, and "reality" of such cognitive devices themselves. This is one fundamental problem the scientist must face. The second problem relates to the degree to which we seek knowledge and understanding beyond simple description. We frequently attempt to understand why the world is the way it appears to be, given the description generated. Scientists carry out their work with essentially two sets of intellectual tools: a conceptual frame of reference or paradigm (Kuhn 1962), and various theories that seek to explain the world as "known" through the use of the paradigm.

The Paradigm—One's Guide to Describing the World

The cognitive frame of reference or paradigm consists of the ideas and concepts with which we approach experience. These condition what one considers relevant to describe or chooses to discuss as of interest. One's cognitive frame of reference may be thought of as the culture of a science. It consists of the concepts in terms of which experience is intellectually assimilated. Despite all the definitional controversy (see Masterman 1970), I follow Kuhn (1977) in viewing paradigm as the intellectual terms upon which one meets experience. The character of one's frame of reference conditions what is considered relevant to describe, what is interesting to discuss, and even how we view the world in terms of problems to be solved. In short, it is what we expect the world to be like. Things become complicated when we recognize that we cannot gain a direct knowledge of the essential properties of the world. Our cognition is neither direct nor objective, but may be indirect and subjective relative to our beliefs about the world (i.e., our paradigm).

We generally defend our claims about what the world is like with inferential arguments. I prefer to call these *warranting arguments:* they are arguments advanced that tend to *warrant to others* the beliefs one has about the world. If done in a robust manner, they make one's claims appear plausible, and acceptable to others. Rarely are such arguments formalized in that the premises are rarely explicitly stated, so conclusions are warranted by appeal to a "common body of knowledge or belief." The more comprehensive the alleged knowledge, or widespread the belief serving as the intellectual context for a warranting argument, the more plausible it appears and therefore the greater likelihood it has of being accepted.

Working within a frame of reference is similar to participation in any other culture; we accommodate experience through our shared cognitive devices. The fact that they facilitate this accommodation appears to us as proof that the world is in fact the way we expect it to be. We may be astonished that others do not see the world the way we do. Anthropologists should be familiar with cultural differences and should be fairly comfortable with the idea that the nature of experience does not necessarily determine the nature of culture. Many persons share identical experiences yet ascribe to them very different meanings; this is essentially the message of anthropology. Cultural man has for all time believed that his beliefs were given by "reality" and were therefore "right," whereas those of other cultures were clearly misguided or "stupid" for not having seen the "truth" inherent in given experience.

Archaeology is perhaps in a fortunate position. Although there is much contemporary "culture" or paradigmatic bias regarding the nature of man and the causes of history, there is very little folk knowledge regarding the formation of the archaeological record. This means that there is little explicit prior development of cognitive devices and frames of reference for accommodating archaeological phenomena in the literal, static sense of the word. For the further development of archaeology, the growth of a paradigm, developing cognitive means for identifying properties of the past or diagnosing the archaeological record and thereby giving meaning to the archaeological record, is crucial.

Much of the time use of a paradigm is viewed as an act of identification. Can we identify a habitation, a hide scraper, a matrilineage, a base camp, agriculture? Or can we diagnose the functions of a site, tool, or element of debris? In most cases we are seeking an unambiguous definition, and realistic concepts with which to partition or diagnose the archaeological record and thereby generate meaningful statements about the past. All such interpretations are dependent on a general, accurate, and unambiguous knowledge of the relationship between statics and dynamics, the formal consequences for organized matter that derive from the operation of a dynamic system. In developed sciences, what is being sought here at the conscious level through "middle-range" research may be taken for granted as paradigmatic:

> The distinction between "empirical" and "theoretical" . . . may be only a relative one. It is relative historically. . . . A scientist who undertakes the study of a particular problem, for example of a biological one, and who uses various scientific instruments constructed on the grounds of different physical theories, is quite aware of the fact that together with the equipment he uses he accepts also these theories. In spite of this fact, however, he will treat the statements he will formulate by means of these instruments as observational. The observational language is, for him, something already present and historically given by the development of science and common knowledge [Amsterdamski 1975:86].

An observational language is essentially nonexistent in archaeology. The concepts and hence paradigmatic characteristic of traditional archaeology are believed to be essentially useless for modern archaeology. Today the archaeological record is not being viewed (by most) as a material manifestation of mental phenomena; it is not being viewed as a preserved past; it is not being viewed as uniquely determined by history; its variability is not being viewed exclusively as a manifestation of past ethnic variability, and so on. As is suggested by Amsterdamski, the instruments that permit and facilitate unambiguous meaningful observations must be developed, demonstrated, and tested, using scientific means. Later, as the science of archaeology becomes more mature, these "instruments for measurement" may be taken for granted and results of their use treated as direct observations of the past.

We are a long way from this level of maturity today. We need to recognize very explicitly the current state of the art and address the growth of a new paradigm as basic and fundamental. Recognizing that this is a historical phase in the growth of the "new archaeology," I began using a special term for this endeavor: *middle-range research* or *middle-range theory building*.[2]

What we are seeking through middle-range research are accurate means of identification, and good instruments for measuring specified properties of past cultural systems. We are seeking reliable cognitive devices; we are looking for "Rosetta stones" that permit the accurate conversion from observation on statics to statement about dynamics. We are seeking to build a paradigmatic frame of reference for giving meaning to selected characteristics of the archaeological record through a theoretically grounded body of research, rather than accepting folk knowledge—let alone implicit folk knowledge—as the basis for describing the past.

Theory—One's Guide to Explaining the World

Theories are the key to the scientific understanding of empirical phenomena, and *they are normally developed only when previous research has yielded a body of information, including empirical generalizations about the phenomena in question.* A theory is then intended to provide deeper understanding by presenting those phenomena as manifestations of certain underlying processes [Hempel 1977:244; emphasis mine].

Given that we have made observations on the archaeological record, offered some generalizations about its properties, and gained considerable experience with the record, I must now ask the crucial question: Why is the archaeological record the way it appears to be? When we seek to reason about the "causes" of the world as known, we are attempting to build theories about the world. "Where it is some event or system of events that is to be explained, explanation has to do with cause [Quine and Ullian 1978:111]."

We are concerned with organizational properties of the world. We seek to understand how the properties of entities and/or events were produced in characteristic ways:

One very central use of "theory" involves an epistemic device which is used to characterize the state-change behavior of isolated systems within a general class of phenomena . . . one can discover that they [theories] invariably postulate a class of states of systems' change over time . . . and are used to characterize how natural classes of phenomena would behave if isolated [Suppe 1977:658].

Quite literally, theories are the answers to the "why" questions of dynamics. They are concerned with understanding variability and how systems proceed from one state to another.

If we are going to build a theoretically informed paradigm for referring observations on the archaeological record to dynamic conditions in the past, where do we begin? It seems to me we must begin with certain fundamental statements of "being as such." *The archaeological record is a static contemporary phenomenon.* It is structured matter motionless and noninteractive in terms of the properties of historical interest to the archaeologist.

Only a universe of energy could have no past. If there is matter, structures grow and differentiate and a past can be recognized and partially reconstructed. It is the problem of durationless non-matter versus enduring matter. . . . At one end of the spectrum is biblical chaos, a past without a past, because no matter exists to convey information. At the other end there is only information and no decisions—static information forever [Margalef 1968:97].

The archaeologist is of course working with static information preserved in structured arrangements of matter. Since there is no energy remaining, there are no culturally relevant interactive relationships to be observed in the archaeological record. Such relationships existed in the past but ceased when system-serving energy was no longer powering the rearrangement and modification of matter—in short, once a static condition was achieved. In a very essential way the contents of the archaeological record must be viewed as products of a complex *mechanical* system of causation. It was mechanical in that the fundamental genesis of the archaeological structure is a situation of forces acting to modify matter in both its organizational and distributional properties. The archaeological record is a structure of relationships between the distribution and form of matter as caused by energy sources acting on matter in the past. In one very important sense, all properties of matter, whether they be chips removed from a flake of flint, mixing of soil betraying the former location of a pit, piles of debris from meals, or the remnants of a construction such as a mud brick wall, are the mechanical consequences of the actions of forces on matter.

I used the term *causal* in the literal sense, that is, to express the idea of a category of generic connections; it refers to the way of producing things. Or, "something, E, is brought forth by something else, C, in a necessary (constant and unique) manner [Bunge 1979:49]."

Clearly if we can isolate causal relationships between things, and if we can understand such relationships in terms of more general principles of necessity, such as the theories of mechanics or some other basic science, then we have a strong warrant for the inference of the cause from the observed effects. We would be building a strong theoretically informed bridge between properties of the contemporary archaeological record and characteristics of the dynamic past.

Insofar as our inferences regarding the past refer to the causal relationships that obtained between dynamics and its static derivatives, then any attempts to discover the character of such causal relationships must reasonably be conducted through the study of living systems where both dynamics and static derivatives may be potentially observed. Taking as an example the problem outlined in Chapter 1, the identification of the agency (energy source) responsible for generating certain patterns remaining in the archaeological record, we might reason as follows:

First, we must attempt to isolate the different agents or forces that might be expected to contribute to or "cause" a given pattern. Second, we would have to conduct studies of these agents or processes in the contemporary world so as to develop criteria of recognition. In short, we need to specify criteria for recognizing traces, "signature patterns" apt to be preserved in the archaeological record, of the agents likely to have contributed to deposits in which hominid remains might also occur. The procedure is similar to that painstakingly worked out over the years for recognizing lithic materials modified by man as opposed to stones modified through other natural processes. The problem is one of pattern recognition linked with the demonstration that the pattern is redundant and unambiguous, a diagnostic signature that discriminates one agent or set of agents from another.

Such a demonstration must be developed by studying phenomena actively generated in a contemporary setting, since there must be little problem of *inference* regarding the identity of the agent producing the patterning or traces that one is demonstrating as a signature pattern sufficient for the unambiguous identification of the agent. The problem is one similar to the development of an identification key for animals through the study of their footprints. The persons who develop the knowledge that permits the recognition of the track, and hence the identification of the animal responsible, *must* study the footprints of identified animals so that the relationship between animal and track is a controlled or known relationship. Given such a control in the contemporary world, and given that one is successful in recognizing and describing diagnostic criteria (constant and unique) between cause and effect, animal and footprint, then when one encounters the diagnostic footprint in the future the inference of the prior presence of the indicated annimal may be considered an inference of high probability.

For an inference about the past to be of high probability, an additional proposition must be met—that the same relationships obtained in the past as obtained in the present between bears and their footprints! Here we introduce the interesting and important, perhaps crucial, problem archaeologists must solve—how do we justify a uniformitarian assumption? This issue is perhaps well illustrated through a discussion of the treatment given the problem by the pioneers of historical geology:

> Lyell's concept of uniformity has four major, and very different, components:
>
> (1) Natural laws are constant (uniform) in space and in time. *As John Stuart Mill showed, this is not a statement about the world; it is an a priori claim of method that scientists must make in order to proceed with any analysis of the past.* If the past is capricious, if God violates natural law at will, then science cannot unravel history.
> (2) Processes now operating to mould the earth's surface should be invoked to explain the events of the past (uniformity of process through time). *Only present processes can be directly observed. Therefore, we are better off if we can explain past events as a result of processes still acting. This again is not an argument about the world, it is a statement about scientific procedure* [S. J. Gould 1977:150; emphasis mine].

As was pointed out by Gould, the remaining two senses in which Lyell used the concept of uniformity were in fact assumptions about the world, existential in character. One has been largely sustained by research (i.e., geologic change was largely uniform in rate, slow, gradual and steady, not cataclysmic). The other claim was also existential, namely that the earth has a uniform configuration, or it has been fundamentally the same since its formation. Most would agree that this has been demonstrated to be quite false as a general descriptive statement.

What is indicated here is that we must make uniformitarian assumptions if we are to gain any understanding of the past. On the other hand, when we do so we are making empirical claims about the past and these must be warranted; they must be subjected to evaluation. The degree to which such uniformitarian assumptions are warranted is a measure of the degree to which our inferences drawn from knowledge of the contemporary world and/or our understanding of its processes in the form of theories and laws are relevant to the past.

Insofar as our inferences regarding the past refer to the dynamics of the past, these inferences must be accomplished by appeals to principles or knowledge about dynamics and how static properties preserved in the archaeological record may be derived from dynamics. Since the only access a researcher has to dynamics is through contemporary experience, all research directed toward the development of principles that serve to make possible inferences about the past must be conducted with documented dynamic situations generally in the present. Such knowledge of "connections" between statics and dynamics must derive from experimental research conducted with documented living systems.

Since knowledge of dynamics derives from experience with living systems, observations of linkage between statics and dynamics must be made on living systems. In order to use these principles of linkage for making statements about the past, we must make a uniformitarian assumption with respect to the properties used in inference. In short, we must assume that knowledge gained from actualistic studies is relevant and applicable to the living systems of the past. This basic proposition must be true if inferences employing principles gained through the study of contemporary dynamics are to be used in inferring the past from patterned statics. This means that the assumption is always conditional and may be false; that is, we could be wrong in our judgments regarding the condition shared by systems or entities of the past and the present.

For instance, any number of "correlates" between statics and dynamics might be observed in the modern world. However, the first question we must ask is whether we are observing an incidence of cause and effect, or whether there is simply correlation or coincidence. The second, and equally important, question to be considered is whether the proposed causation was also characteristic of the past. Both questions must be answered affirmatively before an actualistic observation may realistically serve as a premise for inferences regarding the past.

Although I basically agree with much of Schiffer's (1972, 1976a) general discussion of archaeology and the need for understanding of formation processes, I generally disagree with almost all of his suggestions as to how to solve archaeological problems. He fails to make the critical distinction between description and explanation. This is clear as he cites Nagel for "experimental laws" (i.e., empirical generalizations) and Hempel for "covering laws" (i.e., theoretical laws), as if these were the same thing (see Schiffer 1976a:4). Schiffer also argues that "the subject matter of archaeology is the relationship between human behavior and material culture in all times and places [p. 4]." I might agree that this is one way of viewing the concerns of middle-range research, but find it hard to accept as the central focus for archaeology since the archaeological record contains no direct information on this subject whatsoever!

How do we know what experiences with living systems are relevant to the past? This question is particularly germane with regard to central issues such as identification. Identification, as mentioned earlier, is a key issue in archaeology, since it is this "act" that established the language for discussing the past, and in turn the language carries meanings and provides the units for logical analysis. Identifying things (see Whitehead 1967:144) becomes the act of translating from the domain of matter into the domain of ideas. It is the identities that bridge the gap between the past and the present, that provide, as Whitehead (1967:159) would say, the "eternal objects," the "durables," which serve as the basis for recognizing events, the basis for analyzing events and recognizing transitions from one event to another:

> Whatever passes is an event. But we find entities in nature which do not pass. . . . Factors in nature which are without passage will be called objects . . . recognition is reflected in the intellect as comparison . . . but it is not the events which are compared. For each event is essentially unique and incomparable. What are compared are the objects situated in events [Whitehead 1957:124–125].

It seems to me that uniformitarian assumptions function much like intellectual anchors, for they provide the "points of knowledge" from which we may judge the extent of our ignorance regarding properties of the archaeological record.

What are the durable unchanging characteristics that the events of the present share with the past? As I indicated elsewhere [L. R. Binford 1977a:8],

> We may reasonably ask . . . whether or not there are classes of data remaining from the past which might better support uniformitarian assumptions. In short, are there not classes of phenomena available to us for which a more reliable set of conditions might be projected into the past than for human behavior per se?[3]

I answered the rhetorical question by suggesting that the study of the spatial structure or the arrangement of "objects," in the Whitehead (1957:124) sense of the word, would be a useful area for development. I continue to be of this opinion. On the other hand, I had suggested that ecological and anatomical characteristics of the species still extant with which ancient man interacted were enduring objects for which uniformitarian assumptions might be securely warranted. It is hoped that others will elaborate this list of domains and pursue middle-range research along as many diverse lines as we may be able to justify uniformitarian assumptions.

I began the discussion in Chapter 1 with a demonstration that the "interpretation" of certain archaeological observations was dependent on a basic premise, an assumption about the conditions in the past surrounding the formation of the deposit within which archaeological remains were recovered. I showed that the assumption was generally made that man was the agent responsible for the disposition of all materials found in association with demonstrable artifacts. All the "interpretations"—the postulation of bear cults, cannibalism among early hominid populations, mass killing of elephants at Torralba, systematic hunting of hyena by Neanderthalers at Pin Hole shelter—were inferential arguments consistent with the initial assumptions, the premises upon which the inferences rested. There is an important characteristic of all inferential arguments, simply that *we can never reason in a valid manner from premises to a conclusion that contradicts the premises with which we start*. This fact has important implications for archaeologists:

1. All our statements about the past are inferences relative to observations made on the contemporary archaeological record.

2. The accuracy of our inferential constructions of the past is directly dependent on the accuracy of the assumptions or premises serving as the basis of our inferential arguments.

The conclusion we must draw is that we cannot use either the archaeological record or the inferred past to test our premises or assumptions. Quite literally, all our reasoning is "locked in" by our original premises and observational language. Unless we can take our premises to experience and permit experience to pass judgment on their accuracy, we can never gain a critical perspective with regard to our beliefs about the past. "Can we present historical events as instances or confirmation for a law? We cannot if the very law we wish to test has been presupposed in inferring the event [Kitts 1977:79]."

Put another way, since we construct the past inferentially we cannot use our constructions to test the accuracy of the premises that provided the basis for the characteristics constructed.

Since we cannot use the inferred characteristics of the past to test the basis for our inferential procedures, how do we develop reliable means for knowing the past? The answer, as I have intimated, is that we must engage in middle-range research, which consists of actualistic studies designed to control for the relationship between dynamic properties of the past about which one seeks knowledge and the static material properties common to the past and the present, Whitehead's "eternal objects"—in short, the characteristics about which uniformitarian assumptions may be made, those things which the present shares with the past. These common things provide the basis for a comparison of the events from different times in the past.

The reason that middle-range research must be basically actualistic is that only in the present can we observe the bear and the footprint together, the coincidence of the dynamic and the static derivatives. In more mature disciplines,, where a relatively sound methodology and a sophisticated observational language exist, it may be possible to use inferred conditions about the past as premises for further inferences if the initial premises serving as the basis of the original inference are securely documented and "verified" at the middle-range level of research. As illustrated in Chapter 1, this is probably a very risky strategy, given the lack of sophistication in contemporary archaeology.

The dependence of our knowledge of the past on inference rather than direct observation renders the relationship between paradigm (the conceptual tool of description) and theory (the conceptual tool of explanation) vague, it also renders the "independence" of observations from explanations frequently suspect and commonly standing in a built in relationship, thereby committing the fallacy of "confirming the consequent."

It is this condition that renders it imperative that our methods for constructing the past be intellectually *independent* of our theories for explaining the past. That is, the theories explaining the archaeological record, the work that provides our observational language and conveys meaning to archaeological phenomena, must be intellectually independent of our a priori ideas of the past, or our theories regarding the processes responsible for past events, patterns of change, or stability. *Our middle-range theory must be intellectually independent of our general theory*. Middle-range theory must be tested primarily with documented living systems. Middle-range theory treats the relationship between statics and dynamics, between behavior and material derivatives. General theory may be tested using archaeological phenomena meaningfully operationalized through middle-range research. Stated another way, general theory must be evaluated using instruments for measuring the variables specified in the theory. These instruments must have been developed independently through middle-range research. In the absence of methods for reliably monitoring the variables said to be determinantly operative, no archaeological test of general theory is possible.

The conclusion should be clear: Middle-range research, with particular emphasis of theory building, is crucial to the further development of archaeology. We cannot "know" the past without it, and we cannot evaluate our ideas about the past and why it was the way it appears to have been without means of monitoring the conditions or variables believed to be important. Both of these tasks are dependent upon the development of middle-range research.

Notes

1. References to other chapters refer to the volume in which this originally appeared.

2. This is essentially identical to what David Clarke called *interpretive theory* (Clarke 1973:8) and appears to be what Schiffer (1976a) means by *behavioral archaeology*. (See also Sullivan 1978.)

3. Richard Gould has argued that, since some characteristics appear unlikely to bridge the present and the past, we should avoid uniformitarian assumptions. "The less the archaeologist must depend upon uniformitarian assumptions to infer past human behavior, the more valid his explanations will be [R. A. Gould 1978:255]." This is nonsense, in my view, since any inference, even a simple identification, to the past *must* make a uniformitarian assumption.

Some Thoughts on the Middle to Upper Paleolithic Transition

White's timely and well-organized review of advances in data base and thinking relative to the Middle to Upper Paleolithic transition is welcome. I will arrange my comments in terms of some of his topical headings.

Bone-Working Technology

White accepts Freeman's claim that worked bones in considerable numbers are present in Mousterian Level 17 at Cueva Morín. The specimens illustrated by Freeman (1971, 1978) are without exception indistinguishable from canid-gnawed bone fragments. I have illustrated many "pressure-flaked" bones with the properties he describes, including the diagonal scoring on the external surface (the "pressure flaking" tends to be on the internal face). I have described this scoring as diagnostic of canid gnawing, since it is produced when chips give way on the inside of the bone and the tooth slides down the external face. Most of the "flaking" is produced by animals during the course of collapsing a bone cylinder (Figure 29.1). Once the cylinder splits longitudinally, the "pressure flaking" remains on the ends of the splinters (see Binford 1981b: Figs. 3.19, 3.20). Bones similar to those described by Freeman have been reported by Dart (1960:5) from Makapansgat, by Breuil (1939) from Chou-kou-tien, and by Veyrier and Combier (1952) and de Lumley (1969) from ancient sites in France. In all these cases, the "manufacturers" were most certainly gnawing animals. (For comparative illustrations, see Binford 1981b:Figs. 3.09-3.17.) The "worked" bone reported by Freeman is relevant to the Mousterian only in that it betrays the common use of sites by man and other animals. We need to know much more about the factors conditioning the associations between man and evidence of carnivore occupation at the same site; there are apparently strong geographic variations in such associations. Freeman's misidentifications obscure this interesting research area rather than opening up "traditionally . . . unrecognized" accomplishments by men of the Mousterian era.

Originally published in *Current Anthropology* 23 (2):177–181, 1982. Reprinted by permission from University of Chicago Press. © 1982 by the Wenner-Gren Foundation for Anthropological Research.

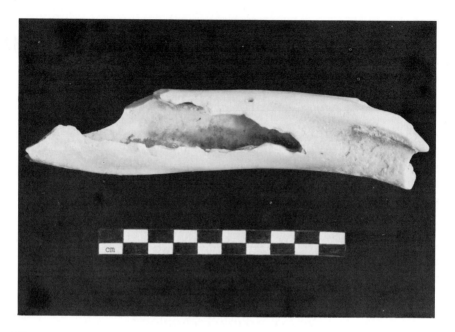

Figure 29.1   Channeled bone gnawed by wolves.

Subsistence Activities

White challenges some of the generalizations offered by Mellars regarding the Upper Paleolithic hunting "specialization" on the basis of recent faunal summaries by Campbell. What he ignores in citing Campbell's summaries is that in only one case (Campbell 1977:75) is there any suggestion that the artifacts referrable to human occupation are not also mixed with the remains of carnivore lairs. Judging from the few tools (7,000-9,000) from the Upper Paleolithic in Great Britain, most of the animal remains observed at the sites where these tools were obtained almost certainly refer primarily to the subsistence activities of animals, not man. I am not surprised that the faunal summaries look like the behavior of predatory generalists.

White further points out that Mellars compares bone counts rather than minimum numbers of individuals, arguing that when MNI's are used the apparent specialization in the Upper Paleolithic "proves illusory." His example, the work of Spiess (1979), is misleading; Spiess assumed that man consumes animal foods in living-animal units, and this is demonstrably not the case most of the time (Binford 1978b:69–72, 478–79). Parts of animals are discarded, transported, stored, and consumed differentially. This means that the presence of a mandible on a site does not mean that a whole animal was consumed there, but probably only that a mandible with attached tongue was used there. For Spiess, "a minimum count of one individual . . . was often made upon the basis of a scrap of one piece of bone" (p. 183). As I have pointed out, this is a fairyland exercise (Binford 1980a:630).

It is true that there are situations in which only a few bones might be transported yet a substantial amount of meat might be introduced to a site—for example, when the meat was stripped from the bones in order to reduce the transport load and the bones discarded at the kill or processing location. The anatomical parts which would be transported in such a situation (Binford 1978b:107–9, 285, 238–45) would be parts of moderate utility with a low meat-to-bone ratio, for example, rib slabs. In the cases cited by White as possibly indicative of a generalist's diet, the parts of large animals represented are predominantly from the head (see Bouchud 1975). This is far from a high-utility part, and certainly not one for which a numerical bias could be expected to arise from the differential transport of processed or stripped meat. The pattern of anatomical-part bias from many of the sites where MNI conversions based on limited bone-counts-to-meat estimates have been made appears bizarre if one assumes the parts were transported incidentally to the introduction of all the meat, presumably removed from the bones at the kill site. For instance, for Level 14 at the Abri Pataud, using a MNI convention leads to the estimate of 1,400 kg of meat, said to represent 37% of the total meat diet, contributed by auroch. This estimate is based on the presence in the level of one upper M2 (Bouchud 1975:134), while reindeer, said to represent 39% of the diet, are represented by 1,481 bones (Bouchud 1975:134). Clearly, a large number of hidden assumptions must stand behind such an inference. We must discard such simple conventions and seek to understand the conditions which might have generated the archaeological patterns.

Hunters and gatherers do not begin eating an animal at the nose and proceed to the tail; they segment the animal and differentially consume parts in different places and at different rates. The archaeological record reflects this differential usage, and we cannot ignore it. Further, both ancient and modern hunter–gatherers used various tactics—hunting, trapping, and scavenging from both the natural death sites of animals and the kill sites of other predators—and at least the latter two are associated with a complicated set of interactions with other predator–scavengers. To equate a set of lower legs and a skull scavenged from the death site of a large bovid with the usable meat in a live animal is naive at best. We must have the methods for identifying the food procurement tactics represented by a faunal assemblage before assuming that all animals were hunted and, further, that all usable parts of hunted animals are represented by a single molar tooth.

Is there any evidence for a contrast between Upper and Middle Paleolithic in degree of hunting specialization? Techniques for identifying hunting tactics are just beginning to appear and have not yet been applied to the relevant materials. This means that, while we may appreciate the inadequacy of interpretive conventions, we must, nevertheless, fall back on impressions and judgments. It is my judgment that, prior to the Upper Paleolithic, (a) scavenging of large body-sized animals was a regular and important part of the food-procurement strategies, (b) gregarious and migratory animals such as reindeer were hunted as if they were territorial game (that is, I see no evidence for large mass kills, but only for the killing of individuals and resumption of hunting after short periods of consumption); and (c) storage of meat was not a regular part of the subsistence strategy. This latter is important because hunting specialization is in my opinion generally linked to storage. Specialization is commonly linked to the periodic aggregation of a species, which renders it a prime target. This is an optimal condition for putting up stores if the schedule of the prey localization and aggregation can be synchronized with the onset of the nongrowing season and reduced temperatures which make storage of meat more reliable (see Binford 1978b:91–133, 1980b).

Storage contrasts, if they can be demonstrated, appear to me to be symptomatic of a still more provocative contrast between the earlier time ranges and the Upper Paleolithic in its "modern man" manifestations. Early adaptations appear to me to be based on tactics which do not require much planning ahead (that is, beyond one or two days): in additon to the absence of storage (assuming for the moment that my impressions are correct) there is an absence of curated technologies (Binford 1976, 1979b) and of the tactical use of such resources as salmon, the exploitation of which in large quantities requires the anticipation from one year to the next of spawning runs, etc. Perhaps of similar relevance is early populations' inability to penetrate the Eurasiatic steppe, where both storage and the anticipation of herd movements would seem prerequisite to adaptation. It is my impression that the *ability to anticipate events and conditions not yet experienced* was not one of the strengths of our ancestors prior to the appearance of clear evidence for symboling, e.g., personal ornaments, graphics in the form of painting, "art," and "notation" (Marshack 1972), graphic decoration of other things, including other persons, etc., things which mark the appearance of "culture" as we know it (cf. White 1949a:363). In my opinion the appearance of symboling is a major change and not one which can be understood by seeking exclusive "social explanations."

White points out that antler is very common in Upper Paleolithic sites, suggesting that this can be understood in terms of an increased demand for antler as a raw material for "artistic and technological" productions. The view that "the desirability of antler as a communicative and technological medium is reflected in a shift to the hunting of large numbers of reindeer" seems to be forcing a "social explanation," to say the least. In the first place, shed antler is almost useless for the manufacture of most kinds of bone tools requiring strength and resiliency. Secondly, a group hunting reindeer for food, particularly one with storage, would have had more antler than it could use for the production of the relatively minor antlerbone component known from Upper Paleolithic sites. This lack of scarcity is illustrated by the variety of functions served by unmodified antler around sites of reindeer-hunters (Binford 1978b:117, 480–81). Far from a situation in which one kills reindeer to get antler for purposes of communicating, the high frequency of antler reflects its abundance where hunters are exploiting reindeer as a focal resource. It is much more likely that the comparative absence of antler in Middle Paleolithic sites reflects the absence of a focus on reindeer.

The societies of early hominids cannot be understood by projecting backwards from what is in many cases a poor understanding of modern hunter–gatherers. This is a point made recently by a number of writers (e.g., Conkey 1980:610). My research on temperate- and cold-environment adaptations will, I feel, greatly aid our understanding of the Upper Paleolithic, but it is only by way of contrast that it directly illuminates the Middle Paleolithic. Figuring out how the Middle Paleolithic was organized remains one of our greatest challenges. I am quite certain that Bordes's arguments about ethnicity are wrong, but I am equally convinced that functional arguments projected from modern logistical hunter–gatherers are likely to be inaccurate.

Dimensions of Settlements

White is correct in pointing out that we have no reliable and unbiased data with which to evaluate the impression that Middle Paleolithic occupations were by small groups for short durations. (It should be kept in mind that some have thought they were large, essentially sedentary groups [Bordes 1968:144].) It remains my *impression* that Middle Paleolithic sites are generally palimpsests composed of numerous small and short-duration episodes of occupation. In the materials known from northern Europe, even the recognizable "levels" are small and yield small inventories. Analysis of the Combe-Grenal data has convinced me that I can demonstrate the composite character of those assemblages, and I will soon present a series of arguments regarding site structure pointing to the conclusion that the Mousterian assemblages as known for Combe-Grenal are *all* palimpsests. My analysis of site-formation observations regarding logistically organized hunter–gatherers (Binford 1982a) shows that there should be assemblage heterogeneity arising from changes in the relative economic potential of different places as a simple consequence of the movement of residential hub locations. This should result in variation even within deposits accumulated under the same general pattern of site use. This type of variation is *not* demonstrable when relatively thick levels like K, L, and M from Combe-Grenal are partitioned vertically and within- and among-sample variance measures calculated; these Mousterian levels are internally homogeneous. I cannot see how this could occur if hunter–gatherers organized into minimally differentiated residential and logistical locations were responsible. A further implication of this pattern is that there are no relative changes in position or activities within a region during long periods of occupation. Given current understanding, this implies that all sites were residential—like those of for-agers—or that there was no fine-grained response by the hominids to minor environmental dynamics within their habitual ranges. Either way, the existence of very different forms of social and economic organization within the Middle Paleolithic is implied. The task remains to figure out what these forms were. Nevertheless, I would be very surprised if Mellars's generalizations were to fall as we develop better methods for inference; both the variance in and the absolute size of settlement achieved are in my opinion greater in the Upper Paleolithic.

White speculates that "aggregation sites" may distinguish Upper from Middle Paleolithic. Upper Paleolithic settlement systems were very different from those of the Middle Paleolithic, but the extent to which the concept of "aggregation site" is useful for describing the nature of the differences is another matter. For instance, Conkey (1980:612) tells us that "an aggregation refers to the concentration of individuals and groups that are otherwise fragmented." She recognizes that the archaeological manifestations of aggregation sites will vary with the "conditions under which aggregation takes place," among them duration of occupation, spatial extent of an occupation, personnel, and context. To my way of thinking, these conditions can be expected to be relevant to almost any type of settlement contrast one might choose to make. The degree to which variation in these conditions permits one to discriminate between an aggregation site and other types is not at all clear. Conkey recognizes the problem (p. 612) when she states that "the real methodological challenge . . . is to develop the test implications for each combination of possible conditions under which an aggregation might take place." Obviously unable to do this, she tells us that "relative diversity is the key; even if a considerable range of activities is indicated we must still investigate the degree to which intrasite variability is greater or less than that between sites, between levels in a site, or between regions." This seems to me to be an unsatisfactory approach. Nowhere is the argument warranted that there is a necessary connection between aggregation and diversity. Many other contexts not particularly associated with aggregation could result in regular and regionally patterned differences in diversity. The potential implications of differences for variations in social organization and settlement system are provocative, but the methods for recognizing such differences from archaeological remains have not yet been developed.

Population Densities

White is correct in pointing out that we have no reliable instruments for measuring even relative population densities across the Middle-to-Upper Paleolithic boundary. Again he is prudent to suggest that the settlement patterns are apt to have been quite different. He fails, however, to acknowledge that even if it were demonstrated that there were absolutely more "Mousterian" sites, particularly undated open-air sites, it could still be quite likely that the Upper Paleolithic sites represented greater numbers of people. The duration of assemblages typologically referrable to the Mousterian from geologically undated contexts is not at all clear. According to the French convention, the Mousterian is an assemblage from the first two stadials of the Würm glaciation; assemblages of Riss age are by definition Acheulian, even when typologically indistinguishable from the Würm assemblages. Thus typologically recognized "Mousterian" assemblages may span as much as 200,000 years, while the Upper Paleolithic sites represents 25,000 to 30,000 years at most. From this perspective, White's objections to the accuracy of Mellars's sample become somewhat less critical to the point at issue.

Differences in Interassemblage Variation

White rightly points out that Bordes and I have both recognized "something different" about the Upper Paleolithic patterning relative to that of the Middle Paleolithic. From the very beginning, the regionally correlated variation seemingly indicated by at least some of the Upper Paleolithic systematics has been much more consistent with the generalizations of previous workers (Wissler 1914, Kroeber 1939) pointing to geo-

TABLE 29.1

Assemblage Variability by Type of Site in the Wabash River Drainage

| | Tool Class | | |
| | --- | --- | --- |
Site Class	General Utility[a]	Weapons[b]	Fabricating, Processing, and Domestic[c]
Settlement	10 ± 5%	15 ± 5%	75 ± 5%
Transient camp	15 ± 5%	30 ± 5%	55 ± 5%
Base camp	15 ± 10%	40 ± 10%	40 ± 5%
Specialized hunting camp	25 ± 5%	55 ± 10%	20 ± 10%
Generalized hunting camp	55 ± 20%	35 ± 10%	10 ± 10%

Source: Winters (1969:35).
[a] Knives, side scrapers, end scrapers, spokeshaves, choppers, and hammerstones.
[b] Projectile points, atlatl weights.
[c] Flakers, punches, awls, and needles; anvils, drills, perforators, gravers, abraders, chisels, and gauges; manos, metates, and shell spoons.

graphical continuity in material-culture "stylistic" markers. At the time of many of my arguments with Bordes I was also aware that when "assemblages" were looked at in a configurational sense—that is, when all tool types were taken as of equal value and the only characteristic deemed important was the pattern of overall assemblage composition—this picture of regional continuity tended to break down. Different *conventions* in comparative study produced very different pictures of the past.

For instance, Winters (1963a, b, 1969) investigated a variety of sites in the Wabash River valley from which the same types of projectile points were regularly recovered. Sites in the same region yielding similar projectile points and/or pottery were conventionally considered as produced by the same or culturally similar peoples, and any differences between them were accepted as referring to conditioners other than cultural identity. The range of variation observed by Winters among sites coming from the same region and judged to be of the same cultural unit is shown in Table 30.1. Bone and shell preservation were good in all of Winters's sites, and therefore it was difficult to visualize the percentages given in the table exclusively in terms of stone tools; nevertheless, it is clear that frequencies among sites vary widely. These differences were shown to covary largely with indicators of seasonal differences, and consequently Winters interpreted them as referrable to seasonally variable structural poses coupled with some seasonal mobility.

Again, Judge (1973) found considerable variation among the assemblages recovered from Rio Grande Valley sites yielding typologically similar projectile points; for example, some sites yielded as low as 2% projectile points and others as high as 23%. Difference of this magnitude is sufficient to qualify the assemblages as different "cultures" by European standards (see Bordes and de Sonneville–Bordes 1970:62–64), yet all the sites were of the Folsom culture, accepted as a "culture" by Bordes himself (1968:216). Like Winters, Judge (1973:318-39) demonstrated a fair correspondence between types of assemblage and the geomorphology of the site locations. This would support the view that the differences in assemblage content and the differential placement of sites of different form could be taken as indicative of similar persons doing different things in different places.

Support for this interpretation can be drawn from a very different pattern in the archaeological record. Irwin and Wormington (1970) described and compared chronologically distinct "cultures" defined by projectile-point styles recovered in stratigraphic order from the Hell Gap site near Gurnsey, Wyoming. This study is of the greater interest for its attempt to utilize the taxonomic principles developed by Bordes (1950, 1961a) for describing the assemblages. Essentially no differences were found between the assemblages associated with Clovis, Folsom, and Midland points. Similarly, there was little difference between the assemblages associated with Hell Gap and Agate Basin points and between Frederick and Cody assemblages. Indeed, by European standards there was very little difference between any of these groupings. There was not as much variation among the assemblages at Hell Gap, regardless of "culture" or time period, as was demonstrated by Judge among assemblages found in association with a single culture as defined by projectile-point styles, yet at Hell Gap the assemblages were associated with very dissimilar projectile-point styles.

Still a more recent example of the seeming lack of assemblage variation in spite of variation in artifact styles in terms of the "typological method" (Krieger 1944) has been described by Vierra (1975). Vierra showed that there was no significant change in the relative frequencies of artifact classes (e.g., end scrapers, projectile points, differing forms of side scrapers, etc.) through a long stratigraphic sequence at Puente (A.D. 158) in the Ayacucho Basin of highland Peru. This was true in spite of considerable directional style shifts in projectile-point types and in susbsistence base for the system as a whole as seen in a regional perspective. (The sequence spanned the origins of agriculture.)

What these studies demonstrate is that when one's typology is developed to measure variation (see Krieger 1944) of the kind characteristic of New World ethnographic data (Kroeber 1939, Wissler 1914), variation as measured by assemblages summarized in ways similar to the "Bordes method" can be shown to be independent of the patterns demonstrable using the "Krieger method." Assemblages from different sites of the same "culture" are shown to be quite varied in content, while asssemblages from the same site but representing different occupational components which were also demonstrably representative of different "cultures" are shown to be roughly the same. There is no escaping the conclusion that variation as measured by assemblage composition conceived in technomorphological terms, as in the Bordean typology for the Middle Paleolithic, does not correspond to variation conceived in ethnic or culture-historical terms. Materials ordered by Bordes "typology" do not vary in the way characteristic of "culture" (that is, little geographical clustering of cultural similarities, with continuity both temporally and spatially between formal varieties of "cultural" products).

It was in the light of all this that I suggested that the varying frequencies among the same artifact types as summarized in assemblage "types" would most likely be informing us about organizational differences arising from the internal dynamics of

Middle Paleolithic systems, not from "cultural" differences among systems. Of equal interest was the seeming inability of taxonomists to isolate modes of variation in the Mousterian which patterned according to "cultural" expectations of temporal and spatial continuity. As much as the Europeans tried, they could not find "historical index" types (Steward 1954:54) as had been discussed by Krieger (1944). I suggested that this "failure" was perhaps telling us that culture as we know it was not manifest in Mousterian materials. Certainly the lack of "continuity" patterning is hard to reconcile with a symbol-based mode of adaptation (including language), if it was actually present (Binford 1972b:161).

While all the attention was seemingly focused on the meaning to be assigned to Middle Paleolithic interassemblage variation, there were clear implications in our arguments for Upper Paleolithic systematics, particularly as it had been developed by the French. These implications had been recognized by de Sonneville–Bordes (1966), and it was her claim that functional variability between assemblages did not characterize the Upper Paleolithic. If this claim was true, then clearly the "interassemblage variation" problem was even greater than imagined. For example, if (a) interassemblage variation, as measured by categories of tools defined in ways similar to Bordes's Middle Paleolithic typology, was demonstrable among relatively recent New World assemblages and (b) this variation patterned in an independent way from variation measured by typical New World "stylistic" typologies, then New World data appeared to be consistent with patterning known from the Middle Paleolithic and earlier time ranges, at least in the form measured by the "Bordes method." If the difference between the earlier and later periods was referrable to the absence of "culture," then in the Upper Paleolithic, where clearly "culture" was present, we should see both forms of patterning: (a) continuity patterning, as illustrated by style-based taxonomies, and (b) interassemblage variation independent of stylistic patterning and analogous in a temporal–geographical sense to that seen in the Middle Paleolithic. The French for years maintained that assemblage systematics as developed under the "Bordes method" worked for the Upper Paleolithic and yielded continuity patterning. This demonstration by White that variation among technofunctional classes of tools is substantial and independent of the generally accepted "cultural" systematics brings Old World material back into line with what was already known from the New World.

The implications, however, will not be appreciated by many Old World workers for some time, since his demonstration implies that Upper Paleolithic systematics is not based on the "Bordes method" (de Sonneville–Bordes 1977:19), but, as was suspected, incorporates many "historical index types" (Steward 1954:54) selected because of their recognized historical patterning. When two different things with different conditioning causalities are treated as the same thing with similar casualities, the picture of the world one obtains is distorted and unrealistic. I think we can expect a general deterioration of the seemingly "clean" cultural picture of Upper Paleolithic times in direct proportion to the degree to which the "Bordes method" is the basis for the systematics.

The question of interassemblage variation remains complex. My work has convinced me that most of the dynamics which have been recently explored—curation (Binford 1976, 1979b), seasonal variability (Yellen 1977, Binford 1978b), activity differentiation among different sites (Binford 1978b, 1980b), and variation arising from the tempo of site reuse (Binford 1982a)—are primarily of direct relevance to logistically organized hunter–gatherers. The Upper Paleolithic societies of Pleistocene Europe were probably so organized. White's demonstration that Upper Paleolithic culture groupings exhibit substantial interassemblage variation is most encouraging. We are gradually building up a body of understanding regarding the processes of site formation among logistically organized hunters which should permit the interpretation of Upper Paleolithic materials.

Our methods of inference are thus far inadequate to provide a picture of Middle Paleolithic systems in organizational terms. We need much more understanding of forager (Binford 1980b) systems and better methods of recognizing the results of subsistence tactics not commonly considered in the past, such as scavenging, hunting small-body-sized prey, and the organization of hunting and scavenging in a forager mode of food procurement. (Even the predominantly forager tactics of such groups as the San Bushmen are not relevant, for their hunting activities are generally organized logistically.) We need to know much more about modern groups that are foraging hunters, among them, apparently, tropical hunters such as the Aché of eastern Paraguay (K. Hawkes, personal communication). In addition, we need to look for further patterned contrasts between the Middle and Upper Paleolithic. For instance, I have noted a general absence of fire-cracked rock from the Mousterian and earlier sites I have examined. This betrays a lack of means for maximizing the radiant potential of fuels. This seems strange when one recognizes that populations were living in near-arctic settings in which, judging from the pollen (a near-absence of arboreal pollen from Levels K, L, and M in Combe-Grenal), fuels must have been a scarce necessity. There was also a general absence of prepared hearths; fires seem to have been mainly kindled directly on the surface, and this would have made draft and heat dissipation hard to control and techniques such as "banking" a fire to last the night difficult at best. In contrast, in the Upper Paleolithic we see extensive use of stone liners and probably a kind of radiant oven in which the hot stones were banked with ash and items buried for cooking over a considerable period of time. In addition, there are large roasting pits such as the entire Perigordian IV (Level 5) "level" at the Abri Pataud (Movius 1977:91) and the feature in Level C at the rockshelter of Le Malpas (Montet-White 1973:20). Almost all the types of hearths recognizable among protohistoric and historic American Indians are represented in the Upper Paleolithic (Movius 1965, 1966).

General Comments

An attitude running through White's writings is consistent with the bias recently expressed by Redman et. al. (1978:14) as "a loosely defined direction toward which many researchers are moving in order to remedy some of the shortcomings of previous research." Clearly implied in the subtitle of the Redman et. al. volume, *Beyond Subsistence and Dating*, the thrust is toward the discussion of "nonmaterial aspects of Paleolithic culture" as causes of the material aspects remaining for us to observe. This was of course the basic point of one of my earliest works (Binford 1962), so I can hardly be in basic disagreement. What the advocates of "social archaeology" seem to ignore, however, is that, as was pointed out by Radcliffe-Brown in 1928 (Srinivas 1958:40–41), there is a big difference between a set of synchronic functional inter-actions and mutual determinacies within a system and the factors which might impinge on a system to modify it through time. We might well observe features in the archae-ological record which are directly referrable to beliefs and/or forms of socially insti-tuted ritual and interaction. These connections refer to the *functional* relationships between the operation of a system and its derivative materials. The existence of such relationships in no way implies that the dynamics operating to bring about change in the organization of the system are to be understood in terms of them. Under-standing the relationships between "material aspects remaining for us to observe" and the internal organization of the nonmaterial aspects of past culture is a matter of understanding the dynamics of roughly synchronic interactions and mutual deter-minacies operative within the organization of a past system.

One of the greatest confusions to have plagued the social sciences is the confusion between regularities in the internal dynamics of cultural systems (synchronic and internal-functional) and the nature of the dynamics which conditioned changes in the organization of systems themselves and in their evolutionary diversification and change (diachronic and external–ecological). I have tried to suggest that with regard to the former problem archaeologists seek to understand the dynamic conditions which produced the statics remaining for us to observe. This may well involve us in many arguments regarding the relationships between "nonmaterial" or "nonpreserved" aspects of past systems and material derivatives of these "nonmaterial" dynamics. I have called this middle-range research, and it is obviously research which would ideally permit the accurate *description* of past conditions. When we turn to the inter-esting job of explaining the nature of past systems, we move into the mode of diachronic patterning and ecological–evolutionary theory building. Functional understandings can never serve as the explanations of evolutionary changes. This fundamental distinction seems to have been overlooked and to be merged in a con-fusing way in the discussions of White and many of his colleagues advocating a "social archaeology."

References

Aikens, C. M.
    1970   Hogup Cave, Salt Lake City: *University of Utah Anthropological Papers* No. 93.

Amsterdamski, S.
    1975   Between experience and metaphysics. *Boston Studies in the Philosophy of Science* 35. Boston: D. Reidel.

Ardrey, Robert
    1961   *African genesis*. New York: Atheneum.
    1976   *The hunting hypothesis*. New York: Atheneum.

Ascher, R.
    1961   Analogy in archaeological interpretation. *Southwestern Journal of Anthropology* 17:317–325.
    1962   Ethnography for Archaeology: A case from the Seri Indians. *Ethnology* 1:360–369.
    1968   Time's arrow and the archaeology of a contemporary community. In *Settlement archaeology*, edited by K. C. Chang. Palo Alto: National Press Books. Pp. 43–52.

Ashmore, W. (editor)
    1981   *Lowland Maya settlement patterns*. Albuquerque: University of New Mexico Press.

Audouze, F., and A. Leroi-Gourhan
    1981   France; a continental insularity. *World Archaeology* 13(2):170–189.

Bacon, F.
    1947   Novum organum (Book 1). In *The world's great thinkers . . . the philosophers of science*, edited by S. Commins and R. N. Linscott. New York: Random House. Pp. 73–154.

Badgley, C., and A. K. Behrensmeyer
    1980   Palaeoecology of Middle Siwalik sediments and faunas, northern Pakistan. *Palaeogeography, Palaeoclimatology, Palaeoecology* 30:133–155.

Bailey, Harry P.
    1960   A method of determining the warmth and temperateness of climate. *Geografiska Annaler* 43(1):1–16.

Baker, C. M.
    1978   The size effect: An explanation of variability in surface artifact assemblage content. *American Antiquity* 43(2):288–293.

Balikci, A.
    1970   *The Netsilik Eskimo*. Garden City, New York: Natural History Press.

Bar-Yosef, O.
    1980   Prehistory of the Levant. In *Annual review of anthropology* (Vol. 9), edited by B. J. Siegel. Palo Alto: Annual Reviews. Pp. 101–133.

Bayard, D. T.
    1969   Science, theory, and reality in the 'new archaeology.' *American Antiquity* 34(4):376–384.

Behrensmeyer, A. K.
    1975   The taphonomy and paleoecology of Plio-Pleistocene vertebrate assemblages of Lake Rudolf, Kenya. *Bulletin of the Museum of Comparative Zoology* 146:473–578.

Behrensmeyer, A. K., and D. E. Dechant-Boaz
    1980   The recent bones of Amboseli Park, Kenya, in relation to East African paleoecology. In *Fossils in the making: Vertebrate taphonomy and paleoecology*, edited by A. K. Behrensmeyer and A. P. Hill. Chicago: University of Chicago Press. Pp. 72–92.

Bennett, John W.
    1976   Anticipation, adaptation and the concept of culture in anthropology. *Science* 192:847–853.

Bicchieri, M. G.
1969   The differential use of identical features of physical habitat in connection with exploitative, settlement, and community patterns; the Bambuti case study. *In* Contributions to anthropology: Ecological essays, edited by David Damas. Pp. 65–72. *National Museum of Canada, Bulletin 230, Anthropological Series* No. 86.
Bidney, David
1946   The concept of cultural crisis. *American Anthropologist* **48**:534-552.
Bietti, A.
1977   Analysis and illustration of the Epigravettian industry collected during the 1955 excavation at Palidoro (Rome, Italy). *Quaternaria* **19**:197–387.
Binford, L. R.
1962   Archaeology as anthropology. *American Antiquity* **28**:217–225
1963   Red ocher caches from the Michigan area: A possible case of cultural drift. *Southwestern Journal of Anthropology* **19**(1):89–107.
1964a   An archaeological and ethnohistorical investigation of cultural diversity. Ph.D. dissertation, Department of Anthropology, University of Michigan, Ann Arbor.
1964b   A consideration of archaeological research design. *American Antiquity* **29**(4):425–441.
1965   Archaeological systematics and the study of culture process. *American Antiquity*, **31**(2):203–210.
1967a   Smudge pits and hide smoking: the use of analogy in archaeological reasoning. *American Antiquity* **32**(1):1–12.
1967b   Reply to K. C. Chang's "Major aspects of the interrelationship of archaeology and ethnology." *Current Anthropology* **8**(3):234–235.
1968a   Archaeological perspectives. In *New perspectives in archaeology,* edited by S. R. Binford and L. R. Binford. Chicago: Aldine. Pp. 5–32.
1968b   Theory and method. In *New perspectives in archaeology,* edited by S. R. Binford and L. R. Binford. Chicago: Aldine. Pp. 1–3.
1968c   Some comments on historical versus processual Archaeology. *Southwestern Journal of Anthropology* **24**(3):267–275.
1968d   Review of K. C. Chang's "Rethinking Archaeology." *Ethnohistory* **15**(1–2):422–426.
1972a   *An archaeological perspective.* New York: Seminar Press.
1972b   Contemporary model building; paradigms and the current state of Palaeolithic research. In *Models in archaeology,* edited by D. L. Clarke. London: Methuen. Pp. 109–166.
1973   Interassemblage variability—the Mousterian and the "functional" argument. In *The explanation of culture change,* edited by Colin Renfrew. London: Duckworth. Pp. 227–254.
1975a   Historical archaeology: Is it historical or archaeological? *Popular Archaeology* **4**(3–4):11–30.
1975b   Sampling, judgment, and the archaeological record. In *Sampling in archaeology,* edited by J. W. Mueller. Tucson: University of Arizona Press. Pp. 251–257.
1976   Forty–seven trips: A case study in the character of some formation processes. *In* Contributions to anthropology, the interior peoples of northern Alaska, edited by E. S. Hall, Jr. Ottawa National Museum of Canada. *National Museum of Man, Mercury Series, Paper* No. **49**:299–351.
1977a   Forty–seven trips: A case study in the character of archaeological formation processes. In *Stone tools as cultural markers: Change, evolution, and complexity,* edited by R. V. S. Wright. Canberra: Australian Institute of Aboriginal Studies. Pp. 24–36.
1977b   General introduction. In *For theory building in archaeology,* edited by L. R. Binford. New York: Academic Press. Pp. 1–10.
1978a   Dimensional analysis of behavior and site structure: Learning from an Eskimo hunting stand. *American Antiquity* **43**:330–361.
1978b   *Nunamiut ethnoarchaeology.* New York: Academic Press.
1979a   Comments on confusion. *American Antiquity* **44**(4)591–594.
1979b   Organization and formation processes: Looking at curated technologies. *Journal of Anthropological Research* **35**:255–273.
1980a   Review of 'Reindeer and caribou hunters' by Arthur E. Spiess. *American Anthropologist* **82**(3):628–631.
1980b   Willow smoke and dogs' tails: Hunter–gatherer settlement systems and archaeological site formation. *American Antiquity* **45**(1):4–20.
1981a   Behavioral archaeology and the 'Pompeii premise.' *Journal of Anthropological Research* **37**:195–208.
1981b   *Bones: Ancient men and modern myths.* New York: Academic Press.
1982a   The archaeology of place. *Journal of Anthropological Archaeology* **1**(1):5–31.
1982b   Objectivity, explanation, and archaeology 1980. In *Theory and explanation in archaeology,* edited by C. Renfrew, M. J. Rowlands, and B. Segraves-Whallon. New York: Academic Press.
1983   *In pursuit of the past.* London: Thames and Hudson.
Binford, Lewis R., and Jack B. Bertram
1977   Bone frequencies—and attritional processes. In *For theory building in archaeology,* edited by L. R. Binford. New York/San Francisco: Academic Press. Pp. 77–156.
Binford, L. R., and S. R. Binford
1966   A preliminary analysis of functional variability, in the Mousterian of Levallois facies. *In* Recent studies in paleoanthropology, edited by J. D. Clark and F. C. Howell. *American Anthropologist* **68**(2):238–295.
1969   Stone tools and human behavior. *Scientific American* **220**:70–84.

Binford, L. R., S. R. Binford, R. Whallon, and M. A. Hardin
1966   Archaeology at Hatchery West, Carlyle, Illinois. *Southern Illinois University Museum Archaeological Salvage Report* No. 25.
Binford, Lewis R., and W. J. Chasko, Jr.
1976   Nunamiut demographic history: A provocative case. In *Demographic anthropology*, edited by Ezra B. W. Zubrow. Albuquerque: University of New Mexico Press. Pp. 63–143.
Binford, L. R., and L. Todd
1982   On arguments for the 'butchering' of giant geladas. *Current Anthropology* 23(1):108–110.
Binford, Sally R.
1966   Mugharet es-Shubbabiq: a Mousterian cave in Israel. *Journal Of The Israeli Exploration Society* 16(1,2):89–108.
1969   Comment on "Culture Traditions and environment of early man," by Desmond Collins. *Current Anthropology* 10(4):299–301.
Binford, S. R., and L. R. Binford (editors)
1968   *New perspectives in archaeology*. Hawthorne, New York: Aldine.
Boas, F.
1938   *General anthropology*. New York: D. C. Heath.
1940   *Race, language, and culture*. New York: Free Press.
1966   *Race, language, and culture* (paperback edition). New York: Free Press.
Bonnichsen, R.
1979   Pleistocene bone technology in the Beringian refugium. *Archaeological Survey of Canada, Mercury Series, Paper* No. 89.
Bordes, François H.
1950   Principes d'une méthode d'étude des techniques de débitage et de la typologie du Paléolithique ancien et moyen. *L'Anthropologie* 54(1–2):19–34.
1952   Stratigraphie du loess et évolution des industries paléolithiques dans l'ouest de bassin de Paris. *L'Anthropologie* 56(1–2):1–30; (5–6):450–452.
1953a   Essai de classification des industries "moustériennes." *Bulletin de la Société Préhistorique Française* 50(7–8):457–466.
1953b   Levalloisien et moustérien. *Bulletin de la Société Préhistorique Française* 50(4):226–235.
1954   Les gisements du Pech-de-l'Azé (Dordogne):1. le Moustérien de tradition acheuléenne. *L'Anthropologie* 58(5–6):401–432.
1955   Le Paléolithique inférieur et moyen de Jabrud (Syrie) et la question du pré-Aurignacien. *L'Anthropologie* 59(5–6)486–507.
1960   Le pré-Aurignacien de Yabroud (Syrie), et son incidence sur la chronologie du Quaternaire et Moyen Orient. *Bulletin of the Research Council of Israel* 9(2–3):91–103.
1961a   Mousterian cultures in France. *Science* 134(3482):803–810.
1861b   Typologie du Paléolithique ancien et moyen. *Institut de Préhistoire de l' Université de Bordeaux, Memoire* No. 1.
1962   Le Moustérien à denticulés. *Arheološki Vestnik* 13:43–49.
1963   Le Moustérien à denticulés. *Acta Archaeologica* 13–145, 43–49.
1968   *The Old Stone Age*. New York: McGraw-Hill. (World University Library.)
1979   Discussion following Mlle. Paquereau's paper. *In* La fin des temps glacieres, edited by D. de Sonneville-Bordes. *Colloques internationaux du Centre National de la Recherche Scientifique* No. 271. Paris: CNRS.
Bordes, F. and D. de Sonneville-Bordes
1970   The significance of variability in Palaeolithic assemblages. *World Archaeology* 2(1):61–73.
Bouchud, J.
1966   *Essai sur le renne et la climatologie du Paleolithique moyen et superieur*. Perigueux: Imprimerie Magne.
1975   Estude de la faune de L'Abri Pataud. *In* Excavation of the Abri Pataud; Les Eyzies (Dordogne), edited by H. L. Movius, Jr. *American School of Prehistoric Research Bulletin* No. 30.
Brain, C. K.
1969   The contribution of Namib Desert Hottentots to an understanding of australopithecine bone accumulations. *Scientific Papers of the Namib Desert Research Station* 39:13–22.
Breuil, H.
1939   Bone and antler industry of the Choukoutien Sinanthropus site. *Paleontologia Sinica*, n.s. D., No. 6. Peking.
Brown, James A. and Leslie G. Freeman, Jr.
1964   A Univac analysis of sherd frequencies from the Carter Ranch Pueblo, eastern Arizona. *American Antiquity* 30(2):162–167.
Bunge, M.
1979   *Causality and modern science*. New York: Dover. (Third revised edition.)
Bunn, H. T.
1982   Animal bones and archaeological inference. *Science* 215:494–495.
Burch, E. S., Jr.
1972   The caribou; wild reindeer as a human resource. *American Antiquity* 37(3):339-368.

Campbell, J. B.
   1977   *The Upper Paleolithic of Britain* (Vol. II). Oxford: Clarendon Press.
Campbell, J. M.
   1968   Territoriality among ancient hunters: Interpretations from ethnography and nature. In *Anthropological archaeology in the Americas,* edited by B. Meggers. Washington, D.C.: Anthropological Society of Washington. Pp. 1–21.
   1970   The hungry summer. In *Culture shock: A reader in modern cultural annthropology,* edited by P. K. Bock. New York: Alfred A. Knopf. Pp. 165–170.
   1978   Aboriginal human overkill of game populations: Examples from interior North Alaska. In *Archaeological essays in honor of Irving B. Rouse,* edited by R. C. Dunnell and E. S. Hall. The Hague Mouton. Pp. 179–208.
Carr, E. H.
   1961   *What is history?* New York: Vintage Books–Random House.
Cartwright, Dorwin (editors)
   1964   *Field theory in the social sciences: Selected papers of Kurt Lewin.* New York: Harper and Row (Harper Torchbook Editions).
Chang, K. C.
   1967   Major aspects of the interrelationship of archaeology and ethnology. *Current Anthropology* **8**(3):227–243.
Chaplin, R. E.
   1969   The use of non-morphological criteria in the study of animal domestication from bones found in archaeological sites. In *The domestication and exploitation of plants and animals,* edited by P. J. Ucko and G. W. Dimbleby. Chicago: Aldine. Pp. 231–245.
Childe, V. G.
   1929   *The Danube in prehistory.* Oxford: Oxford University Press.
   1940   *Prehistoric communities of the British Isles.* London: W. and R. Chambers.
   1956   *Piecing together the past.* New York: Praeger.
   1962   *A short introduction to archhaeology.* New York: Collier Books, Macmillan.
Clark, Grahame
   1977   *World prehistory.* Cambridge; Cambridge University Press. (Third edition.)
Clarke, D. L.
   1968   *Analytical archaeology.* London: Methuen.
   1972   Review of *Explanation in archaeology: An explicitly scientific approach. Antiquity* **46**:237–239.
   1973   Archaeology: The loss of innocence. *Antiquity* **47**:6–18.
Clark, J. D., and C. V. Haynes, Jr.
   1970   An elephant butchery site at Mwanganda's village, Karonga, Malawi, and its relevance for Paleolithic archaeology. *World Archaeology* **1**(3):390–411.
Clastres, Pierre
   1972   The Guayaki. In *Hunters and gatherers today,* edited by M. G. Bicchieri. New York: Holt, Rinehart & Winston. Pp. 138–174.
Coe, M. D.
   1978   The churches on the green: A cautionary tale. In *Archaeological essays in honor of Irving B. Rouse,* edited by R. C. Dunnell and E. S. Hall. The Hague: Mouton. Pp. 75–85.
Collingwood. R. G.
   1956   *The idea of history.* Oxford: Oxford University Press.
Collins, D.
   1969   Culture traditions and environment of early man. *Current Anthropology* **10**(4):267–316.
   1970   Stone artifact analysis and the recognition of culture traditions. *World Archaeology* **2**:17–27.
Collins, M. B.
   1975   Sources of bias in processual data: An appraisal. In *Sampling in archaeology,* edited by J. W. Mueller. Tucson: University of Arizona Press. Pp. 26–32.
Commins, S., and R. M. Linscott (editors)
   1947   *The philosophers of science—man and the universe.* New York: Random House.
Conkey, M. W.
   1980   The identification of prehistoric hunter–gatherer aggregation sites: The case of Altamira. *Current Anthropology* **21**(5):609–630.
Dart, Raymond A.
   1957   The osteodontokeratic culture of *Australopithecus prometheus. Memoirs of the Transvaal Museum* No. 10: Pp. 1–105.
   1959   Further light on australopithecine humeral and femoral weapons. *American Journal Of Physical Anthropology* **17**(1):87–94.
   1960   The bone tool–manufacturing ability of *Australopithecus prometheus. American Anthropologist* **62**(1):134–143.
DeBoer, W. R., and D. W. Lathrap
   1979   The making and breaking of Shipibo–Conibo ceramics. In *Ethnoarchaeology: Implications of ethnography for archaeology,* edited by C. Kramer. New York: Columbia University Press. Pp. 102–138.

de Leguna, F. (editor)
    1960   *Selected papers from the American Anthropologist.* Evanston, Illinois: Row, Peterson.

DeLumley, Henry
    1969   Une cabane acheuléene dan la grotte du Lazaret. *Memoires de la Société Préhistorique Française* (Vol. 7). Paris: CNRS.

de Mortillet, Gabriel
    1885   *Le préhistorique: Antiquite de l' homme.* Paris: Bibliothèque des Sciences Contemporaines. (Second edition).

de Sonneville-Bordes, D.
    1966   L'évolution du Paleolithique supérieur en Europe occidentale et sa signification. *Bulletin de la Société Préhistorique Française* **63**:3–34.
    1975   Discours de Mme. Dénise de Sonneville-Bordes, présidante entrante. *Bulletin de la Société Préhistorique Française* **72**:3–6.
    1977   Les listes types observations de méthode. *Quaternaria* **18**(1):9–43.

Dibble, David S. and Dessamae Lorrain
    1968   Bonfire Shelter: A stratified bison kill site, Val Verde County, Texas. *Texas Memorial Museum, Miscellaneous Papers* No. 1.

Ducos, P.
    1969   Methodology and results of the study of the earliest domesticated animals in the Near East (Palestine). In *The domestication and exploitation of plants and animals,* edited by P. J. Ucko and G. W. Dimbleby. Chicago: Aldine. Pp. 265–275.

Dumond, D.
    1977   Science in archaeology: The saints go marching in. *American Antiquity* **42**(2):330–349.

Duncan, Otis Dudley
    1959   Human ecology and population studies. In *The study of population,* edited by Philip M. Hauser and Otis Dudley Duncan. Chicago: University of Chicago Press.

Dunnell, R. C.
    1971   *Systematics in prehistory.* New York: Free Press.
    1978   Style and function: A fundamental dichotomy. *American Antiquity* **43**(2):192–202.
    1980   Americanist archaeology: The 1979 contribution. *American Journal of Archaeology* **84**:463–478.

Durkheim, E.
    1938   *The rules of the sociological method* (translated by S. A. Solovay and J. H. Mueller), edited by G. E. G. Catlin). Chicago: University of Chicago Press. (Eighth edition.)

Earle, T. K.
    1977   A reappraisal of redistribution: Complex Hawaiian chiefdoms. In *Exchange systems in prehistory,* edited by T. K. Earle and J. E. Ericson. New York: Academic Press. Pp. 213–229.

Eggert, M.
    1976   "Archaeology as anthropology" and its case; remarks on reasoning in prehistoric archaeology. *Western Canadian Journal of Anthropology* **6**(4):42–61.

Elton, G. R.
    1969   *The practice of history.* London: Collins.

Erasmus, C. J.
    1968   Thoughts in upward collapse: An essay on explanation in archaeology. *Southwestern Journal of Anthropology* **24**:170–194..

Feyerabend, P.
    1975   *Against method.* London: Verso.

Flannery, K. V.
    1973   Archaeology with a capital "S." In *Research and theory in current archaeology,* edited by Charles L. Redman. New York: Wiley. Pp. 47–53.
    1982   Review in the Land of the Olmec (Vols. 1 & 2), edited by M. D. Coe and R. A. Diehl. *American Anthropologist* **84**(2):442–447.

Flannery, K. V., and M. D. Coe
    1968   Social and economic systems in formative Mesoamerica. In *New perspectives in archaeology,* edited by S. R. Binford and L. R. Binford. Chicago: Aldine. Pp. 267–283.

Ford, J. A.
    1954   The type concept revisited. *American Anthropologist* **56**:42–54.

Freeman, Leslie G., Jr.
    1964   Mousterian developments in Cantabrian Spain. Ph.D. dissertation, Dept. of Anthropology, University of Chicago (microfilm).
    1968   A theoretical framework for interpreting archaeological materials. In *Man the hunter,* edited by R. B. Lee and I. DeVore. Chicago: Aldine. Pp. 262–267.
    1971   El Huesso Trabajado Musteriense de Cueva Morin. In *Cueva Morin excavationes 1966–1968,* by G. Echegaray and L. G. Freeman, Jr. Santander: Patronato de las Cuevas Prehistoricas. Pp. 135–161.
    1978   Mousterian worked bone from Cueva Morin (Santander, Spain); a preliminary description. In *Views of the past,* edited by L. G. Freeman, Jr. The Hague: Mouton. Pp. 29–51.

Friedman, J.
    1974   Marxism, structuralism and vulgar materialism. *Man* **9**:444–469.

Frison, G.
1968   A functional analysis of certain chipped stone tools. *American Antiquity* **33**:149–155.
1970   The Glenrock Buffalo Jump, 48CO304. *Plains Anthropologist Memoir 7*, **15** (No. 50, Part 2).
1974   Archaeology of the Casper site. In *The Casper site*, edited by G. C. Frison. New York: Academic Press. Pp. 1–112.
Fritz, J. M.
1972   Archaeological systems for indirect observation of the past. In *Contemporary archaeology*, edited by M. P. Leone. Carbondale: Southern Illinois University Press. Pp. 135–157.
Fritz, J. M., and F. T. Plog
1970   The nature of archaeological explanation. *American Antiquity* **35**(4):405–412.
Fruchter, Benjamin
1954   *Introduction to factor analysis*. Princeton: D. van Nostrand.
Gardin, J. C.
1980   *Archaeological constructs; an aspect of theoretical archaeology*. Cambridge: Cambridge University Press.
Gearing, Fred
1962   Priests and warriors. *American Anthropological Association, Memoir* No. 93.
Giddings, J. L.
1964   *The archaeology of Cape Denbigh*. Providence, Rhode Island: Brown University Press.
Gledhill, J., and M. J. Rowlands
1982   Materialism and socioeconomic process in multilinear evolution. In *Ranking, resource and exchange*, edited by C. Renfrew and S. Shennan. Cambridge: Cambridge University Press. Pp. 144–149.
Godelier, M.
1977   *Perspectives in Marxist anthropology*. Cambridge: Cambridge University Press.
Goodyear, A. C.
        Review of "Behavioral archaeology" by M. B. Schiffer. *American Antiquity*. **42**(2):376–377.
Goodyear, A. C., L. M. Raab, and T. C. Klinger
1978   The status of archaeological research design in cultural resource management. *American Antiquity* **43**(2):159–171.
Gould, R. A.
1966   Archaeology of the Point St. George and Tolowa prehistory. *University of California Publications in Anthropology* **4**:1–41.
1969   *Yiwara: Foragers of the Australian Desert*. New York: Scribner's Sons.
1974   Some current problems in ethnoarchaeology. In *Ethnoarchaeology*, edited by C. B. Donnan and C. W. Clewlow. Los Angeles, Institute of Archaeology, University of California Monograph IV: 29–50.
1978   Beyond analogy in ethnoarchaeology. In *Explorations in ethnoarchaeology*, edited by R. A. Gould. Albuquerque: University of New Mexico Press. Pp. 249–293.
1979   Caribou hunters, *Science* **204**:737-739.
1980   *Living archaeology*. Cambridge: Cambridge University Press.
Gould, S. J.
1977   *Ever since Darwin: Reflections in natural history*. New York: Norton.
1980   Is a new and general theory of evolution emerging? *Paleobiology* **6**:119–130.
Griffin, J. B.
1943   *The Fort Ancient aspect; its cultural and chronological position in Mississippi Valley archaeology*. Ann Arbor: University of Michigan Press.
1976   Some suggested alterations of certain portions of *An archaeological perspective*. **American Antiquity** **41**(1):114–119.
Gubser, Nicholas J.
1965   *The Nunamiut Eskimos: Hunters of caribou*. New Haven: Yale University Press.
Guilday, J.
n.d.   The Buffalo Site (46Pu31), Putnam County, West Virginia. Manuscript on file, Carnegie Museum, Pittsburgh, Pennsylvania.
Habermas, J.
1971   *Knowledge and human interest*. Boston: Beacon Press.
Hall, S.
1971   Kangiguksuk: A cultural reconstruction of a sixteenth-century Eskimo site in northern Alaska. *Arctic Anthropology*, viii (1):1–101.
Harmann, H. H.
1961   *Modern factor analysis*. Chicago: University of Chicago Press.
Harpending, H., and J. Bertram
1975   Human population dynamics in archaeological time: some simple models. *American Antiquity* **40**(2) part 2:82–91.
Harris, M.
1968   *The rise of anthropological theory*. New York: Thomas Y. Crowell.
1974   Why a perfect knowledge of all the rules one must know to act like a native cannot lead to the knowledge of how natives act. *Journal of Anthropological Research* **30**(4):242–251.
1979   *Cultural materialism*. New York: Random House.

Harrisson, Tom
   1949   Notes on some nomadic Punans. *Sarawak Museum Journal* **5**(1):130–146.
Harvey, D.
   1969   *Explanation in geography.* London: Arnold.
Hawkes, C.
   1954   Archaeological theory and method: Some suggestions from the Old World. *American Anthropologist* **56**:155–168.
Hayden, B.
   1976   Curation: Old and new. In *Primitive art and technology,* edited by J. S. Raymond. Calgary: University of Calgary Archaeological Association. Pp. 47–59.
   1977   Stone tool functions in the Western Desert. In *Stone tools as cultural markers: Change, evolution, and complexity,* edited by R. V. S. Wright. Canberra: Australian Institute of Aboriginal Studies. Pp. 178–188.
   1978   Snarks in archaeology: Or, inter-assemblage variability in lithics (a view from the Antipodes). In *Lithics and subsistence: the analysis of stone tool use in prehistoric economics,* edited by Dave L. Davis. Pp. 179–198. *Vanderbilt University Publications in Anthropology* **20.**
Heider, K. G.
   1967   Archaeological assumptions and ethnographical facts: A cautionary tale from New Guinea. *Southwestern Journal of Anthropology* **23**:55–64.
Heinz, H. J.
   1972   Territoriality among the bushmen in general and the !ko in particular. *Anthropos* **67**:405–416.
Hemming, J. E.
   1971   The distribution movement patterns of caribou in Alaska. *Wildlife Technical Bulletin* No. 1. Fairbanks, Alaska: Department of Fish and Game.
Hempel, C. G.
   1966   *Philosophy of natural science.* Englewood Cliffs, New Jersey: Prentice-Hall.
   1977   Formulation and formalization of scientific theories, edited by F. Suppe. In *The structure of scientific theories.* Urbana, Illinois: University of Illinois Press. Pp. 244–256. (Second edition.)
Higgs, E. S., and C. Vita-Finzi
   1972   Prehistoric economies: A territorial approach. In *Papers in economic prehistory,* edited by E. S. Higgs. Cambridge: Cambridge University Press. Pp. 27–36.
Hill, J.
   1965   Broken K: A prehistoric society in eastern Arizona. Ph.D. dissertation, Department of Anthropology, University of Chicago. (University microfilms, Ann Arbor.)
   1968   Broken K Pueblo: Patterns of form and function. In *New perspectives in archaeology,* edited by Sally R. Binford and Lewis R. Binford. Chicago: Aldine. Pp. 193–142.
   1969   A processual analysis of non-seasonal population movement in man and other terrestrial mammals. *Anthropology UCLA* **1**(1):49–60.
Hodder, I.
   1977   Some new directions in the spatial analysis of archaeological data at the regional scale. In *Spatial archaeology,* edited by D. L. Clarke. New York/London: Academic Press. Pp. 223–351.
   1982a   The identification and interpretation of ranking in prehistory: a contextual perspective. In *Ranking, resource and exchange,* edited by C. Renfrew, and S. Shennan. Cambridge: Cambridge University Press. Pp. 150–154.
   1982b   *Symbols in action: Ethnoarchaeological studies of material culture.* Cambridge: Cambridge University Press.
Holmberg, Allan R.
   1950   Nomads of the long bow; the Siriono of eastern Bolivia. *Smithsonian Institution: Institute of Social Anthropology Publication* **10.**
House, J. H., and M. B. Schiffer
   1975   Significance of the archaeological resources of the Cache River Basin. In *The Cache River archaeological project: An experiment in contract archaeology,* edited by M. B. Schiffer and J. H. House. *Publications in Archaeology, Research Series* No. 8, Fayetteville: Arkansas Archaeological Survey. Pp. 163–189.
Howells, W. W.
   1960   Estimating population numbers through archaeological and skeletal remains. *In* The Application of Quantitative Methods in Archaeology, edited by Robert F. Heizer and Sherburne F. Cook. *Viking Fund Publications in Anthropology* No. 28.
Ingstad, H.
   1954   *Nunamiut.* London: Allen and Unwin.
Irwin, H. T. and H. M. Wormington
   1970   Paleo-indian tool types in the Great Plains. *American Antiquity* **35**:24–33.
Isaac, G.
   1971   The diet of early man. *World Archaeology* **2**(3):278–298.
   1977   *Olorgesailie: Archaeological studies of a Middle Pleistocene lake basin in Kenya.* Chicago: University of Chicago Press.
Isaac, G., and D. Crader
   1981   To what extent were early hominids carnivorous? An archaeological perspective. In *Omnivorous Primates: Gathering and hunting in human evolution,* edited by R. S. O. Harding and G. Teleki. New York: Columbia University Press. Pp. 37–103.

Isaac, Glynn, and Barbara Isaac
1975   Africa. In *Varieties of culture in the Old World,* edited by Robert Stigler. New York: St. Martins Press. Pp. 8–48.
Jarman, M. R.
1972   European deer economies and the advent of the Neolithic. In *Papers in economic prehistory,* edited by E. S. Higgs. Cambridge: Cambridge University Press. Pp. 125–148.
Jelinek, A. J.
1976   Form, function, and style in lithic analysis. In *Cultural change and continuity: Essays in honor of James Bennett Griffin,* edited by C. E. Cleland. New York: Academic Press. Pp. 19–33.
Jelks, B.
1975   *The use and misuse of random sampling in archaeology.* Normal: Gett Publishing.
Jennings, J. D., A. R. Schroedl, and R. N. Holmer
1980   Sudden Shelter. *University of Utah Anthropological Papers* No. 103.
Jochim, Michael A.
1976   *Hunter–gatherer subsistence and settlement.* New York: Academic Press.
1979   Breaking down the system: Recent ecological approaches in archaeology. In *Advances in archaeological method and theory* (Vol. 2), edited by M. B. Schiffer. New York: Academic Press. Pp. 77–117.
Judge, J.
1973   *Paleoindian occupation of the central Rio Grande Valley in New Mexico.* Albuquerque: University of New Mexico Press.
Kehoe, Thomas F.
1967   Boarding School Bison Drive site. *Plains Anthropologist, Memoir* No. 4.
Kitching, J. W.
1963   *Bone, tooth and horn tools of Paleolithic man.* Manchester: Manchester University Press.
Kitts, D. B.
1977   *The structure of geology.* Dallas: Southern Methodist University Press.
Klimek, S.
1935   The structure of California Indian culture. In *University of California Publications in American Archaeology and Ethnology* 37:1–70.
Knudson, R.
1973   Organizational variability in late Paleo-Indian assemblages. Ph.D. dissertation, Department of Anthropology, Washington State University, Pullman.
Krieger, A.D.
1944   The typological concept. *American Antiquity* 9:271–288.
Kroeber, A. L.
1939   *Cultural and natural areas of native North America,* Berkeley/Los Angeles: University of California Press.
1948   *Anthropology* (second edition) New York: Harcourt, Brace.
Kroeber, A. L., and C. Kluckhohn
1952   Culture: A critical review of concepts and definitions. *Papers of the Peabody Museum of American Archaeology and Ethnology* **47**(1).
Kuhn, T.
1962a   The historical structure of scientific discovery. *Science* **136**:760–764.
1962b   *The structure of scientific revolutions.* Chicago: University of Chicago Press.
1964   *The structure of scientific revolutions.* Chicago: University of Chicago Press (Phoenix Books).
1970   Postscript—1969. In *The structure of scientific revolutions.* Chicago: University of Chicago Press. Pp. 174–210. (Second edition, enlarged.)
1977   Second thoughts on paradigms. In *The structure of scientific theories,* edited by F. Suppe. Urbana, Illinois: University of Illinois Press. Pp. 495–517. (Second edition.)
Kushner, G.
1970   A consideration of some processual designs for archaeology as anthropology. *American Antiquity* **35**(2):125–132.
Lakatos, I.
1976   History of science and its rational reconstructions. In *Method and appraisal in the physical sciences,* edited by C. Howson. Cambridge: Cambridge University Press. Pp. 1–39.
Lamberg-Karlovsky, C. C.
1975   Third millennium modes of exchange and modes of production. In *Ancient civilization and trade,* edited by J. A. Sabloff and C. C. Lamberg-Karlovsky. Albuquerque: University of New Mexico Press. Pp. 341–368.
Lanning, E.
1970   Pleistocene man in South America. *World Archaeology* 2(1):90–111.
Larson, P. A.
1979   Comments on Lewis Binford's "Analysis of behavior and site structure." *American Antiquity* 44(4):590–591.
Laville, H., and J. Ph. Rigaud
1973   The Perigordian V industries in Perigord: Typological variations, stratigraphy and relative chronology. *World Archaeology* 4:330–338.

Laville, H., J. Ph. Rigaud, and J. Sackett
1980   *Rock shelters of the Perigord.* New York/London: Academic Press.
Leach, E.
1973   Concluding address. In *The explanation of culture change: Models in prehistory,* edited by C. Renfrew. London: Duckworth. Pp. 761–771.
Leakey, M. D. L.
1967   Preliminary survey of the cultural material from Beds I and II, Olduvai Gorge, Tanzania. In *Background to evolution in Africa,* edited by W. W. Bishop and J. D. Clark. Chicago: University of Chicago Press. Pp. 417–446.
1971   *Olduvai Gorge.* (Vol. 3). Excavations in Beds I and II, 1960–1963. Cambridge: Cambridge University Press.
Leakey, Richard, and Roger Lewin
1977   *Origins.* London: Dutton.
LeBlanc, Steven A.
1973   Two points of logic concerning data, hypotheses, general laws, and systems. In *Research and theory in current archaeology,* edited by Charles L. Redman. New York: Wiley. Pp. 199–214.
Lee, R. B.
1966   *Kalahari-1: A site report.* Chicago: The Study of Man, Anthropology Curriculum Study Project.
1968   What hunters do for a living, or how to make out on scarce resources. In *Man the hunter,* edited by Richard B. Lee and Irven DeVore. Chicago: Aldine. Pp. 30–48.
1969   !Kung Bushmen subsistence: An input analysis. In *Environment and cultural behavior,* edited by A. P. Vayda, New York: Natural History Press. Pp. 47–79.
1980   Review of *Nunamiut ethnoarchaeology* by L. R. Binford. *American Anthropologist* **82**(3):632–633.
Lee, R. B., and I. DeVore
1968   Problems in the study of hunters and gatherers. In *Man the hunter,* edited by R. B. Lee and I. DeVore. Chicago: Aldine. Pp. 3–12.
Leone, M. P.
1972   *Contemporary archaeology.* Carbondale: Southern Illinois University Press.
Leroi-Gourhan, Andre, and Michael Brezillon
1966   L'habitation Magdalenienne No. 1 de Pincevent Pres Montereau. *Gallia Préhistoire.* (Vol. 9, Part 2). Paris: CNRS.
1972   *Fouilles de Pincevent, essai d'analyse ethnographique d'un habitat Magdalenien.* Paris: CNRS.
Longacre, William
1963   Archaeology as anthropology: A case study. Ph.D. dissertation, Department of Anthropology, University of Chicago (microfilm).
1970   Archaeology as anthropology: A case study. University of Arizona Press, *Anthropological papers of the University of Arizona* No. 17.
Longacre, W., and J. Ayres
1968   Archeological lessons from an Apache wickiup. In *New perspectives in archeology,* edited by S. R. and L. R. Binford. Chicago: Aldine. Pp. 151–159.
Lowie, R. H.
1920   *Primitive society.* New York: Liveright.
1937   *The history of ethnological theory.* New York: Rinehart.
MacNeish, R. S., T. C. Patterson, and D. L. Browman
1975   The central Peruvian prehistoric interaction sphere. *Papers of the Robert S. Peabody Foundation for Archaeology* No. 7.
Margalef, R.
1968   *Perspective in ecological theory.* Chicago: University of Chicago Press.
Marks, A. E.
1977   The Upper Paleolithic sites of Boker Tachtit and Boker: A preliminary report. In *Prehistory and paleoenvironments in the central Negev, Israel,* edited by A. E. Marks. (Vol. 2). Dallas: Southern Methodist University. Pp. 61–80.
Marks, A. E., and D. A. Freidel
1977   Prehistoric settlement patterns in the Avdat/Agev area. In *Prehistory and paleoenvironments in the central Negev, Israel* (Vol. 2), edited by A. E. Marks. Dallas: Southern Methodist University. Pp. 131–158.
Marshack, A.
1972   *The roots of civilization.* New York: McGraw-Hill.
Masterman, M.
1970   The nature of a paradigm. In *Criticism and the growth of knowledge,* edited by I. Lakatos and A. Musgrave. Cambridge: Cambridge University Press.
McHugh, W. P.
1973   "New archaeology" and the old copper culture. *The Wisconsin Archaeologist* **54**(2):70–83.
McMillan, R. B.
1977   Rodgers Shelter: A record of cultural and environmental change. In *Prehistoric man and his environments: A case study in the Ozark Highland,* edited by W. R. Wood and R. B. McMillan. New York: Academic Press. Pp. 111–122.

Mead, M.
1959   Apprenticeship under Boas. In *The anthropology of Franz Boas,* edited by W. Goldschmidt. *American Anthropological Association, Memoir* No. 89: Pp. 29–45.
Meehan, Eugene J.
1968   Explanation in social science. In *A system paradigm.* Homewood, Illinois: Dorsey.
Mellars, P. A.
1965   Sequence and development of Mousterian traditions in southwestern France. *Nature* 205:626–627.
1970   Some comments on the notion of 'functional variability' in stone-tool assemblages. *World Archaeology* 2(1):74–89.
1973   The character of the Middle–Upper Paleolithic transition in south-west France. In *The explanation of culture change: Models in prehistory,* edited by Colin Renfrew. London: Duckworth. Pp. 255–276.
Merton, R. K.
1968   *Social theory and social structure.* New York: Free Press.
Milke, W.
1949   The quantitative distribution of cultural similarities and their cartographic representation. *American Anthropologist* 51:237–252.
Miller, J. G.
1965   Living systems; structure and process. *Behavioral Science* 10(2)337–374.
Montet-White, A.
1973   Le Malpas rockshelter. *University of Kansas Publications in Anthropology* No. 4.
Morgan, C. G.
1973   Archaeology and explanation. *World Archaeology* 4(3):259–276.
Movius, H. L.
1953   Old World prehistory: Paleolithic. In *Anthropology today: An encyclopedic inventory,* edited by A. L. Kroeber. Chicago: University of Chicago Press. Pp. 163–192.
1965   Aurignacian hearths at the Abri Pataud, Les Eyzies (Dordogne). *Symposium in honor of Dr. Li Chi on his seventieth birthday,* Part I. Taipei: Institute of History and Philology, Academia Sinica. Pp. 1–14.
1966   The hearths of the Upper Perigordian and Aurignacian horizons at the Abri Pataud, Les Eyzies (Dordogne) and their possible significance. *American Anthropologist* (special issue) 68(2), Part 2:296–325.
1977   Excavation of the Abri Pataud, Les Eyzies (Dordogne) stratigraphy. *American School of Prehistoric Research Bulletin* No. 31.
Munson, P. J.
1969   Comments on Binford's "Smudge pits and hide smoking; the use of analogy in archaeological reasoning." *American Antiquity* 34(1):83–85.
Murdock, G. P.
1967   Ethnographic atlas; a summary. *Ethnology* 6:109–236.
Murdock, G. P., and Diana O. Morrow
1970   Subsistence economy and supportive practices: Cross-cultural codes 1. *Ethnology* 9:302–330.
Murdoch, J.
1892   Ethnological results of the Point Barrow expedition. In *Ninth Annual Report of the Bureau of Ethnology to the secretary of the Smithsonian Institute 1887–1888,* edited by J. W. Powell. Washington, D. C.: U.S. Government Printing Office. Pp. 3–448.
Nagel, E.
1961   *The structure of science.* New York: Harcourt, Brace and World.
Naroll, Raoul
1962   Floor area and settlement population. *American Antiquity* 27(4):587–589.
O'Connell, J. F.
1977   Aspects of variation in central Australian lithic assemblages. In *Stone tools as cultural markers; change, evolution, and complexity,* edited by R. V. S. Wright. Canberra: Australian Institute of Aboriginal Studies. Pp. 269–281.
O'Connell, J. F., and K. Hawkes
1981   Alyawara plant use and optimal foraging theory. In *Hunter–gatherer foraging strategies: Ethnographic and archaeological analysis,* edited by B. Winterhalder annd E. A. Smith. Chicago: University of Chicago Press. Pp. 99–125.
Oswalt, W. H.
1974   Ethnoarchaeology. In *Ethnoarchaeology,* edited by C. B. Donnan and C. W. Clewlow. Monograph IV Archaeological Survey, Institute of Archaeology. Los Angeles: University of California. Pp. 3–11.
Parkington, J.
1980   Time and place: Some observations on spatial and temporal patterning in the later Stone Age sequence in southern Africa. *Southern African Archaeological Bulletin* 35:43–83.
Perkins, D., and P. Daly
1968   A hunter's village in Neolithic Turkey. *Scientific American* 219(5):97–106.
Petersen, N.
1975   Hunter–gatherer territoriality: The perspective from Australia. *American Anthropologist* 77:73–68.
Peyrony, Denis
1930   Le Moustier: Ses gisements, ses industries. *Revue Anthropologique.* 1(3):48–76.

Plog, F. T.
1974   *The study of prehistoric change.* New York/London: Academic Press.
Pocock, D. F.
1961   *Social anthropology.* London: Sheed and Ward.
Pospisil, L.
1964   Law and societal structure among the Nunamiut Eskimo. In *Explorations in cultural anthropology,* edited by W. H. Goodenough. New York: McGraw-Hill. Pp. 395–431.
Poplin, François
1976   *Les grands vertebres de Gonnersdorf, Fouilles 1968.* Weisbaden: Franz Steiner Verlag GMBH.
Popper, K. R.
1959   *The logic of scientific discovery.* New York: Harper and Row (Harper Torchbooks).
1972   *Objective knowledge: An evolutionary approach.* Oxford: Oxford University Press.
Quine, W. V., and J. S. Ullian
1978   *The web of belief.* New York: Random House. (Second edition.)
Rathje, W.
1978   Archaeological ethnography . . . because sometimes it is better to give than to receive. In *Explorations in ethnoarchaeology,* edited by R. A. Gould. Albuquerque: University of New Mexico Press. Pp. 49–75.
Rathje, W., and M. Schiffer
1982   *Archaeology.* New York: Harcourt Brace Jovanovich.
Rausch, R.
1951   Notes on the Nunamiut Eskimo and mammals of the Anaktuvuk Pass region, Brooks Range, Alaska. *Arctic* **4**(3):147–195.
Read, Dwight W., and Steven A. LeBlanc
1978   Descriptive statements, covering laws, and theories in archaeology. *Current Anthropology* **19**(2):307–335.
Redman. C. L., J. M. Berman, E. V. Curtin, W. T. Langhorne, N. M. Versaggi, and J. C. Wanser (editors)
1978   Social archaeology: The future of the past. In *Social archaeology: Beyond subsistence and dating.* New York: Academic Press. Pp. 1–17.
Reid, J. J. and M. B. Schiffer
1973   Prospects for a behavioral archaeology. Paper presented at the 1973 meeting of the American Anthropological Association, New Orleans.
Renfrew, C.
1969   Trade and culture process in European prehistory. *Current Anthropology* **10**(1)151–160.
1972   *The emergence of civilization: The Cyclades and the Aegean in the third millennium B.C.* London: Methuen.
1973a   *The explanation of culture change: Models in prehistory.* London: Duckworth.
1973b   Monuments, mobilization and social organization in Neolithic Wessex. In *The explanation of culture change.* London: Duckworth. Pp. 539–558.
Rigaud, J-P.
1971   Personal communication.
Roe, D.
1980   Introduction: Precise moments in remote time. *World Archaeology* **12**:107–108.
Rohn, A. H.
1973   A test of density plots and random sampling procedures at the Gilliland site. Paper delivered at the 38th Annual Meeting of the society for American Archaeology, San Francisco, 1973.
Rouse, I.
1964   Archaeological approaches to cultural evolution. In *Explorations in cultural anthropology,* edited by W. Goodenough. New York: McGraw-Hill. Pp. 455–468.
1965   The place of "peoples" in prehistoric research. *Journal of the Royal Anthropological Institute* **95**:1–15.
1972   *Introduction to prehistory: A systematic approach.* New York: McGraw-Hill.
Rust, Alfred
1950   *Die Hohlenfunde von Jabrud (Syrien).* Neumuster, Karl Wacholtz Verlag.
Sabloff, J., T. Beale, and A. Kurland, Jr.
1973   Recent developments in archaeology. *Annals of the American Academy of Political and Social Science* **408**:103–118.
Sabloff, J. A., and G. R. Willey
1967   The collapse of Maya civilization in the southern lowlands: A consideration of history and process. *Southwestern Journal of Anthropology* **23**(4):311–336.
Sackett, J. R.
1982   Approaches to style in lithic archaeology. *Journal of Anthropological Archaeology* **1**(1):59–112.
Sadek-Kooros, H.
1972   Primitive bone fracturing: A method of research. *American Antiquity* **37**(3):369–382.
Sahlins, M.
1976   *Culture and practical reason.* Chicago: University of Chicago Press.
Sahlins, M. D. and E. R. Service
1960   *Evolution and culture.* Ann Arbor: University of Michigan Press.
Salmon, M. H.
1976   "Deductive" versus "inductive" archaeology. *American Antiquity* **41**(3):376–381.

Salmon, W. C.
  1963   *Logic.* Englewood Cliffs, New Jersey: Prentice-Hall.
Sanders, W. T., J. R. Parsons, and R. S. Santley
  1979   *The Basin of Mexico: Ecological processes in the evolution of a civilization.* New York: Academic Press.
Sanders, W. T., and B. J. Price
  1968   *Mesoamerica: The evolution of a civilization.* New York: Random House.
Schebesta, Paul
  1929   *Among the forest dwarfs of Malaya,* translated by A. Chambers. London: Hutchinson.
Schiffer, Michael B.
  1972   Archaeological context and systemic context. *American Antiquity* **37**:156–165.
  1974   On Whallon's use of dimensional analysis of variance at Guila Naquitz. *American Antiquity* **39**(3):490–492.
  1975a   An alternative to Morse's Dalton settlement pattern hypothesis. *Plains Anthropologist* **20**:253–266.
  1975b   Behavioral chain analysis; activities, organization, and the use of space. *In* Chapters in the prehistory of eastern Arizona, IV. *Fieldiana: Anthropology* **65**:103–119.
  1975c   Factors and "toolkits" evaluating multivariate analysis in archaeology. *Plains Anthropologist* **20**(67):61–70.
  1976a   *Behavioral archaeology.* New York: Academic Press.
  1976b   What is archaeology? *South Carolina Antiquities* **8**(2):9–14.
  1979a   The place of lithic use-wear studies in behavioral archaeology. In *lithic use-wear analysis,* edited by B. Hayden. New York: Academic Press. Pp. 15–25.
  1979b   A preliminatry consideration of behavioral change. In *Transformations: Mathematical approaches to culture change,* edited by C. Renfrew and K. L. Cooke. New York: Academic Press. Pp. 353–368.
  1980   Review of "For theory building in archaeology," by L. R. Binford. *American Antiquity* **45**(2):377–378.
  1981   Some issues in the philosophy of archaeology. *American Antiquity* **46**(4):899–908.
  n.d.   Some issues in the philosophy of archaeology. Paper presented at the State University of New York, Binghamton, 1978.
Schiffer, M. B., and J. H. House
  1977   An approach to assessing scientific significance. In *Conservation archaeology: A guide for cultural resource management studies,* edited by M. B. Schiffer and G. J. Gummerman. New York: Academic Press. Pp. 249–257.
Service, Elman R.
  1962   *Primitive social organization.* New York: Random House.
Shipman, P., W. Bosler, and K. Davis
  1981   Butchering of giant geladas at an Acheulian site. *Current Anthropology* **22**(3):257–264.
  1982   Reply to Binford and Todd. *Current Anthropology* **23**(1)110–111.
Silberbauer, George B.
  1972   The G/wi Bushmen. In *Hunters and gatherers today,* edited by M. G. Bicchieri. New York: Holt, Rinehart & Winston. Pp. 271–326.
Skoog, R. O.
  1968   Ecology of the caribou in Alaska. Ph.D. dissertation, Department of Anthropology, University of California, Berkeley.
Smith, P. E. L.
  1967   New investigations in the late Pleistocene archaeology of the Kom Ombo Plain (Upper Egypt). *Quaternaria* **9**:141–152.
Solecki, R. S.
  1950   New data on the inland Eskimo of northern Alaska. *Journal of the Washington Academy of Sciences* **40**(5):137–157.
  1964   Preliminary report of the Columbia University archaeological expedition to Syria, 1964. *Columbia University Anthropologist* **9–12.**
Spaulding, Albert C.
  1960a   The dimensions of archaeology. In *Essays in the science of culture: In honor of Leslie A. White,* edited by Gertrude E. Dole and Robert L. Carneiro. New York: Thomas Y. Crowell.
  1960b   Statistical description and comparison of artifact assemblages. *In* The application of quantitative methods in archaeology, edited by Robert F. Heizer and Sherburne F. Cook. *Viking Fund Publications in Anthropology* No. **28.**
  1968   Explanation in archaeology. In *New perspectives in archaeology,* edited by S. R. Binford and L. R. Binford. Chicago: Aldine. Pp. 33–39.
Spencer, R. F.
  1959   The North Alaskan Eskimo: A study in ecology and society. *Bulletin of the Bureau of American Ethnology* No. 171. Washington, D.C.: U.S. Government Printing Offfice.
Speth, J. D., and G. A. Johnson
  1976   Problems in the use of correlation for the investigation of tool kits and activity areas. In *Cultural change and continuity: Essays in honor of James Bennett Griffin,* edited by C. E. Cleland. New York: Academic Press. Pp. 35–57.
Spiess, A. E.
  1979   *Reindeer and caribou hunters: An archaeological study.* New York: Academic Press.

Srinivas, M. N. (editor)
1958   *Method in social anthropology: Selected essays by A. R. Radcliffe-Brown.* Chicago: University of Chicago Press.
Stanislawski, M. B.
1969a   The ethno-archaeology of Hopi pottery making. *Plateau* **42**(1):27–33.
1969b   What good is a broken pot? An experiment in Hopi–Tiwa ethnoarchaeology. *Southwestern Lore* **35**(1):11–18.
1973   Review of "Archaeology as anthropology," by W. A. Longacre. *American Antiquity* **38**(1):117–122.
1977   Ethnoarchaeology of Hopi and Hopi–Tiwa pottery making; styles of learning. In *Experimental archaeology,* edited by D. Ingersoll, J. E. Yellen, and W. Macdonald. New York: Columbia University Press. Pp. 378–408.
Stanner, W.
1965   Aboriginal territorial organization: Estate, range, domain and regime. *Oceania* **36**:1–26
Steward, Julian
1936   The economic and social basis of primitive bands. In *Essays in honor of A. L. Kroeber,* edited by Robert Lowie. Berkeley: University of California Press.
1954   Types of types. *American Anthropologist* **56**(1):54–57.
1955   *Theory of culture change.* Urbana: University of Illinois Press.
Straus, L. G.
1978   Of Neanderthal hillbillies, origin myths and stone tools: Notes on Upper Paleolithic assemblage variability. *Lithic Technology* **7**:36–39.
1980   Discussion. *Current Anthropology* **21**:624–625.
Straus, L. G., and G. A. Clark
1978   La Riera paleoecological project: Preliminary report, 1977 excavations. *Current Anthropology* **19**:455–456.
Sturdy, D. A.
1975   Some reindeer economies in prehistoric Europe. In *Palaeoeconomy,* edited by E. S. Higgs. Cambridge: Cambridge University Press. Pp. 55–96.
Sullivan, A. P.
1976   The structure of archaeological inference. Manuscript on file, University of Arizona, Tucson.
1978   Inference and evidence in archaeology: A discussion of the conceptual problems. In *Advances in archaeological method and theory* (Vol. 1), edited by M. B. Schiffer. New York: Academic Press. Pp. 183–222.
Sullivan, A. P., and M. B. Schiffer
1978   A critical examination of SARG. In *Investigations of the Southwestern Anthropological Research Group, proceedings of the 1976 conference,* edited by R. C. Euler and G. J. Gummerman. Flagstaff: Museum of Northern Arizona. Pp. 168–175.
Suppe, F.
1977   Afterword—1977. In *The strucutre of scientific theories,* edited by F. Suppe. Urbana: University of Illinois Press. Pp. 617–730. (Second edition.)
Taylor, Walter W.
1948   A study of archeology. *Memoir* No. 69, *American Anthropologist* **50**(3) (Part 2).
1964   Tethered nomadism and water territoriality: an hypothesis. In *Acts of the 35th International Congress of Americanists.* Mexico City: Pp. 197–203.
1972   Old wine and new skins: A contemporary parable. In *Contemporary archaeology,* edited by M. P. Leone. Carbondale: Southern Illinois University Press.
Thomas, David H.
1975   Nonsite sampling in archaeology: Up the creek without a site? In *Sampling in archaeology,* edited by James W. Mueller. Tucson: University of Arizona Press. Pp. 61–81.
Thompson, D. F.
1939   The seasonal factor in human culture. *Proceedings of the Prehistoric Society* **10**:209–221.
Thompson, R. H.
1956   The subjective element in archaeological inference. *Southwestern Journal of Anthropology* **12**(3):327–332.
1972   Interpretive trends and linear models in American archaeology. In *Contemporary archaeology,* edited by M. P. Leone. Carbondale: Southern Illinois University Press. Pp. 34–38.
Toulmin, S. E.
1972   *Human understanding.* Princeton: Princeton University Press.
Trigger, B.
1978   *Time and traditions.* New York: Columbia University Press.
1980   *Gordon Childe: Revolutions in archaeology.* London: Thames and Hudson.
Tringham, R.
1978   Experimentation, ethnoarchaeology, and the leapfrogs in archaeological methodology. In *Explorations in ethnoarchaeology,* edited by R. A. Gould. Albuquerque: University of New Mexico Press. Pp. 169–199.
Tuggle, H. David, Alex H. Townsend, and Thomas J. Riley
1972   Laws, systems, and research designs: A discussion of explanation in archaeology. *American Antiquity* **37**(1):3–12.
Upham, S.
1982   *Polities and power.* New York: Academic Press.

Vanoverbergh, Morice.
   1925   Negritos of northern Luzon. *Anthropos* **20**:148–199; 399–443.
Veyrier, M., and J. Combier
   1952   L'industrie osseuse Mousterienne de la Grotte Neron a Soyons (Ardeche). *L'Anthropologie*
           56(1):383–385.
Vierra, R. K.
   1975   Structure versus function in the archaeological record. Ph.D. dissertation, Department of Anthropology,
           University of New Mexico. (University Microfilms, Ann Arbor.)
Vita-Finzi, C., and E. S. Higgs
   1970   Prehistoric economy in the Mount Carmel area of Palestine: Site catchment analysis. *Proceedings of the*
           Prehistoric Society **36**:1–37.
Voorhies, Michael R.
   1969   Taphonomy and population dynamics of an early Pliocene vertebrate fauna, Knox County, Nebraska.
           University of Wyoming Contributions to Geology, Special Paper No. 1.
Waechter, J. D.
   1952   The excavation of Jabrud and its relation to the prehistory of Palestine and Syria. *Eighth Annual Report of*
           the Institute of Archaeology, University of London. Pp. 10–28.
Wagner, Philip L.
   1960   *The human use of the earth.* Glencoe: Free Press.
Washburn, S. L.
   1957   Australopithecines: The hunters or the hunted? *American Anthropologist* **59**:612–614.
Watson, D.
   1976   Classification in prehistory: A New Guinea case. *Archaeology and Physical Anthropology in Oceania*
           11:81–90.
Watson, Patty Jo, Steven A. Le Blanc, and Charles L. Redman
   1971   *Explanation in archaeology.* New York: Columbia University Press.
Wauchope, R.
   1966   Archaeological survey of northern Georgia, with a test of some cultural hypotheses. *American Antiquity,*
           Memoir No. 21.
Weick, Karl E.
   1968   Systematic observational methods. Handbook of social psychology (Vol. 2). Reading, Massachusetts:
           Addison Wesley. Pp. 357–451. (Revised edition.)
Whallon, Robert C., Jr.
   1963   A statistical analysis of some Aurignacian I assemblages from southwestern France. Master's thesis on file,
           Department of Anthropology, University of Chicago.
   1973   Spatial analysis of occupation floors I; Application of dimensional analysis of variance. *American Antiquity*
           38(3):266–278.
   1974   Reply to Riley and Schiffer. *American Antiquity* **39**(3):492–494.
Wheat, Joe Ben
   1967   A paleo-Indian bison kill. Scientific American **216**(1):44–53.
White, C., and N. Peterson
   1969   Ethnographic interpretation of the prehistory of western Arnhem Land. *Southwestern Journal of*
           Anthropology **25**(1):45–67.
White, L. A.
   1949a   Ethnological theory. In *Philosophy for the future,* edited by R. W. Sellars, V. J. McFill, and M. Farber. New
           York: Macmillan. Pp. 357–384.
   1949b   *The science of culture: A study of man and civilization.* New York: Farrar, Straus and Giroux.
   1959   *The evolution of culture.* New York: McGraw-Hill.
White, T. E.
   1952   Observations on the butchering technique of some aboriginal peoples. *American Antiquity*
           17(4):337–338.
   1953a   A method of calculating the dietary percentage of various food animals utilized by aboriginal peoples.
           American Antiquity **18**(4):396–398.
   1953b   Observations on the butchering technique of some aboriginal peoples. *American Antiquity*
           19(2):160–164.
   1954   Observations on the butchering technique of some aboriginal peoples. Papers 3, 4, 5, 6. *American*
           Antiquity **19**(3):254–264.
Whitehead, A. N.
   1932   *Science and the modern world.* Cambridge: Cambridge University Press.
   1957   *The concept of nature.* Ann Arbor: University of Michigan Press.
   1967   *Science and the modern world: Lowell Lectures, 1925.* New York: Free Press.
Whiting, Beatrice, and John Whiting
   1970   Methods for observing and recording behavior. In *Handbook of methods in cultural anthropology,* edited by
           Raoul Marell and Ronald Cohen. Garden City, New York: Natural History Press. Pp. 282–315.
Wiessner, P.
   1982   Beyond willow smoke and dog's tails: A comment on Binford's analysis of hunter–gatherer settlement
           systems. *American Antiquity* **47**(1):171–178.

Willey, Gordon R., and Phillip Phillips
    1958   *Method and theory in American archaeology.* Chicago: Univesity of Chicago Press.
Willey, Gordon R., and Jeremy A. Sabloff
    1974   *A history of American archaeology.* San Francisco: Freeman.
    1980   *A history of American archaeology.* San Francisco: Freeman. (Second edition.)
Wilson, E. O.
    1975   *Sociobiology, the new synthesis.* Cambridge: Harvard University Press.
Winterhalder, B., and E. A. Smith (editors)
    1980   *Hunter–gatherer foraging strategies: Ethnographic and archaeological analysis.* Chicago: University of Chicago Press.
Winters, H. D.
    1963a   An archaeological survey of the Wabash Valley in Illinois. *Illinois State Museum Reports of Investigations* No. 10.
    1963b   Settlement patterns and settlement systems: a functional model. Paper presented at the Twenty-eighth Annual Meeting of the Society for American Archaeology, Boulder, Colorado, 1963.
    1969   The Riverton Culture. Springfield, *Illinois State Museum, Reports of Investigations* No. 13.
Wissler, C.
    1914   Material cultures of the North American Indians. *American Anthropologist* **16**:447–505.
Wood, Raymond E.
    1962   Notes on bison bone from the Paul Brave, Huff and Demery sites (Oahe Reservoir). *Plains Anthropologist* 7:201–204.
Woodburn, James
    1972   Ecology, nomadic movement and the composition of the local group among hunters and gatherers: An East African example and its implications. In *Man, settlement and urbanism,* edited by P. J. Ucko, R. Tringham, and G. W. Dimbleby. London: Duckworth. Pp. 193–206.
Yellen, John E.
    1972   Trip V itinerary May 24–June 9, 1968. In *Exploring human nature.* Cambridge, Massachusetts: Educational Development Center. (Pilot edition.)
    1977   *Archaeological approaches to the present.* New York: Academic Press.

Index

A

Abbeville, 128
Abri Pataud, 425, 432
Accidents of history, 216, 218
Acculturation, 128
Aché, 432
Acheulian, 103, 126, 127, 128, 132, 150, 196, 204, 428
Activities, 144, 165, 185, 186, 190, 289, 290, 291, 293, 306, 307, 310, 311, 326, 357, 366
 differentiation among, 432
 embedded schedule, 323
 organization of, 181
 structure of, 287
 patterning in, 313
Activity areas, 162, 186, 306, 312, 323
Activity types, 102
 domestic, 304
Activity units, 74
Actualistic context, 162
Actualistic study, 411, 421
Adaptation, 222, 321, 334, 335, 337, 357, 379
Addleman, A., 124
Ad hoc argument, 374
Ad hominem argument, 48
Adoptionist tactics, 206
Aeta, 341
African prehistory, 195
Agate Basin, 430
Aggregation sites, 427, 428
Ahgook, Ben, 174
Ahgook, Bob, 289
Ahgook, J., 272, 275

Ahgook, N., 173
Aikens, C. M., 379
Aïn Métherchem, 110
Alternating industries, 120, 123, 140, 157, 369, 371, 373, 404
Alyawara, 274, 298
Ambiguity, 184
Amsden, C., 176
Amsterdamski, S., 47, 48, 415
Anaktuvuk Pass, 170, 192, 193, 243, 272, 288
Analogy, 320
 argument from, 7, 8, 19
 ethnographic, 10, 61, 202, 392
 negative, 161, 162
 "new," 7
 positive, 161
Andaman Islands, 352, 353
Anderson, D., 324, 356
Andouze, F., 160
Animal Anatomy, 184
Anomaly, 66, 68
Anthropocentric program, 206
Archaeological context, 298
Archaeological theory, 10, 18, 21, 22, 50, 233, 411, 413
Archaeological visibility, 339
Ardrey, R., 196
Argument from elimination, 238
Argument of plausibility, 46
Arguments of relevance, 13, 22, 32, 34, 35, 37, 157, 158, 159, 160, 161, 162, 163, 164, 165, 167, 213, 214, 226, 390, 391, 392
Asch, D., 28
Ascher, R., 7, 229, 230, 232, 233, 241
Ashmore, W., 394

Assemblage,
    composition, 385, 389, 429
    content, 136, 185, 187, 198, 202, 203, 285,
        287
    resolution, 353, 354, 367
    systematics, 357, 371, 377
    types, 132, 319, 430
    variability, 74, 134, 135, 181, 185, 430
Assemblages, 3, 66, 75, 100, 102, 107, 109, 110,
    113, 114, 120, 122, 125, 126, 127, 200,
    261, 269, 357, 361, 368, 373, 376, 401,
    429
Associational relationships, 264
Attritional death pattern, 206
Aurignacian, 374
Australian aborigines, 270, 283
Australopithecus, 37, 187
Ayres, J., 69

B

Backup strategy, 276
Bacon, F., 184, 396, 409
Bagley, C., 205, 206
Bailey, H. P., 349
Baker, C. M., 278
Balikci, A., 352
Bands, 172, 379, 380
Bar Yosef, O., 375
Base camp, 86, 87, 101, 107, 114, 115, 118, 119,
    120, 123, 167, 170, 326, see also Home base
Basehart, H., 410
Baume Bonne site, 129
Bayard, D., 18
Beale, 18, 42
Behavioral archaeology, 165
    context, 220, 229, 239
Behavioral observations, 287, 289, 293, 294,
    295, 297
Behrensmeyer, K., 205, 206
Benfer, R., 28
Bennett, J., 216
Bertram, J., 38, 65, 190, 200, 208, 287
Bicchieri, M. G., 341
Bidney, D., 216
Biette, A., 319
Binford, L. R., 6, 7, 8, 10, 11, 13, 19, 25, 41,
    46, 49, 58, 65, 67, 68, 71, 73, 131, 140,
    147, 148, 157, 160, 161, 163, 167, 170,
    181, 182, 185, 190, 194, 200, 208, 209,
    215, 217, 224, 231, 232, 233, 235, 237,
    238, 239, 241, 256, 269, 270, 273, 277,
    278, 283, 284, 285, 287, 292, 293, 296,
    298, 302, 304, 305, 319, 322, 333, 341,

343, 346, 353, 354, 356, 357, 359, 361,
    364, 366, 369, 370, 375, 376, 380, 382,
    383, 384, 389, 392, 396, 397, 406, 407,
    409, 413, 423, 424, 425, 426, 427, 431,
    432, 433
Binford, S. R., 19, 66, 71, 76, 116, 118, 125,
    131, 140, 148, 160, 170, 171, 182, 184,
    185, 256, 319, 389, 407
Bipolar techniques, 281
Boas, F., 4, 5, 161, 217
Boasian anthropology, 395
Bone breakage pattern, 205, 206, 208
Bone distribution, 315
Bone grease, 250
Bone juice, 250, 278
Bonnichsen, R., 208
Bordes, F., 17, 65, 66, 69, 71, 72, 73, 76, 82,
    87, 91, 97, 102, 103, 104, 105, 107, 109,
    110, 112, 113, 114, 117, 119, 120, 123, 124,
    128, 134, 136, 137, 140, 142, 145, 146,
    148, 149, 157, 158, 159, 163, 166, 172, 182,
    185, 223, 226, 371, 373, 376, 400, 410,
    427, 428, 429, 430
Bosler, W., 205, 206, 207, 209
Bouchud, J., 140, 141, 142, 425
Brain, C. K., 189, 190, 208
Breuil, H., 423
Brezillon, M., 304, 319
Bridging argument, 148
Broken K site, 213
Brown, J. A., 28, 124
Bunge, M., 417
Burch, E. S., 194, 333
Bushman, 320, see also !Kung, and San
Butchering practices, 67, 187
    activities, 83, 91
    frozen meat, 245
    patterns, 207

C

Cache, 144, 172, 176, 245, 258, 270, 271, 272,
    295, 327, 328, 346, 354, 355, 363
Caching strategy, 285
Cagney site, 128
Campbell, J. B., 424
Campbell, J. M., 194, 382
Campsites, 207, 230
Carnivore occupation, 423, 424
Carr, E. H., 59
Cartesian graph, 78, 83, 86, 87
Cartwright, D., 73
Catastrophic death, 206
Catchment analysis, 358
Categorical strategy, 393

Causal,
    dynamics, 163, 385
    patterning, 207
Causation,
    units of, 185, 416, 417
Cautionary tale, 241
Cave, 120, 142, 145, 159, 330, 371
Chang, K. C., 7, 26
Chaplin, R. E., 188, 189
Charlemagne, 374
Chasko, W. J., 194, 287, 333, 383
Chenchu, 352, 353
Cherentian, 129
Cheyenne, 398
Chiefdom, 227
Childe, V. G., 3, 61, 133, 399, 402, 410
Choukoutien site, 126, 423
Clactonian, 126, 127, 128, 132
Clark, G., 204
Clark, G. A., 375
Clarke, D. L., 62, 68, 69, 189, 402
Clastres, 341
Clovis, 430
Coe, M. D., 17, 241, 390, 393
Cognitive,
    categories, 260, 268
    context, 261
    devices, 49, 413, 414
    frame of reference, 414
    map, 35
    structure, 131
Collingswood, R. G., 59, 216
Collins, D., 125, 126, 127, 128, 132, 133, 140,
    161, 166
Collins, M. B., 25, 241
Combe Grenal site, 66, 68, 72, 128, 135, 138,
    143, 149, 151, 171, 172, 186, 187, 427, 432
Combier, J., 423
Compressors, 209
Conceptual inventory, see Observational language
Conjunctive approach, 229
Conkey, M. W., 426, 427, 428
Conspecific competition, 359
Contemporary observations, 152, 179, 412, 416
Contextual empathy, 61
Control,
    cases, 207
    data, 175, 178
    study, 392
    of variables, 178
Conventionalists, 160, 183, 429
Conventions, 7, 17, 19, 32, 33, 35, 36, 65, 68,
    152, 164, 165, 182, 183, 184, 286, 377,
    405, 407, 425
Copper Eskimo, 352

Covering law, 12, 16, 42, 43, 157, 419
Craft activities, 291, 309
Crisis period, 183
Criterion of,
    association, 404, 405, 410
    similarity, 404, 405
Cueva Morín site, 423
Cultural,
    contexts, 60, 61, 229, 230, 231, 394
    decline, 17
    diversity, 219
    evolution, 127
    form, 33
    geography, 358
    norms, 181
    reconstruction, 7
    reproduction, 221
    resource management, 241
    systems, 51, 61, 65, 116, 137, 162, 165, 166,
        217, 221, 223, 231, 236, 264, 357, 368,
        385, 389, 412
    traditions, 125, 133, 146, 218
    transforms, 234, 235
    transmission, 218
Culturally organized systems, 220
Culture, 9, 180, 181, 203, 319, 397, 399, 403,
    413, 414, 430
    change, 404
    emergent, 159
    history, 5, 127, 377, 406
    internally differentiated, 162
    origins of, 412
    repertoires of, 131, 133, 134
    of science, 183
    style, 222
    theory, 22, 260
    traits, 4, 398, 399
    type, 69
    units, 378
Cultures, 46, 429
Culturologist, 216
Cumulative graph, 76, 91, 107, 401, 405
Curated,
    assemblage, 263, 264, 296, 317, 426
    technology, 143, 144, 151, 264, 266, 269, 278,
        283, 285
Curation, 166, 241, 266, 267, 431

D

Daly, P., 188, 189
Dart, R., 187, 190, 196, 208, 423
Darwinian evolution, 237
Davis, 205, 206, 207, 209
De Boer, W., 241

Decision theory, 219
Deductive framework, 8
  method, 31
  nomological, 16, 18
  reasoning, 10, 13, 14, 18, 183, 390, 395
Deep structure, 227, 410
Deetz, J., 22, 423
Definition, 15, 32, 33, 182
  expanded, 11, 12
  operational, 12, 15, 32, 33, 182, 184
Definitional convention, 183
De Laguna, F., 218
De Lumbley, H., 319
Demand curve, 220
Depositional episodes, 366, 384
Descent
  with modification, 222
  without modification, 222
De Sonneville-Bordes, 142, 145, 157, 158, 371,
    372, 373, 400, 429, 431
DeVore, I., 227
Diagnostic criteria, 223
  patterning, 338
Dibble, D., 67, 187, 188, 189
Diehl, R., 393
Differential,
  butchering, 189
  destruction, 189
  transport, 189
Diffusion, 17, 128
Dimensional analysis, 287
Dimensions,
  logistic, 269
  storage, 269
  strategic, 269
Direct historical method, 7
  interpretation, 162
Directional change, 187
  patterning, 204
Dirt archaeology, 240
Discovery, 163, 395
Disposal modes, 287, 298, 302, 320
  dropping, 298, 302
  dumping, 298, 299
  positioning, 298, 299
  resting, 298, 299
  tossing, 298, 299, 302
Distortion, 230
Division of labor, 96, 107
Drop zone, 317
Dry meat, 250, 251, 332, 382
Dumond, D. G., 213
Duncan, O. D., 73
Dunnell, R. C., 17, 51, 52, 241, 358, 376, 401

Duration, 221, 384, 428
Durkheim, E., 399, 400, 410
Dynamics, 6, 14, 15, 36, 39, 51, 67, 157, 162,
    164, 165, 181, 213, 234, 338, 371, 386,
    391, 392, 412, 419

E

Earle, T., 390
Ebert, J., 19, 28
Ecological,
  interaction, 218
  organization, 133
Economic zonation, 358, 359, 360
Eddlehoff, L., 324
Effective temperature, 349, 352
Eggert, M., 6, 17, 51
Elton, G. R., 413
Emic approach, 219, 410
Empathetic understanding, 60, 61, 62
Empirical generalization, 13, 31, 34, 35, 42, 43,
    49, 128, 216, 237, 270, 320, 322, 323, 324,
    392, 403, 416, 419
Empirical law, 42, 43
Empiricist, 6,
  ism, 184
  strict, 17, 52, 395, 396, 408
  view, 160
Enculturative institutions, 222
Entrepreneur, 60
Entropy, 234, 262, 348
Enumeration, argument from, 392
Environmental geography, 358
Environmental stimulus, 131
Erasmus, C. J., 404
Ethnic,
  differences, 189
  distinctions, 140, 152
  identity, 144
  viewpoint, 401
Ethnicity, 139, 145, 147
Ethnoarchaeology, 226, 287, 319, 344, 372, 392,
    393, 410
Ethnographic,
  analogy, see Analogy
  comparisons, 143, 145
  experience, 232
  facts, 158, 164
  viewpoint, 379, 390
Etic approach, 218, 224, 410
Evolution, 182
Evolutionary,
  change, 377
  diversification, 433

dynamics, 233
selection, 232
stages, 126
Excavations, stage, 24
Exchange network, 4
Expedient,
    manufacture, 144, 145, 150, 151, 264
    raw material use, 106, 108, 109, 114
Expediently organized activities, 283
Expendable tools, 296
Experimental law, 42, 419
Explanation, 8, 10, 12, 16, 22, 42, 43, 45, 46,
    49, 58, 68, 157, 160, 164, 172, 183, 184,
    222, 321
Explanation sketch, 215
Extractive activities, 97, 100, 101, 103, 107, 109,
    110, 114, 118, 122, 123, 170
Extractive tasks, 343
Extrasomatic transmission, 222

F

Fabrication plans, 181
    model, 181, 182, 185, 190, 191
Factor analysis, 74, 75, 76, 80, 102, 113, 118,
    120, 122, 138, 139, 213
Falsification, 396
Falsificationists, 165
Faunal assemblage, 66, 67, 124, 149, 171, 186,
    192, 200, 203, 264, 325, 331, 335
    remains, 264, 269, 389
Features, 264
Feyerabend, P., 396
Field camp, 346, 347, 354, 355, 363
Fire-cracked rock, 239, 432
Fishing camp, 224, 328, 329
Flageolet site, 137
Flannery, K. V., 34, 35, 390, 393
Fletcher, R., 18
Flexibility, 227
Foley, R., 344
Folklore, 380
Folsom, 429
Food preferences, 189
    procurement, 425
    sharing, 196
    values, 192
Foragers, 427, 432
Foraging radius, 339, 350, 359, 361, 363, 380
Ford, J. A., 376
Formation processes, 14, 20, 36, 39, 50, 68, 162,
    163, 164, 165, 181, 190, 191, 203, 230,
    234, 238, 239, 241, 243, 262, 268, 269,
    283, 287, 318, 375, 376, 380, 415, 419

Founder effect, 274
Frame of reference, 46, 48
Free enterprise, 62
Free will, 216, 221
Freeman, L., 8, 124, 423
Freidel, D., 376
Freidman, J., 62
Frison, G., 280, 283, 346
Fritz, J., 14, 16, 19, 68
Fruchter, B., 75
Functional argument, 132, 133, 136, 145, 153,
    157
    approach, 151, 223
    differences, 189
    linkage, 234
    problem, 225
    variation, 71, 78, 123, 137, 293, 319, 383
    view, 136, 157, 161
Functional relationships, 50, 433
Functionalism, 45, 51
Functionally specific site, 170, *see also* Special
    purpose sites

G

Garden of Eden, 356
Gardin, J. C., 7
Gear,
    active, 270
    household, 279, 281, 282
    insurance, 270, 271
    passive, 270, 272
    personal, 276, 277, 280, 281, 282, 284, 298
    situational, 276, 279, 280, 281, 282
    trip, 245, 255
    types of, 255, 257
Gearing, F., 100, 181
Gearing up, 282
General systems theory, 393
General theory, 10, 36, 218, 412, 421
Generalizing, 216
Generation gap, 157, 161, 165, 167, 213, 224,
    394
Giddings, J. L., 276
Gilliland site, 27
Gledhill, J., 45, 62
Godelier, M., 62
Goodyear, A. C., 18, 19
Gould, R. A., 7, 18, 59, 68, 219, 241, 275, 283,
    391, 393, 410
Gould, S. J., 207, 418
Graphics, 426
Griffin, J. B., 5
Growing season, 354

Growth, progressive, 17
Guayaki, 341
Gubser, N., 178, 194
Guilday, J., 189
G/wi, 270, 339, 341

H

Habermas, J., 61
Habitation site, 97
Hadza, 341
Harmann, H., 74, 75
Harpending, H., 65, 356
Harris, M., 61, 62, 218
Harrisson, T., 339, 341, 361
Harvey, D., 68
Hawkes, C., 229
Hawks, K., 219
Hayden, B., 226, 280, 283, 343
Haynes, V., 189
Heider, K., 241
Heinz, H. J., 359
Hell Gap site, 430
Hemming, J. E., 207
Hempel, C. G., 16, 18, 42, 43, 49, 320, 416, 419
Higgs, E. S., 358, 359
Hill, J., 6, 10, 11, 12, 16, 17, 19, 33, 124, 162, 166, 167, 213, 382
Historian, 174, 412
Historical,
    archaeology, 169, 178
    causation, 180, 398
    index types, 431
    interpretation, 172
    meaning, 59, 412
    reconstruction, 9
History, 4, 5, 21, 235
    accidents of, 4
Hitchcock, R., 19, 28
Hobbesian contract, 62
Hodder, I., 51, 52, 60, 61, 227, 374, 376, 394, 402
Hogup Cave, 379
Holistic viewpoint, 399
Holmberg, A., 341
Home base, 196, 203, 358
Homo sapiens, 73
Hottentot, 190
Houppeville, 106, 120, 122
House, J., 240, 278
Howells, W., 118
Human,
    choice, 216, 221
    mind, 216, 226, 227
    nature, 59, 60, 196

Hunting,
    blinds, 288
    camp, 177, 239, 279, 284, 325, 328, 329, 330, 335, 365, 366, 367, 371, 384
    parties, 237, 239, 359, 361, 364
    stands, 282, 287, 288, 293, 325, 328, 329, 330
    stations, 170
Hunting and gathering strategies, 337
    collecting, 339, 344, 353
    foraging, 270, 285, 322, 339, 340, 341, 343, 348, 349, 353, 361, 376
    logistically organized, 285
"Hunting hypothesis," 196, 206
Hunting strategies,
    encounter, 287, 361
    intercept, 287
"Hybrid" cultures, 128
Hydrology, 199
Hypothetico-deductive method, 33, 35, 42

I

Idealism, 216, 217
Ideas and values, 255
Identification, 49, 50, 185, 186, 223, 390, 415, 417, 419, 425
Identity, 33, 385
Igloolik, 352
Ignorance, 67, 214, 390, 411
Immunize a theory, 13
Individual psychology, 236
Inductive,
    approach, 31
    argument, 15, 42, 54
    reasoning, 165
    skepticism, 231
    strategy, 35
Inductivists, 229, 230, 231, 232
    strict, 6, 14
Inequality, 57, 59
Inferential argument, 5
Ingalik, 352, 353
Ingstad, H., 172, 174, 178, 194, 276, 277
Innocence, 62
Institutions of cultural reproduction, 222
Instrument for measurement, 33, 49, 126, 129, 138, 139, 146, 392, 394, 415, 421, 428
Insurance cache, 332
Interactionists, 236
Interassemblage variability, 19, 66, 125, 126, 131, 135, 138, 150, 157, 171, 204, 213, 223, 269, 283, 284, 292, 319, 353, 354, 355, 428, 431

Internal site organization, 309
    structure, 357
Internally differentiated system, 232
Interpretative
    conventions, 425
    principles, 67, 68
Intersite variability, 298, 337, 347
Invention, 17
Irwin, H., 377
Isaac, B., 195, 203
Isaac, G., 195, 196, 197, 198, 200, 202, 203, 206

J

Jabrud site, 76, 80, 96, 98, 103, 105, 106, 115, 116, 118, 119, 120, 122, 124, 148
Jabrudian, 103
Jaywa phase, 334
Jelinek, A., 226, 227
Jelks, 24
Jennings, J., 379
Jochim,, M., 215, 241, 319, 360
John, A., 175, 275
Joint site, 238
Judge, J., 28, 377, 429

K

Kakinya, E., 175, 275, 276, 277
Kalambo Falls site, 196
Kehoe, T., 187, 188, 189
Kill sites, 170, 173, 177, 187, 325, 328, 329, 330, 425
Kinematic wave effect, 197, 198
Kitching, J. W., 189
Kitts, D. B., 412, 421
Klimek, S., 402
Kluckholm, C., 180
Knudson, R., 281
Kossinna, G., 399
Krieger, A. D., 376, 398
Kriegerian method, 402, 404, 405, 406
Kroeber, A. L., 180, 218, 374, 428, 430
Kuhn, T., 46, 55, 183, 396, 410, 413, 414
!Kung, 270, 319, 341, 342
Kurland, A., 18, 42
Kushner, G., 227

L

"La Méthode Bordes," 371, 373, 375, 377, 401, 402, 404, 405, 406
La Micoque, 128
Lamarckian, 236, 237

Lamberg-Karlovsky, 227
Land use, 177, 196, 225, 362, 379, 381
Lanning, E., 151
Larson, P. A., 224
Lathrap, D., 241
Laville, H., 374, 375
Lawlike propositions, 243, 266
Laws, 164, 219, 222
    of the mind, 219
Le Malpas site, 432
Leakey, L., 196, 197
Leakey, M., 150, 197
Leakey, R., 198, 204
LeBlanc, S., 15, 33, 34, 41, 43, 49, 68, 69
Lee, R., 227, 241, 358, 391, 393
Leroi-Gourhan, A., 160, 314, 319
Lewin, R., 198, 204
Limitations of the archaeological record, 231, 232
Lipe, W. D., 28
Living floors, 186, 197, 207
Living system, 226, 338, 357
Localizations, 197, 202, 343, 346, 347, 354, 359, 363, 380
Logical positivists, 55, 396, 397
Logico-deductive argument, 157, 184
Logistical
    radius, 359, 363, 380
    routes, 265
    sites, 366
    strategies, 266, 332, 333
    zone, 363
Logistically organized groups, 237, 337, 351, 361, 427
Longacre, W., 6, 16, 17, 69, 96, 162, 166, 167, 213
Lorrain, D., 67, 187, 188, 189
Lowie, R., 5, 68
Lyell, C., 418

M

McHugh, W. P., 6
McMillan, R. B., 379
MacNeish, R., 334
Magdalenian, 374
Maintenance activities, 82, 83, 87, 97, 100, 101, 114, 116, 118, 122, 123, 170, 263
    of tools, 266, 267
    trips, 252, 253
Makapansgat site, 190, 423
Mapping on, 349, 354
Marchiando, P., 324
Margalef, R., 416
Marks, T., 375, 376
Marrow bones, 250, 251, 297, 302

Marshack, A., 426
Martin, P., 124
Mask site, 269, 279, 282, 287, 288, 290, 291, 293, 302, 304, 305, 309, 310, 311, 312, 313, 314, 315, 316, 317, 321
Masterman, 46, 414
Materialist, 216
Matrilocal residence, 162, 167
Matson, R. G., 28
Maximizing, 219
Maya collapse, 9, 222
Mbuti, 341
Mead, M., 219
Meaning, assigned, 179, 358, 396, 413
Meehan, E. J., 34
Mellars, P., 134, 135, 136, 139, 157, 163, 424, 427, 428
Memory, 222
Mendelian theory, 214, 215
Mental science, 216
    templates, 181, 182, 185, 190, 237
Mentalists,
    explanations, 236
    views, 52
Merton, R. K., 19
Metaphysics, 3, 215
Micmac, 352
Middle Paleolithic, see Paleolithic, Middle
Middle Pleistocene, 203, 204
Middle-range research, 10, 14, 18, 48, 49, 54, 58, 223, 225, 389, 390, 408, 411, 415, 419, 421, 433
Middle-range theory, 10, 18, 27, 36, 37, 38
Migration, 17, 121, 373
Milke, W., 374, 402
Minimum number of individuals, 424, 425
Mistassini Cree, 352
Mobile hunter–gatherers, 172, 174, 240
    long-term, 379–386
    residential, 361, 371, 372
    strategies,
        coverage, 361
        positioning, 361
Mobility, 140, 331
    leapfrog, 361
    patterning, 360, 361, 362
Models, 58, 59, 157, 162, 164, 167, 181, 220, 390
Monitoring trips, 252, 253
Montet-White, A., 375, 432
Morgan, B., 356
Morgan, C. G., 16, 19, 166
Morris, C., 28
Mortuary practices, 213

Mother-goddess, 180, 185
Mousterian, 19, 66, 71, 73, 76, 104, 131, 134, 135, 138, 139, 142, 143, 145, 149, 150, 152, 157, 178, 182, 185, 187, 226, 283, 285, 372, 373, 375, 376, 389, 423, 428, 430, 431, 432
    assemblage types, 71, 96, 114, 116, 119, 132, 134, 135, 148, 369, 372
        of Acheulian tradition, 72, 87, 92, 112, 134
        Charentian, 72, 103, 129, 134, 137
        Denticulate, 72, 87, 92, 113, 134, 135, 136, 137, 227
        Ferrassie, 72, 92, 103, 107, 110, 112, 113, 127, 134, 135
        of Levallois facies, 71, 72, 76, 118
        Quina, 72, 127, 132, 134, 136, 226, 227
        Typical, 72, 76, 82, 92, 105, 107, 113, 115, 118, 132, 134, 135, 148
    controversy, 65
    industries, 102
    levels, 159
    problem, 65, 151, 164, 214, 223, 389
    tools, 39
Movius, H., 432
Mueller, J., 26
Mugharet es Shubbabiq site, 76, 96, 106, 116, 119, 120, 122, 123, 148
Multiple working hypotheses, 14, 167
Multivariate
    causality, 73, 74, 123
    techniques, 74
Munson, P. J., 10, 19
Murdoch, J., 277, 278
Murdock, J. P., 348, 349, 352

N

Nagel, E., 413, 419
Naroll, R., 118
Natural law, 418
Neanderthal man, 71, 97, 172, 173, 178, 420
    groups, 99
    tribes, 73, 170
Neff, J. M., 28
Netsilik Eskimo, 352
New Archaeologists, 12, 41
New Archaeology, 3, 6, 14, 16, 17, 18, 19, 31, 39, 42, 43, 67, 160, 161, 213, 214, 233, 239, 240, 389, 390, 396, 407, 415
Newtonian physics, 217
Nomadic bands, 348
Nominal scale, 126
Nomothetic science, 413
Normal science, 162, 183, 410

Normative assumption, 69
  paradigm, 397
  rules, 167
  view, 236, 286
N-transforms, 37, 234
Nunamiut, 68, 143, 145, 149, 151, 152, 166,
    170, 172, 177, 178, 184, 192, 194, 217,
    224, 243, 261, 269, 275, 286, 287, 305,
    317, 321, 325, 326, 327, 328, 331, 333,
    357, 359, 361, 368, 379, 380, 381, 382,
    383, 391, 392, 393

O

Objective evaluation, 47
Objectivity, 6, 45, 47, 48, 52, 54, 55, 61, 378,
    395, 396, 397, 407
  operational, 58
  relative, 390
Observation
  site, 347
  stand, 365, 367, 371
Observational
  language, 48, 57, 58, 240, 378, 403, 406, 420,
    421
  strategy, 412
  tools, 398
  units, 26, 239, 376, 401, 406
Occupational
  duration, 238
  episodes, 366
  periodicities, 397
Occupations, 357, 427
O'Connell, J., 219, 281, 356
Olduvai site, 196, 207
Olmec, 393
Olorgesailie site, 195, 196, 197, 198, 199, 200,
    202, 203, 205, 207, 208
Operational definition, 167
Oppenheim, P., 16
Optimal foraging theory, 219, 220
Optional gear, 255
Ordinal scale, 126
Organization,
  of entropy, 143
  levels of, 232
  site, 24
  of space, 303
  systems, 234
  technological, 67, 223, 263, 264, 265, 268,
    269, 270
Organizational
  differences, 137, 355
  dimensions, 224

features, 22
  properties, 51, 182, 223, 231, 269, 298, 377
  variability, 337
  variables, 213
Overwintering, 351

P

Paleoanthropology, 125
Paleo-Indian, 282
Paleolithic, 159, 162, 327, 372, 374, 375, 377,
    401
  Middle, 65, 136, 137, 138, 140, 146, 147,
    372, 375, 423, 425, 426, 427, 428, 430,
    431
  Upper, 82, 136, 137, 138, 139, 143, 149, 283,
    423, 424, 425, 426, 427, 428
Paneack, S., 172, 173, 175, 271, 275, 329
Paradigm, 35, 45, 46, 47, 48, 54, 55, 57, 68,
    180, 183, 184, 214, 215, 221, 235, 238,
    240, 389, 395, 396, 397, 403, 408, 409,
    413, 414, 415, 421
  change, 55
  growth, 397
Paradigmatic
  bias, 45, 48
  debate, 54
  suggestion, 45, 51
Parallel phyla, 150, 371, 373, 374, 404
Parkington, J., 375
Parsonian idealism, 60
Participant perspective, 218, 219, 221, 223, 232
Particularizing, 216
Parties,
  hunting, 327
  transient, 327
Pattern recognition, 134, 417, 419
Patterning, 66, 176, 192, 255, 268
  signature, 417
  within site, 358
Patterns of association, 4, 198
Pech de l'Azé site, 87, 128
Perigordian, 374, 432
Perkins, D., 188, 189
Permanent sites, 171
  settlements, 238
Personal ornaments, 426
Perspective, 403, 409
  egocentric, 409
  inside, 403, 410
  outside, 403
Perspectives, 389, 397, 407
Peterson, N., 144, 145, 356, 359

Peyrards site, 129
Peyrony, D., 71
Pfeiffer, J., 356
Phillips, P., 21
Piki phase, 334
Pin Hole shelter, 420
Place-centered approach, 224
Plains Cree, 398
Planning, 275, 326, 426
    contingency, 256
    depth, 224
    dimensions, 256
    strategy, 333
Plausible, 414
    view, 181
Plog, F., 14, 15, 16, 19, 68
Polar Eskimo, 352
Pompeii premise, 229, 230, 232, 233, 235, 239,
    240, 241, 406
Poplin, F., 319
Popper, K. P., 183
Portable technology, 265
Positivist, 217
Pospisil, L., 194
Post hoc argument, 8, 46, 53, 67, 167, 373
Pre-Aurignacian, 104
Predictions, 35
Price, B., 380
Primary archaeological context, 198
Process, 217, 268, 358
Processual
    approach, 22, 172, 268
    archaeology, 10
    models, 394
    view, 182
Processualists, 236, 237
Procurement strategy,
    direct, 273
    embedded, 273, 274, 280
Professional competence, 7, 160, 161
Profit motive, 60
Projections, 35
Provenience units, 366
Puente site, 334, 430
Punam, 339, 341, 361
Punctuations, 379, 385
Puntutjarpa rockshelter, 275

Q

Quick time, 232
Quine, W. V., 416

R

Raab, M., 18, 19
Race, 236
Racist position, 216, 217
Range, 359
    annual, 359, 381, 382, 383, 384
    camp, 359
    core area of, 380
    drift, 389
    extended, 359
    home, 382
    lifetime, 383
Ranking, 57, 59, 62
Rathji, W., 227
Rational change, 397
Rausch, R., 194
Ravaged assemblage, 208
Reactionary views, 227
Read, D. W., 41, 43
Received ideas, 408
Reconstructionists, 51, 52, 164, 165, 178, 203,
    204, 219, 230, 231, 235, 239, 406, 411,
    413
Recycling, 263, 279
Redman, C. L., 15, 26, 33, 49, 68, 69, 432
Reference dimension, 192
Refuse,
    de facto, 237, 239, 296, 318
    primary, 237, 302
    secondary, 237
Reid, J., 28, 166, 236, 237
Relevance, 162, 182, 185, see also Arguments of
    problem of, 13
Religion, 180
Renfrew, C., 166, 227, 390
Repertoire of culture, 181
Replacement rates, 144, 264
Reproductive mode, 222
Research program, personal, 389, 390
Residential
    base, 239, 339, 343, 346, 349, 354, 355
    camp, 270, 271, 274, 278, 279, 281, 284,
        358, 359, 360, 362, 363, 364, 369, 382
    location, 263, 264, 319, 427
    mobility, 284, 333, 344, 348, 351, 352, 361,
        371, 372
    occupation, 270
    sites, 325, 328, 329, 365, 383
Rest stops, 328, 329, 364
Revisionist
    New Archaeology, 162, 163

position, 229, 239
Rigaud, J.-P., 137, 324, 375
Riley, T. J., 20, 34
Risk reduction, 219, 227
Ritual, 180
Rock with eyes, 224, 225, 227
Rockshelter, 27, 102, 103, 109, 112, 116, 120, 145, 159, 327, 330, 364
Rodger's rockshelter, 379
Rohn, A., 27
"Rosetta stones," 49, 66, 389, 416
Rouse, B., 52, 241, 401
Rowlands, M., 45, 62
Rulland, F., 329
Rulland, J., 174, 175, 177, 289, 324
Rust, A., 76, 96, 102, 103, 104, 106, 107, 109, 110, 111, 112, 116

S

Sabloff, J., 5, 9, 10, 18, 19, 35, 42, 227, 324, 356
Sabloff, P., 410
Sackett, J., 17, 375
Sadek-Kooros, H., 264
Sahlins, M., 62, 390
Saint Acheul site, 128
Salmon, M., 42
Salvage ethnography, 172
Sampling, 23, 25
    random, 24
    strategies, 24, 25
San, 361, *see also* Bushman and !Kung
Saunders, W., 219, 390
Scavenging, 425, 432
Schebesta, P., 341
Schiffer, M., 18, 19, 37, 42, 50, 162, 163, 164, 166, 215, 224, 227, 229, 230, 232, 233, 234, 235, 236, 237, 238, 239, 240, 241, 296, 298, 302, 367, 392, 419
Schneider, P., 324
Science of culture, 216
Scientific
    procedures, 411
    realism, 215
Seaman, T., 324
Search time, 252
Seating plan, 305, 308, 317
Security, 334, 337
Sedentary settlement, 173, 192
    condition, 237, 239, 370
    groups, 427

Sedentism, 101, 348
Semang, 341
Seminomadic, 348, 352
Semisedentism, 145, 349, 352
Seriation, 6, 69
Service, E., 99, 390
Settlement pattern, 176, 202
Settlement system, 100, 101, 119, 120, 123, 269, 270, 337, 345, 428
Settlement type, 100, 102, 123
Sharing hypothesis, 196, 203
Sheffield Conference, 166
Shipman, P., 205, 206, 207, 209
Signatures, 391
Silverbauer, G., 339
Siriono, 341
Site
    content, 288
    form, 373
    formation, 67, 337, 427
    function, 269, 316, 319, 336, 347
    furniture, 237, 239, 271, 272, 276, 278, 279, 280, 281, 303
    location, 288
    structure, 198, 202, 226, 287, 303, 389, 409, 427
Size effect, 278
Skoog, R., 141, 142
Slave, 352, 353
Smith, Adam, 62
Smith, A. E., 220
Smith, P. E., 375
Social archaeology, 433
Social context, 315
Social organization, 162
Sociobiology, 221
Solecki, R., 102, 124, 194
Solutrean, 374
Space use, 38
Spatial
    organization, 287
    positioning, 358
Spaulding, A. C., 6, 21, 396, 413
Special-purpose sites, 270, 284, 319, 325, 328, 369, 370
Special-use areas, 363
Speiss, A., 215, 216, 241, 424
Spencer, R., 194
Spiral fracture, 208
Staged manufacturing sequence, 282, 284
Stanislawski, M., 226
Stanner, W., 359

State, 227, 412
Statics, 13, 14, 15, 16, 17, 23, 25, 36, 39, 49, 51,
    67, 68, 69, 157, 161, 162, 165, 180, 181,
    213, 214, 223, 338, 368, 370, 389, 390,
    391, 392, 410, 413, 415, 416, 417, 419
Stations, 346, 354, 355, 363
Steward, J., 99
Storage, 270, 333, 351, 425, 426
Storytelling, 206, 209
Straus, L., 285, 324, 375
Structural pose, 100, 101, 181
Structural properties, 38
Structure, spatial, 420
Style
    change, 6
    patterning, 136, 137, 138, 139
Stylistic variation, 73, 78, 144, 147, 167, 429
Subsistence economy, 196
Sudden Shelter, 379, 385
Sullivan, A. P., 241
Systematics, 395, 397, 398, 428
Systemic
    context, 298, 302
    view, 182
Systems,
    components, 182
    functioning, 65, 223
    specific laws, 392

T

Tactical use, 426
Taphonomic agents, 207
Task group, 344
Tasks, 245
Tasmanians, 352
Tautology, 129
Taylor, R., 19
Taylor, W., 3, 5, 61, 229, 231, 233, 241, 341
Technological
    efficiency, 149, 150
    organization, 287, 293, 296, 302
Tenacious cultures, 157, 372, 377
Territoriality, 380
Territory, see also Range,
    annual, 359
    extended, 382
    site, 358
Test implications, 14, 15, 66, 148, 164, 428
Testing, 67, 164, 165, 169, 183, 185, 213, 396
Tethered nomadism, 341
Theoretical hypothesis, 215, 227
Theory, 32, 35, 42, 43, 48, 49, 52, 54, 55, 59,
    183, 214, 321, 329, 378, 393, 396, 407,
    416, 421

Theory building, 12, 18, 27, 34, 35, 36, 38, 43,
    58, 165, 169, 213, 214, 215, 218, 410, 433
Thomas, D. H., 26, 344
Thompson, D., 229, 230, 232
Thompson, R. H., 7, 160
Tikatika, 391
Tool frequencies, 185
Tool kits, 66, 68, 69, 79, 96, 118, 123, 138, 139,
    279
Torralba site, 420
Toss zone, 317
Toulmin, S., 396
Townsend, A., 20, 34
Traditional
    paradigm, 181
    position, 237
    view, 17, 163, 164, 213, 214
Traditional archaeologists, 6, 7, 14, 157, 158
Traditional archaeology, 3, 8, 9, 12, 18, 19, 36,
    48, 52, 147, 152, 161, 162, 163, 214, 236,
    407, 412, 415
Trait list, 182
Transient camp, 101, 328, 329, 364, 365, 367,
    370, 371
Trapping camp, 328, 329
Trigger, B., 26, 399
Tringham, R., 18
Trip gear, 245, 255
Tuggle, H., 20, 34
Type-based systematics, 357

U

Ullian, J. S., 416
Uncertainty principle, 33
Uniformitarian assumption, 5, 37, 38, 50, 58, 59,
    60, 61, 152, 412, 418, 420, 421
Uniformitarianism, 36, 191
Unit of food production, 220
Universal fact, 34, 35
Upham, S., 394
Use area, 310
Upper Paleolithic, see Paleolithic, Upper
Utility
    space, 285, 331
    time, 263, 273, 331, 351

V

Value system, 176
Vanoverbergh, M., 341
Variance, 75, 78
Vértesszöllös site, 126

Veyrier, M., 423
Vierra, R., 334, 356, 370, 377
Vita-Finzi, C., 358, 359
Vital process, 217
Vitalism, 400
Voorhies, M., 189, 190, 205

W

Wagner, P., 99
Warranting argument, 13, 46, 47, 52, 161, 414, 428
Warren, H., 133
Watson, P., 11, 15, 16, 19, 33, 49, 68, 69, 166
Wauchope, R., 52, 160, 230, 241
Weick, K., 289
Whallon, R. C., 124, 166, 167
Wheat, J. B., 346
White, C., 144, 145
White, L., 121, 215, 216, 426
White, R., 423, 424, 425, 426, 427, 428, 433
White, T. E., 187, 189

Whitehead, A. N., 59, 419, 420
Whiting, B., 289
Wiessner, P., 219, 227
Willey, G., 5, 9, 10, 19, 21, 35
Winterhalder, B., 219
Winters, H., 100, 377, 429
Wissler, C., 374, 428, 430
Wood, R., 67, 187, 189
Woodburn, J., 341
Work camp, 101, 103, 107, 111, 112, 114, 115, 116, 120, 123
Work party, 342
Wormington, M., 377
Wright, B., 124

Y

Yahgan, 352, 353
Yellen, J., 42, 224, 226, 274, 287, 304, 312, 313, 319, 320, 321, 322, 341, 342, 343, 361, 431
Yukaghir, 352, 353

STUDIES IN ARCHAEOLOGY

Consulting Editor: Stuart Struever

Department of Anthropology
Northwestern University
Evanston, Illinois

Charles R. McGimsey III. **Public Archeology**

Lewis R. Binford. **An Archaeological Perspective**

Muriel Porter Weaver. **The Aztecs, Maya, and Their Predecessors: Archaeology of Mesoamerica**

Joseph W. Michels. **Dating Methods in Archaeology**

C. Garth Sampson. **The Stone Age Archaeology of Southern Africa**

Fred T. Plog. **The Study of Prehistoric Change**

Patty Jo Watson (Ed.). **Archeology of the Mammoth Cave Area**

George C. Frison (Ed.). **The Casper Site: A Hell Gap Bison Kill on the High Plains**

W. Raymond Wood and R. Bruce McMillan (Eds.). **Prehistoric Man and His Environments: A Case Study in the Ozark Highland**

Kent V. Flannery (Ed.). **The Early Mesoamerican Village**

Charles E. Cleland (Ed.). **Cultural Change and Continuity: Essays in Honor of James Bennett Griffin**

Michael B. Schiffer. **Behavioral Archeology**

Fred Wendorf and Romuald Schild. **Prehistory of the Nile Valley**

Michael A. Jochim. **Hunter-Gatherer Subsistence and Settlement: A Predictive Model**

Stanley South. **Method and Theory in Historical Archeology**

Timothy K. Earle and Jonathon E. Ericson (Eds.). **Exchange Systems in Prehistory**

Stanley South (Ed.). **Research Strategies in Historical Archeology**

John E. Yellen. **Archaeological Approaches to the Present: Models for Reconstructing the Past**

Lewis R. Binford (Ed.). **For Theory Building in Archaeology: Essays on Faunal Remains, Aquatic Resources, Spatial Analysis, and Systemic Modeling**

James N. Hill and Joel Gunn (Eds.). **The Individual in Prehistory: Studies of Variability in Style in Prehistoric Technologies**

Michael B. Schiffer and George J. Gumerman (Eds.). **Conservation Archaeology: A Guide for Cultural Resource Management Studies**

Thomas F. King, Patricia Parker Hickman, and Gary Berg. **Anthropology in Historic Preservation: Caring for Culture's Clutter**

Richard E. Blanton. **Monte Albán: Settlement Patterns at the Ancient Zapotec Capital**

R. E. Taylor and Clement W. Meighan. **Chronologies in New World Archaeology**

Bruce D. Smith. **Prehistoric Patterns of Human Behavior: A Case Study in the Mississippi Valley**

Barbara L. Stark and Barbara Voorhies (Eds.). **Prehistoric Coastal Adaptations: The Economy and Ecology of Maritime Middle America**

Charles L. Redman, Mary Jane Berman, Edward V. Curtin, William T. Langhorne, Nina M. Versaggi, and Jeffery C. Wanser (Eds.). **Social Archeology: Beyond Subsistence and Dating**

Bruce D. Smith (Ed.). **Mississippian Settlement Patterns**

Lewis R. Binford. **Nunamiut Ethnoarchaeology**

J. Barto Arnold III and Robert Weddle. **The Nautical Archeology of Padre Island: The Spanish Shipwrecks of 1554**

Sarunas Milisauskas. **European Prehistory**

Brian Hayden (Ed.). **Lithic Use-Wear Analysis**

William T. Sanders, Jeffrey R. Parsons, and Robert S. Santley. **The Basin of Mexico: Ecological Processes in the Evolution of a Civilization**

David L. Clarke. **Analytical Archaeologist: Collected Papers of David L. Clarke. Edited and Introduced by His Colleagues**

Arthur E. Spiess. **Reindeer and Caribou Hunters: An Archaeological Study**

Elizabeth S. Wing and Antoinette B. Brown. **Paleonutrition: Method and Theory in Prehistoric Foodways.**

John W. Rick. **Prehistoric Hunters of the High Andes**

Timothy K. Earle and Andrew L. Christenson (Eds.). **Modeling Change in Prehistoric Economics**

Thomas F. Lynch (Ed.). **Guitarrero Cave: Early Man in the Andes**

Fred Wendorf and Romuald Schild. **Prehistory of the Eastern Sahara**

Henri Laville, Jean-Philippe Rigaud, and James Sackett. **Rock Shelters of the Perigord: Stratigraphy and Archaeological Succession**

Duane C. Anderson and Holmes A. Semken, Jr. (Eds.). **The Cherokee Excavations: Holocene Ecology and Human Adaptations in Northwestern Iowa**

Anna Curtenius Roosevelt. **Parmana: Prehistoric Maize and Manioc Subsistence along the Amazon and Orinoco**

Fekri A. Hassan. **Demographic Archaeology**

G. Barker. **Landscape and Society: Prehistoric Central Italy**

Lewis R. Binford. **Bones: Ancient Men and Modern Myths**

Richard A. Gould and Michael B. Schiffer (Eds.). **Modern Material Culture: The Archaeology of Us**

Muriel Porter Weaver. **The Aztecs, Maya, and Their Predecessors: Archaeology of Mesoamerica, 2nd edition**

Arthur S. Keene. **Prehistoric Foraging in a Temperate Forest: A Linear Programming Model**

Ross H. Cordy. **A Study of Prehistoric Social Change: The Development of Complex Societies in the Hawaiian Islands**

C. Melvin Aikens and Takayasu Higuchi. **Prehistory of Japan**

Kent V. Flannery (Ed.). **Maya Subsistence: Studies in Memory of Dennis E. Puleston**

Dean R. Snow (Ed.). **Foundations of Northeast Archaeology**

Charles S. Spencer. **The Cuicatlán Cañada and Monte Albán: A Study of Primary State Formation**

Steadman Upham. **Polities and Power: An Economic and Political History of the Western Pueblo**

Carol Kramer. **Village Ethnoarchaeology: Rural Iran in Archaeological Perspective**

Michael J. O'Brien, Robert E. Warren, and Dennis E. Lewarch (Eds.). **The Cannon Reservoir Human Ecology Project: An Archaeological Study of Cultural Adaptations in the Southern Prairie Peninsula**

Jonathon E. Ericson and Timothy K. Earle (Eds.). **Contexts for Prehistoric Exchange**

Merrilee H. Salmon. **Philosophy and Archaeology**

Vincas P. Steponaitis. **Ceramics, Chronology, and Community Patterns: An Archaeological Study at Moundville**

George C. Frison and Dennis J. Stanford. **The Agate Basin Site: A Record of the Paleoindian Occupation of the Northwestern High Plains**

James A. Moore and Arthur S. Keene (Eds.). **Archaeological Hammers and Theories**

Lewis R. Binford. **Working at Archaeology**

in preparation

William J. Folan, Ellen R. Kintz, and Laraine A. Fletcher. **Coba: A Classic Maya Metropolis**